This edition is dedicated to my grandsons, Ben and Will. May their lives be full of good health and happiness.

PATRICK M. DUNNE

This edition is dedicated to my grandsons, John and Jacob. May their lives be full of surprises that challenge them to be among the best.

ROBERT F. LUSCH

Foreword

There has never been a more exciting time to be involved in the world of retailing. The broad expansion of all segments of retailing makes the retail landscape dynamic and extremely competitive. This 6th edition of *Retailing* gives you great insight into all aspects of retailing in a well thought out methodical approach that is sensitive to the constant changes within the industry. Professors Dunne and Lusch have continued the highest level of research to stay current with the industry, and this enables the reader to engage in a well-rounded dialogue about the retail industry. This latest edition covers all major disciplines for retailing including human resources, operations, marketing, multi-channel retailing, finance, and other areas as well, which will help you gain the best possible understanding about the retail industry.

The National Retail Federation (NRF) is the world's largest and most influential retail trade association working to provide thought leadership throughout the retail industry. The NRF co-brands this 6th edition of *Retailing* by Dunne and Lusch to encourage people who may be considering careers in retailing and others who may be beginning their journey into understanding retailing. It is our hope that your study of the retail industry reveals diversified challenges and opportunities for a fulfilling career that can last a lifetime. We encourage you to visit the NRF's Web site to stay current on the issues related to the retail industry at http://www.nrf.com. The NRF Pressroom and Bookstore are areas that may also assist you in your studies.

Daniel Butler
VP Merchandising and Retail Operations
National Retail Federation

Karen Knobloch
Senior Vice President Member Services
National Retail Federation

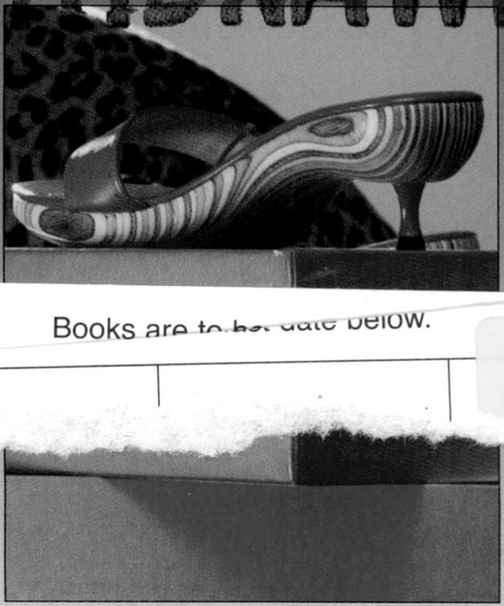

RETAILING

Sixth Edition

Patrick M. Dunne
Texas Tech University

Robert F. Lusch
University of Arizona

THOMSON
SOUTH-WESTERN

ia · Brazil · Canada · Mexico · Singapore · Spain · United Kingdom · United States

THOMSON

SOUTH-WESTERN

Retailing, 6th Edition

Patrick M. Dunne and Robert F. Lusch

VP/Editorial Director:
Jack W. Calhoun

VP/Editor-in-Chief:
Dave Shaut

Publisher:
Neil Marquardt

Developmental Editor:
Elizabeth Lowry

Content Project Manager:
Kelly Hoard

Marketing Manager:
Nicole Moore

Marketing Coordinator:
Sarah Rose

Production Technology Analyst:
Emily Gross

Manager, Editorial Media:
John Barans

Technology Project Manager:
Kristen Meere

Manufacturing Coordinator:
Diane Gibbons

Production House:
LEAP Publishing Services

Compositor:
ICC Macmillan Inc.

Printer:
China Translation and Printing Services, Inc.

Art Director:
Stacy Shirley

Internal Designer:
Thesing Design

Cover Designer:
Thesing Design

Cover Images:
© Getty Images

Photography Manager:
John Hill

Photo Researcher:
Darren Wright

Printed in China
2 3 4 5 08 07

Student Edition
ISBN-13: 978-0-324-36279-4
ISBN-10: 0-324-36279-X
International Student Edition
ISBN-13: 978-0-324-36437-8
ISBN-10: 0-324-36437-7

Library of Congress Control Number:
2006939680

For more information about our products, contact us at:

Thomson Learning Academic Resource Center

1-800-423-0563

Thomson Higher Education
5191 Natorp Boulevard
Mason, OH 45040
USA

Preface

Nearly two decades ago, we joined forces to develop a Retailing text that would describe the exciting challenges that a career in retailing could offer college students. At the same time, we wanted a textbook that students would enjoy reading. Today, as we introduce our 6th edition of this highly regarded text, we seemed to have accomplished our goals. This sixth edition of *Retailing*, like much of retailing itself, has undergone major revisions from prior editions. More than 80 percent of the chapters' story boxes (*Global Retailing*, *Service Retailing*, *What's New*, and *Retailing: The Inside Story*) are new to this edition. We have developed new cases to better reflect Retailing's changing environment. Yet, despite these new and exciting additions, we have sought to maintain the conversational writing style that past adopters have come to appreciate.

Given the influence of the Internet, the continuing growth of the service industry, and the ever-changing global market, we feel that there has never been a more exciting time to study and pursue a career in Retailing. We have tried to capture this excitement with the story boxes and text content. Each chapter of this edition updates retailing changes occurring as well as a behind-the-screen story relating to the chapter's topic. We continue to offer the in-depth coverage of the topics that the readers have come to expect. As a result, we believe that students and instructors will embrace this edition even more than they did the highly successful first five editions.

With retail providing one out of every five jobs in today's economy, we strongly believe that retailing offers the best career opportunities for today's students. Thus, *Retailing* was written to convey that message, not by using boring descriptions of retailers and the various routine tasks they perform, but by making the subject matter come alive by focusing on the excitement that retailing offers its participants, in an easy-to-read conversational style filled with pictures and exhibits. This text demonstrates to the student that retailing as a career choice can be fun, exciting, challenging, and rewarding. This excitement arises from selecting a merchandise assortment at market, determining how to present the merchandise in the store, developing a promotional program for the new assortment, or planning next season's sales in an ever-changing economic environment. And the reward comes from doing this better than the competition. While other texts may make retailing a series of independent processes, this edition of *Retailing*, like the first five editions, highlights the excitement, richness, and importance of retailing as a career choice. *Retailing* provides the student with an understanding of the inter-relationships of the various activities that retailers face daily. To do this, we have attempted to show how retailers must use both creativity and analytical skills in order to solve problems and pursue the opportunities of today's fast-paced environment.

In keeping with our goal of maintaining student interest, *Retailing* focuses on the material that someone entering the retailing field would need to know. We are more interested in telling the student what should happen, and what is happening, than in explaining the academic "whys" of these actions. Thus, when knowledge of a particular theory is needed, we generally have ignored the reasoning behind the theory for a simple explanation and an example or two of the use of the theory.

In presenting these examples, we drew from a rich array of literature sources, as well as our combined 80 years of work in retailing.

Students and teachers have responded favorably to the "personality" of *Retailing* because the numerous contemporary and relevant examples, both in the text itself and in each chapter's various story boxes, provide realistic insights into retailing. One student wrote to say "thanks" for writing a book that was "so interesting and not too long." A faculty member noted she was "so pleased with the writing style because it was easy to understand and the examples used were very appropriate and helped to present the material in a meaningful and easy-to-grasp manner for students." Still another liked *Retailing* because the writing style was "conversational," thus lending itself to very easy reading, so that she felt confident that her students would read the chapters. The content coverage is excellent. Terms are explained in easy-to-understand language. And, although most of the topics of an advanced retailing text are presented, the extent and presentation of the material is very appropriate to an introductory course." Another reviewer was especially pleased that we were able to incorporate so many current examples.

Text Organization

Retailing, which features an attractive, full-color format throughout the entire text, is divided into four parts, which are in turn divided into 14 chapters that can easily be covered over the course of the term. Part 1 serves as an introduction to the study of retailing and provides an overview into what is involved in retail planning. Part 2 examines the environmental factors that influence retailing today: the behavior of customers, competitors, channels, as well as our legal and ethical behavior. The third section examines the role location plays in a retailer's success.

Part 4 deals with the operations of a retail store. This section begins with a chapter on managing the retailer's finances. Special attention in this section is given to merchandise buying and handling, pricing, promotion and advertising, personal selling, store layout and design, and managing people—both customers and employees.

Chapter Organization

Each chapter begins with an **Overview** that highlights the key topic areas to be discussed. In addition, a set of **Learning Objectives** provide a description of what the student should learn after reading the chapter. To further aid student learning, the text material is integrated with the learning objectives listed at the beginning of the chapters and the summaries at the end. In addition, the text features a prominent placement of key term definitions in the margin to make it easier for students to check their understanding of these key terms. If they need a fuller explanation of any term, the discussion is right there—next to the definition.

The body of text will have **photos, exhibits, tables, and graphs** presenting the information and relationships in a visually appealing manner. Each chapter features the following four **Retailing boxes**:

1. *Retailing: The Inside Story*—Covers the inside story on a particular retailing event or decision.
2. *Global Retailing*—Gives insight into what is happening in the international retail market.
3. *What's New*—Discusses the impact of technology, especially the Internet, on retailers.
4. *Service Retailing*—Profiles retailers providing services.

These boxes are typically lengthier real-world examples than can be incorporated into the regular flow of text material. Some of these features are humorous, while others present a unique way to solve problems retailers face in their everyday operations.

Each chapter concludes with a student study guide. The first feature of this addition to the text is a **Chapter Summary by Learning Objective** followed by a list of **Terms to Remember**. These are followed by the traditional **Review and Discussion Questions**, which are also tied to the learning objectives for the chapter, are meant to test recall and understanding of the chapter material, as well as provide students with an opportunity to integrate and apply the text material. Another feature is a set of **Sample Multiple Choice Questions**, which cover each of the chapter learning objectives. The answers to these questions are at the end of the book.

The second half of the study guide is the **Application Section**. This section opens with a **Writing & Speaking Exercise** that is an attempt to aid the instructor in improving the students' oral/written communication skills as well as their teamwork skills. Here the student, or group of students, is asked to write a one-page report and/or make an oral presentation to the class incorporating the knowledge gained by reading the chapters. Some instructors may prefer to view these as "mini-cases."

A **Retail Project** engages the student to either visit a library or a Web site and find an answer to a current retail question.

The next feature of each chapter's Study Guide is a **Case**. Most of the cases are drawn from actual retail situations. The authors believe that the ability to understand the need for better management in retailing requires an explanation of retailing through the use of case studies. These cases cover the entire spectrum of retail operations, including department stores, specialty shops, direct retailing, hardware stores, grocery stores, apparel shops, discount stores, and convenience stores.

Since many of the students taking this class will one day open their own retail business, the next section is for them. **Planning Your Own Retail Business** presents a very specific problem based on the chapter's material that a small business manager/owner will face in his or her day-to-day operations. Importantly, the student, by working the problems, can witness the financial impact of retail decisions.

Finally, **Key Terms and Concepts**, shown in boldface type in the chapter, have their definitions presented in the margins throughout the chapters.

Supplementary Material

The **Instructor's Resource CD-ROM** includes an overview of the chapter, several detailed teaching tips for presenting the material, a detailed outline, the answers to questions for review and discussion, suggestions for handling the writing & speaking exercises, retail projects, cases, and planning your own business. The IRCD also includes:

- The **Test Bank** contains interactive quizzes and is available in Word as well as **ExamView—Computerized Testing Software**. This software is free to instructors who adopt the text.
- A **PowerPoint Presentation** includes a chapter overview, key terms and definitions, charts, tables, and other visual aids by learning objective.
- A **Retail Spreadsheet Project** called The House is a spreadsheet analysis of the financial performance of a family clothing store in a small college town. The project is set up for use with a computer, but it is possible to do all the required computations with a calculator or by hand. The House is about a small retail shop and has two exercises for each chapter.

The **Book Companion Web Site** at www.thomsonedu.com/marketing/dunne contains a section on choosing retailing as a career and 12 to 20 online questions (True/False and Multiple Choice) for each chapter.

A **DVD Supplement** offers a professionally written and produced video case package that provides intriguing, relevant, and current real-world insight into the modern marketplace. Each video is supported with application questions located on the Web site.

ACKNOWLEDGMENTS

Many people contributed to the development of this text. For their helpful suggestions as reviewers of the various editions of this text, we are especially grateful to the following:

Phyllis Ashinger
Wayne State University

Chad W. Autry
Texas Christian University

Steve Barnett
Stetson University

Barbara Bart
Savannah State College

Holly E. Bastow-Stoop
North Dakota State University

Pelin Bicen
Texas Tech University

Jeffrey G. Blodgett
University of Illinois at Springfield

Jerry E. Boles
Western Kentucky University

Elten D. Briggs
University of Texas at Arlington

Doreen Burdalski
University of Philadelphia

Melinda Burke
University of Arizona

David Burns
Xavier University

Doze Yolaine Butler
Southern University

Louis D. Canale
Genesee Community College

Jason M. Carpenter
University of South Carolina

James Carver
University of Arizona

Tim Christiansen
University of Arizona

John Clark
California State University—Sacramento

Victor Cook
Tulane University

Christy A. Crutsinger
University of North Texas

Dennis Degeneffe
University of Minnesota

Roger Dickinson
University of Texas at Arlington

Farrell Doss
Radford University

Janice Driggers
Orlando College

Mary Ann Eastlick
University of Arizona

Joanne Eckstein
Macomb Community College

Jonathan Elimimian
Johnson C. Smith University

Sevo Eroglu
Georgia State University

Kenneth R. Evans
University of Missouri

Ann E. Fairhurst
University of Tennessee—Knoxville

John Fernie
Heriot-Watt University

Robert C. Ferrentino
Lansing Community College

Susan Fiorito
Florida State University

Mark Fish
Ohio University

Judy Zaccagnini Flynn
Framingham State College

Sandra Forsythe
Auburn University

Sally L. Fortenbery
Texas Christian University

Ellen Goldsberry
University of Arizona

D. Elizabeth Goins
University of Illinois at Springfield

Linda K. Good
Michigan State University

Donald H. Granbois
Indiana University

Blaine S. Greenfield
Bucks County Community College

Sejin Ha
The Ohio State University

Jared Hansen
Texas Tech University

Norman E. Hansen
Northeastern University

Jack Hartog
Hanze University

Shelley S. Harp
Texas Tech University

Joseph C. Hecht
Montclair State University

Patricia Huddleston
Michigan State University

Charles A. Ingene
University of Mississippi

Marian H. Jernigan
Texas Woman's University

Julie Johnson—Hillery
Northern Illinois University

Laura Jolly
University of Tennessee—Knoxville

Mary Joyce
Bryant College

Jikyeong Kang
University of Manchester

William Keep
Quinnipiac College

J. Patrick Kelly
Wayne State University

Karen W. Ketch
University of Kentucky

Jiyoung Kim
The Ohio State University

Tammy Lamb Kinley
Western Illinois University

Gail H. Kirby
Santa Clara University

Dee K. Knight
University of North Texas

Jim Kress
Central Oregon Community College

Grace Kunz
Iowa State University

Frederick Langrehr
Valparaiso University

Marilyn Lavin
University of Wisconsin—Whitewater

Marilyn Lebahn
Northwest Technical College

Dong Lee
Fairmont State College

Melody L. Lehew
Kansas State University

Deborah Hawkins Lester
Kennesaw State University

Bruce Klemz
Winona State University

Michael Levin
Texas Tech University

Michael W. Little
Virginia Commonwealth University

John W. Lloyd
Monroe Community College

Dolly D. Loyd
University of Southern Mississippi

Paul MacKay
East Central College

Elizabeth L. Mariotz
Philadelphia University

Shawna L. Mahaffey
Delta College

Louise Majorey
Cazenovia College

Raymond Marquardt
Arizona State University

Nancy McClure
St. Edwards University

Michael McGinnis
University of Southern Alabama

Paul McGurr
Fort Lewis College

Nancy J. Miller
Iowa State University

Diane Minger
Cedar Valley College

Linda Minikowske
North Dakota State University

Marguerite Moore
University of South Carolina

Michelle A. Morganosky
University of Illinois—Urbana

Mark Mulder
Grand Rapids Junior College

David W. Murphy
Madisonville Community College

Lewis J. Neisner
University of Maryland

Elaine M. Notarantonio
Bryant College

Katherine A. Olson
Northern Virginia Community College

Jan P. Owens
Carthage College

Shiretta Ownbey
Oklahoma State University

Charles R. Patton
University of Texas at Brownsville

V. Ann Paulins
Ohio University

John Porter
West Virginia University

Dawn Pysarchik
Michigan State University

Denise Reimer
Iowa Lakes Community College at Emmetsburg

Glenn Richey
University of Alabama

Lynne Ricker
University of Calgary

Jacqueline Robeck
University of Wisconsin—Stout

Robert A. Robicheaux
University of Alabama at Birmingham

Rod Runyan
University of Wisconsin—Stevens Point

Ben Sackmary
State University College at Buffalo

Kare Sandivek
Buskerud University College

Duane Schecter
Muskegon Community College

Jean Shaneyfelt
Edison Community College

Donna Smith
Ryerson University

Leigh Sparks
University of Stirling

Samuel A. Spralls III
University of Tennessee at Chattanooga

Robert Stassen
University of Arkansas

Brenda Sternquist
Michigan State University

Leslie D. Stoel
The Ohio State University

Pauline M. Sullivan
Florida State University

Patrick Swarthout
Central Lakes College

Harriet P. Swedlund
South Dakota State University

William R. Swinyard
Brigham Young University

Paul Thistlewaite
Western Illinois University

Jane Boyd Thomas
Winthrop University

Jeff W. Totten
Southeastern Louisiana University

James A. Veregge
Cerritos Community College

Irena Vida
University of Tennessee

Mary Walker
Xavier University

Mary Margaret Weber
Emporia State University

Scarlett C. Wesley
University of South Carolina

Deborah Whitten
University of Houston

Diane Wilemon
Texas Christian University

Mike Wittmann
University of North Texas

Allen Young
Bessemer State Tech College

Deborah D. Young
Texas Woman's University

We would be remiss if we failed to thank all those in the retailing industry for their input in the text. We particularly want to thank Sue Busch Nehring, Best Buy; Carol J. Greenhut, Schonfeld & Associates, Inc.; Bill Kirk, Weather Trends International; Doral Chenoweth and Marvin J. Rothenberg, both retired consultants; Susan Pistilli, International Council of Shopping Centers; Kevin Coupe, morningnewsbeat.com; Jim Duddleston and Zack L. Adcock, Schick-Wilkinson; Wally Switzer, 4 R's of Retailing, Inc.; Jim Maurer, Pierce's Northside Market; Tom Drake, NARDA; William R. Davidson and Katherine Clarke, Retail Forward; Mark Fallon, Jeffrey R. Anderson Real Estate; Jim Lukens, D.W. Green; Teddy Tenenbaum, Mr. Handyman of Los Angeles; Mickey Reali, Orville's; Chris Gorley, Starbucks; Wayne Copeland, Jr., entrepreneur extraordinaire. We also want to acknowledge our gratitude for permission to use Bob Ridings' story and photos about the birds and to quote from the following individuals' research: Robert Thornton, Lehigh University; Phil Lempert, "Facts, Figures, & the Future" e-Newsletter; Claes Fornell, University of Michigan; Nancy Veatch, National Research Bureau.

A very special thanks go to the following individuals for their significant contributions to this sixth edition. These individuals offered timely suggestions to early drafts of many of these chapters. For their insight and encouragement, we are especially indebted. Thanks again to David Overton, JCPenney's; Dan Butler, National Retailing Federation; Paul Adams, Paul Adams and Associates; James Carver, University of Arizona; and Kathy Mayer. We also want to thank Steve Inman for his assistance on the teaching package and Paul McGurr for updating The House.

To the team at South-Western, we can only say we're glad you let us be a part of the team. These individuals include Neil Marquardt, Acquisitions Editor/Marketing; Mike Roche, former Vice President/Editor-in-Chief and current Senior Project Fixer-Upper; Elizabeth Lowry and Emma Guttler, Development Editors; Nicole Moore, Marketing Manager; Kelly Hoard, Production Manager; and Darren Wright, Photo Editor.

Finally, we want to take this opportunity to thank our wives for their love and understanding, especially as seemingly endless deadlines approached. Thanks, Judy and Virginia.

Patrick M. Dunne — Lubbock, Texas
Robert F. Lusch — Tucson, Arizona

About the Authors

Patrick M. Dunne

Patrick Dunne, a professor at the Rawls School of Business, Texas Tech University, received his M.B.A. and Ph.D. in marketing from Michigan State University and his B.S. from Xavier University.

In over 40 years of university teaching, Dr. Dunne has taught a wide variety of marketing and distribution courses at both the undergraduate and graduate levels. His research has been published in many of the leading marketing and retailing journals. In addition, he has authored nine books. Dr. Dunne was the first academic to receive the Wayne A. Lemburg Award for "conspicuous individual accomplishments" from the American Marketing Association. Dr. Dunne has also been honored with several university teaching awards.

Previously, Dr. Dunne served as Vice President of both the Publications and Association Developmental Divisions of the American Marketing Association. Professor Dunne is an active consultant to a variety of retailers, ranging from supermarkets to shopping malls.

Robert F. Lusch

Robert F. Lusch, a professor at the Eller School of Management, University of Arizona, received his Ph.D. in business administration from the University of Wisconsin and his M.B.A. and B.S. from the University of Arizona.

His expertise is in the area of marketing strategy and distribution systems. Professor Lusch has served as the editor of the *Journal of Marketing*. He is the author of more than 150 academic and professional publications including 15 books. In 1997, the Academy of Marketing Science awarded him its Distinguished Marketing Educator Award and the American Marketing Association presented him the Harold Maynard Award.

Professor Lusch has served as President of the Southwestern Marketing Association, Vice President of Education and Vice President Finance of the American Marketing Association, chairperson of the American Marketing Association, and trustee of the American Marketing Association.

Brief Contents

Contents

Introduction to Retailing

C h a p t e r 1
Perspectives on Retailing

C h a p t e r 2
Retail Strategic Planning
and Operations Management

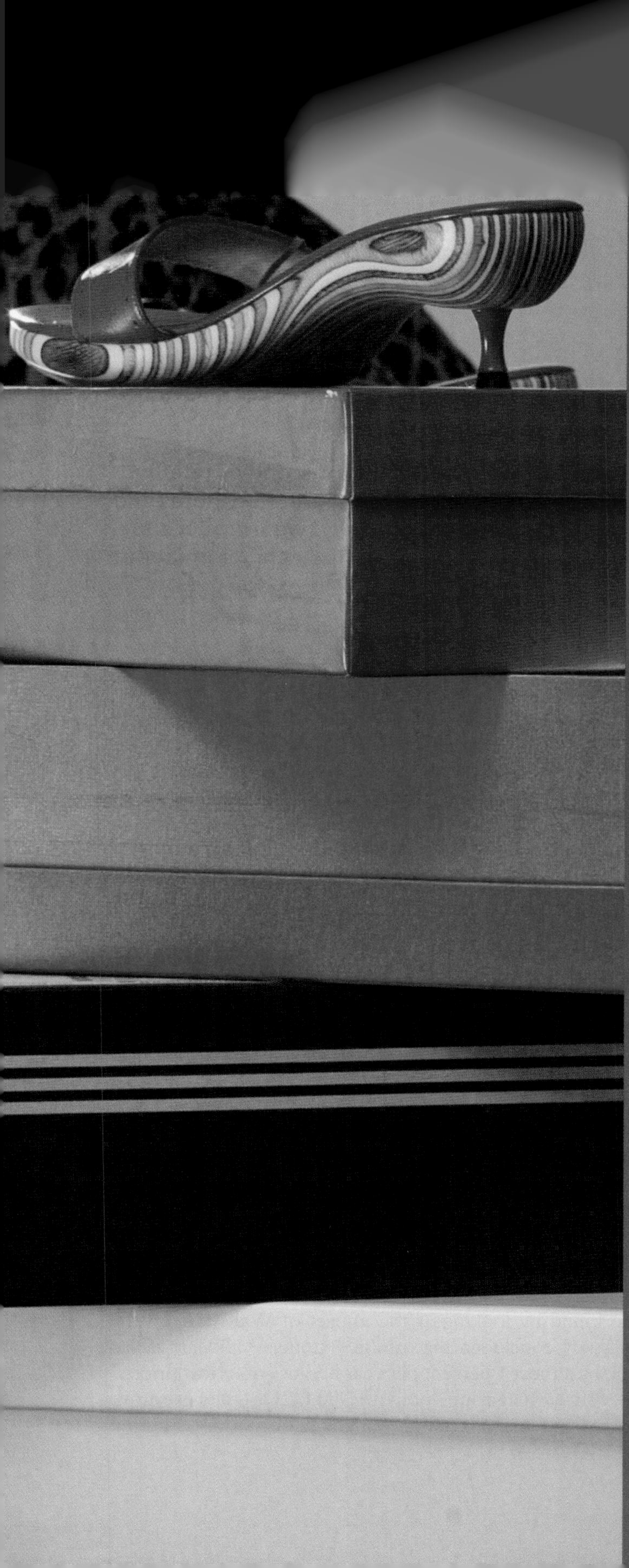

chapter 1

Perspectives on Retailing

Overview:

In this chapter, we acquaint you with the nature and scope of retailing. We present retailing as a major economic force in the United States and as a significant area for career opportunities. Finally, we introduce the approach to be used throughout this text as you study and learn about the operation of retail firms.

Learning Objectives:

After reading this chapter, you should be able to:

1. Explain what retailing is.
2. Explain why retailing is undergoing so much change today.
3. Describe the five methods used to categorize retailers.
4. Understand what is involved in a retail career and be able to list the prerequisites necessary for success in retailing.
5. Explain the different methods for the study and practice of retailing.

LO 1

What Is Retailing?

What is retailing?

It is easy to take for granted the impact retailing has on our lifestyle. In fact, retailing, which is responsible for matching the individual demands of the consumer with vast quantities of supplies produced by a huge range of manufacturers and service providers, has made a significant contribution to the economic prosperity that we enjoy so much. The nations that have benefited from the greatest economic and social progress have been those with a strong retail sector. This statement can be illustrated two ways. First, in 2006, the Nobel Peace Prize was given to Bangladesh economist Muhammad Yunus and the Grameen Bank, a micro-retail bank which he founded decades earlier. The Prize Committee recognized the importance of financing the business aspirations of "millions of small people," with loans as little as $20 to help some of the world's most impoverished people start businesses so that they could work to bring about their own development by establishing a retailing sector.

A second example can be found by looking at the impact of Wal-Mart on the American economy. A recent study concluded that in 2004 alone, Wal-Mart raised consumer discretionary income by almost 1 percent per year because of its low prices.[1] In fact, in both 2003 and 2004, *Fortune* magazine's poll of 1,000 CEOs (chief executive officers) found Wal-Mart, the world's largest retailer, was the nation's most admired

Retailing: The Inside Story

Wal-Mart's Early Use of Computers

Many retail consultants believe that a major factor in Wal-Mart's success can be attributed to its integrated use of the computer, which changed the way retailers now do business. Wal-Mart's early investment in computers to track sales on an individual item level in order to cut costs changed the way retailers today manage their business. But was it insight, luck, or necessity that, in 1980, made Sam Walton undertake his initial investment of $800 million and 1,000 "associates" in a computer division, when competitors thought it was way too expensive?

Folks who knew Sam Walton claim that his greatest asset was his ability to learn from others, so as not to duplicate their mistakes and gain from their successes. Others were using computers in their business. EPOS (electronic point-of-sale) computer systems had already been used in retailing for close to ten years by supermarkets, but only to check prices. Computers weren't used to gather sales and inventory data as they are today. Walton saw these new uses and installed his first system out of necessity to help manage the distribution centers he had been forced by vendors to set up a decade earlier.

In 1970, the year its stock first traded publicly, Wal-Mart established its distribution system. At the time, it had fewer than four dozen stores and many of the big vendors (P&G, General Foods, Lever Brothers, etc.) didn't always call on that small a retailer in the northwestern corner of Arkansas. When they did call on Wal-Mart, the vendors would dictate the purchase terms. Walton's distribution system enabled him to buy in volume and equalize the negotiation terms.

A decade later, Wal-Mart's advanced computers enabled it to not only scan sales but also to make certain that in-bound shipments coming in one side of a distribution center were transferred to the correct dock on the other side of the center for shipment to its then nearly one thousand stores. The computers not only managed product movement within the distribution centers but connected the stores, distribution centers, and vendors via Wal-Mart's headquarters in Arkansas via satellite using EDI (electronic data interchange). This made it possible for Wal-Mart to be the first U.S. retailer to benefit from having a JIT (just-in-time) inventory system and to know what products were moving in which store, significantly lowering operating costs.

Several years later, Walton proposed to Procter & Gamble the idea of setting up a "partnership" that involved not only just sharing sales information through the EDI system but having a real partnership between the companies whereby P&G would tailor its production and shipments to Wal-Mart's sales. Today P&G is Wal-Mart's largest supplier and Wal-Mart is now P&G's largest customer, accounting for nearly a sixth of the manufacturer's sales. Because of the success of this program, nearly 500 other vendors have established a partnership relationship with Wal-Mart whereby they share online information via Wal-Mart's Retail Link system.

In 2005, Wal-Mart showed off the sophistication of its computer system when Hurricane Katrina hit the Gulf Coast. Not only did the computer enable the chain's stores to stock up on bottled water, flashlights, generators, and rodent traps before the storm, but stores had chain saws, mops, and Pop-Tarts (they stay preserved until opened, they taste good, and the whole family can eat them) stored in reserve for after the storm. The news media was amazed that within days, Wal-Mart was able to haul millions of dollars of supplies into the storm-ravaged area before FEMA (Federal Emergency Management Agency) was able to do so.

---

company. (In 2005 and 2006, due to growing criticism of this nonunion company by labor unions and a slumping stock price, Wal-Mart fell to fourth and then 12th position.)[2] When Wal-Mart first achieved this status in 2003, it marked the first time the world's biggest corporation was also its most respected.[3] Wal-Mart was chosen because of its ability to relentlessly focus on three fronts: (a) working with manufacturers to help them produce goods at the lowest possible cost, (b) managing the supply chain so as to bring these goods from those manufacturers to its stores at the lowest possible cost, and (c) using cutting-edge technology to manage its inventory to ensure that it always had the requested merchandise in stock and it didn't incur any unneeded expense by having excess inventory. (This chapter's Retailing: The Inside Story box describes Wal-Mart's early investment into computers.) As a result, economists believe that the retailer's EDLP (Everyday Low Prices) policy has contributed to everyday low inflation, meaning that all Americans benefit from Wal-Mart's efficiency. Warren Buffett, the famous investor, noted that the retailer has "contributed more to the financial well-being of the American public than any institution I can think of." His own back-of-the-envelope calculation of this contribution: $10 billion a year.[4] Still, not everyone likes and admires Wal-Mart. In a survey on advertising done for Advertising Age in 2005, the respondents ranked Wal-Mart the second "most trustworthy company in America" (tied with General Electric and behind Ford Motor) and as the second "least trustworthy company in America" (behind Enron).[5]

On the other hand, nations that fail to develop a powerful retailing system will ultimately have to devise one in order to improve their populations' well-being. One of the reasons Eastern European countries experienced such a low rate of economic growth when they were under Communist control was their lack of a competitive retail structure. Consumers were forced to shop in stores that offered outdated merchandise and were barely the size of a large room. Interestingly, when Benetton, Toys "R" Us, Pizza Hut, and even an IMAX theater opened for business in these countries, they became instant successes.[6] The joy and excitement these new forms of retailing provided illustrates the value people of all cultures place on a retailing system that is responsive to their needs and wants. Even Bulgaria, which was the most depressed of Europe's Soviet bloc nations, has a new 120-store mall in Sofia that has generated great excitement as consumers, especially young people, can now save time and do all their shopping at one place.[7]

Dollars & Sense

Retailers that enter foreign markets and understand the local cultures and customs will be higher profit performers than those who don't understand the local cultures and customs.

retailing
Consists of the final activities and steps needed to place merchandise made elsewhere into the hands of the consumer or to provide services to the consumer.

Retailing, as we use the term in this text, consists of the final activities and steps needed to place a product made elsewhere into the hands of the consumer or to provide services to the consumer. In fact, retailing is actually the last step in a supply chain that may stretch from Europe or Asia to your hometown. Therefore, any firm that sells a product or provides a service to the final consumer is performing the retailing function. Regardless of whether the firm sells to the consumer in a store, through the mail, over the telephone, through the Internet, door to door, or through a vending machine, the firm is involved in retailing.

LO 2 The Nature of Change in Retailing

Why is retailing always undergoing so much change?

Many observers of the American business scene believe that retailing is the most "staid and stable" sector of business. While this observation may have been true in the past, quite the contrary is true today. Retailing, which accounts for 20 percent of the worldwide labor force and includes every living individual as a customer, is the largest single industry in most nations and is currently undergoing many exciting changes. It is important to note that a recent study concluded that the number one reason CEOs were replaced was for "mismanaging change."[8] While this study looked at all types of businesses, this finding would be especially true in retailing. Since managing change is so important, each chapter of this text will have a What's New box just to discuss some of the changes taking place that will impact the future

What's New?

Be Careful What You Wish For

Online airline ticket sales began in the mid-1990s as a way of cutting the expensive middlemen—travel agents—out of the game in order to improve the air carriers' profits. The idea worked so well that today nearly half of all American airline seats are sold on the Internet.

However, little did the airline executives realize the impact of this attempt to improve their bottom line, by eliminating the 10 to 15 percent fees paid to travel agents, would have on the industry. In their rush to cash in on the promise of online commerce, carriers created a marketplace in which every consumer had easy access to every airline's lowest fares. In addition, the explosive growth of discount airlines in an unregulated industry caused more of those cheap seats to be available. The consumer now had all the information (prices, departure and arrival times, available seats, and past performance records) readily available. No wonder that airline profits declined and continued to slide, despite the absence of commissions paid to travel agents, as the Web-surfers' ability to find bargain fares caused average revenue per mile to drop.

Recently, air carriers have attempted to reverse this trend, at least a little, by trying to change the way consumers use the Internet. Their aim is twofold: cut distribution costs even more and increase unit revenue by developing applications that will induce online consumers to pay slightly higher average prices.

As means of cutting costs, the traditional or so-called "legacy" airlines that were in business before the industry was deregulated in the late 1970s (American, Delta, United, Northwest, USAirways, and Continental) are seeking ways to bypass the four big, expensive ticketing networks (Sabre, Galileo, Worldspan, and Amadeus that collectively are known as global distribution systems, or GDSes.) The carriers are backing powerful new third-party search engines, such as kayak.com, mobissimo.com, and sidestep.com. These scan a wide number of airline-operated and third-party travel Web sites—Expedia.com, Orbitz.com, and Travelocity.com—for the best deals. Then, for a modest finder's fee, they transfer consumers directly into the selected airline's Web site and enable the consumer to get that "best" price. These new search engines are called GNEs (GDS-New Entrants or "Genies").

A key difference between these new search engines and the older third-party sites is that older sites buy and resell airline seats, whereas Kayak and the others are merely travel search services that connect customers with airlines. The intent is for GNEs, which run on much less expensive and more efficient network servers, to provide negotiating strength against the older ticketing networks. However, the key argument against these new sites, as well as the older, but popular branded Web sites, such as Travelocity (which is actually owned by Sabre), is that they focus solely on price. Thus, by having such price-focused sites, the airlines have experienced lower revenues per passenger–seat-mile.

Seeking to avoid a total price war, GDSers are seeking to be more hip technologically and narrow the cost gap vs. the GNEs. They also claim they can increase revenue per ticket over GNEs or the airlines' own Web sites by helping them differentiate their services and prices. GDSers also claim that large corporations, whose travelers tend to pay higher fares, still prefer to book their travel through them.

Regardless, airlines and their agents will have to reinvent themselves, and their product offering, over the next few years and they will have to do it with the customer in mind.

Source: "Struggling Upstream," *Forbes*, November 14, 2005: 100–103.

---

of retailing. This box will address the new practices, skills, and strategies that retailers are using to stay ahead of the competition. Sometimes these new approaches don't work as planned. This is illustrated in this chapter's What's New box detailing how, as a result of attempting to improve profits by eliminating the travel agent's commission, airlines have seen their Internet ticket selling systems cause unintended consequences.

According to the Census Bureau, currently just over 1.1 million retail establishments are selling physical or tangible products in the United States, with total annual sales of nearly \$3.8 trillion, or nearly \$11,000 per capita.[9] Ten retail

© Tony Freeman/Photo Edit

Airlines, with the growth of the Internet, are able to bypass retail travel agents and sell direct to airline customers.

establishments exist for every 1,000 households. This equates to average annual sales of nearly $3.45 million per store.[10] Most retailers, however, are smaller, and many have annual sales of less than $750,000.

These figures do not reflect the changes that have occurred behind these dollar amounts. The number of new retail enterprises that were developed in the last two decades is truly amazing. Most of these new businesses have actually been new institutional forms, such as Internet retailing, warehouse retailing, supercenters, and home delivery of both fast food and groceries. Change is truly the driving force behind retailing. Let's explore some of the trends that are affecting retailing today.

E-Tailing

As the What's New box illustrates, the great unknown for retail managers is what the ultimate role of the Internet will be. Most observers recognize the value of online shopping for travel, clothing, cosmetics, and music. But it is still unclear if online shopping will reach its projections for "everyday" needs. Probably the best example of this dilemma is what the future holds for online shopping for books. The Internet, with entrants like Amazon.com, was supposed to destroy the traditional bricks-and-mortar bookstore. Despite such projections, the early returns are mixed.

Yes, the discounters stocked all the best sellers and Amazon offered free delivery and lower prices, but the bookstores are maintaining their profitability. Two possible explanations are given. First, that faced with these threats, bookstore management became more business-oriented. Supply chains were streamlined and some of the "well-read, but not profit-oriented" staff was replaced with stern business-minded types. Special deals on best sellers were used to match competitors, and better sales techniques, especially suggestion selling, were developed so that, once in the store, customers were sold items the competition didn't carry. Second, the traditional retailer stressed the major limitation of the Internet as a retail channel. The bookstores differentiated themselves from the online competition by becoming a retreat from the house. They began to offer coffee, chairs to relax, poetry readings, and lectures. In addition, they conceded the fact that e-tailers can often undercut their bricks-and-mortar rivals, but online customers must wait at least a day for their books to be delivered, often at inconvenient times. This campaign was so successful that Amazon recently announced that it would sell pages of any book for pennies per page, thereby enabling readers to read the first chapter while waiting for delivery.[11]

What the future will bring for online shopping, which now accounts for about three percent of total retail sales, remains to be seen. However, it is the promise of e-tailing's efficiency that has consumers still excited.

Another dramatic change caused by e-tailing is a shift in power between retailers and consumers. Traditionally, the retailers' control over pricing information provided them the upper hand in most transactions. The information dissemination capabilities of the Internet, as highlighted earlier in the What's New box, are making consumers better informed and thus increasing their power when transacting and negotiating with retailers. E-tailers have provided consumers with detailed pricing information about products ranging from autos to office supplies, thus enabling them to negotiate better deals.[12] Some e-tailers, such as Priceline.com, are shifting power to consumers by allowing them to set their own prices and then letting retailers fight for customers. Clearly, e-tailing is adding a new competitive dimension to retailing. However, e-tailers must worry that many consumers will use the Internet for research and then buy the product in neighborhood stores.

Price Competition

Some claim that America's fixation with low prices began after World War II when fair trade laws, which allowed the manufacturer to set a price that no retailer was allowed to sell below, paved the way for America's first discounter, E. J. Corvett. Actually, this revolution more than likely began with the birth of Wal-Mart in Rogers, Arkansas, in 1962. At the time, there were 41 publicly held discount stores and another two dozen privately owned chains already in business.[13] What Sam Walton did that forever changed the face of retailing was to realize before everybody else that most of any product's cost gets added after the item is produced. As a result, Walton began enlisting suppliers to help him reduce these costs and increase the efficiency of the product's movement. Also, as explained in the chapter's Inside Story box, Walton, who had never operated a computer in his life, made a major commitment to computerizing Wal-Mart as a means to reduce these expenses. As a result of the introduction of the computer to retail management, Wal-Mart's selling, general, and administrative costs as a percentage of sales total only 16 percent, while all of its competitors' operating expenses are 3 to 5 percent higher. Simply put, Wal-Mart became the world's largest retailer by relentlessly cutting unnecessary costs and demanding that their suppliers do the same. Those who claim that Wal-Mart is obsessed with its bottom line (PROFITS) miss the point: Wal-Mart is obsessed with its top line (SALES), which it grows by focusing on the consumer's bottom line.[14]

Costco is another retailer that seeks to boost store traffic by getting shoppers to come in for a "super, low price" on key products. Consider gasoline. The chain's goal is to beat the prices at the five nearest gas stations. As a result, its gas is priced

Chris Kleponis/Bloomberg News/Landov

Costco uses low-price gasoline to build store traffic to sell other products.

anywhere from several cents to 30 cents a gallon less than competitors'. Costco keeps costs low by having customers pay at the pump, which eliminates cashiers. Customers also need a membership card, which costs $45 a year and goes straight to the firm's bottom line.[15]

Dollars & Sense

Retailers that outperform their competition in controlling costs incurred after the merchandise is acquired will be higher profit performers.

Demographic Shifts

Significant changes in retailing over the past decade have resulted from changing demographic factors, such as the fluctuating birth rate, the increasing number of immigrants, the growing importance of the 70 million Generation Y consumers (those born between 1978 and 1994), and the fact that Generation Xers are now middle-aged and baby boomers are now reaching retirement. Many people simply failed to realize how these factors, which had profound effects on our society, could also impact retailing. For example, once highly successful retailers like McDonald's are now marginalized because they clearly failed to see the demise of the mass market and the growth of rapidly fragmenting markets.[16] Consider how America's recent immigrants have made once-exotic foods like sushi and burritos everyday options. Also, quick meals of all sorts can now be found in supermarkets, convenience stores, even vending machines. Even supermarkets, which were long thought to be the only retailer capable of catering to all markets, must be aware of the effect of these demographic changes on their business.

Successful retailers must become more service-oriented, offering better value in price and quality; more promotion-oriented; and better attuned to their customers' needs. For example, one of the reasons that Lowe's is threatening Home Depot's dominance in the DIY (do-it-yourself) market is Lowe's awareness of its core customers—women—who are directly responsible for 80 percent of home-improvement sales.[17]

With population growth slowing, retailers are no longer able to sustain their long-term profit projections simply by building new stores to gain additional sales as they did in the past. Profit growth must come by either increasing same-store sales at the expense of the competition's market share or by reducing expenses without reducing services to the point of losing customers. (**Same-store sales** is a retailing term that compares an individual store's sales to its sales for the same month in the previous year. **Market share** refers to a retailer's sales as a percentage of total market sales for the merchandise line or service category under consideration.) As a result, today's retail firms are run by professionals who are able to look at the changing environment and see opportunities, exert enormous buying power over manufacturers, and anticipate future changes before they impact the market, rather than just react to these changes after they occur. After all, whereas in the past retailers drove the market, in today's economy and the economy of the future, it will clearly be driven by the consumer. However, not even the best of these professionals can always agree about what the consumer will want in the future.

same-store sales
Compares an individual store's sales to its sales for the same month in the previous year.

market share
Is the retailer's total sales divided by total market sales.

Retailers who can spot upcoming demographic changes and proactively adapt, rather than merely react after the changes occur, will have higher profit performance.

Dollars & Sense

Store Size

Further insight into the changes occurring in retailing can be obtained by looking at the average store size for various retail categories. The largest increase in store size in recent years has been in drugstores, a reflection of the rapid growth of chains such as Walgreens and CVS. In addition to over-the-counter remedies and prescriptions, these stores sell a variety of general merchandise; in fact, the majority of their sales now comes from many different unrelated items, such as food products, convenience goods, greeting cards, seasonal items (school supplies, gardening supplies, and Christmas decorations), and even clothing. This phenomenon is referred to as **scrambled merchandising** For example, convenience stores are said to be using a scrambled merchandising approach when they sell gasoline, bread, milk, beer, cigarettes, magazines, lottery tickets, and fast food. The same can be said of supermarkets that sell clothing, flowers, and gasoline and offer bank branches and dry cleaners inside their stores. This scrambling of merchandise approach also applies to services, such as ATMs, phone cards, and car washes. Today this practice has gone so far that consumers can now pick up gift cards for home improvement retailers (Home Depot and Lowe's), restaurants (Outback and Olive Garden), and even prepaid debit cards next to the greeting cards in supermarkets, drug stores, and convenience stores. This growth in scrambled merchandising is the result of the pressure being placed on many retailers to increase profits. Consider supermarkets where groceries are a low-margin business. However, the clothing, health and beauty aids (HBA), and floral business not only help attract customers but yield substantially higher margins.

scrambled merchandising
Exists when a retailer handles many different and unrelated items.

Tim Boyle/Getty Images

Convenience stores use scrambled merchandise to enhance sales.

There has also been an increase in average store size by the more traditional general merchandise stores, which in many cases are combining with supermarkets to form supercenters. As a result, the average store size of supermarkets has been shrinking despite increasing the breadth of merchandise carried, reflecting their targeted customer's increased desire for convenience.[18] Likewise, the average department store is now smaller; many of these retailers are closing their downtown locations, which often were their largest stores, because the downtown areas of many cities have become "ghost towns." Thus, retailers today are seeing a trend emerge: Retail stores are now either larger or smaller than their counterparts from the past. In fact, nowhere is this fact of retailing better illustrated than with "category killers." A **category killer** is a mass merchandiser that concentrates on carrying an extensive selection of items in a single or limited number of product categories at low, low prices. Thus, the name derives from its marketing strategy: Carry a large amount of merchandise in a single category at such low prices that it makes it impossible for customers to walk out without purchasing what they need, thus "killing" the competition.

category killer
Is a retailer that carries such a large amount of merchandise in a single category at such good prices that it makes it impossible for the customers to walk out without purchasing what they need, thus killing the competition.

Toys "R" Us, which began operations in 1948 and became publicly traded in 1978, was the first category killer.[19] The company also has the unfortunate distinction of being the largest category killer to fail. In 2005, the entire company, in an attempt to avoid bankruptcy, was sold to a group of investors, as independent toy retailers struggled to recover from the constant, brutal low-price strategy launched by Wal-Mart and Target. During the all-important holiday shopping season, busy parents who were already in the discount stores were pleased to complete their shopping in a single location. The changing tastes of children also contributed to the woes of toy retailers. Today's kids are migrating to electronic and computer games at an earlier age.[20]

Other well-known category killers include Best Buy, Home Depot, Circuit City, Office Depot, CompUSA, PetSmart, and Bed Bath & Beyond. Category killers have diverted business away from traditional wholesale supply houses. For example, Home Depot appeals to the professional contractor and Office Depot to the business owner who traditionally purchased supplies from hardware wholesalers and office supply and equipment wholesalers.

Success in retailing depends on a retail manager's ability to properly interpret what societal changes are occurring and what these changes mean to the store's customers, then building a strategy to respond to those changes. Therein lies the excitement and challenge of retailing as a career. After all, 50 years ago, the Wal-Mart strategy of building a major enterprise in small-town America and offering "everyday low prices" was probably considered foolhardy. This was at a time when retailers thought growth could be achieved only by competing in the big cities where large population bases were located. Yet someone who purchased 100 shares of Wal-Mart when it went public on October 1, 1970, for $16.50 a share and reinvested the dividends would by 2005 be holding more than 200,000 shares worth over $10 million. (This is the reason that the Waltons are the richest family in America;[21] Sam Walton had invested virtually everything he had in this stock. Anyone else who invested a similar amount of money in Wal-Mart stock in 1970 would be equally wealthy.)

Of course, the future can never be predicted with certainty. This text attempts to provide you with the tools to meet these upcoming challenges and be a success in retailing. The answer to what the future will bring lies in the disquieting fact that retailers do not operate in a static, closed environment; they operate in a continuously changing and competitive one. These changes are discussed in greater detail in Chapters 3 through 6. For now, we will concentrate on the following environmental elements: the behavior of consumers, the behavior of competition, the behavior of supply chain members (the manufacturers and wholesalers that the retailer buys from), the legal system, the state of technology, and the socioeconomic nature of society. Exhibit 1.1 depicts these elements.

A final comment about the changing face of retailing: Remember, business entrepreneurs are not obliged to conform to old norms and social standards. They are free to forge new retail approaches that capitalize on emerging market opportunities. In retailing, this is all the more evident when we consider fashion trends; what in the past would have lasted for years now may last only a few months.

Categorizing Retailers

LO 3

Describe the five methods used to categorize retailers.

Categorizing retailers can help the reader understand competition and the changes that occur in retailing. There is no single acceptable method of classifying retail competitors, although many classification schemes have been proposed. The five most popular schemes used today are described in Exhibit 1.2.

Census Bureau

The U.S. Bureau of the Census, for purposes of conducting the Census of Retail Trade, classifies all retailers using three-digit North American Industry

Exhibit 1.1
External Environmental Forces Confronting Retail Firms

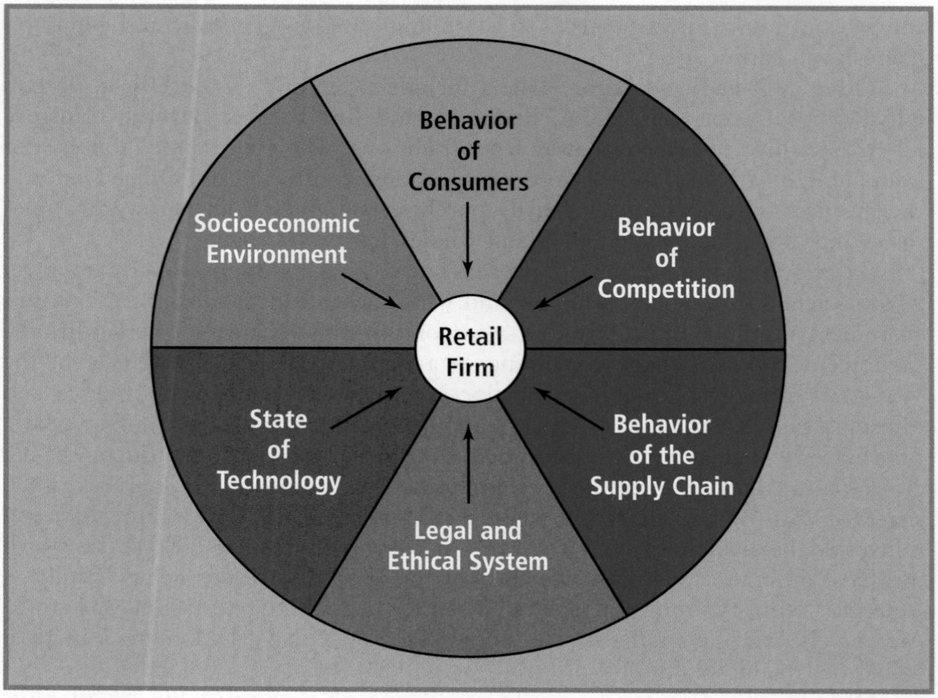

Census Bureau	Number of Outlets	Margin/Turnover	Location	Size
3-digit NAICS code	Single unit	Low margin/low turns	Traditional	By sales volume
4-digit NAICS code	2–10 units	Low margin/high turns	Central shopping districts	
5-digit NAICS code	11+ units	High margin/low turns	Shopping centers	By number of employees
		High margin/high turns	Free-standing nontraditional	

Exhibit 1.2
Categorizing Retailers

Classification System (NAICS) codes. The Web site for locating these codes is http://www.census.gov/epcd. Some examples of these NAICS codes are shown in Exhibit 1.3.

As a rule, these three-digit NAICS codes are too broad to be of much use to the retail analyst. Four-digit NAICS codes provide much more information on the structure of retail competition and are easier to work with. For example, NAICS 454 is non-store retailing, which consists of approximately 56,000 retailers. Within this are NAICS 4541, which consists of 10,000 electronic shopping and mail-order houses (Spiegel and L.L. Bean, for example); NAICS 4542, consisting of 6,000 vending machine operators; NAICS 4543, consisting of 27,000 direct-selling establishments, and so on.[22]

In almost all instances, the NAICS code reflects the type of merchandise the retailer sells. The major portion of a retailer's competition comes from other retailers in its NAICS category. General merchandise stores (NAICS 452) are the

Code	Type of Business	Number of Establishments	Percent of Total	Sales (billions)	Percent of Total	Number of Employees (thousands)	Percent of Total
44-45	Retail Trade	1,111,583	100%	$3,171	100%	15,029	100%
441	Motor vehicle & parts dealers	122,692	11%	$812	26%	1,884	13%
442	Furniture and home furnishings stores	65,088	6%	$94	3%	554	4%
443	Electronics & appliance stores	46,724	4%	$88	3%	418	3%
444	Building material and garden supplies	n/a	n/a	n/a	n/a	n/a	n/a
445	Food & beverage stores	149,802	13%	$488	15%	2,896	19%
446	Health & personal care stores	79,360	7%	$183	6%	1043	7%
447	Gasoline stations	n/a	n/a	n/a	n/a	n/a	n/a
448	Clothing & clothing accessories	149,318	13%	$170	5%	1,425	9%
451	Sporting goods, hobby, book & music stores	63,033	6%	$78	2%	633	4%
452	General merchandise stores	39,846	4%	$451	14%	2,549	17%
453	Miscellaneous store retailers	129,070	12%	$95	3%	849	6%
454	Nonstore retailers	55,764	5%	$171	5%	587	4%

n/a = figures do meet publications standards

Source: U.S. Bureau of Census, *Statistical Abstract of the United States: 2004–2005*, Table 1017, and author calculations.

Exhibit 1.3
Using NAICS Codes (2002)

exception to this rule. General merchandise stores, due to the variety of general merchandise carried, compete with retailers in most other NAICS categories. For example, department stores compete for clothing sales with specialty apparel stores, such as The Gap and The Limited; mail-order retailers, such as L.L. Bean, or off-priced stores, such as T.J. Maxx or Ross's Dress-for-Less. In fact, most retailers must compete to a considerable extent with general merchandise stores, because these larger stores usually handle many of the same types of merchandise that smaller, more limited retailers sell. In a very broad sense, all retailers compete with each other, since they all compete for the same limited consumer dollars.

Another shortcoming of using the NAICS codes, as was pointed out in a footnote earlier in the chapter, is that they do not reflect all retail activity. The Census Bureau definition equates retailing only with the sale of "tangible" goods or merchandise. However, by our definition, selling of services to the final consumer is also retailing. This suggests that retailing is also conducted by businesses such as barber/beauty shops, health clubs, dry cleaners, banks, insurance agencies, funeral homes, movie theaters, amusement parks, maid services, medical and dental clinics, one-hour photo labs, and so on. NAICS 772, which is not classified under retail trade, consists of almost 490,000 eating and drinking establishments. Remember, any time the consumer spends money, whether on tangibles (merchandise) or intangibles (services), retailing has occurred.

Number of Outlets

Another method of classifying retailers is by the number of outlets each firm operates. Generally, retailers with several units are a stronger competitive threat because they can spread many fixed costs, such as advertising and top management salaries, over a larger number of stores and can achieve economies in purchasing. However, single-unit retailers, such as your neighborhood IGA grocery store, do have several advantages. They are generally owner- and family-operated and tend to have harder working, more motivated employees. Also, they can focus all their efforts on one trade area and tailor their merchandise to that area while gaining buying efficiencies by being a member of the IGA group. In the past, such stores were usually able to spot emerging customer desires sooner and respond to them faster than the larger multiunit operations.

Any retail organization that operates more than one unit is technically a chain, but this is really not a very practical definition. The Census Bureau classifies chain stores into two size categories: 2 to 10 stores and 11 or more, thus, when we use the term *chain stores*, this text means 11 or more units. Chain stores account for 41 percent of all retail sales (including 99 percent of all department store sales and 66 percent of all grocery store sales). Though large chain operations account for 58 percent of nondurable goods sales, they account for only about 20 percent of durable goods sales, such as autos and furniture.[23] By the way, McDonald's (13,673 units), H&R Block (11,034), Starbucks (6,409 units), GAP (3,051 units) and Barnes & Noble (2,356 units) are the largest chains in terms of number of outlets.[24]

standard stock list
Is a merchandising method in which all stores in a retail chain stock the same merchandise.

optional stock list
Is a merchandising method in which each store in a retail chain is given the flexibility to adjust its merchandise mix to local tastes and demands.

channel advisor or channel captain
Is the institution (manufacturer, wholesaler, broker, or retailer) in the marketing channel who is able to plan for and get other channel institutions to engage in activities they might not otherwise engage in. Large store retailers are often able to perform the role of channel captain.

private label branding
Also often called store branding, occurs when a retailer develops its own brand name and contracts with a manufacturer to produce the merchandise with the retailer's brand on it instead of the manufacturer's name.

Not all chain operations enjoy the same advantages. Small chains are local and may enjoy some economies in buying and in having the merchandise tailored to their market needs. Large chains are generally regional or national and can take full advantage of the economies of scale that centralized buying, accounting, training, and information systems and a **standard stock list** can achieve. A standard stock list requires that all stores in a retail chain stock the same merchandise. Other national chains such as Wal-Mart, recognizing the variations of regional tastes, use the **optional stock list** approach, which gives each store the flexibility to adjust its merchandise mix to local tastes and demands. This point is driven home by the name of a retail consulting firm composed of former Wal-Mart employees, 4 R's of Retailing, Inc. (Right Merchandise, Right Quantity, Right Place, and Right Time). After all, as one JCPenney executive told the authors, stores in the Rio Grande Valley in Texas sell primarily smalls and mediums in men's shirts, while in Minnesota the chain sells a preponderance of larger sizes.

Both types of stock lists provide scale advantages in other retailing activities. For example, promotional savings occur when more than one store operates in an area and can share advertising, even while tailoring specific merchandise to specific stores.

Finally, chain stores have long been aware of the benefits of taking a leadership role in the marketing supply chain. When a chain store retailer is able to achieve critical mass in purchases, it can get other supply chain members—wholesalers, brokers, and manufacturers—to engage in activities they might not otherwise engage in, and it is then referred to as the **channel advisor** or **channel captain**. For example, the chain store retailer might get other supply chain members to include direct-to-store deliveries, increased promotional allowances, extended payment terms, or special package sizes, all of which help the retailer to operate more efficiently.

In recent years, chains (as will be discussed in greater detail in Chapter 4) have relied on their high level of consumer recognition to engage in **private label branding**.

Private label branding, sometimes called *store branding*, is when a retailer develops its own brand name and contracts with a manufacturer to produce the product with the retailer's brand instead of buying a national brand with the manufacturer's name on it. Today, the whole concept of private label has taken on a new dimension as retailers have made these items, while not nationally advertised, nationally promoted. These private labels are advertised in the newspaper as brands and are heavily promoted in stores.

In the past, private labels were inexpensive knockoffs of popular items. Today, though, some of the best retailers have significantly increased the quality and style of their private merchandise to promote it front and center. Retailers target these private labels, which have their own distinct personality, to specific markets and advertise them in their own promotional pieces.

bricks-and-mortar retailers
Retailers that operate out of a physical building.

Another reason why private labels are so popular with retailers is that the manufacturer's brands, such as Liz Claiborne, Tommy Hilfiger, and Ralph Lauren, are now available in many different stores. Private labels, however, offer the retailer exclusivity by letting the retailer provide unique merchandise, such as JCPenney's Arizona jeans, across the nation. Also important is the fact that a retailer's private label brands can be much more lucrative. Manufacturers of brand names like Hilfiger and Lauren have to share the profits with the famous designer, thus increasing costs. By designing and manufacturing their own labels, retailers can cut out the designer and the middleman. That can translate into profit margins that can be at least 20 percent better than a manufacturer's name-brand label. Some chains, such as Save-A-Lot, a unit of Supervalu, have dropped national brands like Fritos, Dr. Pepper, Pampers, and Coca-Cola, and replaced them with their own brands: Corntitos, Dr. Pop, Waddles, and Bubba Cola. Small retailers, because of their lack of economies of scale, can't use private labels unless they are part of a buying group. Our Global Retailing box looks at the use of private labels across the world.

The major shortcoming of using the number of outlets scheme for classifying retailers is that it addresses only traditional **bricks-and-mortar retailers**, or those operating in a physical building. This scheme thus ignores many nontraditional retailers such as catalog-only and e-tailers. How many outlets does Amazon.com have? One could argue that each new online computer is a potential retail outlet for the e-tailing giant.

When a potential customer connects to Amazon.com, he or she essentially is helping the retailer create a new location—a location with the ultimate in location convenience: the home or office where the user's computer is located.

Retailers who can develop private branded merchandise better than their competition will experience higher profitability.

Dollars & Sense

Global Retailing

The Power of Private Labels

An ACNielsen study in 2005 found that more than two-thirds of global consumers consider private label products to be a "good alternative" to other brands and an "extremely good value for the money;" while nearly as many believe such products offer quality that's "at least as good as that of the usual big brands." As a result, private labels more than doubled the growth rate of manufacturer brands between 2003 and 2005, 5 percent versus 2 percent. In fact, in more than two-thirds of the 38 markets studied, private label sales grew faster than their manufacturer's counterparts.

Europe is most dominant in terms of market share of private label sales, with a 23 percent share across 17 markets and a growth rate of 4 percent. In fact, the top five countries in terms of market share are all European: Switzerland (45%), Germany (30%), Great Britain (28%), Spain (26%) and Belgium (25%). The Emerging Markets (comprised of Croatia, Czech Republic, Hungary, Slovakia, and South Africa) collectively have the fastest growth in private labels at 11 percent, though this is achieved from a much smaller base (6 percent of total sales). Latin America and Asia Pacific, in addition to having the smallest market share, have lower growth rates than the Emerging Markets. In fact, in 2005 Latin America's private labels lost 0.1 percent versus the manufacturer brands. North America is second in market share (16%) and had significant growth rate of 7 percent.

The study also found that nearly everyone in the 38 countries buys private label goods. In fact, 100 percent of households in two-thirds of the markets reviewed had purchased them during the two-year period, and even the "lowest" penetration level was a still strong 77 percent (Singapore).

ACNielsen concluded that while private labels still command only 17 percent of the global marketplace, in many markets that percentage is far higher. As a result, the research firm felt if consumer attitude is any indication, the world would continue to experience substantial growth in the sale of private label products. Supporting this claim, in another study across the same 38 markets, they found that 68 percent of consumers either slightly or strongly agreed with the statement that "Private label brands are a good alternative to other brands."

Source: Based on a study "The Power of Private Labels 2005" by ACNielsen and used with its written permission.

Market Share Percentages of Private Labels by Country

	Country	Region	PL Share
1	Switzerland	Europe	45%
2	Germany	Europe	30%
3	Great Britain	Europe	28%
4	Spain	Europe	26%
5	Belgium	Europe	25%
6	France	Europe	24%
7	Netherlands	Europe	22%
8	Canada	North America	18%
9	Denmark	Europe	17%
10	United States	North America	16%
11	Sweden	Europe	14%
12	Austria	Europe	14%
13	New Zealand	Asia Pacific	12%
14	Italy	Europe	11%
15	Portugal	Europe	11%
16	Hungary	Emerging Markets	10%
17	Slovakia	Emerging Markets	10%
18	Finland	Europe	10%
19	Australia	Asia Pacific	9%
20	Nowray	Europe	8%
21	Ireland	Europe	7%
22	Czech Republic	Emerging Markets	7%
23	Hong Kong	Asia Pacific	4%
24	Brazil	Latin America	4%
25	Greece	Europe	4%
26	South Africa	Emerging Markets	4%
27	Puerto Rico	Latin America	4%
28	Japan	Latin America	4%
29	Israel	Europe	3%
30	Singapore	Asia Pacific	3%
31	Chile	Latin America	3%
32	Argentina	Latin America	3%
33	Colombia	Latin America	2%
34	Croatia	Emerging Markets	2%
35	Thailand	Asia Pacific	1%
36	Mexico	Latin America	1%
37	South Korea	Asia Pacific	1%
38	Philippines	Asia Pacific	<0.5%

Source: "The Power of Private Labels 2005," *ACNielsen Global Services*, September 2005: 9.

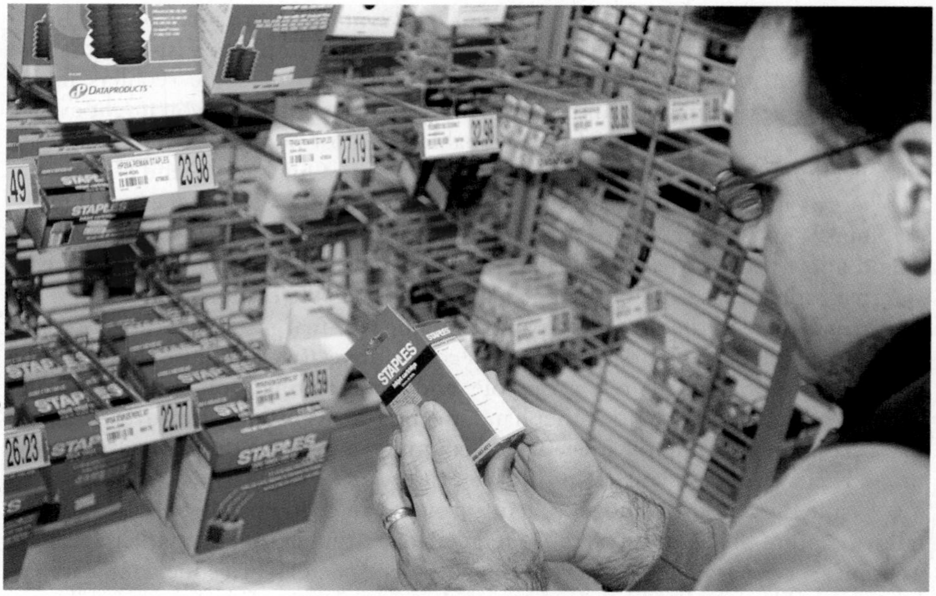
Neal Hamberg/Bloomberg News/Landov

The high price of manufacturer office supplies has driven Staples to develop its own store branded merchandise.

Margins Versus Turnover

Retailers can be classified by their gross margin percent and rate of inventory turnover. The **gross margin percentage** shows how much **gross margin** (net sales minus the cost of goods sold) the retailer makes as a percentage of sales; this is also referred to as the gross margin return on sales. A 40 percent gross margin indicates that on each dollar of sales the retailer generates 40 cents in gross margin dollars. This gross margin will be used to pay the retailer's **operating expenses** (the expenses the retailer incurs in running the business other than the cost of the merchandise, e.g., rent, wages, utilities, depreciation, insurance, etc.). **Inventory turnover** refers to the number of times per year, on average, that a retailer sells its inventory. Thus an inventory turnover of 12 times indicates that, on average, the retailer turns over or sells its average inventory once a month. Likewise, an average inventory of $40,000 (retail) and annual sales of $240,000 means the retailer has turned over its inventory six times in one year ($240,000 divided by $40,000), or every two months.

High-performance retailers, those who produce financial results substantially superior to the industry average, have long recognized the relationship between gross margin percent, inventory turnover, and profit. One can classify retailers into four basic types by using the concepts of margin and turnover.

Typically, the **low-margin/low-turnover** retailer will not be able to generate sufficient profits to remain competitive and survive. Thus there are no good examples of successful retailers using this approach. On the other hand, the **low-margin/high-turnover** retailer is common in the United States. Perhaps the best examples of this retailer type are the discount department stores, the warehouse clubs, and the category killers. Amazon.com is probably the best-known example of low-margin/high-turnover e-tailers. **High-margin/low-turnover** bricks-and-mortar retailers are also quite common in the United States. Furniture stores, high-end women's specialty stores and furriers, jewelry stores, gift shops, funeral homes, and most of the mom-and-pop stores located in small towns across the country are

gross margin percentage
Is the gross margin divided by net sales or what percent of each sales dollar is gross margin.

gross margin
Is net sales minus the cost of goods sold.

operating expenses
Are the expenses the retailer incurs in running the business other than the cost of the merchandise.

inventory turnover
Refers to the number of times per year, on average, that a retailer sells its inventory.

high-performance retailers
Are those retailers that produce financial results substantially superior to the industry average.

low-margin/low-turnover retailer
Is one that operates on a low gross margin percentage and a low rate of inventory turnover.

low-margin/high-turnover retailer
Is one that operates on a low gross margin percentage and a high rate of inventory turnover.

high-margin/low-turnover retailer
Is one that operates on a high gross margin percentage and a low rate of inventory turnover.

clicks-and-mortar retailers
Retailers that sell both online and via physical stores.

high-margin/high-turnover retailer
Is one that operates on a high gross margin percentage and a high rate of inventory turnover.

generally good examples of high-margin/low-turnover operations. Some **clicks-and-mortar retailers**, those that sell both online and in physical stores, that use this approach include Coach and Sharper Image. Finally, some retailers find it possible to operate on both **high margin and high turnover**. As you might expect, this strategy can be very profitable. Probably the most popular examples are convenience food stores, such as 7-Eleven, Circle K, and Quick Mart, and concessions and sports apparel sold at major athletic events. In the early stages of Internet commerce, entrepreneurs are experimenting with different business models that would allow them to have both high margins and high turnover, but to date no Internet retailer has succeeded at achieving this enviable combination.

As indicated in the preceding paragraph, the low-margin/low-turnover retailer is the least able of the four to withstand a competitive attack because this retailer is usually unprofitable or barely profitable, and when competition increases, profits are driven even lower. On the other hand, the high-margin/high-turnover retailer is in an excellent position to withstand and counter competitive threats because profit margins enable it to finance competitive price wars.

While the margin/turnover scheme provides an encompassing classification, it fails to capture the complete array of retailers operating in today's marketplace. For example, service retailers and even some e-tailers, such as Priceline.com, carry no inventory. Thus, while this scheme provides a good way of analyzing retail competition, it neglects an important type of retailing.

Location

Retailers have long been classified according to their location within a metropolitan area, be it the central business district, a regional shopping center or neighborhood shopping center, or as a freestanding unit. These traditional locations will be discussed in greater detail in Chapter 7. However, the last decade saw a major change in the locations that retailers selected. Retailers are now aware that opportunities to improve financial performance can result not only from improving the sales per square foot of traditional sites, but from operating in new nontraditional retail areas.

Dollars & Sense

Retailers that seek out nontraditional locations to reach customers will increase their chances of being highly profitable.

In the past, rather than expand into untested territories, many retailers simply renovated existing stores. Not today. Now retailers are reaching out for alternative retail sites. American retailers today are testing all types of nontraditional locations to expand their businesses. For example, to get more people to eat pizza when they rent videos, Pizza Hut introduced kiosks in video rental stores with direct phone lines to the local Pizza Hut. McDonald's has locations in service stations along interstate highways. Loblaw, a Canadian grocer, has a women's health club in its store near Toronto, and E * Trade, the online brokerage firm, is expanding its non-Internet presence with financial service centers in Target stores. Even the bricks-and-mortar banks, realizing that senior citizens with their high savings account levels and a need for the services of the bank's trust department, have started to install pharmacies in their buildings.

Given the high income levels of many airline travelers, the increasing amount of layover time between flights, and the absence of food on many flights, many

Adam Rountree/Bloomberg News/Londov

Best Buy has added Geek Squad service centers to their stores with the intent of both better serving customers after their computer purchases and increasing margins in the low-margin home computer business.

retailers have opened stores in airports, an idea that originated with and has long been used by European and Asian retailers. Airport retailers have been able to succeed by offering fast service, convenience, pleasant and clean environments, product variety and quality, entertainment, and competitive prices. For example, one of New York City's toniest retail venues today, where shoppers can browse in boutiques featuring merchandise from DKNY, H. Stern Jewelers, and Danish designer Sand, isn't on Fifth or Madison Avenues. It's The Shops at John F. Kennedy International Airport, in Queens, New York. Travelers can also find Brooks Brothers in Pittsburgh's airport and Coach and Body Shop in San Francisco's.[25] Probably the most significant of the new nontraditional shopping locations today are those that combine culture with entertainment or shopping, something that was unheard of a decade ago. Today such locations, including Bass Pro hunting and fishing superstores, have proven that the edges are blurring between shopping and entertainment for the masses.

Retailers do not want to miss out on urban or inner-city neighborhoods, which frequently have high minority populations. It is projected that by 2007 the spending power of Latinos and African-Americans will reach $927 billion and $853 billion respectively.[26] Dollar General, Jewel/Osco, Pathmark, and Von's are leaders in opening stores in urban locations.

The fast-food industry offers another example of nontraditional locations. KFC, Pizza Hut, and Taco Bell, which are all owned by YUM Brands, are opening units near or within several large universities. All three fast-food chains are under one roof, which means employees and facilities (parking lots, restrooms, etc.) can be shared. Other fast-food operators have combined two or more franchisees

George Widman/Associated Press

Many fast food retailers are locating together under one roof to provide customers more convenient selections and locations.

together. One popular example is to combine a "meal" retailer (KFC) with a "dessert" operator (Haagen-Dazs).

Before ending our discussion of location, it is important to point out that this is an area of retailing that may undergo significant changes in the next decade. The Internet suggests that future locations may be as close as a consumer's computer or cell phone. Some retailers are now able to operate out of a home office or car equipped with an iPod.

Size

Many retail trade associations classify retailers by sales volume or number of employees. The reason for classifying by size is that the operating performance of retailers tends to vary according to size. That is, larger firms generally have lower operating costs per sales dollar than smaller firms do. For example, in its most recently available study, the National Retail Federation, which categorizes U.S. department stores into three volume groups, found that operating expenses were 38 percent for firms with sales between $5 and $20 million, 38 percent for stores in the $20 to $100 million range, and only 34 percent for operations of more than $100 million. Most retail trade associations provide similar breakdowns on gross margins, net profits, net markups, sales per square foot of selling space, and so forth. Retailers will find this information meaningful when comparing their results against others of a similar size.

While size has been useful in the past, it is unclear whether the changes brought about by technology will make this classification obsolete. For example, imagine a fully automated retailer where, as a consumer places an order online, an automated stock-picking warehouse packages the selected merchandise and forwards it to the shipping area to be sent by UPS to the customer. Is Wal-Mart comparable to Amazon.com in terms of the number of employees needed?

LO 4

A Retailing Career

What is involved in a retailing career?

Retail is the largest industry in the nation! That means there are many different kinds of retail entities that fuel our nation's economy. Someone once said that "managing a retail store is an easy job. All you have to do is get consumers to visit your store (traffic) and then get these consumers to buy something (convert the traffic into customers) while operating at a lower cost than your competition (financial management)." Assuming this is correct, what type of person is needed to manage a retail store?

Economist	Yes ___	No ___
Fashion expert	Yes ___	No ___
Marketer	Yes ___	No ___

Financial analyst	Yes ___	No ___
Personnel manager	Yes ___	No ___
Logistics manager	Yes ___	No ___
Information system analyst	Yes ___	No ___
Accountant	Yes ___	No ___

In reality, the answer is "yes" to all of these roles. A retail store manager needs to be knowledgeable in all these areas. As we have pointed out, few industries offer a more fast-paced, ever-changing environment where results are quickly seen on the bottom line than retailing. Few job opportunities will train you to become an expert in not just one field, but in all business disciplines. Retailing offers you the economist's job of forecasting sales up to six months in advance, the fashion expert's job of predicting consumer behavior and how it will affect future fashion trends, and the marketing manager's job of determining how to promote, price, and display your merchandise. Further, it offers the financial analyst's job of seeking to reduce various expenses; the personnel manager's job of hiring the right people, training them to perform their duties in an efficient manner, and developing their work schedules; the logistics manager's job of arranging delivery of a "hot item"; the information systems analyst's job of analyzing sales and other data to determine opportunities for improved management practices; and the accountant's job of arriving at a profitable bottom line.

In summary, a retailer is like a master chef. Anyone can buy the ingredients, but only a master chef can make a masterpiece. Over the course of a career, you will have to deal with many issues. Among them are:

1. What product(s) or service(s) to offer.
2. What group of customers to target.
3. Where to locate the store.
4. How to train and motivate your employees.
5. What price level to use.
6. What levels of customer service (store hours, credit, staffing, parking, etc.) to offer your customers.
7. How to lay out the store.
8. How to leverage the Internet to support your mission.

Exhibit 1.4 illustrates the career paths available to the college graduate at a typical retailer. Note the two major paths: store management and buyer. (For a more detailed discussion of the various careers available today in retailing, see http://www.retailology.com/college/career/paths.asp. In addition, CareerBuilders.com provides information on all aspects of the job search. This site offers tips on resumé writing, distributing the resumé, interviewing, and even career assessment.)

If you elect the **store management** path, you will have many decisions to make that affect the store's profitability. Selecting, training, evaluating, and all other aspects of personnel management are your responsibility. This path is very people-skill oriented, as you will be responsible for in-store promotions, displays, customer service, building maintenance, and store security. In addition, there is a need to coordinate your efforts with buyers and department managers in order to meet customers' needs, thus maximizing store sales. This career path does require frequent moves as you increase your responsibilities. Though this path involves working weekends and evenings, it does offer a very rewarding pay package as you advance to store manager and beyond.

store management
The retailing career path that involves responsibility for selecting, training, and evaluating personnel, as well as in-store promotions, displays, customer service, building maintenance, and security.

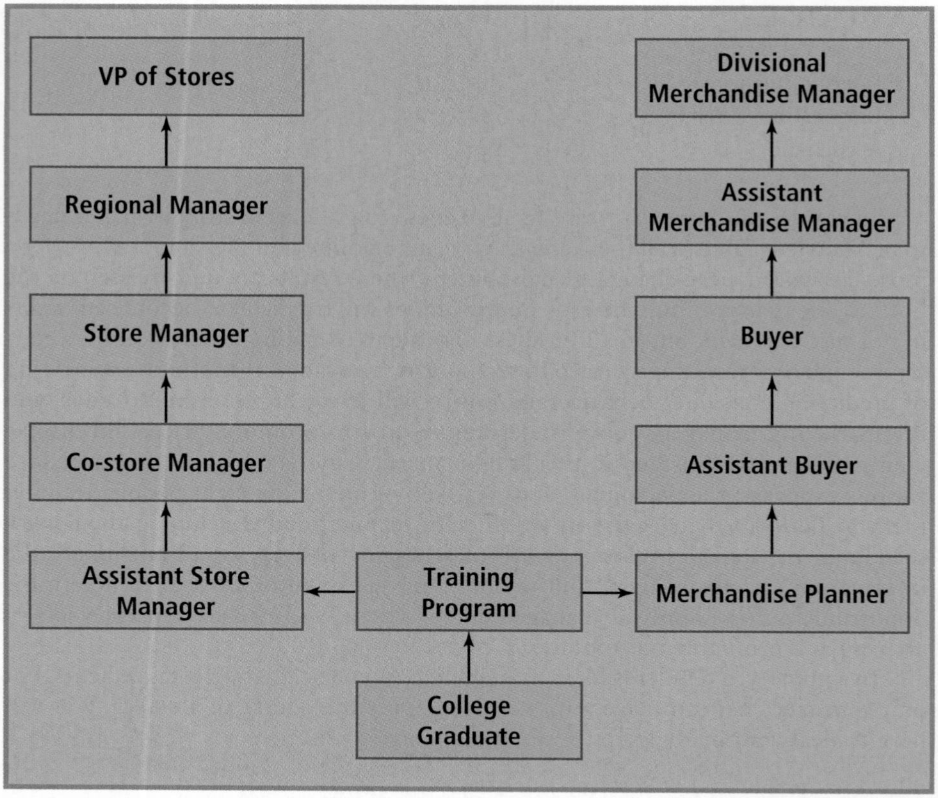

Exhibit 1.4
Retailing's Two Career Paths

buying
The retailing career path whereby one uses quantitative tools to develop appropriate buying plans for the store's merchandise lines.

If your inclination is toward **buying**, you can follow that career path. After spending some time as an assistant buyer, you will be promoted to buyer, or the CEO of a small business unit. Buyers use quantitative tools such as the merchandise budget and open-to-buy, which is the amount of funds a buyer has at any time to commit to merchandise purchses, in their work. Buyers, who usually work out the retailer's main office but do spend a great amount of time traveling, have to develop appropriate buying plans for their merchandise lines. Buyers must not only select the merchandise, but they must select the vendors and negotiate terms with them. Finally, buyers must coordinate with store managers to ensure that they are meeting the customers' needs.

As with any corporation, there are other career paths available in retailing. However, jobs in legal, information systems, human resources, accounting, and advertising are not as abundant as those in the store management and buying fields.

If you consider the list of eight factors on p. 21 that can comprise the ingredients of a retail store there would be more than ten billion possible retail formats. This is because there are 10,000 possible combinations of products and at least ten possible combinations of the other seven issues. No wonder no other occupation offers the immediate opportunities and challenges that retailing does. Yet many students do not consider retailing when exploring career opportunities, or they do not consider all they can do in a retailing career. One of the greatest opportunities for people entering a retailing career is in online retailing, or e-tailing. One particular e-tailing field that is attracting many job seekers is the retailing of online information, which is providing unheralded opportunities to those seeking new challenges.

Common Questions About a Retailing Career

As a student considering your future career, you may have certain questions about what opportunities a career in retailing may offer. To help you understand both the positive and negative sides of retailing, we will examine a few of the most frequently asked questions.

Salary

Are salaries in retailing competitive? Generally, starting salaries in executive training programs will be around $38,000 to $50,000 per year. That, however, is only the short-run perspective. In the long run, the retail manager or buyer is directly rewarded on individual performance. Entry-level retail managers or buyers who do exceptionally well can double or triple their incomes in three to five years, and often within seven to ten years can have incomes twice those of classmates who chose other career fields. It is not uncommon for a college graduate with five to seven years of experience in the supermarket industry to be made a store director or manager and earn a six-figure income. Terry Lundgren, Chairman and CEO of Federated Department Stores, was company president by the age of 35.

Career Progression

Can one advance rapidly in retailing? Yes. Obviously, this answer depends on both the retail organization and the individual. A person capable of handling increasing amounts of responsibility can move up quickly. There is no standard career progression chart. See http://retailindustry.about.com/od/jobs/a/blcareers.htm for career opportunities available with many of the country's leading retailers by geographic area, as well as other fine companies seeking college graduates.

Geographic Mobility

Does a retailing career allow one to live in the area of the country one desires? Yes and no. Retailing exists in all geographic areas of the United States with sufficient population density. In the largest 300 cities in the United States, there will be sufficient employment and advancement opportunities in retailing. In order to progress rapidly, a person must often be willing and able to make several moves, even if the changes may not be attractive in terms of an individual's lifestyle. Rapidly growing chain stores usually find it necessary to transfer individuals, especially those in the store management career path, in order to open stores in new geographic areas. Fortunately, these transfers are generally coupled with promotions and salary adjustments. Finally, a person may stay in one geographic area if he or she so desires. However, this may cost that person opportunities for advancement and salary increases.

Women in Retailing

Has retailing always been viewed as a good career for women? Yes. Today females constitute over 50 percent of all department store executives, making it the profession where women have attained the highest level of achievement. While most female executives are at the lower levels of corporate management, breakthroughs into the retail presidential ranks have recently been made. Prior to agreeing to be sold to an investor group lead by Supervalu and CVS in 2006, Albertsons, with six women on the 11-member board of directors, had the highest percentage of board women, 54.5 percent, among the Global Top 200 companies. A service provider, Wells Fargo, with 35.7 percent female representation on its board, is now the leader.[27] "Women have insight into our customers that no man—no matter how bright, no matter how hard working—can match," said Larry Johnston, Albertsons' former chairman/president/CEO when asked about the high percentage. "That's important when 85 percent of all consumer buying decisions made in our stores are made by women. As we pursue a customer-focused approach to growth, the insight, knowledge and expertise of women is invaluable—at every level in the organization."[28] *Fortune* and the *WSJ* both list eBay's Margaret "Meg" Whittman and Avon's Andrea Jung at the top of their "most powerful women in business" list.[29]

Societal Perspective

Is retailing a respectable profession? Professional merchants are considered respected and desirable members of their community, their state, and their nation. Leading retail executives are well-rounded individuals with a high social consciousness. Many of them serve on the boards of nonprofit organizations, as regents or trustees of universities, as active members of the local chambers of commerce, on school boards, and in other service-related activities. Retailers serve society not only outside their retailing career, but also within it. For example, civic events such as holiday parades are often sponsored by local merchants. In addition, many retail firms support local groups and charities with cash, food, and other goods and services as a means to "reinvest" some of their profits in the communities they serve.

Unfortunately, there are also unscrupulous, deceiving merchants that society can do without. This is true in all professions. Unscrupulous lawyers, doctors, and police officers give their professions a negative image at times. On the other hand, professional and ethical lawyers, doctors, and police officers are good for their professions and for society as a whole. It is not the profession that dictates one's contribution to society, but the soundness of one's ethical principles. Early in your career (preferably as a student), you need to develop a firm set of ethical principles to help guide you throughout your managerial career.

Prerequisites for Success

What is required for success as a retail manager? Let's look at several factors that influence a retailer's success.

Hard Work

Most successful retailers, like any successful individual, will respond to the preceding question with a simple, "Hard work." Beginning retailers have long known that they earn their salary 9 to 5, Monday through Friday, but earn their advancement after 5 o'clock. Still, one can have a balanced and happy life coupled with a retailing career by using good time-management and planning skills.

Analytical Skills

The retail manager must be able to solve problems through numerical analysis of facts and data in order to plan, manage, and control. The retail manager is a problem solver on a day-to-day basis. An understanding of the past and present performance of the store, merchandise lines, and departments is necessary. It is the analysis of these performance data that forms the basis of future actions in the retailing environment. Today's retailer must be able to analyze all the financial data that are available before going to market. The new CEO of Sears Holding Co., Awlwin Lewis, spent three days a week visiting store managers and probing them on such data. Those that know the answers are called "commercial," meaning that

Service Retailing

Creativity and Success

Monday nights have always been a slow night for theaters. Whether it's a night of rest after a long weekend, a continuation of the malaise of going back to work or school, or the attraction of Monday Night Football in the fall, most folks don't want to go out on Monday night. Even when the large theater chains offered "Dollar Night" specials for Monday, attendance didn't increase.

A small theater in Pennsylvania used creativity to attract customers with a "Monday Night is Baby's Night" promotion. Here parents with infants can come in with their baby and watch a movie, at a nondiscounted price, with the knowledge that they are welcome and that their baby will not disturb others in attendance. After all, the others in the theater will be understanding. The only catch is that children over the age of one are not invited, since they want to walk around and tend to be more restless. Other customers may come to watch a movie, but they are warned ahead of time of the presence of the babies.

The theater has bottle warmers ready in the outer lobby and spare diapers, if needed. Since the movies don't start until 7:30 pm, most of the babies actually sleep during the show.

While Mondays are still slow, the theater attendance has doubled on those evenings with this creative promotion. It may prove to have a positive long-term effect as these new parents become accustomed to the idea of relaxing with a night out at the movies.

Expanding upon this idea, a small family-style restaurant in Illinois now offers DVD players to diners with small children. Instead of running around, throwing food, or having a temper tantrum, the kids can watch a cartoon. Thus, instead of being faced with the unhappy choice of going to a typical adult restaurant and risk having a "child problem" or being forced to stay home, parents can take their family to the "sports bar for kids" and everybody can enjoy themselves.

---

they have the sense of how to make money.[30] In addition, quantitative and qualitative analysis of customers, competitors, suppliers, and other constituencies often helps to identify emerging trends and innovations. Combined with current performance results and market knowledge, continual monitoring of these constituencies provides insight into past performance and alerts the retailer to new directions. Many retailers also get information from reading trade journals (such as *Stores*, *Women's Wear Daily*, *Progressive Grocer*, or *Chain Store Age*), discuss current happenings with their buying office, visit markets, and even talk to their competitors as a means to keep current.

Creativity

The ability to generate and recognize novel ideas and solutions is known as creativity. A retail manager cannot operate a store totally by a set of preprogrammed equations and formulas. Because the competitive environment is constantly changing, there is no standard recipe for retailing. Therefore, retail executives need to be idea people as well as analysts. After all, success in retailing is the result of sensitive, perceptive decisions that require imaginative and innovative techniques. Our Service Retailing box illustrates how small, independent service retailers can often use a creative idea to gain an advantage over their competition.

Decisiveness

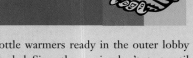

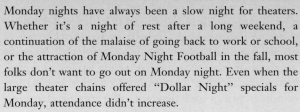

Decisiveness is the ability to make rapid decisions, and to render judgments, take action, and commit oneself to a course of action. A retail manager must be an action person. Better decisions could probably be made if more time were taken to make them. However, more time is frequently unavailable because variables such as fashion trends and consumer desires change quickly. Thus, a manager must make decisions quickly, confidently, and correctly in order to be successful even if perfect information is not always available. For example, buyers often make purchase decisions six months to a year before the merchandise arrives at the store.

Flexibility

The ability to adjust to the ever-changing needs of the situation calls for flexibility. The retail manager must have the willingness and enthusiasm to do whatever is necessary (although not necessarily planned) to get the job completed. Because plans must be altered quickly to accommodate changes in trends, styles, and attitudes, successful retail managers must be flexible. For example, changes in e-tailing occur continuously as retailers adjust prices and product offerings to changing consumer tastes and the competitive actions of other retailers.

Initiative

Retail managers are doers. They must have the ability to originate action rather than wait to be told what to do. This ability is called *initiative*. To be a success, the modern retail manager must monitor the numbers of the business (sales volumes, profits, inventory levels) and seize opportunities for action.

Leadership

Working in retailing is really working on a team. The ability to inspire team members to trust and respect your judgment and delegating, guiding, and persuading this team calls for leadership. Successfully conducting a retail operation means depending on the team to get the work done; in any large-scale retailing enterprise, one person cannot do it all. A manager succeeds when his or her subordinates do their jobs. The concept of the team approach is one of the most important hiring criteria for many retailers.

Organization

Another important quality for retailers is organization. This includes the ability to establish priorities and plans and follow through to achieve these results. Retail managers are often forced to deal with many issues, functions, and projects at the same time. To achieve goals, the successful retailer must be a good time manager and set priorities when organizing personnel and resources.

Risk Taking

Retail managers should be willing to take calculated risks based on thorough analysis and sound judgment; they should also be willing to accept responsibility for the results. Success in retailing often comes from taking calculated risks and having the confidence to try something new before someone else does. For example, no one can say that Jeff Bezos's decision to start Amazon and Sam Walton's decision to start Wal-Mart were not without risk. All successful buyers have at one time or another purchased merchandise that could be labeled as losers. After all, if buyers never made errors, that means they were afraid to take risks and probably passed up many winners. However, they must have the ability to recognize when they made a mistake.

Stress Tolerance

As the other prerequisites to retailing success suggest, retailing is a fast-paced and demanding career in a changing environment. The retailing leaders of the

21st century must be able to perform consistently under pressure and to thrive on constant change and challenge.

Perseverance

Because of the difficult challenges that a retail career presents, it is important to have perseverance. All too often retailers may become frustrated due to the many things they can't control. For example, a blizzard may occur just before Christmas and wipe out the most important shopping days of the year. Others may become exasperated with fellow employees; the long hours, especially the weekends; or the inability to satisfy some customers. The person who has the ability to persevere and take all of this in stride will find an increasing number of career advancement opportunities.

Enthusiasm

Successful retailers must have a strong feeling of warmth for their job; otherwise, they will convey the wrong image to their customers and department associates. Retailers today are training their sales force to smile even when talking to customers on the telephone, "because it shows through in your voice."[31] Without enthusiasm, success in any field will elude you.

Retail stores with managers who possess the twelve prerequisite characteristics of successful retail managers will be more profitable.

Dollars & Sense

The Study and Practice of Retailing

LO 5

Explain the different methods for the study and practice of retailing.

As we have seen, two of the prerequisites to success as a retail manager are analytical skills and creativity. These attributes also represent two methods for the study and practice of retailing.

Analytical Method

The analytical retail manager is a finder and investigator of facts. These facts are summarized and synthesized so a manager can make decisions systematically. In doing so, the manager uses models and theories of retail phenomena that enable him or her to structure all dimensions of retailing. An analytical perspective can result in a standardized set of procedures, success formulas, and guidelines.

Consider, for example, a manager operating a Starbucks shop where everything is preprogrammed, including the menu, decor, location, hours of operation, cleanliness standards, customer service policies, and advertising. This store manager needs only to gather and analyze facts to determine if the preestablished guidelines are being met and to take appropriate corrective action if necessary.

Creative Method

Conversely, the creative retail manager is an idea person. This retail manager tends to be a conceptualizer and has a very imaginative and fertile mind capable of creating a highly successful retail chain. A good example of this is Leslie Wexner, founder and chairman of The Limited. When everyone else (including his father) in the mid-1960s thought he was crazy for selling only a "limited" line of women's apparel focusing on 18- to 35-year-old professional career women, Wexner had a gut feeling he was right. Such a retailer uses insight, intuition, and implicit knowledge, rather than just facts. The result is usually a novel way to approach or solve a retail problem that reflects a deeper understanding of the market. Is it possible to operate a retail establishment, in most part, with just creativity? Yes. However, in the long run, creativity alone will not be adequate. Witness the problem of a slowdown in sales at the Body Shop, a retailer with a very creative pro-environment focus, as other firms, including The Limited, were able to copy its creative focus.[32] Analytical decision making must also be used so that a manager can profitably respond to unforeseen events in the environment.

A Two-Pronged Approach

As shown through the examples of our Starbucks manager and Leslie Wexner, retailing can indeed be practiced from both analytical and creative perspectives. The retailer who employs both approaches is most successful in the long run. Aren't stores like Starbucks successful using only the analytical method? No. The Starbucks manager can operate analytically quite successfully. However, behind the franchisee is a franchisor that is creative as well as analytical. On the creative side was the development of name and logo. On the analytical side was the development of standardized layouts, fixtures, equipment, and employee training. It is the combination of the creative with the analytical that has made Starbucks what it is today.

The synthesis of creativity and analysis is necessary in all fields of retailing. Roger Dickinson, a former retail executive and now a retailing professor, has stated that "many successful merchandisers are fast duplicators rather than originators."[33] To decide who or what to duplicate requires not only creativity but also an analysis of the strategies that retailers are pursuing. This is an exercise in weighing potential returns against risks. Dickinson further states that "creativity in retailing is for the sake of increasing the sales and profits of the firm."[34] If creativity is tied to sales and profits, then one cannot avoid analysis; profit and sales statistics require analysis.

Retailers can't do without either creativity or analytical skills. We will attempt to develop your skills in both of these areas. At the outset, however, you should note that the analytical and creative methods for studying retailing are not that different. Whether you use creativity or analytical skills, they will be directed at solving problems.

Dollars & Sense

Retailers that practice both analytical and creative management will be consistently more profitable.

A Proposed Orientation

The approach to the study and practice of retailing that is reflected in this book is an outgrowth of the previous discussion. This approach has four major orientations: (1) environmental, (2) management planning, (3) profit, and (4) decision making.

Retailers should have an environmental orientation, which will allow them to anticipate and adapt continuously to external forces in the environment. Retailing is not static. With social, legal, technological, economic, and other external forces always in flux, the modern retailer finds it necessary both to assess these changes from an analytical perspective and to respond with creative actions.

Retailers should have a planning orientation, which will help them to adapt systematically to a changing environment. A retailer who wants to have the

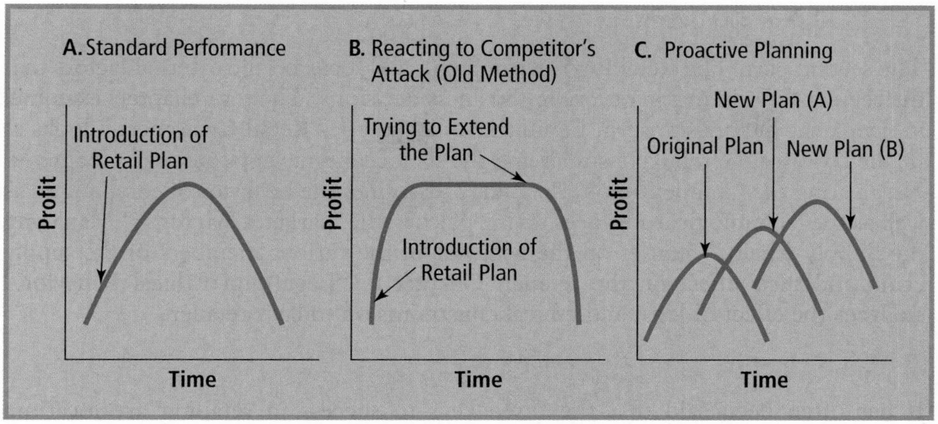

Exhibit 1.5
The Importance of Proactive Planning

competitive edge must plan today for the future. Exhibit 1.5 illustrates the problems facing a retailer that is reactive rather than proactive in its planning. Exhibit 1.5a shows the standard performance for a retailer's plan: The plan is introduced, sales peak as competitors react to the plan, and, finally, the plan becomes obsolete. Exhibit 1.5b shows the old method of reacting to a competitor's attack—the retailer tries to extend the sales peak by matching the competitor's plan until another competitor makes both of their plans obsolete. Exhibit 1.5c shows why this text places special emphasis on the development of creative retail strategies. Here the retailer is proactive and already has another plan ready before either the market changes or the competition attacks its original plan.

Retailers also need a profit orientation, since all retail decisions will have an effect on the firm's financial performance. The profit orientation will focus on fundamental management of assets, revenues, and expenses. Management tools that show how to evaluate the profit impact of retail decisions will be discussed.

Retailers should have a decision-making orientation, which will allow them to focus on the need to collect and analyze data to make intelligent retail decisions. To aid in this process, executives need a retail information system to help program their operations for desired results.

The Book Outline

This book is composed of 14 chapters, each with its own study guide and application section. The chapters are intended to reinforce each other. The end-of-chapter materials provide a way to bring the real world into your studies by launching you into the kinds of situations you might face as a retail manager. Through careful analysis of this material and discussion with fellow students, you will discover retailing concepts that can be vividly retained because of the concrete context. Furthermore, this material will require you to think of yourself as a retail decision maker who must sometimes make decisions with less than perfect information.

Introduction to Retailing

This book is divided into four parts. The first part, Introduction to Retailing, has two chapters. In Chapter 2, "Retail Strategic Planning and Operations Management," you will be exposed to the basic concepts of strategy, administration, and operations planning and management in retailing that will be used in the remaining chapters.

The Retailing Environment

The second part, The Retailing Environment, will focus on the external factors that the retailer faces in making everyday business decisions. The four chapters examine, in detail, the factors shown in Exhibit 1.1. Chapter 3, "Retail Customers," looks at the behavior of the retail consumer and the socioeconomic environment. Chapter 4, "Evaluating the Competition in Retailing," examines the behavior of competitors as well as the technological advances taking place in the market. Chapter 5, "Managing the Supply Chain," focuses on the behavior of the various members of the supply chain and their effect on the retailer. Chapter 6, "Legal and Ethical Behavior," analyzes the effect of legal and ethical constraints on today's retailer.

Market Selection and Location Analysis

It has often been said that the three keys to success in retailing are location, location, and location. In Chapter 7, "Market Selection and Retail Location Analysis," we discuss the various elements to consider in determining the feasibility of targeting a given market segment and entering a given retail market, and then we look at site selection.

Managing Retail Operations

In the fourth part, "Managing Retail Operations," we discuss the merchandising operations of a retail firm. This part deals with the day-to-day decisions facing retailers. Chapter 8, "Managing a Retailer's Finances," discusses various financial statements, the key methods of valuing inventory, and the development of merchandise planning budgets by retailers. Chapter 9, "Merchandise Buying and Handling," looks at how a retailer determines what to buy for its market and how these purchases are made. The appendix following Chapter 9 discusses the merchandising of apparel goods. Chapter 10, "Retail Pricing," discusses the importance to the retailer of setting the correct price. In addition to the various markup methods used by retailers, the chapter also looks at markdowns. Chapter 11, "Advertising and Promotion," provides a complete discussion (with the exception of personal selling, which is covered along with services offered by retailers in Chapter 12, "Customer Services and Retail Selling") of how a retailer can and should promote itself. Chapter 13, "Store Layout and Design," discusses the impact of proper layout and design on retail performance. Chapter 14, "Managing People," examines the role of the two most important groups of people (customers and employees) in the success of a retail firm.

The text concludes with a glossary of all major terms used in this text and an index of the retailers mentioned.

STUDENT STUDY GUIDE

SUMMARY

This chapter seeks to acquaint the reader with the nature and scope of retailing by discussing its impact on the economy, the types of retailers, and its prerequisites for success.

LO 1 **What is retailing?**

Retailing consists of the final activities and steps needed to place a product in the hands of the ultimate consumer or to provide services to the consumer.

LO 2 **Why is retailing always undergoing so much change?**

Retailing is not staid and stable; rather, it is an exciting business sector that effectively combines an individual's skills to make a profit in an ever-changing market environment. That is why some retailers are successful and others, who are either unwilling or unable to adapt to this changing environment, fail.

What are the various methods used to categorize retailers? LO 3

Retailers can be classified in a variety of ways. Five of the more popular schemes are by NAICS code, number of outlets, margins versus turnover, location, and size. None, however, sheds adequate light on competition in retailing.

What is involved in a retailing career? LO 4

In the long run, a retailing career can offer salary comparable to other careers, definite career advancement, and geographic mobility. In addition, a career in retailing incorporates the knowledge and use of all the business activities or disciplines (accounting, marketing, finance, personnel, economics, and even fashion). In retailing no two days are alike; each offers its own set of opportunities and problems. The prerequisites for success in retailing besides hard work include analytical skills, creativity, decisiveness, flexibility, initiative, leadership, organization, risk taking, stress tolerance, perseverance, and enthusiasm. These are all important, but it is especially vital for the retail manager to develop an attitude of openness to new ideas and a willingness to learn. After all, the market is always changing.

What are the different methods for the study and practice of retailing? LO 5

To be successful in retailing, an individual must use both analytical and creative methods of operation. The four orientations to the study and practice of retailing proposed in this text are an environmental orientation, which allows the retailer to focus on the continuously changing external forces affecting retailing; a planning orientation, which helps the retailer to adapt systematically to this changing environment; a profit orientation, which enables the retailer to examine the profit implications of any decision; and a decision-making orientation, which allows the retailer to focus on the need to collect and analyze data for making intelligent creative retail decisions.

TERMS TO REMEMBER

retailing
same-store sales
market share
scrambled merchandising
category killer
standard stock list
optional stock list
channel advisor or **channel captain**
private label branding
bricks-and-mortar retailers
gross margin percentage
gross margin
operating expenses
inventory turnover
high-performance retailers
low-margin/low-turnover
low-margin/high-turnover
high-margin/low-turnover
clicks-and-mortar retailers
high-margin/high-turnover
store management
buying

REVIEW AND DISCUSSION QUESTIONS

What is retailing? LO 1

1. Why is retailing so important to society? Can a nation be prosperous without a well-managed retail system?

STUDENT STUDY GUIDE

LO 2 **Why is retailing always undergoing so much change?**

2. Retailing is often said to be a stable and unchanging sector of the economy since a Subway, Dollar General, or Starbucks seldom change their layout or merchandise categories once they enter a market area. Agree or disagree and defend your answer.
3. Many environmental trends are taking place today that will have an effect on retailing operations over the next decade. Discuss three of these and their effects on retailing.
4. Currently, there is a great deal of debate about the future impact of the Internet on retailing. Which of the following items—a vacation package for spring break, a wedding gift for a friend, a pair of jeans for yourself, or an end table for your apartment—would you be least apt to purchase online? Why?

LO 3 **Describe the five methods used to categorize retailers.**

5. How can a retailer operate with a high-margin/high-turnover strategy? Won't customers avoid this type of store and shop at a low-margin store?
6. Agree or disagree with the following statement and explain your reasoning: "Only locally owned retailers, and not large chains, can tailor their merchandise to the needs of their target markets."

LO 4 **What is involved in a retailing career?**

7. Based on what you read in this chapter, who is a "right fit" for a retailing career? What does career growth look like, and is short-term compensation more important than long-term compensation? Finally, what does it take to succeed in retailing?
8. Is a retail career more about fashion, business, marketing, or consumer behavior? Or something else? What kind of leadership skills does it take to be successful in retailing?

LO 5 **Explain the different methods for the study and practice of retailing.**

9. Jim McCann is often given credit for using his analytical skills to make 800-FLOWERS one of the most successful service e-tailers. McCann was not the individual who started the company. McCann purchased the company from the individual who had the creative idea of having one easy-to-remember phone number, as opposed to having to look up a local FTD florist's number. However, before McCann's buyout, 800-FLOWERS had too small an advertising budget, too many managers, and too large a telemarketing center.

   Does this mean that analytical skills are more important than creative skills for success in retailing? Defend your answer.
10. Visit a local retailer whom you would describe as creative and seek to determine which analytical skills that retailer also possesses.

SAMPLE TEST QUESTIONS

LO 1 **Which of the following statements about retailing is false?**

a. The nations that have enjoyed the greatest economic and social progress have been those with a strong retail sector.
b. Retailing can make a significant contribution to a country's economic prosperity.

c. The development of a retailing sector is the key reason for the economic growth being experienced by the Eastern European countries today.
d. The major retailing problem facing Europe's former Soviet bloc nations is to reduce the huge size of their current stores to match the limited selection available.
e. Retailing consists of the final activities and steps needed to place a product in the hands of the consumer or to provide services to the consumer.

The majority of the 1.1 million retail establishments in the United States are ______ and have actual annual sales of ______. LO 2

a. small, under $750,000
b. large, over $1.5 million
c. medium in size, over $750,000
d. very small, under $150,000
e. extremely large, over $23.0 million

The best way to categorize retailers is by the: LO 3

a. U.S. Bureau of Census three-digit North American Industrial Classification Systems (NAICS).
b. store locations used by the retailer.
c. number of outlets the retailer maintains.
d. retailers' gross margin rate and turnover rate for the past year.
e. There is no single "best" acceptable method of classifying retail competitors.

Due to increased corporate responsibilities, the manager of a bike shop has asked the assistant manager to take responsibility for screening and hiring new sales associates. The manager is allowing the assistant to make the decisions independently but has scheduled weekly meetings for the two to discuss any issues of concern and to provide insight, if needed. The manager is demonstrating which desirable retailing attribute? LO 4

a. Prioritizing
b. Leadership
c. Creativity
d. Laziness
e. Enthusiasm

In attempting to determine if a branch of a sandwich shop should be opened in a small town outside the original trading area, a retailer gathered information on demographics, competitors sales, and available real estate in that area. The retailer was employing the ________ method of retail decision making. LO 5

a. tactical
b. strategic
c. analytical
d. creative
e. intuitive

WRITING AND SPEAKING EXERCISE

Halfway between your apartment and the campus is a small convenience store where you regularly purchase a cup of coffee to get you ready for those early morning classes. Over the last two years, you have become friends with the owner. Late last night, when you filled up your gas tank, you noticed that he was still there working on his books. While visiting with you, he stated that the store has been profitable, but he feels it could do better if he could lower the high rate of employee turnover. He asks you for advice on this problem.

Prepare a short presentation for the owner listing what you think he should look for in hiring part-time employees. Also, list what employee traits he should seek to avoid.

RETAIL PROJECT

How would you use the Internet to purchase your next car? Using the search engine on either your own computer or one at school, select two or three different auto Web sites. List their address, such as http://www.autobytel.com, and make a report describing what they have on their Web site. Which one do you like best? Why? Can you purchase online from each Web site? What is the buying process? Can competitors gain anything from looking at these Web sites? Finally, what is missing from these Web sites that you feel should be on them?

PLANNING YOUR OWN RETAIL BUSINESS

If you think you might want to be a retail entrepreneur, you can use the "Planning Your Own Retail Business" computer exercises at the end of each chapter to assist you in this process. In addition, this text's Web site (www.thomsonedu.com/ . . .) has an exercise called "The House: Understanding A Retail Enterprise Using Spreadsheet Analysis," which can be used to help you understand the dollars and cents of retailing.

This first exercise is intended to acquaint you with how sensitive your retail business will be to changes in sales volume. Let's assume that you plan that your retail business will generate $350,000 per year in annual sales and that it will operate on a gross margin percentage of 40 percent. If your fixed operating expenses are $80,000 annually and variable operating costs are 10 percent of sales, how much profit will you make? {*Hint*: Sales × Gross margin percentage = Gross margin; Gross margin − Fixed operating expenses − Sales × Variable operating expenses as a % of sales = Net profit} Use a spreadsheet program on your computer to compute your firm's net profits; next, analyze what happens if sales drop 10 percent and if sales rise 10 percent. Why are bottom line results (net profits) so sensitive to changes in sales volume?

chapter 2

Retail Strategic Planning and Operations Management

Overview:

In this chapter, we will explain the importance of planning in successful retail organizations. To facilitate the discussion, we introduce a retail planning and management model, which will serve as a frame of reference for the remainder of the text. This simple model illustrates the importance of both strategic planning and operations management. These two activities, if properly conducted, will enable a retail firm to achieve results exceeding those of the competition.

Learning Objectives:

After reading this chapter, you should be able to:

1. Explain why strategic planning is so important and be able to describe the components of strategic planning: statement of mission; goals and objectives; an analysis of strengths, weaknesses, opportunities, and threats; and strategy.
2. Describe the text's retail strategic planning and operation management model, which explains the two tasks that a retailer must perform and how they lead to high profit.

Components of Strategic Planning

LO 1

Explain why strategic planning is so important and describe its components.

In most endeavors, a well-defined plan of action can mean the difference between success and failure. For example, a traveler does not go from Fargo to Kansas City without a well-defined plan of which highways to use. Political candidates and their advisors develop a campaign plan long before the election. Successful college students plan their assignments so that they are not forced to pull an all-nighter just before an assignment is due. Similarly, a clearly defined plan of action is an essential ingredient in all forms of business management. This is especially true in the highly competitive field of retailing, where in the past decade the number of stores has expanded faster than consumer demand.

planning
Is the anticipation and organization of what needs to be done to reach an objective.

Planning is the anticipation and organization of what needs to be done to reach an objective. This sounds simple enough, but as any retail buyer will tell you, it is difficult to know in advance of each upcoming season what styles, quantities, colors, and sizes the customers will want. Superior planning by retailers enables them to offset some of the advantages their competition may have, such as a good location. People not familiar with retailing often wonder how retailers can anticipate what consumers are going to want next season. In reality, success for all retailers, large and small, is generally a matter of good planning and then implementing that plan. For example, years ago the management of Lowe's made the key decision that has defined retailers ever since. After arguing for months about what direction to take the home-improvement chain, they decided to become "our customers' first choice for home improvement in each and every market we serve." Lowe's shifted from opening small stores in small markets to building mega-outlets with brighter lights and wider aisles. And they targeted female customers—important because women make 80 percent of home improvement purchase decisions.[1]

Failure to develop good plans can spell disaster for a retailer. Remember all those "low-carb" items in restaurants during the Atkins Diet craze a couple of years ago? Consider, also, what proved to be a major planning error by Gap Inc. A few years back, the retailer suffered a downturn in sales due in part to having the wrong merchandise mix in its stores and an overlap between its three main divisions—The Gap, Old Navy, and Banana Republic. Without a clear definition of what each store should be, customers headed for low-price Old Navy. Today, there is a clear distinction between the three, as The Gap has returned to basics such as cropped pants, jeans, and khakis and Banana Republic has moved away from basics and towards more fashion-forward merchandise. In addition, Gap has recently added a fourth chain—Forth & Towne—aimed at women age 35 and older, a segment with more money and fewer inhibitions about spending it.[2]

Consider, also, what proved to be a different type of planning error by Barnes & Noble and its Web site—http://www.barnesandnoble.com. The chain made the decision not to integrate the Web site with its stores. Thus, at each of the company's typical bricks-and-mortar stores, there was very little mention of the chain's online alternative. Bricks-and-click integration (using both physical stores and online

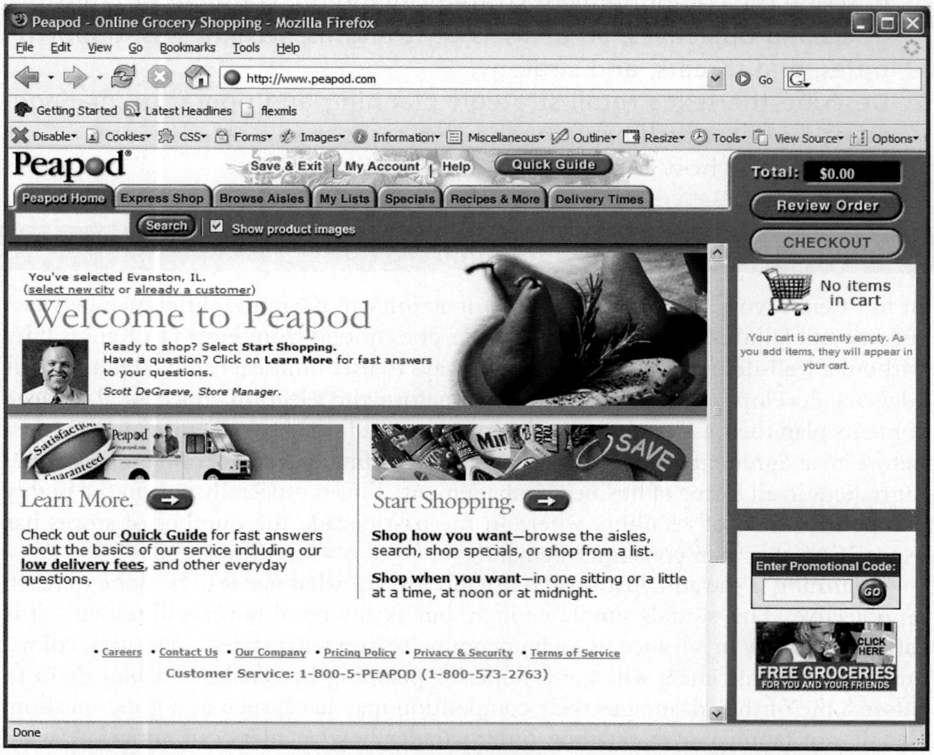

Peapod, LLC., www.peapod.com

Traditional grocery retailers, recognizing the competitive threat of on-line retailers such as Peapod, have responded by launching their own on-line stores.

sales operations) comes at a cost. Cannibalizing their established businesses with the introduction of an e-tailing operation is a risk for large retailers. Barnes & Noble may have had five or six million customers online, but it had tens of millions walking through its stores. Why promote a Web site that offered heavy discounts and, at that point in time, charged no sales tax to consumers who were willing to pay full price? The answer was that if they didn't, many of their customers would eventually switch to Amazon's Web site. This is why Albertson's, Kroger, and Safeway have entered the online grocery battle, even though online grocers account for less than one-half percent of total grocery sales.[3] They didn't want to lose any customers to their rivals (namely, Internet grocers such as Peapod.com and Freshdirect.com) and believed that, while some of their store customers might shift some purchases to their online locations, they would probably increase their total purchases. Instead of just purchasing $400 a month from an Albertson's store, these customers might now purchase $500, $360 in the store and $140 over the Internet.[4] Little wonder that many existing bricks & mortar retailers are developing plans that seek to translate their brand strength to their online venture by vigorously cross-promoting the two ventures, even if that means cannibalizing their existing in-store sales. If they don't pursue this strategy, they risk becoming "forgotten retailers of another era."

Strategic planning involves adapting the resources of the firm to the opportunities and threats of an ever-changing retail environment. Through the proper use of strategic planning, retailers achieve and maintain a balance between resources available and opportunities. Let's take a closer look at the components of the strategic planning process.

strategic planning
Involves adapting the resources of the firm to the opportunities and threats of an ever-changing retail environment.

Strategic planning consists of four components:

1. Development of a mission (or purpose) statement for the firm
2. Definition of specific goals and objectives for the firm
3. An identification and analysis of the retailer's strengths, weaknesses, opportunities, and threats—referred to as SWOT analysis
4. Development of basic strategies that will enable the firm to reach its objectives and fulfill its mission

Mission Statement

The beginning of a retailer's strategic planning process is the formulation of a mission statement. The **mission statement** is a basic description of the fundamental nature, rationale, and direction of the firm. It provides the employees and customers with an understanding of where future growth for the firm is coming from. Not every retailer has a mission statement. In fact, less than 60 percent of all businesses have written mission statements. Because so many businesses don't know where they want to go and how to get there, they end up failing. The lack of a written statement, however, is not itself a cause for failure if the firm has a clearly understood, even if unwritten, plan of action. For example, Wal-Mart doesn't have a written mission statement. Wal-Mart does, however, have a clearly defined sense of direction, which Sam Walton based on Marshall Field's directive to "give the lady what she wants."[5]

mission statement
Is a basic description of the fundamental nature, rationale, and direction of the firm.

While mission statements vary from retailer to retailer, good ones usually include three elements:

1. How the retailer uses or intends to use its resources
2. How it expects to relate to the ever-changing environment

3. The kinds of values it intends to provide in order to serve the needs and wants of the consumer

Consider the mission statement that was developed by Record World, a northeastern chain with more than 100 outlets.

> Record World is in business to provide prerecorded entertainment in all modes desired by consumers. Our target market consists of all viable segments of the population shopping in locations, primarily malls, where our stores are situated in the northeast and mideast regions of the United States. In addition to a broad assortment of merchandise, we strive to provide our customers with both value and personal service. In the long-run, we will have the dominant market share in all the market segments we serve. We endeavor to double our sales in the next five years, primarily through improved market and merchandise development and secondarily through market penetration.[6]

As the above illustration points out, a mission statement really answers the question: What business should the retailer be in? Record World has used its mission statement not to be a record store leader but to be a "value-oriented" retailer of all prerecorded entertainment. The preceding mission statement illustrates how Record World overcame one of the major shortcomings of most retailers' mission statements—defining one's business too narrowly (i.e., being in the record business and not in prerecorded entertainment). A critical issue in defining a retail business is to do it at the most meaningful level of generalization. This is why most mission statements should be general, yet still provide direction, as well as be motivational. Borders, for example, has the following mission:

> to be the best-loved provider of books, music, video, and other entertainment and informational products and services. To be the world leader in selection, service, innovation, ambiance, community involvement, and shareholder value. We recognize people to be the cornerstone of the Borders experience by building internal and external relationships, one person at a time.[7]

As its mission statement implies, Borders did not see itself selling books over the Internet. Therefore, rather than build a separate dot-com business that saps profits, Borders took a more modest approach. That's because Borders believed that online book sales would not capture more than 10 percent of the book market worldwide.[8] Convinced that the opportunities were better in the bricks & mortar world, Borders sought to develop its flagship chain by positioning its Web site as a way to enhance the retail experience and build brand loyalty by offering access to borders.com within its superstores. Borders' own research showed that 80 percent of its customers were already buying online, so management figured it would be wasteful to spend money going after the already established separate online businesses.

Dollars & Sense

Retailers who do a better job of planning than their competition can overcome some of the competition's natural advantages.

As a further example of what makes a good mission statement and what doesn't, consider how a poor mission statement can be improved. The Avon Theater, which was located in downstate Illinois near the author's hometown, claimed it was "in the movie business and would show only PG13 movies at the lowest prices in our trading area." Maybe if they had used a better statement, such as "We are in the entertainment business and we shall seek to show the movies that customers want at prices that reflect the market's price sensitivity," they might still be in business.

As our bookstore examples show, just having a mission statement is not enough in today's business climate. Likewise, the retailer must adhere to its mission and not change with every new fad.

Retailers that have broad missions that motivate employees and focus on customers yet still provide direction will have higher profit performance.

Dollars & Sense

Statement of Goals and Objectives

The second step in the strategic planning process is to define specific **goals and objectives**. These goals and objectives should be derived from, and give precision and direction to, the retailer's mission statement. Goals and objectives should identify the performance results that the retailer intends to bring about through the execution of its major strategies. Goals and objectives serve two purposes. First, they provide specific direction and guidance to the firm in the formulation of its strategy. Second, they provide a control mechanism by establishing a standard against which the firm can measure and evaluate its performance. If the results are less than expected, then it signals that corrective actions need to be taken.

goals and objectives
Are the performance results intended to be brought about through the execution of a strategy.

While these goals and objectives can be expressed in many different ways, retailers will usually divide them into two dimensions: **market performance**, which compares a firm's actions to its competitor's, and **financial performance**, which analyzes the firm's ability to provide a profit level adequate to continue in business. In addition to the market performance and financial performance objectives, some retailers may also establish *societal objectives*, which are phrased in terms of helping society fulfill some of its needs, and *personal objectives*, which relate to helping people employed in retailing fulfill some of their needs.

market performance
Represents how a retailer desires to be compared to its competitors.

financial performance
Represents the profit and economic performance a retailer desires.

Let us examine each type of these goals and objectives in more detail.

Market Performance Objectives

Market performance objectives establish the amount of dominance the retailer has in the marketplace. The most popular measures of market performance in retailing are sales volume and **market share** (retailer's total sales divided by total market sales or the proportion of total sales in a particular geographic and/or product market that the retailer has been able to capture).

market share
Is the retailer's total sales divided by total market sales.

Research has shown that profitability is clearly and positively related to market share.[9] Thus, market performance objectives are not pursued for their own sake but because they are a key profit path.

As retailers increase their market share, their financial performance will also increase in comparison to their competitors.

Dollars & Sense

Financial Objectives

Retailers can establish many financial objectives, but they can all be conveniently fit into categories of profitability and productivity.

Profitability Objectives Profit-based objectives deal directly with the monetary return a retailer desires from its business. When retailers speak of "making a profit," the definition of profit is often unclear. The most common way to define profit is the aggregate total of net profit after taxes, i.e., the bottom line of the income statement. Another common retail method of expressing profit is as a percentage of net sales. However, most retail owners feel the best way to define profit is in terms of return on investment (ROI).[10]

This method of reporting profits as a percentage of investments is complicated by the fact that there are two different ways to define the term *investment*. Return on assets (ROA) reflects all the capital used in the business, whether provided by the owners or by creditors. Return on investment (ROI), also referred to as return on net worth (RONW), reflects only the amount of capital that the owners have invested in the business.

The most frequently encountered profit objectives for a retailer are shown in Exhibit 2.1—the Strategic Profit Model (SPM). The elements of the SPM start at the far left and move right. These five elements include:

net profit margin
Is the ratio of net profit (after taxes) to total sales and shows how much profit a retailer makes on each dollar of sales after all expenses and taxes have been met.

1. **Net profit margin** is the ratio of net profit (after taxes) to net sales, and shows how much profit a retailer makes on each dollar of sales after all expenses and taxes have been met. For example, if a retailer is operating on a net profit margin of 2 percent, it is making two cents on each dollar of sales. In general, retailers operate on lower net profit margins than manufacturers. The net profit margin ratio is derived exclusively from income or operating statement data and does not include any measures from the retailer's balance sheet. Thus, it does not show how effectively a retailer is using the capital at its disposal.

asset turnover
Is total sales divided by total assets and shows how many dollars of sales a retailer can generate on an annual basis with each dollar invested in assets.

2. **Asset turnover** is computed by taking the retailer's annual net sales and dividing by total assets. This ratio tells the retail analyst how productively the firm's assets are being utilized. Put another way, it shows how many dollars of sales a retailer can generate on an annual basis with each dollar invested in assets. Thus, if a retailer's asset turnover rate is 3.0, it is annually generating $3 in sales for each $1 in assets. The asset turnover ratio incorporates key measures from the income statement (sales) and the balance sheet (assets) and, as such, shows how well the retailer is utilizing its capital to generate sales. In

Exhibit 2.1
Strategic Profit Model

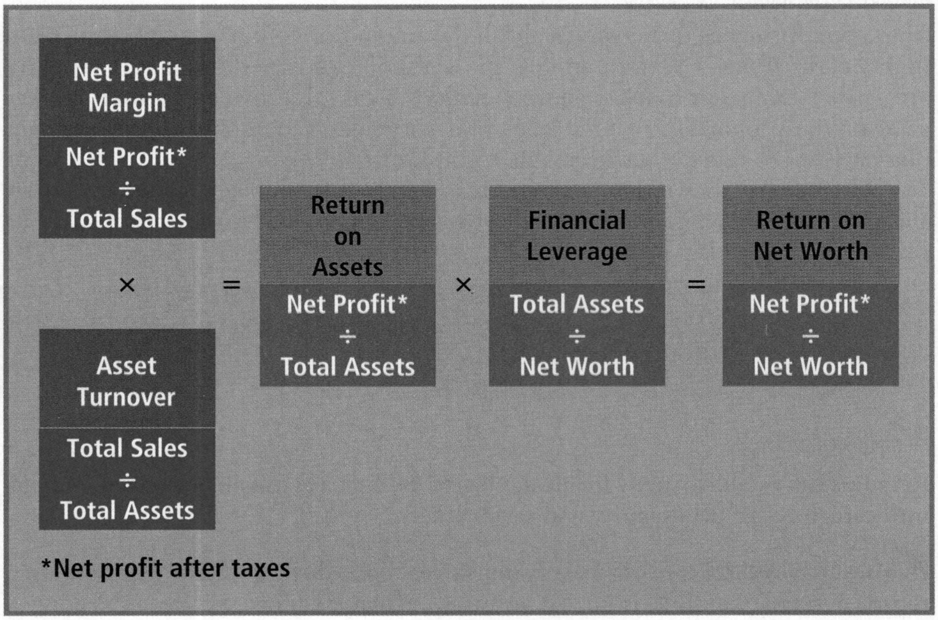

general, retailers experience higher rates of asset turnover but lower net profit margins than do manufacturers.

3. **Return on assets (ROA)** is annual net profit divided by total assets. It depicts the net profit return that the retailer achieved on all assets invested, regardless of whether the assets were financed by creditors or by the firm's owners. As shown in Exhibit 2.1, ROA is the result of multiplying the net profit margin by asset turnover. For example, a retailer with a net profit margin of 2 percent and an asset turnover of 4.0 would have a ROA of 8 percent (2 percent times 4 equals 8 percent).

return on assets (ROA)
Is net profit (after taxes) divided by total assets.

4. **Financial leverage** is total assets divided by net worth or owners' equity. This ratio shows the extent to which a retailer is utilizing debt in its total capital structure. The low end of this ratio is 1.0 times and depicts a situation in which the retailer is using no debt in its capital structure. As the ratio moves beyond 1.0, the firm is using a heavier mix of debt versus equity. For example, when the ratio is 2.0 times, the firm has two dollars in assets for every dollar in net worth, which is equivalent to a mix of 50 percent debt.

financial leverage
Is total assets divided by net worth or owners' equity and shows how aggressive the retailer is in its use of debt.

5. **Return on net worth (RONW)** is net profit divided by net worth or owner's equity. Return on net worth, shown at the far right of the SPM, is usually used to measure owner's performance. Note that, as shown in Exhibit 2.1, the ROA multiplied by financial leverage yields RONW. Thus, if a retailer has a ROA of 8 percent and a financial leverage of 2.0, then its RONW would be 16 percent (8 percent times 2.0 equals 16 percent).

return on net worth (RONW)
Is net profit (after taxes) divided by owners' equity.

The important point to remember from this discussion of profitability is that department or specialty stores, which have higher gross margin (net sales minus cost of goods sold) and lower asset turnover rates, compete differently than discounters, which generally have lower gross margins but higher asset turnover. For discounters, this results in less inventory per dollar of sales and a need for fewer capital assets outside of inventory. Discounters expect to gain a higher asset turnover by reducing their gross margins, and specialty stores expect a lower asset turnover rate with their higher gross margins.

Remember that attempts to increase asset turnover by merely reducing inventory levels can have serious consequences for a retailer. These lower inventory levels may produce higher turnover rates, but they can also lead to stockouts (where products are not available for customers), thus creating a dissatisfied customer who may never return.

Managers are usually evaluated on return on assets, since financial leverage is beyond their control. In addition to the five elements of the SPM, another measure of profitability is the **gross margin percentage**, which is gross margin divided by net sales.

All retailers establish some form of profit objective. The specific profit objectives developed will play an important role in evaluating potential strategic opportunities.

gross margin percentage
A measure of profitability derived by dividing gross margin by net sales.

Productivity Objectives **Productivity objectives** state how much output the retailer desires for each unit of resource input. The major resources at the retailer's disposal are space, labor, and merchandise; productivity objectives for each may be established.

productivity objectives
State the sales objectives that the retailer desires for each unit of resource input: floor space, labor, and inventory investment.

1. *Space productivity*. Space productivity is defined as net sales divided by the total square feet of retail floor space. (In this discussion, whenever we refer to net sales we are talking about annual net sales.) A space productivity objective states how many dollars in sales the retailer wants to generate for each square foot of store space. Even service retailers have a space utilization problem. The chapter's Service Retailing box describes how service retailers are using yield management tools to improve their space productivity.

Service Retailing

Yield Management Tools: Service Retailers' Newest Weapon

Most college students, at one time or another, have experienced a situation where they were flying somewhere and found that the person sitting next to them paid a higher price for the same type of ticket. This surprising experience may have also happened at a hotel, or even on a golf course. Such differentiated pricing is the result of a move towards yield management by service retailers. First introduced in the late 1980s when the airlines started using sophisticated computer programs to balance supply with demand, **yield management** is understanding, anticipating, and reacting to changing customer needs in order to maximize the revenue from a fixed capacity of available services. In the airlines' case, this fixed capacity was seats on the plane. In the case of hotels, the number of rooms is fixed; and for a golf course, it is available tee times.

Yield management strategy is rather simple. Airlines, for example, use it to maximize their **rasm** (**R**evenue per **A**vailable **S**eat **M**ile). The key is optimizing the revenue by balancing sales of the expensive seats, rooms, or tee times with the cheap ones. Your college probably uses such a system for its sporting events, by trying to find the tradeoff between selling discount tickets in order to fill up the arena and selling expensive tickets at midcourt but only filling up a portion of the arena. At the same time, retailers don't want to unduly offend anyone. Since this process involves understanding target customers and analyzing prior purchases, it can be very challenging, yet exciting.

Yield management works best in markets with five characteristics: (1) low marginal costs, (2) fixed capacity, (3) perishable product, (4) fluctuating demand, and (5) different market segments. These are the same five characteristics facing many service retailers. Let's briefly examine each of these characteristics and see how they relate to someone selling a service.

Low Marginal Cost: Service retailers have a low marginal cost, where the cost of selling one more unit doesn't significantly impact total costs, thus making them want to maximize revenue. Therefore, hotel managers, with a low additional cost of cleaning a room, and airlines, which may burn a little extra fuel to carry the additional passenger, will use yield management to "max out" revenue.

Fixed Capacity: If, for example, hotels could add or remove rooms, there would be no reason to try to manage capacity. However, since hotels can't add or subtract rooms on a daily basis to meet demand, they can either max out revenue on their existing rooms or lose revenue by pricing a room too inexpensively, perhaps at $70 when they could have obtained $85 or too expensively, perhaps at $95 when the room goes vacant but could have been sold at $79.

Perishable Product: If, for example, a golf course can't sell all its available tee times one day, the unused inventory can't be stored away for another day. It is lost. Yield management seeks to minimize unused inventory by determining course usage based on prior history so as to maximize revenue.

Fluctuating Demand: All service retailers have peak seasons and slow seasons that may involve months of the year, days of the week, or hours in a day. Airlines, for example, increase their revenues by increasing ticket prices over the summer and lowering prices in slow periods, and by adjusting prices according to the time of the day the flight departs and arrives.

Different Market Segments: To be effective, yield management must be able to segment the market into different segments that can't cross sell to each other. Your college, for example, doesn't want students reselling their athletic tickets to nonstudents. Keeping this in mind, service providers seek a tradeoff between maximum load factor and highest paying customer (big donors) and price-conscious customer (students). One is willing to pay a higher price for seats on the 50-yard line, while the others will settle for cheap end zone seats. Such a strategy allows colleges to fill seats that would otherwise be empty.

Someday soon your college may be using yield management with tuition fees.

---

yield management
The understanding, anticipating, and reacting to changing customer needs in order to maximize the revenue from a fixed capacity of available services.

2. *Labor productivity.* Labor productivity is defined as net sales divided by the number of full-time-equivalent employees. A full-time-equivalent employee is one who works 40 hours per week; typically two part-time workers equal one full-time employee. A labor productivity objective reflects how many dollars in sales the retailer desires to generate for each full-time-equivalent employee.

© James Shaffer/PhotoEdit

Employing the disabled can allow retailers to often meet both labor productivity and societal objectives.

3. *Merchandise productivity.* Merchandise productivity is net sales divided by the average dollar investment in inventory. This measure is also known as the *sales-to-stock ratio*. Specifically, this objective states the dollar sales the retailer desires to generate for each dollar invested in inventory.

rasm
The revenue per available seat mile calculation used by airlines.

Productivity objectives are vehicles by which a retailer can program its business for high profit results. For instance, it would be impossible for a supermarket chain to achieve a respectable return on assets while experiencing dismal space (sales per square foot), labor (sales per full-time employee), and merchandise productivity (sales per inventory dollars). In short, productivity is a key determinant of profit in retailing.

Societal Objectives

While generally not as specific or as quantitative as market and financial objectives, **societal objectives** highlight the retailer's concern with broader issues in our society. The five most frequently cited societal objectives are:

societal objectives
Are those that reflect the retailer's desire to help society fulfill some of its needs.

1. *Employment objectives.* Employment objectives relate to the provision of employment opportunities for the members of the retailer's community. Many times they are more specific, relating to hiring people with disabilities, social minorities, or students.
2. *Payment of taxes.* Paying taxes is the retailer's role in helping finance societal needs, from welfare programs to national parks, that the government deems appropriate.
3. *Consumer choice.* A retailer may have as an objective to compete in a way that gives the consumer a real alternative. A retailer with such an objective desires to be a leader and innovator in merchandising, and thus provide the consumer with choices that previously were not available in the trade area.
4. *Equity.* An equity objective reflects the retailer's desire to treat the consumer and suppliers fairly. The retailer will not price-gouge the consumer in case of

merchandise shortages. Consumer complaints will be handled quickly, fairly, and equitably. The retailer will inform the consumer, to the extent possible, of the strengths and weaknesses of its merchandise. Consider what Dunkin' Donuts is doing to treat its suppliers fairly. The chain offers only Fair Trade Certified coffee, which guarantees that coffee growers and their workers receive a fair price for their product.[11]

5. *Benefactor.* The retailer may desire to underwrite certain community activities. For example, many department store retailers make meeting rooms available for civic groups to use for meetings. Other retailers help underwrite various performing arts, either with cash donations or by hosting social events that, in turn, help draw customers to their stores. Local supermarkets often sponsor food drives at Thanksgiving and Christmas to aid the needy. Nationally, Target and Wal-Mart each contribute over $100 million annually to various causes.[12]

Personal Objectives

personal objectives
Are those that reflect the retailers' desire to help individuals employed in retailing fulfill some of their needs.

The final set of objectives that retailers may establish is personal. **Personal objectives** can relate to the personal goals of any of the employees, managers, or owners of the retail establishment. Generally retailers tend to pursue three types of personal objectives.

1. *Self-gratification.* Self-gratification has as its focus the needs and desires of the owners, managers, or employees of the firm to pursue what they truly want out of life. For example, individuals may have opened up a sporting goods store because they enjoy being around athletically oriented people. These individuals may also be avid amateur golfers, and by operating a sporting goods store they are able to combine work with pleasure. Basically, these individuals are experiencing and living the life they really want.
2. *Status and respect.* All people strive for status and respect. In stating this objective, one recognizes that the owners, managers, and employees need status and respect in their community or within their circle of friends. Recognizing this need, the retailer may, for example, give annual awards to outstanding employees. Not only are Starbucks' employees called "partners," but also the CEO spends hours each week calling store managers to applaud good work.[13]
3. *Power and authority.* Objectives based on power and authority reflect the need of managers and other employees to be in positions of influence. Retailers may establish objectives that give buyers and department managers maximum flexibility to determine their own destiny. They are trusted with the power and authority to allocate scarce resources such as space, dollars, and labor to achieve a profit objective. Many retailers, realizing the importance of keeping customers happy, have empowered their frontline employees with the authority to "make things right" for unhappy customers. Having the power and authority to allocate resources and taking care of customers makes employees feel important and gives them a sense of pride when they excel at making things right.

Exhibit 2.2 is a synopsis of the market performance, financial performance, societal, and personal objectives that retailers can establish in the strategic planning process. This exhibit clearly reveals that all retail objectives, of whatever type, must be consistent with and reinforce the retailer's overall mission.

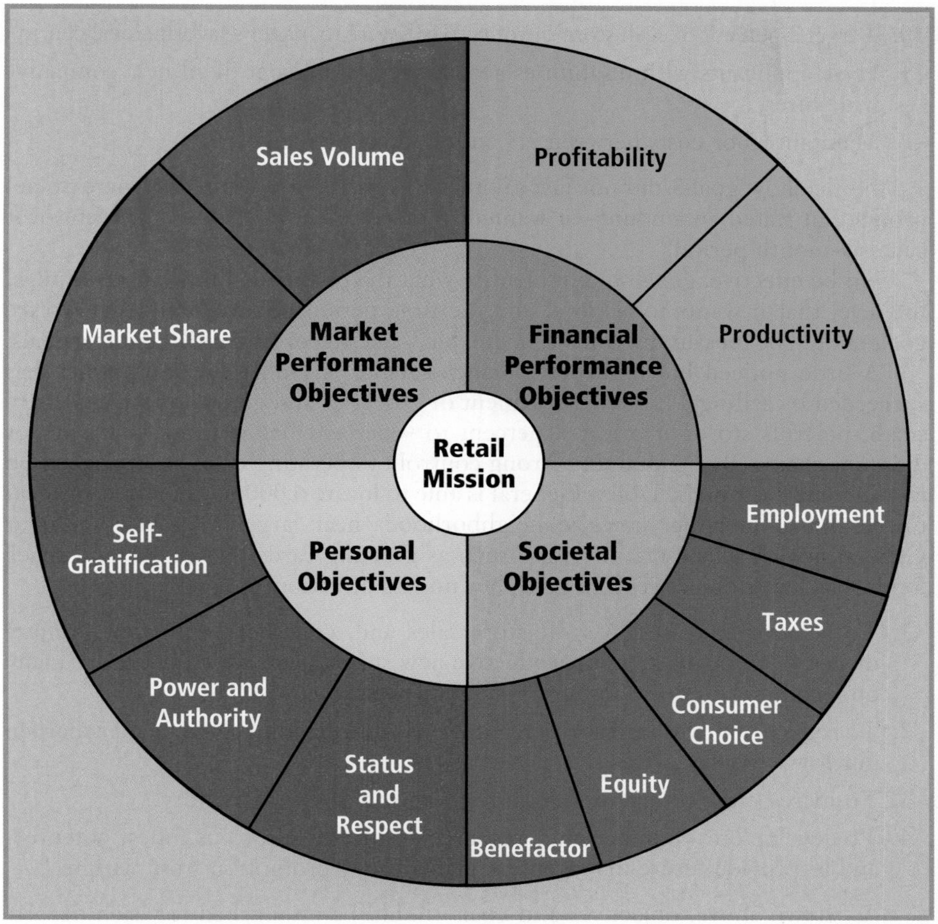

Exhibit 2.2
Retail Objectives

Returning to our earlier discussion, let's now look at Record World's goals and objectives.

1. Open or acquire five to ten new stores over the next year.
2. Remodel six to eight stores over the next year.
3. Increase the net profit margin in each store by 1 percent for each six-month period.
4. Increase video sales in existing stores by 20 percent over the preceding year.
5. Improve sales in classical music by increasing merchandise productivity by 1 percent over the preceding year.
6. Improve the quality of promotion activities, including in-store appearances, publicity, contests, cross-promotions, school promotions, and in-store circulars.
7. Increase awareness/recognition levels of consumers in newer market areas (i.e., Florida) equal to that in the New Jersey/Long Island area.
8. Improve teamwork among top-level executives, especially those at similar management levels.
9. Restructure the buying operation to better interact with other corporate activities.

10. Target 2 percent of each store's profits to the store manager's favorite local charity.
11. Have applicants with disabilities account for 10 percent of all new company-wide hires.
12. Maintain labor costs between 7.5 and 9 percent of sales.

Notice how goal 3 did not just say that Record World wanted to increase net profits, but stated an amount—it wanted to increase net profits by 1 percent over each six-month period.

To be effective, goals should identify what the company wants to accomplish, the level that it wants to achieve, and the time period involved. In other words, goals should be measurable and "schedulable," like Record World's first five goals.

A little noticed but high-performance retailer is Dollar General, which has succeeded by selling a limited assortment of groceries and general merchandise in small, no-frills stores at prices 2 percent to 4 percent below those of the major discount chains. By maintaining strong control of operating costs and focusing on low-income customers, Dollar General is able to locate 6,000-sq.-ft. stores in small towns and/or in larger cities in neighborhoods near larger Wal-Marts. Dollar General, which sells a mix of basics such as greeting cards, motor oil, and snack foods, has fewer objectives and goals but no less direction:

1. To achieve increases in same-store sales and, consistent with that primary objective, to open as many productive new stores as possible. There are many opportunities to do so in our 23-state market.
2. To reduce our overhead as a percentage of sales, enabling us to further sharpen our low everyday prices.
3. To increase the return on our largest financial asset—inventory.
4. To develop our "number one" resource, human assets, to its fullest potential, and to provide future management primarily by promotion from within.[14]

As shown above, objectives and goals should be established for each department or performance area in the business. In the Record World example, goals and objectives 1, 2, 6, 7, 8, and 9 are market performance oriented; numbers 3, 4, 5, and 12 are financial performance oriented; numbers 10 and 11 are societal objectives; and number 10 could be a personal objective (self-gratification) for the store managers. Dollar General's first and fourth goals and objectives are market performance oriented and the second and third are financial performance oriented.

Dollars & Sense

Retailers that develop strategies to build traffic, convert traffic to customers, and lower the costs of serving these customers while maintaining their service level will achieve a high profit.

Strategies

strategy
Is a carefully designed plan for achieving the retailer's goals and objectives.

After developing a mission statement and establishing some goals and objectives, a retailer must develop a strategy. A **strategy** is a carefully designed plan for achieving the retailer's goals and objectives. It is a course of action that when executed will produce the desired levels of performance. Retailers can operate with as few as three strategies:

1. *Get shoppers into your store.* Often referred to as a "retailer's traffic" strategy, many retailers think getting people to visit your Web site or your store is one of the most difficult tasks in retailing. Little wonder then that Wal-Mart hasn't

Global Retailing

Getting Them Into the Store

A couple of years ago, the author traveled to the Rockies for a family vacation and was amazed to notice along the way that the largest, most crowded campgrounds for RVs were not KOA Kampgrounds but Wal-Mart parking lots. In fact, most of the parking lots at the nation's 3,600 Wal-Mart and Sam's Club outlets across the United States (even those with precious little greenery) have become campgrounds for trailers and recreation vehicles.

What turned the world's largest retailer into a camping place? Well, since most of the stores are open all night and they sell gear, groceries, auto supplies, and souvenirs, these locations are more appealing than "spaces for rent" campgrounds outside town that charge between $25 and $40 per night. By catering to these RVers in not-so-subtle ways, Wal-Mart shows it understands the value of getting customers to its stores. From its earliest days in business, when founder Sam Walton held donkey rides in his stores' parking lots to draw traffic, Wal-Mart has always prided itself on having a certain P.T. Barnum quality about it. It isn't an accident that the customized Rand McNally road atlas sold at all Wal-Marts includes the address of each store, its map coordinates, and the availability of RV accessories. RV campers, after all, are profitable customers, as Wal-Mart stores in heavily traveled areas of the country stock extensive recreation-vehicle and camping supplies, which have high profits as a percentage of sales.

No wonder that Wal-Mart, which understands the value of getting consumers into its stores, has adopted this thought process internationally. In China, stores hold live fishing contests on the premises; and in Korea, stores host a kind of cook-off, with variations on a popular dish, *kimchee* (a type of pickled cabbage).

However, it's the chain's German operation that is sparking the most interest with "Singles Shopping." The chain's Dortmund, Germany, store started its singles shopping event in 2003, at the suggestion of workers who thought it might help an unmarried bakery worker at the store who complained about being too old for discos and too proud for Internet dating. Soon, every Friday night became a "singles night" at the store and the event spread to many of the other German Wal-Marts.

The night begins with workers greeting consumers at the store's entrance with a glass of sparkling wine and freshly shucked oysters. Employees take the customers' photos and tack them on a singles bulletin board, along with their age, interests, and the qualities they seek in a prospective partner. Customers are then sent off with a shopping cart outfitted with a bright red bow, denoting their unmarried status.

As Wal-Mart forges into new international markets, it is important that the chain understands local tastes and customer attractions. Despite the strategy described above, Germany and Wal-Mart haven't exactly been a match made in heaven. After making many mistakes during its first decade in Germany, Wal-Mart still isn't profitable. In addition, the American retailer has been hampered by Germany's stringent operating laws that shutter stores by 6 P.M. on weekdays and 4 P.M. on Saturdays, though recently these restrictions have eased, with many stores staying open until 8 P.M. Monday through Saturday. The retailer has also run up against strong unions, and Germany's strict laws against pricing below cost have eroded some of its cost advantages.

However, today the retailer is going back to what Sam Walton used to do, using promotions and ideas from individual Wal-Mart stores, which are then adapted to local needs. The singles shopping nights are a way for Wal-Mart to stand apart from other German discounters and bring in new customers. By the way, Wal-Mart tells women who arrive in groups that they should split up: "Men can be leery of approaching a pack of women."

Wal-Mart has tried the German experiment at a couple of U.S. stores, but it hasn't caught on. However, divisions in Canada and Korea have contacted the German operation for more information.

Source: Based on "Wal-Marts in Germany Redefine the Term 'Checkout Aisle,'" *The Wall Street Journal*, November 9, 2004: B1 & B4; and the author's experiences with Wal-Mart.

---

discouraged college students from coming to its stores late at night, particularly in rural areas, for scavenger hunts, aisle football games, and limbos under the shopping cart stand.[15] Wal-Mart knows the importance of getting consumers into the store. In fact, as this chapter's Global Retailing box illustrates, the chain has made great efforts to attract consumers into its stores.

2. *Convert these shoppers into customers by having them purchase merchandise.* Often referred to as a "retailer's conversion" or "closure" strategy, this means having

the right merchandise, using the right layout and display, and having the right sales force. Each year, the average retailer loses 20 to 40 percent of its customers because it didn't take care of them after they entered the store.[16] The customers may claim that there was "no special reason" that no purchase was made. However, the truth is probably that the retailer neglected the customer. This is particularly important to remember since it costs five times as much money to get a customer into your store as it does to make a sale to someone already there. Today the National Retail Federation considers "customer retention" the major issue facing retailers. This issue will be covered in Chapter 14.

3. *Do this (get shoppers in your shop and convert them into customers) at the lowest operating cost possible that is consistent with the level of service that your customers expect.* This is often referred to as a "retailer's cost management" strategy. Remember, as we pointed out in Chapter 1, most of a product's cost gets added after the item is produced and moves from the factory to the retailer's shelf and finally to the consumer. Thus, good strategies that reduce operating costs while providing the appropriate level of service present significant opportunities for retailers. A great example is a story that Sam Walton loved to tell. He claimed that one of the greatest retail lessons he ever learned, and a major contributor to Wal-Mart's amazing growth rate, came when James Cash Penney visited the Des Moines, Iowa, Penney's store where Sam was a trainee. While Mr. Penney was wandering through the store, a customer approached Sam to buy a set of work clothes for her husband.

   Mr. Penney watched from a distance while Sam took excellent care of the customer. Sam wrapped the work shirt and pants in a package (using paper off a roll and string to tie it), gave the customer her change, and thanked her for shopping at Penney's. Sam was proud of the way he handled the transaction and thought he might even merit praise from Mr. Penney. Sure enough, Mr. Penney came over to Sam and said, "Young man, I want to show you something."

   Mr. Penney proceeded to get a set of work clothes, just like the woman had purchased, and wrapped it with paper from the roll that overlapped by less than an inch. Then using half the string Sam used, he tied the package. After handing the newly wrapped package to Sam to examine, he imparted his wisdom: "Young man, you know we don't make money on the merchandise we sell. We make our profit on the paper and string we save."

   That lesson was never lost on Sam Walton, and today Wal-Mart's executives still preach it. Little wonder then that one executive was recently quoted as telling an investor conference that "the misconception is that we're in the retail business. Actually, we're in the distribution business." Furthermore, the executive added, while it is generally believed that Wal-Mart buys and sells at the lowest price, in fact, Wal-Mart sells at the lowest price because it has the lowest distribution costs.[17]

While the preceding three strategies may seem too simple to be operational, they actually do summarize the tasks that every retailer must perform. Many retailers go further and develop strategies that enable them to differentiate themselves from the competition as they accomplish these three tasks.

One of the greatest failings in retailing today is that too many retailers have concentrated on just one means of differentiation—price. Price promotions usually attract, but rarely hold, customers. Starbucks, for example, has never used a price promotion because it has realized that the customers gained with price promotions are just as apt to switch to another retailer when it cuts its price below theirs. As a result of these constant price deals, retailers have taught consumers that if they wait—and in many cases this wait is only a matter of days—the desired merchandise will go on sale. Unless a retailer has substantially lower operating costs than its competitors, such as Wal-Mart does, this is a very dangerous strategy, since it can easily be copied by the competition and will result in reduced profits or even losses. Some better forms of differentiation for a retailer are:

1. *Physical differentiation of the product.* Target follows this strategy with its brilliant and innovative upscale merchandise that catches trends before the other mass merchandisers. Another example is Torrid, a retailer offering cool clothes for plus-size girls and young women (sizes 12 to 26), who can now match the style, excitement, and selection available at standard-size fashion retailers. Casual Male XL is the men's equivalent of this retailer.
2. *The selling process.* For example, Nordstrom's, Neiman Marcus, and many local jewelers connect with their target customers through their excellent customer service.
3. *After-purchase satisfaction.* Many high-quality bike repair shops and major retailers, such as L.L. Bean Inc., achieve this with their "satisfaction guaranteed" programs, which enable customers to return with their bike or send back the item of clothing, even after years of wear.
4. *Location.* Stores such as Dollar General and Family Dollar excel at this form of differentiation. These stores used to be considered after-thoughts of American retailing, with a marginalized presence in an industry that thrived on larger, more theatrical outlets. Not today. Dollar stores are generating impressive sales increases with a compelling price/value/convenience model. The growing consumer appeal of these stores is that they are usually located in strip centers en route to a nearby supercenter, capturing shoppers who would rather pick up their toothpaste and motor oil quickly instead of searching a cavernous building offering tires and tomatoes, shirts and soup, and bananas and car batteries. In addition, the small size of their stores gives these retailers advantages in negotiating leases in an industry with a surplus of stores, thus reducing their operating costs.

Highly personalized service allows many high-fashion retailers to differentiate their offerings.

5. *Never being out of stock.* This means being in stock with regard to the sizes, colors, and styles that the target market expects the retailer to carry. For example, Nordstrom offers a free shirt if it is out of stock on a basic size.

These means of differentiation will not only get more consumers into your store, but will result in their buying more merchandise once they are there. Note also that in all these examples, the retailers are able to develop their own unique niches in the mind of the consumer, and thus avoid price wars.

So how does a retailer develop a strategy to differentiate itself? This starts with an analysis of the retailer's strengths and weaknesses, as well as the threats and opportunities that exist in the environment. This process, which is often referred to as "SWOT" (strengths, weaknesses, opportunities, and threats) analysis, involves asking the following questions.

Strengths

What major competitive advantage(s) do we have? (These could be lower prices, better locations, better store personnel, etc.)

What are we good at? (This might be the ability to anticipate customer demands better than the competition so that the merchandise is there when the customer wants it.)

What do customers perceive as our strong points? (Customers might perceive that we offer the "best value for the dollar.")

Weaknesses

What major competitive advantage(s) do competitors have over us? (Do they have lower prices, better locations, salespeople, etc.?)

What are competitors better at than we are? (Do they do a better job of selecting merchandise, anticipating demand?)

What are our major internal weaknesses? (Do we do a poor job of employee training? Are our stores in need of remodeling?)

Opportunities

What favorable environmental trends may benefit our firm? (Is our market size growing? Are family income levels rising in our market? Is merchandise priced correctly for the target market?)

What is the competition doing in our market? (Are new firms entering or are existing firms leaving? What is the impact on us?)

What areas of business that are closely related to ours are undeveloped? (Is it possible for us to expand into a related field serving the same customers and take advantage of our good name in the marketplace?)

Threats

What unfortunate environmental trends may hurt our future performance? (Has inflation caused consumers to become more price sensitive, or has it prevented us from raising our prices in order to pass increasing costs on to consumers? How could our competitor's prices, new products, or services; the entrance of new competitors; or the possible loss of suppliers hurt us?)

What technology is on the horizon that may soon have an impact on our firm? (Will some new electronic equipment soon replace our manual way of performing activities?)

In our Retailing: The Inside Story box we look at what could be the SWOT analysis for PetSmart.

Retailing: The Inside Story

SWOT Analysis for PetSmart

Strengths

What major competitive advantages does a PetSmart store have over the competition?

Most other retailers that sell to the pet market simply sell tangible goods or merchandise. *PetSmart* does this at very attractive everyday low prices but has made inroads into selling services such as grooming, pet lodging, pet training, and related services. This business can be expected to grow at double-digit rates for the foreseeable future.

PetSmart sells through multiple channels to include stores, catalog, and the Internet.

What is PetSmart good at?

PetSmart hires only pet parents. Every employee must be a pet owner. It also trains its employees to carry on conversations with customers about their pets.

The company allows customers to bring their well-behaved and leashed pets along on the shopping experience.

The company does not try to skimp on labor, and there are almost always plenty of store personnel to serve customers.

What do customers perceive as PetSmart's strong points?

PetSmart provides special care for abandoned pets. It does not sell pets (except fish) but rather facilitates the adoption of more than one thousand dogs and cats a day. The company donates free space in their stores to humane societies to facilitate adoptions.

Customers perceive PetSmart as a highly trustworthy organization to which they can entrust their pets' welfare.

Weaknesses

What major competitive advantage do mass merchandisers have over a PetSmart?

Grocery stores, discount department stores, and super stores are visited weekly by the typical household; thus, these stores intercept much of the business that could be destined for a *PetSmart*. Some of these competitors are setting up mini pet departments.

What can competitors do better than PetSmart?

Location can be better in most situations. Virtually every supermarket, discount department store, and superstore has the basic commodity pet products. A special trip to a *PetSmart* may not be worth the effort.

What are typical major internal weaknesses of PetSmart?

The company has done a historically poor job at database marketing. Only recently has it established a loyalty or frequent shopper program, but it has a long way to go to develop a highly sophisticated customer relationship management (CRM) program.

Opportunities

What favorable environmental trends may benefit PetSmart?

There are now more dogs and cats in the United States than there are children, and pet count is expected to grow 1 to 2 percent annually. Spending per pet, however, is growing at 3 to 4 percent per year. The total pet supply market is growing at over 6 percent annually vs. most traditional retail merchandise categories, which are growing at 2 percent or less.

Pets are becoming humanized. Over the last 50 years, pets have migrated from the barnyard to backyard to back door to kitchen to living room to bedroom to bed to under the sheets.

Nearly half of U.S. households keep pet dogs or cats, and slightly over 10% have both a dog and cat.

What undeveloped areas are available to PetSmart?

The company estimates that the U.S. market can absorb 1,400 PetSmart stores and, as of 2006, it had just less than 800 stores. Thus, it should have sufficient U.S. growth opportunities through 2014.

The company estimates that its PetsHotels, which in 2006 numbered in the 20s, could eventually be located in 270 PetSmart stores.

A new concept, Doggie Day Camps, has a very large potential. The company is just starting to roll out this service.

PetSmart faces considerable long-run opportunity in its "TLC" or "Total Lifetime Care" model, which strives to provide total lifetime care for every pet and every pet parent, every time.

The growing interest in natural ingredient pet products could be a significant growth vehicle. This growth market also relates to more pet owners being interested in geriatric pet care and pain management for their pets.

Threats

What unfortunate environmental trends may hurt PetSmart's future performance?

Producers such as Procter & Gamble Company are recognizing that they cannot restrict the sale of their premium pet foods, such as Iams, to only pet specialty stores, but must seek to get penetration in big discount mass merchandisers, such as Wal-Mart.

(*continued*)

Global Retailing *(continued)*

How could competitor's actions hurt PetSmart?

As U.S. households move toward more indulgence of their pets in higher-end food, snacks, multivitamins, shampoos and conditioners, and designer collars and leashes, some of the mass merchandisers like Target may start to move into these product categories rather than merely selling low price pet food.

Cat litter accounts for nearly half of pet supplies (nonfood); thus, warehouse clubs and superstores are going aggressively after this largely commodity business.

Wal-Mart has publicly stated that it hopes to grab 30% of the pet supply market during the next five years.

Sources: "PetSmart Focuses on Big Returns by Coming Up with New Services," *The Wall Street Journal*, June 1, 2005: A1; Catherine M. Dalton "A Passion for Pets: An Interview with Philip L. Francis, Chairperson and CEO of PetSmart, Inc.," *Business Horizons*, November-December 2005: 469–475; "PetSmart Tests PetsHotel Concept to Expand Services Business," *DSN Retailing Today*, October 28, 2002: 4; and the author's personal experience with PetSmart.

Now the retailer is ready to develop some strategies to accomplish its objectives. Again, notice the close relationship between a retailer's goals and objectives and its strategies. Objectives indicate what the retailer wants to accomplish, and strategies indicate how the retailer will attempt to accomplish those goals with the resources available.

target market
Is the group or groups of customers that the retailer is seeking to serve.

location
Is the geographic space or cyberspace where the retailer conducts business.

retail mix
Is the combination of merchandise, price, advertising and promotion, location, customer service and selling, and store layout and design.

The retailer must develop a retail marketing strategy with strong financial elements. A fully developed marketing strategy should address the following considerations:

1. The specific target market. A **target market** is the group or groups of customers that the retailer is seeking to serve. It is important for retailers to understand that different target markets demand different product offerings. For this reason, successful retailers must determine which customers make them the most money, segment them carefully, then realign their stores and empower employees to target those favored shoppers with products and services that will encourage them to spend more and come back often. Exhibit 2.3 illustrates Best Buy's targeting process. The left side of the box shows five different target markets that Best Buy is trying to reach. The center shows the offerings or services that Best Buy will feature in the stores catering to those target markets. The far right lists the customer name that the retailer has assigned each target. According to Best Buy, each of their stores will be aimed at one or two of these customer types.
2. A **location(s)**, whether a traditional store in a geographic space, a person's home in relation to a print catalog or television shopping, or a virtual store in cyberspace, that is consistent with the needs and wants of the desired target market.
3. The specific retail mix that the retailer intends to use to appeal to its target market, and thereby meet its financial objectives. The **retail mix**, shown in

Exhibit 2.3
Features Offered by Best Buy to Meet the Needs of Its Various Customer Types

Customer Type	Feature Offering by Store	Customer Name
Affluent tech and home theater enthusiast	Magnolia Home Theater, Geek Squad	Barry
Busy suburban mom	Personal shopping assistant, Geek Squad	Jill
Small business owner	Business pros, Geek Squad	Buzz
Young tech gadget enthusiast	Interactive displays, tailored market assortments, Geek Squad	Ray
Family man seeking good value	Geek Squad, special offers	Mr. Storefront

Source: Used with the written permission of Best Buy.

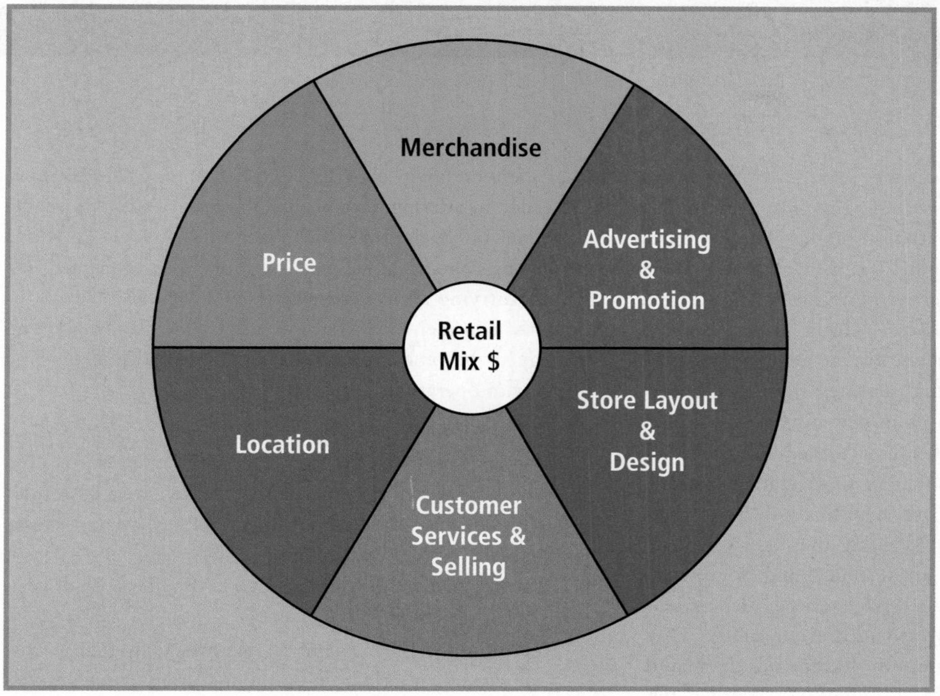

Exhibit 2.4
Retail Mix

Exhibit 2.4, is the combination of merchandise, price, advertising and promotion, location, customer services and selling, and store layout and design that the retailer uses to satisfy the target market.

4. The retailer's **value proposition** is a clear statement of the tangible and/or intangible results a customer receives from shopping at and using the retailer's products or services. It is the difference between the benefits offered by one retailer and those of the competition. A good value proposition answers the question "Why should I buy this product or service from this retailer?"

value proposition
A clear statement of the tangible and/or intangible results a customer receives from shopping at and using the retailer's products or services.

The chapter's What's New box describes the strategy that has made JetBlue Airways, operating as a low-fare, low-cost passenger airline while providing high-quality customer service, America's newest major airline.

The Retail Strategic Planning and Operations Management Model

LO 2

Describe the text's retail strategic planning and operations management model.

Exhibit 2.5, our strategic planning and operations management model, suggests that a retailer must engage in two types of planning and management tasks: strategic planning and operations management. Each of these tasks is undertaken in order to achieve high profit results. Take a few moments to study this model.

As explained in Chapter 1, this book has an environmental orientation, a management planning orientation, a profit orientation, and a decision-making orientation. You will note that the environmental orientation is represented by the

What's New?

JetBlue: Only Unexpected Fuel Prices Can Slow It Down

In 2006, as most of the major airlines (those with more than $1 billion in annual revenue) were emerging from bankruptcy, only Southwest Airlines remained profitable. The high fuel costs associated with hurricanes of 2005 were all that kept the industry's other profitable carrier, JetBlue Airways, from matching Southwest's performance. Both airlines are expected to be the industry leaders for the remainder of the decade because of their customer-oriented strategies. Forget the fact that both are point-to-point operators as opposed to the other major airlines, which followed the "hub & spoke" model. (This concept requires that an airline gather consumers in smaller markets and deliver them to a hub from where they fly to their destinations.) Avoiding the "hub & spoke" model isn't the main reason for JetBlue's and Southwest's success. The key is that both successful service retailers have operating strategies built solely around the consumer.

In 2005, for the third straight year, JetBlue was the market leader in customer satisfaction. Employing a strategy that depends heavily upon technology and innovation to reduce operating costs, and using common sense to treat customers to a better flying experience, JetBlue appears to have succeeded in offering high quality airline service at affordable fares, and in coaxing humanity back to air travel. An added attraction is their leather seats outfitted with individual TV screens carrying 24 live channels.

Let's consider how JetBlue used its retail marketing strategy to become profitable a decade ago during its first full year of operations.

1. ***Target Market:*** JetBlue's CEO, David Neeleman, a former Southwest Airlines executive, recognized, even before targeting any particular market, that customers had become jaded about flying. Thus aging bargain hunters, college kids, young professionals, and affluent consumers have all embraced the airline because of what it offers them.
2. ***Location:*** JetBlue sought to provide high-quality customer service, primarily on point-to-point routes focusing on underserved markets and large metropolitan areas that typically have high average fares.

Emile Wamsteker/Bloomberg News/Landon

3. ***Retail Mix:***

Merchandise: JetBlue's strategy was to use new airplanes with leather seats, an uncommon amount of legroom, and free satellite TV at every seat. All seats would be assigned, unlike Southwest, and all travel would be ticketless; there would be no discount seats, all fares would be one-way with no required Saturday night stay, and over 75% of tickets would be sold on the company's Web site, the cheapest distribution method.

Price: JetBlue's prices were the lowest in the industry, especially for "walk-up" fares. Because it flew longer routes than Southwest and because its fixed costs were spread thinner, with each plane in the air one to three hours more then the competition each day, it faced little competition on price.

Advertising and Promotion: With a limited promotional budget, advertising was the last project completed. Only after getting the product strategy right and teaching the employees to understand the firm's mission did the airline start telling its story through PR. JetBlue chose to build the advertising last so that they could live on realistic budgets. Thus, JetBlue soared on its customers' experiences rather than on big advertising budgets.

Customer Service: The airline's own internal research found that the number one reason people tried JetBlue for the first time was its fares, but the number one reason people recommended the airline to their friends was service. A highlight of the service experience was the friendliness of the employees, especially the reservation agents. The consumers never suspected that all 1,400 of these employees were working at home. Not only did JetBlue save on real estate and coffee supplies, but also the workers saved time and money on commuting. Two other factors keeping employees happy are a no-layoff policy and the fact that over 80 percent are shareholders, the result of a discounted stock-purchasing plan. One stock market analyst noted that because JetBlue customers have lower expectations due to the low prices it charges, the customers are seldom going to be disappointed. This enables Jet Blue to proclaim "We're not going to give you much, but we're going to be cool and sophisticated about it."

Still, JetBlue took extra steps to ensure customer satisfaction. Whenever a flight was delayed for more than four hours for reasons other than weather or traffic, JetBlue would, without being asked, offer a $159 voucher. Similarly, they would give a $25 voucher for misplaced baggage. The airline's Web site (http://www.jetblue.com) is extremely easy to use, an incentive to travelers who book online. Neeleman even went so far as to survey female passengers to see if they preferred a restroom for women only. They didn't.

Layout and Design: Ad Age claims that the affection business professionals and travel snobs share for JetBlue may owe something to the airline's clean but retro styling. The airline used as its inspirations for an image a combination of the warm, fuzzy feelings generated by the recent ads for the Volkswagen Beetle, Starbucks, Target Corp., and the '70s incarnations of Coca-Cola Co.'s Coke.

Sources: Brent Brown and Dean Headley, *2006 Airline Quality Ratings*, published jointly by Wichita State and University of Nebraska at Omaha, April 3, 2006; "Investors Head for the Exit as JetBlue Bleeds Red Ink," *The Wall Street Journal*, February 2, 2006: A2; "Call Centers in the Rec Room," *Business Week*, January 23, 2006: 76–77; "Amid JetBlue's Rapid Ascent, CEO Adopts Big Rivals Traits," *The Wall Street Journal*, August 25, 2005: A1 & A6; and the company's Web site.

top and bottom bars in Exhibit 2.5, the management planning orientation by the first five vertical sections (strategic planning and operations management), the profit orientation by the high profit box at the far right, and the decision-making orientation by all the decisions that the retailer must make throughout this model.

Retailers who develop strategic plans are better able to withstand competitive onslaughts and will have better long-term profitability.

Dollars & Sense

Strategic Planning

Strategic planning, as pointed out at the beginning of the chapter, is concerned with how the retailer responds to the environment in an effort to establish a long-term

Exhibit 2.5
Retail Strategic Planning and Operations Management Model

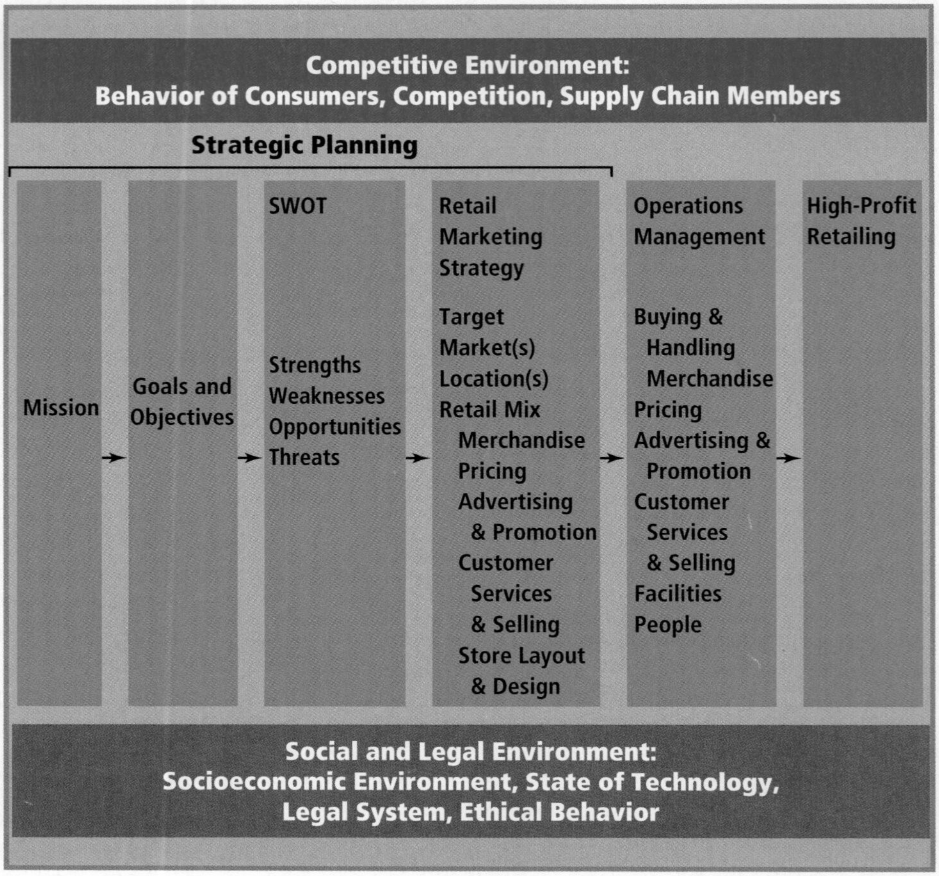

course of action. In principle, the retailer's strategic planning should best reflect the line(s) of trade in which the retailer will operate, the market(s) it will pursue, and the retail mix it will use. Remember, strategic planning requires a long-term commitment of resources by the retailer. An error in strategic planning can result in a decline in profitability, a loss of competitive position, or bankruptcy. On the other hand, effective strategic planning can help protect the retailer against competitive onslaughts.

The initial steps in strategic planning are to define the firm's mission, establish goals and objectives, and perform a SWOT analysis. The next steps are to select the target market and appropriate location(s). It is important to note that most retail managers or executives have very little control over location decisions. A newly appointed manager for a chain department store could change promotional strategy, personnel, service levels, credit policies, and even prices, but in all likelihood would be constrained by a long-term lease agreement. In fact, only the senior management of most chains is ever involved in location decisions. For the small retailer just starting out, however, or retailers considering expansion, location is an important decision. A full discussion of location and site selection appears in Chapter 7.

After selecting the target market and location, the retailer must develop the firm's retail mix. Retailers can best perform this strategic planning only after assessing the external environment. They should be looking for an opportunity to fulfill the needs of a defined group of consumers (i.e., their target market) in a way that sets them apart from the competition. In other words, retailers should strive to seek a differential advantage over the competition. Retailers will rarely discover a means of gaining a differential advantage merely by reviewing their own internal operations or by focusing exclusively on the conventional industry structure. Strategic planning opportunities are to be found in the realities of a constantly changing environment. An effective retail strategy can result only from matching environmental forces with a retail marketing program that satisfies the customer better than anybody else. For example, Foot Locker has found success by concentrating on a very narrow segment of the shoe market but offering a very large selection.

David Zalubowski/Associated Press

Foot Locker's success is largely due to offering highly focused merchandise to serve the needs of its well defined target market.

Exhibit 2.5 profiles the major environmental forces that should be assessed. Briefly, these are as follows:

1. *Consumer Behavior.* The behavior of consumers will obviously have a significant impact on the retailer's future. Specifically, the retailer will need to understand the determinants of shopping behavior so it can identify likely changes in that behavior and develop appropriate strategies.
2. *Competitor Behavior.* How competing retailers behave will have a major impact on the most appropriate strategy. Retailers must develop a competitive strategy that is not easily imitated.
3. *Supply Chain Behavior.* The behavior of members of the retailer's supply chain can have a significant impact on the retailer's future. For example, are certain supply chain members, such as manufacturers and/or wholesalers, always seeking to improve their position in the supply chain by establishing their own Internet sites, thus bypassing retailers? Remember that back in Chapter 1 we discussed the impact of such a move by the airlines as they tried to bypass the travel agents.
4. *Socioeconomic Environment.* The retailer must understand how economic and demographic trends will influence revenues and costs in the future and adapt its strategy according to these changes.
5. *Technological Environment.* The technical frontiers of the retail system encompass new and better ways of performing standard retail functions. The retailer must always be aware of opportunities for lowering operating costs.
6. *Legal and Ethical Environment.* The retailer should be familiar with local, state, and federal regulations of the retail system. It must also understand evolving legal patterns in order to design future retail strategies that are legally defensible. At the same time, the retailer must operate at the highest level of ethical behavior.

Detailed discussions of these environmental forces will be provided in Chapters 3 through 6. For now, realize that although these forces cannot be controlled by a single retailer, the threats emanating from these forces are often translated into opportunities by successful retailers. For example, Macy's was once an independent operation that catered to the working classes of New York, but due to increasing competition and the ability to spot future environmental changes, it is now a trendy boutique store owned by Federated Department Stores catering to the top 25 percent of families.

After reviewing its mission, objectives, and environment, and developing its retail marketing strategy, the retailer should be able to develop alternative uses of resources in order to obtain the highest performance level. Next, the retailer must determine which strategy will yield the best results. Finally, the retailer will concentrate on operations management.

Operations Management

operations management
Deals with activities directed at maximizing the efficiency of the retailer's use of resources. It is frequently referred to as day-to-day management.

Operations management is concerned with maximizing the efficiency of the retailer's use of resources and with how the retailer converts these resources into sales and profits. In other words, its aim is to maximize the performance of current operations.

Most of the retailer's time and energy is devoted to the day-to-day activity of operations management. Our Retail Strategic Planning and Operations Management Model (refer to Exhibit 2.5) shows that operations management involves managing the buying and handling of merchandise, pricing, advertising and promotion, customer services and selling, people and facilities. All of these activities require day-to-day attention. For example, the selling floor must be maintained, customers served, merchandise bought and handled, advertisements run, and pricing decisions made each and every day. In other words, operations management is running the store.

In Part 4, we will focus on operations management, the real "guts" of retailing. In the first several years of a retailing career, your primary concern will be almost exclusively with the operations management side of retailing. The strategic planning duties will be handled by the senior executives. However, if you enter retailing via a small or medium-sized firm, you may be making decisions, even strategic ones, immediately. Regardless, when a retailer is able to do a good job at operations management—that is, efficiently using the resources available—then the retailer is said to be operations effective.

Dollars & Sense

To be a high-profit retailer, the retailer needs strong strategic planning coupled with good operations management.

High-Performance Results

The far right box of the Retail Strategic Planning and Operations Management Model (refer to Exhibit 2.5) suggests that well designed and executed strategic and operations plans will result in high profit. Mistakes in either of these two areas will severely hamper the retailer's performance and prevent it from being among the leaders in its industry. For example, in this chapter you read that The Gap was once hailed as the most successful innovator in the retail apparel industry. However, by 2000, the early baby boomers had already reached age 50 and had all the clothes they needed. Middle-aged consumers quit buying clothes and spent more on their homes. In addition, younger adults, those in their twenties and thirties, found the merchandise at

		Profit Margin	Asset Turnover	Return on Assets	Financial Leverage	Return on Net Worth
Best Buy	BBY	3.7%	2.8x	10.3%	2.3x	23.5%
Wal-Mart	WMT	3.7%	2.4x	8.9%	2.6x	22.7%
Home Depot	HD	7.2%	2.0x	12.8%	1.8x	23.5%
Office Depot	ODP	1.9%	2.2x	4.6%	2.2x	9.9%
Sears Holding	SHLD	2.5%	2.5x	4.4%	2.1x	9.3%
Target	TGT	4.6%	1.6x	7.5%	2.4x	18.0%
Kohl's	KSS	6.3%	1.6x	10.2%	1.5x	15.7%

Exhibit 2.6
Strategic Profit Model for Some of the Country's Leading Retailers

the chain's major divisions—The GAP, Banana Republic, Old Navy, and GAP for Kids—less exciting, not distinctive, and geared too much toward teenagers. Luckily, Gap Inc. was able to turn things around.

The need to strive for a high profit is tied to the extremely competitive nature of retailing. It is still relatively easy to start a retail business in comparison to starting a business in other industries. New retail entrepreneurs are continually entering the marketplace. As competition increases, and more chains use the same format, profit levels naturally deteriorate. Retailers are therefore well advised to set high-profit objectives so that if their planned profits are not reached, they at least have a chance of achieving average profitability. The retailer that aims only for an average profit often finds itself confronting a rather sobering financial performance. Exhibit 2.6 shows how the SPM results of high-performance retailers compare to the median performance for similar retailers. As a general rule of thumb, retailers should strive for the following goals when planning their SPM: net profit margin of 2.5 to 3.5 percent; asset turnover of 2.5 to 3.0 times; and financial leverage of 2.0 to 3.0 times. Achieving such goals would produce a return on assets of 8 to 10 percent and an 18 to 25 percent return on net worth.

SUMMARY

STUDENT STUDY GUIDE

This chapter explains the importance and use of planning in retail management. Toward that end, the chapter introduces a model of retail planning.

LO 1

Explain why strategic planning is so important and describe its components.

Planning and the financial performance of the retailer are intertwined. High-profit performance does not just happen; it is engineered through careful planning. Not all retailers can be leaders, but the ones that are will be those that did the best job of planning and managing. The components of strategic planning include developing a statement of purpose or mission for the firm; defining specific goals and objectives for the firm; identifying the retailer's strengths, weaknesses, opportunities, and threats; and developing basic strategies that will enable the firm to reach its objectives and fulfill its mission.

LO 2

Describe the text's retail strategic planning and operations management model.

Retailers must engage in two types of planning and management tasks: strategic planning and operations management. Strategic planning consists of matching the retailer's mission and goals with available opportunities. The retail marketing strategy that results from this consists of a target market, location(s), retail mix, and value proposition. Operations management consists of planning the efficient use of available resources in order to manage the day-to-day operations of the firm successfully. When retailers succeed at these two levels, they will achieve high-profit results.

TERMS TO REMEMBER

planning
strategic planning
mission statement
goals and objectives
market performance
financial performance
market share
net profit margin
asset turnover
return on assets (ROA)
financial leverage
return on net worth (RONW)
gross margin percentage
productivity objectives
yield management
rasm
strategy
societal objectives
personal objectives
target market
location(s)
retail mix
value proposition
operations management

REVIEW AND DISCUSSION QUESTIONS

LO 1 **Explain why strategic planning is so important and describe its components.**

1. Why is strategic planning so important in retailing today? Has it always been this way, or has the ever-changing retail environment influenced your answer?
2. How do the retail firm's mission statement and its stated goals and objectives statement relate to the retailer's development of competitive strategy?
3. Most college students have unfavorable opinions of their campus bookstore. Suppose you were asked to advise your bookstore. What items would you consider in your SWOT analysis?
4. Is strategic planning more important for a small retailer than for a large retailer? Explain your answer.
5. Choose any two supermarkets operating in your college area or hometown. Compare and contrast their retail mix as they seek to satisfy the needs of their target market given their present location. What changes would you suggest to the management of these retailers as they develop their strategic plans for the coming year?
6. Limited Brands, the operator of over a thousand stores (Victoria's Secret, Express/Women and Men, Bath & Body Works, The Limited, The White Barn Candles, and Henri Bendel), has the following mission statement: "Limited Brands is committed to building a family of the world's best fashion brands to create sustained growth of shareholder value by focusing its time, talent, and capital on the highest return opportunities." Is this mission too restrictive? Would you change this mission statement? If so, how and why?

LO 2 **Describe the text's retail strategic planning and operations management model.**

7. What are the major environmental forces that retailers will face over the next five years? Is any one of these more important than the others?

8. Does strategic planning become more or less important as the uncertainty that the retailer faces increases?
9. When doing the strategic planning and operations management tasks described in our model, does the retailer use creative thinking or analytical problem solving?
10. A wise person once said, "Planning is more important than execution and control." This individual meant that a good plan will always overcome poor operations management. Agree or disagree with this statement and explain your reasoning. Use current examples, if possible, in your answer.
11. Why is it so important for a retailer to seek high profit performance? Isn't it enough to be above average?

SAMPLE TEST QUESTIONS

When a retailer sets goals based on a comparison of its actions against its competitor's, it is establishing _______ goals. LO 1

a. competitive analysis
b. market performance
c. geo-market performance
d. societal performance
e. financial performance

The best way for a retailer to differentiate itself in the eyes of the consumer from the competition is to _______ . LO 2

a. increase advertising of sale items.
b. offer the lowest prices in town.
c. always be well stocked with the basic items that customers would expect to find in your store.
d. not sell any of the brand names the competition is selling.
e. increase its strategic planning effort.

WRITING AND SPEAKING EXERCISE

You are a girls'/women's buyer for a small chain of nine clothing stores operating in seven mid-size southern Ohio and Indiana cites of 60,000 people or less.

As you prepare for your semi-annual trip to the market, you read that plus-size apparel is the fastest-growing market segment in the United States. Yet, despite repeated requests from customers, your chain has avoided carrying these sizes. You feel that there is now a market for this target segment, especially for the upcoming spring/summer season with its need for swimsuits and summer outfits.

In the past, your merchandise manager has felt uncomfortable catering to this market segment. After all, she has repeatedly stated, "These folks don't want to look sexy or updated, and if they did, then the mall stores (Sears and Penney's) would be handling the sizes." She also claimed that the plus-size market didn't have the same taste as regular-sized customers. Finally, your boss felt that having "such large types" around would discourage the fashion-conscious consumers from shopping in your stores.

Because you disagree, you have decided to write a memo to your merchandise manager stating why it isn't a good strategy to ignore this segment of the population. After all, it's a segment that is both growing and underserved, and by targeting it, overall store traffic will increase.

RETAIL PROJECT

Go to the library and either look at the most recent annual reports for four or five of the Top 10 U.S. retailers listed on the inside cover of this text or locate the 10-Ks of those firms on the Internet. [*Note*: All publicly held firms need to file their SEC 10-Ks, a more complete financial analysis of the firm's performance than provided in the firm's annual report to stockholders, electronically. The address for looking up this information is http://www.sec.gov/edgar.shtml. Using the SPM described in Exhibits 2.1 and 2.4, calculate your own SPM numbers for these retailers.

Finally, after calculating these numbers, which retailer do you believe is the best at achieving financial superiority?

PLANNING YOUR OWN RETAIL BUSINESS

In the "Planning Your Own Retail Business" exercise in Chapter 1, you learned how to estimate the net profits that your business might earn. You saw what would happen if your sales estimate was off by 10 percent. Now it is time to analyze the dollar investment in assets you need to support your business and how you might finance these assets.

Your investment in assets needs to cover inventory, fixtures, equipment, cash, customer credit (i.e., accounts receivable), and perhaps other assets. These assets could be financed with debt or by investments you or perhaps other investors make in the business.

Compute the strategic profit model ratios under the assumption that your first year sales are $700,000, net profit is $66,000, total investment in assets is $400,000, and the total debt to finance these assets is $250,000. [*Hint*: Net worth is equal to total assets less debt.] What would happen to these ratios if net profit rose to $75,000?

CASE

The Missed Opportunity: The Sears Takeover of Lands' End*

When Sears bought Lands' End in 2002, many retail observers hailed the purchase. Sears, the troubled department store, had a loyal, more affluent customer for its hard goods lines, but had difficulty sparking interest in its soft goods. In contrast, Lands' End was the #1 specialty apparel catalog. Lands' End's traditional, casually styled merchandise matched Sears' all-American, good-value image, and would attract a more upmarket customer to Sears' apparel. Further, Sears could tap Lands' End's expertise in direct marketing, and its loyal customer database. Lands' End could broaden its customer audience through wider distribution through Sears with its 2,300+ stores.

The results fell short of expectations. By 2005, Lands' End was a relatively small presence in 370 Sears stores. Further, Sears seemed more interested in (or distracted by) its new owner, Kmart; in other private label brand names such as Lucy Pereda; and in developing new store concepts such as Sears Grand, The Great Indoors, and Orchard Supply Hardware.

Most conclude that the Lands' End brand did not live up to its potential in stores, largely due to mismanagement of a well-respected brand. At first, Sears s-l-o-w-l-y rolled out Lands' End merchandise into selected stores. Loyal Lands' End customers who heard about the acquisition ran to their local Sears store for the first time in years, but were often disappointed when the brand was not yet in stock.

When Lands' End finally arrived in local Sears stores, it was poorly publicized. Often, no mention was made in local newspapers except in tiny print at the bottom of a Sears ad. Sears credit card customers received few promotional announcements, even in their bills. In-store Lands' End signage and displays could easily be overlooked. Even today, Lands' End merchandise is buried within the Sears online Web page rather than promoted as a flagship brand.

Sears seems to have underestimated the potential for Lands' End to drive new customers to its stores. Loyal Lands' End customers who decided to revisit Sears in search of their favored brand were often disappointed with the limited selection. Rather than driving differentiation between the brands, Lands' End merchandise often looked mundane and very similar to Sears's basics. Infighting between Sears and Lands' End resulted in many missed opportunities, leading observers to think that fear of cannibalization of Sears's existing brands was a driving issue. Sears claimed that the best-selling Lands' End golf jackets were priced too high for the "typical" Sears customer—forgetting that Sears wanted to attract more than the "typical" Sears clothing customer! In addition, many of the Sears stores did not stock Lands' End sweater sets so popular at holiday time, but stuck with cotton turtlenecks, khakis, and jeans, i.e., what every other mall retailer sold, usually more stylish.

Sears and Lands' End also seemed at odds in their pricing strategies, and ignored the differences in behavior among catalog shoppers and instore customers. While the Lands' End catalog places only limited amounts of merchandise on sale at any given time, bricks & mortar stores have to observe local conditions and sales seasons more carefully. For example, Sears stores in Sunbelt states maintained the full price on Lands' End winter coats through March—when temperatures easily hit the 70s and 80s. One executive stated that "Lands' End should not go on sale right now." This was fine for the upper Midwest, but not the Southern stores!

Recently when Sears executives examined the tepid sales of Lands' End merchandise in many stores, they concluded that an upscale customer was not ready to shop at Sears, and that Lands' End merchandise in stores should be scaled back. Unfortunately, this action will lead to further disappointment for the Lands' End customer base.*

Questions

1. Based on your knowledge of the two retailers, prepare a SWOT analysis for each of them prior to the Sears takeover. Based on your SWOT analysis, what are the pros and cons of the takeover?
2. What is the best strategy for Sears to use with Lands' End?
3. Can a retailer seek to satisfy two different target markets, as Sears tried to do with Lands' End?
4. Should Sears sell off Lands' End?

*This case was prepared by Jan Owens, Carthage College, Kenosha, Wisconsin, and used with her written permission.

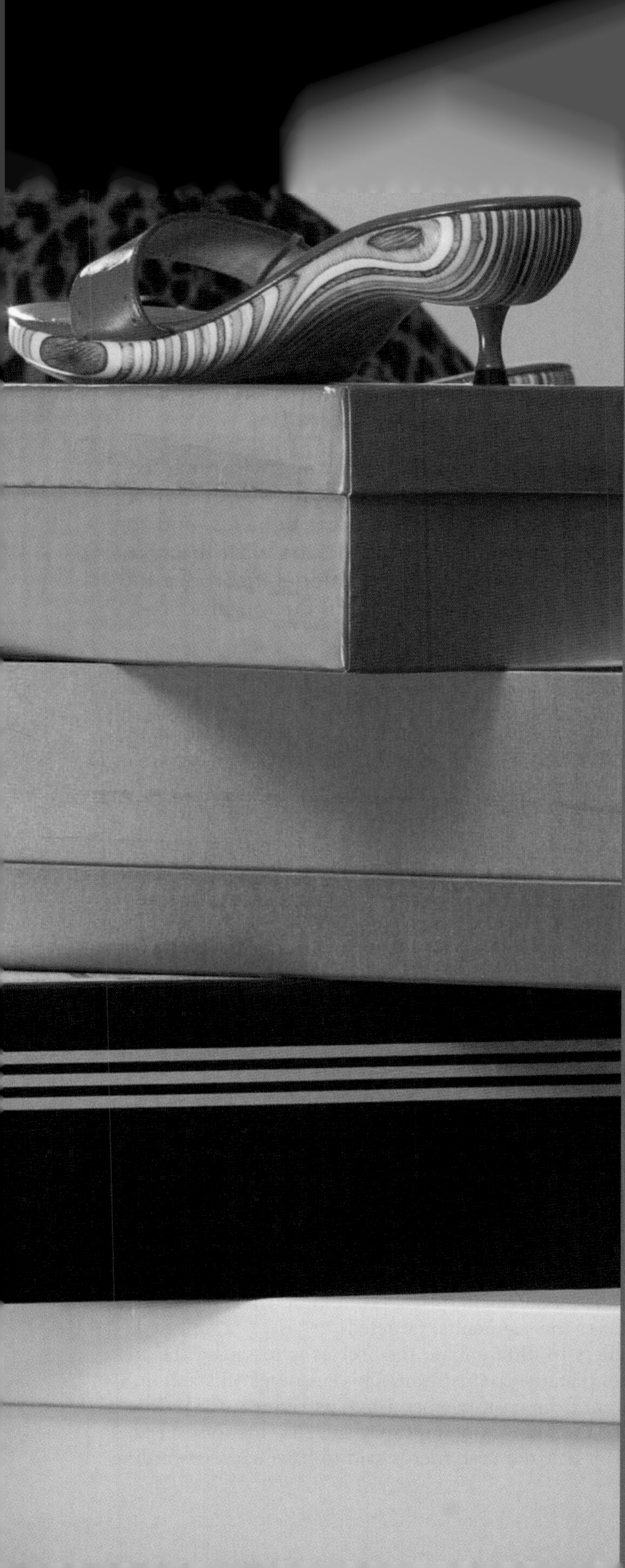

2

The Retailing Environment

chapter

3 Retail Customers

Overview:

In this chapter, we examine the effects of the external environment on retailing. We will discuss the effects of recent changes in the population, social, and economic trends on the way the consumer behaves, and the implications of these changes for retailers. We conclude with the development of a consumer shopping/purchasing model incorporating all of these factors to describe overall shopping and buying practices.

Learning Objectives:

After reading this chapter, you should be able to:

1. Explain the importance of population trends to the retail manager.
2. List the social trends that retail managers should regularly monitor, and describe their impact on retailing.
3. Describe changing economic trends and their effect on retailing.
4. Discuss the consumer shopping/purchasing model, including the key stages in the shopping/purchasing process.

Introduction

In Chapter 1 we said that retailing consisted of the final activities and steps needed to place a product or service in the hands of the consumer. In Chapter 2 we pointed out that to be a high performer, a retailer must be able to differentiate itself from the competition. In doing so, retail managers must realize that, with the possible exception of supermarkets, their stores can't serve all possible customer types. Some consumers will never shop at a nearby Wal-Mart and others will never shop at a Saks Fifth Avenue, Nordstrom, or Neiman Marcus. Therefore, before developing any plans, the successful retailer must first target a specific segment(s) of the overall market to serve and study the environmental factors (competition, the behavior of the other supply chain members, and legal and ethical factors) affecting that segment(s). Only then can retailers decide on a location, format, and retail mix (the combination of merchandise, assortment, price, promotion, customer service, and store layout) that best serves the segment(s) targeted.

customer satisfaction
Occurs when the total shopping experience of the customer has been met or exceeded.

The easiest way for retailers to differentiate themselves is to satisfy the customer's needs and wants better than the competition. This customer satisfaction, as we will use the term, is different from customer service. **Customer satisfaction** is determined by whether or not the total shopping experience has met or exceeded the customer's expectation. If it has, the customer is said to have had a rewarding

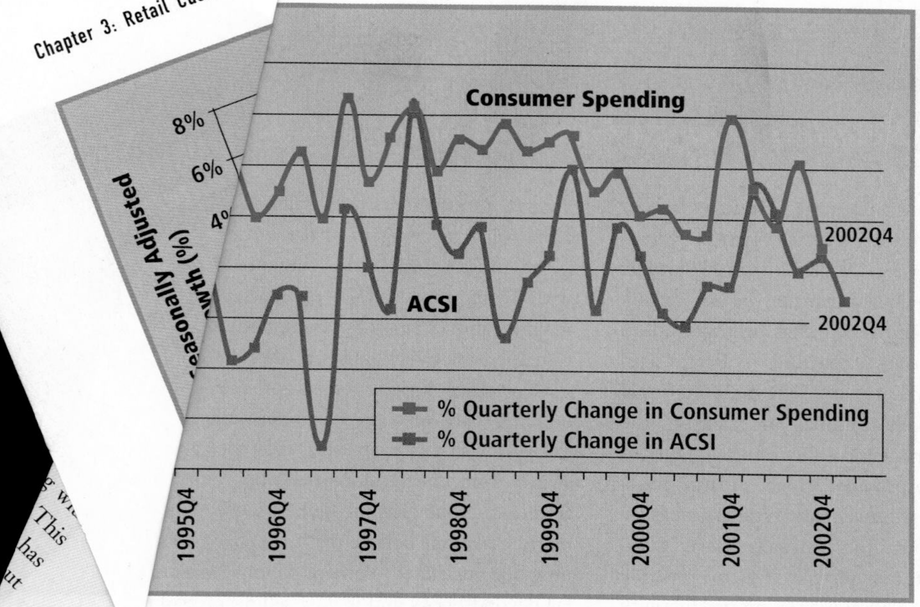

Exhibit 3.1
Consumer Spending (PCE) Growth and Lagged Satisfaction (ACSI)

shopping experience. This is important because it costs the average retailer five times as much money to get a new customer into its store as it does to retain a current customer who may be unhappy. Not only retailers, but also the nation's economy depends upon the customer having a satisfactory shopping experience. Exhibit 3.1 shows the relationship between customer satisfaction and consumer spending. The fact that spending and satisfaction move together should not be surprising since buyer satisfaction leads to repeat business and increased spending. After all, a satisfied buyer will be encouraged to engage in future spending, while the dissatisfied buyer will be more hesitant. Little wonder, then, that many economists feel that the American consumers' desire to spend has prevented the economy from suffering more severe slowdowns in the past decade.[1] This chapter's Retailing: The Inside Story box indicates how retailers have preformed in recent years according to the University of Michigan's American Customer Satisfaction Index.[2]

In addition to the tangible product or intangible service offered for sale, another part of the customer's shopping experience is the services provided by the retailer. These **customer services** are the activities performed by the retailer that influence (1) the ease with which a potential customer can shop or learn about the store's offering, (2) the ease with which a transaction can be completed once the customer attempts to make a purchase, and (3) the customer's satisfaction with the product after the purchase. These three elements are the pretransaction, transaction, and posttransaction components of customer service. Common services provided by retailers (in addition to having the product that satisfies the customer's needs and wants) include alterations, fitting rooms, delivery, gift registries, check cashing, credit, extended shopping hours, short checkout lines, gift wrapping, parking, layaway, and merchandise return privileges, as well as the availability of in-home shopping options such as television, print catalogs, and Internet shopping. It must be remembered that none of these services are actually the merchandise or service being offered for sale; they merely entice the customers whom the retailer is targeting.

customer services
Include the activities the retailer performs that influence (1) the ease with which a potential customer can shop or learn about the store's offering, (2) the ease with which a transaction can be completed once the customer attempts to make a purchase, and (3) the customer's satisfaction with the purchase.

Retailing: The Inside Story

Are Retailers Doing a Good Job Satisfying Their ...rs?

Overall, there has been only a minor decline in customer satisfaction within the retail industry over the past decade as the retail index has gone from a 73.2 ACSI score in 1996 to its most recent score of 72.4. One factor that may be accounting for this decline is that too much pressure has been placed on retail employees to generate sales. According to Prof. Claes Fornell, director of the University of Michigan's National Quality Research Center, which compiles and analyzes the ACSI data, this can have a detrimental effect on the quality of service that the staff is able to provide, which, in turn, has a negative effect on repeat buying. Since many retailers measure and manage productivity, but don't usually have good measures of the quality of customer service, it seems possible that some companies put too much emphasis on productivity at the expense of service. In addition, the overall retail score masks several large changes for both the various retail formats and individual firms.

In the specialty stores industry, The Home Depot posted the biggest decline among any company measured in 2005, with an 8.2 percent drop from 73 to 67. Its major competitor, Lowe's, on the other hand, gained 2.6 percent from 76 to 78 and now leads The Home Depot by 16 percent (78 to 67). Lowe's and The Home Depot both scored 75 when the Index first measured the companies in 2001. Since then, The Home Depot has declined 10 percent, and Lowe's has gone up 4 percent. It is worth noting that since 2001, The Home Depot's stock has declined by 10 percent and Lowe's stock price has grown by 130 percent, mirroring the movement of their ACSI scores.

Kohl's continues to lead in the department and discount store category with a score of 80, up a point from last year. But the biggest positive mover is Target, which climbed 4 percent to 78. Consistent with its improved ACSI score, Target also posted strong sales in 2005. Kmart (70) were again at the bottom of th ment and discount store category. Kmart, with Sears, improved 4.5 percent in 2005, sh making moves to stay competitive. Sears a remained relatively constant over the decade.

Customer satisfaction is of the utmost imp e-tailing. Not only are customer acquisition costs i but also with this format it is easy for an unhappy cust switch from one vendor to another. Amazon.com, alon Barnes & Noble, has the highest score of any retailer (87). might make one believe that the task of book selling online now been mastered. Perhaps so, but Amazon has branched far beyond books and is now selling myriad other products o its way to becoming the first online department store. Can customer satisfaction for Amazon climb higher? That is the question that will be answered over the next few years. The e-tailer has seen its customer expectations climb extremely high. A minor glitch in service or mistakes that are quickly corrected will not dent the satisfaction the company now enjoys, but repeated problems in any aspect of service could have devastating effects on satisfaction and customer retention. Such glitches have hurt Wal-Mart as its sales increase while its score gradually declines.

The relatively new e-tailing format has the highest rating (81 current rating in 2005 versus "not being rated" in 1996), still below its all-time high of 84 in 2003 but definitely on the rebound and maintaining its lead over the ACSI bricks-and-mortar retail sector.

Source: "Retail Trade: Fourth Quarter Scores" and "Commentary by Professor Claes Fornell," *ACSI February 21, 2006 Report*. Used with the written permission of Professor Claes Fornell.

If the customer is dissatisfied with either the product offered or the services provided, that customer is less likely to choose that retailer in the future, thus decreasing future sales. (In the rest of this chapter we will use the term *product* to designate either the physical product or service offered for sale and the term *service* to refer to the services the retailer uses to facilitate that sale. However, in the case of a service retailer, the product offered is in fact the service.) Knowing what products to carry, as well as determining which customer services to offer, is a most challenging problem for retailers as they seek ways to improve the shopping experience. Imagine listening to a radio with no tuning or volume knob. The receiver picks up many different signals, some in harmony, some in conflict, so that the result is noise coming through the speaker. You're getting something, but you can't understand it. To make sense of the confusing array of available information, retailers use

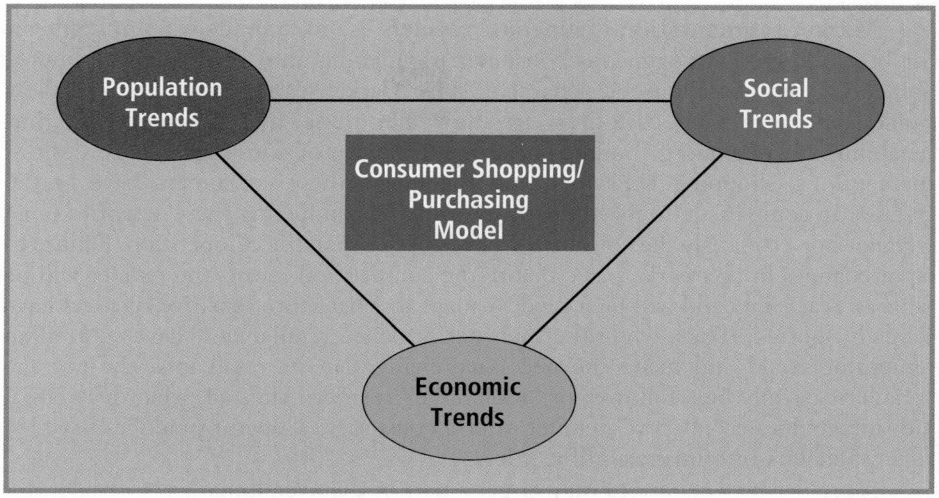

Exhibit 3.2
Current Trends Affect the Way the Consumer Behaves

market segmentation techniques to tune in segments of the population, hoping to hear a series of clear messages that can then be combined into some overall meaning. Exhibit 2.3 (on page 52) pointed out how Best Buy used a segmentation strategy to meet the needs of the target market served by a particular store. The chain customized 20 percent of its merchandise offerings and trained its sales force to meet the demands of a store's target market. Many nonretailers are surprised to find out that 80 percent of the merchandise in most chain stores is the same nationwide. It is only the remaining 20 percent that is tailored to that particular store's market.

Some retailers today claim that the declining level of satisfaction mentioned earlier in the Retailing: The Inside Story box may not actually be a bad sign. They view the decline as a function of rising expectations from the customer. They claim that their merchandise or service is much better today than it was a decade ago, but that customer expectations have increased at a faster rate. They like to point out that today's consumers are fussier and demand perfection. A nearby home improvement store, for example, might have great merchandise and low prices, but the checkout lines may be too long.

Understanding different customer segments and their need for convenience might stimulate the retailer to offer products through its Web site, thus providing a critical service component to enhance the customer's experience. As Exhibit 3.2 points out, it is important that the retailer know and understand its customer.

In Exhibit 3.2 we see the three important types of trends—population, social, and economic—that all retailers must monitor because they will affect the way customers undertake the shopping process. As pointed out in Chapter 2, retailers must perform three strategies:

1. Get as many of the targeted consumers into the store as possible.
2. Convert these consumers into customers by having them purchase merchandise.
3. Perform these first two strategies at the lowest cost possible that is consistent with the level of service that the customers expect.

If the retailer doesn't understand its customer, it won't be able to accomplish the first two strategies.

market segmentation
Is the dividing of a heterogeneous consumer population into smaller, more homogeneous groups based on their characteristics.

Market segmentation is a method retailers use to examine ways to segment, or break down, heterogeneous consumer populations into smaller, more homogeneous groups based on their characteristics. Market segmentation helps retailers understand who their customers are, how they think, and what they do, thus enabling the retailers to build a meaningful picture of consumer needs, desires, perceptions, shopping behaviors, and the image these consumers have of the retailer in comparison to its competitors. Only by conducting these activities can a retailer hope to satisfy the consumers' needs better than the competition. Failure to spot changes in the marketplace before the competition means the retailer will be able to react only and will be forced to adapt to what more sensitive retailers have already spotted. Thus, while the high-performance retailer may have spotted an emerging trend and made the necessary changes in its retail mix, the average retailer can only be a follower or "look-alike" retailer. After all, what differential advantage does a "me-too" retailer offer a consumer? Copycat practices have led many retailers into financial difficulties.

A retailer may choose to only target a part of the overall market. Consider, for example, how the three major membership club operators go after different customer segments. Sam's focuses on small businesses, which are said to spend 50 percent more than individual consumers; Costco aims to meet the needs of upscale consumers by carrying high-end merchandise like gourmet foods and jewelry; and BJ's caters to families by offering larger selections. Each of these merchants has excelled at reaching their target, although they may have excluded the other segments.

Dollars & Sense

Retailers who focus on understanding a well-defined customer niche and serving that market with a differentiated offer will be more profitable than their competitors.

Now, let's begin our study of the changing consumer to see how an understanding of population, social, and economic trends can help a retailer select a market segment to target.

LO 1 Population Trends

Explain the importance of population trends on retail planning.

Retailers often find it useful to group consumers according to **population variables**, such as population growth trends, age distributions, and geographic trends. This is useful for two reasons: First, such data are often linked to marketplace needs; second, the data are readily available and can easily be applied in analyzing markets.

population variables
Include population growth trends, age distributions, and geographic trends.

Population Growth

Retailers have long viewed an expanding population base as synonymous with growth in retail markets. Unfortunately, the nation's overall growth rate has been declining during the past three decades as families have fewer children. If current average projections are correct, the United States population will increase only about 1 percent a year, from 295 million in 2005 to 336 million in 2020 and to 420 million by 2050, or 37 percent over the next 40 years.[3] The majority of this growth will be the result of immigration.

Implications for Retailers

Any increase in domestic population growth will mean an increased demand for goods and services, but nowhere near the 80 percent increase experienced over the last half-century. Still, even minimal growth in the total population will mean opportunities for retailers. However, as population growth slows, retailers will focus on taking market share from competitors, managing gross margin by controlling selling price and cost, and increasing productivity of existing stores.

Some retailers will grow by changes in individual demand for a product. As pointed out in the previous chapter's Inside Story box on PetSmart, the increase demand for pets has resulted in the growth of both pet parents and multiple-pet families. This has resulted in a situation where the growth of the pet population is outstripping the slower growth of the overall population. Another growth opportunity for retailers will be international expansion. However, this may be only a limited time opportunity; demographers are predicting a major decline in worldwide fertility rates. This will lead to a global population decline, which is a radical notion in a world brought up on the idea of overpopulation. While it will take some time, worldwide retailers should be prepared for depopulation.[4]

Age Distribution

The age distribution of the U.S. population is changing significantly. In 1980 the median age was 30, but by 2005 it had risen to over 35 years.[5] The most significant change today is the bulge of early baby boomers moving into their late fifties. This group today accounts for almost 28 percent of the population. Starting January 1, 2008, the first wave of boomers will reach the retirement age of 62. That means that every seven seconds some American, upon entering the demographic group known as the "gray market," will not be spending as freely they did in the past. Many other older citizens are aggressively saving for retirement because of increasing concern over the long-term viability of Social Security and uncertainty about corporate downsizing, which has left many mature adults unemployed. It is assumed that in the future this first wave of boomers will spend less on apparel and clothing and

© Getty Images/PhotoDisc

© Getty Images/PhotoDisc

The graying of America over the next two decades will generate more demand for leisure-oriented as well as medical and health-related goods and services. The retailers that respond to this opportunity will experience a large growth opportunity.

Service Retailing

Growing Old Isn't What It Used to Be

Baby boomers, whose parents were raised during the Great Depression, were taught to focus on saving money for that "rainy day." However, it appears that today's boomers, especially the younger ones, have something different in mind.

The authors are friends with several couples who, like many other 40-something boomers, live in fancy homes that are mortgaged to the hilt, drive leased luxury cars, and purchase apparel at Saks and Neiman Marcus. These couples represent the newest behavioral trend among boomers—being a "waiter." In other words, they are "waiting for their inheritance." Sadly, many are not just waiting but have actually become dependent on what economists say will be the largest amount of money, some $25 trillion, ever set aside for transferring between generations.

These boomers may be disappointed, since family assets have dwindled in recent years as savings are being depleted by the high costs of nursing homes, long-term care, and prescription drugs, increasingly common expenses since Americans are living longer. Fluctuations in the stock market and unpredictable housing values have also taken a toll on family assets.

Making matters worse, as these family assets dwindled, the "old school" parents avoided any discussion with their children about their finances and or what was in their wills. This has led to many a sibling battle over who gets what and when.

As a result, a new type of service retailer has emerged—a combination financial planner and attorney. These professionals seek to avoid family feuds after a parent's death. Their services range from extensive will planning to counseling on how retirees can communicate inheritance decisions to their children. This communication is important since baby boomers have a significantly different attitude toward money than their parents. Because of their Great Depression experiences, the parents were savers, whereas baby boomers grew up in the prosperity of the 1950s and 1960s and never wanted for the basics. Boomers were the spenders who "shopped till they dropped" in the 1980s.

Lifestyle changes also increase the need for these service professionals. The higher divorce rates of recent years and increased number of remarriages have created confusion about the rights of stepchildren and second or third spouses in wills.

Little wonder, then, that these financial planners/lawyers seek to avoid family disputes by placing less emphasis on documenting what a parent wants to say in a will. Instead they spend their time asking detailed questions about the boomer children, such as financial status, living situations, and relationships with siblings. These counselors encourage parents to include their children in estate planning meetings so that everyone involved will understand who is getting what and why, all in an attempt to avoid an extended battle after the parents' deaths.

One word of warning: Over half of the respondents in a recent survey of Americans over 65 stated that they weren't going to divide their assets equally among their children. Instead they plan to give a larger share to the attentive child—the one who provided care, for example.

Source: Based on "I Inherited My Money the Hard Way: I Earned It," *AARP Bulletin*, December 2005: 6; "Not Acting Their Age," *U.S. News & World Report*, June 4, 2001: 54–60; John C. Carver, "Is It Going to Be 'Share the Wealth'?" Texas A&M University, working paper, 1999; "Going Deeper in Debt," *AARP Bulletin*, March 2003: 22–24; Roger M. Williams, "The New Breed and the Mega-Bucks," *Foundation News and Commentary*, September/October 2001: 25; and the authors' observations.

---

more on medicine and recreation. They will focus more on security, good health, comfort, their homes, safety, and most importantly, seeking new experiences.[6]

Today's younger boomers, those between 45 and 55, are unlike the previous generations who, when they reached midlife, would pare debt and begin to save for retirement. As described in this chapter's Service Retailing box, these younger boomers have instead employed a new breed of consultants—a combination of financial planner and attorney—who are equipped to advise parents and their children on how to manage what will be the largest transfer of wealth from one generation to another, some $25 trillion over the next half century.[7]

Seniors should not be viewed as homogeneous. In the past seniors were classified as anyone over age 60. Because people live longer now, more useful categories should be utilized. Octogenarians are people aged 80 to 89, nonagenarians are 90 to 99, and centenarians are 100 and above. In the United States there are more than 70,000 centenarians. By 2010 the number of centenarians is expected to increase by 50 percent.[8] Another useful way to categorize seniors is in terms of their health (good/poor) and wealth (inadequate/adequate). Thus there are four types of seniors: good health/adequate wealth, good health/inadequate wealth, poor health/adequate wealth, and poor health/inadequate wealth. Seniors in general have more wealth than several generations ago due to improved social security benefits, Medicare, and retirement savings, and are relatively healthier than previous generations. The population segment with the largest percentage growth over the past five years has been "active" seniors who have both the health and the wealth to enjoy themselves.

"Baby busters" or "Generation Xers"—those born between 1965 and 1977—are another interesting age group. Unlike the baby boomers, this age group is a declining percentage of the population. Today there are 46 million of these consumers.

"Generation Y," "echo boomers," or the "millennium generation" are those born between 1978 and 1994 and number over 70 million. They are emerging as a major buying and consuming force in the economy. This generation is racially diverse; more than one in three is not Caucasian, and has been pampered, nurtured, and programmed with a slew of activities since they were preschoolers. Three out of four have a working mother, and one out of four is in a single parent household. There is emerging evidence that the Gen Yers' values are more traditional than those of their parents and that they have a conservative lifestyle, as evidenced by their tendency to live separately before marriage. Gen Yers want a professional career but place a higher priority on family and home. Many Generation Yers have never wound a watch, purchased a record, used a typewriter, or dialed a phone; however, they think nothing of using a memory stick to save class assignments, downloading music off the Internet, or having tongue rings.[9] In many ways, they are the most "optimistic" generation in this country's history. They tend to have higher disposable incomes than their age group in prior generations, are interested in good health, and tend not to rely on others for their success. Research has found that Gen Y provides a wealth of potential to employers because of their vigor, enthusiasm, talent, early experience, and high expectations.[10] Exhibit 3.3 illustrates the key differences between these age groups.

Exhibit 3.3
Boomers, Xers, and Yers

	Baby Boomers	Gen X	Gen Y
Also known as	Boomers	Baby busters	Echo boomers Millennium generation Digital generation
Dates of birth	1946–1964	1965–1977	1978–1994
Number in U.S.	76 million	46 million	75 million
Annual spending	Over 900 billion	Over 125 billion	35–100 billion
Experienced	Birth of rock and roll Space exploration Racial divides Sexual revolution	Growing divorce rate Gang violence Pop culture Information explosion	Age of technology Multilayered information Growth in branding Recycling
Respond to	Authority	Creativity	Learning
Perspective on technology	Fearful	Proficient	Indoctrinated
Attitude	Realistic	Pessimistic	Optimistic

Dollars & Sense

Retailers who understand the implications of the country's age distribution will be more apt to identify opportunities to improve their profit performance.

Implications for Retailers

The most significant implication of an aging population is negative for retailers because, especially with regards to the boomers, these consumers' big spending years are behind them. However, retailers must resist the temptation to overlook them since they will still be buying cars, travel, and expensive "toys" for themselves.[11]

Besides understanding the various needs of each age segment, retailers must remember what motivates consumers to spend money. Younger adults are, by their very nature, acquisition-oriented. These first-time renters and home buyers need to acquire material objects and usually judge their progress by such possessions. Older adults tend to conserve what they have already acquired. Thus, as the population ages, a significant driving force for total economic growth may dry up unless retailers provide a reason to shop.[12]

Dollars & Sense

Because consumers change their spending habits as they age, the leading retailers of the next decade will be those that best adapt to these changes.

The changing distribution of the U.S. population poses many challenges and opportunities. Retailers should be aware of what was pointed out earlier—consumers over 60 tend to focus more on their families and finances than those in other age groups. They also spend more on medical services and travel. Thus, the products and services that appealed to boomers as free-spending younger consumers will not necessarily be the ones that appeal to them now as grandparents and homeowners. In addition, this older market is expected to use the services of others more often. The DIY (do-it-yourself) market has begun to soften now that there are more people over 35 than under 35. As the population ages, more people are becoming "do-it-for-me's." This DIFM (do-it-for-me) trend is rapidly growing in the services arena. Two popular emerging do-it-for-me services are home cleaning and yard care. These services have become especially popular among dual-income households over 35, where there is little discretionary time but ample discretionary income. This trend towards DIFM has extended to the financial industry where seniors have shifted to full-service advice firms as they start to withdraw funds from retirement accounts.[13] As the chapter's Global Retailing box illustrates, this trend towards DIFM appears to have spread worldwide, even to undeveloped retail markets.

The "graying of America" will have enormous consequences for business in general, not just retailing, as older consumers tend to be skeptical and less interested in shopping. Retailers must be able to speak the older consumers' language, avoid talking down or patronizing them, shun "phony friendliness," and in a tactful manner recognize that as they age, older consumers have a declining ability to deal with spatial relationships, thus necessitating easy-to-navigate store layouts and clearly labeled merchandise.[14] As shown in our Service Retailing box, it is doubtful that all the baby boomers will behave as their parents did a generation before them. Retailers who make this assumption will be mistaken. A 50-year-old in 2010 will not act like a 50-year-old in 1990. In fact, they may even keep some of the habits of a 30-year-old in 1990 (which is what they were), tempered with the wisdom of

Global Retailing

Home Improvement Is a Worldwide Thing

Consumers around the world are interested in home improvements. While 55 percent of Americans enjoy spending time on home improvement, an even higher percentage of shoppers in other countries, including the less-developed retail markets, also enjoy such projects. Many of these consumers prefer to have others help them with those projects instead of doing them alone.

Driven by an aspiration to achieve a higher standard of living, 75 percent of the consumers in Mexico, 69 percent of those in Russia, 65 percent of Poles, and 64 percent of the residents in India indicate that they enjoy spending time on home improvements projects. These are nations whose retail markets are less developed than those in the United States. China's results (55%) are similar to those of shoppers in a group of developed countries—United States, Canada, France, Germany, and the United Kingdom. Brazil (28%), Japan (37%), and Italy (38%) lag in a 2005 Retail Forward study with the smallest share of shoppers who say they enjoy home improvement projects.

In terms of the DIFM services, China (68%) joins India (76%), Russia (76%), and Mexico (70%) as the countries where shoppers say they prefer to shop at stores that also offer installation services. In contrast, consumers in the developed retail markets of the United Kingdom (24%), Germany (25%), Japan (26%), and Canada (33%) show the least preference for shopping at stores that also offer installation services. The United States is in the middle at 39 percent. One possible explanation for consumers in undeveloped markets having a higher interest in shopping at stores offering installation is that while most of these consumers want to enjoy the benefits of these improvements they lack the technical know-how regarding their use.

Source: Retail Forward's *Global Homegoods Shopper Update*, July 2005; 10–11. Used with the written permission of Retail Forward.

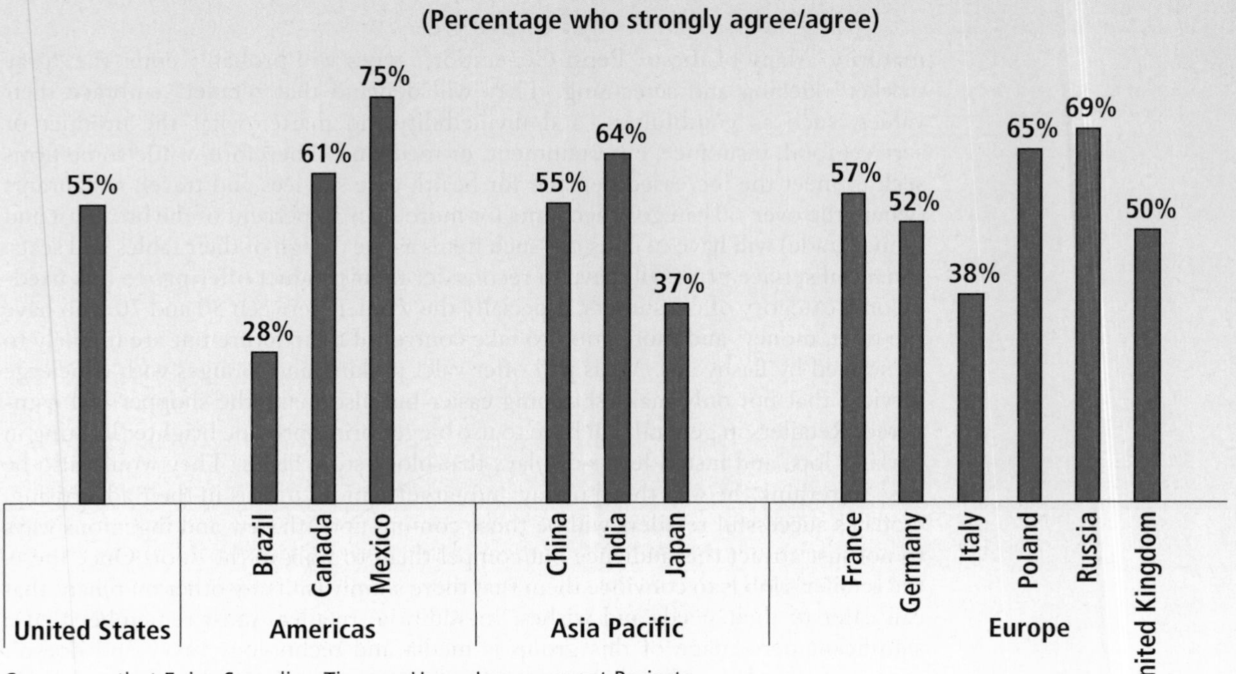

Consumers that Enjoy Spending Time on Home Improvement Projects

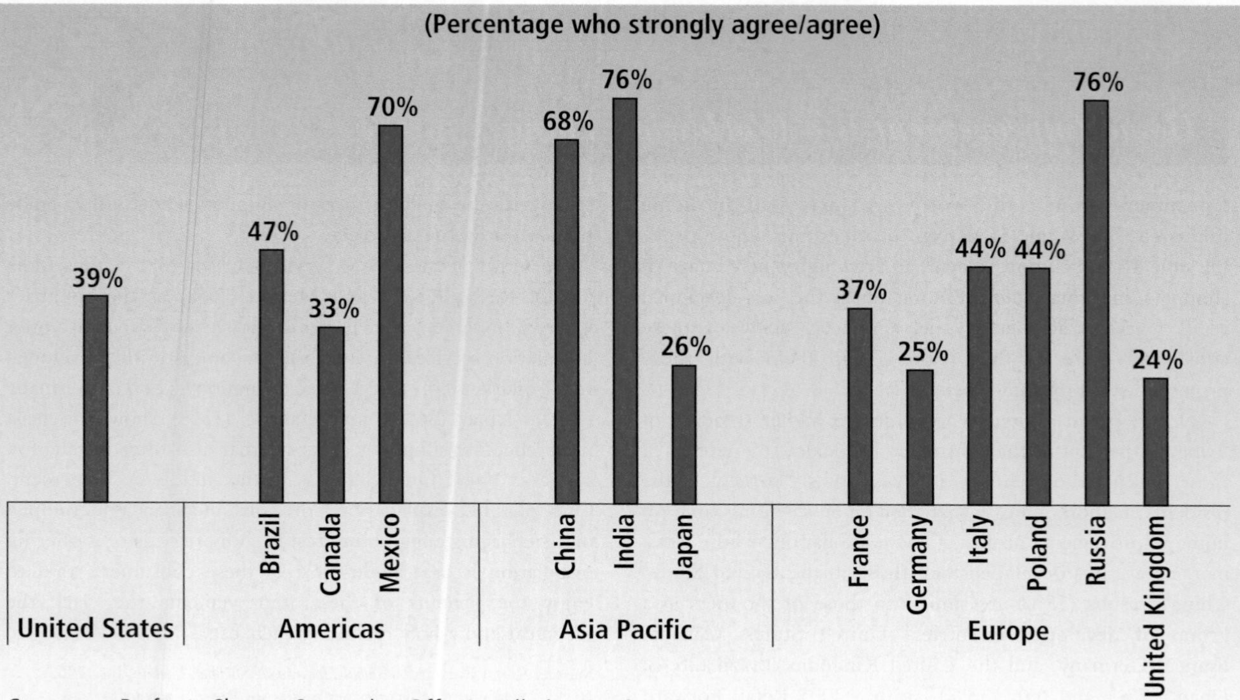

Consumers Prefer to Shop at Stores that Offer Installation Services

maturity. Many of these "Pepsi Generation" types will probably enter the "gray market" kicking and screaming. They will demand that retailers embrace their values, such as youthfulness and invincibility, no matter what the product or service: food, insurance, entertainment, or medicine. Therefore, while some firms seek to meet the increased demand for health care services and travel, restaurants (where the over-60 category accounts for more than 30 percent of the breakfast and dinner trade) will have to consider such items as the design of their tables and seats. Financial service firms will have to reconsider their product offerings to this fixed-income category of consumers, especially the women between 50 and 70 who have the time, money, and motivation to take control of their future but are unlikely to be swayed by flashy ads. Malls will offer valet parking and lounges with concierge services that not only make shopping easier but also make the shopper feel pampered. Retailers in general will have to use bigger print, provide brighter lighting in parking lots, and install fewer displays that block store aisles. They would also be wise to rethink the way they portray and target senior citizens in their advertising. Today's successful retailers will be those coming up with new and ingenious ways to not just attract this audience but compel them to walk in the door. Once there, the retailer's job is to convince them that there simply isn't any other merchant that can cater to their needs and wishes. In addition, retailers must remember that a significant percentage of this group is media and technology savvy and doesn't appreciate condescending behavior.

Retailers haven't forgotten about the Gen Xers and Gen Yers. These two groups are not only different in age but are also significantly different in their

Matthew Staver/Bloomberg News/Landov

Home improvement retailers offer design services that help consumers plan and budget their home improvement projects. If the consumer prefers not to do their own installation, these retailers offer installation services.

buying behavior. They will be difficult for retailers to reach without a well considered effort. Young consumers today don't appreciate conspicuous consumption. In fact, they are more sophisticated than previous generations when it comes to shopping and seem to be turned off by promotions that don't take them seriously. These anti-fashion and anti-establishment consumers still want entertainment or events when they shop.[15] However, these promotions must be relevant to them, funny, and say "we understand." Retailers dealing with this market can't fake it. Marriott, the 2,700-unit hotel chain, is currently in the midst of a major makeover to attract the younger business-casual, iPod-playing traveler. The chain does not need to make a special appeal to Gen X travelers, since they already have established a strong loyalty bond with them.[16] A major problem for retailers seeking to tap this market is that Gen Yers don't turn to newspapers or magazines for information. For them, it is the Internet or television. Since newspaper advertising is the primary vehicle for most retailers, they may have to reexamine their strategy.[17]

Most retailers have made a major mistake by overlooking the "tweeners," those consumers aged 8 to 14. These younger shoppers spend $10 billion annually and influence another $250 billion in purchases. Tweeners now serve as the *de facto* family chief technology officer. Not only do they get consulted before any major family purchase, but also they have probably already done an online search about the item.[18] Retailers of all sorts should target these shoppers as well as their parents. After all, while their parents might cite price as the #1 reason for purchasing a particular item used by their children, "child request" was a close second.[19] Tweeners have trained their parents to know what to buy for them. While many companies analyze which products will appeal to the older generations, retailers seldom think about marketing specifically to children younger than teenagers. Aéropostale, for example, has shifted from targeting teenage males to targeting younger females, because girls buy more clothes; and those goods enjoy higher profit margins. Now instead of going head-to-head with Abercrombie & Fitch and American Eagle Outfitters for the high-school and college-age shoppers, the chain carries clothes which are slightly less sexy and revealing to appeal to tweeners and their parents. Aéropostale found less competition for the younger age group.[20]

Geographic Trends

The location of consumers in relation to the retailer often affects how they buy. In this section we take a closer look at how geographic trends affect retail operations.

Shifting Geographic Centers

Retailers should be concerned not only with the number of people and their ages, but also with where they reside. Consumers, especially as they get older, will not travel great distances to make retail purchases. Consumers want convenience and will therefore patronize local retail outlets. Because the U.S. population for the past 200 years has been moving toward the West and the South, growth opportunities in retailing should be greatest in these areas. Consider that between 2000 and 2003 the eight fastest-growing states were all in the West (Idaho, Nevada, Utah, Arizona, Colorado) and South (Georgia, Florida, and Texas). In fact, between now and 2030, the South's population is expected to grow by 43 percent and the West's by 46 percent, versus only 10 percent for the Midwest and 8 percent for the Northeast.[21] As will be pointed out later in this chapter, there are marked overall differences in the behavior of consumers based on the region where they live.

Implications for Retailers This changing geographic shift means northeastern and midwestern retailers are experiencing slower growth, and national retailers are adding stores and distribution centers (warehouses) in the South and West. A common mistake made by retailers is to assume that all the consumers in a certain geographic area have the same purchasing habits. While households in the Northeast tend to marry later, spend more on education, food, housing, and apparel as a percentage of consumer expenditures, they don't all spend that way. Midwesterners on average spend more on entertainment, tobacco, and smoking supplies; those in the South spend relatively more on transportation and health care, and make more cash contributions. Finally, those in the West spend more on personal insurance and pensions, housing, and entertainment. Exhibit 3.4 contains an important lesson for retailers because it shows that not only do consumers living in one state, Texas, have different consumption patterns than people living in other states, but also that even Texas consumers have dissimilar shopping habits. (Note the amount of lard used in west Texas, the home of one of the authors.) In fact, these same differences have been found to occur in different parts of the same city. As a result, many of the leading retailers have developed "micromarketing" merchandising strategies.

micromarketing
Is the tailoring of merchandise in each store to the preferences of its neighborhood.

Micromarketing involves tailoring merchandise in each store by using the optional stock list approach, discussed in Chapter 1, to match the preferences of its neighborhood. This is made possible by the use of computer software programs that match neighborhood demographics with product demand. Two of the biggest Sears stores in the Chicago area are nearly the same size and do about the same annual sales volume. However, the merchandise makeup of the two stores is different. The urban store, which is close to many gourmet bakeries, doesn't carry bread makers, but bread makers are popular items in the more upscale suburban store 15 miles away.

Exhibit 3.4
Texas Consumers' Percentage of National Average Usage

Product	Dallas/Fort Worth (%)	Houston (%)	San Antonio/ Corpus Christi (%)	West Texas/ New Mexico (%)
Biscuits/Dough	148*	122	103	85
Butter	51	57	39	57
Fresh Eggs	94	112	141	110
Juice/RFG	74	104	76	66
Lard	26	121	**	419
Canned Ham	39	21	22	28
Sausage	134	179	219	73
Baked Beans	82	76	51	60
Cocktail Mixes	118	79	82	112
Pasta	71	80	72	76
Rice/Popcorn Cakes	84	69	58	73
Cosmetics	237	133	329	221
Cold/Sinus Tab/Cough Drops	157	113	125	105
Deodorant	119	118	125	86
Hair Coloring	137	122	238	130
Laxatives	152	116	164	117
Cat Food	88	73	81	67
Diapers	115	135	160	74
Facial Tissue	82	66	64	78
Paper Napkins	71	74	78	68
Motor Oil	112	92	279	114
Shoe Polish & Accessories	147	145	171	147
Tape	163	105	175	149
Hosiery	164	126	156	110

*National average = 100%
**Not measured in this market.
Source: Used with the permission of Information Resources, Inc.

Retailers who develop micromarketing merchandising strategies will have higher profit performance.

Dollars & Sense

Urban Centers

Most of the U.S. population resides in metropolitan areas with populations greater than 50,000, which the U.S. Census Bureau calls **metropolitan statistical areas** (MSAs). The proportion of the population residing in these cities has increased dramatically, from 64 percent in 1950 to 79 percent today. However, the urban or metropolitan population varies considerably by state. For instance California, Massachusetts, and New Jersey are over 90 percent urban/metro; whereas Maine, Mississippi, Vermont, and West Virginia are less than 50 percent urban/metro.[22] This migration to MSAs is directed more to suburban than central city areas.

metropolitan statistical areas
Are freestanding urban areas with populations in excess of 50,000.

Implications for Retailers Every shift in consumer population patterns has major implications for retailers, especially regarding where expenditures are made for

Often in large metropolitan areas, the central cities have clusters of small retailers, especially food and grocery, that cater to various ethnic groups that live nearby.

household products. While these recent shifts have resulted in a slowdown in downtown retail activity, sales increases in freestanding suburban locations have more than offset any decline.

There are also opportunities for retailers in smaller markets. During the past decade, retail activity has grown rapidly in secondary markets, areas with populations less than 50,000. Historically, most chain retailers have ignored these markets. But in addition to their rapid growth, secondary markets are attractive because of the low level of retail competition, lower building costs, cheaper labor, and fewer building and zoning regulations. As MSAs have begun to stabilize, secondary markets have become more attractive.

Mobility

In many countries, people are born, raised, married, widowed, and die in the same city or immediate geographic area. While this was once true in the United States, it certainly is not characteristic of contemporary America. Typically, Americans change residence about a dozen times in a lifetime. This is twice the rate of the British and French and four times as often as the Irish. A major factor for this heightened mobility is the country's divorce rate. Of those that move each year, about 64 percent remain in the same county, about 21 percent move to a new county but stay in the same state, and approximately 18 percent move to a new state.[23] The farther one moves from a prior residence, the more one needs to establish new retail shopping patterns.

Implications for Retailers A study regarding mobility has found that in almost half of large families where the children don't go to college, one child will live within five miles of the parent(s) when the parent(s) reaches age 60; and in more than three-quarters of the cases within 50 miles of the parent(s).[24] Thus, in view of the recent trend toward higher education (discussed in the next learning objective), which results in more job variations, retailers can only expect that mobility will increase. This presents a problem because retailers serve local markets and tend to cater to well-defined demographic groups. If the population moves, the retailer may find that its target market no longer resides in its immediate area. Likewise, retailers in areas undergoing rapid population growth will want to be prepared to serve these new consumers quickly, as many retail-oriented decisions must be made on the spot. After a move, consumers must locate new sources for food, clothing, household goods, and recreation. This presents an advantage for chain operations, since a consumer moving from Des Moines, Iowa, to Baton Rouge, Louisiana, knows what to expect at a Target, Old Navy, Macy's, or Banana Republic.

Social Trends

LO 2

What social trends should be monitored and what are their impacts on retailing?

In this section, we will continue our examination of demographic factors affecting the modern retailer by looking at several social trends: the increasing level of educational attainment, the state of marriage and divorce, the makeup of the American household, and the changing nature of work. To get the most current data regarding these trends, the reader should visit the home page of the Commerce Department's Census Bureau Web site (http://www.census.gov). This site provides easy access to the latest census figures.

Education

The education level of the average American is increasing. In 2003, 85 percent of individuals over age 25 had a high school degree and 27 percent had a college degree. The Gen Xers, who were between the ages 25 and 34 in 2003, are the most educated generation ever. Nearly one in three has completed four years of college. This statistic is almost as high as the 41 percent of those over 25 that had a high school degree in 1960.[25] Currently, more men than women have a college degree.[26] However, this trend is rapidly changing since in 2006 there were 23 percent more women enrolled in college than men.[27] As a result, it is forecast that in the very near future women, who are increasingly pursuing high-paying career fields such as business, psychology, biology/life sciences, and engineering, will earn nearly 60 percent of the bachelor's and master's degrees in U.S. colleges.[28]

Implications for Retailers

Educational attainment is the single most reliable indicator of a person's income potential, attitudes, and spending habits. Thus, college-educated consumers differ in their buying behavior from other workers of the same age and income levels. They are more alert to price, quality, and advertised claims. However, often overlooked when using education to segment the marketplace, are the 32 million Americans over the age of 25 who have some college experience but not a degree. In many ways, people with some college best define the term "average" American.[29] They have more money than high school graduates, but less than college graduates. They also fall between the groups in their propensity to shop in department stores, spend on apparel, buy new cars, travel, read books, watch TV, and invest in stocks and bonds.

Since education levels for the population, in aggregate, are expected to continue to rise, retailers can expect consumers to become increasingly sophisticated, discriminating, and independent in their search for consumer products. They will also demand a staff capable of intelligently dealing with their needs and wants.

Education is a key determinant of the use of the Internet for shopping. Today's 30- and 40-year-olds grew up with the computer and feel comfortable with it. Given their higher level of education, they are more prone to shop electronically because they don't need the assurances or hand holding that some retailers provide. This may present problems for many traditional service providers. For example, as highlighted back in Chapter 1's What's New box (on page 5), travel agencies today may be left out of the loop as cyber shoppers surf the net to purchase airline tickets, hotel rooms, rental cars, and cruises.

State of Marriage

A relatively new social phenomenon has occurred during the past quarter century. In 1970, less than 10 percent of the U.S. male population between the ages of 30 and 34 had never married, and just over 6 percent of the same female population had never married. In 2003, these percentages had increased to 33 and 23 percent, respectively.[30] Married couples are one of the slowest growing household types not only in this country but also worldwide. In 1970, males married at a median age of 23 and females at 21; today the median age for males is about 26 and for females it is 25, however, there are marked regional differences in these numbers.[31] Not only are many people postponing marriage, some are choosing not to marry at all. In the 45- to 54-year-old bracket, 11 percent of males and nine percent of females have never been married.[32]

Implications for Retailers

For the retailer, this trend toward single-person households presents many opportunities because of the increased need for a larger number of smaller houses complete with home furnishings. This is especially true for the young adult market. The retailer may need to adjust its store hours to accommodate the needs of this market. Also, with more men living alone, supermarkets will have to direct promotions toward their needs and habits, since men tend to focus on getting specific items and then getting out of the store as quickly as possible.

Divorce

Since 1960, the U.S. divorce rate has increased by 250 percent. It may be interesting at this point to review the findings of Professor Gary Becker of the University of Chicago. Professor Becker was awarded the 1992 Nobel Prize in economics, theorizing that families, just like businesses, rationally make decisions that maximize benefits. The theory suggests that in the traditional family, working husbands and stay-at-home wives each performed labor that, when combined, provided the greatest payoff for the time involved. However, as women's wages rose, it became more profitable for them to enter the labor force. As a result, spouses became less dependent on each other and divorces increased. An interesting statistic is that the average divorce occurs approximately 7.2 years after marriage, confirming the conventional wisdom about the seven-year itch.

Implications for Retailers

When a divorce occurs, many retail purchases are required. A second household, quite similar to that of the never-married individual, is formed almost immediately. These new households need certain items such as furniture and kitchen appliances, televisions and stereos, and even linens. Divorce may impact the way people shop, once they are settled into their new homes. Retailers must make specific adjustments for divorced, working women with children by adjusting store hours, providing more consumer information, and changing the product assortment.[33]

Makeup of American Households

Because households are the basic consumer unit for most products, household growth and consumer demand go together. Yet, because of the differing sizes and habits of various generations, the change in the makeup of households is notoriously hard to predict. The number of households without children increased 27 percent in the 1970s, 14 percent in the 1980s, and only 7 percent between 1990 and 2001. Most people are unaware of the fact that 52 percent of all households have no children.[34]

Some interesting trends have occurred over the last two decades. For example, between 1980 and 2003, the number of people living alone ("home-aloners") increased by 45 percent.[35] This trend, which represented nearly one-fourth of all households, is the result of an increased desire for privacy, an increase in young adults delaying marriage, an increase in never-marrieds, and a large increase in the number of people who live alone after the death of a spouse. Also, the number of unmarried couples ("mingles") has increased by 167 percent since 1980. This trend, although it represents only 7 percent of all couple households,[36] is significant to the retailer because it represents a purchasing unit that is hard to understand by conventional household or family norms. The retailer, as well as the social scientist, has little knowledge of how much joint decision making occurs in such households.

Finally, there is one more interesting facet about the changing American household formation: the **boomerang effect**—so called because the parents think the children have left for good, but they keep coming back. It is estimated that over the next decade 40 percent of children will return to live with their parents after they have previously left. While this projection is extremely sensitive to future economic conditions, several factors will account for the projected 7 million boomerang households: people who marry in their twenties are just as likely to divorce as those who marry as teens, high school dropouts will not be able to find permanent work, and so on. In addition, with the average college grad owing over $32,000 in student loans, living with the folks helps.[37]

Implications for Retailers

Today, the combination of "home-aloners," "mingles," "singles," "dinks" (dual-income, no-kids households), and "empty nesters" accounts for nearly 75 percent of all U.S. households. This market is not concerned about "back-to-school" sales and other family-oriented retail activities. This segment of the market is more interested in CD and DVD players, high social image, and gourmet foods. However, it is important that retailers recognize the differences within this market. Younger women normally spend more on clothing and men spend more on alcohol, cars, and eating out. As they age, women begin to spend more than men on cars and entertainment while men remain the best customers for eating out. The older segment of the single household market will require special attention from today's retailers. Between now and 2010, the "wild and crazy single guys" of the 1980s and early 1990s will turn into "tired and pudgy older guys" who no longer live like college students.

Changing Nature of Work

In the United States and other industrialized economies, work has become less central to life. In the past, work was often the way people identified themselves and obtained a meaningful life. Perhaps because of deterioration in institutional confidence or perhaps because of the overall prosperity of our economy and our way of life as Americans, we are identifying less with our employment. At the same time, people's hobbies are becoming more work-oriented. People are gardening, investing time and money in learning to cook, and doing projects around the house. There is also a rise of self-employed and home-based workers. In 2003, the most recent year for which data is available, there were nearly 10 million self-employed individuals and an estimated 6 million home-based businesses in the United States.[38] Most of these individuals enjoy the solitude of working at home. These individuals clearly have a distinctive lifestyle. For instance, they are very active in hiking, camping, bird watching, antique shopping, and visiting art museums. They are heavy subscribers to Internet services.

Some consumers are obtaining meaning from consumption. They are literally durable goods junkies collecting RVs, boats, workshops, plasma televisions, swimming pools, and so on. Often, in order to pay for these extras, people hold multiple jobs. In 2003, 7.3 million individuals had multiple jobs.[39] Many of these individuals were starting a small business while holding their main job; others were earning money to purchase something special, saving for future consumption, or saving to retire early so they will not have to work.

Implications for Retailers

Because people are finding less meaning in their work, they are less loyal to their employers. Nearly 30 percent of workers have held their job for less than 12 months and the median length of service in a job is 3.7 years.[40] For entry level personnel in retailing, turnover approaches 75 percent or more per year. Consequently, retailers need to find ways to enrich job experiences and lower turnover. One study found that turnover in the supermarket industry costs $5.8 billion annually. A cashier who departs costs $4,212; a department manager, $9,354; and a store manager, $56,844. Costs of employee turnover include paperwork errors, inventory shrinkage, and improper use of equipment. All of these errors occur due to the lack of experience of new employees. These errors lead to lower levels of customer service, which further leads to lost sales and profits.[41] One major opportunity for retailers is to employ home-based and disabled workers. Home-based workers can handle telephone inquiries and do clerical work or bookkeeping. Likewise, disabled workers may represent a previously untapped pool of talent for the retailer.

Finally, since many individuals are holding multiple jobs, retailers can tap into this pool of individuals for part-time workers. Retailers have done this in the past primarily at the clerk level. Today there are opportunities for retailers to employ part-timers in a variety of positions including accounting, inventory control, merchandising, buying, and store management.

LO 3

Economic Trends

How do changing American economic trends affect retailing?

In this section, we look at the effect on the modern retailer of income growth, the declining rate of personal savings, the increase in the number of working women, and the widespread use of credit in our economy.

Income Growth

In 2002, the median household income was slightly over $51,600, which, after adjusting for inflation, was an increase of less than 4 percent annually since 1980. As total incomes rise, families also tend to have higher disposable incomes. All groups have not shared this income increase equally. African-American, Hispanic, and Caucasian family households experienced a rise in annual income of 4 percent to $33,500, $34,100, and $54,600 respectively from 1980 to 2002. Notably, Asian Pacific Islander family households, which were not tracked in 1980, had the highest household family income, which stood at $60,900 in 2002.[42]

Exhibit 3.5
Share of Aggregate Income Received by Each Fifth and the Top 5% of U.S. Households, 1980–2002

Year	Lowest Fifth	Second Fifth	Third Fifth	Fourth Fifth	Highest Fifth	Top 5%
2002	4.2	9.7	15.5	23.0	47.6	20.8
2000	4.3	9.8	15.4	22.7	47.7	21.1
1990	4.6	10.8	16.6	23.8	44.3	17.4
1980	5.3	11.6	17.5	24.4	41.1	14.6

Source: U.S. Bureau of Census, *Statistical Abstract of the United States: 2004–2005*, Table #672.

There has also been, as shown in Exhibit 3.5, a shifting of incomes among the various classes of Americans. Today, the American upper classes have a higher share of the nation's aggregate income in comparison to 1980. Today, the top fifth of all households by income level accounts for nearly 48 percent of the nation's income, up from 41 percent in 1980, while the bottom two-fifths, or lowest 40 percent of the population, are earning only a seventh (13.9 percent) of the nation's income, down from 16.9 percent in 1980. The distribution of wealth is even more pronounced—1 percent of the population holds 40 percent of the wealth. Thus, it appears that the rich are getting richer and the poor are getting poorer. However, this data is partially misleading because income mobility in the United States is high. A significant proportion of the lowest-income households moves up the income scale over a ten-year period, and similarly, a significant proportion of the richest households moves down the income scale over the same period of time.

Implications for Retailers

The imbalance in income growth across households has created increased demand for value-oriented retailers such as discounters and manufacturers' outlets, and explains why many of the upscale retailers (such as Bergdorf Goodman, Nordstrom, and Neiman Marcus) have not suffered the economic pressures facing many of their lower-scale counterparts. Retailers of luxury automobiles, lavish foreign vacations, and executive-style houses in gated communities have also done well. At the same time, the low income level and low income growth among some segments of the population explains the growth of chains such as Dollar General.

Economists tend to view income from two different perspectives: disposable and discretionary. **Disposable income** is simply all personal income less personal taxes. For most consumers, disposable income is their take-home pay. **Discretionary income** is disposable income minus the money needed for necessities to sustain life, such as minimal housing, minimal food, and minimal clothing. Retailers that sell necessities, such as supermarkets, like to see incomes rise and taxes decrease; they know that, while consumers won't spend all their increased disposable income on the retailer's merchandise, they will nevertheless increase spending. Retailers selling luxury goods want to see disposable income increase and the cost of necessities either decline or at least increase at a slower rate than income increases.

disposable income
Is personal income less personal taxes.

discretionary income
Is disposable income minus the money needed for necessities to sustain life.

Another, often overlooked, implication for retailers is that many Americans now use the Internet, especially eBay, as a source to sell unwanted or unneeded merchandise to increase their income. This is especially evident during the first quarter of the year when many Americans use eBay to get rid of that unwelcome Christmas scarf or tie from Aunt Bessie. In fact, a whole new industry has developed to assist consumers who don't use eBay regularly. Drop shops, which will handle the entire selling process for a fee, are listed on the eBay Web site. Others may re-gift the unwanted merchandise to someone else or donate the item to a charity such as freecycle.org, which is an e-mail list where people can contribute items that they no longer need. All of these activities are variations on garage sales; the seller gets rid of stuff he or she doesn't need and, in many cases, raises spending money.

Personal Savings

A major criticism of the U.S. economic system is that it does not reward personal saving. Savings, expressed as a percentage of disposable income, have dwindled from a post–World War II high of 8.8 percent in 1981 to 4.6 percent in 1995 to a dismal 1.7 percent in 2001. In 2003, the rate was 2.1 percent.[43] While this may seem odd, it is important to note that during the last decade, the economy, stock market, and especially the housing market have experienced exceptionally strong growth. As a result, many people stopped saving and began to invest in the stock market. This might be considered a form of saving, despite its additional elements of risk. It should be noted that the government's numbers regarding the savings rate fail to address the treatment of capital gains. When the government measures disposable income, it counts wages, interest earned, and dividends, but not realized or unrealized capital gains; so the wealth created by increasing home equity values is omitted. It also counts the full cost of purchases made over time, such as cars and appliances. Thus the government's data tends to undermeasure savings because it fails to consider the wealth effect.

The *wealth effect* claims that for every hundred dollars of additional wealth generated in an individual's stock market holdings, the individual will spend $4 (4 percent). Such spending lowers the nation's savings rate because when the stock market rises, spending increases without an increase in wages and salaries. Savings will also be decreased in this example because the government will subtract the taxes on the stock market gains from disposable income. Currently, the net worth of households is a record high of nearly $50 trillion. Obviously, a decrease in property values or stock prices will present problems for retailers.[44]

The national savings rate in the United States is a quarter of those in Europe, Japan, and China.[45] However, given national differences in the measurements of income and savings, comparisons between countries are unclear.

Implications for Retailers

Retailers have enjoyed continued sales growth over the past decade because, even though median household income in fixed dollars has increased only slightly, spending rather than saving has been the focus of the consumer. However, retailers must be prepared for the next decade, when baby boomers and Gen Xers will plan for retirement by reducing their spending and increasing savings. Some economists fear that in another decade, when more boomers retire, they will remove money from the stock market, which could cascade into a declining market. This scenario could result in a reverse wealth effect because as consumers lose money in the stock market, they tend to save about four cents for every dollar lost. Another fear is that because of good health, many boomers may postpone retirement and the extra labor supply could lower overall wages, which could impact retail sales.[46]

Women in the Labor Force

Over the past five decades women have become a dominant factor in the labor force. In 1970, 43 percent of all women over the age of 16 were in the labor force; today it is 60 percent.[47] This trend is true of all age groups, even women age 25 to 34, who might be expected to be raising families. Seventy-six percent of all women age 25 to 34 are currently in the labor force. The percentage of working married women with preschoolers increased from 30 percent in 1970 to 60 percent in 2003.[48] However, just under a third of all female employees are able to make use of flexible schedules at the workplace.[49] As we discussed earlier, more women are obtaining college degrees and over 83 percent of women with college degrees are in the workforce.

This significant rise in the number of working women has protected many households from inflation and recession. In fact, many economists suggest that the working woman has been the nation's secret weapon against economic hardships. For example, the median household income for married households where both spouses were in the work force rose by over 27 percent (after adjusting for inflation) between 1980 and 2002 to over $72,000.[50] In addition to the working wife, another reason for the huge increase in household income for dual-wage-earner families is that, where once a professional man would marry an administrative assistant, nurse, or school teacher (all admirable occupations, but not the highest paid), today many professional men are marrying professional women. As a result, the household income for these couples is increasing faster than the norm. This is not only another cause of the polarization of income shown in Exhibit 3.5, but it is creating a new social phenomenon in America—couples too tired for sex.[51]

High-profit performance retailers will be those that realize that the increase of women in the labor force is a two-edged sword. It will increase disposable income for the family but reduce the time available to spend it, making it imperative that retailers make shopping a pleasant, convenient experience.

Dollars & Sense

Implications for Retailers

The rise in the number of working women has many retail implications. The increase in dual-wage-earner families means that many families have less time for shopping and are more prone to look for convenience and services from retailers. Working men and women are often unable to shop between 8 A.M. and 6 P.M. Monday through Friday, thus preferring that retailers hold sales and special events in the evening or on weekends. Time-pressed shoppers find that price is sometimes less important than convenience, availability, and service. Bricks-and-mortar retailers, in addition to making the shopping experience pleasant, if not exciting, must develop strategies that accommodate these customers' needs. They must extend store hours (early mornings, evenings, and weekends) and offer conveniences (express checkouts). Bricks & mortar retailers should also provide alternatives to in-store shopping, such as catalogs or online shopping, if they want to compete for the time-pressed shopper's store loyalty.

Widespread Use of Credit

Retailers, especially department stores and those selling big-ticket items, have long offered their own credit to customers. However, today the trend is away from the retailer's store-brand credit cards and toward third-party cards (Visa, MasterCard, Discover, American Express, etc.). Spurred on in recent years by active promotional campaigns and low interest rates, consumers in 2006 were staggering under an estimated $2.2 trillion in consumer debt.[52] In the United States, over two-thirds of households now have a credit card and among households with over $50,000 in annual income, more than 90 percent have at least two credit cards.[53] Credit card firms offer promotional incentives such as free airline miles, rebates on new auto purchases, or rebates on future purchases. For the retailer, credit card use has increased sales and profits. Consequently, retailers as varied as supermarkets and the family veterinarian are now forced to accept these third-party cards. Other retailers, such as Kroger, Wal-Mart, Nordstrom, and Toys"R"Us, are now co-branding their names with national card issuers.

Implications for Retailers

Since the growth in credit has been outstripping the growth in personal income, it is evident that as income growth slows or becomes negative, households will face a liquidity crisis. After all, over 25 percent of households rarely pay off their credit card balance and in 11 percent of households debt payments exceed 40 percent of income.[54] Such massive debt loads must be paid off, and that activity will negatively impact future retail sales. Finally, the average 2002 college graduate had accumulated a staggering $22,000 in college loans. No wonder many young people postpone getting married, having children, and buying a first house. All of this may negatively impact retail sales.[55]

LO 4 Consumer Behavior Model

What is involved in the consumer behavior model, including the key stages in the buying process?

Now that we have examined population, social, and economic trends, we can develop a model that describes, and to some degree predicts, how these factors come together to affect consumer buying patterns. We call this the consumer shopping/purchasing model. Consumers are typically confronted with fundamental decisions when it comes to meeting their requirements: What products or brands can potentially fill their need, and where should they purchase these products or brands? Our model is sufficiently general to deal with both of these decisions.

Dollars & Sense

Retailers can use their understanding of their target consumer's buying behavior to improve their profit performance.

Examine the consumer shopping/purchase model in Exhibit 3.6. This model suggests that consumer behavior is a process with a series of stages or steps. The six stages in the model are stimulus, problem recognition, search, evaluation of alternatives, purchase, and post-purchase evaluation.

Exhibit 3.6
Consumer Shopping/ Purchase Model

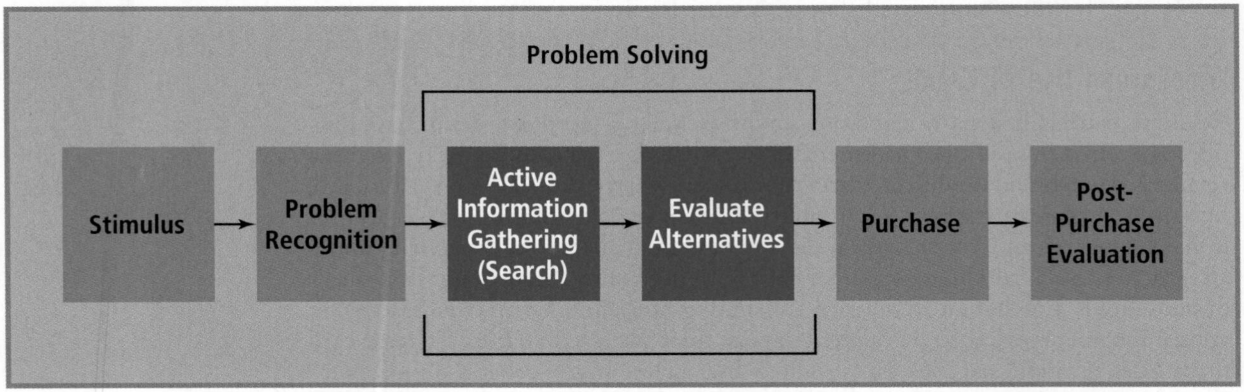

Stimulus

A **stimulus** involves a cue (external to the individual) or drive (internal to the individual). A **cue** is any object or phenomenon in the environment that is capable of eliciting a response. Common examples of retail marketing stimuli are advertisements, point-of-purchase displays, coupons, salespeople, and free samples. All of these examples are cues controlled by the seller or retailer. In addition, there are cues that the retailer does not control. For example, word-of-mouth advertising is common in retailing. Many visits to e-tailing sites are the result of a visitor having a good experience and telling others.

stimulus
Refers to a cue that is external to the individual or a drive that is internal to the individual.

cue
Refers to any object or phenomenon in the environment that is capable of eliciting a response.

A second type of stimulus is internal to the individual and is referred to as a drive. A **drive** is a motivating force that directs behavior. Drives can be physiologically based (hunger and the need to stay warm in the cold) or learned (the desire to spend spring break in Cancun). When drives are strong they are more likely to prompt purchase behavior. The old adage "never go grocery shopping when you are hungry" illustrates this point.

drive
Refers to a motivating force that directs behavior.

Individuals can be exposed to both types of stimuli. For instance, one may see an advertisement (cue) for a restaurant at the same time that one is hungry (drive); a person living in Minnesota may be coping with a long, cold winter and browsing the Internet when she sees an advertisement for a vacation on the sunny beaches of Hawaii.

As consumers move through their daily routines in an information economy they are constantly exposed to hundreds of messages regarding products, services, and where to purchase them. As a result, one of the scarcest resources is human attention. All retailers are competing with virtually all other organizations and individuals for the attention of the consumer. Consequently, the individual is always involved in **passive information gathering**, which is the task of receiving and processing information regarding the existence and quality of merchandise, services, stores, shopping convenience, parking, advertising, and any other factors that a consumer might consider in making a decision of where to shop and what to purchase.

passive information gathering
Is the receiving and processing of information regarding the existence and quality of merchandise, services, stores, shopping, convenience, pricing, advertising, and any other factors that a consumer might consider in making a purchase.

Problem Recognition

Stimuli can often lead to problem recognition. **Problem recognition** occurs when the consumer's desired state of affairs departs sufficiently from the actual state of affairs to place the consumer in a state of unrest so that he or she begins thinking of ways to resolve the difference. Consider a few examples. While driving across town, you notice that your car's gas tank is almost empty; you hear an advertisement for a new Sony CD player and tuner and realize that your ten-year-old stereo needs replacing; you will be graduating from college shortly and do not own any suitable clothes for your new career; or you receive your tax refund and realize you now have money to go to Cancun for spring break.

problem recognition
Occurs when the consumer's desired state of affairs departs sufficiently from the actual state of affairs, placing the consumer in a state of unrest.

Not all problems will stimulate the same level of problem-solving activity. The level of one's desire to resolve a particular problem depends on two factors: the magnitude of the gap between the desired and actual states and the importance of the problem. Consider the example of the gas tank. If a quarter of a tank remained, the problem would be less urgent than if the gas gauge were on empty. Next, compare your recognition of the problem of replacing your old CD player and tuner with your recognition of the problem of acquiring a career wardrobe. In all probability, one of these problems would be more important to you, and thus you would be more motivated to solve it first.

What's New?

Amazon and Food: All About Consumer Opinion and Interaction

While the headlines in the world of Internet food retailing may be focused on the success of Fresh Direct or Albertson's, many shoppers are surfing over to Amazon.com where they can purchase almost any nonperishable food product while exchanging opinions about the items on an open "bulletin board."

Amazon.com only has one toe in the food business water with a "beta" site that serves as a portal for other retailers, processing orders and handling payments but using outside merchants to handle actual fulfillment. Still, there are two facets of its approach that make the company a paradigm that traditional retailers should carefully examine.

One of the more intriguing elements of the Amazon.com offering—and the one that conceivably empowers consumers in a way that can have a profound impact on both retailers and manufacturers—is the ability of purchasers to comment on, recommend, or criticize products sold on the site. This isn't any different from the functions that Amazon offers in other sections of its site; one of the more popular features of its book, CD, and DVD sections is the comment section written by purchasers.

For example, one shopper had this to say:

> I lived in Southern California for many years but moved away in 1995. I forgot about how I used to go to the mall with my best friend and we'd always make a trip to the See's Candy store! I was so happy when I saw Amazon selling See's candy, as I never see it here in Missouri. I bought a TON of candy and have been pigging out! This chocolate is so good! I particularly love this box, with all the nuts and caramel chews. Also, guys, chocolate is almost always a GREAT gift for your girl! I know I am never unhappy receiving a box of chocolate! And See's is one of the best out there!

That would be a rave, and no doubt had an influence on other shoppers.

In essence, these kinds of conversations are replacing the old back fence, where moms used to exchange recipes and household tips and create the most powerful selling tool—word of mouth through personal recommendations! Today the world has changed, and many moms are using the Internet to build relationships and to communicate in this time-starved world.

What should traditional food retailers learn from this? The average supermarket has roughly 50,000 items—and that includes everything from chewing gum sold at the checkout to the most expensive cut of meat. Amazon.com, on the other hand, serves as a retailing portal through which more than 79,000 items are available—many of which would fall into the "gourmet grocery" category.

But it isn't just the range of items that is extraordinary. It is also the ease of navigation, which provides a variety of routes to the desired SKU. You can find products by type of cuisine (there are 304 products identified as African food, 4,018 as low-carb and sugar-free, 316 as Oceania cuisine, and 2,376 as vegetarian). Or you can choose products by brand or retailer, ranging from well-known names such as Dean & Deluca, Godiva, and Harry & David, to more obscure entities such as The Baker's Catalogue or Pacific Rim Gourmet.

You can even shop by price point; Amazon is helpful enough to let customers know that more than 60,000 of its offerings are $24 or less, and that two of them are more than $5,000. For the record, those two happen to be a crystal caviar server that goes for $7,499.95 (a real steal considering its $10,499.00 retail price!), and 12 months of caviar, reduced to $6,749.95 from its list price of $9,449.93.

There's one thing that Amazon isn't offering food shoppers, though, and that's the ability to experience the aromas, colors, and sampling of the in-store experience. Bricks & mortar retailers need to embrace the tools that competitors like Amazon have developed and use these as ways to refocus themselves as the center of their shoppers' communities—both online and off.

Source: *Facts, Figures & the Future*, February 14, 2005: 3–4. Used with Phil Lempert's written permission. (You may sign up for this free monthly newsletter at http://www.factsfiguresfuture.com.)

Problem Solving

The next two stages in the consumer shopping/purchasing model—active information gathering (or search) and evaluation of alternatives—will determine the degree of problem solving that occurs. Individuals solve problems by searching for information and then evaluating their options or alternatives. The search for

Exhibit 3.7
Degrees of Consumer Problem Solving in Shopping/Purchasing

Brand Preference \ Retailer Preference	Strong	None or Weak
Strong	Habitual Problem Solving	Limited Problem Solving
None or Weak	Limited Problem Solving	Extended Problem Solving

information and careful evaluation of alternatives occurs to reduce risk. If consumers do not select the best product, they can incur financial loss (financial risk), personal harm (safety risk), or decline of respect from family and friends (social risk). The importance of understanding how consumers go about this information search is highlighted in the chapter's What's New box. Supermarket guru, Phil Lempert, recently illustrated what sets Amazon apart—its ability to let online shoppers compare notes on products before making a purchase.

The amount of problem-solving activity consumers engage in varies considerably depending on their prior experience and the need to reduce financial, personal, and social risk. Consumers learn quickly, and when they locate the product, brands, and retailers that are good at satisfying their needs at a low or acceptable risk level, the degree of problem solving decreases. Exhibit 3.7 illustrates three levels of problem solving. Note that these levels are determined by whether or not the consumer has a strong preference for a specific brand or retail store.

Habitual Problem Solving

With **habitual problem solving**, the consumer relies on past experience and learns to convert the problem into a situation requiring less thought. The consumer has a strong preference for the brand to buy and the retailer from which to purchase it. Some consumers are not only habitual users of products but also heavy users. For instance, in fast-food restaurants, only one in five persons is a heavy user; however, they account for 60 percent of fast-food restaurant visits.[56] Using past experience, the consumer has arrived at an adequate solution for many consumer problems. Frequently purchased products of relatively low cost and low risk (e.g., toothpaste, milk, bread, soda pop) tend to belong in this category; however, products of higher value may also be in this category. For example, when confronted with the need for a new auto, some people can be loyal to both a particular brand and a specific retailer. Such an individual may be loyal to Ford and may patronize a favorite Ford dealer in their geographic area.

habitual problem solving
Occurs when the consumer relies on past experiences and learns to convert the problem into a situation requiring less thought. The consumer has a strong preference for the brand to buy and the retailer from which to purchase it.

Limited Problem Solving

Limited problem solving occurs when the consumer has a strong preference for either the brand or the store, but not both. The consumer may not have a store choice in mind but may have a strong preference for or have decided on the brand to purchase. Since the brand has been determined, the consumer has, in a sense,

limited problem solving
Occurs when the consumer has a strong preference for either the brand or the store, but not both.

restricted the problem-solving process to deciding which retailer to patronize among those that carry the brand. Because the consumer may not be aware of all the retailers that carry the item, some searching may be required. To illustrate, assume the picture tube on your TV fails and you decide to get a new one. You know that you want a Sony portable color set, but since you are new in town, you do not know where to get the best buy. Also, you recognize that your search does not need to be limited to retailers in your community, and the Internet can help you locate the retailer with the lowest price. You prefer a local retailer who can service your set; however, you have decided that this additional convenience is not worthwhile if the local retailer's price is more than 10 percent higher than an out-of-town retailer's price. Although we refer to this category as limited problem solving, deciding which brand or store to select may still be an extensive process. Problem solving should be viewed as a continuum.

Extended Problem Solving

extended problem solving
Occurs when the consumer recognizes a problem but has decided on neither the brand nor the store.

Extended problem solving occurs when the consumer recognizes a problem but has decided on neither the brand nor the store. For example, a woman in her early twenties has recently received a promotion and a 25 percent raise from the bank that employs her. Over the last year, she has postponed purchasing several major durable goods that she wants—a car, living room furniture, and a DVD player. With the 25 percent raise, she can afford some, but not all, of those items. She has little prior information and experience regarding alternative brands and retailers that sell these products; therefore, she must engage in extensive problem solving to select the products she should buy, determine which brands are appropriate, and learn which retail outlets carry what she wants. Extensive problem solving typically involves infrequently purchased expensive products of high risk. Here, the consumer desires a lot of new information, which implies a need for extensive problem solving.

Problem-Solving Stages

active information gathering
Occurs when consumers proactively gather information.

Once consumers recognize that a problem exists and believe a potential solution involves going to the marketplace to purchase a product or service, then they will engage in problem solving. The first step is **active information gathering**, which is when consumers proactively gather information. In today's Age of the Internet, many consumers begin their active information gathering with a search engine, such as Google, to find out about the desired product or service, its price, and where it is available. Consumers are then confronted with the second stage in problem solving—the evaluation of alternatives. The evaluation of alternatives typically involves three stages:

set of attributes
Refers to the characteristics of the store and its products and services.

1. In the first stage, consumers develop a set of attributes on which the purchase decision will be based. The **set of attributes** refers to the characteristics of the store and its products and services. These can include such things as price, product quality, store hours, knowledgeable sales help, convenient parking, after-sale service, and so on. These attributes are often based on general information sources such as preexisting knowledge, advertising, discussions with friends and relatives, and magazines such as *Consumer Reports*, as well as the many information sources online.
2. In the second stage, consumers narrow the consideration set to a more manageable number of attributes. Although consumers want to think that they have considered a wide range of options so as not to miss a golden opportunity, they do not want to be confused by myriad options. In this phase, consumers

might visit stores or browse online to gather more specific information, such as price ranges, to narrow their list.

3. In the final stage, consumers directly compare the key attributes of the alternatives remaining on their "short list." Here, consumers are very active in their search for specific information and often begin ascertaining actual prices through either store visits, browsing the Web site, or preliminary negotiating when appropriate.

One of the most important variables of problem solving is which information resources consumers use. It is important for retailers to understand what information resources their target market prefers to use and match their communication programs to these resources.

Purchase

Based on information gathered and evaluated in the problem solving stage, the consumer decides whether to purchase and which product and retailer to choose. Of course, a possible outcome of the problem solving stage is a decision not to buy or to delay the purchase. A consumer might conclude that an adequate product or service isn't available or that the cost (financial or otherwise) is greater than previously thought. Although a purchase is not made, the information gathered is often mentally recorded and influences future shopping processes.

The purchase stage may include final negotiation, application for credit if necessary, and determination of the terms of purchase (cash, credit card, etc.). Sometimes last-minute unexpected factors can intervene during the transaction phase and preempt the purchase. For instance, the consumer can become aware of unanticipated costs such as taxes, delivery fees, or other charges and decide not to buy.

The purchase stage is often employed by retailers as an opportunity to use suggestion selling to sell add-on or related purchases, such as extended service warranties, batteries for toys, and impulse merchandise. Both online and bricks & mortar retailers use this technique. For instance, at Amazon.com, once you select books to purchase, the company suggests other titles you might have an interest in buying. If handled properly, consumers view this selling practice as a customer service, as if the retailer were "looking out" for the customer's long-term satisfaction. On the other hand, if handled poorly, the customer can view this as an attempt to gouge them. In extreme cases, the customer may even decide to cancel the initial transaction.

Post-Purchase Evaluation

The consumer shopping and purchase process does not end with the purchase. Ultimately, consumers are buying solutions to their perceived needs, and successful retailers take an active interest in ensuring that customers feel satisfied over the long term that their need has been resolved. The consumer's use and evaluation of a product is therefore a critical, although sometimes overlooked, stage in the consumer behavior process.

The first important moment in the use and evaluation stage is immediately after the transaction, in the first hours and days in which the consumer uses the product or service. During this critical time, consumers form lasting impressions regarding the soundness of their purchase decision that in turn influence all future purchase decisions. If the consumer is dissatisfied, a condition can emerge known as **post-purchase resentment**, in which the consumer's dissatisfaction results in resentment toward the retailer.

post-purchase resentment
Arises after the purchase when the consumer becomes dissatisfied with the product, service, or retailer and thus begins to regret that the purchase was made.

If post-purchase resentment is not identified and rectified by the retailer, it can have a long-term negative influence on the retailer's ability to recapture the consumer as a satisfied customer. A satisfied customer tells a few friends, whereas a dissatisfied customer tells a dozen or more; in an online chat room or Internet complaint site, the unhappy customer can spread his or her story to millions. Consequently, it is less expensive to take care of a dissatisfied customer than it is to convert a noncustomer into a customer. Fortunately, if the retailer is proactive in its customer satisfaction program and responds quickly to budding resentment, it can be overcome. The problem is that many unhappy consumers do not report their dissatisfaction, so retailers must be vigilant in their monitoring of customer satisfaction. This process begins with the establishment of proactive policies such as full-satisfaction guarantees, which should be boldly communicated to the shopper. This tells consumers that if they do have a problem, the retailer wants to hear about and rectify it. Beyond this, many retailers have started customer follow-up programs, such as customer satisfaction reply cards, given out at the time of purchase or mailed to the customer several days later. Electronic cash registers have aided in this process by efficiently gathering the names, addresses, and telephone numbers of customers, recording the merchandise purchased, and automatically mailing the customer satisfaction surveys. It is important that retailers seek to find out why some past customers no longer shop at their stores.

Many large retailers—especially chains in which individual stores are not under central control, such as franchises and dealerships—have taken this customer satisfaction process one step further. They have instituted programs that measure customer satisfaction on an ongoing basis and compare customer service ratings of individual retail locations against preestablished benchmarks or a chain-wide average.

STUDENT STUDY GUIDE

SUMMARY

This chapter has concentrated on how, in order to satisfy the consumer, the retailer must continuously monitor the changes in the environment that affect consumer demand. It should be clear that the rapid changes occurring in our society demand both sensitive management and good retail information systems in the retail industry. Retailers need managers who can provide leadership in meeting the challenges of, and likewise profiting from, the opportunities these changes present.

LO 1 **Explain the importance of population trends on retail planning.**

We began Chapter 3 with a discussion of the major population trends occurring in the United States today and their implications for the future of retailing. These trends include a slowdown in the population growth rate, a changing age distribution as America ages, the geographic shifting of the population to the South and West, the growth of large urban centers, and ever-increasing consumer mobility.

LO 2 **What social trends should be monitored and what are their impacts on retailing?**

Five major social trends and their implications for how retail managers must deal with these changes were discussed. These five trends were the increasing educational levels of consumers, the changing state of marriage (including the expanding never-married population), the effect of higher divorce rates, the changing makeup of the American household, and changes in the nature and importance of an individual's work.

LO 3 **How do the changing American economic trends affect retailing?**

The chapter next considered the effects of income growth, level of personal savings, women in the labor force, and the widespread use of credit retailing in the 21st century.

What is involved in the shopping/purchasing model, including the key stages in the buying process?

LO 4

Shopping and purchasing can be viewed as a six-stage process. A stimulus (stage 1) triggers problem recognition (stage 2); which leads to problem solving. Problem solving consists of two stages: active information gathering or search (stage 3) and evaluation of alternatives (stage 4). The degree of problem solving can vary from habitual, which occurs when the consumer already has a strong preference for the brand and the retailer from which to purchase it, to extended problem solving, which occurs when the consumer has not decided on the brand or the store. Evaluation of alternatives can lead to purchase (stage 5), and purchase is followed by post-purchase evaluation (stage 6).

TERMS TO REMEMBER

customer satisfaction
customer services
market segmentation
population variables
micromarketing
metropolitan statistical areas
disposable income
discretionary income
stimulus
cue
drive
passive information gathering
problem recognition
habitual problem solving
limited problem solving
extended problem solving
active information gathering
set of attributes
post-purchase resentment

REVIEW AND DISCUSSION QUESTIONS

Explain the importance of population trends on retail planning.

LO 1

1. Why isn't customer satisfaction with a retailer equally as important for all customer types? Can you suggest some shopper characteristics that may affect the importance of satisfaction when selecting a retailer?
2. What type of retailers would be most affected by changes in the age distribution of the population?
3. Is it important for a retailer to understand that Gen Xers and Gen Yers are different in their shopping behavior? Is there one example from current events that you can use to emphasize your argument?
4. Given the high mobility rate for Americans today, is it impossible for a local retailer to survive? After all, won't consumers, after they move to a new location, only shop in stores they knew back home?

What social trends should be monitored and what are their impacts on retailing?

LO 2

5. What strategies should retailers develop in the face of the higher level of educational attainment today?
6. Should a retailer care about a changing trend such as the delay or even postponement of marriage by modern Americans? After all, how does this affect apparel retailing? restaurant retailing? home furnishing retailers?
7. Is the "boomerang effect" going to be a short-lived phenomenon? What is the basis for your answer?

8. A recent survey found that employees today are less loyal to their employers. What actions can retailers take to reduce turnover among retail employees?

LO 3

How do the changing American economic trends affect retailing?

9. Why is it more difficult for retailers to manage their businesses in a roller-coaster economy of economic turbulence?
10. Should retailers be concerned about the recent decline in the personal savings rate? Does the behavior of the stock market affect your purchase decisions?
11. How does a trend, such as the increasing number of working women, affect women's apparel retailing? recreational retailing? e-retailing?

LO 4

What is involved in the consumer behavior model, including the key stages in the buying process?

12. Why is the shopping/purchase behavior model presented in the text called a process model? Explain how this would affect a retailer's actions.
13. Does a consumer begin the shopping/purchase process at the need-recognition stage?
14. Why should a retailer care about a customer after a sale has already been made?

SAMPLE TEST QUESTIONS

LO 1

Which of the following statements regarding current U.S. population trends is correct?

a. The baby boomers are now moving into their 30s and 40s.
b. Americans change their residences about a dozen times in their lifetime.
c. Markets with fewer than 50,000 people do not present many opportunities for retailers.
d. The U.S. population is expected to increase about 15 percent a year over the next decade.
e. The country's total population is expected to grow at a record rate during the first half of the 21st century.

LO 2

The "boomerang effect" is a relatively new phenomenon that describes:

a. the recent trend for firms to seek bankruptcy protection.
b. the way styles from years ago come back as today's most popular styles.
c. the recent trend of children returning to live with their parents after having already moved out.
d. the use of price as the main means to attract new customers.
e. the recent trend of having most companies report losses for the current quarter.

LO 3

Discretionary income is:

a. all personal income after taxes and retirement savings.
b. all personal income after savings.
c. all personal income minus the money needed for necessities such as food, clothing, housing, and so on.
d. all personal income after taxes minus the money needed for necessities.
e. all personal income after taxes.

Post-purchase resentment:

a. usually only has short-term negative consequences for the retailer.
b. cannot be fixed.
c. is easily detected.
d. is often transferred from the product to the retailer where it was purchased.
e. is not a problem if the retailer measures customer satisfaction at least every other year.

WRITING AND SPEAKING EXERCISE

You have recently been hired as the assistant manager for a large regional mall in Lexington, Kentucky. One of the first things you notice on an early inspection tour of the mall is a lack of benches in the common areas for the elderly and mothers with babies to sit and rest while shopping. These benches are said to reduce the selling area that the mall can rent to various temporary vendors, such as costume jewelry over the Christmas season.

Last week, you found a memo from your predecessor banning the early opening of the mall commons so that elderly exercise groups cannot use the mall for walking and exercise classes. Such activity would require extra security staff to be present for the walkers in the mall.

Prepare a one-page memo agreeing or disagreeing with the current mall policy and explaining your reasoning.

PLANNING YOUR OWN RETAIL BUSINESS

In this chapter you learned that how broadly or how selectively you define your market is a major determinant of retail performance. In planning your retail business, it will be important that you develop your retail marketing strategy to appeal to a particular market, either broadly or narrowly defined. For example, a women's apparel store could cater to all age groups, professional working women, or teens; it could also target various income groups such as low, moderate, or high income. Further, it could target women of different sizes from petite to full-figured.

Assume for the store you are planning that there are 18,000 households in your community and these are within a reasonable driving distance to your store. You have determined that if you broadly define your store's market, 65 percent of households in the community would be shoppers at the store and would shop there an average of 3.4 times per year. On the other hand, if you define your market much more selectively by focusing on a well-defined niche, you estimate only 28 percent of households would shop at the store, but they would shop an average of 9.2 times annually.

In this situation, would a broadly or more narrowly defined market create more customer visits to the store? (*Hint:* Total store visitors, also referred to as traffic, is equal to the total number of households in the market multiplied by the proportion that would shop the store, multiplied by their average shopping frequency.) What other factors should you consider in deciding how narrowly or broadly to define your market?

CASE

MedExpress Drugstores

There are three locally owned MedExpress Drugstores operating in Rio Bravo, New Mexico, about 20 miles outside of Santa Fe. Until not long ago, Rio Bravo had been basically a "retirement town," with adults over the age of 60 accounting for the largest segment of the population. This situation made it fairly simple for MedExpress to target and serve the senior citizen market. Recently, though, the area has experienced a migration of young families and middle-aged couples who wanted to escape the city life. While at one time 50 percent of the population was in the 60-years and over category, now both the 35- to 45-years age group and the senior citizens group are 35%.

Older consumers were originally attracted to MedExpress Drugstores because they did not have to worry about dealing with many children when shopping, they knew that they would not have to wait in long checkout lines, and they would not have difficulty maneuvering themselves and/or their carts in the extra-wide aisles. Many of these attractions no longer exist. Families with young children have become regular customers of the stores, store traffic has been increasing, and aisle widths have shrunk so that additional shelves can be installed as a means of displaying more merchandise and, ultimately, generating more sales.

Mary Hightower, whose family owns the drugstores, realizes that if the stores continue to operate as they are presently, there is a distinct possibility that older customers will begin shopping elsewhere, especially with the various government-sponsored mail-order health plans available. While she wishes to continue to cater to the loyal senior citizen customers who helped MedExpress Drugstores achieve its current success, she does not want to ignore the potentially lucrative "baby boomer" market that is beginning to form in Rio Bravo. As Ms. Hightower's assistant, you are to consider and answer the following questions:

1. Should MedExpress Drugstores concentrate on only the "baby boomer" or on the senior citizen market? Both? Neither? Explain your position.
2. What types of marketing strategies could MedExpress Drugstores implement that would meet the needs of both age groups?
3. How might the changing marketplace affect MedExpress Drugstores merchandise assortment? What types of merchandise might management want to add, delete, or expand?
4. Should MedExpress Drugstores open an online store to target this market?

chapter 4

Evaluating the Competition in Retailing

Overview:

The behavior of competitors is an important component of the retail planning and management model. Effective planning and execution in any retail setting cannot be accomplished without the proper analysis of competitors. In this chapter, we begin by reviewing various models of retail competition. The types of competition in retailing are described next. We then discuss the evolution of retail competition. Finally, we examine the upcoming retail revolution in nonstore retailing, developing retail formats, global and technological changes, and the use of private labels as a strategic weapon.

Learning Objectives:

After reading this chapter you should be able to:

1. Explain the various models of retail competition.
2. Distinguish between various types of retail competition.
3. Describe the four theories used to explain the evolution of retail competition.
4. Describe the changes that could affect retail competition.

Models of Retail Competition

LO 1

What are the various models of retail competition?

This chapter examines the effects of competition on a retailer's performance. As noted in Chapter 1, retailing in the United States was once a growth industry that was able to increase profits solely on the basis of an increasing population base. Today's slower population growth rates have turned retailing into a business where successful regional and national retailers can grow only by taking sales away from competitors. However, retail competition at the local level is more complex. Depending upon the economic base of the regional economy, it is possible for an area's population and disposable income to grow even while the country's is slowing. For example, Phoenix and Las Vegas are like many Sunbelt communities where a vibrant local economy, combined with attractiveness to retirees and second-home owners, results in a growing sales potential for many retailers. A retailer could grow in such a venue without having to take sales away from a competitor. Just the opposite would occur in areas such as Mansfield and Youngstown, Ohio, which are experiencing a continuing economic slump.

A retailer must always be on the offensive by studying the changing competitive environment, especially its local competition, and differentiating itself from that competition. Only by creating a differential advantage that is extremely difficult to copy in terms of time and money can a retailer hope for continued success. Prime examples of such differentiation are category killers, such as The Home Depot and Lowe's, with their large selection; Wal-Mart, whose technologically advanced distribution system results in significantly lower operating costs than its competitors; Target, with a more fashionable and contemporary merchandise assortment and a more colorful and softer store atmosphere than other mass merchandise discounters; Amazon, with its significant presence on the Internet; and the Walt Disney Company, which is famous for excellent customer service. A retailer's performance will be substandard if it merely copies the actions of others without a lower cost structure or point of differentiation.

A retailer should visit retailers of all sizes in its trading area to learn what merchandise and services the competitors are offering and what they are not, which offerings receive aggressive pricing emphasis, and which promotional tactics are successfully used by competitors. For example, many people believe that local retailers cannot compete with the large discounters. The small appliance store owner would benefit by understanding that these chains usually carry only a limited selection within a product category and provide little personalized and specialized service. Thus, by knowing which televisions the discounter is carrying, and how they are priced, the small retailer can match the price on similar units, offer better services, and stock a more complete range of units. Other chains have created a niche that has worked well against these discounters. Consider, for example, the tactic used by the dollar stores (Dollar General, Family Dollar, and Dollar Tree). These chains successfully operate small stores within the shadow of the large discounters by providing convenience, and low prices on a limited product selection. By enabling their customers to get in and out quickly, these stores are able to compete with the larger chains. Still, the niche served by these dollar stores is risky since they tend to target households earning $25,000 a year or less, a segment that offers little in the way of discretionary spending on high-margin items, and requires that the dollar stores make few, if any, errors, in their merchandise selection.[1]

Small locally owned retailers may also use a tactic like the one tried by a variety store in Viroqua, WI. When Wal-Mart located a store nearby, it gave each of its employees $20 to shop Wal-Mart. Because its employees were local and understood the community, they learned that their store would not be price competitive in health and beauty items or housewares but that Wal-Mart had little offerings for the agricultural community. Further, a new private school in town brought in a number of residents with more sophisticated tastes than those of the typical Wal-Mart customer. By catering to these underserved customer segments, the variety store has thrived.

A small retailer's competition is not just the large discount stores in the area. This retailer would be wise to check the local drugstore, perhaps a Walgreens, that stocks small appliances; the Internet for competitive pricing information and 24/7 shopping convenience; and category killers that might offer a deeper selection and a better level of service than the discounters. For example, Best Buy lured female customers away from traditional discounters and small specialty electronics stores by providing merchandise selections tailored to each local market area and by training its sales associates not to "talk down" to them, as had often happened in other electronics stores.[2]

Dollars & Sense

High-profit retailers want to develop strategic plans that provide a differential advantage that competitors can overcome only with a substantial investment of time and money.

It is important to remember that no retailer, however clever, can design a strategy that will totally insulate it from competition. This is true even if the retailer has done an excellent job in developing and following its mission statement, setting its goals and objectives, and conducting its SWOT analysis; customers still have shopping choices. The rapid growth of discount department stores, convenience stores, and catalog and Internet retailers attest to this fact. Some merchandising innovations can be easily copied and cannot be patented, and the relatively low cost of entry into a retail business, in comparison to other businesses, means that potential retailers can copy a profitable strategy. In retailing, competition is a continuing fact of life.

Competition in retailing, as in any other industry, involves the interplay of supply and demand. One cannot appreciate the nature and scope of competition in retailing by studying only the supply factors—that is, the type and number of competing retailers that exist. One must also examine consumer demand factors, as highlighted in Chapter 3. Let's examine a formal framework for describing and explaining the competitive environment of retailing.

The Competitive Marketplace

One of the most important issues in examining the competitive context is to first decide how you choose to compete as a retailer. Competition can be waged on many fronts, and a retailer must be clear about what advantages it will emphasize and where its resources will have the greatest effect in attracting and satisfying customers.

This framework helps to identify your primary competitors and threats from secondary competitors. For example, a full-line grocery store competes most directly with similar grocery stores—they all try to attract the same type of customer in terms of price sensitivity, preferences in merchandise selection, and geographic convenience. A discount grocery store, such as Rainbow Foods, is also after the grocery store customer, but has a particular appeal to one who puts a higher priority on low prices than on a wide selection of specialty items. However, any business that may win the customer's food dollar should also be viewed as a competitor. Over the past decade, almost a third of a household's food dollar was spent on food consumed outside the home, that is, in restaurants, workplace cafeterias, vending machines, and other venues. The percentage is much higher for certain demographic groups, such as higher-income households who can better afford to eat out, as well as young men who prefer not to cook at home. The fact that the same consumer can and will purchase the same product category (food) at different retailers points to the fact that different retailers are more or less competitive to varying degrees given different consumer buying situations and preferences. The customer may still shop at traditional grocery stores or supercenters for most groceries, but will patronize specialty grocers such as Whole Foods for organically raised meats or Trader Joe's for a particular brand of muesli cereal; eat in a number of restaurant formats for different reasons throughout the week; and purchase grab-and-go foods from convenience stores.[3]

Retailers compete for target customers on five major fronts or factors:[4]

1. The price for the benefits offered
2. Service level
3. Product selection (merchandise line width and depth)
4. Location or access: the overall convenience of shopping the retailer
5. Customer experience (the customer's positive feelings and behaviors in the purchase process)

In any competitive environment, retailers must clear a minimum acceptable threshold on each of these criteria in order to stay in business. Further, they must distinguish themselves in the marketplace by dominating on one key factor, and differentiate themselves on a secondary factor within that primary competitive set. For example, Wal-Mart, Target, and Dollar General compete primarily as general merchandise discounters. However, Wal-Mart emphasizes its excellent prices on a wide selection of top name brands; Target highlights its design-forward private label goods and store atmosphere; and the dollar stores are more convenient than the larger discounters.

Many retailers compete for customers on a local level and must be aware of their direct and secondary competitors in their shopping area. Customers typically will not travel beyond local markets to purchase routine household goods and prefer to shop in the most convenient way possible. When they do travel beyond local markets, however, it is usually because their city or town is too small to support retailers with the selection of merchandise they desire. Some customers will always want to shop out of town, but most cities with a population over 50,000 can provide the consumer with sufficient selection in almost all lines of merchandise. In cities with populations less than 50,000, households generally need to travel to another town or city only for large purchases such as a new automobile, television, furniture, or for a special item of clothing, such as a wedding dress or favored brand name.

Dollars & Sense Retailers that study and respond to the local retail competition will be more profitable when they understand how and when to adapt to national trends, which don't always affect every market in the same way.

Market Structure

Economists use four different economic terms to describe the competitive environment in the retailing industry: pure competition, pure monopoly, monopolistic competition, and oligopolistic competition.

pure competition
Occurs when a market has homogeneous products and many buyers and sellers, all having perfect knowledge of the market, and ease of entry for both buyers and sellers.

Pure competition occurs when a market has:

1. Homogeneous (similar) products.
2. Many buyers and sellers, all having perfect knowledge of the market.
3. Ease of entry for both buyers and sellers; that is, new retailers can start up with little difficulty and new consumers can easily come into the market.

In pure competition, each retailer faces a horizontal demand curve and must sell its products at the going "market" or equilibrium price. To sell at a lower price would be foolish, since you could always get the market price. Of course, you could not sell your merchandise at a higher price because customers know they can buy the item for less.

Pure competition is rare in retailing. Often, neither consumers nor retailers know all the prices in the marketplace without investing extensive time and effort to acquire this knowledge. Further, not all customers value an item similarly. Even in a very good example of pure competition, such as two vendors selling bags of peanuts or bottles of water outside a sporting event, customers seldom explore a number of sites before making a choice.

pure monopoly
Occurs when there is only one seller for a product or service.

The second type of economic environment also does not occur very often in real life. In a **pure monopoly**, the seller is the only one selling a particular product and will set its selling price accordingly. Nonetheless, as the retailer seeks to sell more units, it must lower the selling price. This is because consumers who already have one unit will tend to place a lower value on an additional unit. This is called the "law of diminishing returns" or "declining marginal utility." For example, a hot fudge sundae would taste great right now, but the second, third, or tenth one, purchased and consumed today, would be less desirable. Similarly, not all customers are equally impressed with a product. The monopolist would have to price more aggressively to entice customers who place a lower value on the item than do its target customers. The customer whose favorite color is hot pink might buy the hot pink blazer at full price, but it is unlikely she will buy another one soon. And the retailer will have to discount the remaining blazer to a customer who is less thrilled with hot pink; that is, hot pink had less "utility" for this customer in the first place.

Even so, situations of near-monopoly do exist. The gas station that is many miles from the next competitor, or the only restaurant open late at night on a highway, often controls the commerce for that business in the area. In another example, customers can "self-inflict" a monopoly when a brand name is perceived as unique and highly valued, and a retailer controls its sale. Brand-loyal customers place Harley-Davidson motorcycles and certain luxury-brand goods in a class all their own, and their limited distribution reaps rewards to their retailers.

Monopolistic competition is a market situation that develops when a market has:

monopolistic competition
Occurs when the products offered are different, yet viewed as substitutable for each other and the sellers recognize that they compete with sellers of these different products.

1. Different (heterogeneous) products in the eyes of consumers that are still substitutes for each other. Here two or more retailers may be selling the same product, but one retailer is able to differentiate itself in another dimension. Thus, consumers perceive the retailers to be selling different products, given the total purchase experience.
2. Sellers who may be the only ones selling a particular brand, but who face competition from other retailers selling similar goods and services.

The word *monopolistic* means that each seller is trying to control its own segment of the market. However, the word *competition* means that substitutes for the product are available. For example, a Pepsi-Cola is a substitute for a Coca-Cola. The degree of the seller's control depends on its similarity to the competitor's product from the customer's point of view. This is why the retailer in monopolistic competition attempts to differentiate itself by the products and/or services it offers. Some of the common means of achieving this are by offering: better customer service, credit, more convenient parking, larger or more attractive merchandise selection, cleanliness, free setup and delivery, a more convenient location, and the brand or store image created and developed through marketing communications such as advertising or store events. **Oligopolistic competition** occurs when a market has the following conditions:

oligopolistic competition
Occurs when relatively few sellers, or many small firms who follow the lead of a few larger firms, offer essentially homogeneous products and any action by one seller is expected to be noticed and reacted to by the other sellers.

1. Essentially homogeneous products, such as air travel to the same destination.
2. Relatively few sellers or many small firms who always follow the lead of the few large firms.
3. The expectation that any action by one party is expected to be noticed and reacted to by the other parties in the market.

As in pure competition, oligopolists face a long-run trend toward selling at a similar price since everybody knows what others are doing. Nonprice competition is extremely difficult since consumers view the products and services as essentially similar. This is why the major airlines such as American Airlines and Delta almost always match each other's prices on identical travel routes.

Retailing is often characterized as monopolistic competition or, in rare cases, oligopolistic competition. The distinction lies in the number of sellers. For oligopoly to occur, the top four firms have to account for over 60 to 80 percent of the market. Some national retailers have large market shares. Oligopolistic competition rarely occurs on a national level, but consolidation in many industries has left a few large players in some product categories. For example, The Home Depot and Lowe's often dominate the home improvement retailers; Borders and Barnes & Noble continue their dominance in the walk-in book market; Circuit City and Best Buy increasingly dominate consumer electronics purchases. Oligopolistic competition is more common at a local level, especially in smaller communities, among food stores and department and/or discount department stores. However, if prices become too high, merchandise selection too limited, or services too poor, residents of these communities will travel to larger communities to shop. This is known as **outshopping**. Even when retailing becomes concentrated at the local level, there are several checks on the retailers' power. For example, one of the checks on a retailer at a local level is the Internet. If prices at department and specialty stores become too high, then local shoppers may increase their use of nonstore shopping alternatives. In fact, existing catalog retailers and bricks & mortar stores are proving particularly adept at developing multi-channel strategies to attract customers from a wider geographic area. L.L. Bean has seen its catalog businesses boom with the addition of an online site, and stores such as Wal-Mart have fine-tuned their Internet offerings.

outshopping
Occurs when individuals in one community travel regularly to a larger community to shop.

The Demand Side of Retailing

Most retailers face monopolistic competition, and we assume such a market structure in the remainder of the text. In a monopolistically competitive market, the retailer will be confronted with a negatively sloping demand curve. That is, consumers will demand a higher quantity as price is lowered, assuming the retailer has chosen the merchandise that the customer wants, communicates the value of shopping at his/her store, and makes the product available. The typical retailer thus faces a demand function as shown in Exhibit 4.1.[5]

Again, such customer behavior implies knowledge of the competitive alternatives. Customers who have greater knowledge about their alternatives and about the differences in product features will often patronize a wider range of retailers.[6] There should be little surprise that as retailers become more proactive in their marketing efforts (using such tactics as aggressive advertising, multiple catalogs, and prospecting for new customers), consumers will become aware of a wider range

Exhibit 4.1
Demand as a Function of Price

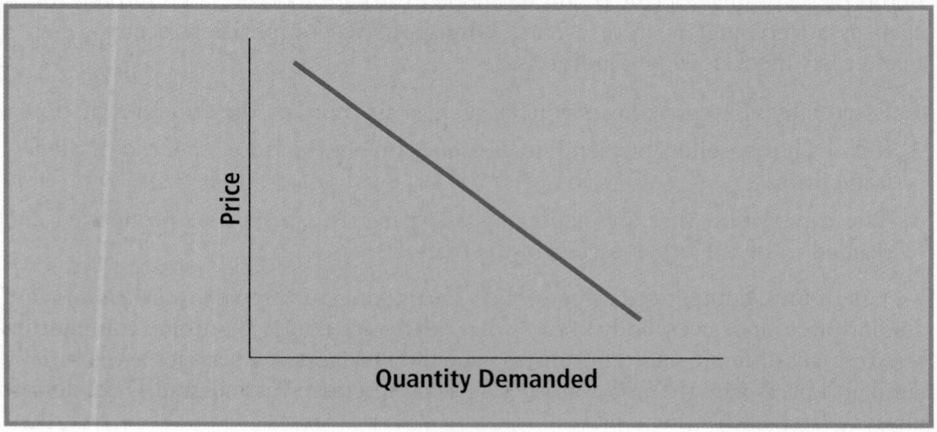

of alternatives and become more demanding customers. Advancements in communication processes, such as comparison shopping on the Internet and expectations of 24/7 (24 hours/7 days a week) customer service, have exacerbated the situation. As customers become more aware of better prices, better service, or better features, they may migrate from the local retailer that does not sufficiently measure up.

Thus, in most cases, higher prices will result in less demand for the retailer, because households have limited incomes and many purchase alternatives. Households will try to shift some of their purchasing power to other retailers with lower prices. This reality should suggest that retailers cannot be profitable by setting prices at the highest possible levels. Retailers will find it necessary to set prices somewhere below the maximum possible price but above zero. Extremely low prices will sell large quantities but not generate sufficient profit to cover costs. A retailer will not be able to meet the maximum customer demand at a profit, and must monitor competitors' prices in its trade area, as well as understand the impact of catalogs and the Internet. The retailer also needs to decide when a drop in a competitor's prices is temporary and inconsequential to long-term competition (i.e., it will be out of business if it prices too low) or when the competitor has set a new permanent pricing standard that requires the retailer to adjust its profit expectations.

Nonprice Decisions

Retailers often believe that they must always match or be lower than the competitor's price. In fact, that is not always the case. Many customers place a value on attributes other than price when selecting a place to shop. Some consumers choose to pick up a loaf of bread at a convenience store or bakery, even when it is cheaper at a supercenter or supermarket. They are willing to pay the higher price because they place a higher value on their time or have a special preference for a certain bakery bread. The chapter's Service Retailing box describes how some spas have used the "experience it" approach to sell their services. Many American retailers find that their most successful and least price-sensitive product lines are those that either save customers time or make them feel better or look younger.[7]

Therefore, the retailer has to make decisions about the other elements (merchandise mix, advertising and promotion, customer services and selling, and store layout and design) of the retail mix in order to influence the quantity of merchandise it sells and the profit level it achieves. If store location is fixed (the retailer has a long-term lease) in a poor location, some of the nonprice variables available are unique (noncomparable) merchandise, advertising, special promotions, personal selling, and store atmosphere. These nonprice variables are directed at enlarging the retailer's demand by drawing in more customers. Research by *Progressive Grocer* found that the most important criterion for selecting a supermarket was "cleanliness." Other essential criteria were low prices and accurate price scanning, which ranked just ahead of all prices clearly labeled; accurate, pleasant checkout clerks; freshness date marked on products; and a good produce department.[8]

Another advantage of competing on nonprice variables is that price is the variable for the competition to copy. Just lowering prices is a no-win situation because it doesn't take long for a competitor to match a low price. A bricks & mortar retailer can simply change the price scanner and the shelf marker; an e-tailer can easily change the price on its Web site. *Advertising Age*, for example, pointed out that when the six major online drugstores mounted a price battle to gain new customers, they wound up spending $2 on ads for every $1 in revenue on products with very low profit margins.[9] They failed to develop a differential advantage that the competition couldn't easily copy. Using price as a weapon to gain loyal customers does not always work. Many

Service Retailing

Service Retailing: The "Experience It" Approach

Today, some retail experts argue that consumers are no longer buying only tangible products and traditional service offerings but that they really want to purchase an experience. Walt Disney is recognized as the pioneer in this "experience it" approach to retailing. Both Disneyland and Epcot Center were built so that consumers could experience the future.

Today we are witnessing this "experience it" facet of retailing in the health spa and resort business. Canyon Ranch in Tucson, which was founded in 1979 by Mel Zuckerman, is considered the pioneer in the high-end health spa and resort business. Zuckerman wanted Canyon Ranch to be more than just a fabulous vacation. It was to be an *experience* that would influence the quality of your life, from the moment you arrived to long after you returned home. Canyon Ranch was a place to explore your potential for a happier, healthier, more fulfilling life. In all promotional material, Canyon Ranch stressed the word "intention" when talking about the experience. Its Web site stated

> . . . we are more intent than ever on motivating our guests to translate their healthiest thoughts into positive, ongoing action—and we do whatever it takes to make that happen . . . Our mission is not selling vacations; it's creating an environment in which you can make a direct, emotional connection between what you know you should do and what you actually do every day.

Over the years, Canyon Ranch has expanded and now has a woodlands health resort in the lush Berkshires of Lenox, Massachusetts. It also has SpaClubs in The Venetian Resort in the Las Vegas Strip, Gaylord Palms Resort in Kissimmee, Florida, and on board the Queen Mary II ocean liner. Nonetheless, as in all competitive markets, innovators are copied. Miraval Spa has entered the Tucson market. Ranked as the #1 resort and spa by the prestigious Zagat Survey and the readers of *Condé Nast*, Miraval has challenged Canyon Ranch and other competitors to provide even more exceptional experiences. Miraval positions itself as helping people create a life-in-balance experience. To accomplish its mission, it offers a variety of workshops such as: Partners, Pleasure and Passion: A Couples Retreat; Power & Passion: Engaging Feminine Sexual Radiance; Partners and Passion: Taking it to the Next Level. In addition, Miraval has recruited well-known holistic and integrative medicine expert Dr. Andrew Weil as Director of Integrative Health & Healing. Dr. Weil personally presents workshops on healthy aging that are targeted to America's fast growing "graying" market segment. Predictably, Canyon Ranch is fighting back with its own new innovative offerings. Even these high-end service providers are not exempt from price competition. Winter is the prime season in the dry Arizona city of Tucson, where the summer temperatures exceed 100 degrees on a daily basis but winter temperatures hover in the 60s and 70s. During this peak demand winter season, price had always been non-negotiable and extremely high. But this changed in 2006 when Miraval offered a special that provided a week-long stay for $4,735 (single occupancy) or $3,780 (double occupancy), which is 15 percent off the regular package price. Others began offering frequent-flyer–style loyalty programs.

Getty Images

Retail service innovators have realized that the spa and resort business is not an exclusively high-end market. In fact, one of the fastest growing areas of service retailing is stand-alone spas. These provide half day to full day treatments with no cost of overnight lodging. Not surprisingly, the cost drops dramatically with many

Service Retailing *(continued)*

treatments costing less than $75. Unless you happen to live in a small town of 25,000 or less, you will see numerous "day" spas in your local business directory.

Another interesting growth area is medical spas. These are spas that provide medical treatments such as dermatology services including Botox or Restylane, certain chemical peels, and intense-pulsed-light skin treatments. Increasingly, the entrepreneurs are medical doctors who are leaving their traditional medical practices with low insurance reimbursements for cash-paying spa customers. In 2000, there may have been a dozen medical spas in the United States; today there are over 1,500, and the number is growing weekly. These spas are successful because they provide a salon-like setting with quick service (sometimes even on a walk-in basis), are conveniently located, and offer attractive prices. They are also open weekends and evenings, unlike a traditional office. Importantly, just as the high-end spas face price competition as the number of competitors increases, so do the medical spas. For example, in December 2005, Lumity MedSpa in West Los Angeles was offering a holiday special of 40 percent off all laser hair removal, and Botox was bargain-priced at $9 a unit.

Sources: "Competition Forces Spas to Offer Big Deals," *The Wall Street Journal*, February 28, 2006: D1 & D7; Joseph B. Pine, II and James H. Gilmore, *The Experience Economy*, Boston, MA: Harvard Business School Press (1999); "Spas in Retail Centers Offer Cosmetic Medical Treatments," *The Wall Street Journal*, January 3, 2006: D1; http://www.canyonranch.

e-tailers, including Amazon, found that offering free shipping meant an unprofitable sale in the short term and little long-term purchase loyalty. Such promotions were expensive, and customer orders dropped substantially once the free shipping was eliminated. Now, many e-tailers require minimum purchase requirements to qualify for free shipping and other price-oriented benefits.

Retailers that are able to remove themselves from price competition by differentiating themselves in some other way will achieve higher profits than those that fail to do this.

Dollars & Sense

Consider some of the ways a retailer could use nonprice competition to achieve a protected niche:

1. The retailer could position itself as different from the competition by altering its merchandise mix to offer higher-quality goods, greater personal service, special-orders handling, or a better selection of large sizes. (In **store positioning**, one identifies a well-defined market segment using demographic or lifestyle variables and appeals to this segment with a clearly differentiated approach.) Such features may increase the maximum price that consumers will pay and also increase the distance consumers will travel to shop for these goods, thereby enlarging the retailer's trade area. Sharper Image, Neiman Marcus, and Nordstrom have done an excellent job of positioning themselves using this strategy.
2. The retailer can offer private label merchandise that has unique features or offers better value than competitors. Exhibit 4.2 lists the private labels for some of the major retailers. The strategy of using private label branding to secure a protected niche is discussed in detail at the end of this chapter.
3. The retailer could provide other benefits for the customer. For example, as gas prices go up, so does the drawing power of retailers who offer cheap fuel. Because shoppers are more likely to consolidate shopping trips as fuel prices increase, many discounters have followed the lead of European grocery stores and warehouse clubs and sacrificed margins on gasoline to increase sales inside of the store.[10]

store positioning
Is when a retailer identifies a well-defined market segment using demographic or lifestyle variables and appeals to this segment with a clearly differentiated approach.

Exhibit 4.2
Some Private Labels of Major Retailers

Kmart
JOE BOXER
Martha Stewart Everyday
Route 66
Sesame Street
Disney
JaclynSmith
Kathy Ireland
Thalia Sodi

Sears apparel brands
American Exchange
Apostrophe
Belongings
Canyon River Blues
c.l.o.t.h.e.s.
Covington
Lands' End
Latina Life
TKS

JCPenney
JCPenney Home Collection (Home Fashions)
St. John's Bay
Arizona
Worthington
Stafford (Men's)
Delicates (Intimate Apparel)

Wal-Mart
Sam's American Choice food & beverage
White Cloud toilet tissue & diapers
Simply Basic HBC premium line
Maxximum
Exceed
Sam's Member's Mark
Great Value
Ol' Roy
Equate
Alcott Ridge Wine
White Stag
Faded Glory
Mary Kate & Ashley
George clothing (ASDA)
GE Small Appliances
EverActive
No Boundaries

Target
Xhileration
Greatland
Merona
Pro Spirit
Archer Farms
Lullaby Club
Mossimo
Michael Graves
Circo
Cherokee

Saks Fifth Avenue
5/48
Real Clothes
SFA Collections

Kohl's
Apt. 9
American Beauty
Bodysource
Croft & Barrow
Good Skin
Sonoma (Private)
Urban Pipeline

Macy's
INC
Alfani
American Rag
Charter Club
Club Room
First Impressions
Green Dog
Hotel
Tasso Elba
Style & Co.

Nordstrom
BP.
Caslon
Classiques Entier
Façonnable
Halogen
JWN Signature
N Kids
Nordstrom
Nordstrom at Home
Nordstrom Lingerie
Nordstrom Rack
Studio 121

Mike Mergen/Bloomberg News/Landov

Kmart uses Martha Stewart to brand many of its houseware products and thus is able to differentiate itself among competing retailers.

4. The retailer could master stockkeeping with its basic merchandise assortment. For example, Nordstrom strives to always have men's dress shirts in stock and will give the consumer a free shirt if they are ever out of the basic sizes. Compare this policy with a competitor who has a similar item in stock only 95 percent of the time. If you go into this store to pick up just five items, the chances are almost one in four that the store will be out of at least one item [$.95 \times .95 \times .95 \times .95 \times .95 = .773$].

A variation is to become a "destination" store for certain products. For example, Hanneford's grocery store in York, Maine, guarantees that it will have hot roasted chickens available every day between 4 and 7 P.M., ready for takeout, or you get a coupon for a free chicken. (Even so, Hanneford's will always have a chicken ready within 30 minutes during this time period if they run out due to unexpectedly heavy demand.) Another example is Bass Pro Shops, which has become a sportsman's paradise by combining merchandise with in-store demonstrations and experiences, including a trout pond. Its flagship store in Springfield, Missouri, is even located adjacent to the American Fish and Wildlife Museum.

Remember, most retail decision variables, whether price or nonprice, are directed at influencing demand. The profitability of the decisions depends on the marginal cost of the action versus the marginal revenue it generates (see Chapter 10 for a discussion of pricing).

Sve Ogrocki/Associated Press

Bass Pro Shops Outdoor World differentiates itself with its merchandise and in-store demonstrations and thus has become a destination store for the active sports-person.

Competitive Actions

We just saw that most bricks & mortar retailers attract customers from a limited geographic area and that as prices are lowered, this area expands. But even at a zero price, households can afford to travel only a certain distance to get the goods and services retailers offer. Therefore, there are several, if not many, retailers in each line of retail trade in most cities.

A good measure of competitive activity in a market is the number of retail establishments of a given type per thousand households. When the number of stores per thousand households gets too large, the market is characterized as **overstored**. These retailers face a major performance imperative because their return on investment is below their cost of capital. Therefore, they will implement both price and nonprice actions in an attempt to increase both sales and profits. This highly competitive situation reduces the average return on investment and lowers the profitability of all retailers. Some will eventually exit the market.

overstored
Is a condition in a community where the number of stores in relation to households is so large that to engage in retailing is usually unprofitable or marginally profitable.

understored
Is a condition in a community where the number of stores in relation to households is relatively low so that engaging in retailing is an attractive economic endeavor.

However, if the number of stores per thousand households is small, in comparison to other markets, the market is **understored**. With too few retailers to adequately service local demand, profits may be high enough to attract new retail competitors, or existing retailers may be enticed to expand. A market is in equilibrium in terms of number of retail establishments if the return on investment is high enough to justify keeping capital invested in retailing, but not so high as to invite more competition.

As just indicated, competition is most intense in overstored markets, since many retailers are achieving an inadequate return on investment. Remember that while e-tailers may not be in close geographic proximity to other e-tailers and retailers, they are easily accessible via a customer's computer. From a customer's perspective, this effectively puts e-tailers in very close proximity, because they can all be shopped at the same location. Thus, the early exit of many e-tailers was the result of the Internet being overstored for the demand at the time, as well as the e-tailers' inability to control back-office costs. Similarly, the online purchases of basic airline tickets, which was discussed in Chapter 1's What's New box, resulted in the demise of many small travel agencies that relied simply on processing tickets, rather than providing value-added services. Agencies that served largely as ticket writers faced an increasingly overstored retail environment.

Suppliers as Partners and Competitors

A retailer's suppliers should be considered both partners and competitors for the customer's dollar. Suppliers, as will be pointed out in Chapter 5, are critical to the retailer's trade, but they are also in competition for gross margins throughout the supply chain. Every extra dollar charged by the supplier is one less for the retailer when retail prices are stagnant. The remedy is for the retailer to develop a loyal group of patrons that encourages the supplier to accommodate the needs of its retail partner. As more manufacturers evaluate their investments and marketing money for retailers and explore their own direct-to-consumer marketing, retailers must determine how they can be most productive for their suppliers, yet still maintain profitability.

When they provide a unique product or promotion, suppliers can be a critical competitive advantage to retailers. Many specialty retailers across categories vie to be the first with the latest products or to stock exclusive merchandise. Saks Fifth Avenue prides itself as the first to carry a new perfume in many retail areas. Further, suppliers can cooperate in improved merchandising and operations, such a developing a package design that is easier to read on the shelf, or in establishing efficient inventory management systems. For example, Office Max has worked with office supply manufacturers to use more informative labeling and packaging. This has greatly reduced the number of packages that customers rip open in the store to learn if the products are right for them. For example, is it the right color of paper? Is a connecting cord included or not?

However, suppliers have learned to become cautious in their relationships with large retailers. Some manufacturers have claimed, off-the-record, that Wal-Mart has been known to stock their product to see how it sells, only to come out with its own private label that directly competes with the manufacturer.

Types of Competition

LO 2

Why is it so important for a retailer to develop a protected niche?

It is possible to merge the preceding discussion of competition in retailing with the classification schemes used by the Department of Commerce in conducting the Census of Retail Trade.

Intratype and Intertype Competition

Intratype competition occurs when two or more retailers of the same type, as defined by NAICS (North American Industrial Classification System) codes in the Census of Retail Trade, compete directly with each other for the same households. This is the most common type of retail competition: Circuit City competes with Best Buy, Avon competes with Mary Kay, Saks Fifth Avenue competes with Neiman Marcus, Family Dollar competes with Dollar General, and Amazon.com competes with bn.com (Barnes & Noble Online).

intratype competition
Occurs when two or more retailers of the same type, as defined by NAICS codes in the Census of Retail Trade, compete directly with each other for the same households.

Due to the changing nature of the retailing environment, retailers are often forced to alter their strategy as their competition changes. For example, in the early 1990s Sears wanted to compete head-on with low-priced discounters such as Wal-Mart and Kmart. Today, after merging with Kmart, Sears is trying to reposition itself against middle-of-the-road merchants JCPenney and May Department Stores by appealing to women, emphasizing apparel, and carrying popular Kmart private labels, such as Martha Stewart. To generate more up-market store traffic, Sears acquired catalog merchant Lands' End (see Chapter 2's Case), whose merchandise is now found in its stores. Sears has also tried to capitalize on the "nesting" trend among many consumers by developing the Great Indoors, large freestanding home centers that offer both deeper selections of home furnishings and housewares and the convenience of at-the-door parking.[11] However, Sears still appears to be trying to find itself—is it a Kmart or Sears? This means that it must determine if it really wants to sell Martha Stewart at Sears stores and Kenmore, Die-Hard, and Craftsman at Kmart.

Every time different types of retail outlets sell the same lines of merchandise and compete for the same limited consumer dollars, **intertype competition** occurs. This is increasingly seen as many retailers compete with a scrambled merchandising strategy. As discussed in Chapter 1, scrambled merchandising occurs when a retailer carries many different unrelated product lines, often outside its traditional product mix, as a means of enhancing one-stop shopping convenience for its customers. Following are some common examples:

intertype competition
Occurs when two or more retailers of a different type, as defined by NAICS codes in the Census of Retail Trade, compete directly by attempting to sell the same merchandise lines to the same households.

- Discounters are handling cosmetics and fragrances that were traditionally the province of traditional department stores.
- Supermarkets (such as Albertson's, Kroger, and Safeway) have taken market share away from fast-food restaurants with their HMRs (Home Meal Replacements). In addition, their floral departments, greeting card sections, banks, and pharmacies have changed the competitive landscape for traditional

florists, card shops, banks, and drugstores, particularly in attracting consumers who place a high priority on convenience.

- Convenience stores (such as 7-Eleven) sell not only motor oil and related auto care products, but have added fast food, lottery tickets, and ATMs.
- Not only are electronic retailers, such as Best Buy and Circuit City, and supermarkets, such as Kroger and Safeway, competing against each other, but they are now engaged in an intertype battle with Wal-Mart, who wants to be the market share leader in all the lines it carries.

In each of the preceding examples, as intertype competition expanded, gross margins on the respective merchandise lines declined. For example, combination mail-order/online pharmacies have gained a growing share of prescription drug sales, and the impact on locally operated or chain-operated retail drugstores has been dramatic in reducing the average gross margin return on drugs. Both types of drug retailers have pressured drug manufacturers for the lowest wholesale prices. As a result, the inflation rate for widely used prescription drugs (those that treat arthritis, ulcers, and other common ailments) is the lowest of any medical category.

Furthermore, new retailers are always entering the marketplace, creating greater intratype and intertype competition. As the chapter's What's New box describes, the eBay Revolution has made it possible for anyone to be an e-tailer. In fact, eBay claims that more than 1.3 million of its members now make their living off the site.[12]

Divertive Competition

divertive competition
Occurs when retailers intercept or divert customers from competing retailers.

Another concept that helps to explain the nature of competition in retailing is **divertive competition**. This occurs when retailers intercept or divert customers from competing retailers. For example, an individual may recognize that she needs to get a birthday card for a relative and plans to do this the next time she visits the local shopping mall, which has a very well-stocked Hallmark card store. However, one day while picking up a prescription at the drugstore, she walks by the card stand and decides to purchase the greeting card at the drugstore. The drugstore retailer has intercepted this customer from the Hallmark store.

Another divertive tactic in use today is to operate a gas station on your property to catch those customers who have already stopped at your store and do not want to make another stop to get gas or, as was mentioned earlier in this chapter, to capture those consumers who need gas and want to consolidate shopping trips. Privately held Meijer now sells gas at 150 of its 170 supercenters in the Midwest, and Wal-Mart operates more than 1,000 gas stations at its supercenters and discount stores. E-tailers use a similar ploy by displaying banners across the top of many information Web sites.

break-even point
Is where total revenues equal total expenses and the retailer is making neither a profit nor a loss.

To comprehend the significance of divertive competition, which can be intertype or intratype competition, one needs to recognize that most retailers operate very close to their **break-even point** (the point where total revenues equal total expenses), but aren't really aware of this fact. For instance, supermarkets, which have extremely low gross margin return on sales, tend to have high break-even points, ranging from 94 to 96 percent of current sales. General merchandise retailers with a higher gross margin return on sales face lower break-even points of 85 to 92 percent of their current sales. In either case, a modest drop in sales volume could make these retailers unprofitable, thus fueling the growth of scrambled merchandising to get more of the customer's share of wallet.

What's New?

eBay: A Retail Revolution

Over the past decade, eBay has transformed from a small dot.com company to one of the largest retailers in America. The online auction house that never sleeps offers such hard-to-find treasures as flight bags from defunct airlines, hat boxes from defunct department stores, out-of-print books, period costume jewelry, an Art Deco dressing mirror, and Pucci scarves. eBay has enabled individuals working from their home to become microretailers reaching a global marketplace. Microretailers are small one- or two-person retail organizations.

Microretailers are not new; for example, microretailers specializing in hot dogs, pretzels, newspapers, and other consumables can be observed operating in the downtown area of any major city. In the past, though, their relatively small trade area (restricted to a few city blocks) and merchandise assortment limited their competitive threat to more traditional retailers. However, the retail world is changing, and eBay, with its 12 million registered users selling merchandise in 4,300 categories, is one of the catalysts. This retailer can compete with any retailer worldwide.

eBay has clearly revolutionized the opportunities available to microretailers. In that sense, eBay can be credited with reinvigorating retailing in the world economy. The tremendous potential for financial freedom, as well as work flexibility, has everyone asking themselves not only, "How much would someone pay for this stuff I don't want?" but, "With the limited investment needed to sell items online, why haven't I become a microretailer already?"

What brings millions of Internet customers to eBay every day? Probably, the lure of a bargain, combined with the excitement of a Las Vegas gamble. Whatever the reason, every time there's a sale, eBay earns a percentage. As a result, eBay, which started as a hobby for Pierre Omidyar, now has a market value higher than May Department Stores, Kroger, and The Gap combined. That's not bad for a company that just over a decade ago was often refereed to as the Beanie Babies Web site.

Today, eBay has become the largest Web site for the buying and selling of used cars, motorcycles, auto parts, and collectibles. In fact, more than $1,000 worth of goods are bought and sold every second.

What is most astounding about this eBay revolution is that this retailer holds no inventory and ships no product. Rather, it is an entirely new concept that took advantage of the Internet and has no direct bricks & mortar competition.

Gary Gardiner/Bloomberg News/Landov

Kroger installs gasoline pumps in many of its new stores, which offer below market gasoline prices, which help to build store traffic and thus enhance the sale of groceries and related merchandise.

Dollars & Sense Retailers should attempt to operate at a sales volume of 20 percent above their break-even point because this will allow them to weather major competitive assaults and thus be able to achieve a higher profit over the long term.

LO 3 Evolution of Retail Competition

What four theories are used to explain the evolution of retail competition?

A discussion of the evolution of retailing not only provides a better understanding of the history of retail formats, but also enhances our ability to make predictions about their future. Several theories have developed to explain and describe the evolution of competition in retailing. We will review three of them briefly, and describe a new concept that helps to explain why a variety of retail formats have the potential to be profitable.

The Wheel of Retailing

wheel of retailing theory
Describes how new types of retailers enter the market as low-status, low-margin, low-price operators; however, as they meet with success, these new retailers gradually acquire more sophisticated and elaborate facilities, and thus become vulnerable to new types of low-margin retail competitors who progress through the same pattern.

The **wheel of retailing theory**, illustrated in Exhibit 4.3, is one of the oldest descriptions of the patterns of competitive development in retailing.[13] This theory states that new types of retailers enter the market as low-status, low-margin, and low-price operators. This entry phase allows retailers to compete effectively and take market share away from the more traditional retailers. However, as they meet with success, these new retailers gradually enter a trading-up phase and acquire more sophisticated and elaborate facilities, often becoming less efficient. This creates both a higher investment and a subsequent rise in operating costs. Today, some academics refer to this stage as the "Big Middle," a market space where the largest number of potential customers reside.[14] Predictably, these retailers will eventually enter the vulnerability phase and must raise prices and margins, becoming vulnerable to new types of low-margin retail competitors who progress through the same pattern. This appears to be the case today with outlet malls. Once bare-bones warehouses for manufacturers' imperfect or excess merchandise, outlet malls quickly evolved into fancy, almost upscale locations where retailers try to outdo each other's accent lighting, private dressing rooms, and generous return policies. As a result, the cost of operating such locations increased and put them in more direct comparison with increasingly competitive department stores.

Exhibit 4.3
Wheel of Retailing

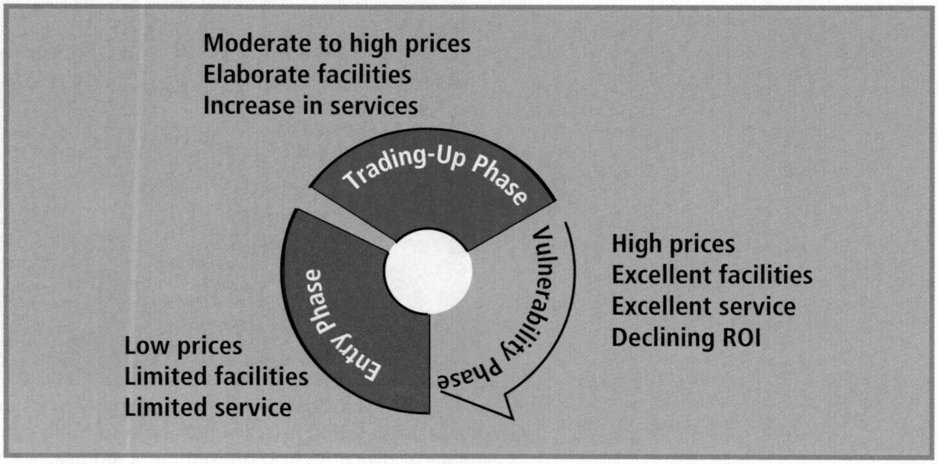

The Pritzker family-owned Hyatt hotel chain maintains a unique price/value positioning. It has developed four distinct hotel/motel formats: Park Hyatt is on top, then Grand Hyatt, Hyatt Regency, and Hyatt Place. Grand Hyatts should be a "hip-hip-hooray hotel" for people who want to be seen, who want to have fun. They drive a Ferrari and wear a big gold clunker watch. The Park Hyatt customer, who's wife dresses in Chanel and likes white wine, drives a Mercedes and has more money than the Grand Hyatt consumer in the Ferrari. The Regency's target customer has traveled on business throughout the world and just wants to sit in his room and work all evening long. Hyatt Place offers a slightly-above-limited-service suite.[15] Realizing that consumers may have different lodging needs depending upon the circumstances, Hyatt has tied these four different formats together with the same loyalty program—the Hyatt Gold Passport.

While the wheel of retailing may explain the evolution of some retail forms, it is less clear about the success of some new niche retailers; retailers that successfully compete on nonprice factors, such as luxury retailers or convenience stores; and the role of cost control on improving customer satisfaction as well as competitiveness, as Wal-Mart and discount clubs have done.

The Retail Accordion

Several observers of the history of retailing have noted that retail institutions evolve from outlets that offer wide merchandise assortments to specialized stores that offer narrow assortments and then return to the wide assortment stores to continue through the pattern again and again. This contraction and expansion of merchandise assortment suggests the term **retail accordion**.[16]

retail accordion
Describes how retail institutions evolve from outlets that offer wide assortments to specialized stores and continue repeatedly through the pattern.

Retail historians have observed that, in the United States, retail trade was dominated by the general store until 1860. The general store carried a broad assortment of merchandise ranging from farm implements to textiles to food. After 1860, due to the growth of cities and roads, retail trade became more specialized and was concentrated in the central business districts of cities. By 1880 to 1890, department and specialty stores were the dominant competitive force. Both carried more specialized assortments than the general store. In the 1950s, retailing began to move again to wider merchandise lines. Typical was the supermarket, which added produce and dairy products, nonfood items such as kitchen utensils, health and beauty aids, and small household appliances. Today specialization in merchandise categories has once again become a dominant competitive strategy. Witness, for example, the success of Foot Locker stores, Barnes & Noble Bookstores, and the spin-offs from The Limited of Intimate Brands (the Victoria's Secret division) and Abercrombie & Fitch Co. Even Wal-Mart is heeding this trend by building freestanding 40,000-square-foot Neighborhood Markets grocery stores in selected markets.

However, the accordion theory is vague about the competitive importance of providing wide assortments for various target customer groups. For example, the customer who wants one-stop shopping convenience has led to success for Wal-Mart's superstores and other retailers using scrambled merchandising. Simultaneously, many category killers have been successful by specializing in a deep but narrow selection of merchandise lines, and specialty stores like Wet Seal and high-end "hot" designers like Gucci have succeeded by offering a highly edited point of view for their customer segments. Again, a major criticism of this theory is its implication that there is one "right" direction for successful retailing, when many are possible if well executed.

The Retail Life Cycle

retail life cycle
Describes four distinct stages that a retail institution progresses through: introduction, growth, maturity, and decline.

The final framework we will examine is the **retail life cycle**. Some experts argue that retailing institutions pass through an identifiable cycle. This cycle has four distinct stages; it starts with (1) *introduction*, proceeds to (2) *growth*, then (3) *maturity*, and ends with (4) *decline*. We discuss each stage briefly.

Introduction

This stage begins with an aggressive, bold entrepreneur who is willing and able to develop a different approach to the retailing of certain products. Most often the approach is oriented to a simpler method of distribution and passing the savings on to the customer. Other times it could be centered on a distinctive product assortment, shopping ease, locational convenience, advertising, or promotion. For example, Jiffy Lube and other quick oil change service retailers offered faster "while you wait" service at more convenient locations with lower prices than conventional service stations and auto dealers and changed the way consumers serviced their cars. During this stage profits are low, despite the increasing sales level, due to amortizing developmental costs.

Growth

During the growth stage, sales, and usually profits, explode. New retailers enter the market and begin to copy the idea. For example, the rapid growth of Starbucks cafes encouraged other "gourmet" coffeehouses to enter the market and capture the growing interest in deeper assortments of coffee beverages and casual "lifestyle" eateries. Toward the end of the growth period, cost pressures that arise from the need for a larger staff, more complex internal systems, increased management controls, and other requirements of operating large, multiunit organizations overtake some of the favorable results. Consequently, late in this stage, both market share and profitability tend to approach their maximum level.

Maturity

In maturity, market share stabilizes and severe profit declines are experienced for several reasons. First, managers have become accustomed to managing a high-growth firm that was simple and small, but now they must manage a large, complex firm in a nongrowing market. Second, the industry has typically overexpanded. Third, competitive assaults will be made on these firms by new retailing formats (a bold entrepreneur starting a new retail life cycle) or more efficient retailers consolidating the industry.

Decline

Although decline is inevitable for some formats (few people get their milk delivered to the door anymore), retail managers will try to postpone it by changing the retail mix. These attempts can postpone the decline stage, but a return to earlier, attractive levels of operating performance is not likely. Sooner or later a major loss of market share will occur, profits fall, and the once promising idea is no longer needed in the marketplace. However, the retailer that can identify a small, but lucrative, customer group that insists on the traditional form (e.g., home delivery of groceries) may be able to extract a premium for its services, and extend its lifetime.

The retail life cycle is accelerating today. New and more competitive concepts now move quickly from introduction to maturity since the leading operators have aggressive growth goals and their investors demand a quick return on equity. In addition, larger retailers with capital and expertise in concept roll-out can acquire

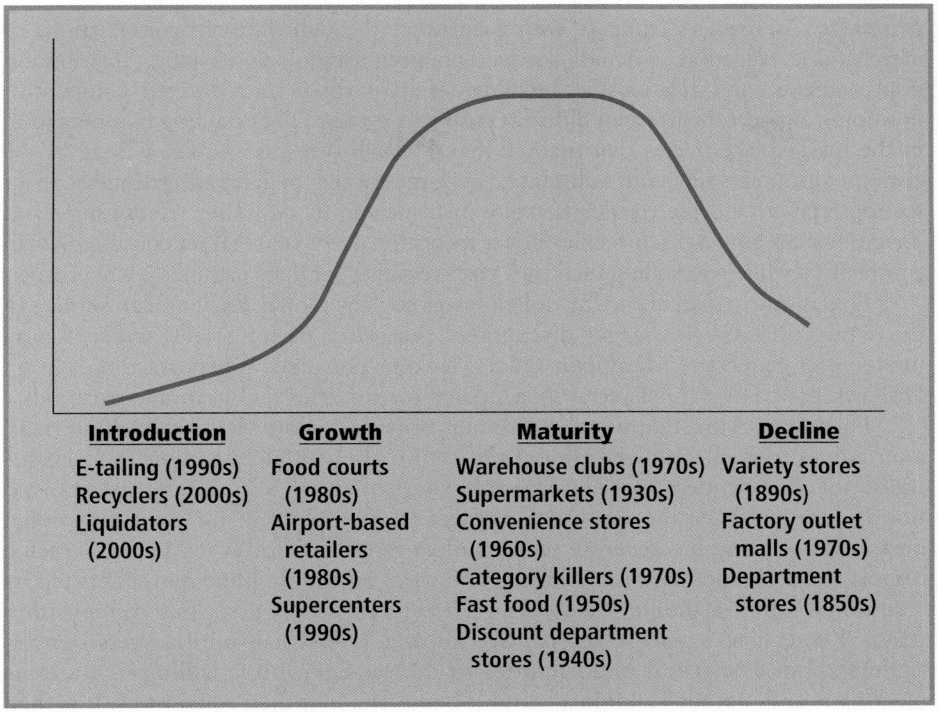

Exhibit 4.4
Retail Institutions in Their Various Stages of the Retail Life Cycle

many entrepreneurs in the early stages of the retail life cycle. Exhibit 4.4 lists the various stages of the retail life cycle for many of our current retail institutions.

Resource-Advantage Theory

The final theory to describe in the evolution of retail competition is resource-advantage.[17] This theory is based on the idea that all firms seek superior financial performance in an ever-changing environment. Retail demand is dynamic because consumer tastes are always changing, and supply is dynamic because, as firm's search for a superior performance, they are forced to change the elements of their retail mix to match changing consumer preferences.

Resource-advantage illustrates two important lessons for retailers:[18]

1. Superior performance at any point in time is the result of achieving a competitive advantage in the marketplace as a result of some tangible or intangible entity (or "resource"). The retailer is able to use this entity, such as an innovation regarding location procedures or merchandise selection, to offer greater value to the market place.
2. All retailers cannot achieve superior results at the same time. The retailer is able to use this entity, such as innovation regarding location procedures or merchandise selection, to offer greater value to the marketplace and/or to operate their firms at a lower cost relative to competitors.

Thus, it is important for currently high-performing retailers to maintain their vigilance over the actions of lower performing competitors, so as not to be overtaken.

The result is ongoing market turbulence, in which new retail forms and offerings continually appear and consumers continually shift their buying preferences and retail patronage. As retailers compete with each other through different combinations of merchandise selection, pricing, service, communication, positioning, distribution improvements, and relationship building, each of these multi-faceted competitive positions can meet the needs of different customer groups. The resulting fragmentation in the marketplace means that many different retail forms are viable, as long as the customer group is sufficiently substantial, i.e. large enough to generate acceptable profit for the retailer, and the retailer is astute in managing its customer relationships and operations. So long as each retailer better meets the needs of its target consumers than competitors while controlling their own costs of satisfying that customer it will prosper.

This is one explanation why dollar stores such as Dollar General can survive in the same markets with larger discounters that offer better prices, wider assortments, and groceries. Many consumers, lacking personal transportation, rely on Dollar General as a quick, convenient place for sundries and grab-and-go foods.

The fact remains that not all customers are equally knowledgeable about retail alternatives; not all retailers are equally astute about understanding their customers; not all customers have similar preferences or access to retail alternatives; and not all retailers have the resources to meet the competition for their traditional customers. Amway has recently seen retailers ranging from Wal-Mart to Tractor Supply make inroads into its suburban and rural base and online merchants tap its traditional "shop-at-home" customers. Therefore, Amway is seeking to reposition itself. These marketplace discrepancies allow for less-than-optimal retail environments, but also reveal opportunities to the retailer who is willing to study its customers and markets, and do a better job in managing their operations. It is then imperative that the retailer communicate its superiority to target customers, thus pushing competition to a new and evolved level.

LO 4

What future changes could affect retail competition?

Future Changes in Retail Competition

Retailers in today's ever-changing marketplace can expect dynamic changes in competition. Trends shaping the retail landscape include an increase in competition from nonstore retailers, the advent of new retailing formats, heightened global competition, the integration of technology into their operations, and the increasing use of private labels.

Nonstore Retailing

Back in Exhibit 1.3 on page 13, it was pointed out that nonstore retail sales—which includes direct sellers, catalog sales, and e-tailing—currently account for five percent of total retail sales. Several retail analysts predict that, as a result of several key forces at work today, nonstore sales (especially those that utilize the Internet) will experience significant growth over the next decade. With accelerated communication technology and changing consumer lifestyles, the growth potential for nonstore retailing is staggering. However, it must be remembered that even a 50 percent increase in sales would mean that nonstore sales would still only account for 7.5 percent of total retail sales. Some of the forces contributing to this expected rapid growth are:

- Consumers' need to save time.
- Consumers' desire to "time-shift," that is, shop when they want, not when a retailer wants to open a store.
- The erosion of enjoyment in the shopping experience.

- The lack of qualified sales help in stores to provide information.
- The explosive development of the telephone, the computer, and telecommunications equipment that facilitates nonstore shopping.
- The consumers' preference for lower prices, which often eliminates or reduces the middleman's profit.[19]

Therefore, traditional retailers need to continuously monitor developments in nonstore retailing.

Direct Selling

direct selling
Engaging in the sale of a consumer product or service on a person-to-person basis away from a fixed retail location.

Direct selling establishments engage in the sale of a consumer product or service on a person-to-person basis away from a fixed retail location, using party plans (The Pampered Chef Ltd.) or one-to-one selling in the home or workplace (Avon Products Inc.). In the United States, more than 13 million independent distributors (also called representatives, consultants, and small business owners), who are not employed by the organization they represent, generate direct sales that total about $30 billion annually. More than 90 percent of all direct sellers operate their businesses part-time. Currently, worldwide sales total slightly over $99 billion, with the United States being the largest of the 45 applicable markets, followed by Japan ($27 billion) and Korea ($8.1 billion). Major product categories include cosmetics and skin care items (Mary Kay Inc., Nu Skin Enterprises), decorative home products (Princess House Inc., Home Interiors and Gifts Inc.), cookware and cutlery (Regal Ware Inc., CUTCO Corp.), and Nutritional Supplements (Herbalife International, Shaklee Corp.). Some of today's direct selling companies are incorporating additional marketing channels, such as catalogs, kiosks, and the Internet to augment sales from traditional direct selling. The major attributes of direct selling remain the same—product quality and uniqueness, knowledge and demonstration of the product by a knowledgeable salesperson, excellent warranties and guarantees, and person-to-person interaction.

Many people are confused by the terms "direct selling" and "multilevel marketing." Direct selling refers to a distribution method, whereas multilevel marketing refers more specifically to a type of compensation plan found in direct selling. A direct selling company that offers a multilevel compensation plan pays its representatives/distributors based not only on his/her own product sales, but on the product sales of that person's "downline" (the people the representative/distributor has recruited into the business, and, in turn, the people the recruits have brought into the business). Eighty-two percent of the direct sellers in the United States use the multilevel compensation plan. Some countries, such as China, have long banned direct selling. However, in late 2005, China permitted direct sellers to enter the country provided that compensation doesn't exceed 30 percent of sales revenue and that the firms use a single level compensation plan. (In a single level plan the representative/distributor is compensated based solely on his/her own product sales.) A multilevel plan should not be confused with a pyramid compensation plan, because in pyramid schemes no product is actually sold. By educating the public, direct sellers are hoping to convince countries like China of the benefits of multilevel plans.[20]

Catalog Sales

catalog sales
Retail sales that occur through catalogs mailed to households.

Catalog sales occur when retailers sell their products primarily through mail-order catalogs. Annual catalog sales to consumers are just under $100 billion. Included in this figure are book and music clubs and retailers, jewelry firms

Exhibit 4.5
The Top 10 Direct-to-Consumer Catalog Retailers

	(in millions)
JCPenney	$2,793.0
Sears Holdings	$1,614.0
Redcats USA	$1,539.0
Williams-Sonoma	$1,135.1
Limited Brands	$1,119.0
LL Bean	$1,100.0 (estimate)
Cabela's	$970.6
Corner Stone Brands	$720.0
1-800 Flowers	$584.9
Neiman Marcus Group	$579.2

This list was provided by *Multichannel Merchant* and used with its written permission.

(Ross-Simon), novelty retailers (Popcorn Factory), specialty merchandisers such as sporting goods (L.L. Bean), ethnic-origin apparel (Eziba, Sundance, and Peruvian Connection), children's apparel retailers (Right Start), kitchenware (Williams-Sonoma), as well as traditional bricks & mortar retailers (Wal-Mart, JCPenney, Best Buy, and Limited) who also offer limited catalogs. Exhibit 4.5 lists the top 10 direct-to-consumer catalog retailers.

E-Tailing

The general belief among retail experts is that electronic, interactive, at-home shopping is definitely the place to be. Every major player in the retail industry, computer industry, telecommunications industry, and the transaction processing industry is committed to this growth. The only prerequisite needed for the Internet's success is having enough homes with PCs. Already 80 percent of American households are connected either at home or at work. More important is the fact that today's teens and twenty-somethings are the first generation to grow up fully wired and technologically fluent. These consumers, especially college students, use social-networking Web sites, such as myspace.com and facebook.com, as a way to establish their identities.

Many believe that these social-networks already have created new forms of social behavior that blur the distinctions between online and real-world interactions to the point that today's young adults largely ignore the differences. Most Gen Xers and Baby Boomers tend to view the Internet as a supplement to their daily lives. They use the Net to gather information, buy items (CDs, books, stocks, and gifts), or link up with others who share passions for a favorite sports team. However, for the most part, their social lives remain rooted in the traditional phone call and face-to-face interaction.

Generation Y folks, by contrast, are able to exist in both worlds at once. Increasingly, America's middle- and upper-class youth use social networks as virtual community centers, a place to go and sit for a while (sometimes hours). While older consumers come and go on the Net for a specific task, Gen Yers are just as likely to socialize online as off. This is partly a function of how much more comfortable young people are on the Web: Fully 87 percent of 12- to 17-year-olds use the Internet, versus two-thirds of adults. For example, as the result of being the first

Web site to allow users to customize their pages any way they wanted, nearly a million Gen Yers sign up as new MySpace members each week.[21]

As the Internet grows, Americans will make increasing use of it as a shopping method. Many shoppers will opt for its convenience and broad selection. Browsing will be easier and the choices more extensive. (Nevertheless, consumers will still want the social experience of shopping outside the home; after all, with so many stores nearby, shopping at a bricks & mortar retailer after doing active information gathering on the computer will become even more convenient.) As a result, Internet shopping is expected to increase from its current level of just over 2 percent of retail sales to around 5 percent over the next decade.

While some so-called experts had once claimed that Internet sales would reach 50 percent of total retail sales, this prediction will never come to pass for the following six reasons.

1. As shown in Exhibit 1.3 on page 13, 26 percent of all retail sales involve automobile dealers. The taxes paid by new car dealers to their state governments will ensure that states will continue to ban Internet sales and protect the current system. Gasoline station sales, which some estimate as almost 5 percent of all retail sales, are not likely to be made over the Internet.
2. Discounters, who account for a third of all general merchandise sales, will have a particularly difficult problem selling via the Internet. After all, consumers looking for bargains won't want to pay for shipping and handling. The same argument could be made for bulky items such as furniture. An IKEA spokesperson recently admitted that the chain's Web site (http://www.ikea.com) was clunky and offered only a narrow selection of products, since many products are simply too large to be shipped cheaply.[22]
3. Half of all food and beverage sales, or over 7 percent of all retail sales, are sold by on-premise restaurants. Regarding off-premise food and beverage sales, this chapter's Inside Story box highlights the two basic business models currently being used for selling groceries online.
4. As mentioned earlier, the United States is currently overstored. Many consumers, after searching the Internet, opt for the instant satisfaction of purchasing from a nearby bricks & mortar retailer, instead of waiting for an overnight delivery.
5. Some items, especially fashion clothing, must be tried on or seen in person before buying. As anyone who has ever seen an array of televisions in a store knows, each set has a different tint. The same can be said for a computer monitor.
6. A final factor limiting e-commerce is the "security issue." Many consumers are afraid of identity theft and, as a result, only 25 percent of Americans purchased even one item on the Internet in 2005.[23]

In addition, it is important to remember that the Internet will not increase overall consumer demand. While online sales will definitely cannibalize store and catalog sales, they will not increase the average consumer spending power. Strategies by clicks & mortar retailers that integrate a single message and seamless operations will be more powerful than a pure e-tailing strategy. This will be especially true once clicks & mortar retailers learn the importance of addressing the total customer experience through any contact point with the customer. For example, while at her home computer, in her "jammies" at 11 P.M., a customer may want to check an order that she placed in the actual (tangible) store earlier that day. A final point to

Retailing: The Inside Story

Business Models for an e-Grocery Operation

There are two basic business models in the e-grocery segment:

1. The **bricks & click approach** (whereby a traditional grocer adds an Internet operation), which has certainly become both more common and less risky
2. The **online only approach**, which seemed in danger of dying off after the failures of Webvan and others at the end of the dot.com bomb (when so many Internet retailers failed), but now has resurfaced with a much smaller presence

Albertsons and Safeway are the most aggressive in their roll-out plans for e-grocery. Albertsons.com currently offers online ordering and delivery in twelve major markets. Safeway.com is serving six markets and, through its Vons.com operation, another ten. According to Nielsen/NetRatings, over a recent year Albertsons.com has increased their unique audience (online) by 54 percent and Safeway.com increased 60 percent. Currently the projected unique audience size for both is approximately 412,000 people.

Kroger has been testing online shopping only in Denver through its King Soopers division since 2003, and after three years, there has been no indication of a further roll-out.

Peapod (acquired by Ahold in 2001) is doing business in eight states mostly under the Giant and Stop & Shop banners, and generated $183 million in sales during the January 2005 year, up 25 percent from the $147 generated the previous year. Bob Clare, a New Jersey ShopRite retailer with a single 80,000 square foot store, has licensed the NetGrocer name and is shipping orders all over the country and even abroad. NetGrocer also is marketing its products through Amazon.com's gourmet food section, though that remains a "test" site that has not received much attention.

In business for seven years now, SimonDelivers.com has put its marketing emphasis on providing fresh foods—produce, meat, and seafood—to shoppers in Minnesota and parts of Wisconsin. The company is an aggressive marketer; one program offered shoppers who spent at least $80 a week for seven weeks $80 worth of groceries free in the 8th week (the equivalent of a 15 percent discount).

New York-based e-grocer FreshDirect.com believes that the way to build sales is to add higher-margin items, including wine and prepared meals—and to position themselves equally against restaurants as supermarkets. FreshDirect generated more than $100 million in revenues, and has more than 250,000 customers, with an average transaction of more than $100 over the 2005 year.

John Catsimatidis, the CEO of privately held Gristede's, has gone on the record as saying that he launched an online business in Manhattan because he saw that FreshDirect had stolen about $20 million of his chain's $300 million in sales. He also has said that if FreshDirect fails, he'll immediately shut down his online operations.

It seemed safe before the dot.com bomb to predict that online grocers would encourage a revolution in how people shop, but the reality is that shoppers are visiting more channels than ever to purchase their foods; having an online resource just adds one more acquisition method, rather than creating a shopping revolution. Online grocery shopping is likely to continue to grow steadily, though not explosively, perhaps reaching as high as $10 billion in annual revenues by the end of the decade.

Source: *Facts, Figures & the Future*, March 14, 2005: 10–11. Used with Phil Lempert's written permission. (You may sign up for this free monthly newsletter at factsfiguresfuture.com.)

---

bricks-and-click approach
An approach that involves a tangible retail store that also offers its merchandise on the Internet.

online only approach
An online only approach is when the retailer only offers merchandise or services via the Internet and not through a tangible retail store.

remember is that e-tailers must pay attention to customer service. Most e-tailers do a good job during busy seasons, such as Christmas. However, in an effort to reduce operating costs, they reduce their service standards at other times. Customers are demanding such basic services as e-mail confirmation of orders and real-time confirmation of available inventory. Since customer service is a particular vulnerability for traditional retailers, e-tailers should seek their niche here.

New Retailing Formats

The practice of retailing is continually evolving. New formats are born and old ones die. Innovation in retailing is the result of constant pressure to improve efficiency and effectiveness in a continual effort to better serve the consumer. The pressure to better serve has also resulted in a shortened life cycle for retail formats. However, just as retailers find it extremely difficult to predict what will be the "hot new item" for an upcoming season, especially Christmas, they have the same trouble predicting the success of new retail formats.

For example, in the late 1980s, most retail experts agreed that hypermarkets (which are one and a half times the size of a supercenter) would be retailing's success story of the 1990s. However, despite their overwhelming success in Europe and their limited success in the United States (Meijer in Michigan and Kroger's Fred Meyer's division in the Northwest), these super-large stores, which resembled airplane hangars, were instead retailing's biggest failure for the 1990s. What happened?

Probably, customers felt that any store that had "rest areas" and stockers wearing roller skates was just too big to shop. Also, shoppers were unnerved by ceilings and shelves that rose several stories high. In addition, category killers, such as Toys"R"Us and Sports Authority, offered greater selection; wholesale clubs offered better prices; and supermarkets, discount drug stores, and other discounters offered more convenient locations. Although hypermarkets were a superior competitive offering in Europe, where the traditional alternatives were small shops with high prices and crowded, in-town locations, they did not have a noteworthy competitive advantage in the overstored American retail landscape.

Another retail format that didn't achieve the success predicted was the off-price retailer. **Off-price retailers** are similar to discounters with one important difference. While discounters offer continuity of brands—that is, they carry the same brands day-in and day-out—off-pricers, which are more opportunistic, carry only brands that they are able to get on special deals from the manufacturer or close-out wholesalers. Thus, the off-price retailers failed because the regular merchants, including discounters, became more price competitive on the brands the off-pricer was currently selling. Moreover, the off-price merchandise brands and selection could be wildly unpredictable as manufacturers became better at planning production and inventories.

off-price retailers
Sell products at a discount but do not carry certain brands on a continuous basis. They carry those brands they can buy from manufacturers at closeout or deep one-time discount prices.

The three primary examples of off-price retailers are factory outlets, independent carriers, and warehouse clubs. Factory outlets, which are owned and operated by the manufacturer, stock the manufacturers' surplus, discontinued, or irregular products. Independent off-price retailers, such as Stein Mart and TJ Maxx, carry an ever-changing assortment of higher-quality merchandise. Warehouse (or wholesale) clubs, such as Costco and Sam's, operate out of enormous, low-cost facilities and charge patrons an annual membership fee. They sell a limited selection of brand-name grocery items, appliances, clothing, and miscellaneous items at a deep discount. Warehouse stores, which have low costs because they buy products at huge quantity discounts and use limited labor, usually have gross margins (gross margin will be explained in detail in Chapter 8) averaging nearly 10 to 12 percent.

Although the hypermarkets and off-pricers have not lived up to expectations, three successful formats developed over the last decade are expected to continue: supercenters; stores that recycle used merchandise in good condition; and liquidators. These three formats have one thing in common: They offer the consumer value by developing an innovative partnership with suppliers.

Supercenters

The **supercenter**—a cavernous combination supermarket and discount department store carrying more than 80,000 to 100,000 SKUs that range from televisions

supercenter
Combine a discount store and grocery store and carry 80,000 to 100,000 products in order to offer one-stop shopping.

to peanut butter to DVDs—should continue to be the key growth format for the mass merchants. These stores offer the customer one-stop shopping (and as a result are capable of drawing customers from a 50-mile radius in some rural areas) and lower the customer's total cost of purchasing in terms of time and miles traveled without sacrificing service and variety. This is exactly what today's time-pressed consumer needs. In contrast, conventional discount department store retailing—barring expansion-minded Target and Kohl's, each with a distinct competitive position in today's marketplace—is facing the end of its life cycle. In fact, according to a recent study by Retail Forward, a major consulting firm specializing in retailing, by 2010 the number of Wal-Mart conventional discount department stores will decline to 688 from the high of 1,995 in 1995. Over the same time period, Wal-Mart's total number of Supercenters will increase to 3,131 from 239.

The significance of supercenters is most evident in the grocery business. Supermarket operators have surrendered peacefully to the supercenters. For example, they joined the other discounters by lowering prices. Supermarkets, which have always operated with paper-thin net profit margins of 1 to 2 percent, matched the supercenters' prices by gaining better control over their inventory to achieve cost savings and tailored their offerings to their own customers' purchasing habits. However, by 2006, Wal-Mart had over 2,000 supercenters and was the nation's leading grocery retailer. Consequently, several large supermarket chains were available for sale.

Not all market segments are equally attracted to the supercenter formats. Target's higher-income customer base is attracted by good value, but is often willing to sacrifice the lowest price for better design, selection, or niche products. Consequently, Target has had more difficulty convincing its customers to shop its groceries than Wal-Mart, which has a price-driven customer base.

The supercenter concept has branched out into the automobile market. Glitzy, computerized auto superstore chains, such as AutoNation, Driver's Mart Worldwide, and CarMax Auto Superstores, are giving nightmares to the nation's 22,000 traditional car dealers. Since its introduction in the mid-1990s, this new breed of retailer has streamlined an industry in which over 20 percent of a car's price consisted of the retailer's expenses, and has made shopping easier for the customer. These massive publicly traded chains sell new and used cars using "cheap" Wall Street money to finance, sell, rent, lease, and repair cars. Just like the supercenters in the grocery industry, these auto superstores are making competition tougher for other auto retailers.

A final issue in the growth of supercenters is their acceptability in a community's landscape. Due to land restrictions, particularly for large-format retailers, Wal-Mart has been forced to buy its way into a number of European countries by acquiring an existing local chain. Further, many U.S. communities prefer to maintain low-profile retail areas and rally against the intrusion of big-box retailers, along with the traffic and environmental impact that is assumed will follow.

Recycled Merchandise Retailers

Due to their very small numbers just a decade ago, recycled merchandisers have experienced the fastest growth of any retail format over the past five years. Originally a product of the Great Depression, the **recycled merchandise retailers** format—which sells gently used children's clothes (Once Upon A Child), teen and adult clothing (Plato's Closet), sporting goods (Play It Again Sports), and even musical instruments (Music-Go-Round)—also includes pawn shops, thrift shops, consignment shops, and flea markets. Even eBay is considered to be a recycler as

recycled merchandise retailers
Are establishments that sell used and reconditioned products.

well as an auction house. As a record number of retailers are seeking bankruptcy protection, these recycled merchandise retailers are growing by 10 percent a year. Three trends are driving this growth. First, conspicuous consumption is no longer chic. With the birth of eBay, consumers would rather gloat about a good buy than an expensive product. Buying used items is appealing to environmentally conscious consumers and selling clothes one no longer needs increases an individual's income. A second trend is that some segments are confined by a lack of money. Teenagers, for example, love fashionable clothes but often can't afford all the new clothes they want. The third major trend focuses on customer groups that have grown to appreciate the design, uniqueness, and quality of "vintage" items of clothing and furniture. It is not unusual to see high-profile celebrities sporting vintage clothing purchased either cheaply at the Salvation Army Thrift Shop or expensively at tony shops like Lilly et Cie in Beverly Hills. Many used furniture shops have reinvigorated themselves as retailers of "period" goods, such as Mood Indigo in New York, which specializes in mid-20th-century items. In addition, Internet sellers, such as eBay, have been instrumental in bringing together widely dispersed sellers and buyers of unique, one-of-a-kind goods.

Now that many preowned clothes shops are using the same media as traditional retailers to advertise their merchandise, shoppers today may find it difficult to distinguish between recyclers and small specialty shops. Because so much of the merchandise is new, nearly new, or gently used, the tattered appearance of traditional thrift stores is no longer expected. Recyclers have developed to serve specific markets, such as pregnant women, people requiring large sizes, and children; or even to offer specific merchandise, such as toys, sporting goods, outerwear, or jewelry. The apparel group accounting for the fewest resale and thrift store sales is men's clothing. It seems that men hang on to their clothes longer than women and children do, leaving much less merchandise available for resale.

Today, there are more than 20,000 secondhand stores nationwide, according to the National Association of Resale and Thrift Shops in St. Clair Shores, Michigan.[24] Recycling is not just an American phenomenon; it is also popular in Europe and Latin America. The flea markets and resale shops of European cities have long been mined for bygone treasures. However, nowhere is it growing faster than in Japan, which reports a growth rate of nearly 20 percent per year. Japanese companies from kimono stores to catalog retailers have jumped on the second-hand bandwagon. One of the most popular stores in Japan is called "Per Gramme Market," which sells items at eight cents a gram. Thus, a secondhand T-shirt would cost around $8.50, but a silk scarf would sell for $2.80.[25]

Liquidators

With more than 15,000 retailers seeking the protection of the bankruptcy courts annually, a new growth industry (albeit another from a very small starting point) has developed: liquidators. Often called retailing's undertakers or vultures, this small and all-but-invisible retail format liquidates leftover merchandise when an established retailer shuts down or downsizes. Firms like DJM Asset Management purchase the entire inventory of the existing retailer and run the "going-out-of-business" (GOB) sale. They make their money by seldom paying more than 30 cents on the dollar for the closeout merchandise. This handful of firms does almost $8 billion in sales annually and earns between 3 and 7 percent of the cash raised.[26]

Some might question why retailers don't do this job themselves, as some manufacturers do with outlet malls. First, the retailers in question usually have problems, or they wouldn't need the liquidator's service in the first place. Second, most liquidators pay cash for the merchandise—a plus for the strapped retailer—and then take all the risks and gain the rewards. Other liquidators will only conduct the sale, but guarantee a minimum payout to the retailer. Finally, by having outsiders run the closeouts, management can focus on operating the continuing stores and moving on to (hopefully) more successful merchandising.

Running closeouts requires some very special retailing skills. Liquidators have a talent for pricing merchandise and estimating the expense of everything from ad budgets and payrolls to utility bills. Since most of the employees know they will be out of a job as soon as the liquidation is complete, liquidators have to develop special incentive plans to make it more profitable for store personnel to stay and work rather than quit or walk off with merchandise.

Heightened Global Competition

The rate of change in retailing around the world appears to be directly related to the stage and speed of economic development in the countries concerned, but even the least-developed countries are experiencing dramatic changes. Retailing in other countries exhibits greater diversity in its structure than it does in the United States. In some countries, such as Italy, retailing is composed largely of specialty houses carrying narrow lines. Finnish retailers usually carry a more general line of merchandise. The size of the average retailer is also diverse, from the massive Harrod's in London and Mitsukoshi Ltd. in Japan, both of which serve more than 10,000 customers a day, to the small one- or two-person stalls in developing African and Latin American nations.

New types of retailing have emerged from all areas of the world. These changing formats can be attributed to a variety of economic and social factors that are the same worldwide: a widespread concern for health, a steady increase in the number of working women and two-income families, inflation, consumerism, and so forth. These factors, and their effects on consumer lifestyles, encourage high-profit retailers around the world to seek new market segments, make adjustments in the retail mix, alter location patterns, and adopt new multisegment strategies. In the process, many new retail concepts and formats have emerged and spread.

Still, it is amazing that retailers from larger countries often do not have the same success when entering a new country that retailers from smaller countries do. Consider, for example, that at the end-of-fiscal year 2006, Wal-Mart was operating 2,640 units in Argentina, Brazil, Canada, China, Germany, Japan, Mexico, Puerto Rico, South Korea, and the United Kingdom.[27] However, during the retailer's 2007 fiscal year, the chain sold its operations in both Germany and South Korea when they failed to meet profit expectations. In Germany, for example, the American retail giant found the discount retail market too tough to crack as homegrown discount retailers already offered very low prices. Wal-Mart also failed to understand the frugal and demanding ways of German shoppers. For similar reasons, Wal-Mart's biggest global competitor, Carrefour SA of France, which operates in 29 countries, never entered the market, citing German regulations restricting store hours, and other retailing basics.[28] Wal-Mart, despite becoming the largest grocery retailer in markets like Brazil, faces a similar challenge from Carrefour and others in Britain. Meanwhile, H & M, the Swedish women's apparel chain, and Zara, the vertically integrated women's apparel chain from Spain, both create excitement and sales in most foreign markets they enter. Yet Kmart, Sears, and JCPenney have all abandoned their foreign expansion plans. Many successful

British merchants, such as Conran's Habitat, a housewares chain, and Laura Ashley, have not been able to replicate their success in the United States.

Retail experts attribute this failure by large-country retailers to two factors. Some think it is a lack of understanding of the new country's culture. Even Wal-Mart made major mistakes when it entered international markets. In Canada, its cultural faux pas was distributing English-language circulars in French-speaking Quebec. Upon entering Mexico, the chain built large parking lots at some stores only to realize that most of their customers rode the bus and then had to cross these large, empty parking lots carrying bags full of merchandise. Wal-Mart responded by creating a shuttle bus service. This error was especially embarrassing for Wal-Mart since one of the key factors for their overall success is the fact that they started and stayed in small rural markets until they completely understood their customers and channel partners.

The late Michael O'Connor, the former president of Super Market Institute, had another explanation. He felt that the failure of many retailers to succeed in international markets was because the larger countries have had successful economies and are used to success. Retailers in smaller countries do not take success for granted and thus tend to take more time and be more careful with key decisions. According to O'Connor, by being a little less sure of themselves, executives from smaller countries sought more counsel and listened to more opinions before developing strategic plans.[29] Along the same lines, smaller country retailers have always had to deal with international issues in order to expand. One smaller country retailer who has made an impact on international retailing is Ingvar Kamprad, president of IKEA, who was the first to successfully develop a warehouse retailing format that could be followed around the world. IKEA is spotlighted in this chapter's Global Retailing box. The firm's warehouse format, which is based on economies of scale in the areas of marketing, purchasing, and distribution, and which utilizes customer participation in the assembly and transportation of the merchandise, generates almost 90 percent of its revenues from global operations—more than any other major worldwide retailer.

Integration of Technology

One of the most significant trends occurring in retailing is that of technological innovation. Technology is having and will continue to have a dramatic influence on retailing. Technological innovations can be grouped under three main areas: (1) supply chain management, (2) customer management, and (3) customer satisfaction.

The plethora of supply chain management techniques such as quick response (QR), just-in-time (JIT), and Efficient Consumer Response (ECR) are already being enhanced by new initiatives such as direct store delivery (DSD) and collaborative planning, forecasting, and replenishment (CPFR) systems.

DSD systems have the potential to fully automate all retail inventory operations, from tracking vendor and item authorization to pricing and order taking. DSD systems provide greater accuracy and increased administrative efficiency, allowing retailers employing such systems to achieve cost advantages. Advancements in DSD systems will create more efficient operations and stronger partnerships and retailers as global competition increases. For example, Giant Food, Inc., eliminated a tremendous amount of paperwork and dramatically increased administrative efficiency with the implementation of a DSD system. Many industry experts believe that DSD is the engine that will drive industry profits. However,

Global Retailing

IKEA: A Global Cult Brand

In November 2005, *Business Week* ran a cover story discussing how IKEA, the world's largest retailer who specializes solely in furniture and home furnishings, has become a cult brand.

Founded by Ingvar Kamprad in Sweden in 1943, IKEA (formed from the founder's initials, I.K., plus the first letters of Elmtaryd and Agunnaryd, the farm and village where he grew up), has identified a global consumer segment for furniture and home furnishings. IKEA's success as a cult is built upon its commitment to the combination of good design, good function, and good quality with prices so low that as many people as possible can afford the products. Emphasizing this singular focus, IKEA has been able to connect with consumers the world over.

Hosting more than 410 million shoppers annually in its 226 stores in Europe, Asia, Australia, and the United States, IKEA is truly a global success.

What makes IKEA so different? A consumer visiting a typical full-line, blue-and-yellow, 300,000-square-foot IKEA store can expect a variety of well over 7,000 items, a third of which are replaced every year. Much like other furniture stores, IKEA offers customers a chance to view product displays of furniture and home furnishings. But that is where the similarity ends. Unlike traditional furniture retailers where a salesperson assists customers with their purchase decisions and schedules delivery, IKEA is completely self-serve. Each product on the display floor has a product identification tag that indicates the item's specific location in the IKEA inventory area. Once a customer has decided on an item, he or she moves to the inventory area, pulls the flat carton containing the disassembled product from the shelf, and proceeds to the checkout counter.

The retailer accounts for 5 to 10 percent of the furniture market in each country in which it operates. More important is the fact that "awareness" of the IKEA brand is much bigger than the size of the company. That's because IKEA is far more than a furniture merchant. It sells a lifestyle that customers around the world embrace as a signal that they've arrived, that they have good taste and recognize value. "If it wasn't for IKEA," wrote British design magazine *Icon*, "most people would have no access to affordable contemporary design." The magazine even voted IKEA founder Ingvar Kamprad the most influential tastemaker in the world today.

There is no doubt that the combination of quality products, convenience, and low prices has allowed IKEA to become one of the world's leading retailers. The retailer has recently expanded with a division offering a line of affordable prefab homes called BoKlok (Swedish for "smart living"). Aimed largely at first-time buyers, BoKlok is proving a big hit, with more than 2,500 units sold in Sweden, Finland, Norway, Denmark, and England since the program was launched in 1997. Thus, it appears that IKEA will continue to successfully respond to the needs of its market.

Source: "Retailers Work To Brand Home Goods," *Advertising Age*, April 5, 2004: S-7; "IKEA: How the Swedish Retailer Became a Global Cult Brand," *Business Week*, November 14, 2005: 96–106; and the authors' experiences with IKEA.

---

gross profit numbers alone don't tell the story and, in fact, can be somewhat misleading when calculating direct and incremental costs of warehouse-delivered products. Rather, it is activity-based costing analyses that demonstrated that in categories with mixed distribution, DSD products consistently outperform those just going through the warehouse.

Other supply chain systems—such as collaborative planning, forecasting, and replenishment (CPFR)—though still in their infancy, have the potential to move retailers and manufacturers far beyond continuous replenishment models in terms of reducing excess inventory levels, cutting out-of-stocks at retail, and efficiently meeting consumer demand. The bottom line is eliminating costly variations and distortions throughout the supply chain. However, technological systems such as DSD and CPFR are only the beginning of the technological revolution occurring within the supply chain. Retailers who continue to use technology in innovative ways within the supply chain will achieve greater efficiency in their operations.

One of the keys to success in retailing is developing the ability to monitor environmental changes, especially those pertaining to technology, and then to adopt the technology that can improve the retailer's profitability.

Dollars & Sense

Retailers on the forefront of using technology to understand their consumers will achieve higher levels of effectiveness. For example, retailers might use technology to better target their customers and provide better service to them. Talbot's employs its catalog information to open retail outlets in locations with the greatest opportunity. Talbot's determines new store locations by examining clusters of ZIP codes that have accounted for sales of $150,000 or more annually in the categories of classic women's and children's apparel. Pier One uses similar information to determine where to incorporate direct mail advertising within the first six months of a new store's opening in order to achieve profitability more quickly.

Believe it or not, some of the most sophisticated users of database technology are casinos. In the past, one had to be a high roller to gain any "comps" (free products or services given to customers, such as free tickets to shows, a free night's stay, etc.). Today, when customers use the casino's gaming facilities (such as gambling at a slot machine), they can insert a card that has been assigned to them and tracks their gaming behavior. Customers then present these cards to the casino to receive individual rewards based on their use of the gaming facilities. Through the use of these cards a casino not only gains a much better understanding of its customers, enabling it to develop more effective retail strategies, but it rewards gamblers at all levels, thus increasing customer satisfaction.

As technology continues to penetrate the retail marketplace, new advancements in customer service and convenience will be evidenced. For example, what replacements are in store for bar code scanners? One cause of long lines at supermarket checkouts is that each item has to be taken out of a shopper's cart, individually scanned, and then bagged. How might technology change this? Recent testing of radio frequency identifiers (RFID) on products might eliminate the item-by-item process completely. The RFID reader generates a low-level radio frequency magnetic field that resonates with the RFID tag's metal coil and capacitor, creating an electrical signal that powers the computer chip, which then transmits its stored data back to the reader. The process works well, but the tags have been expensive—as much as $200 each. However, that cost has recently fallen to less than $1 per tag. Although still too expensive for all but high-priced items, advancements in technology will soon be available, making this system affordable to implement. Imagine bagging your groceries while you shop. Once you have finished, you simply push your cart to the checkout and within a few seconds the cashier scans your entire cart, you pay, and off you go.

These technological advances are but a few of the thousands that will change the nature of retailing. What technological innovations do you see on the horizon for retailers?

Increasing Use of Private Labels

As retailing continues to change, the increased use of private labels has emerged as a key business asset in developing a differential advantage for retailers. Private labels can set the retailer apart from the competition, get customers into their store (or Web site), and bring them back. Today retailers are shifting their emphasis on the development of private label brands into high gear by using a variety of strategies to build the image of their brands, expand brand recognition, and raise their brand images in the marketplace. Further, private label brands often have lower wholesale and marketing costs, resulting in higher levels of profit compared to manufacturers' brands. Retailers must remember, however, that research has shown that for department store shoppers, a product's style is actually more important than the product's brand name.[30]

In the past, retailers believed that national brands drew customers into the store, set the standard, and lent credibility to the retailer. At the same time, retailers felt private label brands could help retailers differentiate their offerings, reach customers seeking lower prices, and boost margins due to the lower costs of private label merchandise.

Today the traditional thinking has changed. Leading retailers, as shown in Exhibit 4.2 on page 108, are focused on developing strong proprietary private label brands as leading brands and supporting them with major advertising and promotional programs. Private brands, such as JCPenney's "The Original Arizona Jean Company," Wal-Mart's "George," and Sears' "Belongings" (which is designed by Liz Claiborne Inc.) and "c.l.o.t.h.e.s." (which is designed by Jones Apparel Group) are now effectively serving as destination draws in their own right while still providing many of the same benefits of traditional private label programs.

Following are some of the private label branding strategies currently being used by retailers.

1. *Develop a partnership with well-known celebrities, noted experts, and institutional authorities.* Celebrity partnerships—or the use of people as private label brands—allow retailers to align with an individual whose personal reputation creates immediate brand recognition, image, or credibility. Target stores feature noted designers Mossimo Giannulli and Todd Oldham; Kmart has Martha Stewart and Joe Boxer.
2. *Develop a partnership with traditionally higher-end suppliers to bring an exclusive variation on their highly regarded brand name to market.* JCPenney is the exclusive distributor of Bisou Bisou line, a trendy line of sexy clothes; Wal-Mart now carries a new, lower-price line of jeans called Levi Strauss "Signature;" and Target has an apparel line called "Isacc Mizrahi for Target."

   These partnerships offer both parties a win-win situation. The retailer gets an exclusive private label with a great image and the opportunity to expand customer appeal, ratchet up price points, and raise margins. The manufacturer builds volume and gains access to a broad new market spectrum.
3. *Reintroduce products with strong name recognition that have fallen from the retail scene.* Old brand names do not die. They get recycled. Retailers can add cachet to their store image by resuscitating former up-market brands that have been discontinued but have not lost their image. Recycled brands can help a retailer achieve differentiation through exclusivity and attract consumers unwilling to risk buying an unknown brand name. By reviving a well-known brand with a pedigree, the retailer is able to leverage the brand's equity while still having a proprietary line.

   Wal-Mart, for example, has purchased the rights from Procter & Gamble to its discontinued White Cloud label on diapers and toilet tissues. They have done the same with Faded Glory denim.
4. *Brand an entire department or business; not just a product line.* In an approach designed to differentiate its supercenter food offerings from others, Target has taken its private label branding strategy one step further by branding its entire supermarket section with the Archer Farms name. Not only does the Archer

©Alan Schein Photography/CORBIS

Target has differentiated and uniquely separated its supercenter food offerings from its general merchandise offering by branding its entire supermarket section with the Archer Farms name.

Farm name readily draw an association with the Target brand (the archer's target or bulls-eye), but it also enables Target to separate the two sections of the store. In fact, many consumers believe it to be a different company entirely. This may be a plus for Target whose customers who might not otherwise shop for groceries in a discount store.

The Archer Farms market positioning strategy leads the consumer to believe that this is an upscale grocer who places more emphasis on quality and freshness than price. Such a strategy reinforces Target's protected niche image as the "discounter for consumers who don't want to be seen in a discount store." A "fresh from the farm" tagline underscores the market positioning message. Store design features, such as green neon perimeter lighting, graphics depicting farm scenes, colorful illustrations of major food categories, and product descriptions and use suggestions all help create a differentiated grocery-shopping environment. The Archer Farms name was also carried into a private label program featuring approximately 100 stock-keeping units (SKUs).[31]

SUMMARY

STUDENT STUDY GUIDE

The behavior of competitors is an important component of the strategic retail planning and operations management model. Effective planning and operations management in any retail setting cannot be accomplished without the proper analysis of competitors.

What are the various models of retail competition?

LO 1

Competition in retailing, as in any other industry, involves the interplay of supply and demand. Various models of retail competition were described to illustrate certain principles of retail competition. These models suggested that retail competition is typically local, but vulnerable to nonstore retailers that provide better selection and convenience; the retail industry is monopolistically competitive and generally not a pure monopoly, pure competition, or oligopoly. Retailers today are in a struggle to develop strategies that allow them to protect themselves from competitive threats by achieving some type of differential advantage over their competition. As a result of this goal, retailers are developing price and nonprice strategies that look at the supply as well as the demand side of retailing. This opening learning objective concluded by looking at how competitive activity can make a market attractive or unattractive.

LO 2 **What are the various types of retail competition?**

Competition is most intense in retailing, and various classification schemes were used to describe this intensity. Intratype and intertype competition describe retailers who compete against each other in the same line of retail trade or in different lines of retail trade, respectively, but still compete for the same customer with similar merchandise lines. Divertive competition describes retailers who seek to intercept customers planning to visit another retailer.

LO 3 **What are the four theories used to explain the evolution of retail competition?**

Retail competition is both revolutionary and evolutionary. Four theories of viewing changing competitive patterns in retailing were reviewed. The Wheel of Retailing proposes that new types of retailers enter the market as low-margin, low-price, less efficient operators. As they succeed, they become more complex, increasing their margins and prices and becoming vulnerable to new types of low-margin competitors, who, in turn, follow the same pattern. The retail accordion theory suggests that retail institutions evolve from outlets offering wide assortments to stores with specialized narrow assortments and then return to wide assortments to repeat the pattern. The retail life cycle theory views retail institutions, like the products they distribute, as passing through an identifiable cycle during which the basics of strategy and competition change. Finally, the theory of resource advantage was discussed. This theory is based on the idea that all firms seek superior financial performance in an ever-changing environment. Retail demand is dynamic because consumer tastes are always changing, and supply is dynamic because as firms search for a superior performance, they are forced to change the elements of their retail mix to match changing consumer preferences. Thus, retail evolution is characterized by a variety of viable retail formats, ever-changing opportunities, and customer demands.

LO 4 **What future changes could affect retail competition?**

Industry analysts contend that nonstore retailing (direct selling, direct marketing, and e-tailing) will be a major competitive force in the future. These various types of nonstore retailing were discussed. We also looked at three examples of possible new retailing formats that have recently evolved: supercenters, recycled merchandise retailers, and liquidators.

Just as the introduction of new retailing formats in one part of the United States will impact retailers in other parts of the country, so it is for international retailing. Retailing in other countries exhibits even greater diversity in its structure than retailing in the United States. The rate of change in retailing appears to be directly related to the stage and speed of economic development in the countries concerned, but today even the least-developed countries are experiencing dramatic changes in retailing, thereby heightening global retail competition. The global analysis section ended with a discussion of why retailers from smaller countries tend to perform better in international competition.

Other changes in retail formats will result from the significant development of technological advances for use in retailing. The chapter concluded with an in-depth discussion of private label branding and the various strategies for its use today.

TERMS TO REMEMBER

pure competition
pure monopoly
monopolistic competition
oligopolistic competition
outshopping
store positioning
overstored
understored
intratype competition
intertype competition
divertive competition
break-even point
wheel of retailing theory
retail accordion
retail life cycle
direct selling
catalog sales
bricks & click approach
online only approach
off-price retailers
supercenter
recycled merchandise retailers

REVIEW AND DISCUSSION QUESTIONS

What are the various models of retail competition? LO 1

1. Can a retailer ever operate in a pure monopoly situation? If you believe that this is possible, provide an example and explain what dangers this retailer faces. If you believe this is not possible, explain why not.
2. Why is it so important for a retailer to develop a protected niche?
3. Why should a retailer treat a supplier as a partner? Aren't they enemies, since they both look out for their own self-interest?

What are the various types of retail competition? LO 2

4. Provide an example of intratype competition that was not mentioned in the text. Provide an example of intertype competition that was not mentioned in the text. Can a retailer face both intratype and intertype competition at the same time? Explain your response.
5. Can divertive competition occur only in intertype competition—that is, where two different types of retailers with a similar product compete with each other?
6. Someone said that "the shift to the supercenter format is providing the greatest competition to grocery retailers." However, aren't other formats also leveraging fast-moving consumer goods, especially food, to draw shoppers, enhance shopping frequency, and increase sales? Provide some local examples in your answer.

What four theories are used to explain the evolution of retail competition? LO 3

7. Describe the wheel of retailing theory of retail competition. What is the theory's major strength and weakness? Does this theory do a good job of explaining what has happened to retailers in your hometown?
8. Describe the retail accordion theory of competition. What is this theory's major strength and weakness?

9. Would strategies for retailers differ in the four stages of the retail life cycle? What strategies should be emphasized at each of the four stages?
10. A friend told you this afternoon that it was almost impossible to find just an ordinary cheeseburger on the menu anymore—that the elegant simplicity of the original McDonald's has given way to a smorgasbord of menu items too complicated to comprehend. What evolution theory of retailing does this suggest?

LO 4

What future changes could affect retail competition?

11. Will nonstore retailing continue to grow? Provide a rationale for your response.
12. Many experts disagree over the future of e-tailing. What is your opinion on the subject?
13. If a new retail format is a hit in one country, it generally will be successful in all countries. Agree or disagree?
14. Several possible explanations were given as to why retailers, such as IKEA, from smaller countries tend to do better when entering foreign markets. Do you agree or disagree with these explanations? Explain your reasoning.
15. Is it better for a retailer to develop a new private label brand or to try to revive a once prestigious brand that has been discontinued? Explain your reasoning.

SAMPLE TEST QUESTIONS

LO 1

What type of competitive structure are most retail firms involved in?

a. horizontal competition
b. monopolistic competition
c. vertical competition
d. pure competition
e. oligopolistic competition

LO 2

When Wal-Mart competes with Kroger, Albertsons, and Safeway by adding groceries to its general merchandise products in its new supercenters, what type of competition is this?

a. extended niche
b. intratype
c. scrambled
d. intertype
e. category killer

LO 3

Walking back to the dorm after class, your roommate complains that she wishes there were a plain old-fashioned hamburger joint, she could go for a simple hamburger, not a fancy triple-decker or one with 17 secret sauces, and not a fast-food restaurant with a playground for 50 kids. Her dilemma describes what theory of retail evolution?

a. retail violin
b. retail life cycle
c. bigger-n-better
d. wheel of retailing
e. compound growth

With regard to international trends in retailing, which of the following statements is true?

a. Because of its sheer size, retailing in the United States is more diverse in its structure than any other country.
b. Success with a retailing format in one country usually guarantees success in all countries.
c. The size of the individual stores does not tend to vary.
d. U.S. retailers haven't been as successful in international expansion as some of their competitors from smaller countries.
e. No new successful retailing format has been developed outside of the United States in the last half-century.

WRITING AND SPEAKING EXERCISE

Over the past summer you worked for your uncle's convenience store in your hometown. As you prepared to return to school, your uncle asked for a report with your impression of the c-store business.

After thinking about it for a couple of days, you are apprehensive to report to your uncle what you really think of the business. Did you really want to tell him that as you see it, c-stores have seven big revenue-generating product categories: prepared food, beer, cigarettes, packaged beverages, fountain drinks, and lottery tickets? However, cigarettes are now too politically incorrect and unhealthy to continue to grow in sales and may even start to decline over the next couple of years. Also, gasoline, which accounts for nearly half of his sales, is under pressure from the likes of Wal-Mart and Costco, which are using fuel as a traffic generator. In addition, the other categories are now seeing low-to-no growth.

You realize that if you tell him this bad news, you need to tell him what to do: sell out or change the business model. What would you tell him to do?

RETAIL PROJECT

You are thinking about buying a Ford Explorer after you graduate this semester. Use the Internet to see if you can get a better deal than the traditional auto retailers offer. All you will have to do is make three online connections, all free.

Start by logging onto DealerNet (http://www.dealernet.com), created by Reynolds & Reynolds, which provides computer services to dealers. You can see a picture of the Explorer and find out how it compares with competitors like the Jeep Grand Cherokee in such key areas as trunk space, fuel economy, and price.

Suppose you settle on a four-door, four-wheel-drive XLT model. Key over to the prices posted by Edmund Publications (http://www.edmunds.com), a longtime compiler of such information. There you discover what the current sticker price is for the XLT and what the dealer pays. You also learn a little-known fact: The XLT carries a 3 percent holdback—essentially a rebate for each Explorer that Ford pays to the dealer at the end of the year. This may help you in evaluating the price your dealer quotes.

When you're ready to order, type in http://www.autobytel.com. There are several buying services on the Web, but Autobytel is free. From here you can buy the car using Autobytel direct or by placing your order, and you'll get a call from a nearby dealer. He will charge you a fixed amount over the invoice and deliver the car. Now, you've saved enough to buy a copy of this valuable text for all your friends.

PLANNING YOUR OWN RETAIL BUSINESS

As a knowledgeable retail entrepreneur you recognize how harmful new retail competitors entering the market can be to your business. You opened your bookstore just 18 months ago and already you have experienced healthy sales. In the year just ended, sales reached almost $782,000. You have estimated that of the 41,000 households in your market, 38 percent visit your store an average of 4.1 times a year. Due to your excellent merchandising and retail displays, 90 percent of visitors to your store make a purchase (referred to as "closure") for an average transaction size of $13.59. Unfortunately, last week you learned that Borders (a category killer bookstore that also sells music tapes and CDs and serves coffee, refreshments, and pastries) has signed a lease to be part of a new shopping mall in a city of 405,000 located 20 miles north of your store. This mall will also house a Lowe's and an Office Depot.

Predictably, you are quite concerned that Borders will take customers from your store. It is hard for you to predict the impact of this new competition; at least they are 20 miles away. Nonetheless, you believe that the percentage of households in your market that will shop your store will decline from 38 percent to 34 percent and average shopping frequency will decline from 4.1 times per year to 3.9 times per year. You believe you can maintain your excellent closure rate and average transaction size. What is the estimated sales impact of gaining Borders as a competitor? [*Hint*: Annual sales can be obtained by multiplying the number of households in the market by the percentage that patronize your store multiplied by their average shopping frequency or number of visits per year. Then multiply this figure by the closure rate, and multiply the result by the average transaction size.]

CASE

Tough Times for Grocers

In search of new ways to woo shoppers, the nation's 24,000 supermarkets have become a marketing battleground. The industry, which is made up of self-service operations providing a full range of departments, is struggling to fight new competition and demographic changes that have been building for years. Baby boomers, one of the largest and most affluent groups of shoppers, have aged and now eat out frequently and shop on the run. The evidence of their life style is ubiquitous: convenience stores and pharmacies now carry an array of groceries, and purveyors of prepared foods are flourishing.

The liberal spending by baby boomers has helped cause food sales to soar. But supermarket shopping sprees have not weighed heavily in the increase. Over the last decade, grocery store sales have climbed 35 percent, in real terms, to $455.5 billion in 2003, according to the Agricultural Department. But spending on food eaten away from home—at fast food restaurants, delis, and other retailers that prepare food—shot up by 76 percent, to $357.1 billion. In addition, research by Retail Forward has found that less than 80 percent of households now visit a supermarket each month, and that percentage is declining. It appears that many shoppers are making major purchases at membership clubs (Costco, Sam's, and BJ's) and supercenters and using the supermarket for replacement items.

This increased competition from supercenters and clubs has forced at least a thousand weaker supermarkets a year to shut down. And, in an attempt to be as attentive to customers' needs as the corner grocers of the past, supermarkets are stocking twice as many products as they did a decade ago, further increasing their costs. Many have added conveniences like in-store restaurants, banks, pharmacies, and delis with hot prepared foods. They are using computer scanners to track individual purchases and to improve their marketing. And some are holding events like sampling extravaganzas to make shopping more exciting.

Service, value, convenience, and quality, rather than price, are the carrots that lure time-pressed shoppers today.

Questions

1. It is important that retailers recognize that they can't compete with everybody. They must pick out one or two competitors and stay ahead of them. Therefore, what strategies should a supermarket adopt to ward off competitive threats from fast-food restaurants and mini-marts?
2. Do you believe the trend in spending for food that is eaten away from home will continue in the future? Explain your response.
3. What can supermarkets do to stay competitive with membership clubs and supercenters?

Source: U.S. Bureau of Census, *Statistical Abstract of the United States: 2004–2005*, Table 1020 and 1033; and author calculations.

chapter

5 Managing the Supply Chain

Overview:

At the outset of this text, we pointed out that retailing is the final movement in the progression of merchandise from producer to consumer. Many other movements occur through time and geographical space, and all of them need to be executed properly for the retailer to achieve optimum performance. Therefore, in this chapter, we will examine the retailer's need to analyze and understand the supply chain in which it operates. After looking at the activities in the supply chain, the chapter then reviews the various types of supply chains and the benefits each one offers the retailer. The chapter concludes with some practical suggestions to improve supply chain relationships, especially the use of a category manager.

Learning Objectives:

After reading this chapter, you should be able to:

1. Discuss the retailer's role as one of the institutions involved in the supply chain.
2. Describe the types of supply chains by length, width, and control.
3. Explain the terms *dependency*, *power*, and *conflict*, and their impact on supply chain relations.
4. Understand the importance of a collaborative supply chain relationship.

LO 1

The Supply Chain

What is the retailer's role as a member of the larger supply chain?

Consider the following example. The final movement of a retail item occurred on March 6 at 10:47 A.M. when a customer brought home a garden hose that she had just purchased at a Wal-Mart Supercenter in Amarillo, Texas. Thirteen months earlier, a sample of that hose had been in a Hong Kong showroom where a Wal-Mart buyer ordered 200,000 hoses for the next year's selling season from the showroom's vendor. The buyer then hired a Chinese agent to represent Wal-Mart after the buyer returned to Arkansas. This agent was to make sure that the factories met Wal-Mart's regulations regarding working conditions and that the hoses and parts met the retailer's quality standards. Over the next nine months, the hoses were assembled in mainland China using nozzles made in Thailand. The hoses were then transported to a warehouse in Mexico to await shipment to a warehouse in El Paso's free trade zone. In late January, three truckloads of these hoses were shipped from

El Paso to the Wal-Mart distribution center in Plainview, Texas, for immediate shipment to the Amarillo Supercenter.

In this example, manufacturing occurred in both China and Thailand, a Mexican warehouse stored the products for several months, and a Mexican motor carrier was used to transport the hoses by truck to the United States, where, after going through customs, the hoses were shipped to the free trade zone. From there, either a U.S. or a Mexican trucking company took the hoses to Wal-Mart's Plainview distribution center. Within an hour of being received at the distribution center, Wal-Mart's own trucks were taking the hoses to Amarillo. Thus, before the final retail transaction could take place, several physical movements were needed that involved many firms other than the retailer. Retailers cannot properly perform their roles without the assistance of these other firms. Retailers are *part* of a supply chain—a valuable component, but not the only one.

It is important to understand the retailer's role in this larger supply chain. A **supply chain**, which is often used interchangeably with the term **channel**, is a set of institutions that moves goods from the point of production to the point of consumption. The supply chain, or channel, might include manufacturers, wholesalers, and retailers. For example, the manufacturer could sell directly to an individual for household usage; sell to a retailer for sale to the individual; or sell to a wholesaler(s) for sale to the retailer, who then sells to the individual. Thus, supply chains consist of all the institutions and all the marketing activities (storage, financing, purchasing, transporting, etc.) that are spread over time and geographical space throughout the marketing process. If the retailer is a member of the supply chain that collectively does the best job, that retailer will have an advantage over other retailers.

supply chains
Is a set of institutions that moves goods from the point of production to the point of consumption.

channel
Used interchangeably with supply chain.

Why should the retailer view itself as part of a larger channel or supply chain? Why can't it simply seek out the best assortment of goods for its customers, sell the goods, make a profit, go to the bank, and forget about the supply chain? The world of retailing is not that easy. Profits sufficient for survival and growth would be difficult, if not impossible, to achieve if the retailer ignored the supply chain. This does not mean that a channel should never be altered. Sometimes an innovative member might break out of the existing supply chain and replace it with a new one. For example, discounters changed their relationship with vendors when they began to buy direct from manufacturers in large quantities, warehoused the merchandise in efficiently run distribution centers, and shipped to their own stores as a means of obtaining lower prices. Prior to this change, retailers had purchased smaller quantities from wholesalers only when the merchandise was needed. Another revolution is currently occurring in the supply chain for prerecorded music. MP3.com, for example, offers music in digital format online, enabling music lovers to get their music by downloading it legally or, in some cases, illegally. MP3.com allows users to purchase music online or through a catalog and listen to it immediately without having to go to a store or wait for delivery of an online order. As a result of this and similar services, CD sales fell about 10 percent in 2005 and were expected to fall even further in 2006.

The supply chain, or channel, is affected by five external forces: (1) consumer behavior, (2) competitor behavior, (3) the socioeconomic environment, (4) the technological environment, and (5) the legal and ethical environment. These external forces cannot be completely controlled by the retailer or any other institution in the supply chain, but they need to be taken into account when retailers make decisions. For example, a change in the minimum-wage law will usually increase the retailer's cost of doing business. Similarly, a rapid rise in fuel prices will result in a shift towards rail transportation versus the use of motor carriers in the retailer's supply chain. The retail strategic planning and operations management model (refer to Exhibit 2.5) dramatizes the importance of these external forces in retail decision making.

Eight marketing functions must be performed by a supply chain or channel: (1) buying, (2) selling, (3) storing, (4) transporting, (5) sorting, (6) financing, (7) information gathering, and (8) risk taking. Whether the economic system is capitalistic, socialistic, or somewhere in between, every supply chain must perform these eight marketing functions. They cannot be eliminated. They can, however, be shifted or divided in differing ways among the different institutions and the consumer in the supply chain.

All forms of retailing were created by rearranging the marketing functions among institutions and consumers. For example, department stores were created specifically to build a larger assortment of goods. They capitalized on the opportunity to perform one or more functions better than the current competition. No longer was it necessary to travel to one store for a shirt and pants, another for shoes, and yet another for cookware; the necessary assortment was available in a single store. Supermarkets increased consumer participation by shifting more of the information gathering, buying, and transporting functions to customers. Before supermarkets, consumers could have the corner grocer select items and deliver them, but with the supermarket came self-service. Consumers had to locate goods within the store, select them from an array of products, and transport them home. For performing more of these marketing functions, the consumer was compensated with lower prices.

A marketing function does not have to be shifted in its entirety to another institution or to the consumer but can be divided among several entities. For example, the manufacturer who does not want to perform the entire selling function could have the retailer perform part of the job through in-store promotions, local advertising, or promotions on the retailer's Web site. At the same time, the manufacturer could assume some of the tasks using national advertising and by developing its own Web site to provide product information such as installation procedures, cleaning directions, and the manufacturer's warranty. The chapter's Service Retailing box describes how a group of service retailers is changing the new car channel for both dealers and customers.

primary marketing institutions
Are those channel members that take title to the goods as they move through the marketing channel. They include manufacturers, wholesalers, and retailers.

Dollars & Sense

Retailers who understand the importance of the eight marketing functions and utilize the abilities of other supply chain members to operate the supply chain most efficiently will tend to be higher-profit performers than those who do not understand their dependency on other supply chain members.

No member of the channel would want to, or would be able to, perform all eight marketing functions completely. For this reason, the retailer must view itself as being dependent on other supply chain members.

The institutions involved in performing the eight marketing functions are usually broken into two categories: primary and facilitating. **Primary marketing institutions** are supply chain members that take title to the goods. **Facilitating marketing institutions** are those that do not actually take title but assist in the marketing process by specializing in the performance of certain functions. Exhibit 5.1 classifies the major institutions participating in the supply chain.

facilitating marketing institutions
Are those that do not actually take title but assist in the marketing process by specializing in the performance of certain marketing functions.

Primary Marketing Institutions

There are three types of primary marketing institutions: manufacturers, wholesalers, and retailers.

Service Retailing

Automobile Sales and the Internet

A recent study by J.D. Power & Associates found that 50 percent of all new vehicle buyers based their purchasing decisions as to make, model, and price on information found on the Internet. The same can be said for other purchasers of expensive products; they are increasingly seeking information on the Net before even approaching the retailer. Therefore, retailers are forced to adapt as the structure of their channel changes and functions shift. Today, for example, new car dealers are forming channel extranet alliances with Internet lead-generating services, such as Autobytel.com, as well as banks and insurance companies. One sales manager at a new car dealership described his relationship with his Internet lead-generating service this way: "GMBuyPower gives me exposure. They have a huge database that is simple and easy to use." He is admitting that even though his dealership has a Web site, it cannot provide the customer with the timely, accurate, and comprehensive information that a lead-generating service, in this case one supported by the manufacturer, can.

Here is how these alliances work for a typical customer. A customer visits a Web site such as http://www.Autobytel.com and requests information about one or more cars shown on the Web site. In many cases, the customer is able to see the exterior, interior, and options that are available with the car. A new car dealer in the area that has signed a service contract with Autobytel.com is sent the sales lead via email. Therefore, Autobytel.com is commonly referred to as a lead-generating service. The new car dealer must respond to the customer, by email, within 24 hours. Most new car dealers say that customers referred to them in this manner are more knowledgeable and receive a 2 to 3 percent discount compared to customers who simply walk in off the street. As a result of contracting with these Internet-based service retailers, new car dealers report sales increases ranging from 5 to 20 percent in the first year.

Some new car dealers, such as AutoNation, have a greater ability to use their channel extranet alliance, which is really a collaboration of channel partners linked to one another in order to communicate, to exchange files, sell or purchase, and perform other business activities. Channel extranet alliances have evolved as a result of a shifting emphasis from conventional distribution supply chains to vertically integrated chains and then to automated data exchanges via proprietary and Internet protocol-based electronic data interchange (EDI) systems. The consequential information advantage is a result of an improved method of coordinating knowledge.

Source: "Half Hit Web Before Showrooms," *Advertising Age*, October 4, 2004: 76; and Samuel A. Spralls III, "Channel Extranet Performance," University of Tennessee-Chattanooga, 2003.

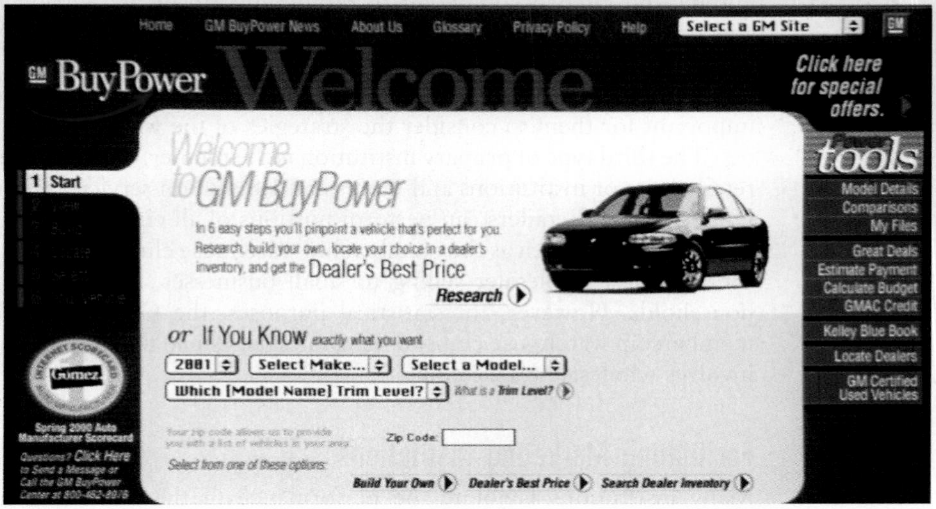

© David Young-Wolff/Photo Edit

Exhibit 5.1
Institutions Participating in the Supply Chain

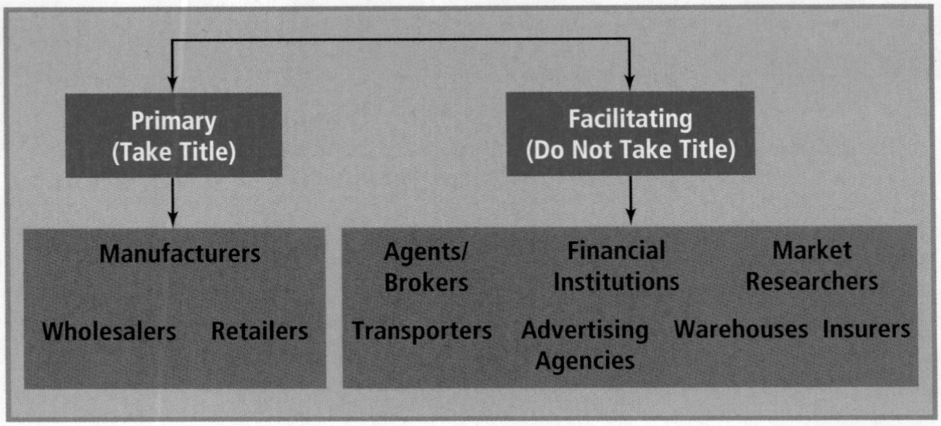

Because they produce goods, we don't often think of manufacturers as marketing institutions. But manufacturers cannot exist by only producing goods; they must also sell the goods produced. To produce those goods, the nation's 400,000 manufacturers must purchase many raw materials, semifinished goods, and components. In addition, manufacturers often need the assistance of other institutions in performing the eight marketing functions.

A second type of primary marketing institution is the wholesaler. Wholesalers generally buy merchandise from manufacturers and resell to retailers, other merchants, industrial institutions, and commercial users. An example of a wholesaler is Houston-based SYSCO Corporation. Through its subsidiaries, SYSCO engages in the distribution and marketing of food and related products primarily to the food service industry in the United States and Canada. It distributes frozen foods, fully prepared entrees, fruits, vegetables, and desserts, as well as various nonfood items, including disposable napkins, plates, cups, tableware, cleaning supplies, and restaurant and kitchen equipment to restaurants, hospitals, nursing homes, schools and colleges, hotels and motels. There are 500,000 wholesalers in the United States, each performing some of the eight marketing functions. Just as it is important for retailers to continuously evaluate their own strategies, it is equally important for them to consider the strategies of the wholesalers in their channel.

The third type of primary institution is the retailer. Today there are 1.1 million retail stores or institutions and more than 1.8 million service establishments in the United States. Retailers can perform portions of all eight marketing functions.

Some firms, such as the membership warehouse clubs (e.g., Sam's, Costco), can act as both a wholesaler selling to small businesses, and as a retailer, selling to households. However, for statistical purposes, the Census Bureau considers all membership warehouse clubs to be wholesalers since the majority of their business involves wholesale transactions.

Facilitating Marketing Institutions

Many institutions facilitate the performance of the marketing functions. Most specialize in one or two functions; *none of them takes title to the goods*. Institutions that facilitate buying and selling in the supply chain, or channel, include agents and brokers, who are independent businesspeople who receive a commission or fee when they are able to bring a buyer and seller together to negotiate a transaction. Seldom do agents or brokers take physical possession of the merchandise. The purchasing agents assist in buying and the others assist in selling for manufacturers.

One of the new breed of e-tailing brokers is Priceline.com, Inc., which pioneered the unique e-commerce pricing channel known as a "demand collection channel" that allows it to act without holding any inventory. Priceline's channel enables consumers to use the Internet to make bids on a wide range of products and services, while enabling sellers to generate incremental revenue. Using its "Name Your Own Price" proposition, Priceline collects consumer demand, in the form of individual customer offers guaranteed by a credit card, for a particular product or service at a price set by the customer. Priceline then either communicates that demand directly to participating sellers or accesses participating sellers' private databases to determine if Priceline can fulfill the customer's offer and earn its brokerage commission. Priceline's business model can be applied to a broad range of products and services and is already being copied.

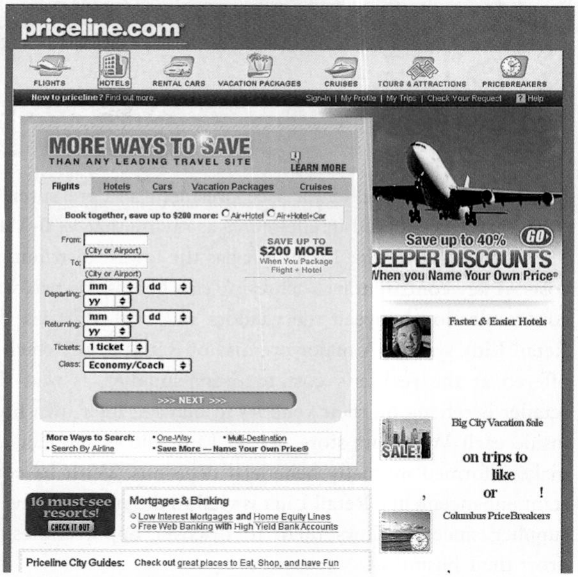

Courtesy of priceline.com

Priceline.com does not take title or possession of goods and services but focuses on bringing buyers and sellers together and thus serves the role of a broker in the supply chain.

Marketing communications agencies, or advertising agencies, also facilitate the selling process by designing effective advertisements and advising management on where and when to place these advertisements.

Institutions that facilitate the transportation function are motor, rail, and air carriers and pipeline and shipping companies. Transporters can have a significant effect on how efficiently goods move through the supply chain. These firms offer differing advantages in terms of delivery, service, and cost. Generally, the quicker the delivery, the more costly it is. However, there is usually a trade-off because faster delivery enables the supply chain to have lower warehousing costs.

The major facilitating institution involved in storage is the **public warehouse**, which stores goods for safekeeping for any owner in return for a fee. Fees are usually based on cubic feet used per time period (month or day). Frequently, retailers take advantage of special promotional buys from manufacturers but have no space for the goods in their stores or storage facilities. As a result, they find it necessary to use public warehouses.

public warehouse
Is a facility that stores goods for safekeeping for any owner in return for a fee, usually based on space occupied.

A variety of facilitating institutions also helps provide information throughout the supply chain. For example, the role of computer specialists, referred to as "channel integrators," in setting up computer channels for transmitting information is evident throughout the business world. Retailers can now order many types of merchandise using an online computer. In fact, many retail analysts believe that Wal-Mart's leap into the #1 spot in retail sales stems directly from its deployment of sophisticated electronics to run a huge supply and distribution network. Wal-Mart's 9,000 suppliers use the Internet to access its Retail Link system about 120,000 times a week, as detailed in the chapter's What's New box. Using Retail Link, suppliers find themselves working and changing in tandem with the giant retailer.

Due to the success of Retail Link, today's major retailers generally require that all their vendors be linked electronically to their computer, thereby permitting the vendors to automatically ship replacements without purchase orders and to receive

What's New?

Wal-Mart's Not So Secret Weapon: The Retail Link

Jay Fitzsimmons, the senior vice president and treasurer at Wal-Mart, was quoted in Chapter 2 as saying that Wal-Mart sells at the lowest price because it has the lowest distribution costs. A key contributor to achieving this goal is the two-way communication between the vendors and Wal-Mart via the Retail Link system. A major premise of Retail Link, which is offered at the retailer's cost to every supplier, is that the retailer is relying on their vendors to manage their own lines inside each Wal-Mart store. Retail Link allows suppliers to make informed mutually beneficial decisions. With its constant enhancements, Retail Link is vital to the success of every supplier since it allows them to discover opportunities to grow their business.

With Wal-Mart's Retail Link a supplier has instant access to such vital information as:

- Percentage of stores currently in stock. (A vendor not meeting the in-stock target assigned by Wal-Mart is in danger of being replaced.)
- The location of any store with low or no stock on hand.
- The sales performance by store for all the vendor's SKUs.
- What other items were purchased when one of the supplier's SKUs was purchased.
- Sales data for all the vendors' SKUs for the past several years. (In addition, most of the suppliers keep records of everything.)
- The current week's of inventory on hand at each store based on that store's sell-through rate.
- The effect of promotional activities on sales.
- Sales by time of day and day of week.
- Current financial projections.

The key to success when using a system like Retail Link is deciding what information is needed by the supplier. Because these reports are built from scratch, suppliers must indicate what level of detail to include in each report. For instance, are they interested in sales units or sales dollars, shipments to the warehouse or shipments to the stores? What about markdowns, current on hand inventory, or gross margin? Also, the suppliers must indicate which stores to include; are they interested in all 3,700 stores or a particular region, district, or specific store? Do they want this information for the current year to date, the current or last month only, just yesterday, last year, or the last ten years? Further, do they want the information reported (aggregated) by the hour, the day, the week, the month, or the year? These questions and others show that the choices result in an almost infinite number of available reports—too much information for anyone to handle. Thus, the most important, and sometimes the hardest, thing for a supplier to do is to decide what information is necessary for the business decision at hand.

Using such data, the category manager and the supplier might see, for example, that a key SKU's sales might taper off late on Sunday afternoons for several weeks in a row only to pick up on Monday afternoons. Such observations might indicate that the current inventory plan isn't adequate. Perhaps sales dropped off on Sunday due to low stock levels and picked up on Monday after the inventory was replenished.

Retail Link is Wal-Mart's internal information system used by the retailer's buyers and replenishment teams to manage the merchandise. Therefore, whether the Retail Link user is a small, locally owned manufacturer, a global consumer package goods company, or Wal-Mart employees, each member of the supply chain will see exactly the same screens and reporting options. This consistency allows Wal-Mart associates to "compare notes" with every manufacturer and ensure that business goals are being met. This usually occurs weekly, if not more often, since most users of Retail Link run several reports every day.

---

payment by electronic funds transfer. By saving on distribution costs, these retailers have been able to hold their selling prices constant despite a slight increase in merchandise costs.

Other facilitating institutions aid in financing, such as commercial banks, merchant banks, stock and commodity exchanges, and venture capital firms. These institutions can provide, or help the retailer obtain, funds to finance marketing functions. Retailers frequently need short-term loans for working capital requirements (e.g., to handle increased inventory and accounts receivables) and long-term loans for continued growth and expansion (adding new stores or remodeling).

Finally, insurance firms can assume some of the risks in the channel. Insurance firms can insure inventories, buildings, trucks, equipment, fixtures, and other assets for the retailer and other primary marketing institutions. They can also insure against a variety of events such as employee and customer injuries, severe weather, changes in interest rates, and the impact of terrorist activity.

Having reviewed the various functions and institutions in the supply chain, we are now ready to examine how the primary marketing institutions are arranged into a supply chain.

Types of Supply Chains

LO 2

What are the different types of retail supply chains?

A large part of the supply chain consists of the marketing functions and the primary marketing institutions that perform them. But how are these functions and institutions arranged into a supply chain? Exhibit 5.2 shows that there are actually three strategy decisions to be made when designing an efficient and competitive supply chain: supply chain length, width, and control.

Supply Chain Length

As shown in Exhibit 5.3, supply chains can be direct or indirect. A **direct supply chain**, or channel, occurs when manufacturers sell their goods directly to the final consumer or end user. In these rare cases, because of the lack of involvement by other middlemen, the manufacturer performs all the functions, although the consumer does make the final purchase. An example of such a channel is when Firestone sells some of its tires through company-owned retail outlets to the consumer. The supply chain becomes **indirect** once independent members (wholesalers and retailers) are added between the manufacturer and the consumer. Indirect chains, as shown in Exhibit 5.3, may include just a retailer or both a retailer and a wholesaler. Consider, for example, your neighborhood Avon or Mary Kay representative. This representative is an independent retailer who purchases cosmetic products from Avon or Mary Kay and then sells them to a consumer. This channel is described as being indirect because it goes from manufacturer to retailer to consumer. When a local independent grocer purchases some Hunt's ketchup

direct supply chain
Is the channel that results when a manufacturer sells its goods directly to the final consumer or end user.

indirect supply chain
Is the channel that results once independent channel members are added between the manufacturer and the consumer.

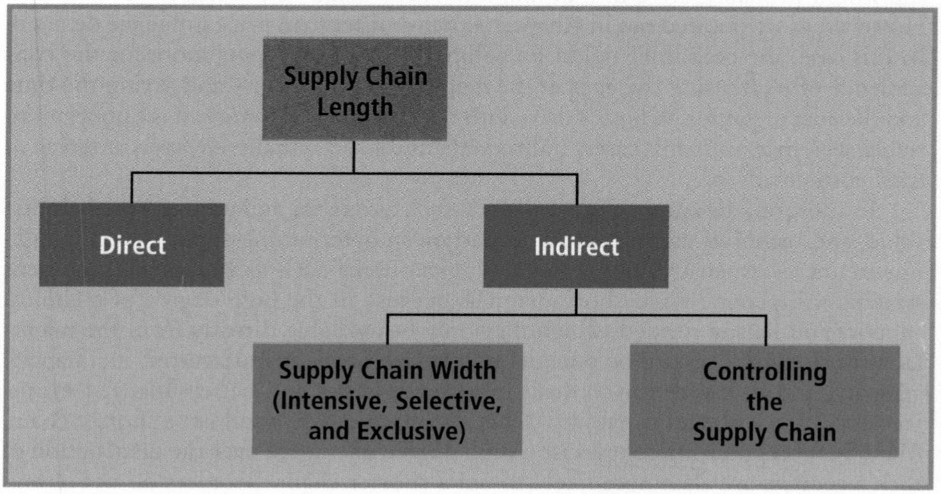

Exhibit 5.2
Strategic Decisions in Supply Chain Design

Exhibit 5.3
Direct and Indirect Supply Chains

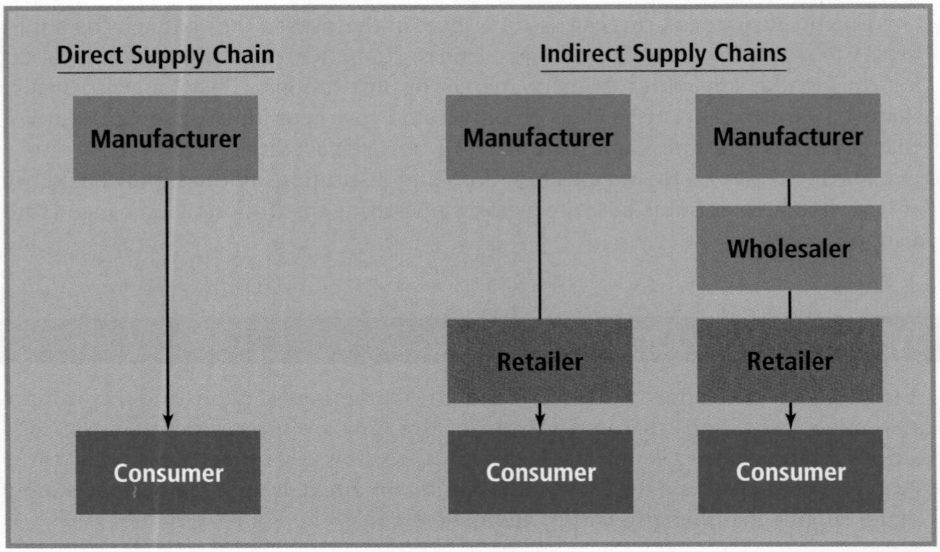

from SuperValu, a large food wholesaler who had already purchased the ketchup from its manufacturer, ConAgra, the channel is also indirect, going from manufacturer to wholesaler to retailer to consumer.

Sometimes the length of a supply chain is hard to determine. For example, when a consumer purchases cosmetics from a manufacturer's Web site and that manufacturer mails the merchandise directly to the consumer, the chain is said to be a direct manufacturer-to-consumer channel. However, if the consumer makes a purchase from a different manufacturer's Web site, such as Avon, and an Avon sales representative delivers the merchandise to the consumer from her own inventory, the channel would actually be an indirect one—manufacturer to retailer (remember that the Avon or Mary Kay lady is an independent businessperson) to consumer.

The desired length is determined by many customer-based factors, such as the size of the customer base, geographical dispersion, behavior patterns such as purchase frequency and average purchase size, and the particular needs of customers. For example, if the consumer were concerned *only* about product costs, he or she would probably drive to a farmer's roadside stand to purchase a dozen eggs. However, as we pointed out in Chapter 4, items other than price influence demand. In this case, the consumer might be willing to pay a few cents more for the convenience of purchasing the eggs at the neighborhood grocer—and saving the time and the cost of gas for an hour's drive into the country. Therefore, it is important to remember that, in many cases, indirect channels are actually cheaper in terms of total costs involved.

In addition, the nature of the product, such as its bulk and weight, perishability, value, and technical complexity, is important in determining supply chain length. For example, expensive, highly technological items such as home entertainment systems will generally use short channels because of the high degree of technical support and liaison needed, which may only be available directly from the manufacturer. Length can also be affected by the size of the manufacturer, its financial capacity, and its desire for control. In general, larger and better-financed manufacturers have a greater capability to bypass intermediaries and use a shorter chain. Manufacturers desiring to exercise a high degree of control over the distribution of their products are also more likely to use a shorter chain. Retailers do not always have a lot of control over their channel length. For example, retailers entering Japan will find that their channel's long length is, to a great extent, predetermined. Japan's channel structure (often referred to as a multitiered distribution channel) was formed in feudal times and is the accepted method of doing business in that country. Sometimes the retailer must learn to operate as efficiently as possible within an inefficient channel.

Supply Chain Width

Supply chain width, or channel width, shown in Exhibit 5.4, is usually described in terms of intensive distribution, selective distribution, or exclusive distribution. **Intensive distribution** means that all possible retailers are used to reach the target market. **Selective distribution** means that a smaller number of retailers are used, while **exclusive distribution** means only one retailer is used in the trading area. Although there are many exceptions, as a rule, intensive distribution is associated with the distribution of convenience goods, which are products that are frequently purchased; those for which the consumer is not willing to expend a great deal of effort to purchase. Selective distribution is associated with shopping goods, items for which the consumer will make a price/value comparison before purchasing. Exclusive distribution is identified with specialty goods—products that the consumer expressly seeks out. Thus, soft drinks, milk, and greeting cards (convenience goods) tend to be carried by a very large number of retailers; home appliances and apparel (shopping goods) are handled by relatively fewer retailers; and specialty goods such as Rolex watches are featured by only one dealer in a trading area. Some of these specialty goods are so exclusive, Rolls Royce automobiles for example, that many trade areas may not have a retailer handling them.

intensive distribution
Means that all possible retailers are used in a trade area.

selective distribution
Means that a moderate number of retailers are used in a trade area.

exclusive distribution
Means only one retailer is used to cover a trading area.

Control of the Supply Chain

The previous discussion was concerned with the length and width of a supply chain. However, a more pressing issue is who should control the supply chain. Many chains consist of independent business firms who, without the proper leadership, may look out solely for themselves, to the detriment of the other members. For this reason, experts agree that *no supply chain will ever operate at a 100 percent efficiency level.* Supply chain members must have as their goal "to minimize the sub-optimization" of the supply chain.

Exhibit 5.4
Width of Marketing Supply Chain

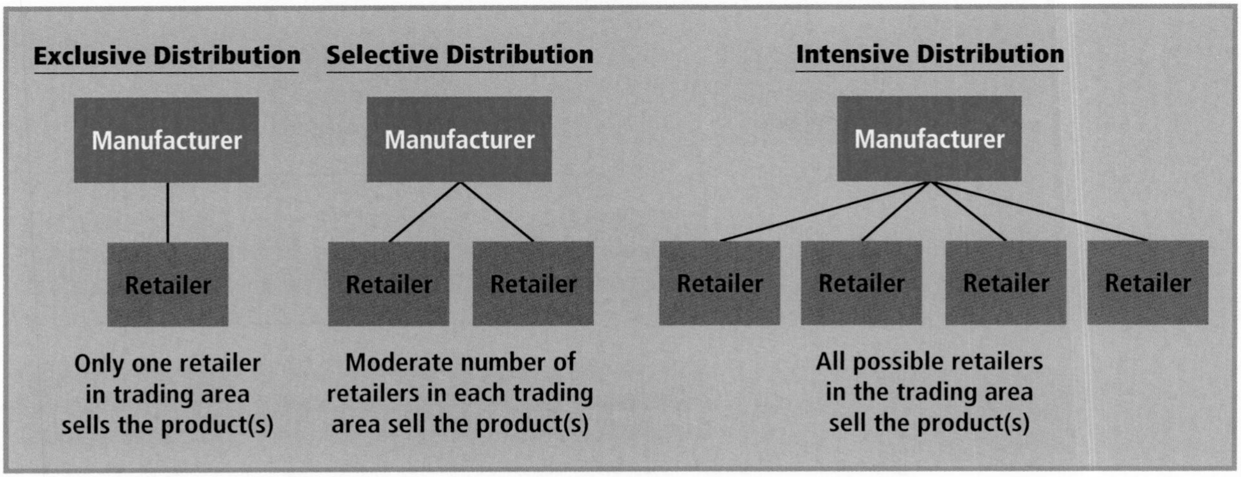

Supply chains follow one of two basic patterns: the conventional marketing channel and the vertical marketing channel. Exhibit 5.5 provides an illustration of these major channel patterns.

Conventional Marketing Channel

conventional marketing channel
Is one in which each channel member is loosely aligned with the others and takes a short-term orientation.

A **conventional marketing channel** is one in which each member of the channel is loosely aligned with the others and takes a short-term orientation. Predictably, each member's orientation is toward the subsequent institution in the channel. The prevailing attitude is "what is happening today" as opposed to "what will happen in the future." The manufacturer interacts with and focuses efforts on the wholesaler, the wholesaler is primarily concerned with the retailer, and the retailer focuses efforts on the final consumer. In short, all of the members focus on their immediate desire to close the sale or create a transaction. Thus, the conventional marketing channel consists of a series of pairs in which the members of each pair recognize each other, but not necessarily the other components of the supply chain.

The conventional marketing channel, which is historically predominant in the United States, is a sloppy and inefficient method of conducting business. It fosters intense negotiations within each pair of institutions in the supply chain. In addition, members are unable to see the possibility of shifting or dividing the marketing functions among all the participants. Obviously, it is an unproductive method for marketing goods and has been on the decline in the United States since the early 1950s.

vertical marketing channels
Are capital-intensive networks of several levels that are professionally managed and centrally programmed to realize the technological, managerial, and promotional economies of a long-term relationship orientation.

Vertical Marketing Channels

Vertical marketing channels are capital-intensive networks of several levels that are professionally managed and rely on centrally programmed systems to realize the technological, managerial, and promotional economies of long-term relationships. The basic premise of working as a system is to operate as close as possible to that

Exhibit 5.5
Marketing Channel Patterns

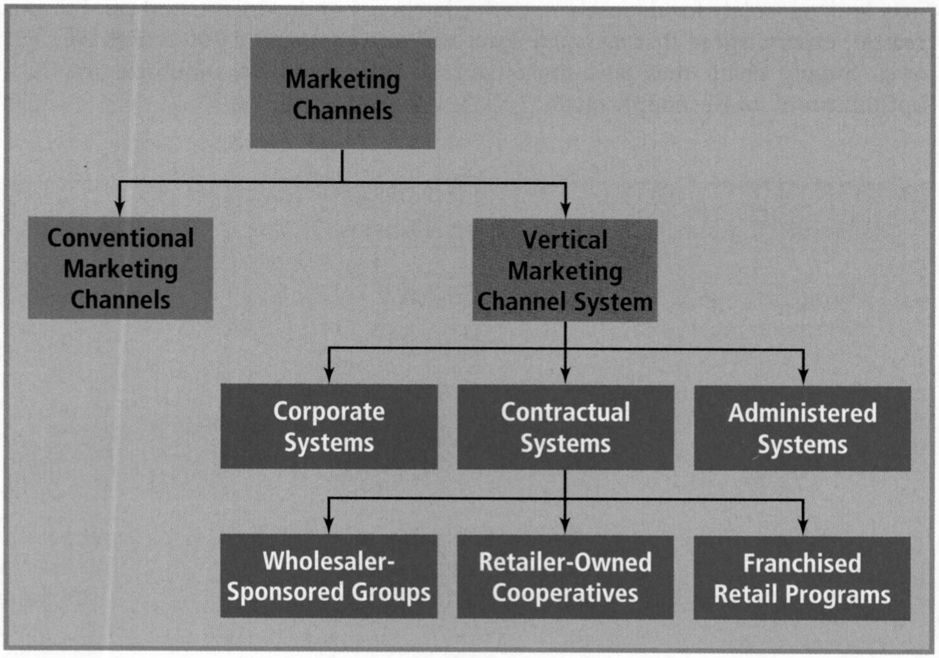

elusive 100 percent efficiency level. This is achieved by eliminating the suboptimization that exists in conventional channels and improving the channel's performance by working together.[1]

Virtually every high-profit performance retailer in the U.S. economy is part of a vertical marketing channel.

Dollars & Sense

Formerly adversarial relationships between retailers and their suppliers are now giving way to new vertical channel partnerships that minimize such inefficiencies.[2] Because vertical channel members realize that it is impossible to offer consumers value without being a low-cost, high-efficiency supply chain, they have developed either **quick response (QR) systems** or **efficient consumer response (ECR) systems**. These systems, which are identical despite the differing names adopted by various retail industries, are designed to obtain real-time information on consumers' actions by capturing SKU (**stock-keeping units** are the lowest level of identification of merchandise) data at point-of-purchase terminals and then transmitting this information through the entire supply chain. This information is used to develop new or modified products, manage channel-wide inventory levels, and lower total channel costs. The final section of this chapter discusses category management, which is accomplished when all the members—who in a conventional channel would have acted independently—work as a team to apply the ECR concept to an entire category of merchandise.

quick response (QR) systems
Also known as **efficient consumer response (ECR) systems,** are integrated information, production, and logistical systems that obtain real-time information on consumer actions by capturing sales data at point-of-purchase terminals and then transmitting this information back through the entire channel to enable efficient production and distribution scheduling.

There are three types of vertical marketing channels: corporate, contractual, and administered. Each has grown significantly in the last 50 years.

stock-keeping units
Are the lowest level of identification of merchandise.

Corporate Channels **Corporate vertical marketing channels** typically consist of either a manufacturer that has integrated vertically forward to reach the consumer, or a retailer that has integrated vertically backward to create a self-supply network. The first type includes manufacturers such as Sherwin Williams, Polo Ralph Lauren, Coach, and Liz Claiborne, which have created their own warehousing and retail outlets. The second type includes Holiday Inn, which for years was vertically integrated to control a carpet mill, furniture manufacturer, and numerous other suppliers needed to build and operate its motels. To illustrate this point, consider that Holiday Inn recently conducted research to overcome manufacturing problems encountered with the production of cinnamon rolls—the trademark of its Holiday Inn Express units.

corporate vertical marketing channels
Exist where one channel institution owns multiple levels of distribution and typically consists of either a manufacturer that has integrated vertically forward to reach the consumer or a retailer that has integrated vertically backward to create a self-supply network.

In corporate channels it is not difficult to program the channel for productivity and profit goals, since a well-established authority structure already exists. Independent retailers that have aligned themselves in a conventional marketing channel are at a significant disadvantage when competing against a corporate vertical marketing channel.

Contractual Channels **Contractual vertical marketing channels,** which include wholesaler-sponsored voluntary groups, retailer-owned cooperatives, and franchised retail programs, are supply chains that use a contract to govern the working relationship between the members. Each of these variations allows for a more coordinated, systemwide perspective than conventional marketing channels. However, they are more difficult to manage than corporate vertical marketing channels because the authority and power structures are not as well defined.

contractual vertical marketing channels
Use a contract to govern the working relationship between channel members and include wholesaler-sponsored voluntary groups, retailer-owned cooperatives, and franchised retail programs.

Channel members must give up some autonomy to gain channel economies of scale and greater market impact.

wholesaler-sponsored voluntary groups
Involve a wholesaler that brings together a group of independently owned retailers and offers them a coordinated merchandising and buying program that will provide them with economies like those their chain store rivals are able to obtain.

Wholesaler-Sponsored Voluntary Groups. **Wholesaler-sponsored voluntary groups** are created when a wholesaler brings together a group of independently owned retailers (*independent retailers* is a term embracing anything from a single mom-and-pop store to a small local chain), grocers for example, and offers them a coordinated merchandising program (store design and layout, store site and location analysis, inventory management channels, accounting and bookkeeping channels, insurance services, pension plans, trade area studies, advertising and promotion assistance, employee-training programs) and a buying program that will provide these smaller retailers with economies similar to those obtained by their chain store rivals. In return, the independent retailers agree to concentrate their purchases with that wholesaler. It is a voluntary relationship; that is, there are no membership or franchise fees. The independent retailer may terminate the relationship whenever it desires, so it is to the wholesaler's advantage to build competitive merchandise assortments and offer services that will keep the voluntary group satisfied.

AP Photo/Tom Gannam

Ace Hardware is one of the oldest and largest retailer-owned cooperatives in the United States.

In the past, local food wholesalers got practically all of their business from independent grocers. Recently, however, as transportation costs have risen, major chains operating over a wide geographic area have also started using local or regional wholesalers. While welcoming this new business, wholesalers have attempted to keep their independents happy (since they still account for over 40 percent of their business) by offering them additional services.

Wholesaler-sponsored voluntary groups have been a major force in marketing channels since the mid-1960s. They are now prevalent in many lines of trade. Independent Grocers' Alliance (IGA) and National Auto Parts Association (NAPA) are both examples of wholesaler-sponsored voluntary groups.

Retailer-Owned Cooperatives. Another common type of contractual vertical marketing channel is **retailer-owned cooperatives,** which are wholesale operations organized and owned by retailers and are most common in hardware retailing. They include such familiar names as True Value, Ace, and Handy Hardware. They offer scale economies and services to member retailers, allowing their members to compete with larger chain-buying organizations.

retailer-owned cooperatives
Are wholesale institutions, organized and owned by member retailers, that offer scale economies and services to member retailers, which allows them to compete with larger chain buying organizations.

It should be pointed out that, in theory, wholesale-sponsored groups should be easier to manage since they have only one leader, the wholesaler, versus the many owners of the retailer-owned group. One would assume that in retailer-owned wholesale cooperatives, individual members would desire to keep their autonomy and be less dependent on their supplier-partner for support and direction. In reality, however, just the opposite has been true. A possible explanation is that retailers belonging to a wholesale co-op may make greater transaction-specific investments in the form of stock ownership, vested supplier-based store identity, and end-of-year rebates on purchases that combine to erect significant exit barriers from the cooperative.[3]

Franchises. The third type of contractual vertical marketing channel is the franchise. A **franchise** is a form of licensing by which the owner of a trademark, service mark, trade name, advertising symbol, or method (the franchisor) obtains distribution through affiliated dealers (franchisees). Each franchisee is authorized by the franchisor to sell their goods and/or services either in a retail space or a designated geographical area. The franchise governs the method of conducting business between the two parties. Generally, a franchisee sells goods or services supplied by the franchisor or that meet the franchisor's quality standards. The Federal Trade Commission and often individual state laws regulate this relationship. In many cases the franchise operation resembles a large chain store. Franchises operate with standardized logos, uniforms, signage, equipment, storefronts, services, products and practices—all as outlined in the franchise agreement. The consumer might never know that each location is independently owned.

franchise
Is a form of licensing by which the owner of a product, service, or business method (the franchisor) obtains distribution through affiliated dealers (franchisees).

Franchising is a convenient and economic means of fulfilling an individual's desire for independence with a minimum amount of risk and investment, and maximum opportunities for success. This is possible through the utilization of a proven product or service and marketing method. Consider that one of the benefits of franchising is that it permits a franchisee to select a location in a somewhat sophisticated manner based upon the various professional forecasting models that use data from earlier units. Another advantage is in the purchasing of key items. Holiday Inn, for example, knows more about how to buy mattresses and furniture than most of its franchisees. Many franchisors provide a full range of services, including site selection, training, product supply, marketing plans, and even assistance in obtaining financing.

However, a franchisee/franchisor relationship requires an ongoing commitment, with each party expected to uphold its end of the contract though active communication, solidarity, and mutual trust. In those cases where a franchisee/franchisor relationship does not work, it is usually the result of either a franchisee misunderstanding the franchising model or the franchisor failing to set expectations and/or the franchisee not understanding them at the outset. Remember that a franchisee gives up some freedom in business decisions that the owner of a nonfranchised business would retain. The most common franchise mistakes result from a franchisee's incorrect perception of himself as a traditional entrepreneur. In order to maintain uniformity of service and to ensure that the operations of each outlet will reflect favorably on the organization as a whole, the franchisor must exercise some degree of control over the operations of franchisees, requiring them to meet stipulated standards of product and service quality and operating procedures. Exhibit 5.6 lists some of the major advantages and disadvantages of franchising for both parties.

There are some 1,600 franchisors in the United States today, and they can be found at any position in the marketing channel; about 60 percent of them have startup costs of less than $250,000.[4] The franchisor could be a manufacturer, such as Chevrolet and Midas Mufflers; a service specialist, such as Sylvan Learning, The UPS Store, AAMCO Transmissions, H&R Block, Lawn Doctor, Merry Maids, Mr. Handyman, Supercuts, and Century 21 Real Estate; a retailer, such as Gingiss Formalwear; or a fast-food retailer, such as McDonald's, Dunkin' Donuts, Subway, Domino's Pizza, and KFC. A more complete list can be found at the International Franchise Association Web site, http://www.franchise.org.

Franchisors that focus their expansion efforts internationally have a higher profit potential.

Dollars & Sense

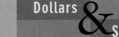

Graham Barclay/Bloomberg News/Landov

Domino's Pizza, by using the franchise marketing channel, has been able to expand rapidly.

Exhibit 5.6
Advantages and Disadvantages of Franchising

ADVANTAGES TO FRANCHISEE	ADVANTAGES TO FRANCHISOR
1. Access to a well-known brand name, trademark, or product	1. Since franchisee is the owner, more motivated managers on site
2. Assistance in location decisions	2. Local identification of the owner
3. Assistance in buying decisions	3. Economics of scale
4. Being part of a successful format	4. Franchisee must make royalty payments regardless of profitability
5. Acquiring rights to well-defined trade area	5. The rapid rollout of a successful concept requires less capital
6. Lower risk of failure	
7. Standardized marketing and operational procedures	
8. By borrowing from the franchisor, the franchisee has access to a lower cost of capital	

DISADVANTAGES TO FRANCHISEE	DISADVANTAGES TO FRANCHISOR
1. Higher costs because of fees due franchisor	1. Loss of some profits
2. Must give up some control of the business	2. Loss of some control
3. Franchisor may not fulfill all promises	3. Franchisee may not fulfill all parts of the agreement
4. Can be terminated or not renewed	

Although only a third of U.S. franchisors are currently operating in foreign countries, another third are looking to expand internationally within the next five years. After all, why compete in overcrowded U.S. markets when many foreign markets are available? Although franchising is seen as an economic-development tool for poor countries, the most widely considered foreign markets are the most prosperous markets of Canada, Japan, Mexico, Germany, the United Kingdom, and, more recently, Southeast Asia—the Philippines, Thailand, Taiwan, Singapore, and Indonesia.

Administered Channels The final type of vertical marketing channel is the administered channel. **Administered vertical marketing channels** are similar to conventional marketing channels, but one of the members takes the initiative to lead the channel by applying the principles of effective interorganizational management, which is the management of relationships between the various organizations in the supply chain. Administered channels, although not new in concept, have grown substantially in recent years. Frequently, manufacturers initiate administered channels because they have historically relied on their administrative expertise to coordinate the retailers' marketing efforts. Suppliers with dominant brands have predictably experienced the least difficulty in securing strong support from retailers and wholesalers. However, many manufacturers with "fringe" items have been able to elicit such cooperation only through the use of liberal distribution policies that take the form of attractive discounts (or discount substitutes), financial assistance, and various types of concessions that protect resellers from one or more of the risks of doing business.[5]

administered vertical marketing channels
Exist when one of the channel members takes the initiative to lead the channel by applying the principles of effective interorganizational management.

Some of the concessions manufacturers offer retailers are liberal return policies, display materials for in-store use, advertising allowances, extra time for merchandise payment, employee-training programs, assistance with store layout and design, inventory maintenance, computer support, and even free merchandise.

Manufacturers that use their administrative powers to lead channels include General Electric (on both major and small appliances), Sealy (on its Posturepedic line of mattresses), Villager (on its dresses and sportswear lines), Scott (on its lawn-care products), Norwalk (on its upholstered furniture), Keepsake (on diamonds), and Stanley (on hand tools). Retailers can also dominate the channel relationship. For example, Wal-Mart, one of the earliest adopters of ECR systems, administers the relationship with almost all of its suppliers by asking that all money designated for advertising allowances, end display fees, and so forth be, instead, taken off the price of goods.

Managing Retailer-Supplier Relations

LO 3

How do dependency, power, and conflict influence channel relations?

Retailers that are not part of a contractual channel or corporate channel will probably participate in different channels, since they will need to acquire merchandise from many suppliers. Predictably, these channels will be either conventional or administered. If retailers want to improve their performance in these channels, they must understand the principal concepts of interorganizational management. In this case, it involves a retailer strategically managing its relations with wholesalers and manufacturers.

What are the basic concepts of interorganizational management that a retailer needs to understand? They are dependency, power, and conflict.

Dependency

As we mentioned earlier, every supply chain needs to perform eight marketing functions, which can be performed by any combination of the members. None of the respective institutions can isolate itself; each depends on the others to do an effective job.

Retailer A is dependent on suppliers X, Y, and Z to make sure that goods are delivered on time and in the right quantities. Conversely, suppliers X, Y, and Z depend on retailer A to put a strong selling effort behind their goods, displaying them properly and maybe even helping to finance consumer purchases. If retailer A does a poor job, each supplier can be adversely affected; if even one supplier does a poor job, retailer A can be adversely affected. In all these alignments, each party depends on the others to do a good job.

When each party is dependent on the others, we say that they are *interdependent*. Interdependency is at the root of the collaboration and the conflict found in channels today. To better comprehend this interdependency, an understanding of channel power is necessary.

Power

power
Is the ability of one channel member to influence the decisions of the other channel members.

We can use the concept of dependency to explain power; but first we must define power. **Power** is the ability of one member to influence the decisions of the other channel members. The more dependent the supplier is on the retailer, the more power the retailer has over the supplier. For example, a small manufacturer of grocery products would be very dependent on a large supermarket chain, such as Kroger, if it wanted to reach the most consumers. Therefore, that supermarket has power over the small manufacturer. Likewise many suppliers to Wal-Mart are very dependent on Wal-Mart because it is their biggest customer. For example, Wal-Mart accounts for 18 percent of Rayovac's annual sales and 14 percent of Newell Rubbermaid's annual sales, making Rayovac and Newell highly dependent on Wal-Mart to make their brands as dominant as those of other major manufacturers.[6] Thus, the power one member has over another channel member is a function of how dependent the second member is on the first member to achieve its own goals.

There are six types of power:

reward power
Is based on B's perception that A has the ability to provide rewards for B.

expertise power
Is based on B's perception that A has some special knowledge.

referent power
Is based on the identification of B with A.

coercive power
Is based on B's belief that A has the capability to punish or harm B if B doesn't do what A wants.

legitimate power
Is based on A's right to influence B, or B's belief that B should accept A's influence.

1. **Reward power** is based on the ability of A to provide rewards for B. For instance, a retailer may offer a manufacturer a prominent endcap display in exchange for additional advertising monies and promotional support.
2. **Expertise power** is based on B's perception that A has some special knowledge. For example, Midas Muffler (a franchisor) has developed an excellent training program for store managers. Thus franchisees view the franchisor as an expert.
3. **Referent power** is based on the identification of B with A. B wants to be associated or identified with A. Examples of this are auto dealers that want to handle BMWs or Mercedes because of the cars' status, or a manufacturer that wants to have its product sold in Neiman Marcus because of the image that retailer projects.
4. **Coercive power** is based on B's belief that A has the capacity to punish or harm B if B does not do what A wants. A franchisor, Burger King, for example, has the right to cancel a franchisee's contract if it fails to maintain standards concerning restaurant cleanliness, food, hours of operation, and employees.
5. **Legitimate power** is based on A's right to influence B, or B's belief that B should accept A's influence. The appearance of legitimate power is most obvious in contractual marketing channels. A manufacturer may, for example, threaten to cut off a retailer's supply if the retailer does not properly display the manufacturer's products. Also, if the retailer accepts co-op advertising dollars, the manufacturer may control the minimum retail price, since this subject is usually covered in the agreement. Absent such an agreement, the retailer is free

to set the selling price. To do otherwise would be a violation of certain federal antitrust laws, which we will discuss in the next chapter.

6. **Informational power** is based on A's ability to provide B with factual data. Not to be confused with expertise power, informational power is when the factual data is provided independently of the relationship between A and B. An example of this power would be a small retail store sharing scanner data with a vendor.

informational power
Is based on A's ability to provide B with factual data.

Retailers and suppliers that use reward, expertise, referent, and informational power can foster a healthy working relationship. On the other hand, the use of coercive and legitimate power tends to elicit conflict and destroy cooperation in the channel.

Conflict

Conflict is inevitable in every channel relationship because retailers and suppliers are interdependent; that is, every channel member is dependent on every other member to perform some specific task. Interdependency has been identified as the root cause of all conflict in marketing channels. There are three major sources of conflict between retailers and their suppliers: perceptual incongruity, goal incompatibility, and domain disagreement.

Perceptual incongruity occurs when the retailer and supplier have different perceptions of reality. A retailer may perceive that the economy is entering a recession and therefore may want to cut inventory investments, while the supplier may believe that the economy will remain strong and therefore may feel that inventory investments should be maintained or possibly increased. For example, consider the following areas that the retailer and supplier might perceive differently: the quality of the supplier's merchandise, the potential demand for the supplier's merchandise, the consumer appeal of the supplier's advertising, and the best shelf position for the supplier's merchandise. Recently, Burger King and its franchisees have had differing views of the chain's promotional campaign featuring a freaky mute plastic-head king and a fictional heavy-metal band. Franchisees felt the campaign was too skewed to male teens.[7] Privately held Quizno's dropped its spongmonkey campaign after franchisees started posting signs on their doors saying they "had nothing to do with the ads."[8]

perceptual incongruity
Occurs when the retailer and supplier have different perceptions of reality.

A second source of conflict is **goal incompatibility**, a situation in which achieving the goals of either the supplier or the retailer would hamper the performance of the other. For example, Nike and Foot Locker have fought over the retailer's goal of gaining sales with its liberal use of "BOGOs"—industry jargon for "Buy One, Get One At Half-Off" sales. Such sales encourage consumers to buy two pairs at a single outing, thereby reducing the chance the consumer would buy the second pair elsewhere, and also harming Nike's brand image by the use of deep discounts.[9]

goal incompatibility
Occurs when achieving the goals of either the supplier or the retailer would hamper the performance of the other.

Another example of incompatibility between retailer and supplier goals is a situation known as dual distribution. **Dual distribution** occurs when a manufacturer that sells to independent retailers decides to also sell directly to the final consumer through its own retail outlets and/or through an Internet site. Thus the manufacturer manages a corporately owned vertical marketing channel that competes with independent retailers, which it also supplies through a conventional, administered, or contractual marketing channel. Retailers tend to become upset about dual distribution when the two channels compete at the retail level in the same geographic area. However, as consolidation continues among department stores, some manufacturers, such as Liz Claiborne, have opened stores selling their

dual distribution
Occurs when a manufacturer sells to independent retailers and also through its own retail outlets.

"power brands"—Juicy Couture, Lucky, Sigrid Olsen, and Mexx. This practice has angered traditional retailers that buy from these manufacturers and can have an adverse effect on manufacturer-retailer relationships. Recently, Tupperware pulled its products out of Target's 1,200 stores. The attempt at dual distribution was meant to reach shoppers too busy to attend sales parties or deal with door-to-door salespeople. However, the easy availability of Tupperware products in the giant retailer's stores had a detrimental effect on Tupperware parties.[10]

When Wal-Mart sold its McLane's wholesaling subsidiary to Warren Buffett's Berkshire Hathaway Inc., many retailing experts felt that this action would ultimately enable Wal-Mart to expand into the convenience store market. If the giant retailer had entered the convenience store market without selling McLane's, which is the nation's largest wholesaler serving c-stores, it would have established a dual-distribution network whereby Wal-Mart would operate its own retail outlets in competition with its McLane's division wholesale customers. In such a case, the convenience store operators likely would have dropped McLane. Why would they want to financially support a competitor? The same thing occurred in 2006 when Supervalu was part of the group buying Albertsons. Within a year the company announced plans to spend nearly $1 billion to open new stores and remodel existing Albertsons units. The independent grocers using Supervalu as their wholesaler got very uncomfortable, and competing wholesalers opened the door for them to switch wholesalers.

The problem of goal incompatibility is not necessarily one of profit versus image goals. Even if the retailer and supplier both have a return on investment (ROI) goal, they can still be incompatible, because what is good for the retailer's ROI may not be good for the supplier's ROI. Consider the price element in the transaction between the supplier and the retailer. If the supplier obtains a higher price, its ROI will be higher, but the ROI of the retailer will be lower. Similarly, other key elements in the transaction between the retailer and supplier, such as advertising allowances, cash discounts, order quantity, and freight charges, can result in conflict.

domain disagreements
Occur when there is disagreement about which member of the marketing channel should make decisions.

A third source of conflict is **domain disagreements**. *Domain* refers to the decision variables that each member of the marketing channel feels it should be able to control. When the members of the marketing channel agree on who should make which decisions, domain consensus exists. When there is disagreement about who should make decisions, domain disagreement exists.

Consider the case of an automobile manufacturer and an automobile dealer. The dealer believes it should be able to make decisions regarding employees, advertising, retail pricing, hours of operation, and remodeling and expansion. However, the manufacturer believes that it is the best judge of these concerns. Recently, the GM dealers in Miami complained that they were never consulted on GM national ad program. As a result, on Christmas Day, Miami viewers saw ads featuring GM products driving in snow or Spanish versions of ads featuring a woman in a Mexican dress in front of the Alamo, not an ad aimed at Miami's mostly Cuban-Hispanic market. GM executives claimed that they alone had control over all national ad campaigns.[11]

diverter
Is an unauthorized member of a channel who buys and sells excess merchandise to and from authorized channel members.

Another controversial domain disagreement practice in today's retail marketing channels occurs when retailers sell merchandise purchased from the vendor to discounters the manufacturer does not want selling its products. A **diverter** is an unauthorized member of a channel who buys and sells excess merchandise to and from authorized channel members. For instance, suppose a retailer could buy a name-brand appliance intended to retail for $389 at $185 if it purchases 100 units. However, if the retailer orders 200 units it can purchase the item at $158. What does the retailer do? Some retailers will purchase 200 units even though they need only 100. They in turn sell the 100 extra units at a slight loss, say $155, to a discount store that may retail the item for $219. The net result is that the retailer loses $3 a unit on 100 units or $300; however, it bought the remaining 100 units at $27 a unit less, for a savings of $2,700. As a result of this price arbitrage, the retailer is $2,400 ahead on the transaction. However, the manufacturer is upset because the appliance has been diverted into a retail channel it did not intend and over which it has no direct control.

Similar to diverting is a practice known as **gray marketing**, where genuinely branded merchandise flows through unauthorized channels that cross national boundaries. Gray market channels develop when global conditions are conducive to profits. For example, over 200,000 autos are brought into the United States annually by importers from Canada. These cars are nearly identical to U.S. models that are priced $3,000 to $7,000 higher, due to the lower value of the Canadian dollar and a weaker economic situation in Canada, which has forced manufacturers to "price to the market." The lower prices are all the market will bear, the car manufacturers claim. Yet, under these circumstances, should American dealers be responsible for warranty work?[12] Another example can be seen in the retailing of prescription drugs. Since Americans pay on average 67 percent more than Canadians do for these drugs, the gray market, especially from Canada, has increased substantially.[13] Recently, as the chapter's Global Retailing box describes, many college textbooks, including earlier editions of this text, were being gray marketed back to the United States.

gray marketing
Is when branded merchandise flows through unauthorized channels.

Diverting and gray marketing can lead to another problem for the channel–free-riding. **Free-riding** occurs when consumers seek product information and usage instructions about products, ranging from computers to home appliances, from a full service specialty store. Then, armed with the brand's model number, the consumers purchase the product from a limited-service discounter or over the Internet.

free-riding
Is when a consumer seeks product information, usage instructions, and sometimes even warranty work from a full-service store but then, armed with the brand's model number, purchases the product from a limited-service discounter or over the Internet.

Not all conflict in a channel is bad. Low levels of conflict will probably not affect any channel member's behavior and may not even be noticed. A moderate level of conflict might even cause the members to improve their efficiency, much the same as happens with some of your classmates when you are working on a team project. However, high levels of conflict will probably be dysfunctional to the channel and lead to inefficiencies and channel restructuring.

Collaboration in the Channel

LO 4

Why is collaboration so important in supply chains today?

Although all channels experience some degree of conflict, the dominant behavior in successful channels is collaboration. Collaboration, where both parties seek to solve all problems with a "win-win" attitude, is necessary and beneficial because of the interdependency of retailers and suppliers. Retailers and suppliers must develop a partnership if they want to deal with each other on a long-term and continuing basis. As a result, many channel members have begun to follow a set of best practices as listed in Exhibit 5.7. This vendor partnership is often a critical factor for the retailer who does not want to confuse the final consumer with constant adjustments in product offerings resulting from constant changes in suppliers.

Retailers who treat their fellow channel members as partners rather than enemies will tend to have a better profit performance over the long term than those who do not.

Dollars & Sense

Global Retailing

Why Textbooks Are Cheaper Abroad

As will be pointed out in Chapter 10, pricing strategies by manufacturers, wholesalers, and retailers are complicated and complex enough already without having to account for differences in international economic systems. Add to this complexity the possibility of instant awareness of pricing differences and gray markets can appear overnight. Consider the book that you are now reading. It can be purchased new or used at your campus bookstore, an off-campus store, or online from Amazon. In all cases, the prices will be similar depending on the book's condition. This wasn't always the case. You could have purchased a copy of the 5th edition of this book for around $50 from several U.K. Internet sites, at the same time that the retail price for that edition in the United States was in the $120 range. Is the prospect of saving over 50 percent on textbooks enough of an incentive for you to wait the week or so for shipping? For many students the answer is yes.

The simple question is, "Why are textbooks priced differently in different parts of the world?" The answer is that channels are market driven. In the United Kingdom, for instance, textbook use is different from that in the United States and Canada, where books are adopted for use in a course and the syllabus directs students to read specific chapters and complete specified problems and cases. Although there might be several competing books for any area of study, the students are "prescribed" one book for use in the course. In the United Kingdom and in other parts of the world, professors assign a reading list with several potential books to be read.

Consider the following scenario. In the United States, a student taking a principles of marketing class is told to buy Douglas Hoffman's *Marketing Principles*, 3rd edition. The student can either purchase a new or used hardback or softback copy of the book at the campus bookstore or buy the book from an online merchant. On the other hand, a student in the United Kingdom would be assigned four possible intro to marketing books from which to choose. The student can go to a nearby bookstore and examine the four books. Since the selection is in the hands of the consumer, and all the books are intellectually equal, the lowest-priced textbook is often selected. Compare this market to the market for music CDs where the distribution supply chain is the same in both the United States and the United Kingdom. As a result, you will find that prices are similar in both markets.

Western economies value intellectual property and are fortunate to have a fairly wealthy population. In other areas of the world, such as Southeast Asia and India, there is much less respect for intellectual property and the population is not as wealthy. This presents publishers with a dilemma: Should they price their products at the same level as they do in the United States and see lowered sales because the merchandise is priced higher than consumers can afford? High prices also open up the possibility of illegal counterfeit and knock-off products that cut into the publisher's market share. For example, several years ago, the authors of this text were approached by a foreign university and asked to visit there to present a series of seminars on retailing. Yet, the publisher never sold any textbooks in that country. All of the textbooks in use were cheap black & white reproductions of sample copies provided to faculty members.

Today, as a means to combat such problems, publishers and wholesalers have undertaken several significant changes in their channels. Some publishers have instituted one global price for their products; others have restricted sales of new editions in the international markets for a set period. This practice allows publishers to protect their domestic higher-priced markets for a limited time before releasing their products in lower-priced areas of the world. Publishers have also begun differentiating their products by producing "International Student Editions," which are produced as adapted versions of textbooks for different regions of the world. The adapted books are differentiated by the use of local examples and data and can be priced to local conditions without risking leakage back into the domestic market. A fourth possibility is to lower the U.S. price by 20 to 25 percent, but charge that same price internationally and hope no one illegally reproduces the book. Without such changes, authors have little incentive to write the books.

1. All supply chain members must remember that satisfying the retail consumer is the only way anyone can be successful.
2. Successful partners work together in good times and bad.
3. Never abandon a supply chain partner at the first sign of trouble.
4. Work together with your partners to offer products at appropriate prices. No one will win if either partner is dishonest or unfair with the other or with the retail customer.
5. Never abuse power in negotiations. Rather, understand your partner's needs prior to negotiations and work to satisfy those needs.
6. Share profits fairly among partners.
7. Limit the number of partners for each merchandise line. By doing so you can signal greater commitment and trust to your partners, thus building stronger relationships.
8. Set high ethical standards in your business transactions.
9. Successful partners plan together to help the supply chain operate efficiently and effectively.
10. Treat your partner as you would wish to be treated.

Exhibit 5.7
Supply Chain Management Best Practices

Facilitating Channel Collaboration

Three important types of behaviors and attitudes facilitate collaboration in channel, or supply chain, relations. These are mutual trust, two-way communication, and solidarity.

Mutual Trust

Mutual trust occurs when the retailer trusts the supplier and the supplier trusts the retailer. In continuing relations between retailers and suppliers, mutual trust, which is built on past and present performance between the members, is critical. This trust allows short-term inequities to exist. If mutual trust is present, both parties will tolerate these inequities because they know that in the long term they will be fairly treated.[14] For example, a vendor suggests that the retailer purchase a certain product. The retailer does not believe that the product will be successful in its market. However, the vendor insists that many buyers in other markets are purchasing that particular item and even agrees to "make it good" if the product does not sell. The buyer will probably buy the merchandise knowing that the supplier can be trusted to make an appropriate adjustment on the invoice amount, provide markdown money, or make up this inequity some other way in the future if the product does not sell.

mutual trust
Occurs when both the retailer and its supplier have faith that each will be truthful and fair in their dealings with the other.

Without mutual trust, retail supply chains would disintegrate. On the other hand, when trust exists, it is contagious and allows the channel to grow and prosper. This occurs because of reciprocity. If a retailer trusts a supplier to do the right thing and the supplier treats the retailer fairly, then the retailer develops more trust and the process of mutual trust continues to build.

Two-Way Communication

As noted earlier, conflict is inevitable in retail channels. Consequently, two-way communication becomes the pathway for resolving disputes, which allows the channel relationship to continue. **Two-way communication** occurs when both parties openly communicate their ideas, concerns, and plans. Because of the interdependency of the retailer and supplier, two-way communication is necessary to coordinate actions. For example, when Jockey decides to run a national

two-way communication
Occurs when both retailer and supplier communicate openly their ideas, concerns, and plans.

promotion on its underwear, it needs to coordinate this promotion with its retail channels so that when customers enter stores to shop for the nationally advertised items, they will find them displayed and in stock. Two-way communication is critical to accomplishing this coordination.

Communication is not independent of trust. Disputes can be resolved by good two-way communication, and this improves trust. Furthermore, trust facilitates open two-way communication. The process is circular and builds over time.

Solidarity

solidarity
Exists when a high value is placed on the relationship between a supplier and retailer.

Solidarity exists when a high value is placed on the relationship between a supplier and a retailer.[15] Solidarity is an attitude and thus is hard to explicitly create. Essentially, as trust and two-way communication increase, a higher degree of solidarity develops. Solidarity results in flexible dealings where adaptations are made as circumstances change. When solidarity exists, each party will come to the rescue of the other in times of trouble. For example, several years ago Wal-Mart had a problem with shoplifting. It discovered that several Procter & Gamble products were easy to steal. Because of the relationship that existed between the retailer and supplier, P&G soon altered the packaging of the vulnerable products. Among the changes it made were enlarging and adding an extra layer of plastic to the Crest Whitestrips package and using a clamshell, a flat piece of cardboard covered with plastic, on its Oil of Olay products.[16] In probably the most extraordinary example of solidarity, several large toy manufacturers created a number of toys for the 2004 Christmas season to be sold exclusively at Toys "R" Us stores. In addition, the suppliers also footed the bill to advertise them on television, all in an attempt to save the financially troubled retailer from bankruptcy.[17] As mentioned in Chapter 1, despite these efforts, the retailer was sold to a group of private investors the following year.

Nowhere is this collaboration in today's channels exhibited more clearly than in the shift toward category management.

Category Management[18]

category management (CM)
Is a process of managing all SKUs within a product category and involves the simultaneous management of price, shelf space, merchandising strategy, promotional efforts, and other elements of the retail mix within the category based on the firm's goals, the changing environment, and consumer behavior.

category manager
Is an employee designated by a retailer for each category sold in their store. The category manager leverages detailed knowledge of the consumer and consumer trends, detailed point-of-sales information, and specific analysis provided by each supplier to tailor a store's offerings to the specific needs of each market. The category manager works with the suppliers to plan promotions throughout the year.

Category management involves the simultaneous management of price, shelf space merchandising strategy, promotional efforts, and other elements of the retail mix within the category based on the firm's goals, the changing environment, and consumer behavior. The task of category management is accomplished by members of a channel working as a team, not acting independently, to apply the ECR concept to an entire category of merchandise, such as all hand tools, and not just a particular brand, such as Stanley. The manager's goal is to enable the retailer to meet specific business goals such as profitability, sales volume, or inventory levels.

Retailers designate a **category manager** from among their employees for each category sold. The retailer begins the process by defining specific business goals for each category. The category manager then leverages detailed knowledge of the consumer and consumer trends, detailed POS (point-of-sales) information, and specific analysis provided by each supplier to the category. With this information, the category manager creates specific modulars, which may have different facings for different stores as the retailer tailors its offerings to the specific needs of each market. In addition, category managers work with suppliers to plan promotions throughout the year to achieve the designated business goals for the category.

In cases where the solidarity of the channel partners is high, a supplier may serve as the retailer's category manager. In this case, the chosen supplier takes on the designation of category advisor. Wal-Mart, for example, uses this strategy wherein the category advisor works closely with the Wal-Mart buyer to ensure that the category achieves peak performance in all stores. Normally a supplier is chosen to become a category advisor because it is a trend leader in the specific category and can contribute merchandising and market analysis. Oftentimes, this supplier is also the dominant provider within the specific category, but not always. As each buyer has responsibility for several related product categories, each category may have a separate category advisor, depending on need. And while a supplier may be recognized as a trend leader in one category, a different supplier may be recognized as the trend leader in another.

At one point, category advisers were called category captains. While the responsibilities have not changed, retailers have adopted the new terminology (category advisors) to avoid speculation and confusion about who has "decision-making responsibilities." Also, to ensure fairness, the individual fulfilling the category advisor position is not supposed to have any sales relationships with Wal-Mart. In fact, this person is not supposed to report to anyone with selling responsibility to Wal-Mart. The category advisor receives access to the sales information for all items/suppliers in the designated category. To keep business confidentiality, they do not receive access to data on profitability. Also, they are not allowed to share the information with anyone in their company. Given these boundaries, the question arises, why would a vendor want to pay for the category advisor? Most companies would agree that the ability to better understand the retailer's merchandise direction (or thinking and strategy) is enough of a benefit to justify the cost.

The category captain and/or the category advisor, working closely with the retail buyer, must make sure that the retailer has the best assortment for each store in order to achieve the greatest sales possible. This includes carrying the competition's merchandise. As a result, the supplier's role as the category captain or category advisor has changed greatly in recent years. Whereas in the past the supplier sought to get as many of its items into the retailer's store as possible, today that supplier has to understand how its products help the retailer achieve its objectives, even if this means selecting a competitor's product over its own. For retailers using a single advisor, a yearly review and possible reassignment of the advisor's role to another supplier helps to keep the category captain's recommendations objective.

To survive strong competition from other retailers, the advising supplier(s) must stay ahead of consumer trends and meet the ever-changing tastes of the consumer. To aid the supplier who serves as a category advisor, the retailer provides the same POS information (except the competition's prices) that it would give its own employee serving as the category manager.

Category managers must be ready to constantly adjust the space given to each item so that the right merchandise is in the right stores, at the right time, and in the right amount. Over the last decade, category management has enabled retailers to do a better job of staying in stock on the best-selling items and avoid being overstocked on merchandise with a lower turnover rate. The category manager must be able to recognize what critical items need to remain in stock at all times to make the assortment complete. In addition, as will be explained in Chapter 13, the category manager tries to create a shelf layout based on how the consumer shops.

Retailers, however, are far from passive when it comes to accepting a supplier's recommendation. They usually run the supplier's category plan by a second supplier, known as the "validator." Thus Unilever, for example, will run a reality check for supermarkets using Procter & Gamble as its category advisor or captain. Even more important, retailers must insist that category captains adhere to the retailer's strategy with regards to pricing, promotions, etc.

Category management is now standard practice at nearly every U.S. supermarket, convenience store, mass merchant, and drug chain. Its use is growing

Retailing: The Inside Story

Why Do All the Stores Look Alike?

Some retail experts are beginning to question the concept of category management. These experts claim that its practice is the driving force behind a cookie-cutter marketplace in which Safeway looks like Kroger and The Home Depot looks like Sutherlands. In their view, category management is retail's Faustian bargain: Lured by the savings and convenience of getting manufacturers to mind the store, retailers have ceded not only responsibility for their shelves but also any hope of differentiating themselves. What is to prevent a manufacturer of one product category from leasing a giant building, putting a big sign on the front claiming "RETAILER," and then subleasing the extra space to manufacturers of other categories?

Some small suppliers claim that category management systematically denies them shelf space because they have less access to the ever-important POS data. These small suppliers believe that the big supplier managing the category will include competitive items to complete the line only if it doesn't currently offer a similar product. They ask, "Who besides the dominant player in the industry would a retailer choose to manage the category?" They feel that since collaboration between the big supplier and the retailer is the key to maximum efficiency, the big supplier tends to keep the competition out.

Thus, the battle in retailing today has become a war between retailer efficiency and consumer choice. Some question whether category management is a salvation for retailers or a Trojan horse whereby manufacturers are quietly co-opting the point of purchase. Consider, for example, the tools section at Wal-Mart. Black & Decker provides over 90 percent of the tools carried, since it is the market leader and can supply nearly any tool that Wal-Mart might need. Therefore, whenever you find a non-B&D tool at Wal-Mart, there is a fairly good chance B&D doesn't make that tool. Little wonder, then, that the shelves in many retailers' stores are beginning to look alike.

Most manufacturers want to be category captains so as to ensure themselves a seat at the retailer's table when key decisions are made. After all, they may be able to spin the discussion toward their product. And the more retailers the category captain can spin, the more of its products the category captain can sell. However, as one leading business journal pointed out, "Any retailer who lets their vendors run the show is doomed to fail the blindfold test."

The blindfold test: You lead a blindfolded shopper to aisle five, remove the blindfold, and see if he or she can identify the store. Retailers who flunk this test might as well rent their store to that manufacturer mentioned above.

Source: "Who's Minding the Store?" *Business 2.0*, February 2003: 70–74; and information obtained from many suppliers and retailers.

---

because the results of this collaboration benefit both retailer and supplier. Retailers using category management report an increase in sales for both parties, a decrease in markdowns, better in-stock percentages on key items for the retailer, an increase in turnover rates and a decrease in average inventory for both retailers and wholesalers, and an increase in both members' ROI and profit.

However, as the Retailing: The Inside Story box above illustrates, when all retailers begin to use the same category management approach to optimize each store's layout in order to maximize the gross margin dollars produced per unit of space, many times their stores tend to look just like their competitors. It was as a result of these problems that Wal-Mart replaced the "captain" with "advisors," to gain the benefits of different approaches.

SUMMARY

LO 1

What is the retailer's role as a member of the larger supply chain?

In reality it is the retailer's supply chain, or marketing channel, rather than its outlet that competes against other retailers. If the retailer ignores the supply chain in order to maximize short-run profits, then in the long run the chain will work against the retailer. And if the supply chain overlooks the retailer, profits sufficient for survival and growth will vanish. In learning to work within the channel, the retailer needs to recognize the eight marketing functions necessary in all marketing channels: buying, selling, storing, transporting, sorting, financing, information gathering, and risk taking. The retailer can seldom perform all eight functions and therefore must rely on other primary and facilitating institutions in the supply chain. Although marketing functions occur throughout the supply chain, they can be shifted or divided in different ways among the institutions in the marketing channel.

What are the different types of retail supply chains?

LO 2

Supply chains can be arranged by length, width, and control. Length is concerned with the number of primary marketing institutions in the chain. The supply chain or channel is said to be direct if it involves only the manufacturer and the consumer. An indirect channel adds either a retailer or a wholesaler or both to the channel. The channel's width measures the number of retailers handling the product in a given trading area.

Control looks at the two primary marketing channel patterns—conventional and vertical. A conventional marketing channel is one in which each member of the channel is loosely aligned with the others, each member recognizing only those it directly interacts with and ignoring all others. Conventional marketing channels are on the decline in the United States and vertical marketing channels are becoming dominant. In the vertical marketing channel, all parties to the channel recognize each other and one party programs the channel to achieve technological, managerial, and promotional economies. The three types of vertical marketing channels are corporate, contractual, and administered.

How do dependency, power, and conflict influence channel relations?

LO 3

In order to operate efficiently and effectively in any marketing channel, the retailer must depend on other channel members for assistance. When a retailer becomes highly dependent on other channel members, they gain power over the retailer. However, other channel members (manufacturers and wholesalers) also depend upon the retailer, resulting in interdependency and a sharing of power. Although power and interdependency can lead to conflict, they are more likely to create a high desire for cooperative relationships.

Why is collaboration so important in supply chains today?

LO 4

Because all supply chains experience some degree of conflict, most supply chains today seek to resolve it by using some form of collaboration. Collaboration is necessary and beneficial because of the interdependency of the members and because most retailers and suppliers must nurture a partnership if they want to deal with each other on a long-term basis. This is the only way to perform the marketing functions effectively and efficiently for the benefit of the consumer.

Category management is one of the ways collaboration is used in channels today. Category management, where an entire category is managed as a unit, involves the simultaneous management of price, shelf space merchandising strategy, promotional efforts, and other elements of the retail mix within the category based on the firm's goals, the changing environment, and consumer behavior.

STUDENT STUDY GUIDE

TERMS TO REMEMBER

supply chains
channel
primary marketing institutions
facilitating marketing institutions
public warehouse
direct supply chain
indirect supply chain
intensive distribution
selective distribution
exclusive distribution
conventional marketing channel
vertical marketing channels
quick response (QR) systems
efficient consumer response (ECR) systems
stock-keeping units
corporate vertical marketing channels
contractual vertical marketing channels
wholesaler-sponsored voluntary groups
retailer-owned cooperatives
franchise
administered vertical marketing channels
power
reward power
expertise power
referent power
coercive power
legitimate power
informational power
perceptual incongruity
goal incompatibility
dual distribution
domain disagreements
diverter
gray marketing
free-riding
mutual trust
two-way communication
solidarity
category management (CM)
category manager

REVIEW AND DISCUSSION QUESTIONS

LO 1

What is the retailer's role as a member of the larger supply chain?

1. If the eight marketing functions (buying, selling, storing, transporting, sorting, financing, information gathering, and risk taking) can be shifted between supply chain members, why can't they be eliminated?
2. Must a retailer be involved in performing all the marketing functions? If it can rely on other members of the channel, what functions can they perform and which members can perform them?
3. Facilitating marketing institutions, since they don't take title to the goods, add no value to a supply chain. Agree or disagree with this statement and explain your reasoning.

LO 2

What are the different types of retail supply chains?

4. What factors contribute to the determination of the desired length of a supply chain?
5. Your roommate says he can save money by eliminating the middleman, in this case the retailer, and purchasing his potato chips at Costco in 8-pound boxes. He says you pay too much by purchasing chips at the nearby 7-Eleven in 4-ounce bags. According to your roommate, the more direct the channel is, the cheaper the item. Who is correct?
6. What is a vertical marketing channel? What is the primary difference between a conventional marketing channel and a vertical marketing channel?

How do dependency, power, and conflict influence supply chain relations? LO 3

7. You are a manufacturer of a popular consumer product that is sold through independent retailers and some department store chains. Today a large "big box" chain approaches you and wants to carry your line. What should you do? How will this affect your relationship with your current retailers?
8. What are the major types of conflict in a channel? Are all these conflicts the fault of retailers?
9. Can a small retailer ever achieve power in the channel?
10. How can conflict improve channel performance?

Why is collaboration so important in supply chains today? LO 4

11. Why is trust so important in a channel?
12. With the advent of category management, how has the role of the supplier changed?

SAMPLE TEST QUESTIONS

Facilitating institutions may best be described as specialists that: LO 1

a. take title but not possession of the merchandise.
b. take title to the merchandise in order to facilitate the transaction.
c. manage the supply chain so as to increase overall efficiency above 100 percent.
d. facilitate the transaction by performing all eight marketing functions.
e. perform certain marketing functions in which they have an expertise for the other supply chain members.

A supply chain in which each member is loosely aligned with the others is a LO 2

a. highly efficient supply chain.
b. contractual channel.
c. supply chain capable of achieving 100 percent efficiency.
d. supply chain based on the ideals of cooperation and partnership.
e. conventional marketing channel.

The basic root of all conflict in a supply chain is that LO 3

a. each member wants all the power.
b. each member is dependent on the other members of the supply chain.
c. each member is fully capable of performing all eight marketing functions.
d. partnership agreements tend to expire after a year.
e. everybody wants to work independently of the other members.

The key to efficient supply chain management and the minimization of conflict is: LO 4

a. considering all members as part of the same team and collaborating with each other.
b. letting the retailer run the supply chain.
c. never using coercive power.
d. allowing all members to make at least a 10 percent profit.
e. allowing the manufacturer to make all the decisions.

WRITING AND SPEAKING EXERCISE

In 2001, your sister opened a backpacking store in Durango, Colorado. Since then, she has added four more bricks-and-mortar stores (two in suburbs of Denver, one in Santa Fe, New Mexico, and one in Cheyenne, Wyoming), and an online Web site (thus increasing her trading area). Up to now, your sister has handled almost all of the marketing functions internally. However, because of the tremendous success of her bricks-and-click strategy, it seems unfeasible for this practice to continue. Your sister does not believe that she has adequate personnel to perform all of the related duties, nor does she think that she is carrying out the functions at the highest level of efficiency and effectiveness. During a discussion with her on a recent visit, you promise to send her a one-page memo making some suggestions concerning what to do and what marketing functions she could have other marketing institutions perform.

RETAIL PROJECT

In Chapter 4 we discussed divertive competition and introduced the topic of the break-even point, or the point where total revenues equal total expenses. Let's see how this topic will help us determine whether to join a franchise or stay independent.

Assume that you own a sandwich shop. In looking over last year's income statement you see that the annual sales were \$250,000, with a gross margin of 50 percent, or \$125,000. The fixed operating expenses were \$50,000; the variable operating expenses were 20 percent of sales, or \$50,000; and your profit was \$25,000, or 10 percent of sales.

In discussions with your spouse, you wonder if joining a franchise operation, such as Subway or Blimpie, would improve your results. Your research has determined that Subway requires a \$10,000 licensing fee in addition to an 8 percent royalty on sales and a 2.5 percent advertising fee on sales. Blimpie, while requiring an \$18,000 licensing fee, charges only a 6 percent royalty and a 3 percent advertising fee.

Assuming that you wanted to break even, what amount of sales would you have to generate with each channel during the first year, since both your fixed and variable expenses would increase?

Remember, the break-even point (BEP) is where gross margin equals total operating expenses, or in equation form:

$$\text{Gross Margin} = \text{Fixed Operating Expenses} + \text{Variable Operating Expenses}$$

Thus with Subway, your fixed expenses would increase from \$50,000 to \$60,000 and your variable expenses would increase from 20 percent of sales to 30.5 percent (20% + 8% + 2.5%). Blimpie's would increase fixed expenses by \$18,000 and variable expenses by 9 percent. Using the equation, we can calculate the BEP for both.

Subway's BEP:

$$50\% \text{ (net sales)} = \$60{,}000 + 30.5\% \text{ (net sales)}$$
$$\text{Net sales} = \$307{,}692$$

Blimpie's BEP:

$$50\% \text{ (net sales)} = \$68{,}000 + 29\% \text{ (net sales)}$$
$$\text{Net sales} = \$323{,}809$$

As a result of the increased franchisee expenses, you would have to increase sales over 20 percent just to break even. To make the same profit you are already making, you would have to add that profit figure to the equation.

Gross Margin = Fixed Operating Expenses + Variable Operating Expenses + Profit

Subway's BEP with a $25,000 profit:

$$50\%\ (\text{net sales}) = \$60{,}000 + 30.5\%\ (\text{net sales}) + \$25{,}000$$
$$\text{Net sales} = \$435{,}897$$

Blimpie's BEP with a $25,000 profit:

$$50\%\ (\text{net sales}) = \$68{,}000 + 29\%\ (\text{net sales}) + \$25{,}000$$
$$\text{Net sales} = \$442{,}857$$

Thus, to keep the same profit that you currently make, a franchise would have to help you increase sales by over 75 percent. There is no doubt the image of the franchise will draw additional customers, and its management may even help cut some of your other expenses. However, as these numbers point out, joining a franchise channel is not always a sure-fire guarantee of success.

Now, either by using a franchise directory in the library (e.g., the International Franchise Association at http://www.franchise.org) or by using a franchisor's Web site home page on the Internet, look up two competing franchise channels in the same line of retail trade. After locating the information about these franchises, do the same cost analysis we just did and determine if, based on these figures, joining a franchise is a good investment.

PLANNING YOUR OWN RETAIL BUSINESS

Upon graduation you decide that you wish to get in on the ground floor of the e-tailing revolution and develop your own online business. You decide that a large opportunity exists in providing private label apparel to a niche segment of Generation Y consumers. In the process of planning your business, your preliminary sales forecasts lead you to believe that your first year's sales will be $500,000. You have identified two major manufacturers who can make the merchandise you want to sell online. One manufacturer is in a distant city and is able to promise seven-day delivery on orders of more than $5,000. The second manufacturer is located only 80 miles away and provides next-day delivery on orders of more than $500 placed by 1 P.M. Unfortunately, the nearby manufacturer has slightly higher prices. Consequently, you estimate that by purchasing through this source your gross margin would be 41 percent, versus 43 percent by purchasing from the more distant manufacturer. However, because the nearby manufacturer is able to provide more frequent and smaller deliveries, you estimate that your average inventory would be $25,000 versus $30,000 if you used the more distant manufacturer as a supply source. Each manufacturer sells on terms of 2 percent/10 net 30. This means that if the invoice is paid within 10 days, a 2 percent discount can be taken; if not, the net invoice is due within 30 days. Which supply source should you select? [*Hint*: Compute the gross margin return on inventory investment which is defined as the gross margin dollars divided by average inventory investment.]

CASE

Who Should Pay for Product Recalls?

While going to college, you have been working for a local vending machine company. Your job, which entails about 20 hours a week, requires you to replenish the candy and cigarettes in 213 machines at 86 locations each week. These locations range from beauty/barber shops to small offices. The money is good, as you are paid a commission, and on average, you earn over $200 a week.

Last Monday morning, just before you left for class, you received a phone call from your boss. You had to go to every one of your candy dispensing machines carrying FunTime* candy bars (46 locations) and remove them. It seems that over the weekend, four possible cases of salmonella were reported across a three-state area. The health department associated the illnesses with the almonds in the candy bars; however, no problems were reported in your trading area. Your company had been distributing some of the suspected infected candy during the past two weeks, and your boss knows that several route people, such as yourself, have distributed the product.

You know the consequences of selling a product containing salmonella, an organism that can bring about serious and sometimes fatal infections in young children, frail or elderly people, and others with weakened immune systems. You also know that even healthy individuals infected with salmonella can become quite ill. Thus, you skipped class on Monday and stopped by all your accounts and removed the FunTime candy bars. While doing this, you made some quick calculations and assumed that since no one locally had been reported as sick, the infected bars must still be in the machines, or if a bar had been sold, a healthy person ate it and wasn't seriously affected.

Later that week, the FunTime vendor came by to replace the recalled product. Your boss handed him a bill to cover the cost of the recall. After all, the route employees hadn't been able to handle any of the other tasks on Monday. They just took out all the FunTime bars before anyone got sick. The vendor apologized but said that was a cost of doing business as a distributor and his company couldn't pay. Besides, if they reimbursed you, every manufacturer would have to pay every retailer for every recall. Your boss became upset and claimed that he was totally justified in recovering the costs associated with this recall. Pulling product from the machines, isolating it in the warehouse, and exchanging it costs time and money. And this didn't count the missed sales that resulted from the time and attention the route paid to handling a recall and not refilling other fast-selling products.

Questions

1. Should the manufacturer pay for the costs of a recall?
2. If the manufacturer must pay for the legitimate costs of a recall, who would determine the legitimacy of each cost and see that it was not creating an opportunity for middlemen to make an extra profit?
3. If the manufacturer must pay for the recall, would this cause some manufacturers to be more careful so as to avoid recalls? Or would it cause them to hesitate longer before deciding that a recall is necessary?

*This is not a real name. The authors didn't want to single out any one product.

chapter 6

Legal and Ethical Behavior

Overview:

In this chapter, we will discuss how the legal and ethical environment influences the retailer in making decisions. The discussion covers the legal aspects of decisions made on pricing, promotion (including the use of credit), products or merchandise, and marketing supply chains and concludes with a discussion of the major ethical decisions facing the retailer today.

Learning Objectives:

After reading this chapter, you should be able to:

1. Explain how legislation constrains a retailer's pricing policies.
2. Differentiate between legal and illegal promotional activities.
3. Explain the retailer's responsibilities regarding the products sold.
4. Discuss the impact of government regulation on a retailer's behavior with other supply chain members.
5. Describe how various state and local laws, in addition to federal regulations, must be considered in developing retail policies.
6. Explain how a retailer's code of ethics will influence its behavior.

In addition to studying the changing consumer (Chapter 3), competition (Chapter 4), and supply chain environments (Chapter 5), the dynamic nature of retailing requires that retailers monitor the legal environment. Large retailers, especially those operating in many states where local laws and regulations are sometimes different, maintain legal departments and lobbyists to keep abreast of, interpret, and even influence government regulations. Such activities are usually beyond the resources of small businesses. However, governments and the business press do a reasonably good job of keeping retailers informed of pending and new legislation. For example, the reader might want to visit the Federal Trade Commission's Web site, http://www.ftc.gov, and review some basic primers on the various activities related to the United States to be discussed in this chapter. In addition, there are retailer associations, such as the National Retail Federation (NRF), in most major countries and in every state in the United States that help keep retailers abreast of proposed changes in state laws and attempt to protect the retailers' interests.

We will now explore the final set of external constraints that affect retail decisions: legal and ethical decision making. These forces are shown in Exhibit 6.1. Consider the impact on convenience stores when the U.S. Food and Drug Administration (FDA), seeking to cut down on underage smoking, required a photo

Exhibit 6.1
Ethical and Legal Constraints Influencing Retailers

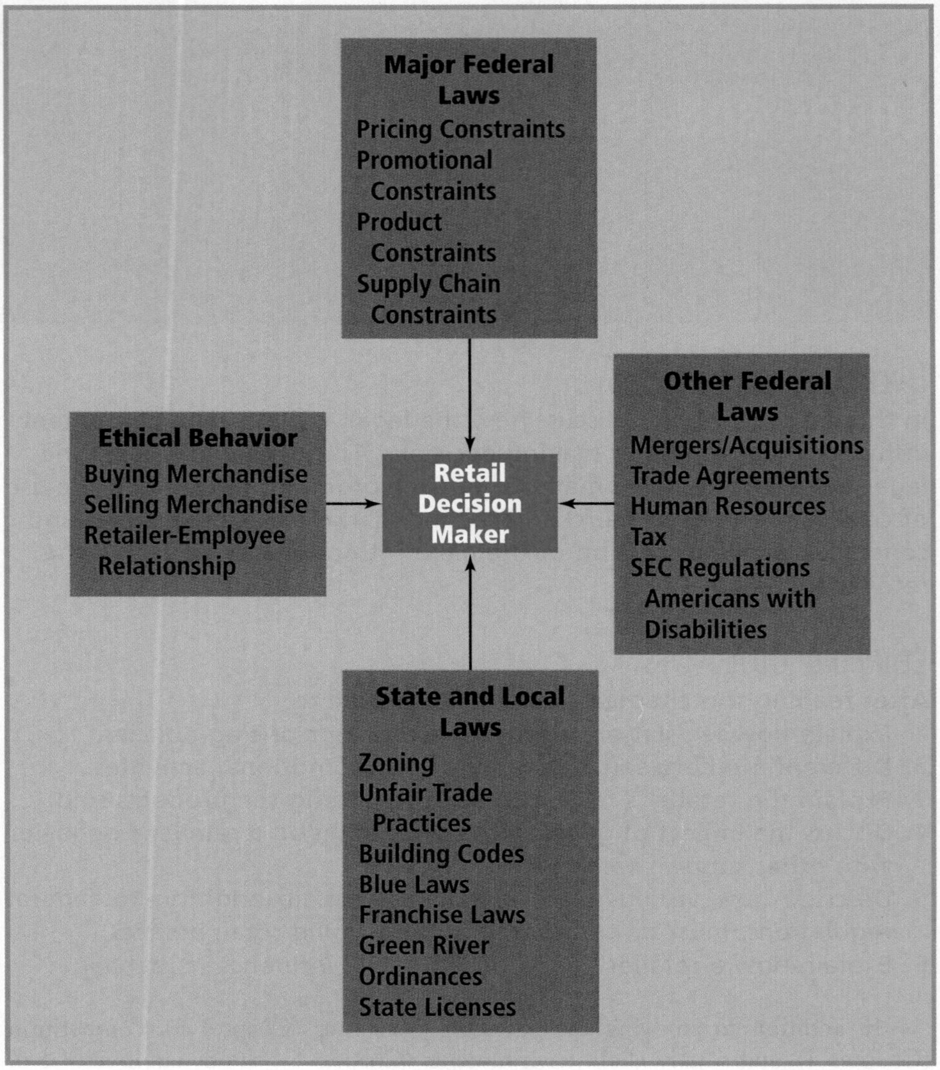

ID from any person appearing to be less than 18 years of age who wanted to buy cigarettes or smokeless tobacco. Think about the impact of various local laws that prevent smoking in restaurants and bars. Consider the communities and states that regulate the sales of over-the-counter cold medicines containing pseudoephedrine, an ingredient used in the illegal manufacture of methamphetamine, or crystal meth. What about those cities that have "sign ordinances" regulating the retailer's use of billboards and even the signage on the retailer's building? What about state regulations restricting the retailer's use of product samples? All these laws control the ability of retailers to serve the needs of their target market. In addition, ethical issues influence retailers' decisions.

Dollars & Sense

Retailers who are familiar with the various laws regulating business will be less apt to make costly mistakes and thus more likely to be higher-profit performers.

Global Retailing

Retailers Going International Face a Quagmire of Laws

Each nation's legal system reflects and reinforces its brand of capitalism—predatory in the United States, paternal in Germany, and protected in Japan—and its social values. As a result of these different philosophies, government regulations in foreign nations can sometimes confuse retailers. In fact, regulations can even be different in various regions of the same country. For example, Scotland, although part of the United Kingdom, has been more liberal when regulating retailers on issues such as Sunday openings.

Regulations in France, for example, require that products be sold to all retailers—big and small alike—for the same price, thus making it tough for discounters to get any kind of pricing advantage. Discounters have circumvented these rules by offering private-label products. Also, the size of a store in France is limited to 1,000 square meters (almost 11,000 square feet) if it is located in a city with a population of less than 40,000. If the city is larger, the size may increase to 1,500 square meters (just over 16,000 square feet). French law protects manufacturers of major brand-name products several ways. It permits a three-year prison term for shoppers buying fake products and it limits the penetration of private label products by not allowing French distributors to advertise on TV.

A recently enacted Korean law relaxes the restrictions on store registration qualifications, store size, and store construction for the large discount stores. The law also provides new financial and/or administrative support to small and medium-sized distribution businesses to build communal logistic centers. Also, both Korean and Japanese retailers, in an attempt to protect the environment from imprudent business developments, must conduct an environmental impact report when building within a city's green zones.

A Norwegian law allows only small food stores (less than 100 square meters) to be open nights and weekends. It also permits gas stations and video stores to offer grocery items. As a result, some larger stores close down most of their store area after 9 P.M. and only keep a 100-square-meter area open. The justification for this regulation is two-fold: To allow "mom-and-pop" shops to survive and to limit the cost of operation for larger food stores that otherwise probably would be forced to offer longer store hours.

In Australia, store hours are regulated separately by each state, resulting in confusion across the country. These laws are designed to protect small and medium-sized retailers from the larger "category killers" that could easily afford to operate 24/7 if the laws permitted. Some states, like Queensland, have highly restrictive laws making many retail categories unavailable in the evenings and on weekends. Others, like New South Wales, have moved to a more liberal approach where 24-hour shopping is common among supermarkets and variety discount stores.

Quebec, a Canadian province that is 80 percent French-speaking, allows English on commercial signs only if French words dominate. Also, textiles sold in Canada must specify the point of origin and the contents, or makeup, of all items.

Retailers in Germany are also restricted in the number of hours they may be open. The law allows a retail store to operate until 8 P.M. on weekdays and to 4 P.M. on Saturday, but not to be open on Sunday with the exception of bakeries which can be open for three hours. Also, certain transportation terminals are permitted to be open longer hours during the week and on Sunday for the convenience of travelers.

The Netherlands sets minimum selling prices for goods produced within the country, but none for imported items. Shops in the Netherlands are only allowed to be open past 6 P.M. on one night per week. In tourist areas retailers are allowed to be open every Sunday. Outside of these areas, retailers are only allowed to be open a maximum of 12 Sundays (jointly chosen by government and retailers).

Countries in the Middle East are closed for business on Fridays to allow for Friday prayers. Friday is the Muslim holy day. In Saudi Arabia, for example, business hours vary in different parts of the country. Retail stores close for the noon prayer and reopen around 4 P.M. The normal workweek runs from Saturday through Wednesday, with many companies required to take a half or full day off on Thursdays. The sale of alcohol is banned in Saudi Arabia, and any kind of advertising that doesn't show women conservatively dressed is also prohibited.

A final country to consider is India, where only four percent of its 15 million retail establishments (a number 15 times greater than in the United States) are over 500 square feet in size. Only recently has India relaxed some of its laws aimed at protecting these small retailers, because the government is afraid that removing its ban on FDI (foreign direct investment) would enable Wal-Mart and its British and French counterparts, Tesco and Carrefour, to open efficient large operations and close millions of the small retail shops.

Clearly, while it is probably more difficult to open and operate retail outlets in these other countries than in the United States, it

(continued)

Global Retailing *(continued)*

is still easier to open a branch bank in most countries than in all but a few states here. However, this is rapidly changing as more and more banks are merging, thus forcing branch banking. In addition, an international retailer seeking to open a store in the United States must be prepared for some of our own unusual local laws. For example, a law in Kansas City allows the sale of shotguns to children, but not cap guns.

Source: "Special Report: Retailing in India," *The Economist,* April 15, 2006: 69–71; "As Luxury Industry Goes Global, Knock-Off Merchants Follow," *The Wall Street Journal,* January 31, 2006: A1 & A13; and current information supplied by Jack Hartog, Hanze University; John Fernie, Heriot-Watt University; Sigurd Troye, Norwegian School of Economics and Business Administration; Charles Areni, University of Sydney; Sejin Ha, Ohio State University; and Lynne Ricker, University of Calgary.

To avoid costly blunders, the retailer needs to understand the potential legal and ethical constraints within not only each country in which it does business, but also each state and city. Some of the philosophical concepts used in developing laws and regulations in other countries are described in this chapter's Global Retailing box. In fact, as the box indicates, the differences in the laws of each nation can drive global retailers crazy. However, they also present some interesting opportunities for the retailer who is alert enough to take advantage of the situation.

Due to the myriad of country-specific laws described in the Global Retailing box, this chapter will deal mainly with the various federal constraints that can affect the retailer's decision-making process with regard to pricing, promotion, products, and supply chain relationships in the United States.

However, due to their sheer number, we will not be able to discuss all of the other federal laws that impact retailers. Also, since state and local laws are quite varied and often complex, we will make only general comments on some of them. We will, for the most part, leave it up to you and your class discussions to investigate the impact of state and local laws on retail activities in your state and community.

As shown in Exhibit 6.2, most federal laws affecting retailing seek to "promote competition." These fall into several categories. First, the Sherman Antitrust Act,

Exhibit 6.2
Primary U.S. Laws That Affect Retailing

Legislation	Impact on Retailing
Sherman Act, 1890	Bans (1) "monopolies or attempts to monopolize" and (2) "contracts, combinations, or conspiracies in restraint of trade" in interstate and foreign commerce.
Clayton Act, 1914	Adds to the Sherman Act by prohibiting specific practices (e.g., certain types of price discrimination, tying clauses) "whereas the effect . . . may be to substantially lessen competition or tend to create a monopoly in any line of commerce."
Federal Trade Commission Act, 1914	Establishes the Federal Trade Commission, a body of specialists with broad powers to investigate and to issue cease-and-desist orders to enforce Section 5, which declares that "unfair methods of competition in commerce are unlawful."
Robinson-Patman Act, 1936	Amends the Clayton Act, adds the phrase "to injure, destroy, or prevent competition." Defines price discrimination as unlawful (subject to certain defenses) and provides the FTC with the right to establish limits on quantity discounts, to forbid brokerage allowances except to independent brokers, and to ban promotional allowances or the furnishing of services or facilities except when made available to all "on proportionately equal terms."
Wheeler-Lea Amendment to the FTC Act, 1938	Prohibits unfair and deceptive acts and practices regardless of whether competition is injured.
Lanham Act, 1946	Establishes protection for trademarks.
Celler-Kefauver Antimerger Act, 1950	Amends Section 7 of the Clayton Act by broadening the power to prevent corporate acquisitions where the acquisition may have a substantially adverse effect on competition.
Hart-Scott-Rodino Act, 1976	Requires large companies to notify the government of their intent to merge.

Legislative Action	Examples of Laws Designed to Protect Consumers
Mail Fraud Act, 1872	Makes it a federal crime to defraud consumers through use of the mail.
Pure Food & Drug Act, 1906	Regulates interstate commerce in misbranded and adulterated foods, drinks, and drugs.
Flammable Fabrics Act, 1953	Prohibits interstate shipments of flammable apparel or material.
Automobile Information Disclosure Act, 1958	Requires auto manufacturers to post suggested retail prices on new cars.
Fair Packaging and Labeling Act, 1966	Regulates packaging and labeling; establishes uniform sizes.
Child Safety Act, 1966	Prevents the marketing and selling of harmful toys and dangerous products.
Truth in Lending Act, 1968	Requires lenders to state the true costs of a credit transaction; established a National Commission on Consumer Finance.
Fair Credit Report Act, 1970	Regulates the reporting and use of credit information; limits consumer liability for stolen credit cards to $50.
Consumer Product Safety Act, 1972	Created the Consumer Product Safety Commission.
Magnuson-Moss Warranty/ FTC Improvement Act, 1975	Empowers the FTC to determine rules concerning consumer warranties and provides for consumer access to means of redress, such as the "class action" suit; expands FTC regulatory powers over unfair or deceptive acts or practices.
Equal Credit Opportunity Act, 1975	Prohibits discrimination in credit transactions because of gender, marital status, race, national origin, religion, age, or receipt of public assistance.

Exhibit 6.3
Examples of Laws Designed to Protect Consumers

the Clayton Act, the Federal Trade Commission Act, the Celler-Kefauver Antimerger Act, and the Hart-Scott-Rodino Act were passed to ensure a "competitive" business climate. Second, the Robinson-Patman Act was designed to regulate pricing practices. Third, the Wheeler-Lea Amendment was created to control false advertising. Although some may question whether all these regulations are bleeding the economy, many do believe that they sometimes boost competitiveness. Other laws have been passed to protect consumers and innocent third parties. A sampling of these consumer protection laws is shown in Exhibit 6.3.

Note that all aspects of retailing—price, promotion, product, and supply chain membership—are regulated. We will begin our discussion of how federal laws affect a retailer's decision-making ability by looking at pricing regulations.

Pricing Constraints

LO 1

Does legislation constrain a retailer's pricing policies?

Retailers continuously establish prices for the many items they sell. Pricing laws also influence retailers in determining what price they should pay for a product. In making these decisions, retailers have considerable, but not total, flexibility. The major constraining factors are summarized in Exhibit 6.4.

Horizontal Price Fixing

horizontal price fixing
Occurs when a group of competing retailers (or other channel members operating at a given level of distribution) establishes a fixed price at which to sell certain brands of products.

Horizontal price fixing occurs when a group of competing retailers establishes a fixed price at which to sell certain brands of products. For example, all retail grocers in a particular trade area may agree to sell eggnog at $2.49 a quart during the Christmas season. Regardless of its actual or potential impact on the competition or the consumer, this price fixing by the retailers would violate Section 1 of the Sherman Antitrust Act, which states that "every contract, combination in the form of trust or otherwise, or conspiracy, in restraint of trade or commerce among the several

Exhibit 6.4
Pricing Constraints

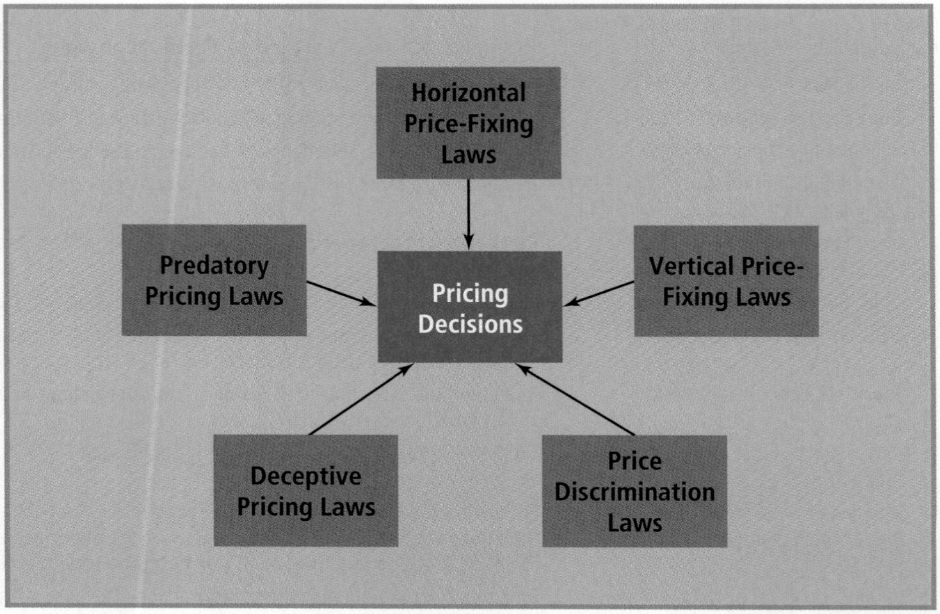

states, or with foreign nations is declared to be illegal."[1] It is also illegal for retailers to reach agreements with one another regarding the use of double (or triple) coupons, rebates, or other means of reducing price competition in the marketplace.

Occasionally, retailers have argued that the Sherman Act does not apply to them, since they operate locally, not "among the several states"—the definition of interstate commerce. However, because the merchandise that retailers purchase typically originates in another state, the courts view retailers as involved in interstate commerce even if all their customers are local. Also, most states have laws similar to the Sherman Act, prohibiting such restraints of trade as horizontal price fixing on a strictly local level.

Vertical Price Fixing

vertical price fixing Occurs when a retailer collaborates with the manufacturer or wholesaler to resell an item at an agreed-on price.

Vertical price fixing occurs when a retailer collaborates with the manufacturer or wholesaler to resell an item at an agreed-upon price. This is also often referred to as resale price maintenance or "fair trade." These agreements are illegal and have been viewed as a violation of Section 1 of the Sherman Act. This does not mean that manufacturers cannot recommend to retailers a price at which they would like to see an item sold. However, in cases where the retailer has signed a "co-op" advertising agreement, whereby the manufacturer gives the retailer advertising money, the retailer may be required to not sell above a specific price. Without a co-op agreement, manufacturers cannot legally threaten retailers with supply cutoffs if they sell above a recommended price. Resale price maintenance agreements, which made a previously illegal act (the fixing of a price) legal, were allowed in the United States between 1937 and 1976. These agreements were established as a means for small retailers to combat the price advantages of the chain stores during the depression of the 1930s. They were finally banned in 1976.

Today some manufacturers and smaller retailers are seeking the reintroduction of "fair trade laws" as a means to combat the inroads of discounters, such as Wal-Mart, Target, and Kohl's, as well as the warehouse clubs. However, the FTC tends to "treat vertical price fixing as per se illegal." Thus even if the retailer accepts co-op advertising dollars, the manufacturer may obviously not control the *minimum* retail price. The FTC is concerned about a policy called MAP, minimum (not the maximum) advertised price that kept the prices of CDs artificially high and stifled competition. With MAPs, a record company might have funded a retailer's entire ad budget for a top CD. In return, the retailer agreed not to advertise or sell the CD for a price below that stated on the label. Such action was an attempt to make sure that CDs were never discounted. While the intent may have been good, that is the small retailer wanted to prevent discounters from slashing the prices on CDs as an attempt to lure customers into the store and then sell them other higher gross margin items, it nevertheless limited competition.

Although manufacturers or franchisors cannot require that their retailers or franchisees sell their products at an established price, the U.S. Supreme Court has ruled that they are allowed to cap retail prices. This is not identical to strict vertical price fixing because retailers or franchisees can sell at lower than the capped retail prices that manufacturers or franchisees establish. Also, the U.S. Supreme Court decided that alleged violations would be decided by a "rule of reason" analysis, which means that each price cap should be evaluated on its own merits to determine if it unreasonably restrains competition.

Price Discrimination

Laws can also influence the price that the retailer has to pay for the merchandise it wants to sell. **Price discrimination** occurs when two retailers buy identical amounts of "like grade and quality" merchandise from the same supplier but pay different prices. However, these laws do not mean that the retailer cannot sell identical products, for example, a new car, to two different customers at different prices. These laws are meant to protect competition by making sure that the retailers are treated fairly by suppliers.

price discrimination
Occurs when two retailers buy an identical amount of "like grade and quality" merchandise from the same supplier but pay different prices.

Not all forms of price discrimination are illegal, however. Federal legislation addressed the legality of price discrimination in the Clayton Act, which made *certain forms* of price discrimination illegal. The Clayton Act was amended and strengthened by the passage of the Robinson-Patman Act. The latter act had two primary objectives: (1) to prevent suppliers from attempting to gain an unfair advantage over their competitors by discrimination among buyers either in price or in providing allowances or services and (2) to prevent buyers from using their economic power to gain discriminatory prices from suppliers so as to gain an advantage over their own competitors.

For price discrimination to be considered illegal, it must meet two conditions. First, the transaction must occur in interstate commerce. Trade between states, which is the definition of interstate commerce, covers all retailers, because the items they produce or market generally originate in another state. Second, while competition does not actually have to be lessened, the potential for a substantial lessening of competition must exist. In addition, the act provides that any buyer who knowingly receives the benefit of discrimination is just as guilty as the supplier granting the discrimination.

Considerable attention has been given to the phrase "commodities of like grade and quality." What does this phrase mean? To begin with, commodities are goods and not services. This implies that discriminatory pricing practices in the sale of advertising space or the leasing of real estate are not prohibited by the act. For example, shopping center and mall developers frequently charge varying rates for equivalent square footage depending on the tenant, the type of merchandise to be sold, and its ability to draw customers to the center.

AP Photo/J. Pat Carter

Charging different rent per square foot to different retailers in the same shopping center is not an illegal form of price discrimination.

"Like grade and quality" has been interpreted by the courts to mean identical physical and chemical properties. This implies that different prices cannot be justified merely because the labels on the product are different. Therefore, private labeling of merchandise does not make it different from identical goods carrying the seller's brand. However, if the seller can establish that an actual physical difference in grade and quality exists, then a differential in price can be justified.

The preceding discussion may have led you to believe that the illegality of price discrimination is clear cut and that retailers no longer have to fear being discriminated against. This is not always the situation. Buyers and sellers use a variety of defenses that enable some types of price discrimination to occur. These defenses include cost justification, changing market conditions, and meeting competition in good faith.

Dollars & Sense

Retailers effectively using legal price discrimination to purchase merchandise will be more profitable.

1. *Cost justification defense*. Such a defense would attempt to show that a differential in price could be accounted for on the basis of differences in cost to the seller in the manufacture, sale, and/or delivery arising from differences in the method or quantities involved. The burden of such a defense is with the seller.
2. *Changing market defense*. This defense would attempt to justify the price differential based on the danger of imminent deterioration of perishable goods or on the obsolescence of seasonal goods.
3. *Meeting competition in good faith defense*. The seller can attempt to show that its lower price to a purchaser was made in good faith in order to meet an equally low price of a competitor, provided that this "matched price" did actually exist and was lawful itself.

Therefore, it is legally possible that one retailer, a large warehouse club purchasing 10,000 cases, for example, might have a lower cost per case than a smaller retailer purchasing only 15 cases. However, the retailer that knowingly receives a discriminatory price from a seller (assuming the goods are of like grade and quality) should be relatively certain that the seller is granting a defensible discrimination based on any of the three preceding criteria. Although the Robinson-Patman Act is mainly concerned with illegal activities of the sellers, if a buyer knowingly misrepresents to the seller a price that another seller is willing to offer and the seller meets that "factious" offer, the buyer and not the seller is liable.

Sellers are not only prohibited from discrimination in price; they are also banned from providing unequal services and payments to different retailers. These services and payments frequently include advertising allowances, displays and banners to promote the goods, in-store demonstrations, and distribution of samples or premiums. The Robinson-Patman Act deals specifically with these practices and states that such services and payments or consideration must be made available on proportionately equal terms to all competing customers. Finally, it is important to point out that most of the United States' trading partners do not have laws, such as the Robinson-Patman Act, that ban price discrimination, as well as many of the other regulations to be discussed in this chapter. As a result, many United States retailers have been shocked by what they perceived as an "unfair" playing field when they entered foreign markets. For example, price and quality of product are not always the most important issue when setting up a supply chain in some foreign countries.

Deceptive Pricing

Retailers should avoid using a misleading price to lure customers into the store. Advertising an item at an artificially low price and then adding hidden charges is **deceptive pricing**, which is an unfair method of competition. The Wheeler-Lea Amendment of the Federal Trade Commission Act made illegal all "unfair or deceptive acts in commerce." Not only is the retailer's customer being unfairly treated when the retailer uses deceptive pricing, but the retailer's competitors are being potentially harmed because some of their customers may deceitfully be diverted to that retailer. In addition, FTC Guide 233.1 prohibits the advertisement of an inflated former price to emphasize a price reduction (a clearance or sale). The FTC is also concerned with the comparisons between a retailer's price and supposedly that of a competitor when the comparison price is higher than the competitor's actual price. The chapter's Retailing: The Inside Story box describes another concern of the FTC and state regulators—the misuse of rebates in promoting a price.

deceptive pricing
Occurs when a misleading price is used to lure customers into the store; usually there are hidden charges or the item advertised may be unavailable.

Seeking to avoid any charges of deceptive pricing, some retailers have asked manufacturers not to use the word "free" on special packs of merchandise. These retailers feel the word "free" is often misleading after they received customer complaints that merchandise marked "free" really should be free of charge, not just a bigger size at the same price. Recently these retailers have expanded this policy to also apply to shrink-wrapping in an extra product, as in a "two-for-the-price-of-one" package.[2]

Predatory Pricing

Predatory pricing exists when a retailer charges different prices in selected geographic areas in order to eliminate competition in those areas. This is a violation of the Robinson-Patman Act, which also forbids the sale of goods at lower prices in one area for the purpose of destroying competition or eliminating a competitor, or the sale of goods at unreasonably low prices for such purpose. Generally, predatory pricing charges are difficult to prove in federal court.

predatory pricing
Exists when a retail chain charges different prices in different geographic areas to eliminate competition in selected geographic areas.

Retailing: The Inside Story

Rebates: Fair or Not?

Introduced by consumer-product maker Procter & Gamble in the 1970s, rebates serve as an easy way to cut price and thus trigger a sale on everyday necessities and new items without actually marking the products down. Retailers and manufacturers both know that rebates give the perception of saving money, yet in reality many of these rebates are never claimed.

The problem is simple "consumer inertia" in a system where shoppers treat rebates as a discount in the store but seldom find the motivation to mail in the original cash register receipt, the UPC code from a 12-pack of soda, and a correctly filled-out claim form to collect a $1.00 rebate on the 12-pack. Never mind the 39 cents stamp required to mail in the claim. Also, complaints to the FTC by consumers claimed that redemptions are slow in coming or rejected by the payer because of some violation of the rules, such as not having two original receipts when two rebate items are purchased together.

According to *Business Week*, Americans are eligible for 400 million rebates each year worth nearly $6 billion. However, fully 40 percent of these rebates never get redeemed because consumers fail to apply for them or their applications are rejected. *Business Week* quoted one fulfillment house that was publishing a "Rebate Redemption Guide" several years ago as claiming that companies hiring them could expect just a 10 percent redemption rate for a $10 rebate on a $100 product, and only a 35 percent rate for a $50 rebate on a $200 product.

Others complain that rebates are deceptive because the customer really paid $2.99 (not the $1.99 "after-rebate" price that was posted above the display) for the 12-pack of soda mentioned above. Not surprisingly, some retailers, such as Best Buy, have dropped rebates, and others, such as Walgreens, have gone online with theirs.

In view of all this, are rebate programs unfair? Actually, rebates are probably a good deal for everybody and will continue to be part of the American marketplace, although probably in a different form than used today.

Retailers: This is an easy way for retailers to offer a "sale" without having to raise prices after the "sale" is over.

Manufacturers: This is a game with great appeal for manufacturers, since they get the benefits of a price reduction, and anything with less than a 100 percent redemption rate is free money. Not to mention the information that can be obtained from the completed rebate forms.

Consumers: Provided that they are motivated enough to send in the required forms and proofs, they can save money.

Source: "The Great Rebate Runaround," *Business Week*, December 5, 2005: 34–37; and "The Long Rebate Wait," *AARP Bulletin*, April 2004: 21.

LO 2

Promotion Constraints

Is there a difference between legal and illegal promotional activities for a retailer?

The ability of the retailer to make any promotion decision is constrained by two major pieces of federal legislation, the Federal Trade Commission Act and the Wheeler-Lea Amendment of the FTC Act. The retailer should be familiar with three promotional areas that are potentially under the domain of the FTC Act and the Wheeler-Lea Amendment. These areas are deceitful diversion of patronage, deceptive advertising, and deceptive sales practices. Exhibit 6.5 depicts these three areas of constraint.

Deceitful Diversion of Patronage

If a retailer publishes or verbalizes falsehoods about a competitor in an attempt to divert patrons from that competitor, the retailer is engaging in an unfair trade practice. The competitor would be afforded protection under the FTC Act but also could receive protection by showing that the defamatory statements were libel or slander. In either case, the competitor would have to demonstrate that actual damage had occurred.

palming off
Occurs when a retailer represents that merchandise is made by a firm other than the true manufacturer.

Another form of deceitful diversion of patronage that occurs in retailing is **palming off**. Palming off occurs when a retailer represents merchandise as being

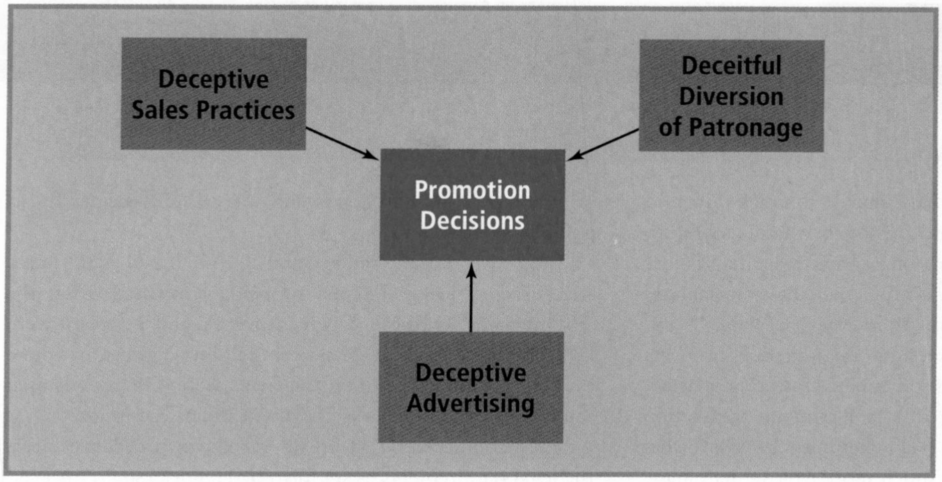

Exhibit 6.5
Promotional Constraints

made by a firm other than the true manufacturer. For example, an exclusive women's apparel retailer purchases a group of stylish dresses at a bargain price and replaces their labels with those of a top designer. This is deception as to source of origin, and litigation can be brought under the FTC Act and the Wheeler-Lea Amendment. Also, if the designer's dress label were a registered trademark, protection would also be afforded under the major piece of federal trademark legislation, the Lanham Act (1946).

According to the World Customs Organization, counterfeiting accounts for 5 percent to 7 percent of global merchandise trade, equivalent to lost sales of as much as $512 billion a year.[3] The scale of the threat (for example, an estimated 67 percent of all copyrighted material sold in Russia is pirated[4]) is prompting new efforts by multinationals to stop, or at least curb, the spread of counterfeits. Companies are deploying detectives around the globe in greater force than ever, pressuring foreign governments to crack down, and trying everything from electronic tagging to redesigned products to aggressive pricing in order to thwart the counterfeiters. Even China, where some 85 percent, or over $400 million, of recorded music sold in 2005 was pirated, is getting into the act.[5] Hundreds of different products, ranging from counterfeit Avian Flu vaccines to fake bottles of Hennessy cognac, have been copied overseas and shipped to the United States for retail sale, sometimes even by the authorized manufacturer of the product.[6] The top categories for counterfeit products are video games and other electronic software, apparel, watches, and golf clubs. Not all the blame for such actions should be placed on retailers. After all, a great deal of the merchandise sold in the United States is produced in foreign countries. In many of these foreign countries, trademark law is relatively new and the concept of such protection is not always clear to the workers. In fact, many of the billions of dollars in sales were probably unwittingly sold by United States retailers despite their use of purchase orders stating explicitly that "the products being purchased do not infringe on anyone's patent, trademark, trade name, or copyright interests."[7] When informed of questionable merchandise being sold in their stores, most retailers will discontinue all future purchases and work out some type of agreement with the injured party to sell any remaining stock. After all, the retailers know their reputation is on the line.[8]

The chapter's Retailing: What's New box describes a situation in which a court will be asked to determine the liability of Internet retailers, such as eBay, regarding

What's New?

Are eBay's Days Numbered?

Recently some manufacturers have started to crack down on not only the people selling knockoffs of their famous brands, but also their landlords. The manufacturers' reasoning is that anyone making money illegally off their valuable name should be sued. The legal terms involved are "vicarious" and "contributory" liability. These suits are targeting property owners for aiding and abetting someone committing a crime, even if the owners are engaged in a legitimate transaction such as renting out property. Manufacturers are aware that wealthy property owners have much more to lose than many of their renters who are actually selling the counterfeits.

Today, however, knockoff artists don't need to operate in parking lots, flea markets, or other retail buildings. They have the Internet. Its anonymity and reach make it perfect for selling knockoffs. However, the question facing the courts in late 2006 or early 2007 will be "if landlords can be held responsible for the actions of their tenants, can eBay be held to the same standard?"

From its beginning, eBay claimed that by using a hands-off approach to its auctions, it was a marketplace and not a retailer. Thus, it was not guilty of any deception. Whether some sales involved outright fraud, unfair bidding practices, or brand theft, eBay maintained that it simply provided a service, and it should not be asked to monitor its site of 180 million members and 60 million items for sale at any one time for knockoffs.

eBay had already successfully used this "service provider" defense in a 2001 landmark case (*Hendrickson v. eBay*). Here the courts ruled that eBay was protected from copyright claims by the Digital Millennium Copyright Act (DMCA), provided that the site removed copyright-protected material upon notification by the copyright holder. Such notification is called a "takedown notice."

However, this stance—the heart of eBay's business model—was challenged by Tiffany & Company in 2004, when it sued eBay for facilitating the trade of counterfeit Tiffany items. Tiffany alleged that eBay profited from the sale of counterfeit Tiffany goods and was willfully neglectful in policing the problem.

In 2004, Tiffany anonymously purchased 186 items advertised as being Tiffany, or being advertised using the Tiffany name. Of these, 5 percent were real, 73 percent were fake, and the remaining 22 percent fell into a gray area where the sellers didn't claim that the items were Tiffany but used the company's trademarks heavily in their descriptions.

eBay countered by saying its takedown procedure meets the legal requirements as set forth by Hendrickson. However, Tiffany used a novel legal argument. The retailer did not claim a copyright infringement. Rather, it claimed trademark abuse. As a result, eBay could not hide behind the safe harbor provided by the DCMA takedown procedure. The basis for Tiffany's argument was that eBay both directly and indirectly assisted the counterfeiters by elevating counterfeit items to its home page for spotlight treatment—as potential Mother's Day gifts, for example. eBay was also said to have placed special advertisements on Yahoo and Google, which highlighted the Tiffany items that ultimately proved to be fakes. That, according to Tiffany, directly promotes fraud.

While most experts don't expect eBay to lose this case, they are in agreement that the question of whether or not eBay is a facilitator of fraud is a critical issue that could affect not only eBay's future, but Internet commerce generally. If eBay were to lose, or if the case was settled out of court and word of the settlement's terms got out, it would mean Internet retailers would have to begin policing everything sold on their Web sites for all brand names and trademarks. The cost impact of such action could directly destroy the business models of many Internet retailers.

Source: "O.K., Knockoffs, This Is War," *New York Times*, March 30, 2006: E1 & E2; "Bagging Fakers and Sellers," *The Wall Street Journal*, January 31, 2006: B1 & B2; "Seeing Fakes, Angry Traders Confront eBay," *New York Times*, January 29, 2006: Section 1, 1, 12; Hendrickson v. eBay, 165 F. Supp. 2d 1082 (C. D. Cal. 2001) and Tiffany (NJ) Inc. et al v. eBay Inc. civ doct #104-cv-04607-nrb.

---

the sale of fakes. The future existence of these firms and their business models will depend on that outcome.

Not only are product trademarks an issue, but the trademark of a retailer's name may be as well. The U.S. Supreme Court ruled recently that Victoria's Secret was not damaged by an Elizabethtown, Kentucky, store named "Victor's Little Secret." According to the court, the use of the name neither confused any consumers or potential consumers, nor was it likely to do so since the Kentucky store sold adult-themed items in addition to lingerie. While the court unanimously agreed that Victoria's Secret had a valid interest in protecting its name, it resupported the notion that trademark law requires evidence that the competitor actually caused harm to a retailer by using a sound-alike or knockoff name.[9]

Another potential problem area for retailers concerns patents. Most retail buyers assume that the wholesaler or manufacturer dealing with them has a valid patent on the merchandise being offered. As a rule, if the patent is ever questioned, a retail buyer will discontinue the product. After all, it is easier and involves less court time to replace the "questionable" item with a substitute.

Deceptive Advertising

Deceptive advertising occurs when a retailer makes false or misleading advertising claims about the physical makeup of a product, the benefits to be gained by its use, or the appropriate uses for the product. Deceptive advertising is illegal. However, it is often difficult to distinguish between what is false or misleading and what is simply "puffery" or "laudatory language," which retailers can legally use. Puffery occurs when a retailer or its spokesperson states what is considered to be an opinion or a judgment about a product, not a statement of fact. An example is a salesperson saying, "This is an excellent buy, and you cannot afford to pass it up." Probably most important for the retailer to recognize is that the FTC's concern is not the intent of the advertiser but whether or not the consumer was misled by the advertising. When the FTC challenges any claim contained in advertising or promotional material, several requirements must be met before the commission can find actionable deception: (1) the FTC must prove that the challenged claim is contained in the advertisement; (2) the claim must be deceptive; and (3) the deceptive claim must be material.[10]

deceptive advertising
Occurs when a retailer makes false or misleading advertising claims about the physical makeup of a product, the benefits to be gained by its use, or the appropriate uses for the product.

AP Photo/Monty Davis

Pizza Hut unsuccessfully used the Federal Courts to challenge Papa John's advertising slogan "Better Ingredients. Better Pizza." Pizza Hut claimed the slogan was misleading and denigrated Pizza Hut products.

The application of the above requirements is never as clear as some would like. The Pizza Hut versus Papa John case supports this point. In this instance, Pizza Hut claimed that Papa John's ran a misleading advertisement that denigrated Pizza Hut products. The ad in question was Papa John's use of the advertising slogan "Better ingredients, better pizza." The 5th Circuit Court of Appeals found that the slogan amounted to nothing more than puffery given that it so exaggerated the company's product. As such, it could not by itself be considered misleading. The court also noted that if Pizza Hut could have proven that consumers were swayed by the ad and as a result lost sales, then the court would have viewed the slogan as misleading and would have ruled against Papa John's.[11]

Dollars & Sense

Retailers who engage in any type of deceptive promotional activities will damage their reputations and be unable to achieve long-term high profits.

bait-and-switch
Advertising or promoting a product at an unrealistically low price to serve as "bait" and then trying to "switch" the customer to a higher-priced product.

Bait-and-switch advertising is another type of deceptive advertising. Bait-and-switch advertising is promoting a product at an unrealistically low price to serve as "bait" and then trying to "switch" the customer to a higher-priced product. However, the scope of the FTC's ban on bait-and-switch is much broader than the typical bait-and-switch scenario, and this strictness could, at least theoretically, pose problems for many retailers. For example, federal regulations outlaw all acts or practices by an advertiser that would discourage the purchase of the advertised merchandise as part of a bait scheme to sell other merchandise. Among those forbidden acts or practices are:

1. Refusing "to show, demonstrate, or sell the product offered."
2. Disparaging, by word or deed, the advertised product or the "guarantee, credit terms, availability of service, repairs or parts, or in any other respect, in connection with it."
3. Failing to have sufficient quantities of the advertised product to meet "reasonable anticipated demands" at all outlets listed in the advertisement, unless the ad clearly discloses that supply is limited or available only at certain locations.
4. "The refusal to take orders for the advertised merchandise to be delivered within a reasonable period of time."
5. The "use of a sales plan or method of compensation for salesmen . . . designed to prevent or discourage them from selling the advertised product."[12]

Deceptive Sales Practices

There are basically two illegal deceptive sales practices. These practices are (1) failing to be honest or omitting key facts in either an ad or the sales presentation and (2) using deceptive credit contracts.

Deceptive activities included in the first practice involve not only the failure to tell the customer vital facts during the sales presentation, but repackaging a used product and reselling it as new. All retailers expect customer returns. Rather than ship the product back to the manufacturer, most retailers resell these items as "open." However, to avoid frustrating or deceiving purchasers of these "open items" because parts are missing or there are different processes that come into play for warranties and service plans, retailers must have procedures in place to ensure that "open item" products are labeled as such, which includes a list of missing or damaged parts or documentation of what has been repaired.[13]

With regard to deceptive credit, federal laws attempt to "assure a meaningful disclosure of credit terms so that the consumer will be able to compare more readily the various credit terms available to him and avoid the un-informed use of credit."[14] These laws were the result of unscrupulous practices on the part of retailers attempting to hide the true cost of merchandise in unrealistically (and sometimes illegal) high credit terms. For example, the retailer might sell a car at a very low price but then tack on a high (and often hidden) finance charge. Many states have laws limiting these hidden charges.

Product Constraints

LO 3

What responsibilities does a retailer have regarding the products sold?

A retailer's major goal is to sell merchandise. In order to accomplish this goal, the retailer must assure customers that the products they purchase will not be harmful to their well being and will meet expected performance criteria. Three areas of the law have a major effect on the products a retailer handles: product safety, product liability, and warranties. They are highlighted in Exhibit 6.6.

Product Safety

Retailers are in a difficult position when it comes to product safety. Most retailers do not produce the goods they sell but purchase them from wholesalers or manufacturers. Retailers have little to say about product quality or safety. Their only weapon is choosing reputable suppliers so as not to carry merchandise they consider unsafe. You might therefore conclude that retailers are not responsible for the safety of products they sell; this is definitely not the case.

A retailer who does not recognize that it is responsible for the safety of products it sells will have lower long-term profits than a retailer that ensures it sells safe products to its customers.

Dollars & Sense

According to the Consumer Product Safety Act (1972), the retailer has specific responsibilities to monitor the safety of consumer products.[15] Specifically, retailers (as well as manufacturers, other intermediaries, and importers) are required by law to report to the Consumer Product Safety Commission any

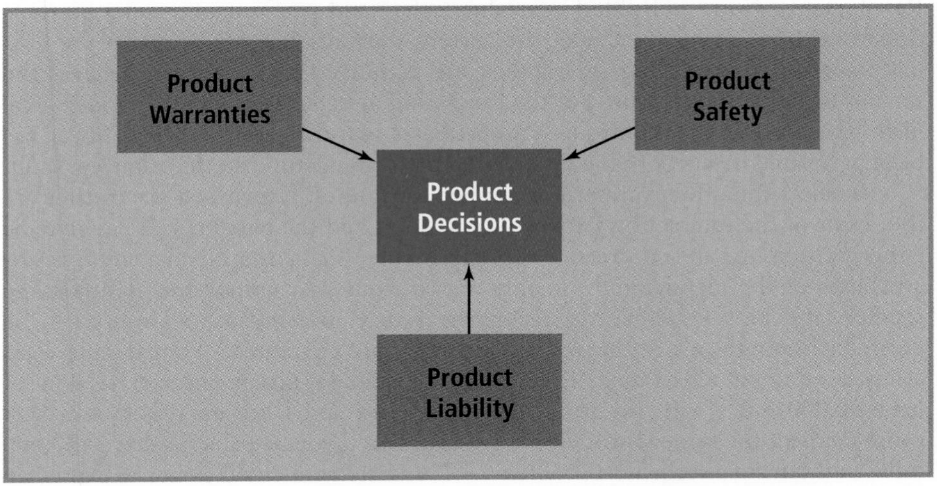

Exhibit 6.6
Product Constraints

Jeff Kowalsky/Bloomberg News/Landov

McDonald's cautions customers that its coffee drinks are hot.

possible "substantial product hazard." For example, Wal-Mart paid a $750,000 fine to the Consumer Product Safety Commission to settle allegations that it failed to report safety problems with some exercise equipment it sold, and agreed to create a system for monitoring information about such safety issues. According to the U.S. Justice Department, this was the first time a retailer had been held accountable in such a case.[16] Some retailers today worry that they are being held responsible for the safety issues created by products they sell even if they are ignorant of the problems involved. After all, what is to prevent a convenience store operator from being sued for illnesses caused by tobacco, alcohol, or products, such as potato chips laden with trans fat?

Furthermore, a retailer may violate the law by not cooking its meals to a required temperature. Retailers may also violate the law by failing to repurchase from customers nonconforming products sold after the effective or expiration date of a health standard or for a number of other reasons. Examples abound. For instance, although an appeals court substantially reduced a lower court award of $2.9 million against McDonald's, the retailer was still found guilty of serving a "too hot" cup of coffee.

Product Liability

product liability laws
Deal with the seller's responsibility to market safe products. These laws invoke the foreseeability doctrine, which states that a seller of a product must attempt to foresee how a product may be misused and warn the consumer against the hazards of misuse.

Product liability laws invoke the "foreseeability" doctrine, which states that a seller of a product must attempt to foresee how a product may be misused and warn the consumer against the hazards of misuse. The courts have interpreted this doctrine to suggest that retailers must be careful in how they sell their products. This is of particular importance to restaurant, nightclub, and bar owners who fail to consider the consequences of serving a consumer who appears intoxicated. In addition to the federal laws covering product liability, all states have their own regulations.

Warranties

Retailers are also responsible for product safety and performance under conventional warranty doctrines. Under the current warranty law, the fact that the ultimate consumer may bring suit against the manufacturer in no way relieves the retailer from its responsibility for the fitness and merchantability of the goods. The disheartening fact that confronts the retailer is that in many states the buyer has been permitted to sue both the retailer and the manufacturer in the same legal suit.

expressed warranties
Are either written or verbalized agreements about the performance of a product and can cover all attributes of the merchandise or only one attribute.

Retailers can offer expressed or implied warranties. **Expressed warranties** are the result of the interaction between the retailer and the customer. They may be either written into the contract or verbalized. They can cover all characteristics or attributes of the merchandise or only one attribute. An important point for the retailer (and its salespeople) to recognize is that an expressed warranty can be created without the use of the words "warranty" or "guarantee." For example, a car salesperson might tell a buyer, "Everybody we've sold this type of car to has gone at least 60,000 miles with no problems whatsoever, and I see no reason why you cannot expect the same. I would not be surprised if you are able to drive 100,000 miles without any mechanical problems." This statement could create an expressed warranty. The court would, however, be concerned with whether this was just sales talk (puffery) or a statement of fact or opinion by the salesperson.

Implied warranties are not expressly made by the retailer but are based on custom, norms, or reasonable expectations. There are two types of implied warranties (which overlap a bit): an implied warranty of merchantability and an implied warranty of fitness for a particular purpose.

Every retailer selling goods makes an **implied warranty of merchantability**. By offering the goods for sale, the retailer implies that they are fit for the ordinary purpose for which such goods are typically used. The notion of implied warranty applies to both new and used merchandise. For example, imagine that a sporting goods retailer located close to a major lake resort sells used inner tubes for swimming and a customer purchases one. The tube bursts while the person is floating on it, and the person subsequently drowns. This retailer may be held liable. Because of the potential legal liability that accompanies an implied warranty, many retailers, especially many online operators, will expressly disclaim at the time of sale any or all implied warranties and seek to mark a product "as is."[17] This is not always legally possible; some retailers will not be able to avoid implied warranties of merchantability.

implied warranty of merchantability
Is made by every retailer when the retailer sells goods and implies that the merchandise sold is fit for the ordinary purpose for which such goods are typically used.

The **implied warranty of fitness** for a particular purpose arises when the customer relies on the retailer to assist or make the selection of goods to serve a particular purpose. Consider a customer who is about to make a cross-country moving trip and plans to tow a 4-foot-by-4-foot, two-wheel trailer behind her SUV. She needs a pair of tires for the rear of the SUV and thus goes to a local tire retailer and asks the salesperson for a pair of tires that will allow her to tow the loaded trailer safely. The customer in this regard is ignorant and is relying on the expertise of the retailer. If the retailer sells the customer a pair of tires not suited for the job, then the retailer is liable for breach of an implied warranty of fitness for a particular purpose. This is true even if the retailer did not have in stock a pair of tires to safely perform the job but instead sold the customer the best tire available.

implied warranty of fitness
Is a warranty that implies that the merchandise is fit for a particular purpose and arises when the customer relies on the retailer to assist or make the selection of goods to serve a particular purpose.

Consumer product warranties frequently have been confusing, misleading, and frustrating to consumers. As a consequence, the Magnuson-Moss Warranty Act was passed. Although nothing in federal law requires a retailer to warrant a product under this act, anyone who sells a product for more than $15 must provide a written warranty (while only written warranties are covered by federal laws, many types of warranties are subject to state laws) to the consumer is required to provide the consumer with all the details of the warranty.[18]

Supply Chain Constraints

LO 4

How does government regulation influence a retailer's behavior with other supply chain members?

Retailers are restricted in the relationships and agreements they may develop with supply chain, or channel, partners. These restrictions can be conveniently categorized into four areas, as shown in Exhibit 6.7.

Territorial Restrictions

As related to retail trade, **territorial restrictions** can be defined as attempts by a supplier, usually a manufacturer, to limit the geographic area in which a retailer may resell its merchandise. The courts have viewed territorial restrictions as potential contracts in restraint of trade and in violation of the Sherman Antitrust Act. Thus, even though the retailer and manufacturer may both favor territorial restrictions, because of the lessening of competition between retailers selling the brand in question, the courts will often frown on such arrangements. The law does

territorial restrictions
Are attempts by the supplier, usually a manufacturer, to limit the geographic area in which a retailer may resell its merchandise.

Exhibit 6.7
Channel Constraints

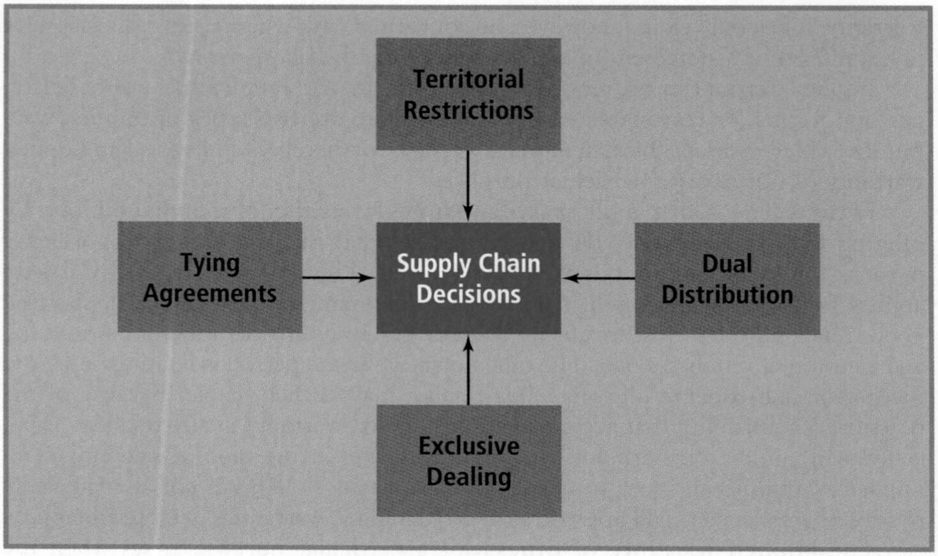

not, however, prevent manufacturers and retailers from establishing territorial limits as long as they do not exclude all other retailers or restrict the sale of the manufacturer's products. Franchise agreements have long had territorial restrictions that provide a protected zone for the franchisee. Because of these zones, the franchisee is able to develop a primary demand for the product without fear of cannibalization by another entry in the protected zone. In cases where the franchisor has permitted another franchisee to invade the "exclusive territory" of another franchisee as outlined in a contract, the original franchisee could sue the parent chain under a breach of contract claim. However, a federal appeals court ruling found that when a franchise contract expressly spells out that a franchisee does not have an exclusive territory, the franchisor has the power to place other outlets nearby.[19]

Dual Distribution

dual distribution
Occurs when a manufacturer sells to independent retailers and also through its own retail outlets.

As discussed in the previous chapter, a manufacturer that sells to independent retailers and also through its own retail outlets is engaged in **dual distribution**. Thus the manufacturer manages a corporately owned vertical marketing system that competes with independent retailers, which it also supplies through a conventional, administered, or contractual marketing channel. Retailers tend to become upset about dual distribution when the two supply chains compete at the retail level in the same geographic area. For example, Ralph Lauren operates wholly owned retail stores and, in addition, uses major independent retailers as outlets. Such supply chain strategy can have an adverse effect on manufacturer-retailer relationships. Independent retailers will argue that dual distribution is an unfair method of competition and thus is in violation of the Sherman Act. As indicated in Chapter 5, the Internet has created new opportunities for dual distribution, which has increased the levels of channel conflict. Dual distribution also takes place when manufacturers sell similar products under different brand names for distribution through different channels, as with private labels.

Ralph Lauren has a dual distribution strategy where it markets its Polo brand apparel through its own retail stores as well as through traditional department stores.

© Steve Raymer/CORBIS

Retailers who view the supply chain as a partnership and abide by the law in their relations with their partners will have higher long-term profits.

Dollars & Sense

The courts have not viewed dual-distribution arrangements as antitrust violations. In fact, they have reasoned that dual distribution can actually foster competition. For example, the manufacturer may not be able to find a retailer to represent it in all trade areas, or the manufacturer may find it necessary to operate its own retail outlet to establish market share and remain competitive with other manufacturers. The courts will apply a rule-of-reason criterion. Thus the independent retailer suing a manufacturer for dual distribution will have to convince the court that it was competed against unfairly and damaged. The retailer's best bet would be to show that the manufacturer-controlled outlets were favored or subsidized (for instance, with excessive advertising allowances or lower prices) to an extent that was detrimental to the independent retailer.

Exclusive Dealing

Retailers and their suppliers occasionally enter into exclusive dealing arrangements. In a **one-way exclusive dealing** arrangement, the supplier agrees to give the retailer the exclusive right to sell the supplier's product in a particular trade area. The retailer, however, does not agree to do anything in particular for the supplier; hence the term "one-way." For example, a weak manufacturer often has to offer one-way exclusive dealing arrangements to get shelf space at the retail level. Truly one-way arrangements are legal.

A **two-way exclusive dealing** agreement occurs when the supplier offers the retailer the exclusive distribution of a merchandise line or product if the retailer

one-way exclusive dealing
Occurs when the supplier agrees to give the retailer the exclusive right to merchandise the supplier's product in a particular trade area.

two-way exclusive dealing
Occurs when the supplier offers the retailer the exclusive distribution of a merchandise line or product in a particular trade area if in return the retailer will agree to do something for the manufacturer, such as heavily promote the supplier's products or not handle competing brands.

agrees to do something for the manufacturer in return. For example, the retailer might agree not to handle certain competing brands. Two-way agreements violate the Clayton Act if they substantially lessen competition or tend to create a monopoly. Specifically, the courts have generally viewed exclusive dealing as illegal when it excludes competitive products from a large share of the market and when it represents a large share of the total sales volume for a particular product type.

Tying Agreements

tying agreement
Exists when a seller with a strong product or service requires a buyer (the retailer) to purchase a weak product or service as a condition for buying the strong product or service.

When a seller with a strong product or service forces a buyer (the retailer) to purchase a weak product or service as a condition for buying the strong one, a **tying agreement** exists. For example, a large national manufacturer with several very highly demanded lines of merchandise may try to force the retailer to handle its entire merchandise assortment as a condition for being able to handle the more popular merchandise lines. This is called a *full-line policy*. Alternatively, a strong manufacturer may be introducing a new product and, in order to get shelf space or display space at the retail level, may require retailers to handle some of the new products before they can purchase better-established merchandise lines.

Tying arrangements have been found to be in violation of the Clayton Act, the Sherman Act, and the FTC Act. Tying is not viewed as a violation per se, but it is generally viewed as illegal if a substantial share of commerce is affected. The most serious problems involving tying arrangements are those associated with franchising. Quite often, franchise agreements contain provisions requiring the franchisee to purchase all raw materials and supplies from the franchisor. The courts generally consider tying provisions of a franchise agreement legal as long as there is sufficient proof that these arrangements are necessary to maintain quality control. Otherwise, they are viewed as unwarranted restraints of competition.[20]

LO 5

Other Federal, State, and Local Laws

What are the various state and local laws, in addition to federal regulations, considered in developing retail policies?

Several other federal laws also affect retailers, but a detailed discussion of their impact is beyond the scope of this text. However, some limited comments follow. One such set of these laws, which is shown in Exhibit 6.1 on page 170, is extremely important today because it deals with mergers and acquisitions. As retailers seek to consolidate their operations by selling off unprofitable stores, expand into new markets, or acquire the outlets of other retailers, they must consider the impact on the competitive environment.[21]

Various U.S. trade agreements regulating the amount of importing and exporting American firms can conduct with firms in various countries sometimes limit, if not totally forbid, a retailer's ability to purchase merchandise from certain foreign countries. At one extreme, America bans all merchandise from countries sponsoring terrorist organizations, while at the other extreme our NAFTA membership attempts to reduce all barriers to trade with Mexico and Canada.

Retailers must be aware of the laws that deal with minimum wages and hiring practices, since labor is a retailer's largest operating expense. Chapter 14, "Managing People," will cover the major laws affecting employment and personnel decisions. Chapter 13 will consider how the Americans with Disabilities Act affects the layout and design of the retailer's store. Finally, Chapter 7's Case will discuss the issues relating to the 2005 Supreme Court's ruling that permitted eminent domain powers to be used in New London, Connecticut, for economic development purposes.[22] The city wanted to confiscate waterfront homes to build an office

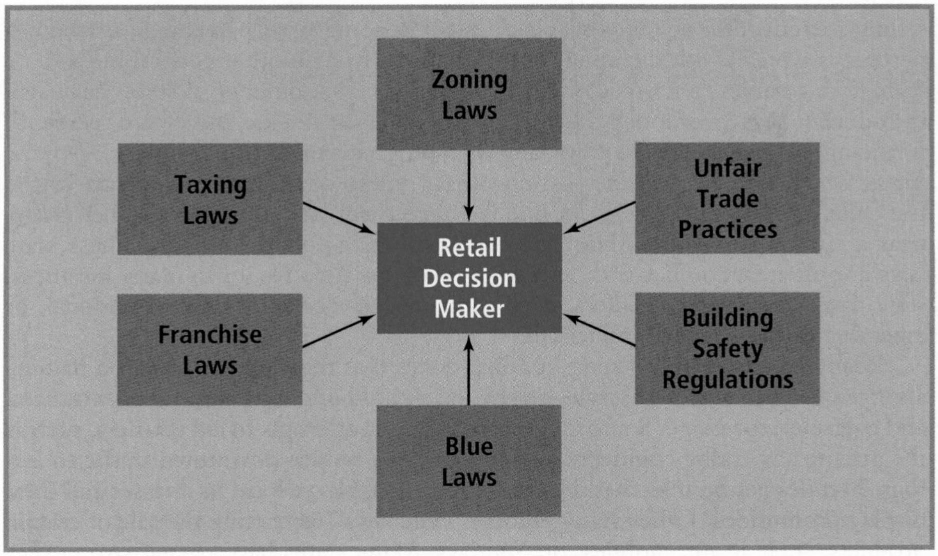

Exhibit 6.8
State and Local Regulations Affecting Retailers

complex and condominiums. This 5-4 ruling prompted property rights advocates to take their case to state, as well as local governmental bodies.[23] Tax laws and Securities and Exchange Commission (SEC) rules and regulations that deal with the legal form of ownership (sole proprietorship, partnership, or corporation) and shareholder disclosure requirements are not covered in this text.

In addition to federal laws, many states and municipalities have passed legislation regulating retail activities. Exhibit 6.8 illustrates how state and local laws affect the retailer. Zoning laws, for example, prohibit retailers from operating in certain locations and require building and sign specifications to be met. Many retailers have found these codes to be highly restrictive, especially since some existing firms have been able to influence this type of legislation, thereby protecting their already established local businesses. For example, several states ban the sale of caskets over the Internet. Their laws dictate that coffins can be provided to the public only by licensed funeral directors. And a Louisiana statute prohibits flower selling without a license. The excluded competitors claim these laws are a deliberate attempt by legislators to protect the entrenched businesses that fear competition.[24]

Retailers must abide by local and state laws regulating retail trade or their profitability performance will be hampered.

Dollars & Sense

With regard to unfair trade practices, most states have established their own set of laws that prevent one retailer from gaining an unfair advantage over another retailer. As a general rule, "unfair trade practices" laws regulate the competitive behavior (usually relating to pricing, advertising, merchandise stocked, and employment practices) of retailers. For example, because shoppers are more likely to consolidate their trips when gas prices are high, some retailers that sell general merchandise along with gasoline may seek to sell gas below cost. Thirteen states have laws against such pricing strategies. The specific content of these laws varies, but usually they prohibit the retailer from seeking unfair advantages from vendors, selling merchandise below cost (or at cost plus some fixed percentage markup, 6 percent is typical) with the intent of using profits from another geographic area or from cash reserves to destroy or hurt competition.[25] A number of states have also introduced laws preventing both "zero down" car leases and "zero percent" financing programs because they claim such programs mislead consumers. Also, the franchise laws in many states assume that, unless otherwise spelled out in the franchise agreement, there is an implied agreement not to locate another outlet near a current location without the current franchisee's permission. These state laws are often in conflict with federal regulations. As a result, in many instances, state laws regulating retailers have either been declared unconstitutional or amended to meet federal guidelines.

Many localities have strong building codes that regulate construction materials, fire safety, architectural style, height and size of buildings, number of entrances, and even elevator usage. Some local ordinances are attempts to aid retailers, such as the attempt by traffic engineers in some cities to reduce downtown traffic to less than 20 miles per hour so that the consumers can observe local businesses and their display promotions. Other states enforce "blue laws" restricting the sale of certain products, such as automobiles, on Sundays. Many states have passed strong regulations on topics not covered by federal regulations governing the relationship between franchisors and franchisees in order to protect the individual businesspeople of their states. These laws require a full disclosure of all the pertinent facts involved in owning a local franchise. Many experts believe that these state franchise laws protect the current antiquated and inefficient automobile dealerships from newer, more efficient forms of competition because the dealers provide 20 percent of state sales tax revenues and are usually the largest advertisers in the local media. Given such a concentration of political clout, most state governments will make it difficult for discounters and Internet sellers to enter the new-car business or for Detroit to control the pricing and promotion of its own products. However, Internet businesses that serve as automotive brokers are emerging. These businesses bring together purchasers and franchised dealers, who will sell the car to the purchaser at a price the Internet broker negotiates. Many state and local governments, which must operate with balanced budgets, view the Internet as a cash pirate. After all, the lost revenue in unpaid sales tax from online transactions is estimated to be as high as $33.7 billion by 2008.[26]

Sometimes states pass laws that don't fit into any of the categories listed in Exhibit 6.8 but that may present problems for retailers. One such issue is what is to be done with the unused portion of gift cards. Customers often leave a little money on the plastic cards and sometimes lose them altogether. Roughly 10 percent of all cards are unredeemed, allowing many stores and restaurants to keep the spare change, which adds up to an estimated $5 billion a year or more and is growing. While most retailers continue to carry the value of the unredeemed cards as a liability on their books, The Home Depot and Best Buy recently increased their profits by recording unredeemed cards that expired as income. Since introducing their cards, Best Buy and The Home Depot have realized $43 million and $29 million worth of income from such cards.[27]

With budgets to balance and with so much unclaimed money at stake, many states are seeking these funds for their treasuries. Since all states have laws that allow them to take custody of funds abandoned by their residents and hold them until the rightful owner can claim them, it is not surprising that every state regards unredeemed gift cards as unclaimed property. Retailers disagree with these laws, arguing that when the state "escheats" an unused gift card, the retailer is deprived of the profit it expected to earn when the card was redeemed for merchandise. They further point out that retailers actually lose money on the gift card because they have to cover the expense of issuing and accounting for the card, but then turn the value of the card over to the state. Today about half the states claim the full value of gift cards or some portion (such as 60 percent). Some retailers have tried to avoid turning the unredeemed money over to states by imposing conditions on gift cards, such as expiration dates or monthly service fees that whittle away the value of the gift card. That way, the card has no value by the time the state would lay claim to its unredeemed value. However, expiration dates that diminish the value of gift cards are unpopular with consumers. A dozen states now regulate the imposition of an expiration date and/or service fees. For the most current summary of the various state regulations regarding gift cards, visit http://www.consumersunion.org/pdf/gift-factsheet.pdf.

In addition, state court systems sometimes make rulings that affect retailers operating across the country. For example, supreme courts of two states are deciding whether or not to hear cases involving injury to a customer when the retailer's employee did not follow a robber's demands as directed by the retailer's rules. Another state court is currently deciding if a retailer discriminated against a female by claiming that only men could be employed as the store's Santas. Also, various cities have passed laws governing retailing, such as the "Green River Ordinances"—named after the town in Wyoming that first passed them—restricting door-to-door selling. Other communities restrict the excessive use of garage sales, lottery promotions, or sale of obscene materials and dangerous products. In addition, states and cities might require licenses to operate certain retail businesses, such as liquor stores or massage parlors.

For further information about these various laws, a retailer should consult the local Better Business Bureau, the National Retail Federation, state and local retail trade associations, or state and local regulatory agencies.

ethics
Is a set of rules for human moral behavior.

explicit code of ethics
Consists of a written policy that states what is ethical and unethical behavior.

Ethics in Retailing

LO 6

How does a retailer's code of ethics influence its behavior?

Ethics is a set of rules for moral human behavior. These rules or standards of moral responsibility often take the form of dos and don'ts. Some retailers have an **explicit code of ethics**, which is a written policy that states what constitutes ethical and unethical behavior. However, most often an implicit code of ethics exists. An **implicit code of ethics** is an unwritten but well understood set of rules or standards of moral responsibility. This implicit code is learned as employees become socialized into the organization and the corporate culture of the retailer.

Retailers who abide by a strong set of ethical guidelines are more likely to achieve higher profits.

Dollars & Sense

Regardless of whether the code of ethics is explicit or implicit, it is an important guideline for making retail decisions. Shortly we will review some retail decision areas where ethical considerations are common. However, before doing so, note that legal behavior and ethical behavior are not necessarily the same. Unethical actions may be legal. Laws, after all, represent a formalization of behavioral standards through the political process into rules or laws. Therefore, a retailer needs to behave legally since laws represent a "formalized" set of ethical rules. In addition, retailers need to look beyond laws and engage in practices that

implicit code of ethics
Is an unwritten but well understood set of rules or standards of moral responsibility.

are also ethical. One problem, though, is that "reasonable" people may disagree as to what is "right" and "wrong" behavior. For this reason retailers should develop explicit codes of ethical behavior for their employees to provide a formal indication of what is right and wrong.

Let's look at three retail decision areas that involve ethical considerations:

1. Buying merchandise
2. Selling merchandise
3. Retailer-employee relationships

In each of these situations, the retailer faces an ethical dilemma. Note that in each of these situations, what is legal may not necessarily represent the best ethical guideline.

Ethical Behavior in Buying Merchandise

When buying merchandise the retailer can face at least four ethical dilemmas; these relate to product quality, sourcing, slotting fees, and bribery.

Product Quality

Should a retailer inspect merchandise for product quality or leave that to the customer? Although the law does not require such inspections, most retail buyers want to ensure that their merchandise meets the expectations of the store's customers. As a result, some retailers have developed laboratory testing programs to verify quality of not only their private label products but of manufacturers' brands as well.

Sourcing

Should a retailer inspect the working conditions at all plants producing products sold by the retailer? What about foreign merchandise sources using child labor or failing to pay a fair level of wages? The only way United States retailers can be sure that they are not buying illegal merchandise is to inspect all suppliers, down to the smallest subcontractors. However, some retailers are also having troubles with American suppliers. A program of careful vigilance to overcome such activities can be expensive and it is doubtful that American consumers would be willing to bear the cost. Seeking to overcome such complaints, many retailers have begun using private investigators to check out vendors to make sure they are not buying from unsavory characters. Many other major American retailers have agreed to allow independent observers, including human rights officials, to monitor working conditions in their foreign factories. Consumers can check the U.S. Department of Labor's Web site (http://www.dol.gov) to see if a particular retailer is involved in the program. In an unusual display of corporate candor, Gap Inc. in 2004 issued a "social responsibility" report acknowledging that many of the overseas workers making the retailer's clothes are mistreated, and it vowed to improve often shoddy factory conditions by cracking down on unrepentant manufacturers. Gap's commitment is particularly significant because thousands of factories were involved.[28] Gap's report can be found at http://www.gapinc.com/public/SocialResponsibility/sr_report.shtml.

slotting fees (slotting allowances)
Are fees paid by a vendor for space or a slot on a retailer's shelves, as well as having its UPC number given a slot in the retailer's computer system.

Slotting Fees

Should a retailer demand money from a manufacturer for agreeing to add a new product to its inventory? **Slotting fees** (also called **slotting allowances**) are fees paid by a vendor for space, or a slot, on a retailer's shelves, as well as for having a slot in the retailer's computer system for its UPC number. After all, if an item's UPC code is not in the system, individual stores cannot stock it. Retailers claim that such fees help defray the extra expenses of adding warehouse space, replacing existing items in the store, and placing the new items in the inventory control system, and provide a form of insurance by guaranteeing at least some profit from carrying the new item. It is estimated that these fees now account for over 16 percent of new product introduction costs. In the only major academic study to date on the subject, the authors found support for the rationale that slotting allowances help enhance market efficiency by optimally allocating scarce retail shelf space to the most successful products. They also concluded that the fees do not thwart competition but helped balance the risk of new product failure between manufacturers and retailers, helped manufacturers signal private information about potential success of new products, and served to widen retail distribution for manufacturers by mitigating retail competition.[29] However, most manufacturers still claim that such fees are only an attempt by retailers to make money buying goods rather than selling goods that meet their customers' needs. Thus, smaller food manufacturers complain that slotting fees limit competition and translate into higher prices for consumers. The competition to get a product into a store is fierce, given that a typical grocery store has room for only about 40,000 items, and more than 100,000 grocery items are available for consideration. Still the question remains, are slotting fees really necessary?

Bribery

Should a retailer, or its employees, be allowed to accept a bribe? Bribery occurs when a retail buyer is offered an inducement (which the IRS considers to have a value greater than $25) for purchasing a vendor's products. Such inducements, it should be noted, are legal in many foreign countries. The reader may want to visit the document and publication section at the Transparency International Web site (http://www.transparency.org) to see in which countries bribes are still considered part of normal business behavior. However, in the United States, the Foreign Corrupt Practices Act bans bribes as anticompetitive. It is, after all, hard to develop a healthy relationship between a retailer and supplier when bribes are expected.

Wal-Mart, which as the world's largest retailer is also the largest purchaser, has probably the strictest employee standard in the industry. Wal-Mart's employees are not allowed to accept any gifts (including samples) from vendors, not even a cup of coffee or a soft drink when visiting a supplier's showroom. Today, many of the nations' top retailers require not only all their managers and buyers, but also their vendors, to sign an integrity pledge.

Since retail buyers are often compensated based on their buying performance, a modern version of bribery occurs when retailers shakedown vendors for markdown money. **Markdown money** is the funds that retailers arbitrarily deduct from vendors' payments when the merchandise doesn't sell briskly enough. This topic will be covered in greater detail in Chapter 10.

markdown money
Markdown money is what retailers charge to suppliers when merchandise does not sell at what the vendor intended.

Ethical Behavior in Selling Merchandise

Ethics can also influence the selling process with regards to the products sold and the various selling practices that salespeople use.

Products Sold

Should a retailer sell any product, as long as it is not illegal? For example, should a convenience store operator located near a school carry cigarette paper for those few

Service Retailing

Privacy and Search Engines

A popular urban legend revolves around the college student who used an Internet search engine to have someone write a term paper for him. After all, the student reasoned, if American companies can go online to outsource their work, why can't students outsource their homework? However, in this case, the term paper writer, who charged only $100, was the student's professor.

Search engines have become so popular for this type of activity that *The Wall Street Journal* reports that today it is as easy to buy 10 pages about the causes of the Civil War as it is to buy a song on iTunes. To combat this problem, companies, such as TurnItIn and Ithenticate, help professors in attempting to stop such plagiarism.

A simpler solution to this problem might be to allow professors to check with the search engines to find out who used their services. Sound far-fetched? After all, wouldn't this be an invasion of privacy and thus illegal? Many people thought so until recently.

Worse yet is the question of how private are the records of your online use of search engines, such as Yahoo or Google. Can someone get them? In 2005, Yahoo was suspected of supplying information to China's government, which led to the jailing of a journalist. His crime was sending the text of an internal Communist Party memo to foreign-based Web sites. Yahoo said it was only complying with China's laws.

An even more important case occurred in 2006, here in the United States, when Google resisted a Justice Department effort to force the company to turn over data on customers' Web searches for certain types of porn. The Justice Department wanted the California-based company to turn over 1 million random Web IP addresses and records of all Google searches from any one-week period. The issue at hand was to see if online pornography sites were accessible by minors. Google, while not a party to the lawsuit, resisted on privacy grounds and said it would "vigorously" oppose the subpoena for Web search information.

The government responded by saying it only requested "anonymous data" (the computer's IP address) and that Google's rivals, including Time Warner's AOL, Microsoft's MSN, and Yahoo, already complied. However, the refusal by Google—whose guiding philosophy is "don't be evil"—overlooked an important issue: "Why was a search engine keeping so much information at all?" While a final court decision on this privacy issue is not expected until 2007 or later, the broader question remains: "Are search engines' inquiries really private?"

Source: "Google's Reputation at Stake in Fight with Government," *Business Week*, January 23, 2006: 2B; Locatecell.com's Web site, January 27, 2006; "Cracks in the Wall," *Fortune*, February 27, 2006: 90–96; "About That Motto," *The Wall Street Journal*, January 21, 2006: A2; and "China: Yahoo 'Helped Jail China Writer'," a news release by CorpWatch dated September 7, 2005.

customers who prefer to roll their own and risk selling the paper to students who might use it for smoking marijuana? Others have questioned Wal-Mart's decision not to sell adult-themed sex magazines. Long before actions by some states and communities, many drug store and general merchandise chains banned the sale of pseudoephedrine, an ingredient found in most popular over-the-counter cold medicines, and lithium batteries, because both pseudoephedrine and lithium are used in the production of crystal meth (methamphetamine). Other retailers have chosen not to sell "unrated" movie DVDs, the ones with raunchy humor and explicit sex scenes, despite the fact that they tend to outsell the original versions.[30]

Sometimes not carrying products can add to a retailer's profit. For example, Trader Joe's, the California-based specialty food retailer, performed a sales analysis on all its cigarettes by company and brand and found that only Marlboro merited the space allocated. Therefore, rather than carry just that one brand, the retailer dropped all cigarettes.[31] Today, the topic of what products should be sold has reached the Internet's service providers. The chapter's Service Retailing box highlights the issue of what happens to all that information that Internet search engines, such as Google, gather about their users.

Selling Practices

Can a salesperson, while not saying anything false, be allowed to conceal certain facts from the customer? Also, should selling the "wrong" product for the customer's needs be permitted? Many retailers have ethical standards against such practices. However, as long as salespeople are paid on commission, we can expect such behavior to occur. Some highly successful retailers, such as The Home Depot and Best Buy, have sought to overcome this dilemma by never putting their employees at odds with their own code of ethics. Bernie Marcus, the founder of The Home Depot, has been quoted as saying: "The day I'm laid out dead with an apple in my mouth is the day we'll pay commissions. If you pay commissions, you imply that the small customer is not worth anything."[32] When Best Buy switched from commissions to salary in 1989, manufacturers like Toshiba and Hitachi that depended on salespeople to push premium-priced items were opposed. However, customers liked the no-pressure atmosphere and sales soon outpaced all rivals.[33] It should be pointed out, however, that paying commissions could be difficult in self-service operations like The Home Depot and Best Buy.

Ethical Behavior in the Retailer-Employee Relationship

Ethical standards can also influence the retailer-employee relationship in three ways: misuse of company assets, job switching, and employee theft.

Misuse of Company Assets

Most people would agree that the stealing of merchandise is illegal, but what about other types of stealing? What about an employee who surfs the Web or trades stock on company time? Also, what about taking an extra break or using the retailer's phone for a personal long-distance call? All of these, while not subject to criminal prosecution, are forms of employee theft and should be considered when an employee develops his or her code of ethics.

Advancements in computer technology and the growth of the Internet have recently challenged one of the most treasured of American rights—the right to privacy. Most retailers have an asset that would have been unheard of a generation ago. In a situation similar to that described above regarding Google, retailers today have databases that contain heretofore private information about nearly every American, and most consumers do not even know it exists. These databases are constructed in a number of ways, including computer cookies and purchased information from state governments (for example, driver's license bureaus or voting records). As a result, current laws provide for consumers to opt out of such databases.

Many e-tailers, for example, know not only what purchases you made from them, but also what sections of their Web site you visited. The majority of e-tailers disclose their privacy policy on their Web site. Exhibit 6.9 shows the National Retail Federation's Principles on Customer Data Privacy. In general, most of the major retailers in this country adhere to the NRF's principles. However, the shakeout in e-tailing during the early part of this decade showed just how consumers' rights to privacy could be violated by retailers who had no intention of doing so.

Job Switching

Do employees have the right to work for whomever they want? Of course, but employees have a responsibility to their previous employers. These firms provided them with training and access to confidential information, such as vendor costs, customer lists, and future plans. When an employee leaves one retailer for another, the employee should respect the previous employer's right to retain the confidentiality of this information.

GENERAL RULE

The privacy of information collected by a retailer about its customers during the course of transactions with those customers should be maintained with the degree of confidentiality that the retailer reasonably anticipates would be expected of it by the typical shopper purchasing that type of merchandise from the retailer. Departures from this standard should be disclosed to customers at or before each time of occurrence, unless previously consented to by the customer or otherwise expressly permitted by law.

PRACTICE PRINCIPLES

Each retailer should adopt a customer privacy policy explaining its practices with respect to the information it collects about its customers.

Policies could either be corporate-wide or divisional depending upon the manner in which the company believes customers view its retail operations.

A retailer should make reasonable efforts to inform its customers of the existence of its customer privacy policies, and make the substance of such policies available, on a regular basis.

At a minimum, a customer privacy policy should allow a customer to elect whether he or she wishes to prevent the marketing of his or her name to other unaffiliated corporations, or to "opt out" of future promotional solicitations from the company(s) to which the policy applies, or both.

Retail companies should develop procedures to reasonably ensure that customer information is not accessible to, or used by, its employees or others in contravention of its policies and customer elections, and that access to personally identifiable data for non-promotional purposes is limited to those individuals with a customer servicing need to know.

Exhibit 6.9
National Retail Federation Principles on Customer Data Privacy

At the same time, the retailer should not seek to replace an employee, usually a manager or executive, with a lower-paid, younger person, just because the employee reaches the so-called 20-40-80 plateau (20 years or more with the firm; 40 years or older; and making over $80,000 a year).

Employee Theft

Even as the misuse of company assets is actually a type of theft, outright stealing by employees is an even more serious issue. After all, just as employers have a responsibility to be fair to their employees, so do employees have a responsibility to be honest and fair with their employers. However, at a time when retailers attribute 47 percent of their missing inventory to employee theft,[34] many workers admit to "stealing" from their employers. Employee theft is most prevalent in food stores, restaurants and bars (which is discussed in greater detail in Exhibit 9.6, on page 313), department stores, and discount stores. Considering that these types of stores are usually larger in size, sales volume, and number of employees, the lack of close supervision might contribute to this problem. Some retailers, such as Wal-Mart, are trying to address this problem by offering cash bonuses just before Christmas if the store not only makes its profit goal but also keeps shrinkage under a predetermined limit.

The above discussion is not meant to be an all-inclusive list of the ethical dilemmas facing retailing today. It does, however, provide the reader with a big picture of the role of ethics in retailing.

SUMMARY

We began this chapter by describing the multifaceted legal environment that confronts retailers in the United States. We identified constraints on retailers' activities in six broad categories: (1) pricing, (2) promotion, (3) products, (4) supply chain relations, (5) other federal laws, and (6) state and local regulations. Within each of these broad constraints, we summarized some specific activities that are regulated.

Does legislation constrain a retailer's pricing policies?

LO 1

With regard to pricing—the issue that most frequently confronts retailers—the retailer should first be familiar with two methods of price fixing: with other retailers (horizontal) and with supply chain members (vertical). In addition, the retailer must consider all the ramifications of price discrimination when purchasing merchandise. In setting retail prices, two other areas of concern are deceptive pricing and predatory pricing.

Is there a difference between legal and illegal promotional activities for a retailer?

LO 2

The retailer should focus on three areas that constitute illegal promotional activities: deceitful diversion of patronage, which includes selling counterfeit or fake products; deceptive advertising, including making false claims about a product and using bait-and-switch tactics; and deceptive sales practices, which include not being completely honest in discussions about merchandise and use of deceptive credit contracts.

What responsibilities does a retailer have regarding the products sold?

LO 3

With regard to product constraints, the retailer should be aware of legislation dealing with product safety, product liability, and both expressed and implied warranty requirements as they relate to retailing.

How does government regulation influence a retailer's behavior with other supply chain members?

LO 4

Since all retailers are members of some type of supply chain, it is important to understand supply chain relationships in terms of the legality of territorial restrictions, dual distribution, exclusive dealing, and tying agreements.

What is the impact of various state and local laws, in addition to federal regulations, in developing retail policies?

LO 5

The retailer must be aware of state and local laws, which include regulations on zoning, unfair trade practices, building safety, blue laws, and franchises.

How does a retailer's code of ethics influence its behavior?

LO 6

Laws and regulations do not cover every situation a retailer might face in the day-to-day operations of a business. In such cases, codes of ethics for both retailer and employee behavior will provide guidance. A code of ethics is particularly important in buying merchandise, selling merchandise, and managing the retailer-employee relationship.

TERMS TO REMEMBER

horizontal price fixing
vertical price fixing
price discrimination
deceptive pricing
predatory pricing
palming off
deceptive advertising
bait-and-switch
product liability laws
expressed warranties
implied warranty of merchantability
implied warranty of fitness
territorial restrictions
dual distribution
one-way exclusive dealing
two-way exclusive dealing
tying agreement
ethics
explicit code of ethics
implicit code of ethics
slotting fees (slotting allowances)
markdown money

STUDENT STUDY GUIDE

REVIEW AND DISCUSSION QUESTIONS

LO 1

How does legislation constrain a retailer's pricing policies?

1. It has been said that vertical price fixing harms only the consumer. Agree or disagree and explain your reasoning.
2. The Service Retailing box in Chapter 2 discussed yield management. Some contend that the use of such a strategy causes retailers to engage in price discrimination, which is unfair to the customers paying the higher price. Agree or disagree and explain your reasoning.
3. Deceptive pricing harms not only the consumer but also competition. Agree or disagree and explain your reasoning.

LO 2

What is the difference between legal and illegal promotional activities for a retailer?

4. If a student downloads a song from a file-swapping site, is this an example of "deceitful diversion of patronage"? Would your answer be the same if the student purchased a preloaded iPod? Explain your reasoning.
5. Should all types of "puffery" be removed from ads? Explain your reasoning.
6. Describe what is meant by the term "bait-and-switch." Is this a legal or an illegal retailing tool?

LO 3

What responsibilities does a retailer have regarding the products sold?

7. Should a retailer be held liable for selling tobacco? Alcohol? Products laden in fat? Firearms?
8. Should a retailer be held liable for statements made by its sales staff, even if the staff was instructed not to make such statements? Explain your reasoning.

LO 4

How does government regulation influence a retailer's behavior with other supply chain members?

9. Could a decision by a manufacturer to engage in dual distribution be harmful to the consumer and members of the supply chain? Explain your reasoning.
10. Discuss the concept of exclusive dealing. Are exclusive dealing arrangements in the retailer's best interest? Are they in the consumer's best interest?

LO 5

What is the impact of various state and local laws, in addition to other federal regulations, in developing retail policies?

11. Should a retailer be allowed to sell products below cost in an attempt to increase store traffic? Why or why not?
12. In a free market system, such as the one we have in the United States, should cities be allowed to use zoning laws to prevent big-box discounters from entering their market?

LO 6

How does a retailer's code of ethics influence its behavior?

13. Retailers should abide by the philosophy that "as long as it is legal, it is ethical." Agree or disagree and explain your reasoning.
14. Because of religious or personal beliefs, a retailer may not want to stock a particular product, say cigarettes or condoms, that is normally sold by its

category of store. Can government force the retailer to carry a full line of merchandise, if that retailer is the only store in a community?

15. Many retailers face the problem of small amounts of unredeemed money that remain on a gift card. Does this "breakage" belong to the retailer as part of its profit, does it belong in the state's treasury, or should it go into the state's unclaimed money fund to the consumer? Explain your reasoning.

SAMPLE TEST QUESTIONS

Ben Cooper's Pontiac charges two different customers (one a man, the other a woman) two different prices for identical automobiles. This is in all probability a violation of the LO 1

a. Clayton Act.
b. your state's Unfair Trade Practices Act.
c. Robinson-Patman Act.
d. Sherman Act.
e. This is not illegal since it involved a sale to a final consumer, not just sales between supply chain, or channel, members.

An example of deceitful diversion of patronage would be LO 2

a. spreading rumors about a competitor, even if the rumors do not hurt the competitor's business.
b. telling the truth about a competitor that will hurt the competitor's business.
c. advertising a product at a very low price and then adding hidden charges.
d. putting extra large signs in your store's front window offering lower prices than your competitor next door.
e. illegally using another company's trademark or brand name that results in the loss of sales for the other company.

When a customer relies on the retailer to assist the customer or to select the right goods to serve a particular purpose, the retailer is establishing: LO 3

a. an implied warranty of fitness.
b. an implied warranty of merchantability.
c. a price discrimination defense.
d. an expressed warranty of fitness.
e. an expressed warranty of merchantability.

D-A Pet Products Company has an extremely popular line of cat food. The company has recently started insisting that retailers who carry its cat food must also carry its rather overpriced cat litter. Due to its price, the litter is not a big seller, and it takes away shelf space from more profitable products. Requiring stores that stock the cat food to also stock the litter is an example of: LO 4

a. a consent agreement.
b. a tying contract.
c. unfair advertising.
d. monopolistic competition.
e. power marketing.

APPLICATIONS

LO 5 **The most stringent laws governing franchises are typically enacted at the ___ level.**

a. federal
b. state
c. county
d. local
e. international

LO 6 **Which of the following is not an ethical dilemma that a retailer faces when buying merchandise?**

a. whether or not the retailer believes he/she can sell the merchandise
b. the source of the merchandise
c. the issue of product quality
d. whether or not to demand a slotting fee
e. whether or not to ask for a bribe

WRITING AND SPEAKING EXERCISE

You are the assistant manger of an electronics store and this morning a local television station came in and asked for an interview. They are doing a story on how electronics retailers planned on a great Christmas selling season. After all, thanks to the introduction of another new version of Xbox, retailers expected high traffic counts to result in sales of many high markup impulse items. However, that wasn't the case, as most retailers forgot about the eBay effect, which compounded the inability of Microsoft to produce enough new versions of Xbox in time for Christmas.

After Thanksgiving when consumers started hunting for the popular game, they could not find any in the stores. However, there were plenty on eBay available for over $800 each (double the retail price). Advance planning by the eBayers enabled them to stock up on the hot game.

These "mom & pop" retailers went into action by purchasing all the Xboxes whenever they arrived at neighborhood stores. eBay became the merchant of last resort because it encouraged its microretailers to scour stores and other potential sources long before the masses began shopping after Thanksgiving. As a result, consumers became angry with the traditional retailers and had no reason to shop in their stores. They also attacked the actions of the eBayer for allowing such price gouging. What especially angered consumers was the fact that eBayers were allowed to take such high markups even though they were operating with a very low overhead and really were not taking a big risk on being stuck with excess inventory.

Now the television station wants you to comment on this situation. How would you respond?

RETAIL PROJECT

Each year the United States government's Consumer Information Center publishes the *Consumer Action* handbook. This book is designed to help consumers make informed decisions and address any problems they may have if they think they were cheated, swindled, or treated unfairly. In addition, the book lists other pamphlets and the phone numbers for all government agencies dealing with consumer issues, such as credit, door-to-door selling, car repairs (including what to do if you purchased a "lemon"), and insurance.

You can order a copy of the handbook and get a list of all other pamphlets by writing the CIC at P.O. Box 100, Pueblo, CO 81002 or contacting the center online at http://www.pueblo.gsa.gov.

PLANNING YOUR OWN RETAIL BUSINESS

You are the general manager/partner for a local Ford dealership with a net worth of $1,800,000. At your regular Friday morning meeting with the sales force, you congratulate them on being ahead of their sales quota for the year.

Things could not be better, you think to yourself as you leave the meeting and return to your office. You are going to exceed your $8.5 million sales goal for the year. Your cost of merchandise sold is expected to average 88 percent of sales, and your fixed operating costs are being held to $30,000 a month. With variable costs averaging 5 percent of sales, you are expecting to produce almost a quarter of a million dollars in profit before taxes this year.

Just when things are looking so great, your partner calls to ask if you read the article in the morning newspaper about last night's city council meeting. It seems that in order to reduce local property taxes and thus keep voters happy, a council member has suggested that the city increase the sales tax by 1 percent. This tax would cover everything sold in the city, including automobiles.

While you hate to see any type of sales tax increase since it raises the price of your automobiles, this one in particular could present your dealership with a major problem. Just last year, several dealers representing most major domestic and foreign car manufacturers moved to a nearby suburban location, creating a sort of "car mall" where shoppers could easily move from one dealership to another and compare the various offerings. One of those "car mall" dealers was the city's other Ford dealer. This dealer's customers would not have to pay this additional sales tax since the suburb's government planned to keep local sales taxes at the current level and instead reap the benefits of an increase in retail sales as consumers flocked to suburban merchants to get lower prices.

What should you do? Should you absorb the additional tax to keep your prices competitive? What would this do to your profits? Or should you lobby city hall to persuade the council to see the errors of this tax increase?

CASE

The Changing Face of Tobacco Retailers[35]

Over the last half-century, Americans have become accustomed to the idea of being able to buy cigarettes at a variety of retail outlets ranging from vending machines in bars, restaurants, airports, supermarkets, convenience stores, gas stations, and discount stores. However, federal legislation may soon change the way tobacco is sold in the United States.

Wal-Mart was one of the first major retailers to address the tobacco issue. In 1990 Sam Walton admitted in a letter to a consultant that he was "still in a quandary (sic) on our direction for this very important issue."[36] The next year the retailer announced the banning of smoking on all Wal-Mart property, including the stores, as well as the removal of any cigarette vending machines. At the time, Walton was not aware of any vending machines, but as a precaution, he issued the "ban" order. Later, when Wal-Mart expanded into Canada by purchasing 127 Woolco stores, Walton met with the pharmacists from the newly acquired stores. At their request, Wal-Mart dropped the sale of tobacco in its Canadian stores. Members of the chain's executive committee decided to continue with the sale of cigarettes after Mr. Walton's death.

At the same time, various state and local agencies began to enforce age restrictions on the sale of cigarettes and other products, such as firearms, spray paint (which was used for painting gang slogans), and even glue. Wal-Mart even introduced a program into its scanners that froze the cash register when the SKU for one of these products was recorded until the clerk ascertained the age of the purchaser. As a result of the increased enforcement, some retailers, especially supermarkets and drug stores, began to drop tobacco. How would this affect the sale of these legal products, which accounted for over $60 billion in sales per year?

If such a change were to occur, what retailers would benefit? Some experts think that one of the retailers best prepared, should cigarettes be dropped by the mass sellers, is John Roscoe's family-owned Cigarettes Cheaper chain. This is a 400-store operation already doing $50 million in sales each year.

Cigarettes Cheaper, which sells only cigarettes in 1,200-square-foot outlets located primarily in strip malls and is second only to Wal-Mart in total cigarette sales, is a spin-off of Roscoe's Customer Company convenience store chain. The name Customer Company was a reflection of Roscoe's appreciation for his consumers. As a result, he offered the lowest possible prices on everything in the store. His tobacco stores follow the same philosophy by charging 20 percent less than the nearby competitors on the average pack or carton of cigarettes.

The chain is able to charge such prices by taking advantage of every manufacturer discount available and realizing that its customers are not apt to buy just a pack or even a carton, but will more likely purchase 10 to 12 cartons at a time. But low prices are not the only attraction. Roscoe's stores (and similar operations) have a broader range of brands and packaging than other retailers, a regular diet of promotions, and a welcoming attitude towards smokers that is not always the case elsewhere.

These facts about Roscoe's operation are most impressive:

1. No member of John Roscoe's family smokes, nor do they encourage anyone to smoke.
2. The stores put a great deal of effort into controlling "underage" customers. All stores have a large sign stating "NO MINORS ALLOWED INSIDE," and a manager could lose his/her job for violating this rule.

Many retail experts think this might be the way all cigarettes are sold in the future. What do you think?

Roscoe says his stores are just there to serve the market. Do you agree with his right to do this? Do you agree with his decision to do this?

3

Market Selection and Location Analysis

Chapter 7

Market Selection and Retail Location Analysis

chapter 7

Market Selection and Retail Location Analysis

Overview:

In this chapter, we will review how retailers select and reach their target markets through the choice of location. The two broad options for reaching a target market are store-based and nonstore-based locations. The chapter's major focus is the decision process for selecting store-based locations. We describe the various demand and supply factors that must be evaluated for each geographic market area under consideration. We conclude with a discussion of alternative locations that retailers consider as they select a specific site.

Learning Objectives:

After reading this chapter, you should be able to:

1. Explain the criteria used in selecting a target market.
2. Identify the different options, both store-based and nonstore-based, for effectively reaching a target market and identify the advantages and disadvantages of business districts, shopping centers, and freestanding units as sites for retail location.
3. Define geographic information systems (GIS) and discuss their potential uses in a retail enterprise.
4. Describe the various factors to consider in identifying the most attractive geographic market for a new store.
5. Discuss the various attributes to consider in evaluating retail sites within a retail market.
6. Explain how to select the best geographic site for a store.

LO 1

Selecting a Target Market

What criteria are used in selecting a target market?

Many retailing experts consider the most critical determinants of success in retailing to be first, selecting a target market, and second, evaluating alternative ways to reach this target market.

Traditionally, for retailers desiring to reach a given target market, this has meant selecting the best location for a store. In fact, according to an oft-repeated story, a famous retailer once said that the three major decisions in retailing are location, location, and location. There is truth in that statement because, while the other elements of the retail mix are also important, if the customer cannot reach your store conveniently, those elements become secondary. The easier it is to reach the store, the more store traffic a store will have and this will lead to higher sales.

Today, however, retailers are finding alternative ways to reach customers, and location refers to more than just a store's physical location. For example, Dell sells computers and peripherals through the mail, over the Internet, in kiosks in airports and shopping malls, and by phone; the University of Phoenix offers an MBA online via a computer in the student's home or place of business; eBay has 180 million members/users; and Tupperware, after its problems with selling its products in Target stores that was discussed in Chapter 5, continues to sell most of its kitchenware via in-home parties.

As noted in earlier chapters, the Internet is becoming a major force in retailing. The equivalent of a store on the Internet is a retailer's site on the World Wide Web (WWW). When stopping at an e-tailer's Web site, visitors first view the firm's **home page**, which can be compared to a storefront. From the home page a person visiting the retailer can be linked to other pages that provide more detailed information about merchandise, credit, warranties, terms of trade, and so forth. The total collection of all the pages of information on the retailer's Web site is known as its **virtual store**. Whereas a traditional store is located in geographic space, a virtual store is located in cyberspace.

The cyberspace counterpart to location is the "ease of access" a consumer has to the site. **Ease of access** refers to the consumer's ability to find a Web site in cyberspace easily and quickly. To gain access to a site, a consumer can use a retailer's name (for example, http://www.target.com) or a search engine, such as Google or Yahoo. Exhibit 7.1 illustrates that as the number of Web sites increases, the importance of easy access also increases.

home page
Is the introductory or first material viewers see when they access a retailer's Internet site. It is the equivalent of a retailer's storefront in the physical world.

virtual store
Is the total collection of all the pages of information on the retailer's Internet site.

ease of access
Refers to the consumer's ability to easily and quickly find a retailer's Web site in cyberspace.

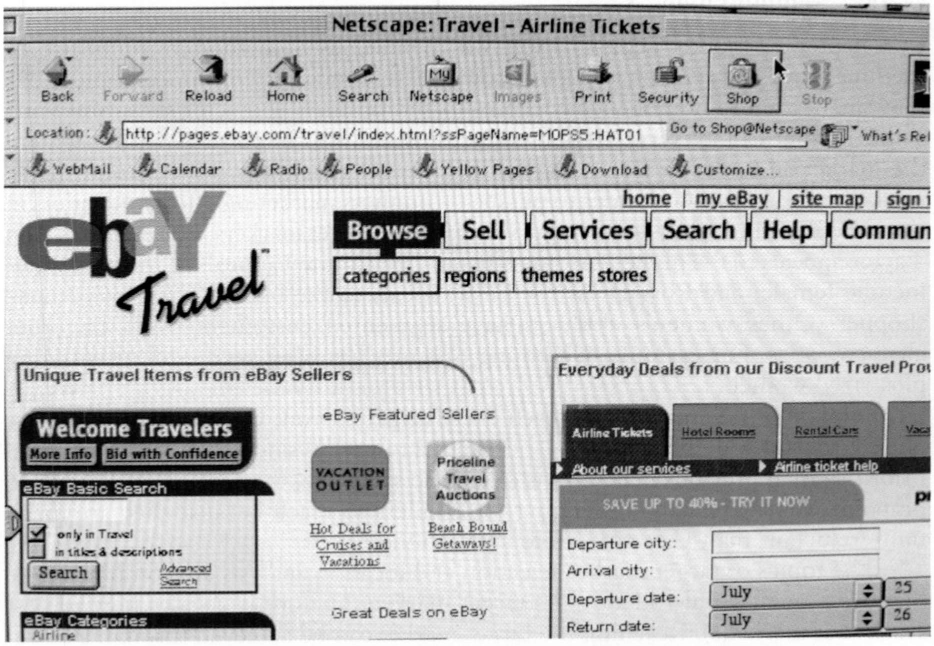

eBay is within easy reach of any person with access to a computer and the Internet.

Exhibit 7.1
Ease of Access

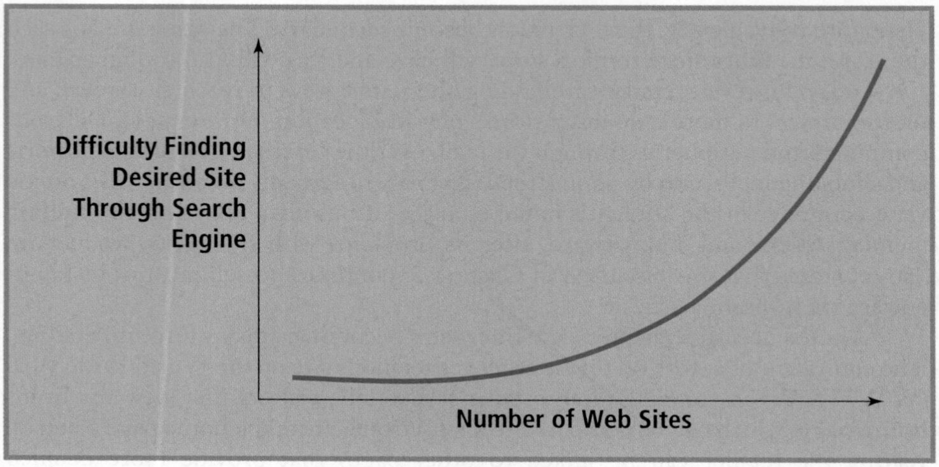

Dollars & Sense

Retailers who select high-traffic geographic or cyberspace sites will be able to generate higher profits.

Regardless of whether retailers are planning a traditional store in geographic space or a virtual store in cyberspace, their first step is to develop a cost-effective way to reach the household and individual consumer that they have identified as their target market. It is important to realize that failure to clearly identify the target market will result in a significant waste of marketing expenditures.

Market Segmentation

target market
Is the group of customers that the retailer is seeking to serve.

In Chapter 3, market segmentation was defined as a method retailers use to examine ways to segment, or break down, heterogeneous consumer populations into smaller, more homogeneous groups based on their characteristics. Since any single retailer cannot serve all potential customers, it is important that it segment the market and select a target market(s). A **target market** is that segment of the market that the retailer decides to pursue through its marketing efforts. Retailers in the same line of retail trade often pursue different target markets. For example, Ann Taylor appeals to the higher-income female, The Limited appeals to the moderate-income female, and Ross Dress for Less appeals to the budget-conscious female shopper. Other women's clothiers have segmented customers based on other characteristics. For example, Charming Shoppes has been successful in targeting plus-sized women.

Sometimes it is not easy to reach every target market. Generation Y types are poised to reshape the cultural landscape. However, since they have different priorities than previous generations did at the same age, they are more difficult to pinpoint. Canadians are challenging for e-tailers to reach because they are much more reluctant than U.S. citizens to shop online.

The topics of target market selection and location analysis are combined here because a retailer must identify its target market(s) before it decides how to best reach that market(s). Reaching the target market can be achieved through a store-based location in which the consumer travels to the store, or through a nonstore retailing format in which products and services are offered to the consumer at a

AP Photo/Paul Sakuma

The Limited locates its stores in shopping centers with trade areas that capture The Limited's target market.

more convenient or accessible location. These are related topics because individuals of different characteristics are not randomly spread over geographic space. In fact, it has been repeatedly demonstrated that people of similar backgrounds live near each other and have similar media habits, consumption habits, activities, interests, and opinions. Because of this, retailers such as Nordstrom know where to geographically locate their stores, and merchants such as Williams Sonoma (which has a very successful mail-order catalog for high-quality kitchenware) know which ZIP codes, geographic areas, or specific households should receive their catalogs.

Identifying a Target Market

To reach a target market successfully, three criteria should be met. First, a retailer should be able to describe the selected market segment using objective measures for which there is data available, such as age, gender, income, education, ethnic group, religion, and so on. The most commonly available objective data is demographic, which the U.S. Census Bureau provides for businesses at little cost. Conversely, a subjective variable such as personality is more difficult to determine. For example, how can a retailer reasonably or cost-effectively measure the number of compulsive shoppers in the United States?

A second criterion is accessibility, or the degree to which the retailer can target its promotional or distribution efforts to a particular market segment. Do individuals in the target market watch certain television programs, listen to particular radio programs or podcasts, frequently visit the same Web sites (i.e., cluster in cyberspace), or cluster together in neighborhoods? As we will see in this chapter, the location decision is largely determined by identifying the most effective way to reach a target market. Finally, successful target marketing requires that the segment be substantial enough to be profitable for the retailer. When Joe Albertson opened the first Albertsons grocery store in 1939, he drove through neighborhoods looking for diapers on clotheslines and tricycles in driveways. He knew that these were the signs of families with many mouths to feed and neighborhoods that promised future growth, and therefore a place to build a grocery store.[1]

Clearly, a retailer could develop a store to appeal to any market segment regardless of size, such as a store for fans of the Green Bay Packers; however, the retailer would have to ask whether enough Packer fans lived within its trade area to make the store profitable. While there are surely enough Packer fans in Wisconsin to support such a retailer, a nonstore location such as a Web site on the Internet would be a more effective way to market to Packers fans worldwide.

Dollars & Sense

Retailers that select markets that are measurable, accessible, and substantial will be able to generate higher profits.

LO 2 Reaching Your Target Market

Identify the different options, both store-based and nonstore-based, for effectively reaching a retailer's target market and identify the advantages and disadvantages of business districts, shopping centers, and freestanding units as sites for retail location.

As noted above, once a retailer identifies its target market, it must identify the most effective way to reach this market. Exhibit 7.2 illustrates the two basic retail formats that can be used to reach target markets: store-based and nonstore-based retailers. **Store-based retailers** operate from a fixed store location that requires that customers travel to the store to view and select merchandise and/or services. Essentially, the retailer requires that the consumer perform part of the transportation function, which is one of the eight marketing functions discussed in Chapter 5. **Nonstore-based retailers** reach the customer at home, at work, or at a place other than a store where they might be open to purchasing. As mentioned earlier, many retailers now reach customers on the Internet.

Exhibit 7.2
Retail Formats for Accessing a Target Market

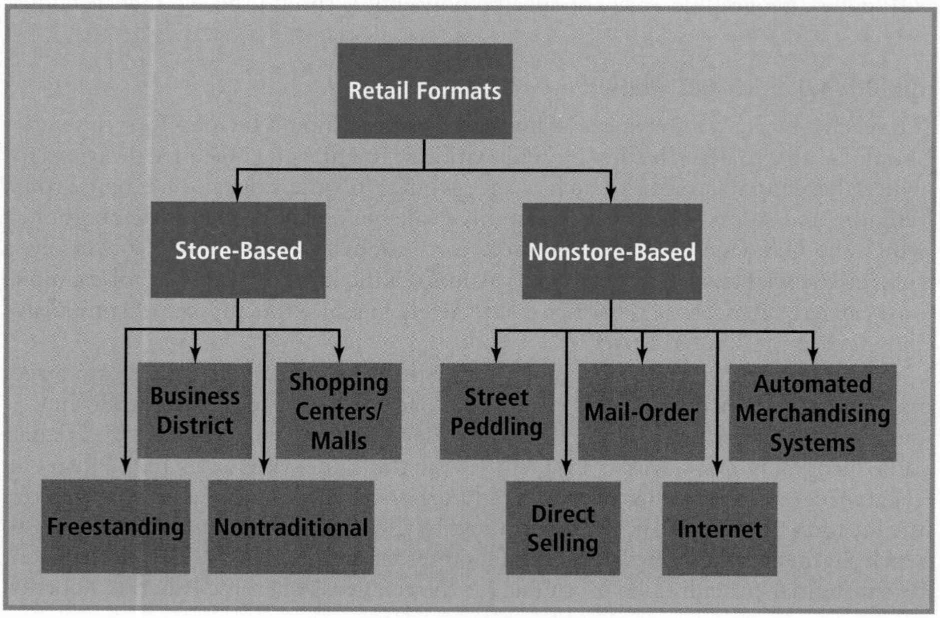

Location of Store-Based Retailers

As shown in Exhibit 7.2, there are four basic types of store-based retail locations: business districts, shopping centers/malls, freestanding units, and nontraditional locations. No one type of location is inherently better than the others. Many retailers, such as McDonald's, have been successful in all four location types. Each type of location has its own characteristics relating to the composition of competing stores, parking facilities, affinities with nonretail businesses (e.g., office buildings, hospitals, universities), and other factors.

store-based retailers
Operate from a fixed store location that requires customers to travel to the store to view and select merchandise or services.

nonstore-based retailers
Intercept customers at home, at work, or at a place other than a store where they might be susceptible to purchasing.

central business district (CBD)
Usually consists of an unplanned shopping area around the geographic point at which all public transportation systems converge; it is usually in the center of the city and often where the city originated historically.

Business Districts

Historically, many retailers were located in the **central business district (CBD)**, usually an unplanned shopping area around the geographic point at which all public transportation systems converge. Many traditional department stores are located in the CBD along with a good selection of specialty shops. The makeup or mix of retailers in a CBD is generally not the result of any advance planning, but depends on history, retail trends, and luck. Recently, traditional department stores have been challenged—on one side by mass merchants, such as Kohl's and Wal-Mart, and category killers, and on the other side by focused specialty retailers. As a result, their market attraction has declined, which in turn has hurt the rest of the CBD. Some communities have tried to reinvigorate their city center by enhancing the shopping experience or using other nonshopping attractions. To date, however, the success of these efforts has been mixed.

However, some towns wish to protect their town center from nonlocal retailers that want to locate there.[2] For example, as of February, 2006, 277 cities were listed on the http://www.sprawl-busters.com Web site as victories.[3] The consumers in these cities believe that the introduction of big-box stores would destroy their

Barnes & Noble not only locates in suburbs but in central business districts such as shown here in Fort Worth, Texas.

Retailing: The Inside Story

Sam Walton's Own Thoughts

One of the most interesting facets of Wal-Mart's expansion strategy can be seen in a letter Sam Walton wrote to Bob Kahn, a member of the Wal-Mart board of directors and a retail consultant, on May 4, 1988. It read:

> Dear Bob,
> I am replying to your letter of the 19th concerning the Wal-Mart monopoly of communities. I have realized for some time and, I suspect, many folks have in the company, as well, how fortunate we are to have very little competition in some of the larger communities in the country. That hasn't always been the case, as you well know. The history of our company has been that we have had more competition early on than almost any regional discounter in the United States. However, one by one, our competitors weakened, were mis-managed, and have fallen out in many of the cities that we practically now have to ourselves. That has been the case generally with Howard's, TG&Y, Gibson, Kuhn's, Magic Mart, and certainly some of the variety chains which were once active in this area. These competitors, plus Alco, Pamida, and the group in Indiana, are on the ropes now and I don't choose to believe those companies disappeared because of our effectiveness. Rather, I choose to believe, for most part, they were mis-managed and, had they been managed well, there could and would have been enough business in their areas for them and for us. That hasn't been the case, as the evidence is now in, *and certainly, we now have a heavy responsibility of taking care of our customers in the best possible way without having the direct competition from a competing discounter in some very sizable markets.* [Italics added].

As the letter indicates, Sam Walton realized the importance of ensuring that the lack of competition would not cause Wal-Mart to lose sight of its objective of being the best it could be. At the same time, Walton wanted to give the consumer fair and honest choices and not have Wal-Mart take advantage of its power.

Today, with Wal-Mart's annual sales exceeding a third of a trillion dollars, its number of employed "associates" approaching 1.7 million, some experts contend the chain has grown too big. Others, however, call it the savior of the economy, as described in Chapter 1.

Source: Letter from Sam Walton to Robert Kahn, May 4, 1988. Used with the permission of the Kahn family.

---

quaint, close-knit downtown business districts that feature coffee shops, boutiques, clothing stores, and maybe even a small department store. This action is not limited to only the United States. Recently when one of the authors was visiting New Zealand, the editorial page and letters to the editor section were devoted to the issue of stopping a Mitre 10 MEGA store in Dunedin.[4] This chapter's Retailing: The Inside Story box illustrates that Sam Walton recognized that Wal-Mart would not be welcome in every city it desired to enter, but once there, it had a responsibility to treat its customers fairly.

The CBD has several strengths and weaknesses. Among its strengths are easy access to public transportation; wide product assortment; variety in images, prices, and services; and proximity to commercial activities. Some weaknesses to consider are inadequate (and usually expensive) parking, older stores, high rents and taxes, traffic and delivery congestion, potentially high crime rate, and the often-decaying conditions of many inner cities. However, despite these disadvantages, The Home Depot joined Best Buy, Toys "R" Us, Burlington Coat Factory, Staples, and The Container Store by deviating from their historical suburban location policies and adapting their formulas to the most urban-of-urban environments—New York City. Despite the high costs and other disadvantages of such locations, the chain felt the high traffic and the more than double their national average in sales per square foot of space, made these locations economically viable.[5]

Often, the weaknesses of CBDs have resulted in a retail situation known as inner-city retailing. This occurs when only the poorest citizens are left in an urban area. Despite the fact that such areas annually contribute two to three percent of all retail spending, product and service offerings in these areas have decreased, while prices have held steady or even increased. Although many consumers are aware that basketball great Magic Johnson has found success opening movie theaters in Harlem as well as in the inner cities of Los Angeles, Cleveland, and Houston, they may not be knowledgeable about the success of other retailers in these urban areas. Retailers such as Dollar-General, Vons, Stop & Shop, Supermarkets General, Jewel/Osco, Kroger, First National Supermarkets, A&P, American Stores, Pathmark, and even service retailers like Sterling Optical have used good merchandise selection and heavy public relations to find success in previously underserved inner-city areas. One of the key reasons for their success in these markets is that they have tailored their inventories to the special needs and tastes of inner-city residents. In addition, these retailers have leveraged an underutilized workforce with high retention in an overall tight labor market.[6]

In larger cities, secondary and neighborhood business districts have developed. A **secondary business district (SBD)** is a shopping area that is smaller than the CBD and revolves around at least one department or variety store at a major street intersection. A **neighborhood business district (NBD)** is a shopping area that evolves to satisfy the convenience-oriented shopping needs of a neighborhood. The NBD generally contains several small stores, with the major retailer being either a supermarket or a variety store, and is located on a major artery of a residential area. An increasing number of national retail chains are finding the neighborhood business district an attractive location for new stores. These chains include retailers such as Ann Taylor, The Body Shop, Starbucks, Crate & Barrel, Williams-Sonoma, Wolf Camera, and Pottery Barn.

secondary business district (SBD)
Is a shopping area that is smaller than the CBD and that revolves around at least one department or variety store at a major street intersection.

neighborhood business district (NBD)
Is a shopping area that evolves to satisfy the convenience-oriented shopping needs of a neighborhood, generally contains several small stores (with the major retailer being a supermarket or a variety store), and is located on a major artery of a residential area.

The single factor that distinguishes these business districts from a shopping center or mall is that they are usually unplanned. Like CBDs, the store mixture of SBDs and NBDs evolves partly by planning, partly by luck, and partly by accident. No one plans, for example, that there will be two department stores, four jewelry stores, two camera shops, three shoe shops, twelve apparel shops, and one theater in an SBD.

Shopping Center/Mall

For nearly a century, America has had a love affair with the shopping center. A **shopping center, or mall**, is a centrally owned and/or managed shopping district that is planned, has balanced tenancy (the stores complement each other in merchandise offerings), and is surrounded by parking facilities. A shopping center has one or more **anchor stores** (dominant large-scale stores that are expected to draw customers to the center) and a variety of smaller stores. In the past these anchors were department stores. However, the recent consolidation of department store companies has reduced the number of stores, either chain or independent, available to serve as the magnets to draw consumers to the center. Today, as a result, many centers are now anchored by a single department store, along with a Cheesecake Factory, Barnes & Noble, and maybe an Embassy Suites or Linens' n Things. In fact, the current retailing move towards entertainment and lifestyle has seen a movement away from the traditional mall or shopping center and towards the lifestyle center concept described in the chapter's What's New box.

shopping center (or mall)
Is a centrally owned or managed shopping district that is planned, has balanced tenancy (the stores complement each other in merchandise offerings), and is surrounded by parking facilities.

anchor stores
Are the stores in a shopping center that are the most dominant and are expected to draw customers to the shopping center.

To ensure that these smaller stores complement each other, the shopping center often specifies the proportion of total space that can be occupied by each

What's New?

Changing the World One Lifestyle Center at a Time!

A Lifestyle Center is a new physical grouping of retailers that is designed to address the needs of today's time-pressed consumer. This new genre emerged earlier this decade and has evolved into a true competitive threat to the traditional enclosed mall. Currently, it is the preferred development vehicle for both developers and retailers.

Lifestyle Centers are open air, as opposed to the traditional enclosed mall, architecturally pleasing shopping and entertainment groupings designed to meet the needs of specific consumers within an edited mix of venues. The targeted consumer is female, between 25 and 55 years of age. She is pressed for time and makes 75percent of the purchasing decisions for her household. She has more reasons to dislike the mall experience than to like it. This consumer seeks out a lifestyle center because it addresses her desire for a safe and, most importantly, convenient shopping and entertainment environment that she can identify with.

Architecture is a key component to the Lifestyle Center development process. Reminiscent of the old "town square" or "Main Street" look—stores and restaurant facades bear a resemblance to an earlier, simpler period of time in American history. Adding to the ambience are a plethora of fountains, public gathering areas, beautiful landscaping, and street-side entertainment. Music is piped in to add the final touch of atmosphere—all of which is presented in a less confined venue than the traditional center court of any local mall.

Competitively, it is most important for the Lifestyle Center to exude convenience. Historically, enclosed regional malls required large parcels of ground and would typically locate at the edge of the suburbs next to larger commercial parcels of land, which were still available for sale. The Lifestyle Center takes a completely different approach, seeking to locate close to where the consumer lives. The amount of land needed to develop a Lifestyle Center is generally only 35-50 acres, thus making Lifestyle Centers a great opportunity for redevelopment of deteriorating areas that are located adjacent to older, more established and affluent consumer neighborhoods. Often times Lifestyle Centers are located within 2 to 5 miles of the highest percentage of wealth in their particular market. Designed with abundant parking that is partially located directly in front of the shops or restaurants, the convenience factor is realized when the consumer can leave their home and be inside the desired store within minutes. Contrast that pleasant scenario with the regimen of the anxiety-producing mall trip. The consumer leaves the house dreading the highway drive to the mall, searching for a parking spot in the parking garages, followed by a long and winding walk through a department store where she is unable to avoid the perfume counter which aggravates her allergies, through the food court with its masses of unsupervised teenagers, and, finally (!), 20 minutes later to her store—clearly, not convenient.

The venue of the Lifestyle Center has two required components: (1) the name-brand appeal of specialty retail shops and (2) high volume, experienced-based, customer service-oriented dining. Attractive components that can be added, based on the market and the needs of the consumer, include a department store or two, a movie theater, or other niche anchors specializing in categories such as home furnishings, gourmet groceries, pet care supplies, beauty salons and spas, shoes, and sporting goods. The common denominator of these components is that they are all, individually, desired destinations that target the affluent female shopper. Together this "varsity team" line-up and combination of smaller niche tenants creates a Lifestyle Center with approximately 70 tenants. (Traditional malls can have over 200 tenants.)

A successful recipe for a Lifestyle Center would be one anchored by Bed Bath & Beyond, Wild Oats or Whole Foods Grocery, DSW Shoes, and Dick's Sporting Goods. The surrounding streetscape would consist of Pottery Barn, Williams-Sonoma, PetSmart, Banana Republic, Talbot's, Chico's, Coldwater Creek, Ann Taylor Loft, Gymboree, and a central outdoor parking area that features a variety of sit-down restaurants such as PF Chang's, Brio Restaurant, and J. Alexander's, topped off with a great steakhouse. Sprinkle the rest of the center with accessory stores, fast "casual" dining, various children's stores, and jewelers, and you've created just the right mixture of the most sought-after retailers and eateries for your target consumer. You've made your Lifestyle Center a place for one-stop shopping and leisure activities—eliminating any reason for her (your customer) to go to the mall other then to drop off her teenager.

The eclectic mix of tenancy, the sense of place, and the safety and convenience of parking gives more than a competitive edge. It provides a great reason for traditional mall developers, who up until a few years ago argued that Lifestyle

What's New (*continued*)

Centers were an "unproven passing fad," to change their attitude and restructure their existing properties in an attempt to compete with the now proven entity, the Lifestyle Center.

With fewer than 200 Lifestyle Centers open and operating across the country in diverse communities, research on their success is still limited. One study found that Lifestyle Center shoppers typically spend 57 minutes per visit as compared to 78 minutes at a mall. They visit, on average, once a week, and their median household income is $85,000, almost double that of the national median.

Retailers have found that sales per square foot are nearly 25 percent higher at Lifestyle Centers than at traditional malls. We should expect a huge push in development of this category and a resulting pull back from traditional mall development.

Source: This box was prepared by Mark Fallon, vice president of real estate, Jeffrey R. Anderson Real Estate, Inc., Cincinnati.

©Jeff Greenberg/PhotoEdit

Lifestyle Centers are expected to experience rapid growth over the next decade.

type of retailer. Similarly, the center's management places limits on the merchandise lines that each retailer may carry. For example, several years ago Old Navy's now-defunct Torpedo Factory, which sold coffee and submarine sandwiches, wanted to locate in a center with a Starbucks. However, Starbucks had a coffee exclusive that prevented Torpedo Factory's entry.[7] In addition, all the retailers in the center follow a unified, cooperative advertising and promotional strategy. Because of the many advantages shopping centers/malls can offer the retailer, they are a fixture of American life and account for 55 percent of all retail sales in the United States. Some of the advantages a shopping center offers over a CBD location are:

1. Heavy traffic resulting from the wide range of product offerings
2. Cooperative planning and sharing of common costs

3. Access to highways and availability of parking
4. Lower crime rate
5. Clean, neat environment

Despite these favorable reasons for locating in a shopping center, the retailer operating in a mall does face several disadvantages:

1. Inflexible store hours (the retailer must stay open during mall hours and cannot be open at other times)
2. High rents
3. Restrictions as to what merchandise the retailer may sell
4. Inflexible operations and required membership in the center's merchant organization
5. Possibility of too much competition and the fact that much of the traffic is not interested in a particular product offering
6. An anchor tenant's dominance of the smaller stores

Shopping center image, preferences, and personality all attract various subsets of consumers, giving retailers located at a center a competitive advantage over other retailers. Therefore, it is extremely important that a retailer considering a shopping center location be aware of the makeup, image, preferences, and personality of the center under question. For example, the open-air Rookwood Commons and Pavillion in Cincinnati developed a whole new trade area for retailers. Prior to its development in the economically depressed area of Norwood, retailers located either in downtown Cincinnati or in the more distant suburbs.

Courtesy of Jeffrey R. Anderson Real Estate, Inc.

Type	Concept	Sq. Ft. Incl. Anchors	Acreage	Number of Anchors	Typical Anchor(s) Type	Anchor Ratio*	Primary Trade Area**
Neighborhood Center	Convenience	30,000–150,000	3–15	1 or more	Supermarket	30%–50%	3 miles
Community Center	General merchandise; convenience	100,000–350,000	10–40	2 or more	Discount dept. store; supermarket; drug; home improvement; large specialty/discount apparel	40%–60%	3–6 miles
Regional Center	General merchandise; fashion (mall, typically enclosed)	400,000–800,000	40–100	2 or more	Full-line dept. store; jr. dept. store; mass merchant; disc. dept. store; fashion apparel	50%–70%	5–15 miles
Superregional Center	Similar to regional center but has more variety and assortment	800,000	60–120	3 or more	Full-line dept. store; jr. dept. store; mass merchant; fashion apparel	50%–70%	5–25 miles
Fashion/Specialty Center	Higher-end, fashion-oriented	80,000–250,000	5–25	N/A	Fashion	N/A	5–15 miles
Power Center	Category-dominant anchors; few small tenants	250,000–600,000	25–80	3 or more	Category killer; home improvement; discount dept. store; warehouse club; off-price	75%–90%	5–10 miles
Theme/Festival Center	Leisure; tourist-oriented; retail and service	80,000–250,000	5–20	N/A	Restaurants, entertainment	N/A	N/A
Outlet Center	Manufacturers' outlet stores	50,000–400,000	10–50	N/A	Manufacturers' outlet stores	N/A	25–75 miles
Lifestyle Center	Open-air configuration	150,000–500,000	10–40	1 or more	Upscale department store	N/A	5–10 miles

* The share of a center's total square footage that is attributable to its anchors

** The area from which 60%–80% of the center's sales originate

Source: Used with the permission of the International Council of Shopping Centers

Exhibit 7.3
ISCS Shopping Center Definitions

As Exhibit 7.3 shows, according to the International Council of Shopping Centers, there are nine different types of shopping centers/malls, each with a distinctive function.

Shopping centers and malls now account for one-half of all retail sales, excluding automotive, in the United States. Seniors engage in their daily exercise, families find malls a good source of low-cost entertainment, and teens use them as social outlets. In many cases the loyalties of shoppers toward a specific center or mall have, over time, become equal to or greater than their loyalties to a particular retailer. While shopping centers and malls have become a fixture of American social and economic life and are popular locations for retailers, they haven't reached that status in all developed countries. The chapter's Global Retailing box indicates that despite their overwhelming success in much of the world, malls are just now entering the Moscow market.

Global Retailing

Moscow Is Beginning Its Love Affair with the Mall

Malls in many European countries are experiencing the pains of being in mature markets similar to those in America. However, privatized (non-government owned) Western-style shopping centers and malls are a recent addition to the Moscow retail scene.

Retail Forward places Russia just behind China as the next big frontier for retail development. After all, with an economy closely tied to higher global oil prices, an increasing level of political stability, a rising level of disposable income, and a rapidly growing middle class, Russia, and particularly Moscow, may be one of the last undeveloped but attractive markets remaining. The fact that Russia is ranked by Retail Forward as the world's third most attractive market for apparel retailers is indication of the need for future mall development. In addition, the fact that the country's gross domestic product has been growing by 7 percent over the past half decade highlights the urgency of the issue. Furthermore, dollar income per capita has risen by nearly 29 percent annually over the same period, a much faster rate than China's. In addition, *Business Week* reports that 70 percent of a Russians' income is disposable, versus around 40 percent for a typical Western consumer. (Russians pay a 13 percent flat income tax, are offered subsidized housing and utilities, and save 10 percent of their income. Thus the majority of their earnings are available for spending.) Little wonder, then, that the world's most frequented shopping center, with 52 million visitors annually, is Moscow's new Mega-1 mall. This mall, which opened in December 2002, features a French-owned Auchan hypermarket, an IKEA from Sweden, and dozens of boutiques selling everything from Yves Rocher cosmetics to Calvin Klein underwear.

Still, Moscow has a long way to go before it catches up to the retail supply levels of neighboring countries. At the beginning of the 21st century, Moscow had only about 15 percent of the mall selling space per capita of that in Western Europe and less than 10 percent of that in the United States. The opportunities for retail shopping development in Russia are even better outside of Moscow. The country has 13 other cities with populations over 1 million, but only six have a modern shopping center. However, the lack of modern malls has not limited the Russian consumers' knowledge of international brands. Russians know and desire such merchandise. Moscow, however, is the only city with western retail franchise stores. These include Adidas, Baskin-Robbins, Benetton, Tommy Hilfiger, IKEA, Levi Strauss, Mothercare, Nike, Promodes, Reebok, and Swatch. There are even "wild" rumors that despite denials, Wal-Mart is looking into the Russian market.

Experts agree that Moscow is one of the most promising retail markets from Tokyo to Europe. It has Europe's largest concentration of people, 8.5 million (some estimates put this number over 10 million) compared to London's 7 million, and its residents, besides being willing and able to spend money, are quick to adapt to Western-style products. Annual beer consumption, for example, has increased from 15 liters per person to 60 liters over the past decade. Between 2000 and 2005, mobile-phone ownership jumped from 3 million users to 80 million.

The primary factor that is limiting further American expansion into Russia continues to be the negative images of Russia presented by the media. While American chains, such as Abercrombie & Fitch, Old Navy, The Gap, The Limited, and Foot Locker would be welcomed in Russia, that will not happen until the American retailer's perception of Russia as an unfavorable place to do business changes. The government must prove its ability to guarantee to investors that Russia is politically, logistically, and socially a safe place to invest and that corruption and lawlessness are things of the past.

Source: *Retailing in China*, an industry outlook report published by Retail Forward in January 2006; "Shoppers Gone Wild," *Business Week*, February 20, 2006: 46–47; "When Will Wal-Mart Say *da* to Russia?" *Shopping Centers Today*, May 2005, 112; Linda Good, Patricia Huddleston, and Leslie Stoel, "Retailing in the New Russia," *Discount Merchandiser*, April 1995: 58–61; and information supplied by former students from Russia.

---

freestanding retailer
Generally locates along major traffic arteries and does not have any adjacent retailers to share traffic.

Freestanding Location

Another location option is to be freestanding. A **freestanding retailer** generally locates along major traffic arteries without any adjacent retailers selling competing products to share traffic. Freestanding retailing offers several advantages:

1. Lack of direct competition

2. Generally lower rents
3. Freedom in operations and hours
4. Facilities that can be adapted to individual needs
5. Inexpensive parking

Freestanding retailing does have some limitations:

1. Lack of drawing power of complementary stores
2. Difficulties in attracting customers for the initial visit
3. Higher advertising and promotional costs
4. Operating costs that cannot be shared with others
5. Stores that may have to be built rather than rented
6. Zoning laws that may restrict some activities

The difficulties of drawing, and then holding, customers to an isolated or freestanding store is the reason that only large, well-known retailers should attempt it. Small retailers may be unable to develop a loyal customer base since customers are often unwilling to travel to a freestanding store that does not have a wide assortment of products and a local or national reputation. Discounters and wholesale clubs, with their large selections, are most often thought of when discussing this location strategy. When these large national chains acquire land for a freestanding store, they are seeking to acquire land in areas in which they expect the community will grow in the future. As a result, they often acquire more than they need and then "out-parcel" (i.e., sell) the remaining land to smaller retailers. Some astute local retailers and small regional chains have found it quite attractive to buy this excess land and build stores, even at a premium price, because of the traffic a large discounter like Wal-Mart generates. Many convenience stores and gasoline stations, due to the nature of their product offerings, have been able to use the freestanding location strategy successfully in the past.

Nontraditional Locations

Increasingly, retailers are identifying nontraditional locations that offer greater convenience. Recognizing, for example, that a significant number of travelers spend several hours in airports (especially since 9/11/2001) and can use this time to purchase merchandise they might otherwise purchase in their local communities, many airport concourses now look like real regional malls, complete with national brands, casual dining, service kiosks, and entertainment-infotainment venues. There are even pâté sandwiches at Philadelphia International Airport, a winery in Dallas/Fort Worth International Airport, a Gallagher's Steak House in Newark, and a couple of offbeat bars (of the oxygen and sushi variety) to belly up to at the not-so-blue-collar Detroit Metropolitan Wayne County Airport.[8]

Retailers that seek to develop stores in nontraditional locations will enhance their opportunities for achieving high profits.

Dollars & Sense

On college campuses there are increasing numbers of food courts in student unions and cosmetic counters in campus bookstores. Truck and travel stops along interstate highways are incorporating food courts. Some franchises, such as Taco

Roslan Rahman/AFP/Getty Images

The concourses of large airports have become popular shopping centers for many frequent travelers that spend a lot of time waiting in airports.

Bell and Dunkin' Donuts, are putting small food service units in convenience stores, university libraries, and classroom buildings. Embassy Suites, a Hilton Hotels chain, saw an opportunity to offer guests additional entertainment, dining, and shopping amenities and, as a result, built new units in shopping centers.[9] Hospitals are building emergency-care clinics near where people live in the suburbs and away from the hospital, lawyers are opening storefront offices wherever there is high pedestrian traffic, and dry cleaners and copying services are locating in major office buildings. Today, some Wells Fargo banks have mini-marketplaces featuring Starbucks coffee bars, dry cleaners, delis, and postal centers. Other banks have opened branch offices in retirement centers.

Some service retailers are an exception, however, since their products are delivered to consumers at home. For example, plumbers, house painters, repair services, maid services, carpet cleaners, and lawn-care firms may not be concerned with their location. Enterprise Rent-A-Car will even deliver your rental car to you.

Nonstore-Based Retailers

There is a great diversity and variety of nonstore-based retailers. Perhaps the oldest form is the street peddler who sells merchandise from a pushcart or temporary stall set up on a street. Street peddling is still common in some parts of the world such as Mexico, Turkey, Pakistan, India, and many parts of Africa and South America. But it is also seen in this country in such places as New York City and San Francisco, where street-corner vendors sell T-shirts, watches, books, magazines, tobacco, candy, hot dogs, and other products. Peddlers also operate in many other United States cities, oftentimes using family members to operate kiosks and carts in heavily traveled areas, such as malls and the parking lots at sporting events. These "mom & pop" retailers are supplied both by manufacturers and by franchisors.[10]

In Chapter 4, "Evaluating the Competition in Retailing," we discussed several popular forms of nonstore retailing which are depicted in Exhibit 7.2 on page 208 (direct sellers, catalog sales, and e-tailing). Because retailing in the United States for the next 20 years and perhaps beyond will continue to be predominantly store-based, we will focus our attention on location analysis for these retailers. However, note that some innovative retailers are using multiple retail formats to reach their target markets. For example, JCPenney not only continues to build and remodel traditional stores but also has extensive mail and online operations where different catalogs are developed to target specific customer segments. In fact, most experts predict that over the next few years virtually every traditional store-based retailer will have developed multiple retail formats to reach its target market(s). Interestingly, while catalog sales have dropped slightly for these retailers, online sales have shown tremendous growth. Experts feel that this is the natural outgrowth of consumers searching for merchandise in stores and in catalogs, but ordering online at their convenience. However, although consumers are increasing their online shopping, Consumer WebWatch states that only 29 percent of users making a purchase from an online only retailer actually trust the sites. They feel much safer purchasing from sites run by conventional bricks & mortar retailers.[11] Even widely used online operators, (refer to the eBay discussion in the What's New box on page 180 in Chapter 6) must constantly address this consumer confidence issue.

Retailers who understand the need for multiple retail formats to reach their target market will be the star profit performers of the next decade.

Dollars & Sense

Geographic Information Systems

LO 3

Define geographic information systems (GIS) and discuss their potential uses in a retail enterprise.

One recent technological innovation in retailing is geographic information systems. A **geographic information system (GIS)** is a computerized system that combines physical geography with cultural geography. Physical geography is the latitude (north/south) and longitude (east/west) of a specific point in physical space and its related physical characteristics (water, land, temperature, annual rainfall, etc.). Cultural geography consists of the things that people have put in place in that space. To understand this one needs to appreciate that **culture** is the buffer that humankind has created between itself and the raw physical environment. It includes characteristics of the population such as age, gender, and income and man-made objects placed in that space, such as fixed physical structures (factories, stores, apartment buildings, schools, churches, houses, highways, railroads, airports, etc.) and mobile physical structures (e.g., cars and trucks). In reality, culture includes anything that humans can put onto a physical space, which then becomes an attribute of the physical space. For example, Scottsdale, Arizona, has become known for its very high density of golf courses, but these golf courses were put there by people, not by nature. Other areas are known as high-crime areas, but nature did not put crime there, people did. Recent advancements in GIS have allowed the retail analyst to also describe the lifestyle (activities, interests, opinions) of the residents of geographic areas. This can be quite helpful in selecting locations for stores that are highly lifestyle sensitive, such as Pittsburgh-based Dick's Sporting Goods, Inc. Dick's is a category killer in the sporting goods area, with over 255 stores in 34 states. Executives speaking at an ICSC (International Council of Shopping Centers) Research Conference noted that with increased user-friendliness of GIS mapping technology, they have become more research driven in locating stores. They no longer have to rely on real estate brokers to supply information that

geographic information system (GIS)
Is a computerized system that combines physical geography with cultural geography.

culture
Is the buffer that people have created between themselves and the raw physical environment and includes the characteristics of the population, humanly created objects, and mobile physical structures.

Exhibit 7.4
GIS Components

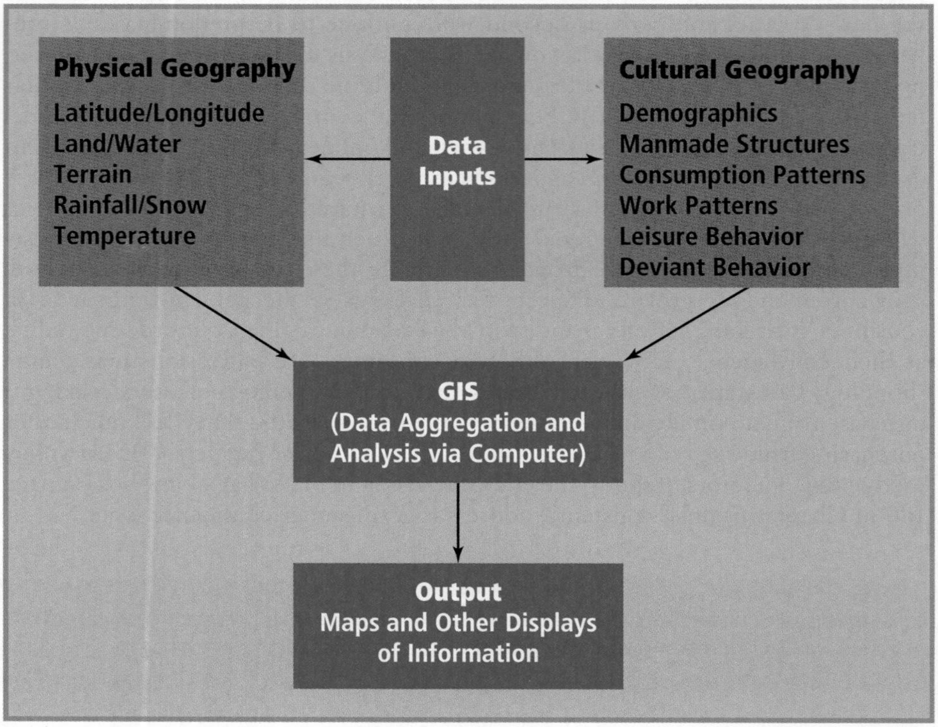

may or may not be relevant to their business, such as the fact that the supermarket across the street is doing $30 million in sales annually.[12] Exhibit 7.4 shows the key components of geographic information systems.

Thematic Maps

Historically, it was not unusual for a retailer to push pins into a map of a city where it was located. Each pin represented where a customer lived. An even more sophisticated retailer might have colored the map to represent different areas of the city in terms of income levels or ethnic composition. This was an early form of thematic mapping. **Thematic maps** are area maps that use visual techniques such as colors, shading, lines, and so on to display cultural characteristics of the physical space. Thematic maps can be very useful management tools for retailers. They can help the retailer visualize a tremendous amount of information in an easy-to-understand format. Today, thematic maps are an important feature of geographic information systems and are fully computerized, making them easy for retailers to develop.

thematic maps
Use visual techniques such as colors, shading, and lines to display cultural characteristics of the physical space.

Uses of GIS

As a management technology, GIS has a variety of important uses in retailing. Some of the more popular uses are identified as follows.

1. *Market selection*. A retailer with a set of criteria in mind, such as the demographics of its target market and the level of over- or understoring in a market, can have the GIS identify and rank the most attractive cities, counties, or other geographic areas to consider for expansion.

2. *Site analysis*. If a retailer has a particular community in mind, a GIS can identify the best possible site or evaluate alternative sites for their expected profitability.
3. *Trade area definition*. If the retailer develops a database of where its customers reside, a GIS can automatically develop a trade area map and update this daily, weekly, monthly, or annually.
4. *New store cannibalization*. A GIS can help the retailer evaluate how the addition of another store in a community might cannibalize sales from its existing store(s).
5. *Advertising management*. A GIS can help the retailer allocate its advertising budget to different stores based on the market potential in their respective trade areas. Similarly, a GIS can help the retailer develop a more effective direct-mail campaign to prospective customers.
6. *Merchandise management*. A GIS can help the retailer develop an optimal mix of merchandise based on the characteristics of households and individuals within its trade area.
7. *Evaluation of store managers*. A GIS can provide an important human resource function. It can help assess how well a store manager is performing based on the trade area characteristics. Consider that two stores of the same size could be performing quite differently because of the demographics and competitive conditions in the two trade areas. Thus it would be inappropriate to either reward or punish a manager for things over which the manager has no control.

Retailers that use GIS technology are able to improve their store profitability.

Dollars & Sense

Although most large retailers are using a combination of mapping and demographics to create a basic site-selection process, many small to medium-sized retailers are not using GIS technology to its full advantage. This may be due to the lack of technical expertise in using complicated software. If a program isn't easy, many firms won't use it. Visualization of these maps is improving, but it isn't possible to make a perfect model of the world. A mall, for example, has to have anchors that draw traffic for the other stores. As soon as an anchor leaves, the economics of the GIS model are changed. This is happening with more frequency today as the consolidation of department store chains and mall saturation has caused malls to seek a new type of anchor. Not only are Circuit Cities and Best Buys now anchoring regional malls, as discussed earlier in this chapter, but so are Linens'n Things and hotels.

Market Identification

LO 4

What factors should be considered in identifying the most attractive retail market?

The location decision for store-based retailers involves three sequential steps. First, the retailer must identify the most attractive markets in which to operate. Some retailers, such as Carrefour, The Home Depot, Wal-Mart, and Benetton, are international, and thus when they think of adding new locations, they consider the attractiveness of geographic expansion into foreign countries. Perhaps the most global of all retailers is McDonald's, which currently operates in over 100 countries.[13] Over the last decade retailers such as Pier 1 and Sharper Image have identified Mexico as an attractive market for expansion. However, most retail analysts contend that China,

AP Photo/Eugene Hoshiko

Retail analysts view China as the most lucrative growth market for retailers over the next two decades.

with the world's third-largest consumer market (the United States and Japan are larger) is the most lucrative market in the early 21st century. China has the world's largest population. Its economy is expected to exceed 10 percent annual growth heading into the 2008 Olympics. Furthermore, growth in China's technological infrastructure has been matching its economic growth. Already U.S. retailers such as Amazom.com, Amway, and Wal-Mart (which is the country's 19th largest retailer) have entered China with aggressive expansion plans.[14]

On the other hand, many retailers such as County Seat Jeans, Kohl's, and Kroger, as well as most smaller merchants, concentrate on the United States, and when considering new locations they evaluate the attractiveness of domestic markets only. Still other retailers concentrate on a small region of the United States, possibly a single state or city.

The second step in the retail location decision is to evaluate the density of demand and supply within each market and identify the most attractive sites that are available within each market. Essentially, this means identifying the sites most consistent with the retailer's target market and then identifying those for which the market is not already overstored or in which competition is not overly intense.

The third step is selecting the best site (or sites) available. This stage involves estimating the revenue and expenses of a new store at various locations and then identifying the most profitable new locations. These three steps are illustrated in Exhibit 7.5.

trading area
Is the geographic area from which a retailer, or group of retailers, or community draws its customers.

As stated earlier, the first step in making a good retail location decision is to identify the most attractive market or **trading area**—the geographic area from which a retailer, group of retailers, or community draws its customers—in which the retailer could locate. For instance, Dollar General, which only recently has been entering larger cities, had been very successful in the past by concentrating its expansion in small towns (generally those with populations under 10,000), which have less competition, easier zoning and building regulations, and lower wages and operating costs.

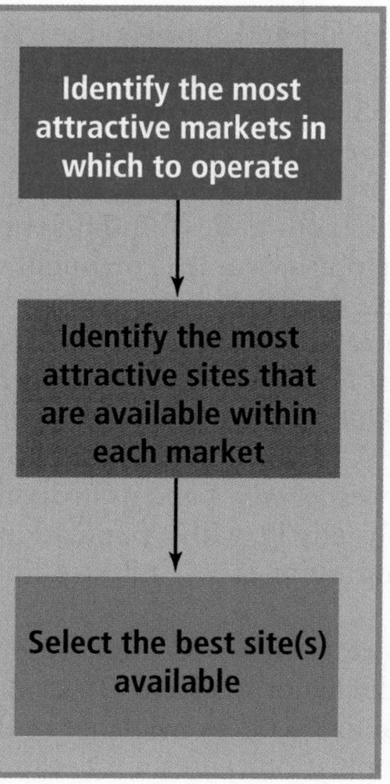

Exhibit 7.5
Selecting a Retail Location

Retail Location Theories

The most attractive retail markets are not necessarily the largest. A variety of other factors need to be considered in identifying attractive markets. To start, three methods are especially useful for identifying the best markets.

Retail Gravity Theory

Retail gravity theory suggests that there are underlying consistencies in shopping behavior that would yield to mathematical analysis and prediction based on the notion or concept of gravity. **Reilly's law of retail gravitation,**[15] named after its developer, William Reilly, dealt with how large urbanized areas attracted customers from smaller communities. In effect, it stated that two cities attract trade from an intermediate location approximately in direct proportion to the population of the two cities and in inverse proportion to the square of the distance from these two cities to the intermediate place. That is, people will tend to shop in the larger city if travel distance is equal, or even somewhat farther, because they believe that the larger city has a better product selection and will be worth the extra travel.

retail gravity theory
Suggests that there are underlying consistencies in shopping behavior that yield to mathematical analysis and prediction based on the notion or concept of gravity.

Reilly's law of retail gravitation
Based on Newtonian gravitational principles, explains how large urbanized areas attract customers from smaller rural communities.

Two decades later, Reilly's original law was revised in order to determine the boundaries of a city's trading area or to establish a point of indifference between two cities.[16] This **point of indifference** is the breaking point at which customers would be indifferent to shopping at either city. The new formulation of Reilly's law can be expressed algebraically as:

$$D_{ab} = \frac{d}{1 + \sqrt{\frac{P_b}{P_a}}}$$

where D_{ab} is the breaking point from A, measured in miles along the road to B;
d is the distance between A and B along the major highway;
P_a is the population of A; and
P_b is the population of B.

point of indifference
Is the extremity of a city's trading area where households would be indifferent between shopping in that city or in an alternative city in a different geographical direction.

For example, if Levelland and Norwood are 65 miles apart and Levelland's population is 100,000 and Norwood's is 200,000, then the breaking point of indifference between Levelland and Norwood would be 26.9 miles from Levelland and 38.1 miles from Norwood. This means that if you lived 25 miles from Levelland and 40 miles from Norwood, you probably would choose to shop in Levelland since it is within your zone of indifference for Levelland and is beyond your zone of indifference for Norwood. (You might want to figure this out yourself, using Norwood as A and Levelland as B.)

Exhibit 7.6 shows how Reilly's law can be used to determine a community's trading area. As shown in Exhibit 7.6, city A has a population of 240,000. City B, with a population of 14,000, is 18 miles north of A and its breaking point is 14.5 miles north of City A (point X on Exhibit 7.6). City C, with a population of 21,000, is 14 miles southwest of city A and its breaking point is 10.8 miles southwest of city A (point Z). Finally, city D, with a population of 30,000, is 5 miles southeast of city A and its breaking point is 3.7 miles southeast of city A (point Y on the diagram).

Retail gravity theory rests on two assumptions: (1) the two competing cities are equally accessible from the major road and (2) population is a good indicator of the differences in the goods and services available in different cities. Consumers are attracted to the larger population center not because of the city's size, but because of the larger number of stores and wider product assortment available, thereby making the increased travel time worthwhile. However, in its simplicity, retail

Exhibit 7.6
Trading Area for City A

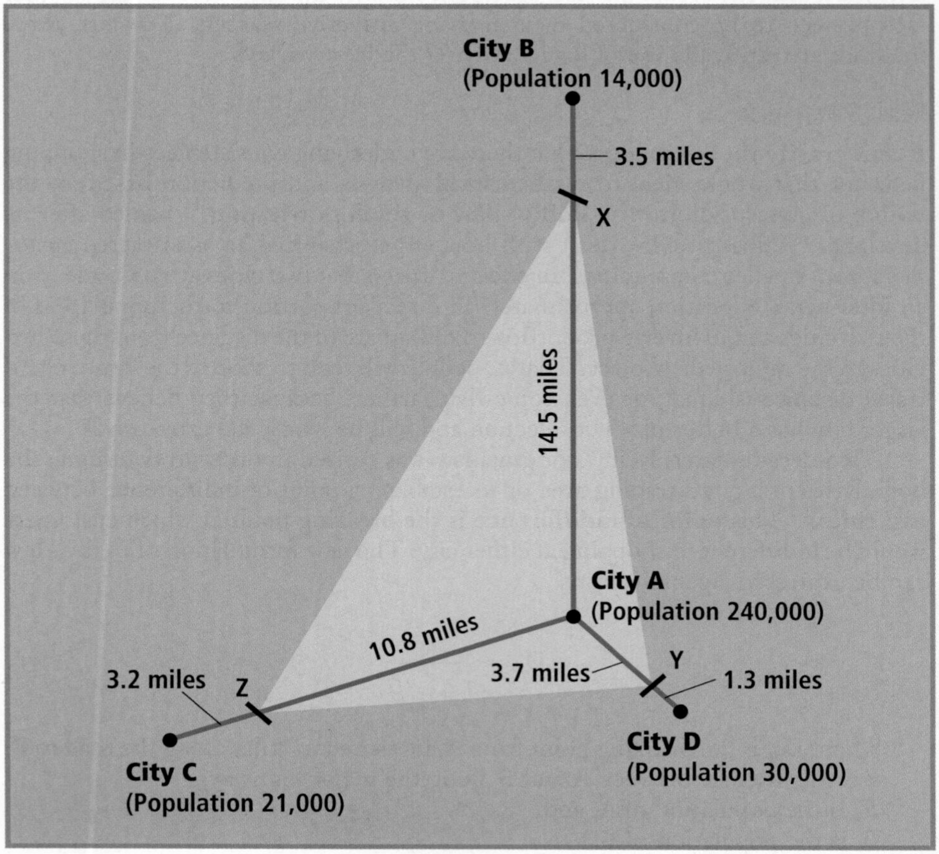

gravity theory does have several limitations. First, city population does not always reflect the available shopping facilities. For example, two neighboring cities, each with a population of 20,000 and similar demographics, would not be reflected equally if one of the cities had a shopping center with Target as the anchor store and the other did not. Second, distance is measured in miles, not the time involved for the consumer to travel that distance or the consumer's perception of that distance or time involved. Given our present highway system, this limitation is extremely important. Traveling 20 miles on an interstate highway to a mall located at an exit may be easier than the stop-and-start travel involved in going six miles through downtown traffic. Therefore, some retailers will substitute travel time for mileage. Finally, while the theory works reasonably well in rural areas, where distance is a major decision factor, it is not flawless.

Research on **outshopping**—that is, leaving your community to shop—from rural areas suggests that factors other than those considered by retail gravity theory are important. For example, several years ago when Canada enacted high sales taxes, the 70 percent of Canadians living near the border began to shop in the United States. As a result, the Canadian government was forced to repeal the tax. Americans are great outshoppers, as described in Chapter 5's Global Retailing box, on page 158, discussed how American college students purchase textbooks from European online retailers. Purchasing merchandise online is probably the most common form of outshopping for most Americans. As mentioned in Chapter 6, this results in states losing $33 billion in lost sales taxes.[17]

outshopping
Outshopping occurs when a household leaves their community of residence to shop in another community; it usually occurs when people leave a smaller community to shop in a larger community.

Some other factors that the retail gravity theory fails to consider include perceived differences between local and other trading centers, variety-seeking behavior, and other services provided, including medical services and/or entertainment facilities. Also, gravity theory is less useful in metropolitan areas where consumers typically have a number of shopping choices available within the maximum distance they are willing to travel.

Saturation Theory

Another method for identifying attractive potential markets is based on retail saturation, which examines how the demand for goods and services in a potential trading area is being served by current retail establishments in comparison with other potential markets. Such analysis produces three possible outcomes:

1. **Retail store saturation** is a condition under which existing store facilities are utilized efficiently and meet customer needs. Retail saturation exists when a market has just enough store facilities for a given type of store to serve the population of the market satisfactorily and yield a fair profit to the owners.
2. When a market has too few stores to satisfactorily meet the needs of the customer, it is **understored**. In this setting average store profitability is quite high.
3. When a market has too many stores to yield a fair return on investment, it is **overstored**.

retail store saturation
Is a condition where there are just enough store facilities for a given type of store to efficiently and satisfactorily serve the population and yield a fair profit to the owners.

understored
Is a condition in a community where the number of stores in relation to households is relatively low so that engaging in retailing is an attractive economic endeavor.

overstored
Is a condition in a community where the number of stores in relation to households is so large that engaging in retailing is usually unprofitable or marginally profitable.

Saturation theory, therefore, implies a balance between the number of existing retail store facilities (supply) and their use (demand). As indicated in Chapter 4, one typically measures saturation, overstoring, and understoring in terms of the number of stores per thousand households. The consensus among retail location experts is that the United States is currently highly saturated or overstored with retail establishments, and thus retailers are taking a second look at some long-ignored markets such as older downtown areas.

index of retail saturation (IRS)
Is the ratio of demand for a product (households in the geographic area multiplied by annual retail expenditures for a particular line of trade per household) divided by available supply (the square footage of retail facilities of a particular line of trade in the geographic area).

A possible indicator of understored versus overstored markets is the **index of retail saturation (IRS)**,[18] which is the ratio of demand for a product or service divided by available supply. The IRS can be measured as follows:

$$IRS = (H \times RE)/RF$$

where IRS is the index of retail saturation for an area; H is the number of households in the area; RE is the annual retail expenditures for a particular line of trade per household in the area; and RF is the square footage of retail facilities of a particular line of trade in the area (including square footage of the proposed store). If you multiply the two terms in the numerator together (households and retail expenditures per household), you obtain dollar sales. Recalling that the denominator is square footage of retail space, it is easy to see that the IRS is essentially the sales per square foot of retail space in the marketplace for a particular line of retail trade.

Dollars & Sense

Retailers who identify and locate in markets where the index of retail saturation is high will be able to achieve a higher profit.

When the IRS takes on a high value in comparison with the line of trade in other cities, it indicates that the market is understored, and therefore a potentially attractive opportunity exists. When it takes on a low value, it indicates an overstored market, which precludes the potential of a significant opportunity. The Home Depot, for example, monitors its sales per square foot for a store because it recognizes that if this ratio is too high, customers may not be well served and competition may be invited into the market. In fact, if sales per square foot are over \$400, it believes it is advantageous to close a thriving store and open two smaller stores. Although this cannibalizes the existing store, it better serves customers and discourages competition from entering the market.[19]

As an example of how the index of retail saturation is used, consider an individual planning to open a dry cleaner in either city A or city B. This individual has the following information: Residents of both cities spend \$12.56 per month on dry cleaning. The total number of households in both cities is also the same—17,000. City A, however, has 2,000 square feet of dry-cleaning facilities, and city B has 2,500 square feet; and our proposed square footage is 500 square feet. Given this information and using our formula for IRS, we can find the IRS for each city:

$$IRS\ (City\ A) = (17{,}000 \times 12.56)/(2{,}000 + 500) = 85.41$$
$$IRS\ (City\ B) = (17{,}000 \times 12.56)/(2{,}500 + 500) = 71.17$$

Thus, based solely on these two factors of demand (number of households and average expenditure for products by each household) and one factor of supply (the square footage of retail space serving this demand), the individual would choose to locate in city A, since its value of \$85.41 is higher than city B's \$71.17.

As nonstore-based retailing continues to grow, retailers need to recognize that the index of retail saturation may become less useful. That is because it incorporates only store-based retailing in the supply component of the index. This is not a problem in the preceding dry cleaner example, but it may be a problem for apparel retailers and computer retailers because many households use mail-order catalogs and e-tailers.

Buying Power Index

Sales & Marketing Management magazine annually publishes the Survey of Buying Power. This survey reports on current data for metropolitan areas, cities, and states. It provides some data that are not readily available from other sources such as the Census Bureau. These data include retail sales by specific merchandise categories, effective buying income, and total retail sales by area, and population.

The population, retail sales, and buying income data provide the retail manager with an overview of the potential of various trading areas. By comparing one trading area to another, the retailer can develop a relative measure of each market's potential. For each area, the retailer can develop a **buying power index (BPI)**, which is a single weighted measure combining effective buying income (personal income, including all nontax payments such as social security, minus all taxes), retail sales, and population size into an overall indicator of a market's potential. Generally, business firms use a formula for BPI that was developed by *Sales & Marketing Management*. The BPI is weighted in the following manner:

buying power index (BPI)
Is an indicator of a market's overall retail potential and is composed of weighted measures of effective buying income (personal income, including all nontax payments such as social security, minus all taxes), retail sales, and population size.

$$\begin{aligned} \text{BPI} = {} & 0.5(\text{the area's percentage of U.S. effective buying income}) \\ & + 0.3(\text{the area's percentage of U.S. retail sales}) \\ & + 0.2(\text{the area's percentage of U.S. population}) \end{aligned}$$

It is obvious that effective buying income is the most important factor, followed by retail sales and population. This formula can be further refined by breaking down these general figures into more specific figures geared toward the consumers of the retailer's products.

For example, XYZ Corporation, a retail chain specializing in general merchandise goods, is considering expansion into one of two different trading areas. The proposed trading areas are the Alton-Granite City, Illinois, or Hamilton-Middletown, Ohio, markets. XYZ aims its general merchandise at the 25- to 34-year-old market with incomes over $35,000. Therefore, this age group will substitute for population, the general merchandise sales will substitute for total retail sales, and households with income over $35,000 will replace effective buying income.

Using data that can be easily obtained from *Sales & Marketing Management*, XYZ can develop the BPI for each city:

$$\text{BPI (Alton-Granite City)} = 0.5\,(.000386) + 0.3\,(.00083) + 0.2\,(.00012) = .000466$$

$$\text{BPI (Hamilton-Middletown)} = 0.5\,(.000717) + 0.3\,(.00063) + 0.2\,(.000112) = .000570$$

As you can see, the BPI of Hamilton-Middletown is almost 25 percent greater than that of Alton-Granite City, even though the cities are nearly equal in size. Therefore, XYZ would probably choose to expand its Ohio market rather than the Illinois market.

Remember that the BPI is broad in nature and reflects only the demand levels for the two proposed trading areas and not the supply level. Therefore, it does not reflect the saturation levels of these two markets. This can be easily taken care of by dividing the BPI for each area by the area's percentage of U.S. retail selling space for general merchandise (the supply factors) to determine each area's attractiveness:

$$\text{IRS (Alton-Granite City)} = .000466/.000452 = 1.03$$

$$\text{IRS (Hamilton-Middletown)} = .000570/.000483 = 1.18$$

In this case the Ohio trading area is again chosen. This IRS formula does not reflect the availability of competing products or stores in nearby larger cities: Cincinnati, in the case of Hamilton-Middletown, and St. Louis, Missouri, in the case of Alton-Granite City.

Other Demand and Supply Factors

In addition to using retail gravity theory, the index of retail saturation, and the buying power index in evaluating various potential markets, the successful retailer will also look at some other demand and supply factors for each market.

Market Demand Potential

In analyzing the market potential, retailers identify certain criteria that are specific to the product line or services they are selling. The criteria chosen by one retailer might not be of use to a retailer selling a different product line. The major components of market demand potential are as follows.

1. *Population characteristics*. Population characteristics are the criteria most often used to segment markets. Although total population figures and their growth rates are of primary importance to a retailer in examining potential markets, the successful retailer can obtain a more detailed profile of a market by examining school enrollment, education, age, sex, occupation, race, and nationality. Retailers should seek to match a market's population characteristics to the population characteristics of people who desire their goods and services.
2. *Buyer behavior characteristics*. Another useful criterion for analyzing potential markets is the behavioral characteristics of buyers in the market. Such characteristics include store loyalty, consumer lifestyles, store patronage motives, geographic and climatic conditions, and product benefits sought. These data, however, are not as easily obtainable as population data.
3. *Household income*. The average household income and the distribution of household incomes can significantly influence demand for retail facilities. Further insight into the demand for retail facilities is provided by Engel's laws, which imply that spending increases for all categories of products as a result of an income increase, but that the percentage of spending in some categories increases more than for others. Thus, as average household income rises, the community will exhibit a greater demand for luxury goods and a more sophisticated demand for necessity goods.
4. *Household age profile*. The age composition of households can be an important determinant of demand for retail facilities. In communities where households tend to be young, the preferences for stores may be different from communities where the average household is relatively old. For example, consumers over 55 spend almost four times as much at drugstores as do 30-year-olds.
5. *Household composition*. If we hold income and age constant and change the composition of the household, we will be able to identify another determinant of the demand for retail facilities. After all, households with children have different spending habits than childless households with similar incomes.
6. *Community life cycle*. Communities tend to exhibit growth patterns over time. Growth patterns of communities may be of four major types: rapid growth, continuous growth, relatively stable growth, and finally, decline. The retailer should try to identify the communities that are in a rapid or continuous growth pattern, since they will represent the best long-run opportunities.
7. *Population density*. The population density of a community equals the number of persons per square mile. Research suggests that the higher the population density, the larger the average store should be in terms of square feet and thus the fewer the number of stores that will be needed to serve a population of a given size.

Demographic Characteristic	Desired Target Market	Community A	Community B
Population per square mile	over 400	375	423
Median family income	over $31,000	$28,024	$32,418
% population 14–54	over 60%	48%	63%
% white collar	over 50%	38%	54%
% people living in 1–3 person units	over 70%	61%	72%
% workforce traveling 0–14 minutes to work	over 75%	49%	74%
Average annual household expenditure on eating out	over $600	$521	$619

Exhibit 7.7
Identifying Communities with High Demand Potential for a Fast-Food Drive-In Restaurant

8. *Mobility*. The easier it is for people to travel, the more mobile they will be.[20] When people are mobile they are willing to travel greater distances to shop. Therefore, there will be fewer but larger stores in the community. That is, in a community where mobility is high, there will be a need for fewer retailers than in a community where mobility is low.

The most attractive market areas are those in which the preceding criteria are configured in such a way that they represent maximum market potential for a particular retailer. This will vary by the type of retailer and the product lines it handles. In assessing different market areas a retailer should first establish the market demand potential criteria that characterize the target market it would like to attract. Exhibit 7.7 illustrates this concept with a fast-food drive-in chain that sells hamburgers, hot dogs, and drinks. This fast-food chain with over 3,000 units from coast to coast is a 1950s-style drive-in where people usually order burgers and drinks in their autos and in which car-hops provide service.

Exhibit 7.7 shows that the chain has determined that there are seven demographic factors that have a positive impact on fast-food restaurant sales. One of these factors may need explanation. Through research the chain has determined that its restaurants do better when at least 75 percent of the workforce travels less than 14 minutes to work. When people have to travel longer to work, they get tired and frustrated about being in their cars and thus are not likely to be interested in eating in their autos at a drive-in restaurant. You might examine the other six demographic factors and develop an explanation for why they would be related to the success of a fast-food drive-in restaurant. The information in Exhibit 7.7 shows the desired target market and data on the seven demographic factors for two possible communities. From analyzing this data, you should conclude that community B is the most attractive market to enter from a demand potential basis. Exhibit 7.8 shows the Top 10 Developed Markets and Top 10 Least Developed Markets in terms of shopping center space.

Market Supply Factors

In deciding to enter a new market, the successful retailer will spend time analyzing the competition. The retailer should consider square feet per store and square feet per employee, store growth, and the quality of competition.

1. *Square feet per store*. It is helpful to obtain data on the square feet per store for the average store in the communities that are being analyzed. These data will indicate whether the community tends to have large- or small-scale retailing. And, of course, this is important in terms of assessing the extent to which the retailer's standard type of store would blend with the existing structure of retail trade in the community.

Exhibit 7.8A
Top Developed Markets (CBSA Metros by 2005 GLA per Capita)

Rank	CoreBased Statistical Area—Metro	2005 GLA per Capita	2005–2010 Proj Annl Population Growth	2005–2010 Proj Annl Income Growth
1	Myrtie Beach-Conway-North Myrtie Beach, SC	40.86	2.05%	4.94%
2	Sandusky, OH	34.01	−0.31%	2.03%
3	Cape Coral-Fort Myers, FL	33.16	3.17%	7.04%
4	Raleigh-Cary, NC	31.10	2.84%	5.81%
5	Denver-Aurora, CO	29.86	1.39%	4.53%
6	Elmlra, NY	28.78	−0.24%	2.21%
7	Salisbury, MD	28.54	0.92%	3.58%
8	Charlotte Gastonia-Concord, NC-SC	28.07	2.17%	5.10%
9	Phoenix-Mesa-Scottsdale, AZ	27.43	2.72%	5.58%
10	Atlanta-Sandy Springs-Marletta, GA	27.09	2.25%	4.96%
10	Naples Marco Island, FL	27.09	3.87%	6.70%
	National CBSA Metro Average	**18.19**	**1.10%**	**3.81%**

Source: National Research Bureau Shopping Center Database, subsidiary of CoStar Property Group, Inc. 2005/2010 Population and Income Esxtimates from Clarites, Inc.

Gross leasable area represents shopping center space and not total retail space. Shopping centers are retail properties with three of more stores and marketed as a shopping center.

Exhibit 7.8B
Least Developed Markets (CBSA Metros by 2005 GLA per Capita)

Rank	CoreBased Statistical Area—Metro	2005 GLA per Capita	2005–2010 Proj Annl Population Growth	2005–2010 Proj Annl Income Growth
1	Yaklma, WA	4.33	0.58%	3.01%
2	McAllen-Edinburg-Pharr, TX	5.71	3.05%	6.25%
3	Longview, TX	6.60	0.62%	3.59%
4	Hinesville-Fort Stewart, GA	7.14	−1.08%	1.26%
5	Madera, CA	7.40	2.10%	5.03%
6	Corvallis, OR	7.61	0.77%	3.88%
7	Farmington, NM	7.82	2.19%	5.61%
8	Yuba City, CA	7.96	1.60%	4.38%
9	St. George, UT	7.96	3.82%	7.42%
10	Merced, CA	7.98	2.28%	5.05%
	National CBSA Metro Average	**18.19**	**1.10%**	**3.81%**

Source: National Research Bureau Shopping Center Database, subsidiary of CoStar Property Group, Inc. 2005/2010 Population and Income Estimates from Clarites, Inc.

Gross leasable area represents shopping center space and not total retail space. Shopping centers are retail properties with three or more stores and marketed as a shopping center.

2. *Square feet per employee.* A measure that combines two major supply factors in retailing, store space and labor, is square feet of space per employee. A high number for this statistic in a community is evidence that each employee is able to handle more space. This could be due to either a high level of retail technology in the community or more self-service retailing. Since retail technology is fairly constant across communities, any difference in square feet

per employee is most often due to the level of service being provided. In communities currently characterized by retailers as offering a high level of service, there may be a significant opportunity for new retailers that are oriented toward self-service.

3. *Growth in stores.* The retailer should look at the rate of growth in the number of stores for the last one to five years. When the growth is rapid, then on average the community will have better-located stores with more contemporary atmospheres. More recently located stores will coincide better with the existing demographics of the community. Their atmosphere will also better suit the tastes of the marketplace, and they will tend to incorporate the latest in retail technology. All of these factors hint that the strength of retail competition will be greater when the community has recently experienced rapid growth in the number of stores. Retailers, as well as entrepreneurs, can obtain the information needed for computing the square feet per store, square feet per employee, and growth in stores from the Urban Land Institute's *Dollars and Cents of Shopping Centers*, the National Mall Monitor's *Store Retail Tenant Directory*, and Lebhar-Friedman's *Chain Store Guide*.
4. *Quality of competition.* The three preceding supply factors reflect the quantity of competition. Retailers also need to look at the strength or quality of competition. They should attempt to identify the major retail chains and local retailers in each market and evaluate the strength of each. Answers to questions such as the following would be insightful: What is their market share or profitability? How promotional- and price-oriented are they? Are they customer-oriented? Do they tend to react to new market entrants by cutting price, increasing advertising, or improving customer service? A retailer would think twice before competing with Wal-Mart on price, Saks Fifth Avenue on fashion, and Nordstrom's on service or shoe selection.

Quite often when a discounter enters a small community and adds 80,000 to 100,000 square feet of retail space, existing small-town retailers feel they cannot compete and must close down. This is undoubtedly true for the already poor-performing retailers. However, despite the discounter's enormous buying advantages, small-town retailers can compete head-on with the out-of-towners by providing better customer service, adjusting prices on products carried by the discounters, and remaining open Sundays and evenings. Customers will appreciate the increased standard of living that the discounter's prices make possible, and as a result the trading area will increase. The apparel retailer, for example, should cut down on basic stock items like socks and underwear, but increase its inventory of specialty or novelty items. The sales lost on basic items will be overcome with these newer items and the larger trading area the discounter provides.

site analysis
Is an evaluation of the density of demand and supply within each market with the goal of identifying the best retail site(s).

Site Analysis

LO 5

What attributes should be considered in evaluating retail sites within a retail market?

Once a retailer has identified the best potential market, the next task is to perform a more detailed analysis of the market. Only after careful analysis of the market can the retailer choose the best site (or sites) available. **Site analysis** consists of an evaluation of the density of demand and supply within each market. It should be augmented by an identification of the most attractive sites that are currently available within each market. The third and final step, site selection, is the selection of the best possible site.

Site analysis begins by evaluating the density of demand and supply of various areas within the chosen market by using census tract, ZIP code, or some other meaningful geographic factor, and then identifying the most attractive sites, given the retailer's requirements, that are available for new stores within each market. One of the advantages of using census tract data is the ready availability of such data from the Census Bureau.

Census tracts are relatively small statistical subdivisions that vary in population from about 2,500 to 8,000 and are designed to include fairly homogeneous populations. They are most often found in cities and counties of metropolitan areas—that is, the more densely populated areas of the nation.

Size of Trading Areas

Earlier we discussed the general trading area of a community. Our attention will now shift to how to determine and evaluate the trading area of specific sites within markets. In other words, we will attempt to estimate the geographic area from which a store located at a particular site will be able to attract customers.

At the same time that Reilly was developing retail gravity theory to determine the trading area for communities, William Applebaum designed a technique specifically for determining and evaluating trading areas for an individual store. Applebaum's technique was based on customer spottings. For each $100 in weekly store sales, a customer was randomly selected or spotted for an interview. These spottings usually did not require much time since the interviewer requested only demographic information, shopping habits, and some pertinent consumer attitudes toward the store and its competitors. After the home addresses of the shoppers were plotted on a map, the analyst could make some inferences about trading area size and the competition.[21] Exhibit 7.9 is an example of a map generated using customer spottings.

Thus, it is relatively easy to define the trading area of an existing store. All that is necessary is to interview current customers of the store to determine where they reside. For a new store, however, the task is not so easy. There is a fair amount of

Exhibit 7.9
Customer Spotting Map for a Supermarket

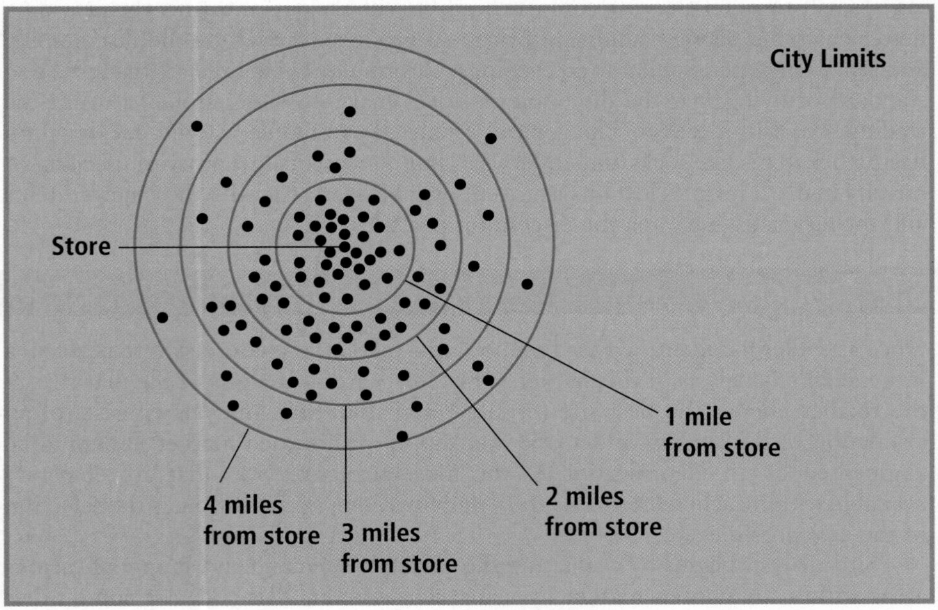

conventional wisdom that has withstood the test of time about the correlation of trading area size, which can be summarized as follows:

1. Stores that sell products the consumer wants to purchase in the most convenient manner will have a smaller trading area than so-called specialty stores.
2. As consumer mobility increases, the size of the store's trading area increases.
3. As the size of the store increases, its trading area increases because it can stock a broader and deeper assortment of merchandise, which will then attract customers from greater distances.
4. As the distance between competing stores increases, their trading areas will increase.
5. Natural and manmade obstacles such as rivers, mountains, railroads, and freeways can abruptly limit the boundaries of a trading area.

Description of Trading Area

Retailers can access, at relatively low cost, information concerning the trading area for various retail locations and the buyer behavior of the trading area. If you use your search engine to locate the Web sites of any of the firms providing geographical information services, you will see how readily available this information is to the typical retailer. For example, consider the work of MapInfo (http://www.mapinfo.com).

MapInfo is a global software company that integrates software, data, and services to help customers make more insightful location decisions. As a market research firm specializing in developing psychographic or lifestyle analyses of geographic areas, it produces solutions that are available in 20 languages in 60 countries. MapInfo's PSYTE, which breaks down all neighborhoods in the United States into 65 different clusters, is based on the old adage that birds of a feather flock together. In other words, even though the total makeup of the American marketplace is very complex and diverse, neighborhoods tend to be just the opposite. People tend to feel most comfortable living in areas with others who are like them. Think for a moment of the place where you are living now as a student, and of your parent's home, and you will most likely see the truth of this adage.

Consumers may live in homogeneous neighborhoods for many possible reasons. The most obvious is income level, since people must be able to afford the homes. However, income is probably not the only answer, since many neighborhoods have similar income levels. Factors such as age, occupation, family status, race, culture, religion, population density, urbanization, and housing types can all distinguish between very different types of neighborhoods that have similar incomes. Therefore, these other factors are usually more important for the retailer to consider than income alone.

In distinguishing between neighborhood types, PSYTE and similar products use two basic criteria. First, each type of neighborhood must be different enough from all the others to make it a distinct marketing segment. Second, there must be enough people living in each type of neighborhood to make it a worthwhile segment to retailers. Utilizing a variety of databases, including U.S. census data and proprietary computer software, MapInfo found 65 neighborhood types in the United States. These types are distinguished from each other in many ways. Some are based primarily on income, some are family-oriented, some are race-oriented, some are urban, some suburban, and some rural. Most combine two or more distinguishing demographic characteristics. The reason MapInfo settled on 65, and not some other number of clusters, was that in "solution after solution this number afforded the maximum amount of discrimination with the fewest number of clusters."[22] Exhibit 7.10 identifies these 65 neighborhood types or clusters.

Exhibit 7.10
PSYTE USA Cluster Demographics

			Cluster Size		Household Characteristics				Socio-Economic Indexes					
Group	No.	Cluster Name	% Pop	% HHs	HH Size	% HH Married	% HH with Kids	% HH Owned	Age Ratio 45+ / <45	Mgr/Prof Tech	College Educated	Income	Financial Assets	Wealth
		United States	100.0%	100.0%	2.6	55.2	36.2	64.2	100	100	100	100	100	100
U1	03	Ivory Towers	0.32%	0.52%	1.6	27.2	9.0	33.8	89	213	307	297	296	223
	18	Hi Rise Hustle	0.72%	1.05%	1.8	30.7	13.0	38.2	102	172	213	130	98	138
	24	Gliterati	0.50%	0.78%	1.6	19.6	9.1	19.8	44	182	276	117	38	47
U2	29	Old Metro Rows	0.88%	0.91%	2.5	50.8	30.5	45.1	117	98	92	97	99	150
	37	Big City Boomers	1.03%	1.33%	2.0	31.6	20.6	26.0	84	123	139	87	78	37
	39	East Goes West	0.98%	0.98%	2.6	50.4	33.1	48.9	101	112	129	107	197	251
U3	53	Latino del Sol	0.74%	0.66%	2.9	49.3	40.5	40.3	118	64	55	55	19	40
	54	Cross Roads	0.80%	0.77%	2.7	39.7	36.6	17.7	77	70	76	64	11	14
	55	City Services	1.69%	1.50%	3.0	36.4	46.7	49.9	99	67	48	70	12	16
	64	San Juan Norte	0.79%	0.68%	3.0	31.9	49.7	16.2	75	50	30	49	6	10
	65	Urban Stress	1.12%	0.97%	3.0	22.1	53.4	22.0	77	46	21	38	6	10
F1	05	Euro-Boomers	0.86%	0.85%	2.6	66.4	36.0	81.7	117	178	249	199	511	299
	07	Hi-Rent Swank	0.57%	0.68%	2.2	51.7	22.6	65.1	145	176	227	189	489	330
	08	Mortgage Heights	1.51%	1.27%	3.1	81.2	53.0	91.2	93	156	206	193	208	145
	11	Execu-Twins	1.46%	1.72%	2.2	54.0	24.9	69.1	123	169	224	161	626	263
F2	12	Homebodies	2.27%	2.12%	2.8	68.5	36.8	86.7	147	102	92	124	89	124
	23	Metro Managers	2.05%	2.31%	2.3	49.2	29.6	57.7	79	139	168	118	90	102
	26	Pacific Medley	0.82%	0.63%	3.5	66.7	52.5	69.4	88	97	106	119	65	112
	27	Solidarities	2.24%	2.47%	2.4	53.9	28.6	73.7	148	88	67	86	44	56
F3	43	Changing Places	1.55%	1.57%	2.6	50.0	38.3	64.6	111	55	32	62	14	22
	45	Yankee Blues	1.80%	2.03%	2.3	41.7	29.1	44.7	106	82	66	76	11	38
	50	Growing Pains	2.01%	2.49%	2.1	34.1	26.2	35.5	81	91	87	61	10	50
	51	Night Lights	0.77%	1.00%	2.0	24.1	17.8	18.4	37	117	175	57	26	24
F4	52	Factory Hands	2.12%	2.03%	2.7	44.1	42.0	41.4	78	61	44	57	14	51
	59	Solo Tenements	0.47%	0.41%	1.7	19.2	15.6	16.6	162	78	42	41	5	9
	62	Church Fans	1.36%	1.42%	2.5	25.4	35.8	40.9	158	52	29	41	4	8
	63	Borderlands	2.49%	1.74%	3.8	54.0	57.2	45.3	84	39	23	53	5	8
S1	01	Tuxedo Park	0.66%	0.63%	2.7	75.0	34.9	90.2	206	199	300	485	572	514
	02	Business Barons	0.93%	0.96%	2.5	70.5	30.5	87.9	212	190	271	303	296	291
	04	Power Hitters	0.90%	0.77%	3.1	82.2	49.9	93.0	117	184	272	270	272	232
	09	Rolling Acres	1.79%	1.73%	2.7	69.9	41.8	80.2	81	158	205	165	270	197

S2	10	Empty Nesters	2.04%	2.00%	2.7	72.0	33.1	90.0	187	143	166	157	267	234
	16	Silver Linings	0.94%	1.31%	1.9	49.2	12.2	69.8	315	122	118	101	199	180
	17	Winding Down	2.93%	3.31%	2.3	56.1	27.6	70.4	137	124	126	104	202	138
	21	Senior Circles	1.11%	1.41%	2.1	60.6	16.0	84.2	310	81	60	64	61	67
S3	15	Team-Mates	2.25%	2.00%	3.0	73.1	53.8	81.8	44	144	179	143	162	138
	19	Kids, Dogs, Vans	2.68%	2.30%	3.1	73.3	54.4	82.7	58	103	100	119	43	75
	20	2nd City Gentry	1.76%	1.79%	2.6	60.3	38.7	67.5	72	119	129	104	50	62
S4	28	America First	2.51%	2.52%	2.6	63.6	36.8	79.4	121	76	55	89	47	66
	34	Capital Singles	1.42%	1.97%	1.9	31.6	18.4	28.9	50	141	188	96	32	42
	36	Middle-dale	1.89%	1.89%	2.6	55.8	40.4	64.5	86	86	73	85	26	41
	40	Omni-Boomers	2.47%	2.05%	3.2	65.4	53.8	71.1	65	82	65	88	12	57
	49	Gen X Scramble	2.40%	2.66%	2.4	43.2	35.6	36.5	51	96	98	81	19	74
X1	06	Country Manors	1.34%	1.30%	2.7	73.5	36.6	86.3	139	155	203	211	161	204
	13	Trailblazers	2.57%	2.38%	2.8	72.8	41.7	85.9	110	118	121	134	217	301
	14	Highlanders	2.19%	1.99%	2.9	75.3	45.2	86.3	93	106	108	131	609	275
X2	22	Rods & Rifles	3.02%	2.86%	2.8	70.4	43.1	84.2	93	86	71	97	96	63
	30	Country Roads	1.50%	1.56%	2.5	59.6	35.0	73.0	117	90	80	80	58	81
	31	Outback Elders	2.80%	3.07%	2.4	60.2	29.4	78.4	169	79	59	68	16	47
	32	Upper Dogpatch	2.82%	2.75%	2.7	66.4	42.0	82.3	92	67	46	78	18	94
X3	46	Midland Blues	1.76%	1.66%	2.5	50.2	37.6	59.0	81	73	54	64	12	57
	48	Old River Towns	2.90%	3.32%	2.3	46.6	30.1	58.9	130	66	45	60	15	58
	57	Gerber-ville	0.31%	0.24%	3.3	81.0	69.2	15.1	12	92	89	66	49	36
	60	Dixie Flatlands	1.92%	1.78%	2.8	38.9	44.7	57.4	117	48	31	46	4	7
R1	25	Leafy Hamlets	1.95%	1.79%	2.9	73.3	43.3	83.1	100	69	58	92	36	51
	33	Nordic Rustics	2.08%	2.03%	2.7	67.6	40.0	82.1	112	59	40	72	42	103
	35	Wheat & Timber	1.47%	1.43%	2.7	70.9	38.1	78.3	128	52	49	75	23	55
	38	Mill Towners	1.98%	2.01%	2.6	66.2	38.1	82.2	124	49	29	62	21	50
R2	41	Old Homesteads	0.86%	0.82%	2.7	58.7	40.0	76.4	121	64	43	59	14	66
	42	Stars & Bars	1.63%	1.50%	2.9	63.4	46.4	80.4	89	50	29	63	11	33
	44	Market Gardens	1.13%	0.91%	3.2	64.0	48.8	69.0	97	57	41	64	17	60
	47	Mines & Wells	1.37%	1.37%	2.6	58.5	39.1	74.3	131	48	25	48	16	43
	56	Amer-Indians	0.24%	0.18%	3.4	51.7	57.4	70.0	88	74	36	49	10	7
GQ	58	Military Bases	0.43%	0.18%	3.4	85.8	75.3	6.8	9	95	84	69	10	17
	61	Alma Maters	1.13%	0.68%	2.2	28.5	16.8	26.3	36	110	231	85	19	9

Cluster Group Legend
U—Urban; F—Fringe; S—Suburban; X—Exurban; R—Rural; GQ—Group Quarters
Source: PSYTE is a trademark of MapInfo Corporation. This exhibit is used with the written permission of MapInfo Corporation, One Global View, Troy, NY 12180-8399 (http://www.mapinfo.com).

The neighborhood names attempt to capture the essence of the neighborhood and provide an easy way of remembering distinctions. Also associated with the neighborhoods are demographics, lifestyle, retail opportunities, and financial and media habits. Still, in some cases the information about a cluster may be confusing. Consider, for example, cluster 61, which is "Alma Maters." This segment's behavior cannot be based solely on household income because half of the cluster's population lives in group quarters, such as college dorms. This neighborhood type, which is typical of neighborhoods surrounding college campuses across the country, can be characterized by the fact that two-thirds of its population is between the ages of 18 and 24. Without considering the fact that mom and dad are supporting the kids, the makeup of cars owned and amount of travel would seem contradictory to the cluster's income level.[23]

Demand Density

demand density
Is the extent to which the potential demand for the retailer's goods and services is concentrated in certain census tracts, ZIP code areas, or parts of the community.

The extent to which potential demand for the retailer's goods and services is concentrated in certain census tracts, ZIP code areas, or parts of the community is called **demand density**. To determine the extent of demand density, retailers need to identify what they believe to be the major variables influencing their potential demand. One such method of identifying these variables is to examine the types of customers who already shop in the retailer's present stores. The variables identified should be standard demographic variables such as age, income, and education, since data will be readily available. Let us construct an example.

A retailer is evaluating the possibility of locating in a community that has geographic boundaries as shown in Exhibit 7.11. It is comprised of 23 census tracts. The community is bordered on the west by a mountain range, on the north and south by major highways, and on the east by railroad tracks. The retailer has decided that three variables are especially important in determining the potential demand: median household income of over $35,000, households per square mile in excess of 1,200, and average growth in population of at least 3 percent per year over the last three years. In Exhibit 7.11, a thematic map shows the extent to which these three conditions are met for each of the 23 census tracts in the community undergoing evaluation. Thus you can easily visualize the density of potential demand in each tract. Note that only three tracts (6, 10, and 17) meet all three conditions.

Another method of looking at potential demand for a retailer's product could incorporate the data mentioned earlier when discussing neighborhood types. In this example, suppose a retail computer chain wanted to enter the Atlanta market. The chain would first determine, from its own records, which neighborhood types accounted for the largest sales in comparison to the national average of its product categories. In this case, higher levels of income and education, under age 45, and percentage of "executive/managers/professional/technical" households were the most important factors. Thus, the neighborhood types "Ivory Towers," "Mortgage Heights," "Night-Lights," and "Team-Mates" may be among the most attractive locations for a computer store (see Exhibit 7.10).

Supply Density

While the demand-density map allows you to identify the area within a community that represents the highest potential demand, the location of existing retail establishments should also be mapped. For example, for nearly three decades, ZIP code 07652 in Paramus, NJ has had the largest dollar volume in retail sales of any ZIP code in the United States. The 600,000-plus residents of 07652 have a buying

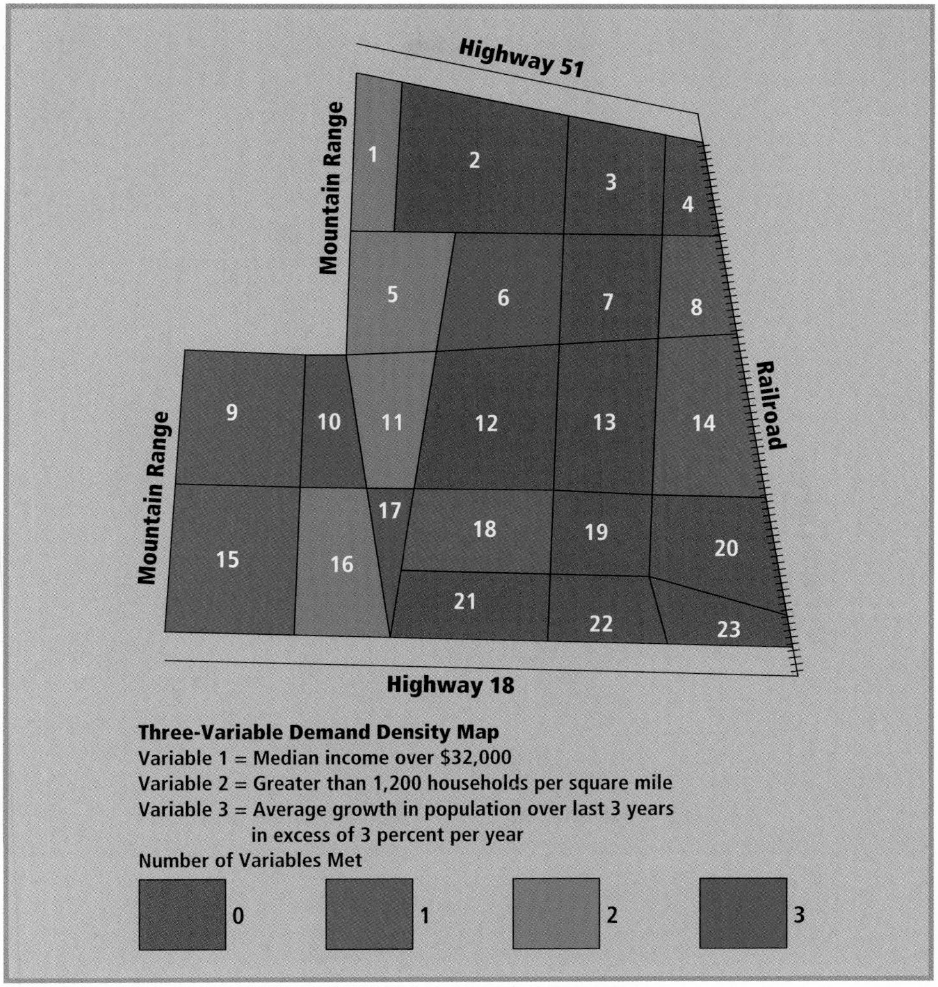

Exhibit 7.11
Demand Density Map

power exceeding $15 billion. Paramus's demographics are highly desirable and so is its location. The ZIP code also benefits from its lack of a state sales tax on clothing and shoes, enabling it to draw shoppers from nearby "high-taxed" New York City. In addition, Paramus is located in Bergen County, which has a population over a million and is ranked among the Top 20 American counties in terms of household income. Not surprisingly, Paramus has five major enclosed shopping malls nearby and over seven million square feet of retail space. This space has few vacancies and also commands some of the highest rents for retail space in the country. This last piece of information about the lack of available space and the number of retailers already serving the market is most important because it allows the retailer to examine the density of supply—that is, the extent to which retailers are concentrated in different areas of the market under question.

Exhibit 7.12 shows the density of stores in the community we saw in Exhibit 7.11. Exhibit 7.12 reveals that two census tracts (10 and 17) out of the three most attractive ones have a lack of stores. Also, in the census tracts with fairly attractive demand density (two of the three conditions met); there are currently no retail outlets (see tracts 1 and 5).

Exhibit 7.12
Store Density and Site Availability Map

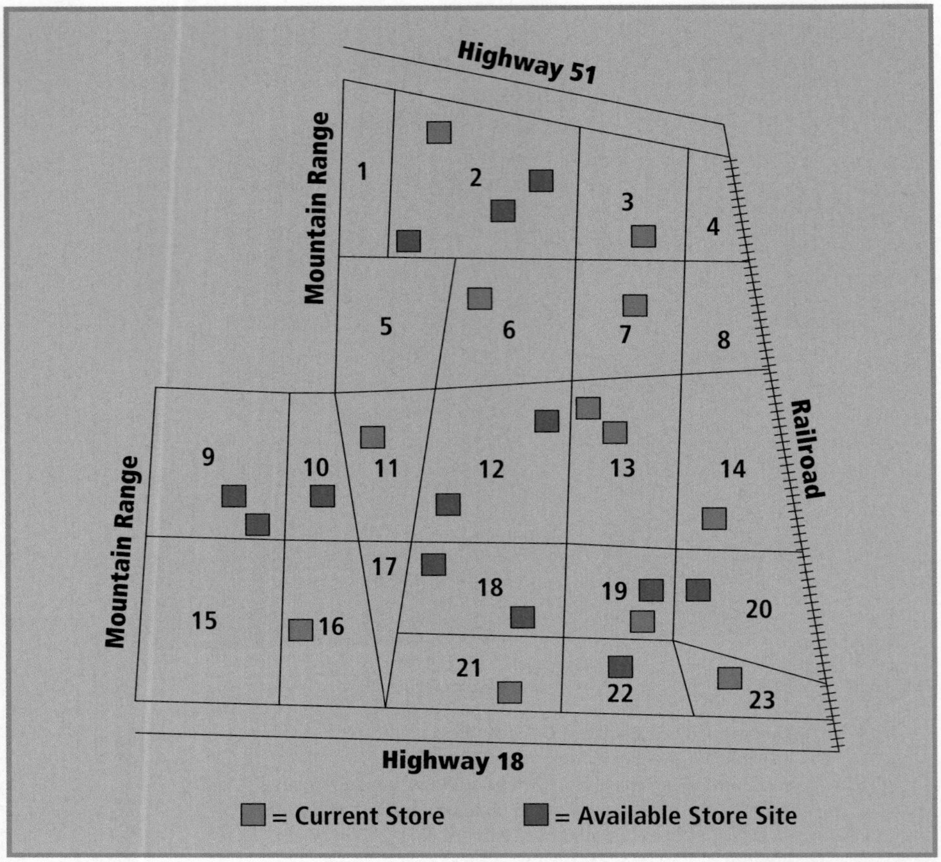

Site Availability

Just because demand outstrips supply in certain geographic locations does not immediately imply that stores should be located in those locations. Sites must be available.

A map should be constructed of available sites in each community being analyzed. We have done this in conjunction with the supply-density map in Exhibit 7.12. The only available site in the top six census tracts (in terms of demand density) is in census tract 10. In tracts 1, 5, and 17, which currently have no retail outlets, no sites are available, which may explain the present lack of stores in these areas. Perhaps these tracts are zoned totally for residential use.

Although Exhibit 7.12 seems to show only one good potential site, several more may exist. Census tract 9 borders the high-density tract 10, in which there are no present stores and in which only one site is available for a new store. Tract 9, however, has two available sites. Furthermore, tract 12 has an available site that is close to the borders of tracts 11 and 17, which are both attractive but lack available sites. This same kind of analysis can be done with a high-fashion chain in looking over the Los Angeles market. Some retailers have developed a checklist of all the items they want to consider during the site analysis stage. One such list is shown in Exhibit 7.13.

Local Demographics
Population and/or household base
Population growth potential
Lifestyles of consumers
Income potential
Age makeup
Educational makeup
Population of nearby special markets, that is, daytime workers, students, and tourists, if applicable
Occupation mix

Traffic Flow and Accessibility
Number and type of vehicles passing location
Access of vehicles to location
Number and type of pedestrians passing location
Availability of mass transit, if applicable
Accessibility of major highway artery
Quality of access streets
Level of street congestion
Presence of physical barriers that affect trade area shape

Retail Competition
Number and types of stores in area
Analysis of key players in general area
Competitiveness of other merchants
Number and location of direct competitors in area
Possibility of joint promotions with local merchants

Site Characteristics
Number of parking spaces available
Distance of parking areas
Ease of access for delivery
Visibility of site from street
History of the site
Compatibility of neighboring stores
Size and shape of lot
Condition of existing building
Ease of entrance and exit for traffic
Ease of access for handicapped customers
Restrictions on sign usage
Building safety code restrictions
Type of zoning

Cost Factors
Terms of lease/rent agreement
Basic rent payments
Length of lease
Local taxes
Operations and maintenance costs
Restrictive clauses in lease
Membership in local merchants association required
Voluntary regulations by local merchants

Exhibit 7.13
Checklist for Site Evaluations

Site Selection

LO 6

How is the best geographic site selected?

After completing the analysis of each segment of the desired market and identifying the best available sites within each market, retailers are now ready to make the final decision regarding location: selecting the best site (or sites) available. Small- to medium-sized retailers without an in-house real estate department are well advised to use the assistance of a real estate professional at this stage. Even if the retailers or their staff have done all the analysis to this point, the assistance of a real estate professional is important. In fact, more and more large retail firms set up separate corporations just to handle their real estate transactions.

100 percent location
Is when there is no better use for a site than the retail store that is being planned for that site.

In principle, all retailers should attempt to find a **100 percent location** for their stores. A 100 percent location is one where there is no better use for the site then the retail store that is being planned. Retailers should remember that what may be a 100 percent site for one store may not be for another. The best location for a supermarket may not be the best location for a discount department store.

How is the 100 percent location or site identified? Unfortunately, there is no best answer to this basic question. There is, however, general agreement on the types of things that the retailer should consider in evaluating sites: the nature of the site, traffic characteristics, type of neighbors, and the terms of purchase or lease.

Nature of Site

Is the site currently a vacant store, a vacant parcel of land, or the site of a planned shopping center? Many of the available retail sites will be vacant stores. This is because 10 to 15 percent of stores go out of business each year. This does not mean that because a men's apparel store failed in a particular location that a bookstore is doomed to do likewise. However, sometimes a piece of property becomes known as "jinxed" or "snakebit" because of the high number of business failures that have occurred there. Every town usually has one or more such areas. Restaurants, which are one of the toughest businesses to get off the ground, seem to try these locations the most. Therefore, when the retail site that appears to be best suited to the retailer's needs is a vacant parcel of land, the retailer needs to investigate why it is vacant. Why have others passed up the site? Was it previously not for sale or was it priced too high? Or is there some other reason?

Finally, the site may be part of a planned shopping center. In this case, the retailer can usually be assured that it will have the proper mix of neighbors, adequate parking facilities, and good traffic. Sometimes, of course, the center has not been properly planned, and the retailer needs to be aware of these special cases. It is difficult to succeed in a shopping center in which a high percentage of space is not rented. As described in the chapter's Service Retailing box, many service retailers are moving into vacant locations at shopping centers and malls.

Traffic Characteristics

The traffic that passes a site, whether it is vehicular or pedestrian, can be an important determinant of the potential sales at that site. However, factors other than traffic flow must be considered. The retailer must determine if the population and traffic are of the type desired. For example, a retailer of fine furs and leather coats may be considering two alternative sites; one in the central business district and the other in a group of specialty stores in a small shopping center in a very exclusive residential area. The CBD site may generate more total traffic, but the alternative site may generate more of the right type of traffic.

The retailer should evaluate two traffic-related aspects of the site. The first is the availability of sufficient parking, either at the site or nearby. One of the advantages of shopping centers/malls is the availability of adequate parking space. If the site is not a shopping center, then the retailer will need to determine if the parking space will be adequate. It is difficult to give a precise guideline for the space that will be needed. Generally, it is a function of four factors: size of the store, frequency of customer visits, length of customer visits, and availability of public transportation. As a rule of thumb, shopping centers estimate that there should be five spaces for every 1,000 square feet of selling space in medium-sized centers and ten spaces per 1,000 square feet in large centers.

A second traffic-related aspect the retailer should consider is the direction of traffic relative to the shopping area. Many shoppers prefer not to have to make left-hand turns from a busy roadway into a shopping area. A third consideration is the ease with which consumers can reach the store site. Are the roadways in good shape? Are there traffic barriers (rivers with a limited number of bridges, interstate highways with limited crossings, one-way streets, high level of street usage resulting in congestion that limits exits to the site)? Remember, customers normally avoid heavily congested shopping areas and shop elsewhere in order to minimize driving time and other difficulties.

Service Retailing

They're Back!

Banks, medical offices, day spas, nail salons and real estate offices are among a group that has just made a comeback to malls and shopping centers. Their reasoning is as diverse as the services they provide. An early example of this trend is the strategy of placing branch bank locations within big box retailers and grocery stores with their more convenient operating hours. Let's look at this strategy in more detail.

As they seek a competitive advantage in the fierce Internet banking world, financial institutions have recommitted to placing branches in locations where they will be in close proximity to their customers, once again making banking services convenient. Banks have returned to malls to serve those who cannot or will not work personal financial transactions over a computer. Such locations are especially helpful for the many senior citizens who are not "computer savvy." Locating banks and stock brokerage offices near specialty retailers allows older consumers to handle their personal financial needs face to face with a bank employee or broker. For some, this provides a level of comfort. The red-hot residential real estate market and the many Americans seeking to start Roth IRAs to provide for their retirement years have produced a large group of banking customers needing a significant amount of personal attention. Others simply desire a comfortable place for a face-to-face interaction when dealing with mortgages, stock purchases, or money wiring services.

Following the banks' example, many "service" sector retailers are migrating to mall developments frequented by their customers. It is more common now to find the presence of a nail salon, a noninvasive cosmetic surgery office, day spa, or a residential estate office when visiting your local enclosed mall, lifestyle center, or other shopping venue. The idea is that if these services are within walking distance of your favorite department store, specialty shop, etc., then you are more likely to commit to frequenting those specific locations. In a sense this strategy plays off the mentality of "don't come to us—we'll come to you." Traditionally these types of service retailers were often relegated to a 2nd level space in downtown city centers or to a 3rd generation space after the previous owner had shifted elsewhere. Today, developers try to differentiate their retail centers from the traditional competitor by being "everything to everyone," thus giving their already time-starved customer a place for one-stop shopping and thereby allowing a win-win situation for the customer and the development's retailers.

Mall occupancy charges may be higher for these service-based providers than they were in their traditional venues. However, these providers may be able to afford more as most of their businesses do not have plans to expand overseas, to manufacture products, incur shipping or trucking costs to deliver products, or have the need to maintain a large inventory area. These service-based providers are also not fearful of someone copying their product design and selling it cheaper on eBay. Their success is generally dependent on the quality of the service being provided to the individual customer.

Source: This box was prepared by Mark Fallon, Vice President of Real Estate, Jeffrey R. Anderson Real Estate, Inc., Cincinnati.

Type of Neighbors

What neighboring establishments surround the site? There can be good and bad neighbors. What constitutes a good or bad neighbor depends on the type of store being considered at the site. Suppose that you plan to open a children's apparel store and are considering two alternative sites. One site already has a toy store and a gift shop; the other site has a bowling alley and an adult bookstore. Obviously, in this case, you know who the good and bad neighbors are.

However, determining the good and bad neighbors may not always be that easy, especially for an entrepreneur. A good neighboring business will be one that is compatible with the retailer's line of trade. When two or more businesses are compatible, they can actually help generate additional business for each other. For example, a paint store, hardware store, and auto parts store located next to one another may increase total traffic and thus benefit them all.

store compatibility
Exists when two similar retail businesses locate next to or nearby each other and they realize a sales volume greater than what they would have achieved if they were located apart from each other.

Research has found that retailers experience a benefit from **store compatibility**. That is, when two compatible, or very similar, businesses (e.g., two shoe stores) locate near each other, they will show an increase in sales volume greater than what they would have achieved if they were located separately.[24] For example, when Lowe's opened a store near a Home Depot in Lewisville, Texas, The Home Depot store went from a category B to a category A store. This meant that the addition of a nearby competitor increased The Home Depot's sales by 20 percent. Another example is PetSmart, which doesn't mind locating near a Petco outlet. PetSmart likes to "shove their stores down the competition's throat," unless they have PetSmart beat on convenience.[25] PetSmart believes that if it can't outposition rivals by being closer to its target demographics, it will compete head-to-head with them and both will do better. A final case is Big Lots, a closeout specialist, which likes being near Wal-Mart. In fact, the large discounter is not only a competitor for Big Lots, but also its biggest landlord. Today, Big Lots operates 40 stores on sites where Wal-Mart shut down to open a larger unit nearby. An executive for the smaller chain told a real estate conference that many of our customers "like to comparison shop, and if the competition is across the parking lot rather than across town, we feel like we'll win."[26]

Clustering dates back to the 1950s when the choicest location for a gas station was believed to be an intersection that already had three other stations. It is seen today with shoe stores in malls, auto dealerships, furniture stores, and restaurants. The major benefit of clustering is that it allows customers to walk from store to store, comparing prices, products, and service. However, grouping of stores doesn't always benefit competitors. Consider membership retailers, such as wholesale clubs and fitness centers. After all, if consumers have already paid to use one of the retailers, it is doubtful that they would pay to shop at the other. In such cases, one of three things would happen:

1. The retailers would fight it out to the death and both would lose.
2. The trade area could expand to become big enough so that both could succeed.
3. One retailer would be forced to completely differentiate itself from the other, and even then they might not both survive.

Terms of Purchase or Lease

Another consideration for the retailer at this point is the lease terms. The retailer should review the length of the lease (it could be too long or too short), the exclusivity clause (whether or not the retailer will be the only one allowed to sell a certain line of merchandise), the guaranteed traffic rate (a reduction in rent should be offered if the shopping center fails to achieve a targeted traffic level), and an anchor clause (which would also allow for a rent reduction if the anchor store in a developing center does not open on time or when you open). Lease arrangements generally call for either a fixed payment, in which the rental charge is usually based on a fixed amount per month, or a variable payment, in which rent is a specified percentage of sales with a guaranteed minimum rent. It is important for the retailer to choose the one that is best under the circumstances—perhaps a combination of the two methods.

When the retailer decides to locate in a shopping center, it usually has no other choice than to lease. However, in the case of a freestanding location, an outright purchase is often possible. Purchase and lease costs should be factored into the site's expected profitability.

Expected Profitability

The final step in site selection analysis is construction of a pro forma (expected) return on asset model for each possible site. The return on asset model comprises three crucial variables: net profit margin, asset turnover, and return on assets.

For purposes of evaluating sites, the potential return on equity is not relevant. This is because the financial leverage ratio (total assets divided by equity) is a top-management decision; it represents how much debt the retail enterprise is willing to assume. Most likely, the question of how to finance new store growth has already been answered or at least contemplated. The retailer should already have determined that it has or can obtain the capital to finance a new store. It is therefore reasonable and appropriate to evaluate sites on their potential return on assets and not return on equity.

If the retailer is to evaluate sites on their potential return on assets, it will need at least three estimates: total sales, total assets, and net profit. Each of these is likely to vary depending on the site. Sales estimates will be different for alternative sites because each will have unique trade area characteristics, such as the number and nature of households and the level of competition. Estimated total assets could vary because the alternative sites will likely have different prices; the cost of construction could also vary. Finally, estimated profits could vary not only due to varying sales for the different sites but different operating costs. For example, some sites may be in areas where labor expenses, taxes, or insurance rates are higher.

STUDENT STUDY GUIDE

SUMMARY

Selecting a target market and determining which retail format will most effectively reach this market are two of the most important decisions a retailer will make. The retailer can reach potential customers through both store-based retail locations and nonstore retail formats. Geographical information systems can help the retailer gain knowledge of its potential customers and where they reside and how they behave. This can help the retailer better determine how to reach its target market.

Most of the chapter discussed how to select a location for a store-based retailer. The choice of retail location involves three decisions: (1) market identification, or identifying the most attractive markets; (2) site analysis, or evaluating the demand and supply within each market; and (3) site selection, selecting the best site (or sites) available.

Explain the criteria used in selecting a target market.

LO 1

We began this chapter by stating that an effective target market must be one that is measurable, accessible, and substantial. Measurability concerns whether or not objective data exists on the attributes of the target market. Accessibility deals with the extent to which marketing efforts can be uniquely targeted at a particular segment of the market. Substantiality. relates to whether the target market is large enough to be economically worth pursuing.

Identify the different options, both store-based and nonstore-based, for effectively reaching the retailer's target market and identify the advantages and disadvantages of business districts, shopping centers, and freestanding units as sites for retail location.

LO 2

We next reviewed the four store-based location alternatives available to the retailer: the business district, the shopping center/mall, the freestanding unit, and the nontraditional store location. The business district is generally an unplanned shopping area around the geographic point where a city originated and grew up. As cities have grown, we have witnessed an expansion of two newer types of business districts: the secondary business district and the neighborhood business district.

A shopping center or mall is a centrally owned and/or managed shopping district that is planned, has balanced tenancy, and is surrounded by parking facilities. It has one or more anchor stores and a variety of smaller stores. Because of the many advantages shopping centers can offer the retailer, they are a fixture of America and account for 55 percent of all retail sales in the United States.

A freestanding retailer generally locates along major traffic arteries. There are usually no adjacent retailers selling competing products with which the retailer will have to share traffic.

The retailer also has five nonstore-based options: street peddling, mail order, automatic merchandising machines, direct selling, and the Internet.

LO 3 **Define geographic information systems (GIS) and discuss their potential uses in a retail enterprise.**

Higher-quality market selection and retail location decisions can be made with the use of geographic information systems, which are computerized systems combining physical geography with cultural geography. The GIS technology can be used not only for market selection, site analysis, and trade area definition, but also to evaluate new store cannibalization, advertising management, merchandise management, and store managers.

LO 4 **What are the various factors that should be considered in identifying the most attractive retail market?**

We began our analysis of market selection by looking at a trio of theories that can aid in the location decision. Retail gravitation theory assumes that the population of a community serves as a drawing power for the community and draws customers into its business district. The index of retail saturation reflects the total demand for the product under question and if the area is overstored or understored (i.e., the availability of current retailers to service or supply current demand). The buying power index enables us to develop an overall indicator of a market's potential. We concluded our discussion on market identification by looking into other factors that could influence a community's supply (square feet per store, square feet per employee, growth in stores, and quality of competition) or demand (market population; buyer behavior; household income, age, and composition; community life cycle; density; and mobility) for goods and services.

LO 5 **What attributes should be considered in evaluating retail sites within a retail market?**

After reviewing the three location theories, we discussed the second of our three steps in the location process: site analysis, which is an evaluation of the density of demand and supply within each possible market. This process begins by determining the size, description, and density of demand and supply of various areas within the chosen market and then identifying the most attractive sites, given the retailer's requirements, that are available for new stores within each market.

LO 6 **How is the best geographic site selected?**

Finally, the retailer should conduct a site selection analysis of the top-ranking sites in each market. The goal is to select the best site or sites. Retail site analysts suggest that the following factors should be considered at this stage: nature of the site, traffic characteristics, type of neighbors, terms of lease or purchase, and, finally, the expected profitability or return on assets.

TERMS TO REMEMBER

home page
virtual store
ease of access
target market
store-based retailers
nonstore-based retailers
central business district (CBD)
secondary business district (SBD)
neighborhood business district (NBD)
shopping center, or mall
anchor stores
freestanding retailer
geographic information system (GIS)
culture
thematic maps
trading area
retail gravity theory
Reilly's law of retail gravitation
point of indifference
outshopping
retail store saturation
understored
overstored
index of retail saturation (IRS)
buying power index (BPI)
site analysis
demand density
100 percent location
store compatibility

REVIEW AND DISCUSSION QUESTIONS

What criteria are used in selecting a target market? LO 1

1. Why should retailers be concerned about selecting the right target market? How are target market selection and location related?
2. What three criteria should be met to successfully target a market?

Identify the different options, both store-based and nonstore-based, for effectively reaching the retailer's target market and identify the advantages and disadvantages of business districts, shopping centers, and freestanding units as sites for retail location. LO 2

3. What types of retailers would be best suited for locating in a central business district?
4. Why are some shopping centers/malls now using big-box stores, such as The Home Depot and Linens 'n Things, as anchors? Aren't anchor stores supposed to be department stores?
5. What lines of retail trade do you believe will be most affected by the growth of retailing on the Internet?

Define geographic information systems (GIS) and discuss their potential uses in a retail enterprise. LO 3

6. How have improvements in the user-friendliness of GIS mapping technology caused retailers to become more research-driven in locating stores?
7. Identify and discuss the seven uses of geographic information systems in retailing.

What factors should be considered in identifying the most attractive retail market? LO 4

8. Someone once said that if "you build a better mousetrap, they will come." If this is true, why is it important for a retailer to select the correct site within a trading area? Explain your answer.

9. According to Reilly's law of retail gravitation, cities attract trade from an intermediate place based on what two factors? How are these factors used in making a location decision?
10. Calculate the Buyer Power Indexes for the following three cities:

U.S. City	Percent of Effective Buying Income	Percent of U.S. Retail Sales	Percent of U.S. Population
Mansfield	.006	.004	.006
Springfield	.009	.007	.009
Carlyle	.007	.005	.007

11. Compute the index of retail saturation for the following three markets.The data for restaurants is:

Market	A	B	C
Annual retail expenditures per household	$789	$875	$943
Square feet of retail space	600,000	488,000	808,000
Number of households	121,000	102,000	157,000

Based on this data, which market is most attractive? What additional data would you find helpful in determining the attractiveness of the three markets?

LO 5 **What attributes should be considered in evaluating retail sites within a retail market?**

12. Identify the factors you would consider most important in locating a fast-food restaurant. Compare these factors with the factors you would use in selecting a site for a supermarket.
13. Explain the concepts of demand density and supply density. Why are they important to retail decision making?

LO 6 **How is the best geographic site selected?**

14. Why is it so hard to find that 100 percent retail location?
15. Why do some stores cluster around each other? Doesn't being so close to their competition hurt their profitability?

SAMPLE TEST QUESTIONS

LO 1 **Which of the following is not a criterion used to successfully reach a target market?**

a. The market segment should be measurable.
b. Promotional efforts can be directed at the market segment.
c. The market segment should create high sales.
d. The market segment should be profitable.
e. Distribution efforts can be directed at the market segment.

LO 2 **Freestanding retailers offer which of the following advantages?**

a. lack of direct competition
b. high drawing power from nearby complementary stores
c. higher traffic than shopping malls
d. lower advertising costs
e. stores must be leased

Geographic information systems can be used for which of the following purposes? LO 3

a. site analysis
b. trade area definition
c. advertising management
d. merchandise management
e. all of the above

The three sequential stages involved in selecting a location for a store-based retailer are LO 4

a. Identify the most understored markets, identify the most attractive sites that are available within each market, select the best site(s).
b. Identify most attractive markets, identify the most attractive sites that are available within each market, select the best site(s).
c. Identify most attractive markets, identify the vacant parcels of real estate within each market, select the best site(s).
d. Identify the most understored markets, identify the vacant parcels of real estate within each market, negotiate terms for best site.
e. Identify most attractive markets, identify the most attractive sites that are available within each market, negotiate for the lowest priced site.

Site analysis consists of LO 5

a. establishing purchase or lease terms.
b. consideration of the type of neighbors.
c. analyzing sources of financing for the site (i.e., debt or equity financing).
d. determining the expected profitability from operating a store at the site.
e. evaluating the density of demand and supply within each market.

Which of the following is not an important consideration in selecting the best site for a new retail store? LO 6

a. nature of the site
b. traffic characteristics of the site
c. alternative investments available to the retailer
d. potential profitability of the site
e. type of neighbors

WRITING AND SPEAKING EXERCISE

You are doing a summer internship with Table Rock Jewelers, a family-held concern located in the central business district of a resort community in southwest Missouri with a summer population of 200,000. Thomas Frey, the owner, has a problem and wants you to help him solve it. Around 10 o'clock this morning, a street peddler showed up in front of the store and began selling fake famous-name brand watches (Rolex, Ebel, Piaget) from a pushcart for $10 to $20 each. After first asking the peddler to find another street corner and being told no, Mr. Frey called the police to have the peddler removed. However, the police informed Mr. Frey that according to the city code street peddling was not illegal. Frey then called his city council representative, Sarah Inman, explaining that he believes it was unfair for him to pay city taxes and have to compete with someone who paid no taxes. Besides, he wondered, did the street peddler have to purchase a sales permit from the city as all the regular downtown merchants were required to do? Ms. Inman told Frey that she wasn't sure about the permit and asked Frey to send her a memo explaining the situation and proposing a solution(s). Now Mr. Frey wants you to write the memo for him.

RETAIL PROJECT

Small as well as large retailers can benefit immensely from knowing the trade area of their store. Identify a small local retailer such as a florist, pet store, gift store, or restaurant. Contact the store owner or manager and say that you are a student studying retailing and would like to volunteer to construct a map of his or her trade area. To do this you need to obtain the addresses of all the patrons over a one-week period and plot these on a map. Review the customer spotting map for a supermarket in Exhibit 7.9 on page 232. Develop a method to collect the needed data and construct the map of the trade area. What percentage of customers are within one mile of the store: within three miles, within five miles?

PLANNING YOUR OWN RETAIL BUSINESS

The retail store you are planning has an estimated circular trade radius of four miles. Within this four-mile radius there is an average of 1,145 households per square mile. In a normal year you expect that 47 percent of these households would visit your store (referred to as *penetration*) an average of 4.3 times (referred to as *frequency*). Based on those figures, what would you expect to be the traffic (i.e., number of visitors to your store per year)? (*Hint*: Traffic can be viewed as the square miles of the trade area multiplied by the household density multiplied by penetration, which is in turn multiplied by frequency.)

Once you answer this question, do some sensitivity analysis, which is an assessment of how sensitive store traffic is to changes in your assumptions about penetration and frequency. What happens if penetration drops to 45 percent or rises to 50 percent? What happens if frequency drops to 4.0 times annually or rises to 4.5 times annually? In this analysis, change only one thing at a time and hold all other assumptions constant.

CASE

Eminent Domain: Fair or Foul?

Prior to 2005, state and local governments had primarily used eminent domain to confiscate private land to build roads, schools, hospitals, and other public facilities. However, a 5–4 ruling by the U.S. Supreme Court (*Kelo v. City of New London*, 125 S. Ct. 2005) in June 2005, permitted eminent domain powers to be extended to confiscate waterfront homes in order to build an office complex and condominiums. As a result, some local and state governments are now using eminent domain to foreclose on private property so that real estate developers can build shopping malls that will pay more in property taxes to the community than the homes and small businesses they replaced.

These cities favor this expanded use of eminent domain to replace "blighted or deteriorating" private properties for "public use" by explaining that such action will benefit the general public by creating jobs and adding needed tax revenue to the area.

Many responsible city leaders acknowledge that eminent domain is not a power to be used lightly. Cities must be sensitive to those who will be displaced. However, as part of a legislative process, with citizen input and discussion, the use of eminent domain is one of the most powerful tools city officials have to cure neighborhood ills and rejuvenate city budgets. While government officials admit to feeling sympathy for the existing property owners, they have a legal obligation to consider all of their citizens who will benefit from the job creation these projects bring. In addition, they point out that economic development is really cutthroat competition between neighboring communities. If one city or town doesn't offer incentives, its neighbors will.

Existing property owners oppose such action by claiming that the use of eminent domain to wipe out good, clean neighborhoods merely to increase tax revenues is a blow to the rights of all property owners. Theoretically, no property is now safe if some government body concludes that a developer can make better use of it. What is to become of the small business owner who has been at her current location for years and has built a loyal customer following? Others claim that once a city threatens the use of eminent domain, honest negotiations between the parties are over.

After hearing both sides of the argument, some state and local governments today are considering limits on the power of local governments to condemn private property and transfer it to real estate developers merely to improve a community's economic welfare. How can a community be better off if some of its citizens are made to suffer? Among the actions being considered are:

1. *Defining economic benefit*. This involves setting up a procedure to show that the economic benefits gained by the use of eminent domain far out-weigh the negative consequences to the existing property owners. This alternative would make it harder for governmental units to declare a neighborhood "blighted or deteriorating" strictly for economic development.
2. *Total ban*. This entails a complete ban on the use of eminent domain for economic development. This can be accomplished by specifically banning economic development as a reason for permitting eminent domain or by listing what end results can be sought by the use of eminent domain.
3. *Over compensation.* In an attempt to make eminent domain less desirable, local and state governments would have to pay 25 percent to 100 percent above "fair" market value when they confiscate private property for economic development.
4. *Do nothing.* Don't establish separate rules for economic development. Government leaders must consider the benefits to society as whole and not just a few individuals. They must not enact one law for building highways and schools, a second law to eliminate "blight and/or deterioration," and a third law for economic development. After all, aren't all three situations the same?

Questions

1. Should local and state governments be allowed to use eminent domain for any reason? Explain your reasoning.
2. Should local and state governments be allowed to use eminent domain for economic development? Explain your reasoning.
3. When weighing the benefits of economic development, how can you measure the pain and suffering of the displaced property owners?
4. Of the four possible legislative solutions, which one do you favor? Why?

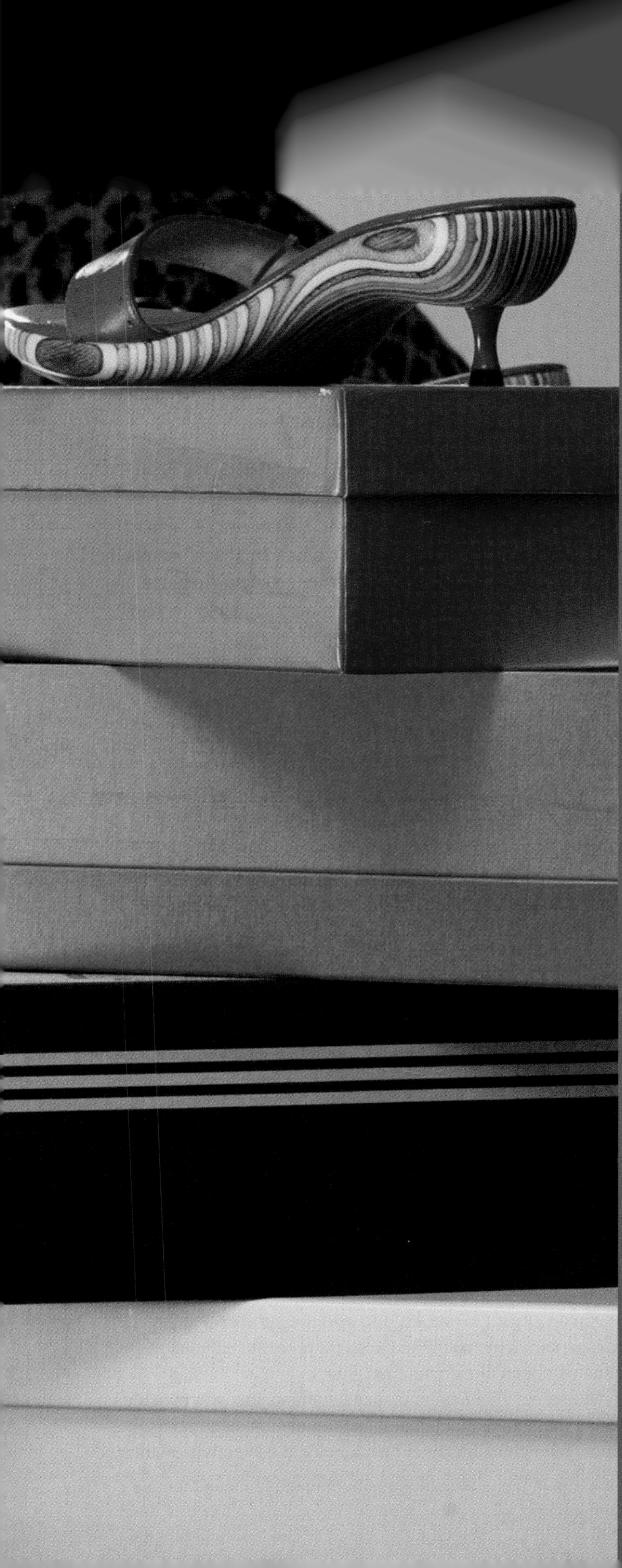

4

Managing Retail Operations

chapter 8

Managing a Retailer's Finances

Overview:

In this chapter, we will begin by looking at how a merchandise budget is prepared and how it is used in making plans for an upcoming merchandise season. Next, we will describe the basic differences among an income statement, balance sheet, and statement of cash flow, as well as how a retailer uses these accounting statements in controlling its merchandising activities. Finally, we will discuss the accounting inventory systems and pricing methods available to value inventory.

Learning Objectives:

After reading this chapter, you should be able to:

1. Describe the importance of a merchandise budget and know how to prepare a six-month merchandise plan.
2. Explain the differences among and the uses of these three accounting statements: income statement, balance sheet, and statement of cash flow.
3. Explain how the retailer is able to value inventory.

LO 1

The Merchandise Budget

Why is a merchandise budget so important in retail planning and how is a merchandise budget prepared?

In Chapter 7 we described the role location plays in a retailer's success. Location is important and was discussed before the other elements of the retail mix because for most new retailers, it is the first decision made. Also, once the location decision is made, it is difficult and costly to change.

Another important retail mix element is merchandising, including pricing. Some experts agree that all the other retail mix elements revolve around merchandising, especially if we consider chain store operators. After all, the merchandise in a JCPenney store in Grand Rapids, Michigan, looks much the same, with only slight variations due to the different climates, as that in Tulsa, Oklahoma. The same may be said about a Carrefour store in Buenos Aires, Argentina, or one in Paris, France. Only after these merchandising decisions are made can retailers concern themselves with the other retail mix elements: promotion, store layout and design, and customer service. However, before we can explain how to make these merchandise decisions we must discuss the retailer's means of controlling these activities.

merchandising
Is the planning and control of the buying and selling of goods and services to help the retailer realize its objectives.

Many people believe that the terms *retailing* and *merchandising* are synonymous. They are not. Retailing includes all the business activities that are necessary to sell goods and services to the final consumer. **Merchandising** is only one of these activities and is

AP Photo/John Russell

Music is a merchandise category where it is difficult to budget far in advance because it is virtually impossible to predict the top selling musical artists and new releases. New releases are only known about one month before release.

concerned with the planning and control involved in the buying and selling of goods and services to help the retailer realize its objectives. Success in merchandising requires total financial planning and control. This chapter is divided into three sections: the merchandise budget, retail accounting statements, and inventory valuation.

Successful retailers must have good financial planning and control of their merchandise. The retailer invests money in merchandise for profitable resale to others. A poor choice of merchandise will result in low profits, or maybe even a loss. Therefore, in order to be successful in retailing, as in any other activity, an individual must have a plan of what is to be accomplished. In retailing this plan of operation is called the merchandise budget. A **merchandise budget** is a plan of projected sales for an upcoming season, when and how much merchandise is to be purchased, and what markups and reductions will likely occur. The merchandise budget forces the retailer to develop a formal outline of merchandising objectives for the upcoming selling season.

merchandise budget
Is a plan of projected sales for an upcoming season, when and how much merchandise is to be purchased, and what markups and reductions will likely occur.

Retailers who thoroughly analyze and project all the factors in developing a merchandise budget for an upcoming season will be more profitable.

Dollars & Sense

In developing the merchandise budget the retailer must make five major merchandising decisions:

1. What will be the anticipated sales for the department, division, or store?
2. How much stock on hand will be needed to achieve this sales plan, given the level of inventory turnover expected?
3. What reductions, if any, from the original retail price must be made in order to dispose of all the merchandise brought into the store?
4. What additional purchases must be made during the season?
5. What **gross margin** (the difference between sales and cost of goods sold) should the department, division, or store contribute to the overall profitability of the company?

gross margin
Is the difference between net sales and cost of goods sold.

When preparing the merchandise budget, a retailer must employ the following four rules.

First, a merchandise budget should always be prepared in advance of the selling season. The original plan is often prepared by the buyer for a particular department for approval by the divisional merchandising manager and/or the general merchandising manager. Therefore, most retail firms selling apparel and hard goods begin the process of developing the merchandise budget three to four months in advance of the budget period. This is not always the case with some specialty retailers, for example, fine restaurants that can easily order special selections such as fresh fish on a daily basis. However, most retailers have only two seasons a year: (1) spring/summer, usually February 1 through July 31, and (2) fall/winter, August 1 through January 31. (Some small retailers may use a three-month budget where the four seasons begin in February, May, August, and November.) The buyer for a particular department will usually begin to prepare merchandise budgets on or about March 1 and September 1 for the upcoming seasons.

Second, since the budget is a plan that management expects to follow in the upcoming merchandise season, the language must be easy to understand. The merchandise budget illustration contained in this chapter has only 11 items, although the number of items contained in a budget may vary by companies due to their particular merchandise and market characteristics. Remember, the budget serves no useful purpose if it cannot be understood by all the decision makers.

Third, because the economy today is constantly changing, the merchandise budget must be planned for a relatively short period of time. Six months is the norm used by most retailers, although some retailers use a three-month, or even shorter, plan. Forecasting future sales is difficult enough without complicating the process by projecting for a time period too far into the future. The firm's upper management should be concerned with long-term trends. The firm's buyers are involved in the more short-term decisions that may influence the merchandise budget.

Fourth, the budget should be flexible enough to permit changes. All merchandise budgets are plans and estimates of predicted future events. However, competition and consumers are not always predictable, especially in regard to fashion preferences. Thus, any forecast is subject to error and will need revisions.

Keeping in mind this discussion of merchandising decisions and rules, review the blank six-month merchandise budget for the Housewares Department of a major department store shown in Exhibit 8.1. Do not be alarmed if Exhibit 8.1 is not clear to you at this time. In the following discussion, as well as in the next chapter, we will describe why the budget is set up in this form. Additionally, we will explain all the analytical tools used by the retailer to calculate the numbers required in developing a six-month merchandise budget or plan.

Exhibit 8.1 appears to be more confusing than it really is because each element is broken into four parts: last year, plan for the upcoming season, revised plan, and actual. This is merely a means to provide the decision maker with complete information. Last year refers to last year's sales for the period; plan for the upcoming season is what the original plan projected; revised plan is the result of any revisions caused by changing market conditions after the plan was accepted; and actual is the final results.

Exhibit 8.2 presents the same material in a simpler form. Here we will only attempt to show you how and why a retailer develops a six-month merchandise plan. Exhibit 8.3 is a summary of how all the numbers in the merchandise budget are determined. Exhibit 8.2 shows the spring/summer season, February through July, for the Two-Seasons Department Store, Department 353, with projected sales of $500,000, planned retail reductions of $50,000 or 10 percent of sales, planned initial markup of 45 percent, and a planned gross margin on purchases of $208,750.

Exhibit 8.1
Sample Six-Month Merchandise Budget

		SIX-MONTH MERCHANDISE BUDGET Housewares Department						
		FEBRUARY	MARCH	APRIL	MAY	JUNE	JULY	Total
BOM Stock	Last Year							
	Plan							
	Revised							
	Actual							
Sales	Last Year							
	Plan							
	Revised							
	Actual							
Reductions	Last Year							
	Plan							
	Revised							
	Actual							
EOM STOCK	Last Year							
	Plan							
	Revised							
	Actual							
RETAIL PURCHASES	Last Year							
	Plan							
	Revised							
	Actual							
PURCHASES @ COST	Last Year							
	Plan							
	Revised							
	Actual							
INITIAL MARKUP	Last Year							
	Plan							
	Revised							
	Actual							
GROSS MARGIN DOLLARS	Last Year							
	Plan							
	Revised							
	Actual							
BOM STOCK/SALES RATIO	Last Year							
	Plan							
	Revised							
	Actual							
SALES PERCENTAGE	Last Year							
	Plan							
	Revised							
	Actual							
RETAIL REDUCTION PERCENTAGE	Last Year							
	Plan							
	Revised							
	Actual							

STOCKTURN: Last Year ____________ Plan ____________ Actual ____________
ON ORDER – BEGINNING OF SEASON ____________ Plan ____________ Actual ____________
EOM INVENTORY FOR LAST MONTH ____________ Plan ____________ Actual ____________
REDUCTION PERCENTAGE ____________ Plan ____________ Actual ____________
MARKUP PERCENTAGE ____________ Plan ____________ Actual ____________

	February	March	April	May	June	July	Total
1. Planned BOM Stock	$225,000	$300,000	$300,000	$250,000	$375,000	$300,000	–
2. Planned Sales	75,000	75,000	100,000	50,000	125,000	75,000	$500,000
3. Planned Retail Reductions	7,500	7,500	5,000	7,500	6,250	16,250	50,000
4. Planned EOM Stock	300,000	300,000	250,000	375,000	300,000	250,000	–
5. Planned Purchases at Retail	157,500	82,500	55,000	182,500	56,250	41,250	575,000
6. Planned Purchases at Cost	86,625	45,375	30,250	100,375	30,937.50	22,687.50	316,250
7. Planned Initial Markup	70,875	37,125	24,750	82,125	25,312.50	18,562.50	258,750
8. Planned Gross Margin	63,375	29,625	19,750	74,625	19,062.50	2,312.50	208,750
9. Planned BOM Stock-to-Sales Ratio	3	4	3	5	3	4	–
10. Planned Sales Percentage	15%	15%	20%	10%	25%	15%	100%
11. Planned Retail Reduction Percentage	10%	10%	5%	15%	5%	21.67%	10%

Planned Total Sales for the Period	$500,000
Planned Total Retail Reduction Percentage for the Period	10%
Planned Initial Markup Percentage	45%
Planned BOM Stock for August	$250,000

Exhibit 8.2
Two-Seasons Department Store, Dept. 353, Six-Month Merchandise Budget

Exhibit 8.3
Formulas for the Six-Month Merchandise Budget

Determining Planned Sales for the Month

(Planned Sales Percentage for the Month) × (Planned Total Sales) = (Planned Sales for the Month)

Determining Planned BOM Stock for the Month

(Planned Sales for the Month) × (Planned BOM Stock-to-Sales Ratio for the Month) = (Planned BOM Stock for the Month)

Determining Planned Retail Reductions for the Month

(Planned Sales for the Month) × (Planned Retail Reduction Percentage for the Month) = (Planned Retail Reductions for the Month)

Determining Planned EOM Stock for the Month

(Planned BOM Stock for the Following Month) = (Planned EOM Stock for the Current Month)

Determining Planned Purchases at Retail for the Month

(Planned Sales for the Month) + (Planned Retail Reductions for the Month) + (Planned EOM Stock for the Month) − (Planned BOM Stock for the Month) = (Planned Purchases at Retail for the Month)

Determining Planned Purchases at Cost for the Month

(Planned Purchases at Retail for the Month) × (100% − Planned Initial Markup Percentage) = (Planned Purchases at Cost for the Month)

Determining Planned Initial Markup for the Month

(Planned Purchases at Retail for the Month) × (Planned Initial Markup Percentage) = (Planned Initial Markup for the Month)

or

(Planned Purchases at Retail for the Month) − (Planned Purchases at Cost for the Month) = (Planned Initial Markup for the Month)

Determining Planned Gross Margin for the Month

(Planned Initial Markup for the Month) − (Planned Retail Reductions for the Month) = (Planned Gross Margin for the Month)

Determining Planned Sales

The initial step in developing a six-month merchandise budget is to estimate planned sales for the entire season and for each month. The buyer begins by examining the previous year's sales records. Adjustments are then made in the planning of sales for the upcoming merchandise budget. When comparing this year's sales to last year's sales, retailers do not always compare to the exact date (i.e., comparing February 10, 2008, sales to February 10, 2007) since February 10th will fall on a different day of the week each year. For instance, as shown in Exhibit 8.4, February 10th in 2008 is on a Sunday, when the retailer might be closed, and on a Saturday in 2007. In 2009, because of the leap year in 2008, February 10th is on a Tuesday, normally a slow day in terms of retail sales. Therefore, retailers use a Retail Reporting Calendar (see Exhibit 8.4), which divides the year into two seasons, each with six months. Thus, February 4, 2008, the first Monday of the spring season (and the first Monday of February for a retailer using the calendar) would be compared to February 5, 2007, which was the first Monday of 2007's spring season. In the year 2009, the first Monday of the spring season is February 2nd.

Exhibit 8.4
Retail Reporting Calendar

SPRING 2007

Month	S	M	T	W	T	F	S
FEB	4	5	6	7	8	9	10
	11	12	13	14	15	16	17
	18	19	20	21	22	23	24
	25	26	27	28	1	2	3
MARCH	4	5	6	7	8	9	10
	11	12	13	14	15	16	17
	18	19	20	21	22	23	24
	25	26	27	28	29	30	31
	1	2	3	4	5	6	7
APRI	8	9	10	11	12	13	14
	15	16	17	18	19	20	21
	22	23	24	25	26	27	28
	29	30	1	2	3	4	5
MAY	6	7	8	9	10	11	12
	13	14	15	16	17	18	19
	20	21	22	23	24	25	26
	27	28	29	30	31	1	2
JUNE	3	4	5	6	7	8	9
	10	11	12	13	14	15	16
	17	18	19	20	21	22	23
	24	25	26	27	28	29	30
	1	2	3	4	5	6	7
JULY	8	9	10	11	12	13	14
	15	16	17	18	19	20	21
	22	23	24	25	26	27	28
	29	30	31	1	2	3	4

FALL 2007

Month	S	M	T	W	T	F	S
AUG	5	6	7	8	9	10	11
	12	13	14	15	16	17	18
	19	20	21	22	23	24	25
	26	27	28	29	30	31	1
SEPT	2	3	4	5	6	7	8
	9	10	11	12	13	14	15
	16	17	18	19	20	21	22
	23	24	25	26	27	28	29
	30	1	2	3	4	5	6
OCT	7	8	9	10	11	12	13
	14	15	16	17	18	19	20
	21	22	23	24	25	26	27
	28	29	30	31	1	2	3
NOV	4	5	6	7	8	9	10
	11	12	13	14	15	16	17
	18	19	20	21	22	23	24
	25	26	27	28	29	30	1
DEC	2	3	4	5	6	7	8
	9	10	11	12	13	14	15
	16	17	18	19	20	21	22
	23	24	25	26	27	28	29
	30	31	1	2	3	4	5
JAN	6	7	8	9	10	11	12
	13	14	15	16	17	18	19
	20	21	22	23	24	25	26
	27	28	29	30	31	1	2

SPRING 2008

Month	S	M	T	W	T	F	S
FEB	3	4	5	6	7	8	9
	10	11	12	13	14	15	16
	17	18	19	20	21	22	23
	24	25	26	27	28	29	1
MARCH	2	3	4	5	6	7	8
	9	10	11	12	13	14	15
	16	17	18	19	20	21	22
	23	24	25	26	27	28	29
	30	31	1	2	3	4	5
APRI	6	7	8	9	10	11	12
	13	14	15	16	17	18	19
	20	21	22	23	24	25	26
	27	28	29	30	1	2	3
MAY	4	5	6	7	8	9	10
	11	12	13	14	15	16	17
	18	19	20	21	22	23	24
	25	26	27	28	29	30	31
JUNE	1	2	3	4	5	6	7
	8	9	10	11	12	13	14
	15	16	17	18	19	20	21
	22	23	24	25	26	27	28
	29	30	1	2	3	4	5
JULY	6	7	8	9	10	11	12
	13	14	15	16	17	18	19
	20	21	22	23	24	25	26
	27	28	29	30	31	1	2

FALL 2008

Month	S	M	T	W	T	F	S
AUG	3	4	5	6	7	8	9
	10	11	12	13	14	15	16
	17	18	19	20	21	22	23
	24	25	26	27	28	29	30
SEPT	31	1	2	3	4	5	6
	7	8	9	10	11	12	13
	14	15	16	17	18	19	20
	21	22	23	24	25	26	27
	28	29	30	1	2	3	4
OCT	5	6	7	8	9	10	11
	12	13	14	15	16	17	18
	19	20	21	22	23	24	25
	26	27	28	29	30	31	1
NOV	2	3	4	5	6	7	8
	9	10	11	12	13	14	15
	16	17	18	19	20	21	22
	23	24	25	26	27	28	29
DEC	30	1	2	3	4	5	6
	7	8	9	10	11	12	13
	14	15	16	17	18	19	20
	21	22	23	24	25	26	27
	28	29	30	31	1	2	3
JAN	4	5	6	7	8	9	10
	11	12	13	14	15	16	17
	18	19	20	21	22	23	24
	25	26	27	28	29	30	31

SPRING 2009

Month	S	M	T	W	T	F	S
FEB	1	2	3	4	5	6	7
	8	9	10	11	12	13	14
	15	16	17	18	19	20	21
	22	23	24	25	26	27	28
MARCH	1	2	3	4	5	6	7
	8	9	10	11	12	13	14
	15	16	17	18	19	20	21
	22	23	24	25	26	27	28
	29	30	31	1	2	3	4
APRI	5	6	7	8	9	10	11
	12	13	14	15	16	17	18
	19	20	21	22	23	24	25
	26	27	28	29	30	1	2
MAY	3	4	5	6	7	8	9
	10	11	12	13	14	15	16
	17	18	19	20	21	22	23
	24	25	26	27	28	29	30
JUNE	31	1	2	3	4	5	6
	7	8	9	10	11	12	13
	14	15	16	17	18	19	20
	21	22	23	24	25	26	27
	28	29	30	1	2	3	4
JULY	5	6	7	8	9	10	11
	12	13	14	15	16	17	18
	19	20	21	22	23	24	25
	26	27	28	29	30	31	1

FALL 2009

Month	S	M	T	W	T	F	S
AUG	2	3	4	5	6	7	8
	9	10	11	12	13	14	15
	16	17	18	19	20	21	22
	23	24	25	26	27	28	29
SEPT	30	31	1	2	3	4	5
	6	7	8	9	10	11	12
	13	14	15	16	17	18	19
	20	21	22	23	24	25	26
	27	28	29	30	1	2	3
OCT	4	5	6	7	8	9	10
	11	12	13	14	15	16	17
	18	19	20	21	22	23	24
	25	26	27	28	29	30	31
NOV	1	2	3	4	5	6	7
	8	9	10	11	12	13	14
	15	16	17	18	19	20	21
	22	23	24	25	26	27	28
DEC	29	30	1	2	3	4	5
	6	7	8	9	10	11	12
	13	14	15	16	17	18	19
	20	21	22	23	24	25	26
	27	28	29	30	31	1	2
JAN	3	4	5	6	7	8	9
	10	11	12	13	14	15	16
	17	18	19	20	21	22	23
	24	25	26	27	28	29	30

Michael Bradley/Getty Images

The month when Easter falls each year makes prior year sales comparisons difficult.

By using this calendar, retailers are able to make direct comparisons to prior years. Office supply retailers, such as Staples and Office Depot, can compare sales for their two nontraditional key seasons (late summer/early fall for "back to school" supplies and January, when businesses tend to open new budgets and everyone prepares for the tax season) to those for the previous years. Some retailers, such as fashion/apparel retailers, may have problems making direct comparisons. They will be affected once each season by the movement of Easter (April 8th in 2007, March 23rd in 2008, and April 12th in 2009) and Thanksgiving. For example, in both 2007 and 2008 Easter sales occur during the March reporting period. In 2009, however, Easter falls on the eighth day of the retailers' April reporting period. March's sales will probably suffer in comparison to 2007 and 2008, but April's apparel sales should benefit. In addition, the expected warmer weather should also improve Easter sales, as many consumers in northern climates don't want to put a coat over a new Easter outfit. During the fall season, the period between Thanksgiving and Christmas can vary in length by as much as a week. Since Thanksgiving is the fourth Thursday of November, it can fall between November 22 and 28. As a result, the number of days in the Christmas shopping season will differ from year to year. For example, in 2008 and 2009 there are four weekends (Christmas is on a Thursday in 2008 and on a Friday in 2009) and 27 and 28 shopping days, respectively, between Thanksgiving and Christmas, while in 2007 there were five full weekends and 32 days between November 22 and Christmas Day.

The use of a retail reporting calendar cannot overcome many of the uncontrollable and unexpected variables retailers encounter when forecasting sales. Retailers are just now learning how to deal with the greatest uncontrollable variable they must face—the weather. As the chapter's Service Retailing box describes, the consequences of weather can have a major impact on a retailer's planned sales projections. In February 2006 apparel retailers were hurt by two weather events: (1) an East Coast blizzard just before Valentine's Day that closed the stores and (2) significantly colder temperatures than normal. February's average nationwide temperature was seven degrees lower than January's. To make matters worse, these events occurred after a warm "Indian summer" in fall of 2005 that hurt autumn sales of sweaters and coats.

Sometimes weather can produce unusual consequences for retailers. When Texans in 2003 experienced 12 straight days of 100-degrees-plus heat, the tanning salons were surprisingly busy. The outdoor heat was simply too intense for many Texans, resulting in record business for the air-conditioned tanning salons. At the same time, the volume at local putt-putt courses was off nearly 50 percent. Conversely, in other parts of the country, cooler weather led to different results. Community Health Systems, one of the nation's largest rural hospital groups, explained that lower admittance figures were due to the weather.[1] (The cooler summer meant fewer respiratory problems.) In each of these situations, retailers were caught off-guard by uncharacteristic changes in consumer behavior. Today, in view of the above-mentioned weather effects, even the smallest retailer should review the Weather Bureau's long-range forecast before making buying plans. Large retailers, including JCPenney, Wal-Mart, Sam's Club, ASDA, Kohl's, Lowe's, Saks Inc., Carson Pirie

Service Retailing

How Weather Forecasts Can Improve Retail Performance

Consider the case of auto service retailers and car battery sales. As anyone who has lived above the Mason-Dixon Line knows, finding your car battery dead on a cold morning is one of life's most unpleasant surprises. While all consumers know that frigid weather is the #1 cause of dead batteries, many car owners tend to postpone replacing their battery and are often unprepared when a battery problem occurs.

How can retailers use this information when forecasting sales? To start, it is imperative that they know the most conducive weather for a product's sales, in this case car batteries, before developing a merchandising budget or planning promotional events.

The figure below, for example, shows the deviation from average automotive battery sales in Minneapolis, Minnesota,

AUTOMOTIVE BATTERY SALES VS WEATHER
Minneapolis, MN

Precipitation	0° to 4°	5° to 9°	10° to 14°	15° to 19°	20° to 24°	25° to 29°	30° to 34°	35° to 39°	40° to 44°	45° to 49°	50° to 54°	55° to 59°	60° to 64°	65° to 69°	70° to 74°	75° to 79°	80° to 84°
Very Dry	150%	44%	30%	−2%	−23%	−10%	−21%	18%	1%	3%	0%	−6%	3%	0%	16%	23%	16%
Dry	195%			−7%	−1%	−2%	−6%	15%	−12%	−12%	−8%	23%	5%	14%	10%	11%	35%
Average			52%	−11%	−35%	−51%	−9%	−5%	−41%	−19%	11%	−12%	4%	−6%	24%	29%	46%
Wet	17%	8%		−21%	−45%	−30%	−44%	−19%	7%	−26%	35%	−15%	−12%	−16%	13%	33%	13%
Very Wet			142%	−24%	−3%	−15%	−63%	−15%	−31%	−16%	−8%	0%	−7%	4%	16%	6%	10%
Deviation From Average Annual Unit Sales	106%	38%	52%	−14%	−16%	−9%	−25%	5%	−12%	−9%	−1%	−3%	−1%	−1%	14%	20%	25%

5°F Temperature Intervals (Weekly Mean Temperature)

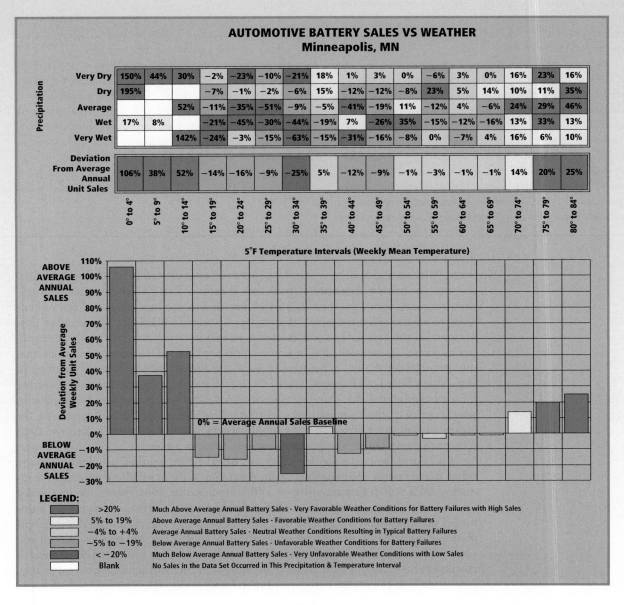

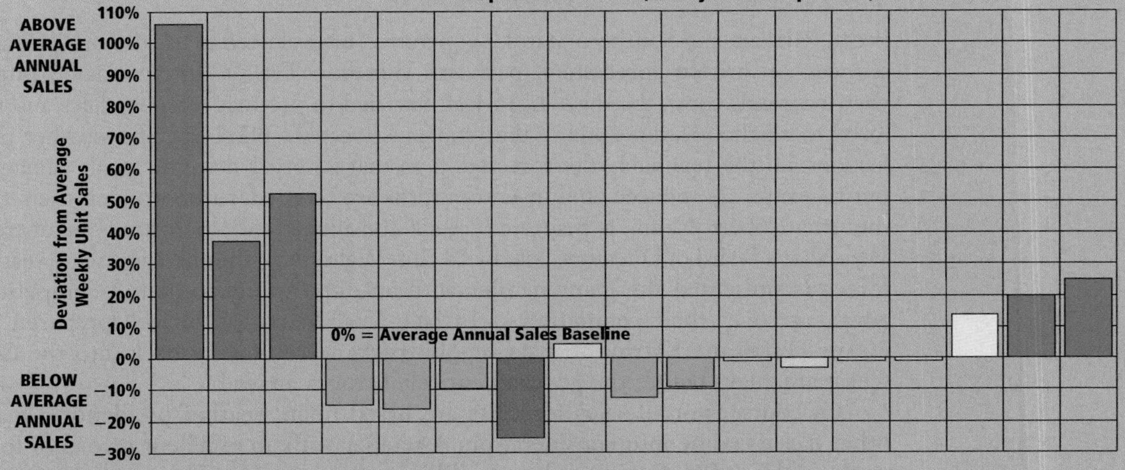

LEGEND:

- >20% — Much Above Average Annual Battery Sales - Very Favorable Weather Conditions for Battery Failures with High Sales
- 5% to 19% — Above Average Annual Battery Sales - Favorable Weather Conditions for Battery Failures
- −4% to +4% — Average Annual Battery Sales - Neutral Weather Conditions Resulting in Typical Battery Failures
- −5% to −19% — Below Average Annual Battery Sales - Unfavorable Weather Conditions for Battery Failures
- < −20% — Much Below Average Annual Battery Sales - Very Unfavorable Weather Conditions with Low Sales
- Blank — No Sales in the Data Set Occurred in This Precipitation & Temperature Interval

(continued)

Service Retailing *(continued)*

in 5° Fahrenheit temperature intervals across five precipitation categories. Temperatures are defined as a weekly mean temperature. Therefore, when it is really cold, with weekly mean temperatures below 14° (implying high temperatures in the middle 20°s and low temperatures in the middle single digits) there is a 52 percent increase in battery sales due to weather-driven failures. (Notice that there is a 66 percent swing in sales with just a 5° drop from 19° to 14°.)

Consider the problems of a retailer who planned a battery promotion for a particular winter week in Minneapolis, only to see temperatures rise unexpectedly to a balmy weekly mean of 32° (high temperatures in the 40°s) that week. There probably wouldn't be an increase in battery sales, and the advertising dollars would be wasted!

The figure on the previous page illustrates the importance of using weather forecasts when projecting sales. Historically, when the Minneapolis area has a weekly mean of 32° along with very wet conditions (200 percent above average rain or snowfall), battery sales will fall 63 percent below average sales. Conversely, if colder weather is predicted, say 0° to 4°, sales should increase by 106 percent over average. The product-weather matrix also illustrates that temperatures between 15° and 49° generally result in fewer battery failures and resulting lower sales. Between 50° and 69°, battery sales are near average, with little impact due to weather. However, when temperatures are 70° or higher, failures increase 14 percent to 25 percent above average and extremely hot weather—above 80° with average precipitation—results in peak summer sales of nearly 50 percent above average. (High temperatures would be in the middle 90°s in Minneapolis.) Precipitation has little impact on this product category in this part of the country.

Therefore, using a reliable weather forecast to determine the most likely really cold, or really hot, weeks would allow retailers to strategically plan to have more battery inventory during these key periods and enable them to craft effective retailing plans.

Battery retailers located in southern cities, which do not get cold enough in winter months to result in failures, should make forecasts based on hot summer weather.

The product-weather matrix can be done for any category by assessing weekly unit sales against past weather conditions for several years to identify the optimal combination of temperature and precipitation for sales of a particular product. Sales can then be grouped by temperature and precipitation intervals, and expressed as a unit value or deviation from average annual sales.

Source: Based on Bill Kirk, "Better Business in Any Weather," *ICSC Research Review*, v. 12, No. 2, 2005: 28–34; and used with Mr. Kirk's written permission.

Scott, Parisian, and Southern States Cooperative, have elected to use the sophisticated services of private forecasters, such as Weather Trends International (http://www.wxtrends.com), that have historical data tied to product category sales and tailored to all the locations where the retailer is located. These specific weather projections aid the retailer's sales forecasting so that its gross margins aren't damaged, out-of-stocks are reduced, and inventory turns are boosted. Little wonder, then, that the late Robert Kahn, a respected retail consultant and long-time member of Wal-Mart's Board of Directors, convinced Sam Walton that the effective use of weather forecasts presented the giant retailer with an opportunity to gain a competitive advantage over their competitors.[2] In fact, Wal-Mart was so well prepared for 2005's Hurricane Katrina that its supply trucks were moving back into the Gulf Coast area days before the government relief trucks arrived.[3]

Of course, not all sales forecasts are based upon weather predictions; many other factors come into consideration. A retailer with an excellent record of forecasting sales is San Francisco-based Williams-Sonoma, best known for its *Catalog for Cooks*. Williams-Sonoma's secret for forecasting sales rests on its highly automated mailing lists. Its database of 5 million customers tracks up to 150 different pieces of information per customer. With a few keystrokes, the retailer can tell you what you've bought from each of its five annual catalogs (an estimated 60 percent of customers have bought from more than one), what time of the year you tend to buy, how often you buy, what category of merchandise you lean toward, and so forth.

Through a complex cross-referencing of the data, Williams-Sonoma's two full-time statisticians are able to project, to 5 percent accuracy on average, each catalog's sales.

Forecasting is most important for service retailers because their services are perishable. Services present unique forecasting problems for retailers because, unlike physical products, they cannot be produced or manufactured, boxed, stored, and shelved. In fact, services theoretically perish the moment they are produced. This perishability is not a problem when demand is steady. However, when demand fluctuates, service retailers have problems. As a result, service retailers often try to balance their demand and supply by continually altering their retail mix in an attempt to better manage sales. Many restaurant chains now seek to balance their supply and demand with the aid of a computer program that tracks the sales of every menu item on an hourly basis and sets cooking schedules based on the program. After consulting the printout, the restaurant's manager can determine how many baked potatoes to cook and when to put them in the oven to meet the expected demand. While it's not completely accurate, the computer bats close to 90 percent according to one Texas steakhouse manager. The same program can also be used to order merchandise and schedule hourly employees. The computer program alone saves the retailer more than 25 hours a week in hand calculations. Another group of service retailers for whom proper forecasting can make the difference between profit and loss is the travel industry. These retailers need to know how many customers on each flight will not show up. As described in Chapter 2's Service Retailing box on page 42, by accurately estimating who will really be on any given flight, airlines can avoid offending their valued frequent business flyers.

Return now to the example in Exhibit 8.2. After reviewing the data available, the buyer for Department 353 forecasts that $500,000 was a reasonable total sales figure for the future season. June, with a projected 25 percent of the total season's sales, and April, with 20 percent, are expected to be the busy months. May, with only 10 percent, is expected to be the slowest month. The remaining months will have equal sales. Since April, May, and June account for 55 percent of total sales, then February, March, and July's total must be 45 percent, or 15 percent per month since they are equal. The buyer is able to determine planned monthly sales by multiplying the planned monthly sales percentage by planned total sales. Since we know February's planned monthly sales are 15 percent of the total planned sales of $500,000, February's planned sales must be $75,000 ($15\% \times \$500{,}000 = \$75{,}000$).

It is important to use recent trends when forecasting future sales. All too often retailers in no-growth markets merely use last season's figures for the current season's budget. This method overlooks two major influences on projected sales volume: inflation and competition. If inflation is 10 percent and no other changes have occurred in the retail environment, then the retailer planning on selling the same physical volume as the previous year should expect a 10 percent increase in this season's dollar sales. Similarly, if the exit of a competitor across town is expected to increase the number of customer transactions by 5 percent, this increase should be reflected in the budget. Suppose that last year's sales were $100,000, inflation is 10 percent, and the retailer expects its market share to increase by 8 percent while the total market remains stable. What should the projected sales be? A simple equation used in retail planning is

$$\text{Total sales} = \text{Average sales per transaction} \times \text{Total transactions}$$

In the preceding example, average sales would increase by the 10 percent level of inflation to 1.10 times last year's sales, and total transactions would increase by the 8 percent gain in market share to 1.08 times last year's total transactions, for an increase in total sales of 1.188 times (or 1.10 × 1.08), resulting in a total sales increase of $18,800 or budgeted total sales of $118,800.

Dollars & Sense

Since planning future sales is the most important part of developing a merchandise budget, the retailers that do the best job of forecasting sales will be the most profitable.

Determining Planned BOM and EOM Inventories

Once the buyer has estimated seasonal and monthly sales for the upcoming season, plans can be made for inventory requirements. In order to achieve projected sales figures, the merchant will generally carry stock or inventory in excess of planned sales for the period, be it a week, month, or season. The extra stock or inventory provides a merchandise assortment deep and broad enough to meet customer needs. A common method of estimating the amount of stock to be carried is the **stock-to-sales ratio**. This ratio depicts the amount of stock to have on hand at the beginning of each month to support the forecasted sales for that month. For example, a ratio of 5:1 would suggest that the retailer have $5 in inventory (at retail price) for every $1 in forecasted sales. Planned average beginning-of-the-month (BOM) stock-to-sales ratios can also be calculated directly from a retailer's planned turnover goals. For example, a retailer wants a target turnover rate of 4.0. By dividing the annual turnover rate into 12 (the number of months in a year), the average BOM stock-to-sales ratio for the year can be computed. In this case, 12 divided by 4.0 equals 3.0. Thus the average stock-to-sales ratio for the season is 3.0. Generally, stock-to-sales ratios will fluctuate month to month because sales tend to fluctuate monthly. Nevertheless, it is important to always review these ratios because if they are set too high or too low, too much or too little inventory will be on hand to meet the sales target. Remember, it is just as bad to have too much inventory on hand as it is to have too little. Stocking too much inventory could result in inventory-holding costs that outweigh the gross margins to be made on sale of the merchandise.

stock-to-sales ratio
Depicts the amount of stock to have at the beginning of each month to support the forecasted sales for that month.

Retail trade associations such as the National Retail Federation (NRF) in the United States (http://www.nrf.com) and the Australian Retailers Association (http://www.ara.com.au) conduct surveys and publish industry average stock-to-sales ratios. For example, based on available data, the buyer for Department 353 in Exhibit 8.2 used a planned stock-to-sales ratio of 3.0 for February, April, and June; a ratio of 4.0 for March and July; and a ratio of 5.0 for May. The buyer was able to determine that $300,000 worth of merchandise was needed beginning March 1 due to a planned stock-to-sales ratio of 4.0 and planned sales of $75,000 (line 1). Two things should be noted. First, stock-to-sales ratios always express inventory levels at retail, not cost. Second, the beginning-of-the-month (BOM) inventory for one month is the end-of-the month (EOM) inventory for the previous month. This relationship can be easily seen by comparing the BOM figures (line 1) for one month with the EOM figures for the previous month (line 4).

Determining Planned Retail Reductions

All merchandise brought into the store for sale to consumers is not actually sold at the planned initial markup price. Therefore, when preparing the six-month budget, the buyer should make allowances for reductions in the dollar level of inventory that results from non-sale events. Generally, these planned retail reductions fall into three types: markdowns, employee discounts, and stock shortages. These reductions must be planned because as the dollar value of the inventory level is reduced, the BOM stock that is planned to support next month's forecasted sales will be inadequate unless adjustments are made this month. A buyer must remember that reductions are part of the cost of doing business.

Retailers who recognize that reductions are part of the cost of doing business and plan appropriately will achieve higher profits.

Dollars & Sense

A small number of retailers do not include planned reductions in their merchandise budgets. They simply treat them as part of the normal operation of the store and feel they should be controlled without being a separate line item in the budget. This gives management an understated, conservative planned-purchase figure, thereby having the effect of holding back some purchase reserve until the physical inventory reveals the exact amount of reductions. We have chosen to include planned reductions in this text for two reasons: (1) to reflect the additional purchases needed for sufficient inventory to begin the next month and (2) to point out that taking reductions is not bad. Too often, inexperienced retailers believe that taking a reduction is an admission of error and therefore they fail to mark down merchandise until it is too late in the season. A buyer must remember that reductions are part of the cost of doing business. Methods available to the retail buyer for minimizing retail reductions caused by retailer mistakes are discussed in Chapter 10.

Note that the reductions in our six-month budget are listed as a percentage of planned sales. The buyer in our example has estimated monthly retail reduction percentages as shown on line 11. To determine planned retail reductions for March (line 3), planned monthly sales are multiplied by the planned monthly retail reduction percentage to yield the planned monthly retail reduction of \$7,500 (\$75,000 × 10% = \$7,500).

Reductions are one of the major items in the merchandise budget subject to constant change. One reason is that the planned reductions may prove inadequate in light of actual conditions encountered by the retailer. If retailers delay too long in taking reductions, especially those resulting from unexpected weather, they may be forced to take even larger price cuts later as the merchandise style depreciates even more in value. Alternatively, consider what happens when the department manager does such an effective merchandising job that not all the reduction money is needed for the period. The solution to both these dilemmas is found in the rules for developing a budget; namely, keeping it flexible so it can be intelligently administered.

Determining Planned Purchases at Retail and Cost

We are now ready to determine whether additional purchases must be made during the merchandising season. The retailer will need inventory for (1) planned sales, (2) planned retail reductions, and (3) planned EOM inventory. Planned BOM inventory represents purchases that have already been made. In the six-month merchandise budget shown in Exhibit 8.2, the March planned purchases at retail for Department 353 are \$82,500 (line 5). This figure was derived by (1) adding planned sales, planned retail reductions, and planned EOM inventory and (2) subtracting planned BOM inventory:

$$\$75{,}000 + \$7{,}500 + \$300{,}000 - \$300{,}000 = \$82{,}500$$

Once planned purchases at retail are determined, planned purchases at cost can be easily calculated. The retail price always represents a combination of cost plus markup. If the markup percentage is given, the portion of retail attributed to cost, or the cost complement, can be derived by subtracting the markup percentage from the retail percentage of 100 percent. Given that the markup percentage is 45 percent of retail for Department 353, the cost complement percentage must be 55 percent (100% – 45% = 55%). Planned purchases at cost for March (line 6), must be 55 percent of planned purchases at retail or $45,375 ($82,500 × 55% = $45,375). Planned initial markup for March (line 7) must be 45 percent of planned purchases or $37,125 ($82,500 × 45% = $37,125).

Determining the Buyer's Planned Gross Margin

The buyer is accountable for the purchases made, the expected selling price of these purchases, the cost of these purchases, and the reductions that are involved in selling merchandise the buyer has previously purchased. Therefore, the last step in developing the merchandise budget is determining the buyer's planned gross margin for the period. As already discussed, the buyer, in making plans, recognizes that the initial selling price for all the products will probably not be realized and that some reductions will occur. Referring to Exhibit 8.2, the buyer's planned gross margin for February (line 8) is determined by taking planned initial markup (line 7) and subtracting planned reductions (line 3) ($70,875 – $7,500 = $63,375).

LO 2

Retail Accounting Statements

What are the differences among and the uses of these three accounting statements: income statement, balance sheet, and statement of cash flow?

Successful retailing also requires sound accounting practices. The number and types of accounting records needed depend on management's objectives. Large retailers generally require more detailed information, usually based on merchandise lines or departments. Smaller retailers may be able to make first-hand observations of sales and inventory levels and make decisions before financial data are available. For example, a retailer in a developing country owning and operating a 100-square-foot store can easily use observation to obtain a general idea of the store's inventory. Still, the small retailer should consult the accounting records to confirm personal observations.

Properly prepared financial records provide measurements of profitability and retail performance. In addition, they show all transactions occurring within a given time period. However, these financial records must provide the manager not only with a look at the past but also a preview of the future so the manager can plan. Financial records not only indicate if a retailer has achieved good results, they also demonstrate what growth potential and problem areas lie ahead:

1. Is one merchandise line outperforming or underperforming the rest of the store?
2. Is the inventory level adequate for the current sales level?
3. Is the firm's debt level too high (does the firm owe too much money)?
4. Are reductions, including markdowns, too high a percentage of sales?
5. Is the gross margin adequate for the firm's profit objectives?

These are a few of the questions that the financial data must answer for the retailer. The authors know of one company where merchandise line "X" was generating an annual profit of $800,000, and merchandise line "Y" was losing money at the rate of $600,000 a year. Management was totally unaware of the situation, just happy to be making $200,000! They were astounded when a little accounting work revealed the true situation.

Let's look at the three financial statements most commonly used by retailers: the income statement, the balance sheet, and the statement of cash flow.

Income Statement

The most important financial statement a retailer prepares is the income statement (also referred to as the *profit and loss statement*). The **income statement** provides a summary of the sales and expenses for a given time period, usually monthly, quarterly, seasonally, or annually. Comparison of current results with prior results allows the retailer to notice trends or changes in sales, expenses, and profits. However, given the accounting scandals earlier this decade at Enron and Krispy Kreme,[4] the mere fact that a company reports increased earnings each year and the income statement looks great should not lead one to believe that everything is fine. New government regulations have resulted in some restoration of that confidence. However, there are still some unclear areas regarding the reporting of income and expenses.

income statement
Is a financial statement that provides a summary of the sales and expenses for a given time period, usually a month, quarter, season, or year.

Income statements can be broken down by departments, divisions, branches, and so on, enabling the retailer to evaluate each subunit's operating performance for the period. Exhibit 8.5a shows the basic format for an income statement and Exhibit 8.5b shows the income statement for TMD Furniture.

gross sales
Are the retailer's total sales including sales for cash or for credit.

Gross sales are the retailer's total sales, including sales for cash or for credit. **Returns and allowances** are reductions from gross sales. Here the retailer makes a financial adjustment for customers who became dissatisfied with their purchases and have returned the merchandise to the retailer. Since these reductions represent cancellations of previously recorded sales, the gross sales figure must be reduced to reflect these cancellations.

returns and allowances
Are refunds of the purchase price or downward adjustments in selling prices due to customers returning purchases, or adjustments made in the selling price due to customer dissatisfaction with product or service performance.

Net sales, gross sales less returns and allowances, represent the amount of merchandise the retailer actually sold during the time period. Sometimes it is difficult to determine what figure to report for net sales. As the chapter's Retailing: What's New box illustrates, retailers often have problems determining how to account for rebates when reporting net sales.

net sales
Are gross sales less returns and allowances.

Cost of goods sold is the cost of merchandise that has been sold during the period. While this concept is easy to understand, the exact calculation of the cost of goods sold is somewhat complex. For example, like their own customers, retailers may obtain some return privileges or receive some allowances from vendors. Also, there is the issue of determining how inventory levels will be carried on the company's books. This will be fully discussed in the next section of this chapter.

cost of goods sold
Is the cost of merchandise that has been sold during the period.

Exhibit 8.5A
Retailers' Basic Income Statement Format

Gross Sales		$________
– Returns and Allowances	$________	
Net Sales		$________
– Cost of Goods Sold	$________	
Gross Margin		$________
– Operating Expenses	$________	
Operating Profit		$________
±Other Income or Expenses	$________	
Net Profit Before Taxes		$________

Exhibit 8.5B
Sample Income Statement

TMD Furniture, Inc.
Six-Month Income Statement
July 31

				Percentage
Gross Sales			$393,671.79	
Less: Returns and Allowances			16,300.00	
Net Sales				
Less: Cost of Goods Sold			$377,371.79	100%
Beginning Inventory		$ 98,466.29		
Purchases		218,595.69		
Goods Available for Sales		$317,061.98		
Ending Inventory		103,806.23	213,255.75	56.5%
Gross Margin			$164,116.04	43.5%
Less: Operating Expenses				
Salaries & Wages:				
Managers	$18,480.50			
Selling	17,755.65			
Office	7,580.17			
Warehouse & Delivery	6,685.99	50,502.31		
Advertising		$ 15,236.67		
Administration and Warehouse Charge		800.00		
Credit, Collections, and Bad Debts		1,973.96		
Contributions		312.50		
Delivery		1,434.93		
Depreciation		5,398.56		
Dues		23.50		
Employee Benefits		566.26		
Utilities		3,738.74		
Insurance		3,041.75		
Legal and Auditing		1,000.00		
Merchandise Service & Repair		1,439.16		
Miscellaneous		602.00		
Rent		9,080.00		
Repairs & Maintenance		1,576.99		
Sales Allowances		180.50		
Supplies, Postage		1,135.40		
Taxes:				
City, County, & State	$ 2,000.00			
Payroll	3,902.90	5,902.90		
Telephone		1,520.09		
Travel		404.92		
Warehouse Handling Charges		12,216.86	118,088.00	31.3%
Operating Profit			$ 46,028.04	12.2%
Other Income:				
Carrying Charges		$ 3,377.48		
Profit on sale of parking lot		740.47	4,117.95	1.1%
Net Profit Before Taxes			$ 50,145.99	13.3%

What's New?

How Rebates Affect Net Sales

Rebates are agreements to refund a portion of a purchase price to the consumer. They are offered by both vendors and retailers to encourage sales. During 2006, it is estimated that over $6 billion of rebates were offered. (This figure doesn't include automobile rebates.)

The financial community has struggled with how to account for rebates. Should rebates be considered a reduction of sales or a cost of selling the product? Also, should the dollar amount of the rebate be recognized at the time of the sale or when the rebate is actually redeemed?

The Emerging Issues Task Force (EITF) is the part of the Financial Accounting Standards Board (FASB) that develops consensus concerning newer or unusual types of financial transactions. When the EITF was asked to review the way that retailers accounted for rebates, it issued a conclusion (EITF 01–09) that required rebates to be recognized as a reduction of sales (rather than a selling expense). In addition, they required that the reduction be recognized at the time the sale was made.

For example, suppose that during a three month promotion period a retailer sells $1 million of "special" merchandise offering a 20 percent rebate. Even though the company collects $1 million in sales, they are allowed to recognize sales of only $800,000 and a liability (known as a "Liability for Rebate Claims") for $200,000. As customers redeem the rebates, the liability is reduced.

However, determining the amount of the liability may be complicated by rebates the customer does not claim or what is referred to as *breakage*. Oftentimes these rebates are not redeemed because the customer either forgets or does not consider the effort of processing the rebate worthwhile. If the company can estimate the amount of breakage, the company may reduce the liability by the amount of expected breakage. For example, if the company believes that 50 percent of the rebate offers will be redeemed, they will recognize $900,000 in sales and a liability of $100,000.

Collections	$1,000,000
Liability for Rebate Claims	– 200,000
Expected Breakage	+ 100,000
Sales Recognized	$ 900,000

Critics of this accounting method claim that companies can increase their sales by purposely overestimating the expected breakage. For example, by using a 75 percent breakage in the above example, the retailer can increase sales recognized by $50,000 to $950,000. In addition, as was pointed in Chapter 6's Retailing: The Inside Story box on page 178, others claim that retailers make redeeming rebates difficult so that only 40 percent of all rebates are actually redeemed. As a result of this low redemption rate, they feel that rebates are deceptive because the customer is really paying something closer to the $4.99 regular price (not the $3.99 "after the 20% rebate" price that was posted above the display).

Source: Prepared by Dr. William Pasewark, Texas Tech University.

Gross margin is the difference between net sales and cost of goods sold or the amount available to cover operating expenses and produce a profit.

Operating expenses are those expenses that a retailer incurs in running the business other than the cost of the merchandise (e.g., rent, wages, utilities, depreciation, advertising, and insurance).

operating expenses
Are those expenses that a retailer incurs in running the business other than the cost of the merchandise.

Retailers must consider not only Generally Accepted Accounting Principles (GAAP) regulations when presenting their income statement, but also Internal Revenue Service (IRS) rulings. The IRS provided a tax break for retailers by ruling that they may estimate inventory shrinkage (the loss of merchandise through theft, loss, and damage).[5] This enables retailers to reduce ending inventory and thus taxable earnings. Prior to this change, which resulted from court cases involving Kroger and Target, the IRS did not permit retailers to estimate shrinkage from the last physical inventory to the end of the retailer's tax year, usually the end of January. Since it is not feasible for most retail chains to count all their inventory in a single day in late January, most chains check inventory on a rotating basis throughout the year and can now estimate their losses without being challenged by the IRS.

operating profit
Is gross margin less operating expenses.

other income or expenses
Includes income or expense items that the firm incurs which are not in the course of its normal retail operations.

net profit
Is operating profit plus or minus other income or expenses.

Operating profit is the difference between gross margin and operating expenses.

Other income or expenses includes income or expense items that the firm incurs other than in the course of its normal retail operations. For example, a retailer might have purchased some land to use for expansion and after careful deliberation, postponed the expansion plans. Now the retailer rents that land. Since renting land is not in the normal course of business for a retailer, the rent received would be considered other income. Likewise, many convenience stores place income from selling money orders under other income and supermarkets report the rent received from banks and pharmacies operating in their buildings as other income.

It is also on this line of the income statement that most grocery chains report the revenue from their non-selling activities such as slotting fees, promotional allowances, and free goods, because this revenue is considered to be earned by buying merchandise, rather than selling it.

Net profit is operating profit plus or minus other income or expenses. Net profit is the figure on which the retailer pays taxes and thus is usually referred to as net profit before taxes.

Many retailers actually divide the income statement into two sections: the first, or top half, being those elements above the gross margin total and the second, or bottom half, being those elements below the gross margin total. Sales and cost of goods sold are essentially controllable by the buying functions of the retail organization. In more and more retailing operations today the buying organization is separated from the store management team who is primarily concerned with the operating expenses that are shown below gross margin. As a result, store managers often look at gross margin from the bottom up and use this formula:

$$\text{gross margin} = \text{operating expenses} + \text{profit}$$

Sometimes retailers use the terms "top line" (sales), "gross" (gross margin), "line above the bottom" (other income), and "bottom line" (profit) when referring to the key elements of their income statement.

Finally, it is important to point out that, just as they do in the reporting of revenues, GAAP allow for variations in how retailers report certain expenses. Pre-opening expenses, for example, can be expensed as they occur, during the month the store opens, or capitalized and written off over several years. Advertising can be written off when the ad runs or when payment is made. Store fixtures can be depreciated over 5 years, 40 years, or some increment in between. Thus, when comparing the financial statements of different retailers, it is important to know how each retailer treated these and other expenses.

Balance Sheet

The second accounting statement used in financial reporting is the balance sheet. A balance sheet shows the financial condition of a retailer's business at a particular point in time, as opposed to the income statement, which reports on the activities over a period of time. The balance sheet identifies and quantifies all the firm's assets and liabilities. The difference between assets and liabilities is the owner's equity or net worth. Comparing a current balance sheet with one from a previous time period enables a retail analyst to observe changes in the firm's financial condition.

A typical balance sheet format is illustrated in Exhibit 8.6. As Exhibit 8.6a shows, the basic equation for a balance sheet is

$$\text{Assets} = \text{Liabilities} + \text{Net worth}$$

Hence, both sides always must be in balance. Exhibit 8.6b shows the balance sheet for TMD Furniture.

Current Assets			Current Liabilities		
Cash	$____		Accounts Payable	$____	
Accounts Receivable	$____		Payroll Payable	$____	
Inventory	$____		Current Notes Payable	$____	
Prepaid Expenses	$____		Taxes Payable	$____	
Total Current Assets		$____	Total Current Liabilities		$____
Noncurrent Assets			Long-term Liabilities		
Building (less depreciation)	$____		Long-term Notes Payable	$____	
Fixtures and Equipment (less depreciation)	$____		Mortgage Payable	$____	
Total Noncurrent Assets		$____			
Goodwill		$____	Total Long-term Liabilities		$____
			Net Worth		
			Capital Surplus	$____	
			Retained Earnings	$____	
			Total Net Worth		$____
Total Assets		$____	**Total Liabilities** and **Net Worth**		$____

Exhibit 8.6A
Retailers' Basic Balance Sheet Format

asset
Is anything of value that is owned by the retail firm.

current assets
Are assets that can be easily converted into cash within a relatively short period of time (usually a year or less).

accounts and/or notes receivable
Are amounts that customers owe the retailer for goods and services.

TMD Furniture, Inc.
Balance Sheet
July 31

Current Assets			Current Liabilities		
Cash	$ 11,589		Accounts Payable	$57,500	
Accounts Receivable	71,517		Payroll Payable	1,451	
Inventory	103,806		Current Notes Payable	14,000	
			Taxes Payable	1,918	
Total Current Assets		$186,912	Total Current Liabilities		$ 74,869
Noncurrent Assets			Long-term Liabilities		
Building (less depreciation)	$ 61,414		Long-term Notes Payable	$52,750	
Fixtures and Equipment (less depreciation)	11,505		Mortgage Payable	38,500	
Total Noncurrent Assets		72,919	Total Long-term Liabilities		$ 91,250
Goodwill		100	Net Worth		93,812
Total Assets		$259,931	**Total Liabilities** and **Net Worth**		$259,931

Exhibit 8.6B
Sample Balance Sheet

An **asset** is anything of value that is owned by the retail firm. Assets are broken down into two categories: current and noncurrent.

Current assets include cash and all other items that the retailer can easily convert into cash within a relatively short period of time (generally a year). Besides cash, current assets include accounts receivable, notes receivable, prepaid expenses, and inventory. **Accounts and/or notes receivable** are amounts that customers owe the retailer for goods and services. Frequently, the retailer will reduce the total

AP Photo/Elaine Thompson

Nordstrom has created a high degree of brand equity for the Nordstrom name by focusing on high levels of personalized customer service. Nonetheless, accounting standards in the United States do not allow this brand equity to be recorded on Nordstrom's balance sheet.

prepaid expenses
Are those items for which the retailer has already paid, but the service has not been completed.

retail inventories
Comprise merchandise that the retailer has in the store or in storage and is available for sale.

noncurrent assets
Are those assets that cannot be converted to cash in a short period of time (usually 12 months) in the normal course of business.

goodwill
Is an intangible asset, usually based on customer loyalty, that a retailer pays for when buying an existing business.

total assets
Equal current assets plus noncurrent assets plus goodwill.

receivables by a fixed percentage (based on past experience) to take into account those customers who may be unwilling or unable to pay. **Prepaid expenses** are items such as trash collection or insurance for which the retailer has already paid but the service has not been completed. **Retail inventories** comprise merchandise that the retailer has in the store or in storage and is available for sale.

Noncurrent assets are those assets that cannot be converted into cash in a short period of time (usually 12 months) in the normal course of business. These noncurrent or long-term assets include buildings, parking lots, the land under the building and parking lot, fixtures (e.g., display racks), and equipment (e.g., air conditioning system). These items are carried on the books at cost less accumulated depreciation on everything except the land. Depreciation is necessary because most noncurrent assets have a limited useful life; the difference between the asset and depreciation is intended to provide a more realistic picture of the retailer's assets and prevent an overstatement or understatement of these assets. However, as every retailer has learned, the value of real estate can fluctuate greatly over time.

Dollars & Sense

Although noncurrent assets and fixed assets are important in retailing, the high-profit retailer recognizes that current assets (primarily inventory) are usually more critical to achieving outstanding performance.

liability
Is any legitimate financial claim against the retailer's assets.

current liabilities
Are short-term debts that are payable within a year.

Some retailers also include goodwill as an asset. **Goodwill** is an intangible asset, usually based on customer loyalty, that a retailer pays for when purchasing an existing business. Usually the dollar value assigned to goodwill is minimal.

Total assets equal current assets plus noncurrent assets plus goodwill.

The other part of the balance sheet reflects the retailer's liabilities and net worth. A **liability** is any legitimate financial claim against the retailer's assets. Liabilities are classified as either current or long term.

Current liabilities are short-term debts that are payable within a year. Included here are accounts payable, notes payable that are due within a year, payroll payable, and taxes payable. **Accounts payable** are amounts owed vendors for goods and services. Payroll payable is money due employees on past labor. Taxes due the government (federal, state, or local) are also considered a current liability. Some retailers also include interest due within the year on long-term notes or mortgages as a current liability.

Long-term liabilities include notes payable and mortgages not due within the year. **Total liabilities** equal current liabilities plus long-term liabilities.

Net worth, also called **owner's equity**, is the difference between the firm's total assets and total liabilities and represents the owner's equity in the business. The figure reflects the owner's original investment plus any profits reinvested in the business less any losses incurred in the business and any funds that the owner has taken out of the business.

In actuality, the balance sheet does not reflect all the retailer's assets and liabilities. Specifically, items such as store personnel can be an asset or a liability to the business. These items might not appear on the balance sheet but are extremely important to the success of a high-performance retailer. Other items that could be either assets or liabilities, although not in the strict accounting sense, are goodwill, customer loyalty, and even vendor relationships. Each of these items can contribute to the success or failure of a retailer.

accounts payable
Are amounts owed vendors for goods and services.

long-term liabilities
Are debts that are due in a year or longer.

total liabilities
Equal current liabilities plus long-term liabilities.

net worth (owner's equity)
Is total assets less total liabilities.

Statement of Cash Flow

A third financial statement that retailers can use to help understand their business is the statement of cash flow. A statement of cash flow lists in detail the source and type of all revenue (cash inflows) and the use and type of all expenditures (cash outflows) for a given time period. When cash inflows exceed cash outflows, the retailer is said to have a positive cash flow; when cash outflows exceed cash inflows, the retailer is said to be experiencing a negative cash flow. Thus the purpose of the statement of cash flow is to enable the retailer to project the cash needs of the firm. Based on projections, plans may be made to either seek additional financing, if a negative flow is projected, or to make other investments if a positive flow is anticipated. Likewise, a retailer with a positive cash flow for the period might be able to take advantage of "good deals" from vendors.

Retailers who do the best job of managing cash flow will have higher long-term profitability.

Dollars & Sense

A statement of cash flow is not the same as an income statement. In a statement of cash flow, the retailer is concerned only with the movement of cash into or out of the firm. An income statement reflects the profitability of the retailer after all revenue and expenses are considered. Often expenses will be incurred in one time period but not paid until the following time period. Thus, the retailer's income statement and statement of cash flow are seldom identical. Consider the example of TMD Furniture for the month of August, as shown in Exhibit 8.7a.

August is a slow month for furniture sales because many customers are taking vacations, and as a result TMD is expecting sales of only $40,000 for the month. $15,450 of that amount will be for cash and TMD expects to collect $24,998 on its account receivables. Along with a tax refund check due from the state for $97, TMD has projected a cash inflow of $40,545 for August. However, because August is the month that several notes and accounts payable are due, TMD Furniture is expecting to have to pay out $48,372 during August. This will result in a negative cash flow for the month of $7,827. TMD has prepared for this by having cash on

Exhibit 8.7A
Sample Cash Flow Statement

TMD Furniture, Inc.
Cash Flow Statement
August 31

Cash Sales	$15,450	
Collection of Accounts Receivable	24,998	
Refund on State Taxes	97	
Total Cash Inflow		$40,545
Cash Outflow		
Rent	$ 1,513	
Purchases at Cash	5,750	
Salaries	8,483	
Utilities	1,450	
Advertising	2,300	
County Taxes	173	
Supplies	921	
Telephone	150	
Paying Off Accounts Payable	20,632	
Paying Off Notes Payable	7,000	
Total Cash Outflow		$48,372
Total Cash Flow		($ 7,827)

Exhibit 8.7B
Typical Cash Inflow and Outflow Categories

Cash Inflows	Cash Outflows
Cash sales	Paying for merchandise
Collecting accounts receivable	Rent expenses
Collecting notes receivable	Utilities expenses
Collecting other debts	Wages and Salary expenses
Sale of fixed assets	Advertising expense
Sale of stock	Insurance premiums
	Taxes
	Interest expenses
	Supplies and other expenses
	Purchase of other assets
	Paying off accounts payable
	Paying off notes payable
	Buying back company stocks
	Paying dividends

hand (as reported on the July 31 balance sheet) of $11,589. In reality, many retailers forget about cash and realize the difference between cash flow and profit only after the coffers are empty. In the case of TMD Furniture, paying off the notes and accounts payable had no effect on the income statement. Likewise, the statement of cash flow considered only that part of purchases that were paid for with cash, not those placed on account. These credit purchases had no direct effect on the cash flow. Exhibit 8.7b lists the typical retailer's cash inflow and outflow items. It should be noted that retailers who decide to use major credit cards, instead of handling their own credit operations, are able to convert sales much more quickly to cash because they do not need to wait for customers to pay for their purchases—some other party such as a bank assumes this financing function.

An increasing number of retailers are becoming aware of the critical nature of cash flow. In fact, the #1 cause of retailing bankruptcies in recent years has been cash flow problems. A retailer can be growing quickly and be profitable yet fail due to inadequate cash flow.

The lack of a sufficient cash flow is not limited to those large troubled chains you hear about on television. Many a small entrepreneur has come up with a brilliant idea for a retail operation, only to fall short. In fact, more than a quarter of all retail operations fail during the first two years. The entrepreneur's problems usually start by overestimating revenues and underestimating costs, resulting in a negative cash flow. By not ensuring they have enough cash on hand to withstand a rocky two-year start-up period, many retailers are assuring themselves of failure. In fact, according to one of the author's mentors, the first thing to look for when examining a retailer's financial records to determine its ability to survive is accounts payable, particularly government payroll taxes. It seems that when retail firms get into a cash bind, they tend to postpone payments to the government so that they can pay their suppliers and employees. After all, they believe that they can always pay the taxes later. Unfortunately, the government does not always agree with such thinking.[6] As a result, some of these unsuccessful retailers often resort to questionable tactics to improve their financial statements. Besides changing the breakage rate for rebates described earlier in this chapter, some other methods used to inflate retail accounting statements are described in the chapter's Retailing: The Inside Story box.

Inventory Valuation

LO 3

How does a retailer value its inventory?

Due to the many different merchandise lines carried, inventory valuation is quite complex. Yet the retailer must have information such as sales, additional purchases not yet received, reductions for the period, gross margin, open-to-buy, stock shortages, and inventory levels in order to operate profitably.

A retailer must make two major decisions with regard to valuing inventory: (1) the accounting inventory system and (2) the inventory pricing method to use.

Accounting Inventory System

Two accounting inventory systems are available for the retailer: (1) the cost method and (2) the retail method. We will describe both methods on the basis of the frequency with which inventory information is received, difficulties encountered in completing a physical inventory and maintaining records, and the extent to which stock shortages can be calculated.

The Cost Method

cost method
Is an inventory valuation technique that provides a book valuation of inventory based solely on the retailer's cost of merchandise including freight.

The **cost method** of inventory valuation provides a book valuation of inventory based solely on the retailer's cost, including freight. It looks only at the cost of each item as it is recorded in the accounting records when purchased. When a physical inventory is taken, all the items are counted, the cost of each item is taken from the records or the price tags, and the total inventory value at cost is calculated.

One of the easiest methods of coding the cost of merchandise on the price tag is to use the first ten letters of the alphabet to represent the price. Here A = 1, B = 2, C = 3, D = 4, E = 5, F = 6, G = 7, H = 8, I = 9, J = 0. A product with the code HEAD has a cost of $85.14. The cost method is useful for those retailers who sell big-ticket items and allow price negotiations by customers. Sales personnel know from the code how much room there is for negotiation and still cover the cost of the merchandise plus operating expenses.

Retailing: The Inside Story

Dressing Up Financial Statements

Accounting rules give companies wide discretion in calculating their earnings. By accruing, or allotting, revenues and expenses to specific periods, retailers aim to allocate income to the month, quarter or year in which it was effectively earned. This "accrual accounting" method is supposed to provide a more accurate picture of what's happening in a business at a given time, and often it does. However, retailers, especially small retailers, have learned that lenders judge the worth and creditability of a business by its financial statements. Thus, today many retailers are using aggressive accounting methods to make their statements look as good as possible. Listed below are several methods retailers have used to window-dress their books.

Adjust Inventory

Retailers using the standard LIFO (last-in, first-out) inventory accounting know when the older and less costly goods are sold at today's inflated prices, profits look better. Therefore, today's earnings can be improved by reducing the basic stock level, the minimum amount of an item to be carried at all times. (Basic stock will be discussed in greater detail in the next chapter.) This will therefore result in some less expensive older inventory being sold. However, the retailer's future earnings could be hurt when it replaces the inventory at higher prices.

Improving The Current Ratio

Since using an analysis of a retailer's **current ratio** (current assets divided by current liabilities) is probably the easiest and most common way for lenders to analyze a balance sheet, some retailers try to improve their ratios by paying off even a small portion of their current debt before the review. For example, suppose a retailer has $20,000 in cash, $30,000 in other current assets, and $30,000 in current liabilities, for a current ratio of 1.67:1. Lenders prefer to see the current ratio closer to 2:1. Therefore, if $10,000 of the cash is used to reduce debt, the ratio improves significantly to 2:1.

Massage Cash

Another simple method for retailers to pump up their cash is to sell some of their receivables to a third party.

Convert Short-Term Loans to Long-Term Loans

A few years ago, some retailers took advantage of another method of improving the financial statements when long-term interest rates declined quickly and closely approached short-term rates. (In normal times, long-term rates are one to two percentage points higher than long-term rates.) With so many willing lenders offering extremely low long-term interest rates, these retailers were able to refinance a portion of their short-term debt for long-term debt.

Extend the Payment Time

Another method troubled retailers use to improve the appearance of their balance sheet is to have vendors agree to a slower repayment schedule, enabling the retailer to build up its cash balance.

---

current ratio
Current assets divided by Current Liabilities.

The cost method of inventory valuation does have several limitations:

1. It is difficult to do daily inventories (or even monthly inventories).
2. It is difficult to cost out each sale.
3. It is difficult to allocate freight charges to each item's cost of goods sold.

The cost method is generally used by those retailers with big-ticket items and a limited number of sales per day (e.g., an expensive jewelry store or an antique furniture store), where there are few lines or limited inventory requirements, infrequent price changes, and low turnover rates.

retail method
Is an inventory valuation technique that values merchandise at current retail prices, which is then converted to cost based on a formula.

The Retail Method

The **retail method** of inventory values merchandise at current retail prices. It overcomes the disadvantages of the cost method by keeping detailed records of

	Cost	Retail
Beginning Inventory	$199,000	$401,000
Net Purchases	70,000	154,000
Additional Markups		5,000
Freight-in	1,000	
Total Inventory Available for Sale	$270,000	$560,000

Exhibit 8.8
Inventory Available for Whitener's Sporting Goods Sales, Fall Season

inventory based on the retail value of the merchandise. The fact that the inventory is valued in retail dollars makes it a little more difficult for the retailer to determine the cost of goods sold when computing the gross margin for a time period.

There are three basic steps in computing an ending inventory value using the retail method: calculation of the cost complement, calculation of reductions from retail value, and conversion of the adjusted retail book inventory to cost.

Step 1. Calculation of the Cost Complement. Inventories, both beginning and ending, and purchases are recorded at both cost and retail levels when using the retail method. Exhibit 8.8 shows an inventory statement for Whitener's Sporting Goods for the fall season.

In Exhibit 8.8, the beginning inventory is shown at both cost and retail. Net purchases, which are the total purchases less merchandise returned to vendors, allowances, and discounts from vendors, are also valued at cost and retail. Additional markups are the total increases in the retail price of merchandise already in stock which were caused by inflation or heavy demand and are shown at retail. Freight-in is the cost to the retailer for transportation of merchandise from the vendor and is shown in the cost column.

Using the information from Exhibit 8.8, the retailer can calculate the average relationship of cost to the retail price for all merchandise available for sale during the fall season. This calculation is called the cost complement:

$$\begin{aligned}\text{Cost complement} &= \text{Total cost valuation/Total retail valuation}\\ &= \$270{,}000/\$560{,}000 = .482\end{aligned}$$

Since the cost complement is .482, or 48.2 percent, 48.2 cents of every retail sales dollar is composed of merchandise cost.

Step 2. Calculation of Reductions from Retail Value. During the course of day-to-day business activities, the retailer must take reductions from inventory. In addition to sales, which lower the retail inventory level, retail reductions can lower retail inventory levels. These reductions include markdowns (sales and reduced prices on end-of-season, discontinued, or damaged merchandise), discounts (employee, senior citizen, student, religious, etc.), and stock shortages (employee and customer theft, breakage). Markdowns and employee discounts can be recorded throughout an accounting period, but a physical inventory is required to calculate stock shortages.

In Exhibit 8.8, it was shown that Whitener's had a retail inventory available for sale of $560,000 for the upcoming fall season. This must be reduced by actual fall season sales of $145,000, markdowns of $12,000, and discounts of $2,000. This results in an ending book value of inventory with a retail level of $401,000. This is shown in Exhibit 8.9.

Exhibit 8.9
Whitener's Sporting Goods Ending Book Value at Retail, Fall Season

	Cost	Retail
Inventory Available for Sale at Retail		$560,000
Less Reductions:		
Sales	$145,000	
Markdowns	12,000	
Discounts	2,000	
Total Reductions		159,000
Ending Book Value of Inventory at Retail		$401,000

Once the ending book value of inventory at retail is determined, a comparison can be made to the physical inventory to compute the actual stock shortages; if the book value is greater than the physical count, a stock shortage has occurred. If the book value is lower than the physical count, a stock overage has occurred. Shortages are due to thefts, breakages, overshipments not billed to customers, and bookkeeping errors—the most common cause. These errors result from the failure to properly record markdowns, returns, discounts, and breakages. Many retailers have greatly reduced their original shortage estimate by reviewing the season's bookkeeping entries. A stock overage, an excess of physical inventory over book inventory, is also usually the result of bookkeeping errors, either miscounting during the physical inventory or improper book entries. Exhibit 8.10 shows the results of Whitener's physical inventory and the resulting adjustment.

Because a physical inventory must be taken in order to determine shortages (overages) and retailers take a physical count only once or twice a year, shortages (overages) are often estimated in merchandise budgets as shown in Exhibits 8.1 and 8.2. As a rule of thumb, retailers may estimate monthly shortages between .5 and 3 percent.

Step 3. Conversion of the Adjusted Retail Book Inventory to Cost. The final step to be performed in using the retail method is to convert to cost the adjusted retail book inventory figure in order to determine the closing inventory at cost. The procedure here is to multiply the adjusted retail book inventory ($398,000 in the case of Whitener's) by the cost complement (.482 in the Whitener's example):

$$\text{Closing inventory (at cost)} = \text{Adjusted retail} \times \text{Cost complement book inventory}$$
$$= \$398{,}000 \times .482 = \$191{,}836$$

Although this equation does not yield the actual closing inventory at cost, it does provide a close approximation of the cost figure. Remember that the cost complement is an average. Now that ending inventory at cost has been determined, the retailer can determine gross margin as well as net profit before taxes, if operating expenses are known. We will discuss expenses in more detail later. In the

Exhibit 8.10
Whitener's Sporting Goods, Stock Shortage (Overage) Adjustment Entry, End of Fall Season

	Cost	Retail
Ending Book Value of Inventory at Retail		$401,000
Physical Inventory (at retail)		398,000
Stock Shortages		3,000
Adjusting Ending Book Value of Inventory at Retail		$398,000

Whitener's example, let's use $30,000 for salaries, $1,000 for utilities, $19,000 for rent, and $2,200 for depreciation. These figures are shown in Exhibit 8.11.

The retail method has several advantages over the cost method of inventory valuation:

1. Accounting statements can be drawn up at any time. Inventories need not be taken for preparation of these statements.
2. Physical inventories using retail prices are less subject to error and can be completed in a shorter amount of time.
3. The retail method provides an automatic, conservative valuation of ending inventory as well as inventory levels throughout the season. This is especially useful in cases where the retailer is forced to submit insurance claims for damaged or lost merchandise.

A major complaint against the retail method is that it is a "method of averages." This refers to the fact that closing inventory is valued at the average relationship between cost and retail (the cost complement), and that large retailers offer many different classifications and lines with different relationships. This disadvantage can be overcome by computing cost complements for individual lines or departments.

Another limitation is the heavy burden placed on bookkeeping activities. The true ending book inventory value can be correctly calculated only if there are no errors in recording beginning inventory, purchases, freight-in, markups, markdowns, discounts, returns, transfers between stores, and sales. As noted earlier, many of the retailers' original shortages have later been determined to be bookkeeping errors. Most retailers today use the retail method of inventory valuation, which was created in the early 1900s.

Inventory Pricing Systems

Two methods of pricing inventory are FIFO and LIFO. The **FIFO** (first in, first out) method assumes that the oldest merchandise is sold before the more recently

FIFO
Stands for first in, first out and values inventory based on the assumption that the oldest merchandise is sold before the more recently purchased merchandise.

	Cost	Retail
Sales		$145,000
Less: Cost of Goods Sold:		
Beginning Inventory (at Cost)	$200,000	
Purchases (at Cost)	70,000	
Goods Available for Sale	$270,000	
Ending Inventory (at Cost)	191,836	
Cost of Goods Sold		78,164
Gross Margin		$ 66,836
Less: Operating Expenses		
Salaries	$ 30,000	
Utilities	1,000	
Rent	19,000	
Depreciation (Fixtures + Equipment)	2,200	
Total Operating Expenses		52,200
Net Profit Before Taxes		$ 14,636

Exhibit 8.11
Whitener's Sporting Goods Income Statements August 1–January 31

LIFO
Stands for last in, first out and values inventory based on the assumption that the most recently purchased merchandise is sold first and the oldest merchandise is sold last.

purchased merchandise. However, merchandise on the shelf will reflect the most current replacement price. During inflationary periods this method allows "inventory profits" (caused by selling the less expensive earlier inventory rather than the more expensive newer inventory) to be included as income.

The **LIFO** (last in, first out) method is designed to cushion the impact of inflationary pressures by matching current costs against current revenues. Costs of goods sold are based on the costs of the most recently purchased inventory, while the older inventory is regarded as the unsold inventory. During inflationary periods, the LIFO method results in the application of a higher unit cost to the merchandise sold and a lower unit cost to inventory still unsold. In times of rapid inflation most retailers use the LIFO method, resulting in lower profits on the income statement, but also lower income taxes. Most retailers also prefer to use LIFO for planning purposes, since it accurately reflects replacement costs. The Internal Revenue Service permits a retailer to change its method of accounting only once.

Let's study an example of the effect of the LIFO and FIFO methods of inventory valuation on the firm's financial performance. Suppose you began the year with a total inventory of 15 home theater packages, which you purchased on the last day of the preceding year for $500 each. Thus, if these home theater packages were the only merchandise you had in stock, your beginning inventory was $7,500 (15 × $500). Suppose also that during the year you sold 12 packages for $900 each, for total sales of $10,800; that in June you purchased 8 new home theater packages (same make and model as your old ones) at $525; and that in November you bought 4 more at $550. Thus, your purchases were $4,200 in June and $2,200 in November for a total of $6,400, and you would still have 15 home theater packages in stock at year end. Under the LIFO inventory approach, your ending inventory would be the same as it was at the beginning of the year ($7,500), since we would assume that the 12 packages sold were the 12 purchased during the year. However, using the FIFO approach, we would assume that we sold 12 of the original $500 packages and had 3 left. These three home theater packages, along with June's and November's purchases, result in an ending inventory of $7,900 [(3 × $500) + (8 × $525) + (4 × $550)]. Now let's see how these approaches can affect our gross margins.

	LIFO	FIFO
Net sales	$ 10,800	$10,800
Less: Cost of goods sold		
Beginning inventory	$ 7,500	$ 7,500
Purchases	6,400	6,400
Goods available	$ 13,900	$13,900
Ending inventory	7,500	7,900
Cost of goods sold	6,400	6,000
Gross margin	$ 4,400	$ 4,800

The issue of which inventory valuation method (LIFO or FIFO) to use is just one of the key issues facing retailers and accountants around the world as they seek to find a common method of reporting financial transactions. As described in the Global Retailing box, there are major differences in the way retailers in different countries can report their financial performances.

Global Retailing

International Accounting Rules

The International Accounting Standards Board (IASB), formerly the International Accounting Standards Committee (IASC), has been working to achieve uniformity in accounting principles since 1973. Today the organization has representatives from approximately 100 countries and has issued 47 international accounting standards. These standards address a number of topics, including goodwill, inventory valuation, and business combinations.

The treatment of goodwill, which is the premium over book value that a retailer pays when it acquires another retail company, varies greatly between different countries. According to international accounting standards, goodwill should be amortized over a period of 5 to 20 years, although the IASB strongly recommends that companies use the 5-year period. Several countries have complied with this standard, including Australia, Mexico, Spain, Japan, and Brazil. However, there is still a great deal of variation among other countries. Switzerland, for example, allows companies to immediately expense goodwill. Hong Kong allows companies to choose whether they want to immediately expense goodwill or amortize it over a period of 5 to 20 years. The United States does not allow for the amortization of goodwill. Instead, in the United States, goodwill is tested annually for possible impairment. Because of a European mandate, United Kingdom companies no longer expense goodwill but must amortize it. China has not yet addressed the treatment of purchased goodwill. The problem with such wide variations in the area of goodwill is that it makes the comparison of financial statements very difficult.

In 1991, the IASC issued exposure draft E32, which would have eliminated LIFO as an alternative method of valuing inventory. The IASC argued that the LIFO method did not assign the most current costs to ending inventories and therefore distorted the balance sheet. It also would have generated higher tax revenues. However, due to public sentiment, the IASC reversed its E32 position and has continued to allow LIFO. This was good news to the United States and other countries that use the LIFO method, since revaluing their inventories with the FIFO or weighted average method would have resulted in higher ending inventory values and a higher tax liability.

Accounting for business combinations has also been addressed by the IASC. It provides two methods for accounting for mergers and acquisitions. The purchase method of accounting for business combinations effectively reports the earnings of two separate businesses as one business through the use of consolidated financial statements. The net assets of the acquired company are carried on these statements at their cost to the acquiring company. The other method of accounting for mergers and acquisitions is the pooling of interests method. This method may be used only when the transaction is principally an exchange of voting common shares or if all of the net assets and operations of the two entities are combined into one entity. The pooling of interests method effectively reports the earnings of only one business, and the net assets of the acquired company are carried on the combined entity's financial statements at their premerger value. The reporting requirements of each country essentially result in a difference in the valuation of the acquired companies' net assets. The pooling of interests method will typically result in a lower net asset figure than the purchase method.

Currently, standards issued by the IASB are not mandatory unless a particular country adopts them. This explains the wide variation in reporting requirements. The European Union and Australia mandated the use of international standards for consolidated reporting beginning in 2005. That mandate has gone a long way towards standardizing worldwide practices.

Still, while U.S. retailers may complain about GAAP and IRS rules, it could be worse. *The Wall Street Journal* reported that a Chinese premier reminded Chinese taxpayers that "tax evasion can result in death by execution."

Source: The authors acknowledge the assistance of Dr. Linda Nichols, Texas Tech University, with this box.

SUMMARY

LO 1

Why is a merchandise budget so important in retail planning and how is a merchandise budget prepared?

The purpose of this chapter was to introduce you to the major financial statements and their importance in retail planning. We began our discussion with the six-month merchandise budget. This statement projects sales, when and how much new merchandise should be ordered, what markup is to be taken, what reductions are to be planned, and the target or planned gross margin for the season. The establishment of such a budget has several advantages for the retailer:

1. The six-month budget controls the amount of inventory and forces management to control markups and reductions.
2. The budget helps to determine how much merchandise should be purchased so that inventory requirements can be met.
3. The budget can be compared with actual or final results to determine the performance of the firm.

We concluded our discussion of the six-month merchandise budget by showing how each of the figures is determined. We illustrated how to estimate sales, inventory levels, reductions, purchases, and gross margin.

LO 2

What are the differences among and the uses of these three accounting statements: income statement, balance sheet, and statement of cash flow?

The second section of this chapter explained how the retailer uses three important accounting statements: the income statement, the balance sheet, and the statement of cash flow. The income statement gives the retailer a summary of the income and expenses incurred over a given time period. A balance sheet shows the financial condition of the retailer at a particular point in time. The statement of cash flow lists in detail the sources and types of all revenue and expenditures for a given time period.

LO 3

How does a retailer value its inventory?

The final section of this chapter described two decisions a retailer must make with regard to inventory recordkeeping: Which accounting system (cost or retail) to use and whether to use the LIFO or FIFO valuation method.

The cost system is the simplest, but the retail system is the most widely used because of these advantages:

1. Accounting statements can be drawn up at any time.
2. Physical inventories using retail prices are less subject to error and can be completed in a shorter amount of time.
3. The retail method provides an automatic, conservative valuation of ending inventory as well as inventory levels throughout the season.

The FIFO method assumes that the oldest merchandise is sold before the more recently purchased merchandise, so merchandise on the shelf more accurately reflects the replacement cost. During inflationary periods this method allows "inventory profits" to be included as income. The LIFO method is designed to cushion the impact of inflationary pressures by matching current costs against current revenues. Cost of goods sold is based on the costs of the most recently purchased inventory, while the older inventory is regarded as the unsold inventory. In times of rapid inflation most retailers use the LIFO method, resulting in lower profits on the income statement, but also lower income taxes. Most retailers also prefer to use LIFO for planning purposes, since it accurately reflects replacement costs.

TERMS TO REMEMBER

merchandising
merchandise budget
gross margin
stock-to-sales ratio
income statement
gross sales
returns and allowances
net sales
cost of goods sold
operating expenses
operating profit
other income or expenses
net profit
asset
current assets
accounts and/or notes receivable
prepaid expenses
retail inventories
noncurrent assets
goodwill
total assets
liability
current liabilities
accounts payable
long-term liabilities
total liabilities
net worth (owner's equity)
cost method
current ratio
retail method
FIFO
LIFO

REVIEW AND DISCUSSION QUESTIONS

Why is a merchandise budget so important in retail planning and how is a merchandise budget prepared? LO 1

1. What are the components of a merchandise budget? Which one is the most difficult to predict? Why?
2. It costs money to carry inventory, yet retailers must carry an amount of inventory in excess of planned sales for an upcoming period. Why?
3. What is a stock-to-sales ratio?
4. Why should a retailer be allowed to change its merchandise budget after the start of a season? If changes can be made, what would cause such changes?
5. A retailer who last year had sales of $100,000 plans for an inflation rate of 3 percent and a 4 percent increase in market share. What should planned sales for this year be?
6. A retailer believes that because a major competitor has just entered the local market, the number of transactions for this year's upcoming season will decrease by 2 percent; but because of inflation, the value of the average sale will increase by 4 percent. If sales last year were $500,000, what will they be this year?

What are the differences among and the uses of these three accounting statements: income statement, balance sheet, and statement of cash flow? LO 2

7. In what ways are the balance sheet and the income statement different? How do retailers use these two financial statements?

8. What is the difference between a statement of cash flow and an income statement?
9. How would the following activities affect a retailer's balance sheet and income statement for the current year?
   a. The retailer over-estimates the amount of year-ending inventory that is obsolete, thus reducing inventory.
   b. The retailer under-estimates the breakage on a current rebate program.
   c. The retailer switches from LIFO to FIFO.
10. The Candy Wrapper is trying to determine its net profit before taxes. Use the following data to find the Candy Wrapper's net profit.

Rent	$ 25,000	Salaries	$ 74,000
Purchases	$300,000	Sales	$486,000
Ending inventory	$123,000	Utilities	$ 45,000
Beginning inventory	$108,000	Other income	$ 5,300

11. A hardware store with sales for the year of $572,000 and other income of $32,000 has operating expenses of $234,000. Its cost of goods sold is $307,000. What are its gross margin, its operating profit, and its net profit in dollars?

LO 3

How does a retailer value its inventory?

12. List the advantages and disadvantages the retail method of inventory valuation has over the cost method.
13. Define FIFO and LIFO and the reasons for using one or the other.
14. Why is it difficult to determine the exact value of inventory when preparing financial statements?

SAMPLE TEST QUESTIONS

LO 1

Which one of the following factors is not found on a six-month merchandise budget?

a. planned gross margin
b. current liabilities
c. planned sales percentage
d. planned BOM stock
e. planned purchases at retail

LO 2

The ______ provides the retailer with a picture of the organization's profit and loss situation.

a. expense report
b. index of inventory valuation
c. statement of cash flow
d. income statement
e. statement of gross margin

LO 3

The total cost valuation of a retailer's inventory is $120,000, while the total retail valuation of sales was $200,000. Approximately how much of every retail sales dollar is composed of merchandise cost?

a. 12 cents
b. 40 cents
c. 60 cents
d. $1.20
e. $1.50

WRITING AND SPEAKING EXERCISE

Over the last few years the inflation rate has held steady around 3 percent. However, due to the rapid increase in oil prices, new economic forecasts predict that the inflation rate will be 6 percent next year. The cost of goods sold at your family-owned menswear shop, and also your retail prices, mirror the country's inflation rate, so you expect both your costs and sales to increase by 6 percent. Your father asks you to prepare a memo detailing how this new information will impact the profitability of the business, if it continues to use a LIFO method of valuing inventory. Also, how will this inflation affect the inventory carried on the balance sheet?

RETAIL PROJECT

Go to the library and look at the most recent annual reports of some retailers. (If you are using the Internet, go to the retailer's home page or to http://finance.yahoo.com. Enter the retailer's stock symbol, then click "profile.") Using the financial data from these reports, compare the net cash flow to the net income for each of the retailers you chose and explain the reason for the differences.

PLANNING YOUR OWN RETAIL BUSINESS

You are unsure of what level of sales to forecast for your new drugstore, which you plan to open on New Year's Day. Consequently, you have decided to make some assumptions. You believe that it is reasonable to assume that your trade area will encompass about 25 square miles. The city planning department has told you that within this area the population density is 1,157 people per square mile. You conservatively estimate that 40 percent of these individuals will visit your store an average of 4 times annually and that 85 percent will purchase something on a typical visit. You expect them to purchase an average of $25 per visit. Information from industry sources suggests that drugstores do more business in the fall and winter. In fact, you expect sales during each of the months of November, December, January, and February to be 10 percent of your annual volume. The remaining eight months will share equally the 60 percent of remaining sales. You believe for your business to be profitable you need to have a beginning-of-month inventory-to-sales ratio of 3.0 for October through November and 2.5 for the remaining months. You want to plan your beginning-of-month inventory for each of the next 12 months. You also want to begin the first month of your second year of business with $250,000 in inventory at retail prices. Please compute the beginning-of-the-month inventory for each of the next 12 months.

CASE

Dolly's Place

After years of teaching retailing and marketing at the University of Southern Mississippi, Dolly Loyd decided to retire and return to her first love—running an apparel store on the Gulf Coast. Because she used to run such a department for a major retail chain before teaching, she kept up with the current trends in the industry. Dolly gained the support of an ex-high school classmate who, after making millions with an Internet startup, financed her new endeavor.

Today Dolly is beginning to make plans for the upcoming three-month spring season. Dolly anticipates planned sales of $250,000 for the season based on a planned initial markup of 45 percent. Within the season, planned monthly sales are projected to be as follows: 33 percent in February, 27 percent in March, and 40 percent in April (Easter is April 12th). To ensure a profitable season, trade association records were consulted. The records indicated: (1) The stock-to-sales ratios need to be 3.0 for February, 5.0 for March, and 6.0 for April; (2) reductions can be planned at 5 percent for February, 10 percent for March, and, in an attempt to clear the store of old merchandise before her tourist season apparel arrives, a 20 7percent reduction is planned for April; and (3) with the tourist season approaching, an inventory of $400,000 will be necessary to begin the summer season. Complete a three-month merchandise budget for Dolly.

Dolly's Place **Date: January 7, 2009**
Three-Month Merchandise Budget **Season: Spring 2009**

Spring	February	March	April	Seasonal Total
1. Planned BOM Stock				
2. Planned Sales				
3. Planned Retail Reductions				
4. Planned EOM Stock				
5. Planned Purchases @ Retail				
6. Planned Purchases @ Cost				
7. Planned Initial Markup				
8. Planned Gross Margin				
9. Planned BOM Stock/Sales Ratio	3.0 ×	5.0 ×	6.0 ×	—
10. Planned Sales Percentage	33%	27%	40%	100%
11. Planned Retail Reduction	5%	10%	20%	11.05%

Planned total sales for the period	$250,000
Planned total retail reduction percentage for the period	11.05%
Planned initial markup percentage for the period	45%
Planned BOM stock for May	$400,000

chapter 9

Merchandise Buying and Handling

OVERVIEW:

In this chapter, we explain the planning that retailers must do regarding their merchandise selection. We also analyze how a retailer controls the merchandise to be inventoried. The selection of and negotiations with vendors are also discussed, as well as the security measures used when handling the merchandise.

LEARNING OBJECTIVES:

After reading this chapter, you should be able to:

1. Explain the differences between the four methods of dollar merchandise planning used to determine the proper inventory stock levels needed to begin a merchandise selling period.
2. Explain how retailers use dollar merchandise control and describe how open-to-buy is used in the retail buying process.
3. Describe how a retailer determines the makeup of its inventory.
4. Describe how a retailer selects proper merchandise sources.
5. Describe what is involved in the vendor-buyer negotiation process and what terms of the contract can be negotiated.
6. Discuss the various methods of handling the merchandise once it is received in the store, so as to control shrinkage, including vendor collusion, and theft.

Dollar Merchandise Planning

LO 1

What is the difference between the four methods of dollar merchandise planning used to determine the proper inventory stock levels needed to begin a merchandise selling period?

According to an old retailing adage, "goods well bought are half sold." In this chapter, we will look at merchandise management—the merchandise buying and handling process and its effect on a store's performance.

Merchandise management is the analysis, planning, acquisition, handling, and control of the merchandise investments of a retail operation. *Analysis* is used in our definition because retailers must be able to correctly identify their customers before they can determine the needs and wants of their consumers. *Planning* occurs because merchandise must be purchased six to twelve months in advance of the selling season. The term *acquisition* is used because, with the exception of service retailers, merchandise needs to be bought from others, either distributors or manufacturers. In addition, all retailers, even those selling only services, must acquire the equipment and fixtures needed to complete a transaction. Proper

AP Photo/Ted S. Warren

The Gap needs to carefully consider its merchandising and buying practices so that its other two divisions—Old Navy and Banana Republic—have merchandise offerings differentiated from The Gap.

merchandise management
Is the analysis, planning, acquisition, handling, and control of the merchandise investments of a retail operation.

handling assures that the merchandise is where it is needed and in the proper shape to be sold. *Control* of the large dollar investment in inventory is important to ensure an adequate financial return on the retailer's merchandise investment.

In fact, many retailing experts agree that it was the failure to properly manage merchandise that caused Gap, one of the most successful retail operations for over a decade in the 1990s and early 2000s, to stumble recently. First, the chain failed to spot major changes in consumer trends. Second, similar merchandise selections in the chain's three divisions, Gap, Old Navy, and Banana Republic, confused customers and resulted in interstore cannibalization of customers.[1]

Whatever career path you decide to take in retailing, you cannot avoid some contact with the firm's merchandising activities. This is because merchandising is the day-to-day business of all retailers. As inventory is sold, new stock needs to be purchased, displayed, and sold once again. Clearly then, as we explained in Chapter 8, merchandising, though only a subfunction of retailing, is its heartbeat. Therefore, retailers that do a superior job at managing their inventory investment will be the most successful. If a retailer's inventory continues to build up, then either the retailer has too much money tied up in inventory or is not making the sales it was expecting and is heading for trouble. Likewise, a retailer who is frequently out of stock will quickly lose customers. Now you know why the business trade press and retailers take such an interest in inventory levels as retailers approach different seasons. For example, Christmas, which traditionally accounts for 25 to 30 percent of annual sales[2], can be ruined by the lack of inventory to support sales. On the other hand, if the inventory is not sold, the costs involved in carrying excess inventory can force the retailer into taking extra markdowns, in addition to having to pay interest on the inventory investment.

gross margin return on inventory
Is gross margin divided by average inventory at cost; alternatively it is the gross margin percent multiplied by net sales divided by average inventory investment.

Because inventory is the largest investment that retailers make, high-performance retailers use the gross margin return on inventory model when analyzing the performance of their inventory. **Gross margin return on inventory** (GMROI) incorporates how quickly inventory sells and profit into a single measure. It can be computed as follows:

$$(\text{Gross margin/Net sales}) \times (\text{Net sales/Average inventory at cost}) = (\text{Gross margin/Average inventory at cost})$$

Here the gross margin percentage (gross margin/net sales) is multiplied by net sales/dollars invested in inventory to get the retailer's gross margin dollars generated for each dollar invested in inventory. Net sales are typically computed on an annual or 12-month basis. (Note, however, that sales/dollars invested in inventory is not the same as inventory turnover. Inventory turnover measures sales/inventory at retail. In the GMROI equation, we are using inventory at cost to reflect the investment in carrying the merchandise.) Thus, if a particular item has a gross margin of 45 percent and sales per dollar of inventory investment of 4.0, its GMROI would be $1.80 ($.45 × 4). That is, for each dollar invested in inventory, on average the retailer obtains $1.80 in gross margin annually. Gross margin dollars are used to first pay the store's operating expenses (both fixed and variable), with the remainder being the retailer's profit. In an extreme example of the use of GMROI, Eddie Lampert, the head of Sears Holding, has declared that he will sacrifice some lost sales by reducing inventory levels in Sears and Kmart stores, if such action improves the firm's GMROI.[3]

Retailers that use the GMROI model when planning inventory and evaluating inventory decisions will be more profitable.

Dollars & Sense

Before we continue our discussion of merchandise management, you may want to review a couple of earlier chapters. Because all retailing activities are aimed at serving the customer's needs and wants at a profit, you may want to revisit Chapter 3 on the customer. Likewise, because merchandise management is concerned with the acquisition of inventory from other supply chain members, you may also want to review Chapter 5 on the behavior of the different supply chain members.

As we pointed out in Chapter 8, successful merchandise management revolves around planning and control. It takes time to buy merchandise, have it delivered, record the delivery in the company records, and properly display the merchandise; therefore, it is essential to plan. Buyers need to decide today what their stock requirements will be weeks, months, a merchandising season, or even a year in advance.

As planning occurs, it is only logical that the retailer exercise control over the merchandise (dollars and units) that it plans to purchase. A good control system is vital. If the retailer carries too much inventory, the costs of carrying that inventory might outweigh the gross margin to be made on the sale, especially if the retailer is forced to reduce the selling price. After concluding our discussion on the dollar amount of inventory needed for stock requirements, the remainder of this chapter will look at the other merchandising decisions facing the retailer: calculating the dollar amount available to be spent, managing the inventory, choosing and evaluating merchandise sources, handling vendor negotiations, handling the merchandise in the store, and evaluating merchandise performance.

Buyers, working with upper management, are responsible for the dollar planning of merchandise requirements. In the previous chapter, we described the various factors that must be considered in making the sales forecast, the first step in determining inventory needs. Once planned sales for the period in question have

Service Retailing

This Hotel Has Gone to the Dogs (and Cats)

It used to be a bad sign when it was said that a hotel "went to the dogs." Not anymore. Today PetSmart, which was highlighted in Chapter 2's Retailing: The Inside Story box on page 51, has identified a large group of pet owners that they refer to as "pet parents," not "pet owners." Pet parents were found to be passionately committed to their pets. As a result, the retailer focuses on providing these customers with a one-stop shopping destination that offers everything needed for these family members in an easy-to-shop, full-service specialty environment. One of these needs was a unique market segment not being met by the competition—pet boarding.

As a result PetSmart introduced PetsHotels, a boarding and daycare for dogs and cats that caters to their every need—even if this includes frequent TLC. Each hotel provides three daily meals prepared just the way the four-legged guest likes them, free DVDs, and a daily dose of lactose-free ice cream. In addition, PetsHotel offers its guests many amenities not offered by traditional kennel such as 24-hour supervision, an on-site veterinarian, air-conditioned rooms and suites, daily specialty treats, and play time. On holidays, the hotel serves a special meal designed especially for pets. On Thanksgiving, for example, dogs feast on turkey and stuffing, followed by a cranberry apple crumb dessert. Felines indulge in turkey and giblets, followed by kitty milk and cookies. Each dinner is served on special turkey-shaped plates.

All service retailers must use forecasting tools to adjust their retailing mix and make preparations, especially regarding personnel, to satisfy their customers' wants. This is especially difficult for PetsHotel's management. While a regular hotel might experience some fluctuations in demand based on a multitude of factors, it can always count on an occupancy level of between 40 and 100 percent. Therefore, it will always need someone at the front desk and to work in maintenance/repairs overnight. This is not so with PetsHotel. There will be many days, especially during the school year when family travel is limited, when no guests will require their services. However, during holidays and summer months there will probably be many days when they reach capacity. Even the slightest change in a weather pattern can affect occupancy rates as pet parents may decide to leave the four-legged "child" outside while they go on a two-day business trip. Thus, it is very important for service retailers, especially those offering a new type of service, to manage their merchandise mix and personnel needs. However, with careful planning, success is quite possible.

Source: Based on both of the authors' experiences as "pet parents."

---

been projected, buyers are then able to use any one of four different methods for planning dollars invested in merchandise: basic stock, percentage variation, weeks' supply, and the stock-to-sales ratio method.

While our discussion in this chapter will focus on retailers who sell tangible goods, the same basic principles may be applied to service retailers, with one exception. Whereas tangible products are first produced, then sold, and then consumed, services are first sold, then produced and consumed simultaneously. Thus service retailers, be they beauty parlors or hospitals, are prevented from stockpiling their inventories, be it a hair highlighting process or a heart by-pass operation, in anticipation of future demand. Given the inability to stockpile inventories, service retailers must pay special attention to forecasting demand. In addition, as shown in the Service Retailing box on PetsHotel, these service retailers must adjust their retailing mix and make preparations, especially regarding personnel, to satisfy their customers' wants.

basic stock method (BSM)
Is a technique for planning dollar inventory investments and allows for a base stock level plus a variable amount of inventory that will increase or decrease at the beginning of each sales period in the same dollar amount as the period's expected sales.

Basic Stock Method

The **basic stock method (BSM)** is used when retailers believe that it is necessary to have a given level of inventory available at all times. It requires that the retailer always have a base level of inventory investment regardless of the predicted sales volume. In addition to the base stock level, there will be a variable amount of inventory that will increase or decrease at the beginning of each sales period (one month in the case of our merchandise budget) in the same dollar amount as the period's sales are expected to increase or decrease. The BSM can be calculated as follows:

Average monthly sales for the season	=	Total planned sales for the season/ Number of months in the season
Average stock for the season	=	Total planned sales for the season/ Estimated inventory turnover rate for the season
Basic stock	=	Average stock for the season – Average monthly sales for the season
Beginning-of-month (BOM) stock at retail	=	Basic stock + Planned monthly sales

To illustrate the use of the basic stock method, let's look at the planned sales for Department 353 of the Two-Seasons Department Store, shown in Exhibit 8.2 on page 256. Assume that the inventory turnover rate for the six months, or the number of times the average inventory is sold, for the season is 2.0.

Average monthly sales for the season	= Total planned sales/Number of months
	= \$500,000/6 = \$83,333
Average stock for the season	= Total planned sales/Inventory turnover
	= \$500,000/2 = \$250,000
Basic stock	= Average stock – Average monthly sales
	= \$250,000 – \$83,333 = \$166,667
BOM @ retail (February)	= Basic stock + Planned monthly sales
	= \$166,667 + \$75,000 = \$241,667
BOM @ retail (March)	= \$166,667 + \$75,000 = \$241,667
BOM @ retail (April)	= \$166,667 + \$100,000 = \$266,667
BOM @ retail (May)	= \$166,667 + \$50,000 = \$216,667
BOM @ retail (June)	= \$166,667 + \$125,000 = \$291,667
BOM @ retail (July)	= \$166,667 + \$75,000 = \$241,667

It is obvious that \$166,667 of basic stock is added to each month's planned sales to arrive at the BOM stock. In those cases where actual sales either exceed or fall short of planned sales for the month, the retailer can easily adjust the amount of overage or shortfall to bring the next month's BOM stock back in line by buying more or less stock. Therefore, the basic stock method works best if a retailer has a low inventory turnover rate (that is, less than six times a year) or if sales are erratic.

Percentage Variation Method

A second commonly used method for determining planned stock levels is the **percentage variation method (PVM)**. This method is used when the retailer has a high annual inventory turnover rate—six or more times a year. The percentage variation method assumes that the percentage fluctuations in monthly stock from average stock should be half as great as the percentage fluctuations in monthly sales from average sales.

percentage variation method (PVM)
Is a technique for planning dollar inventory investments that assumes that the percentage fluctuations in monthly stock from average stock should be half as great as the percentage fluctuations in monthly sales from average sales.

BOM stock = Average stock for season × 1/2[1 + (Planned sales for the month/Average monthly sales)]

Since the PVM utilizes the same components as the BSM, we can use the data from the previous example.

BOM (February)	= $250,000 × 1/2[1 + ($75,000/$83,333)]	=	$237,500
BOM (March)	= $250,000 × 1/2[1 + ($75,000/$83,333)]	=	$237,500
BOM (April)	= $250,000 × 1/2[1 + ($100,000/$83,333)]	=	$275,000
BOM (May)	= $250,000 × 1/2[1 + ($50,000/$83,333)]	=	$200,000
BOM (June)	= $250,000 × 1/2[1 + ($125,000/$83,333)]	=	$312,500
BOM (July)	= $250,000 × 1/2[1 + ($75,000/$83,333)]	=	$237,500

Weeks' Supply Method

weeks' supply method (WSM)
Is a technique for planning dollar inventory investments that states that the inventory level should be set equal to a predetermined number of weeks' supply, which is directly related to the desired rate of stock turnover.

A third method for planning inventory levels is the **weeks' supply method (WSM)**. Generally, the WSM formula is used by retailers such as grocers where inventories are planned on a weekly, not monthly, basis and where sales do not fluctuate substantially. It states that the inventory level should be set equal to a predetermined number of weeks' supply. The predetermined number of weeks' supply is directly related to the inventory turnover rate desired. In the WSM, inventory level in dollars varies proportionally with forecast sales. Thus, if forecast sales triple, then inventory in dollars will also triple.

To illustrate the WSM, let's return to our earlier problem and use the following formulas:

Number of weeks to be stocked = Number of weeks in the period/Stock turnover rate for the period

Average weekly sales = Estimated total sales for the period/Number of weeks in the period

BOM stock = Average weekly sales × Number of weeks to be stocked

Thus,

Number of weeks to be stocked = 26/2 = 13

Average weekly sales = $500,000/26 = $19,231

BOM stock = $19,231 × 13 = $250,000

Having determined the number of weeks' supply to be stocked (13 weeks) and the average weekly sales ($19,231), stock levels can be replenished on a frequent or regular basis to guard against stockouts.

Stock-to-Sales Method

stock-to-sales method (SSM)
Is a technique for planning dollar inventory investments where the amount of inventory planned for the beginning of the month is a ratio (obtained from trade associations or the retailer's historical records) of stock-to-sales.

The final method for planning inventory levels, and the one used in Chapter 8, is the **stock-to-sales method (SSM)**. This method is quite easy to use but requires the retailer to have a beginning-of-the-month stock-to-sales ratio. This ratio tells the retailer how much inventory is needed at the beginning of the month to support that month's estimated sales. A ratio of 2.5, for example, would tell retailers that they should have two and one-half (2 1/2) times that month's expected sales on hand in inventory at the beginning of the month.

Stock-to-sales ratios can be obtained from internal or external sources. Internally, the statistics can be obtained if the retailer has designed a good accounting system and has properly stored historical data so that the figures can be readily retrieved. Externally, the retailer can often rely on retail trade associations, such as the Menswear Retailers Association, or on national groups, such as the following:

1. National Retail Federation (http://www.nrf.com) in the United States
2. Australian Retailers Association (http://www.ara.com.au)

3. Retail Merchants Association of New Zealand (http://www.retail.org.nz)
4. Retail Council of Canada (http://www.retailcouncil.org)
5. Japan Retail Association (http://www.japan-retail.or.jp)
6. Hong Kong Retail Management Association (http://www.hkrma.org)

These and other trade associations collect stock-to-sales ratios from participating merchants and then compile, tabulate, and report them in special management reports or trade publications.

These ratios should only be used as a guide to determine how much inventory to have on hand at the beginning of each month. Successful chain store retailers have long known that even stores located near each other require not only different merchandise mixes, but also different inventory levels per sales dollars. This is a reflection of the store's trading area, layout, and competition. However, inventory turnover remains a key factor in a retailer's financial performance. Planned average beginning-of-the-month stock-to-sales goals can be easily calculated using turnover goals. If you divide the number of months in the season by the desired inventory turnover rate, an average BOM stock-to-sales ratio for the season can be computed. For example, if you desired an inventory turnover rate of 2.0 for the upcoming six-month season (4.0 annually), your average BOM stock-to-sales ratio would be 3.0 (6/2.0 = 3.0).

Retailers who realize that the various dollar merchandise plans are not hard and fast rules to be followed at all times for all stores will have higher profits.

Dollars & Sense

Dollar Merchandise Control

LO 2

How does a retailer use dollar merchandise control and open-to-buy in the retail buying process?

Once the buyer has planned the dollar merchandise to have on hand at the beginning of each month (or season), it becomes essential that the buyer does not make commitments for merchandise that would exceed the dollar plan. In short, the dollars planned for merchandise need to be controlled. This control is accomplished through a technique called open-to-buy. **Open-to-buy (OTB)** represents the dollar amount that a buyer can currently spend on merchandise without exceeding the planned dollar stocks discussed previously. When planning for any given month (or season), the buyer will not necessarily be able to purchase a dollar amount equal to the planned dollar stocks for that month (or season). This is because some inventory may be already on order but not yet delivered. To illustrate this point more succinctly, let's compute the open-to-buy for an upcoming month.

open-to-buy (OTB) Refers to the dollar amount that a buyer can currently spend on merchandise without exceeding the planned dollar stocks.

Assume that at the beginning of February the buyer for Department 353 of the Two-Seasons Department Store (see Exhibit 8.2 on page 256) has already ordered, but not yet received, $15,000 worth of merchandise at retail. Keeping planned EOM stock at $300,000 and planned reductions for February at 10 percent of planned sales, the buyer's planned purchases for February will remain $157,500. However, the open-to-buy for the month will be only $142,500 at retail since we are now accounting for that $15,000 of merchandise already ordered but not yet received. The computations would look like this:

1. Planned sales for February	+ $ 75,000
2. Plus planned reductions for February	+ 7,500
3. Plus end-of-month (EOM) planned retail stock	+ 300,000
4. Minus beginning-of-month (BOM) stock	− 225,000

5. Equals planned purchases at retail	$157,500
6. Minus commitments at retail for current delivery	– 15,000
7. Equals open-to-buy	$142,500

The OTB figure should not be set in stone because it can be exceeded. Consumer needs are the dominant consideration. If actual sales exceed planned sales, additional quantities should be ordered above those scheduled for purchase according to the merchandise budget. This should not be a common occurrence, however. If this is the case, the sales planning process is flawed. Either the buyers are too conservative in estimating sales or they are buying the wrong merchandise. In any case, the buyer, along with management, should always determine the causes of OTB adjustments. Some common buying errors include:

1. Buying merchandise that is priced either too high or too low for the store's target market.
2. Buying the wrong type of merchandise (i.e., too many tops and not enough skirts) or buying merchandise that is too trendy.
3. Having too much or too little basic stock on hand.
4. Buying from too many vendors.
5. Failing to identify the season's hot items early enough in the season.
6. Failing to let the vendor assist the buyer by adding new items and/or new colors to the existing mix. (All too often, the original order is merely repeated, resulting in a limited selection.)

Merchandise planning is a dynamic process subject to many changes. Consider the implications that could arise in planning your stock levels as a result of: (1) sales for the previous month that are lower or higher than planned, (2) reductions that are higher or lower than planned, and (3) shipments of merchandise that are delayed in transit. Understanding the consequences of each of these situations can show you the interrelationship of merchandising activities with the merchandise budget. Such occurrences serve to make retailing a challenging and exciting career choice.

Dollars & Sense

Retailers who realize that their OTB, which is an important planning tool, can be adjusted in order to meet changing market conditions will be higher-profit performers.

LO 3

Inventory Planning

How does a retailer determine the makeup of its inventory?

merchandise line
Is a group of products that are closely related because they are intended for the same end use (all televisions); are sold to the same customer group (junior miss clothing); or fall within a given price range (budget women's wear).

The dollar merchandise plan is only the starting point in merchandise management. Once the retailer has decided how many dollars can be invested in inventory, the dollar plan needs to be converted into an inventory plan. On the sales floor, items, not dollars, are sold. The assortment of items that will comprise the merchandise mix must then be planned.

Optimal Merchandise Mix

Exhibit 9.1 shows the three dimensions of the optimal mix: variety, breadth, and depth. Each of these dimensions needs to be defined; however, we need first to define merchandise line or category. A **merchandise line** consists of a group of products that are closely related because they are intended for the same end use (all televisions), are sold to the same customer group (junior miss clothing), or fall within a given price range (budget women's wear). Today, as was discussed in

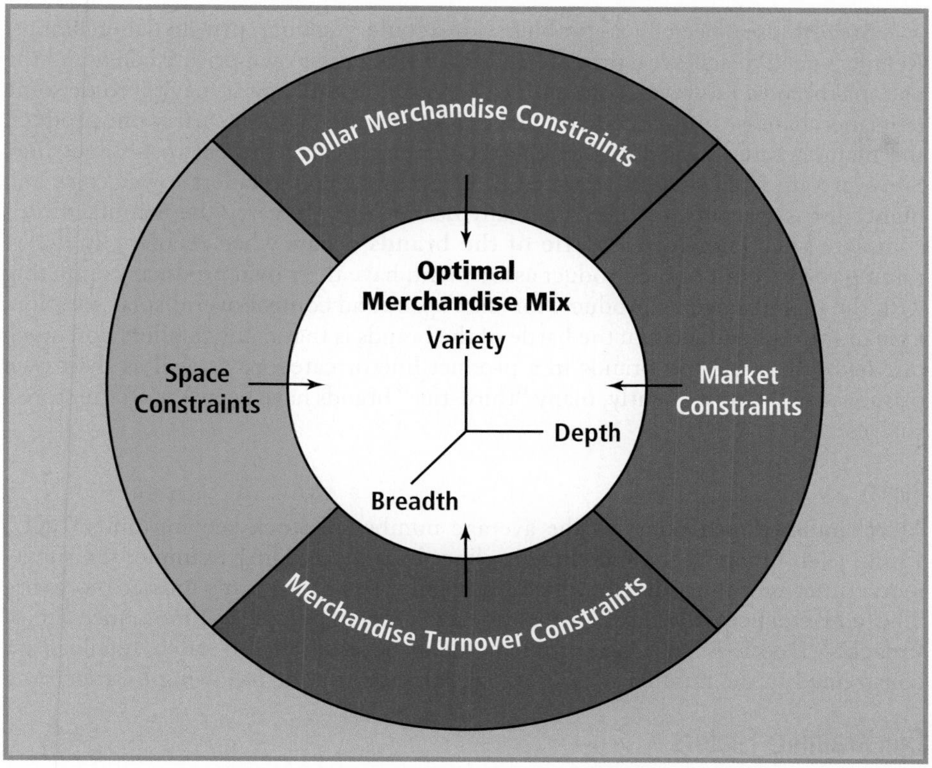

Exhibit 9.1
Dimensions of and Constraints on Optimal Merchandising Mix

Chapter 5, over 90 percent of grocery retailers use the term **category management** to refer to their management of categories as a strategic business unit. That is, a supermarket buyer using category management would no longer be concerned with GMROI for just the Tide® or Cheer® detergent. Instead, that buyer would be concerned with the GMROI for the entire detergent line or category. For that buyer, the line or category is his or her strategic business unit.

category management
Refers to the management of merchandise categories, or lines, rather than individual products, as a strategic business unit.

Variety

The **variety** of the merchandise mix refers to the number of different lines the retailer stocks in the store. For example, department stores have a large variety of merchandise lines. Some have more than 100 departments, carrying such lines as menswear, women's wear, children's clothing, infant's wear, toys, sporting goods, appliances, cosmetics, and household goods.

variety
Refers to the number of different merchandise lines that the retailer stocks in the store.

On the other hand, PetSmart carries only one basic merchandise line: pet supplies. In the middle of these two would be a retailer like Sports Authority, selling a complete range of sporting apparel and equipment.

Breadth

Breadth, also called **assortment**, refers to the number of merchandise brands that are found in the merchandise line. For example, a supermarket will have a wide breadth, or assortment, in the number of different brands of mustard that it carries: six or seven national or regional brands, a private brand, and a generic brand. A 7-Eleven convenience store, however, will offer very little breadth in that it will generally carry only one or two brands in any merchandise line.

breadth (or assortment)
The number of merchandise brands that are found in a merchandise line.

Breadth is especially a problem for retailers selling private label brands. Retailers need to achieve a proper balance between their own private labels and the national brands. However, sometimes a powerful manufacturer may try to tie some of its merchandise lines together. That is, if the retailer wishes to carry one product, the manufacturer stipulates that the retailer must carry the entire product line. Since private label brands, as noted in Chapter 4, offer retailers lower costs and higher gross margins, retailers generally do not want to carry the manufacturer's complete line. Therefore a **battle of the brands** occurs when retailers, in determining the breadth of the product assortment, have their own products competing with the manufacturer's products for shelf space and control over display location. One of the consequences of the battle of the brands is that many retailers now stock one or both of the top brands in a product line or category as well as their own private brand. Consequently, many "third-tier" brands have been left off the store's shelves.

battle of the brands
Occurs when retailers have their own products competing with the manufacturer's products for shelf space and control over display location.

Depth

Merchandise **depth** refers to the average number of stock-keeping units (SKU) within each brand of the merchandise line. In the preceding example, the supermarket manager must decide which sizes and types of French's mustard to carry. The convenience store will probably carry only the regular nine-ounce jar of French's. Depth is an acute problem today because all too often retailers are constrained in the number of SKUs they can carry by the following four factors.

depth
Is the average number of stock-keeping units within each brand of the merchandise line.

Constraining Factors

Research indicates that the merchandise mix, in addition to satisfying customer wants, can actually shape those wants and impact whether and what customers purchase.[4] Exhibit 9.1 details the four constraining factors that may restrict the retailer's design of the optimal merchandise mix. Remember, just as the trading areas for each store in a chain are different, the optimal mix will be different for every store. Merchandise mix decisions are a blend of financial plans that consider the retailer's dollar and turnover constraints, the store's space constraints, and the constraints caused by the actions of competitors.[5]

Dollar Merchandise Constraints

There seldom will be enough dollars to emphasize variety, breadth, and depth. If the decision is made to emphasize variety, it would be unrealistic to expect also to have a lot of breadth and depth.

For instance, assume for the moment that you are the owner/manager of a local gift store. You have $70,000 to invest in merchandise. If you decide that you want a lot of variety in gifts (jewelry, crystal, candles, games, cards, figurines, ashtrays, clocks, and radios), then you obviously cannot have much depth in any single item, such as crystal glassware.

Some retailers try to overcome this dollar constraint by shifting the expense of carrying inventory back on the vendor. When a retailer buys a product on **consignment**, the vendor retains the ownership of the goods, usually establishes the selling price, and is paid only when the goods are sold. Or the retailer might try to get extra dating, where the vendor allows the retailer some extra time before paying for the goods. For example, most textbook publishers either sell their books on consignment or give the bookstores an extra 60 days in which to pay. In this way your campus bookstore orders its books in early July for an early August delivery. The bookstore then sells the books in late August or early September. However,

consignment
Is when the vendor retains the ownership of the goods and usually establishes the selling price; it is paid only when the goods are sold by the retailer.

because the books were sold on consignment, or with extra dating, the bookstore does not have to pay the publisher until October.

Space Constraints

The retailer must also deal with space constraints. If depth or breadth is wanted, space is needed. If variety is to be stressed, it is also important to have enough *empty* space to separate the distinct merchandise lines. For example, consider a single counter containing cosmetics, candy, fishing tackle, women's stockings, and toys. This would obviously be an unsightly and unwise arrangement. As more variety is added, empty space becomes necessary to allow the consumer to clearly distinguish among distinct product lines.

Retailers, especially in the grocery business, have been able to turn this space constraint into an advantage by charging manufacturers slotting fees, which were discussed in both Chapters 6 and 8, to carry their products.

Merchandise Turnover Constraints

As the depth of the merchandise is increased, the retailer will be stocking more and more variations of the product to serve smaller and smaller segments. Consequently, inventory turnover will deteriorate and the chances of being out of stock will increase. One does not have to minimize variety, breadth, and depth to maximize turnover, but one must know how various merchandise mixes will affect inventory turnover.

Market Constraints

Market constraints also affect decisions on variety, breadth, and depth of the merchandise mix. The three dimensions have a profound effect on how the consumer perceives the store, and consequently on the customers the store will attract. The consumer perceives a specialty store as one with limited variety and breadth of merchandise lines but considerable depth within the lines handled. An individual searching for depth in a limited set of merchandise lines such as formal menswear will thus be attracted to a menswear retailer specializing in formal wear. On the other hand, the consumer perceives the general merchandise retailer such as Target as a store with lots of variety and breadth in terms of merchandise lines, but with more constrained depth. Therefore, someone who needs to make several purchases across several merchandise lines, and who is willing to sacrifice depth of assortment, would be more attracted to the general merchandise retailer.

The constraining factors make it almost impossible for a retailer to emphasize all three dimensions. However, retailers can take some comfort in the fact that greater product selection does not necessarily mean that the consumer will get more enjoyment from the shopping experience. Research has found that retailers can cut SKUs without lowering consumer perceptions of selection. In fact, Procter & Gamble claims that in the laundry category 40 percent of SKUs could be eliminated, yet 95 percent of consumer needs would still be met.[6] Some consumers may even be more satisfied with the smaller selection.[7] This is important for retailers using the category management system to remember. After all, category management, in its effort to increase profits, typically reduces the number of SKUs as it seeks to increase inventory turnover. Nevertheless, if you are going to lose customers, you should seek to lose the less profitable ones by properly mixing your merchandise in terms of variety, breadth, and depth within the dollar, space, turnover, and market constraints.

©Tony Freeman/PhotoEdit

Retailers are not only concerned about the GMROI for each sku in its merchandise mix but also the GMROI for each category of merchandise.

Dollars & Sense

High-profit retailers are those who realize that it is impossible to emphasize all three dimensions of the merchandise mix and therefore adjust their merchandise mix to satisfy the most profitable market segments.

Managing the Inventory

After you decide the relative emphasis to be placed on the three dimensions of the merchandise mix, you need to decide when to order and reorder the desired merchandise lines and items. Ideally, as shown in Exhibit 9.2, a retailer selling a basic stock item (one that was always to be in stock) would receive the reordered merchandise just as it is needed. However, a retailer selling a seasonal item, as shown in Exhibit 9.3, would want to be completely sold out at the planned out-of-stock date.

Exhibit 9.2
Inventory Management for a Retailer Selling a Basic Stock Item

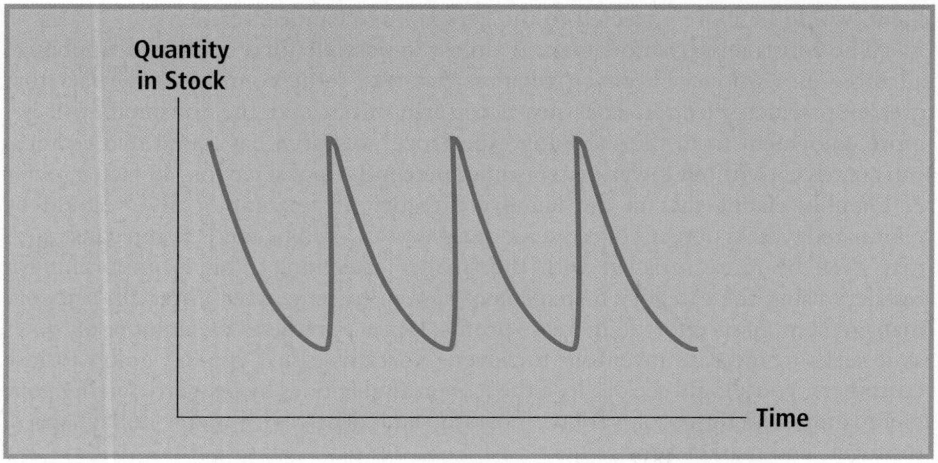

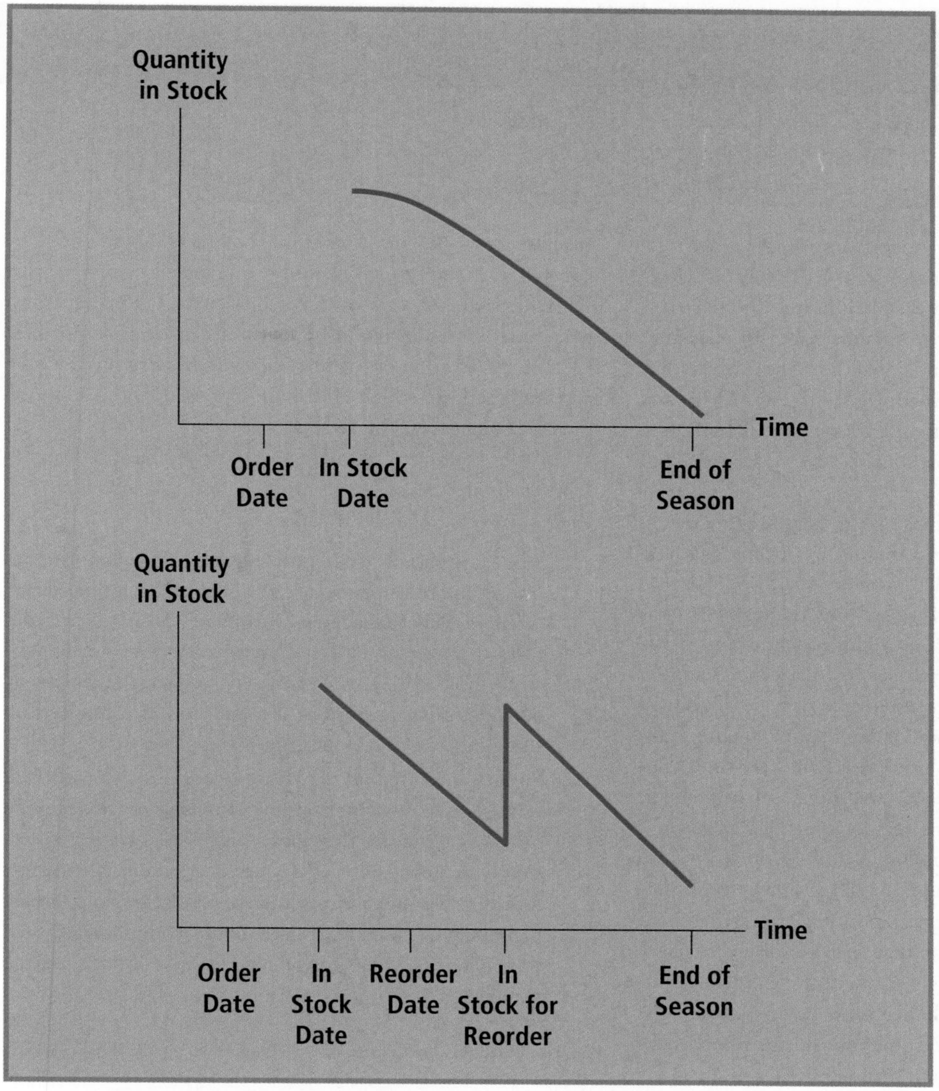

Exhibit 9.3
Inventory Management for a Retailer Selling a Seasonal Item

Both Exhibits 9.2 and 9.3 recognize the fact that it annually costs the retailer between 20 and 25 percent to carry inventory. Some of these costs are direct, such as interest on the money borrowed to pay for the inventory or insurance and warehousing expenses, and other costs may be indirect, such as what the retailer could have made elsewhere when it uses its own money to pay for the inventory.

The retailer tries to achieve the optimization of its inventory dollars by closely monitoring its inventory using RFID (radio frequency identification) or barcode data. That means as the merchandise is being sold, reorders are submitted. However, this is extremely difficult when fast-moving or high-turnover items are involved. This chapter's Retailing: What's New box describes what may be a revolutionary method to overcome this long-standing problem.

Retailers should not always allow past sales results to determine future stocking patterns. Consider, for example, how relying solely on past records to determine

What's New?

Will Radio Frequency Identification (RFID) Tags Benefit Retailers?

Every major retailer's CIO (Chief Information Officer) believes that the widespread adoption of RFID tags is a sure thing and that it will ultimately enable him/her to track every single product, from point of manufacture to checkout. Already the biggest names in global retailing—Carrefour, The Home Depot, Marks & Spencer, Metro AG, Tesco and Wal-Mart—have lined up behind RFID's promise of absolute inventory control and its consequent cost reductions and profit margin improvements.

However, before realizing these advantages, RFID tagging will require a high initial investment in technology and training costs. RFID tagging will produce reams of information ranging from when and where the merchandise was produced to its current location in the supply chain to the customer profile of the purchaser of that merchandise. Without a proper information system the data provided will create mountains of paperwork for retailers to handle. This data will have to be stored, transmitted in real-time, and shared with store management, warehouse management, inventory management, and the retailer's financial systems.

As an innovative retail technology, RFID is infinitely more powerful than barcodes, although it still has a few drawbacks. For one, while RFID offers a great advantage to retailers that sell high-ticket merchandise or that wish to tag at the case, carton, or pallet level, there is a major technical obstacle to widespread adoption that still needs to be overcome—the radio waves used by the tags to communicate are absorbed by liquids and distorted by metal, making RFID useless for tracking, say, cans of soda or jugs of milk.

A second obstacle is that some consumer privacy groups have expressed concerns that products could even be tracked to customers' homes. Therefore, before being accepted by consumers, retailers will have to convince consumers that RFID tags are not a threat to personal privacy. Retailers must overcome the issues raised by consumer associations such as CASPIAN (Consumer Against Supermarket Privacy Invasion and Numbering), which is strongly opposed to the adoption of RFID technology by retailers.

While research regarding overcoming such consumer fears is limited, one recent study offers the following two suggestions for retail RFID adopters:

1. Since attitude is the most powerful characteristic to impact the consumer's perception of risk, it is crucial that retailers help consumers formulate positive attitudes toward RFID. Retailers should create ways to demonstrate how RFID can positively impact consumers by demonstrating its ease of use and how it can speed up shopping and check out time.
2. Surveys indicate that the greatest consumer fear of RFID is having the retailer share post-purchase usage data with others. Therefore, this study suggested that if retailers simply removed the RFID tag at checkout, this worry would be eliminated. In addition, retailers should display their privacy statements and should communicate such statements to their consumers in an effort to reduce perceived risks.

Source: Based on a tour of the University of Arkansas's RFID lab, April 6, 2006; and Ji-Young Hwang and Linda Good, "Consumers' Perceptions of RFID Technology and the Role of Providing Information," a paper presented at the ACRA 2006 Spring Conference, Springdale, Arkansas, April 7, 2006.

---

what sizes to purchase would have produced a problem, given that demand for larger women's sizes has increased in recent years. In fact, the only women's apparel class to experience sales growth over the past decade has been the larger-sized clothing. Retailers, manufacturers, and even fashion magazines have finally realized that more than 40 percent of all American women now wear some clothing that is plus-sized, usually size 14 to 24.[8] "Plus sizes" now generate nearly $20 billion in annual sales as these customers demand style and quality. Retailers such as Lane Bryant no longer hide baggy, cheaply made tent-like smocks in a "fat ladies'" section in the basement. Instead, today's successful retailers are disregarding past sales records and offering larger selections of plus sizes featuring the latest looks, including the same designer-made fitted dresses and coats worn by fashion models. Saks, Bloomingdale's, and Macy's are experiencing record sales for this market by lavishing prime floor space and advertising dollars on plus sizes. However, while 21 percent of women (and 10 percent of men) acknowledge that they are quite a bit overweight, one retailer is catering to a different market. Banana Republic has added a size "double zero." This new size is aimed at sylphs who can't fill out a size 0 and fits a woman with a 31-inch bust, 23-inch waist, and 32-inch hips. (By the way, the average woman wears a size 12 and is 39-31-41.)[9]

At the same time, men's clothing sales have declined. Two reasons may account for this change:

1. The workplace has become more casual. (Since 1997, the percentage of American men wearing a suit to work has declined from 14 percent to 5 percent.)[10] Also, there have been few interesting new ideas in casual fashions.
2. More women are working outside the home and are otherwise increasingly busy, causing men to shop for themselves. Many retailers have failed to realize that men have different shopping styles. For example, while women prefer to see 40 pairs of black slacks on a rack, men prefer to see 3, and then have help matching a shirt and tie. Men tend to be less interested in clothes and thus rush through the shopping process.

Some retailers, such as Jos. A. Bank believe that the men's suit market is showing signs of life as businesses revive dress codes and more Americans suit up to compete for jobs.[11] Either way, failing to follow current trends or looking only at last year's merchandise purchases will lead to major inventory problems. A decade ago suits comprised half of Jos. A. Bank's sales; now they are 27 percent.[12] Other examples abound. From 1960 to 1998 men's and women's apparel showed continued growth in sales as baby boomers matured and retailers planned accordingly. However, this has not been true over the last decade. An even more stunning change involves the sale of watches. In 2005, sales of watches that cost between $30 and $150—those usually purchased by teens and young adults—declined by 10 percent from the previous years as this market segment used their cell phones, iPods, and other gadgets to tell time.[13] Finally, after nearly 50 years of being a top seller, the worldwide sales of Barbie have hit the skids, dropping nearly 20 percent in 2005.[14]

Probably the biggest misjudgment in forecasting retail sales occurred during the Christmas 2004 season. "Shrek 2" was predicted to be the greatest selling DVD of all time, especially when its first week's sales were reported. However, the old formula for forecasting sales (first week sales will equal one-fourth of total sales for animated movies and sales would climb steadily for months) no longer worked. Now first week sales can account for up to 70 percent of total sales. The reason for the big change is the intense competition for shelf space as movie producers and television producers release a flood of new DVDs every week. Based on the first week's sales, retailers across the country re-ordered and double-ordered the DVD. However, today when sales of a once popular disc slow, retailers now ship back unsold copies and use their shelf space for a new faster-moving release. Therefore, while the retailers didn't hit their sales target, the studio took the real hit.[15]

Retailers who realize that in addition to past sales records they must also be aware of changing market conditions when purchasing merchandise will be more profitable.

Dollars & Sense

AP Photo/Douglas C. Pizac

Retailers adding new items have to carefully consider space needed for these items or which items to delete to provide space.

Conflicts in Stock Planning

Stock planning is an exercise in compromise and conflict. The conflict is multidimensional because not everything can be stocked. The conflicts are summarized as follows:

1. Maintain a strong in-stock position on genuinely new items while trying to avoid the 90 percent of new products that fail in the introductory stage. The retailer wants to carry the new products that will satisfy customers. If the consumer is sold a poor product, it hurts the retailer as much as, if not more than, the manufacturer. The problem becomes one of screening out poor products before they reach the customer. Any screening device, however, has error; the retailer might end up stocking some losers and turning down winners. Thus a basic conflict arises, but even the best of buyers will make some mistakes and be forced to use markdowns to unload slow-selling merchandise.
2. Maintain an adequate stock of the basic popular items while having sufficient inventory dollars to capitalize on unforeseen opportunities. Many times, if the retailer fills out the model stock with recommended quantities, there is little, if any, money left over for the super buy that is just around the corner. But if the retailer holds out that money and cuts back on basic stock, customers may be lost, and that super buy may never surface. For this reason, it is important that retailers realize that they should never be out of stock on staples and best-selling products.
3. Maintain high inventory turnover goals while maintaining high gross margin goals. This is perhaps the most glaring conflict. Usually, items that turn over more rapidly have thinner gross margins. Therefore, developing an inventory plan that will accomplish both objectives is surely challenging.
4. Maintain adequate selection for customers while not confusing them. If customers are confronted with too many similar items, they will not be able to make up their minds and may leave the store empty-handed and frustrated. On the other hand, if the selection is inadequate, the customer will again leave empty-handed. Thus, a delicate balance needs to be struck between too little and too much selection.

5. Maintain space productivity and utilization while not congesting the store. Take advantage of buys that will utilize the available space, but avoid buys that cause the merchandise to spill over into the aisles. Unfortunately, some of the best buys come along when space is already occupied.

As should be readily evident at this point, inventory management is no easy task. Equally challenging is the selection of vendors from whom to buy the merchandise.

Selection of Merchandising Sources

LO 4

How do retailers select proper merchandise sources?

After deciding on the type and amount of inventory to be purchased, the next step is to determine where the retailer is to obtain the merchandise. All too often people have misconceptions about how retailers choose and negotiate with vendors. In reality, with proper planning and control, it can be a very rewarding experience, especially when your customers react positively to your merchandise selection. However, no matter how rewarding your buying experience is, it will also be grueling. Not only must the retail buyers determine what merchandise lines to carry, but they also must select the best possible vendor to supply them with these items and then must be able to negotiate the best deal possible with that vendor.

Unless the retailer owns a manufacturing and/or wholesale operation, the retailer must consider many criteria when selecting a merchandise source. These criteria are dependent on the retailer's type of store and merchandise sold. Generally the following criteria, which may vary across merchandise lines, should always be considered: selling history, consumers' perception of the manufacturer's or wholesaler's reputation, reliability of delivery, trade terms, projected markup, quality of merchandise, after-sale service, transportation time, distribution center processing time, inventory carrying cost, country of origin, fashionability and net cost.

Country of origin is becoming a more important issue every day as governments use trade agreements to limit the amount of merchandise that can be imported from various countries. As described in this chapter's Global Retailing box, consumers are becoming aware of sweatshops and the use of child labor in certain countries and rebel against buying products manufactured there. While laws regulating country of origin have long applied to apparel, one of the many initiatives found in the Farm Security and Rural Investment Act requires country of origin labeling by 2007 for beef, lamb, pork, fish, perishable agricultural commodities, and peanuts. Although consumers say they want to know where their food comes from, most are unaware of the costs associated with tracking these products, the amount of recordkeeping needed, and loss of sales resulting from the higher prices. The Grocery Manufacturers of America (GMA) claim such a law is unworkable, and will do little to maintain the safety and purity of the U.S. food supply.

Even something as seemingly minor as the number of units in a pack can be a significant factor in choosing a vendor. Wal-Mart, for example, once asked a vendor to ship some school supplies in packs of 10 instead of 80. Working with vendors in this way allowed the retail chain to increase inventories by only 4 percent while increasing sales by over 12 percent. The $1.4 billion saved by such vendor negotiations was made available for other uses.[16] In 2006, Wal-Mart went a step further and changed the way store employees ordered merchandise. It pruned the assortment of merchandise available in stores to emphasize the items that sell best in each category. Thus, many consumers were surprised not to find some of their favorite products in the new streamlined Wal-Mart. The retailer's reasoning was

Global Retailing

Retailers Are Using Their Clout to Improve Working Conditions Around the World

As a result of consumer outcries during the last decade, exposés about American retailers selling merchandise made in foreign sweatshops are seldom seen today. High-profile manufacturers and retailers such as Nike, Mattel, The Home Depot, Wal-Mart, and Gap have joined 2,000 other firms in the United Nations Global Compact. This accord urges a socially responsible approach for business operations by embracing labor, human rights, and environmental practices ranging from banning child and forced labor to using environmentally sound technologies.

Hundreds of other company and voluntary industry codes have been developed regarding electronics, jewelry, and apparel and toy manufacturing. For example, Wal-Mart in 2005 reinforced all agreements with its suppliers by making them even more accountable for environmental and social standards. The Home Depot, which sells over 8,000 wood products, has not made purchases since the late 1980s from suppliers who obtain wood from endangered trees and rain forests. Gap, with more than 3,000 factories scattered across roughly 50 countries, is probably the retailer at the forefront of this movement. The San Francisco-based owner of the Gap, Old Navy, and Banana Republic stores had been addressing this issue since 1992. However, in an unusual display of corporate candor, in 2004 the retail giant acknowledged that many of the overseas workers making its clothes were mistreated and vowed to improve on their shoddy factory conditions by cracking down on unrepentant manufacturers.

Today, you can go to the retailer's Web page and see the full extent of its efforts. Some of the key points include:

1. Gap has a global network of more than 90 full-time employees to ensure that garment manufacturers are in compliance with the firm's Code of Vendor Conduct and that the manufacturers respect the workers' rights and provide acceptable working conditions.
2. The retailer has implemented guidelines to help protect rights of foreign contract garment workers, including freedom to return to their home country.
3. It has invited Social Accountability International (SAI) to conduct external reviews of its factory monitoring program.
4. In 2005, the retailer held a Global Vendor Summit in San Francisco to build closer relationships and develop a set of expectations among top garment manufacturers.
5. Its Code of Vendor Conduct agreement spells out a set of principles and operating standards that factory owners and operators must follow regarding:
   - Prohibition of child labor
   - Adherence to local labor laws
   - Requirements for working conditions
   - Assurance of workers' freedom of association
   - Prohibition of forced labor
   - Prohibition of discrimination
   - Requirements for wages and work hours
   - Environmental practices and policies

Source: Gap's Web page. (http://www.gapinc.com/public/SocialResponsibility/socialres.shtml); Wal-Mart's press release on the subject, October 20, 2005; and "How Barbie Is Making Business a Little Better," *USAToday*, March 27, 2006: 1B, 2B.

that focused, "uncluttered" stores will produce more sales than those laden with merchandise. The resulting drop in inventory costs will bolster the retailer's margins. As a result, some Wal-Mart suppliers, notably Procter & Gamble, had to reduce sales forecasts while Wal-Mart sold off its excess P&G inventory.[17]

Likewise, in cases where a manufacturer offers to co-op some expense—for example, advertising or display support—the amount of price reduction has been shown to have a significant effect on the purchase decision.[18] Some retailers also check to see whether the same merchandise will be made available to a nearby competitor; in such cases, it may be advantageous for the retailer to use a private label or they may choose not to purchase the merchandise. As a result, some discounters which try to offer lower prices by carrying only the "hottest" toys, claimed that some vendors would not sell them the "hot" toys for fear of losing business to smaller chains and independents that sell toys year-round and not just at Christmas.

Recent research concludes that the use of private label brands (a) increases as the perceived consequences of making a buying mistake decrease, (b) increases when the different brands in the category are perceived to have a wide variance in quality, and (c) decreases if the category benefits are deemed to require actual trial/experience rather than being assessable through a search of package label information.[19]

One of a retailer's greatest assets when dealing with a vendor is the retailer's past experiences with that vendor. Whether you are a small retailer doing all the buying yourself or a new buyer for a large chain, you should always approach vendors with two important pieces of information: the vendor profitability analysis statement and the confidential vendor analysis. The **vendor profitability analysis statement** (see Exhibit 9.4) provides a record of all the purchases you made last year, the discount granted you by the vendor, transportation charges paid, the original markup, markdowns, and finally, the season-ending gross margin on that vendor's merchandise.

The **confidential vendor analysis** (see Exhibit 9.5) lists the same information as in the profitability analysis statement but also provides a three-year financial summary as well as the names, titles, and negotiating points of the entire vendor's sales staff. This last piece of information is based on the notes taken by the buyer after the previous season's buying trip.

vendor profitability analysis statement
Is a tool used to evaluate vendors and shows all purchases made the prior year, the discount granted, the transportation charges paid, the original markup, markdowns, and finally the season-ending gross margin on that vendor's merchandise.

confidential vendor analysis
Is identical to the vendor profitability analysis but also provides a three-year financial summary as well as the names, titles, and negotiating points of all the vendor's sales staff.

Dollars & Sense

Retailers who maintain and review both a vendor profitability analysis and a confidential vendor analysis statement before going to market will be more profitable.

Exhibit 9.4
Two-Seasons Vendor Profitability Analysis

	Purchases		Discount and Anticipation	Freight	Markup % Landed	Markdown		Gross Margin	
Vendor Name	Cost	Retail	(%)	(%)	Loaded	$	%	Percentage	Vendor No.
Anderson Sports	62,481	129,861	7.1	1.4	50.7	20,211	15.6	46.2	273359
Jack Frost, Inc.	26,921	53,962	8.0	1.3	49.4	3,233	6.0	50.5	818922
Sue's Fashions	25,572	51,930	8.1	1.8	49.9	6,667	12.8	47.1	206284
Jana Kantor Asso.	14,022	29,434	8.0	0.8	52.0	481	1.6	55.1	050187
Pierce Mills	12,761	25,438	9.5	1.7	49.8	7,858	30.9	33.1	132886
Ray, Inc.	2,196	4,416	8.0	1.8	49.4	754	17.1	43.8	148296
Dusty's Place	2,071	4,332	8.0	1.3	51.6			55.4	662411
Lady Carole	1,050	2,100	8.0	2.1	48.9			52.9	676841
Jill Petites	740	1,584	10.4	0.5	54.2	640	40.5	29.2	472977
Andrea's	198	410	8.0	0.8	51.1			55.0	527218

Cost: your cost
Retail: your original selling price
Discount and anticipation %: discount received for early payments
Freight %: your shipping expenses
Markup % Landed Loaded: [Retail selling price − (Cost + Freight)]/Retail selling price
Markdown: Amount original selling price is reduced
Gross Margin %: [Actual selling price − (Cost + Freight − Discount and Anticipation)]/Actual selling price

Trip Dates Fall Market City Dallas Buyer's Name Cooper Dept. Name Women's Wear Dept. No. 491

Vendor/Address Phone No./Floor No.		Volume History 200X	200X	200X	Markup History 200X	200X	200X	Markdown History 200X	200X	200X	Vendor Executives & Titles	Remarks
West Texas Blouse	Spring	590.5	719.4	330.8	47.5	47.7	46.7	2.4	5.3	4.4	Larry Wilcox (VP)	Cash Discount
	Fall	1002.8	706.7		47.3	47.5		3.4	7.8		Julie Davin	Prone to co-op
	Year	1593.3	1426.1		47.4			3.1			Ted Rombach	ads
	Objectives:											
	Results As of 5/22:											
Flatland Fashions	Spring	224.5	230.2	210.8	47.7	50.0	47.2	6.5	8.5	3.8	Joe Hall (P)	
	Fall	175.8	230.5		47.3	47.6		17.0	9.0		Richard Reel	Will deal on
	Year	400.3	460.7		47.5	48.8		11.1	8.7			transportation
	Objectives:											
	Results As of 5/22:											
Southern	Spring	-0-	42.3	50.7		48.4	45.4	-0-	9.1	4.2	Jackie Poteet (SM)	
	Fall	37.0	69.2		47.1	42.3		7.7	7.8		Boonie Hanley	"Quantity"
	Year	37.0	112.5		47.1	44.7		7.7	8.2		Carol Little	
	Objectives:											
	Results As of 5/22:											
Gallo	Spring	21.7	195.0	55.6	46.9	50.0	48.3	1.3	0.2	1.2	Ruth Wilson (P)	
	Fall	-0-	13.9		-0-	46.7		-0-	2.0		John Murphy	Easier of the
	Year	21.7	33.4		46.9	48.6		1.3	0.9			two
	Objectives:											
	Results As of 5/22:											

Exhibit 9.5
Confidential Vendor Analysis

Based on the information obtained in the previous two reports, some retailers classify vendors into five categories.

1. **Class A vendors** are the vendors from whom the retailer purchases large and profitable amounts of merchandise. The retailer may distinguish these vendors

from others by purchasing a certain minimum quantity from them. These vendors and the retailer work together as partners. Because of the retailer's sheer size, every vendor selling to Wal-Mart is a Class A vendor. For example, nearly 30 percent of Dial Corporation's total sales are to Wal-Mart. The numbers for some other vendors are Unilever (Home and Personal Care), 28 percent; Clorox, 24 percent; Procter & Gamble, 16 percent; Energizer, 16 percent; and 12 percent for Kellogg, General Mills, Gillette, and Kraft Foods.[20]

class A vendors
Are those from whom the retailer purchases large and profitable amounts of merchandise.

2. **Class B Vendors** are those who generate satisfactory sales and profits for the retailer. They occasionally develop a strong product offering for the retailer.
3. **Class C Vendors** are vendors who carry outstanding lines but do not currently sell to the retailer. This is the type of vendor that the store buyer desires as a supplier.
4. **Class D Vendors** are those from whom the retailer purchases small quantities of goods on an irregular basis. Because of the expense of the small orders, it is doubtful if the purchases from these vendors produce any profits for either the retailer or the vendor.
5. **Class E Vendors** are vendors with whom the retailer has had an unfavorable experience. Only after the approval of top store officials can orders be placed with these vendors.

class B vendors
Are those that generate satisfactory sales and profits for the retailer.

class C vendors
Are those that carry outstanding merchandise lines but do not currently sell to the retailer.

class D vendors
Are those from whom the retailer purchases small quantities of goods on an irregular basis.

class E vendors
Are those with whom the retailer has had an unfavorable experience.

Even buyers who do not go to market, but have the vendors come to them, evaluate their vendors. For years, many grocers felt that firms like Procter & Gamble treated retailers poorly. These grocers needed the many products that P&G manufactured, but they did not appreciate P&G's "we win, you lose" attitude, which forced retailers to purchase the complete line of P&G products in order to earn merchandising money. P&G was a Class B vendor, at best. Recently, however, P&G has developed a program in which it helps all its customers in formalizing their merchandise plans for the coming months and no longer requires grocers to purchase slow-moving products. This new attitude of "let's both win" has seen many supermarket managers reclassify P&G as a Class A vendor. P&G has obviously determined that it can only be as successful as its retailers let it be.

After selecting the vendor(s), the retailer still must make decisions on the specific merchandise to be bought. Some products, such as the basic items for the particular department in question, are easy to purchase. Other products, especially new items, require more careful planning and consideration. Retailers should concern themselves with several key questions:

1. Where does this product fit into the strategic position that I have staked out for my department?
2. Will I have an exclusive with this product or will I be in competition with nearby retailers?
3. What is the estimated demand for this product in my target market?
4. What is my anticipated gross margin for this product?
5. Will I be able to obtain reliable, speedy stock replacement?
6. Can this product stand on its own, or is it merely a "me-too" item?
7. What is my expected turnover rate with this product?
8. Does this product complement the rest of my inventory?

LO 5

Vendor Negotiations

What is involved in the vendor-buyer negotiation process and what terms of the contract can be negotiated?

negotiation
Is the process of finding mutually satisfying solutions when the retail buyer and vendor have conflicting objectives.

The climax of a successful buying plan is active **negotiation**, which involves finding mutually satisfying solutions for parties with conflicting objectives. The effectiveness of this buyer-vendor relationship depends upon the negotiation skills of both parties and the economic power of the firms involved.

The retail buyer must negotiate price, delivery dates, discounts, shipping terms, and return privileges. All of these factors are significant because they affect both the firm's profitability and cash flow.

Manufacturers as well as retailers have in recent years become increasingly aware of the cost of carrying excess inventory. Likewise, both parties have become more concerned with the time value of money and the resulting effect on each firm's cash flow. Since both parties to the negotiation process are aware of these cost factors and are trying to shift them to the other party, most negotiations produce some conflict. However, successful negotiation is usually accomplished when buyers realize that the vendors should serve as their partners during the upcoming merchandising season. Both the buyer and the vendor are seeking to satisfy the retailer's customers better than the competition. Therefore, buyers and vendors must resolve their conflicts and differences of opinion, remembering that negotiation is a two-way street and a long-term profitable relationship is the goal. After all, the vendor wants to develop a long-term relationship with the retailer as much as the retailer does with its customers.

What can be negotiated? There are many factors to be negotiated (prices, freight, delivery dates, method of shipment and shipping costs, exclusivity, guaranteed sales, markdown money, promotional allowances, return privileges, and discounts), and life is simplest when there are no surprises. Therefore, the smart buyer leaves nothing to chance and discusses everything with the vendor before purchase orders are signed. The buyer and seller together work out future plans using the buyer's merchandise budget and planned turnover. Therefore, the buyer and seller should seek to make negotiations a win-win situation where neither side feels like a loser, such as P&G and its retailers are doing today. The essence of negotiation is to trade what is cheap to you but valuable to the other party for what is valuable to you but cheap to the other party.

The smart buyer puts all the upcoming areas of negotiations and previous agreements in letter form and sends it to vendors before going to market. This helps to eliminate any misunderstandings afterward. Price, of course, is probably the first factor to be negotiated. Buyers should attempt to purchase the desired merchandise at the lowest possible net cost, but should not expect unreasonable discounts or price concessions. However, the buyer can try to bring about a price concession that is legal under the Robinson-Patman Act.

The buyer must be familiar with the prices and discounts allowed by each vendor. This is why past records are so important. However, the buyer must remember that his or her bargaining power is a result of his or her planned purchases from the vendor. As a result, a large retailer may be able to purchase goods from a vendor at a lower price than a small mom-and-pop retailer. Five different types of discounts can be negotiated.

trade discount
Is also referred to as a **functional discount** and is a form of compensation that the buyer may receive for performing certain wholesaling or retailing services for the manufacturer.

Trade Discount

A **trade discount**, sometimes referred to as a **functional discount**, is a form of compensation that the buyer may receive for performing certain wholesaling and/or retailing services for the manufacturer. Because this discount is given for the performance of some service, the size of the discount will vary with that service. Thus, variations in trade discounts are legally justifiable on the basis of the different costs associated with doing business with various buyers.

Trade discounts are often expressed in a chain, or series, such as "list less 40-20-10." Each figure in the chain of discounts represents a percentage reduction from the list price of an item. Assume that the list price of an item is $1,000 and that the chain of discounts is 40-20-10. The buyer who receives all these discounts would actually pay $432 for this item. The computations would look like this:

List price	$1,000
Less 40%	– 400
	600
Less 20%	– 120
	480
Less 10%	– 48
Purchase price	$ 432

To illustrate how the various chains of discount permit a vendor to compensate the members of the supply chain for their marketing activities, let's look at the preceding example. Assume that the manufacturer sells through a supply chain that includes manufacturer's agents, service wholesalers, and small retailers. The purchase price of $432 is accorded to the manufacturer's agent who negotiates a sale between the manufacturer and the service wholesaler. The manufacturers' agent then charges the service wholesaler $480 for the item, thus realizing $48 for rendering a number of marketing activities. The service wholesaler, in turn, charges a retailer $600 for the item, thus making $120. The retailer then sells the item at the suggested list price of $1,000, thus making $400 in gross margin to cover expenses and a profit.

Trade discounts are legal where they correctly reflect the costs of the intermediaries' services. Sometimes, large retailers want to buy directly from the manufacturer and pay only $432, instead of $600. This action would enable the large retailer to undercut the competition and is illegal, unless one of the three defenses of the Robinson-Patman Act explained in Chapter 6 can be applied.

Quantity Discount

A **quantity discount** is a price reduction offered as an inducement to purchase large quantities of merchandise. Three types of quantity discounts are available:

1. **Noncumulative quantity discount**: a discount based on a single purchase
2. **Cumulative quantity discount**: a discount based on total amount purchased over a period of time
3. **Free merchandise**: a discount whereby merchandise is offered in lieu of price concessions

The manufacturer can legally justify noncumulative quantity discounts if costs are reduced because of the quantity involved or if the manufacturer is meeting a competitor's price in good faith. Cumulative discounts are more difficult to justify since many small orders may be involved, thereby reducing the manufacturer's savings.

quantity discount
Is a price reduction offered as an inducement to purchase large quantities of merchandise.

noncumulative quantity discount
Is a discount based on a single purchase.

cumulative quantity discount
Is a discount based on the total amount purchased over a period of time.

free merchandise
Is a discount whereby merchandise is offered in lieu of price concessions.

For an example of how a quantity discount works, consider the following schedule:

Order Quantity	Discount from List Price
1 to 999	0%
1,000 to 9,999	5%
10,000 to 24,999	8%
25,000 to 49,999	10%

If a retailer that had already purchased 500 units wanted another 800 units, it would have to pay list price if the vendor uses a noncumulative policy. However, the retailer would receive a 5 percent discount on all purchases if the vendor uses a cumulative pricing policy.

Quantity discounts might not always be in the seller's best interest and should always be viewed by the buyer as an invitation for further negotiations. Consider the following price schedule published by a computer manufacturer:[21]

Quantity	Unit Price
1–19	$795
20–49	$749
50–149	$699
150–249	$659

Let's say that as a buyer for a retail chain you want 19 of these computers and your cost is $15,105 (19 × $795). But 20 would cost only $14,980 (20 × $749). What do you do?

You actually have four choices:

1. Tell the manufacturer to ship 20 computers for $14,980 and you keep the extra one.
2. Tell the manufacturer to ship you 19 computers at $14,980 and have them keep the other one.
3. Order 20 but tell the manufacturer to ship you only 19 and to credit you for the other computer at $749.
4. Negotiate a purchase price.

Whenever quantity discounts are offered, buyers should always check to see if by ordering more, the total purchase price might be lower.

Many times, retailers can make a quick profit from utilizing quantity discounts by selling the extra merchandise to a diverter to sell in a gray market. The diverter, who is not an authorized member of the marketing supply chain but still functions as an intermediary, will be able to purchase these goods cheaper from the retailer than it can from the manufacturer and will then sell this excess merchandise to other retailers. Also, such discounts allow the manufacturer to have its products sold in discount stores without offending all of its authorized retailers. However, many authorized retailers are upset when diverters provide discounters with such merchandise. Some department stores have dropped cosmetic lines when discounters, most of whose cosmetics are diverted, started to carry the lines. Costco acknowledges that they will try to buy directly from manufacturers, but in instances where the manufacturers refuse, Costco will make a legal purchase through a third party. Little wonder that Costco has a vice president of "diverting" who purchases over $200 million worth of merchandise from unauthorized vendors.[22]

Consider the previous retailer that needed only 19 computers and purchased 20. Here the retailer sold the extra computer to a diverter for $600. As a result, the retailer was better off by $725 (the $125 difference in price between ordering 20 versus 19 units plus the $600 from the diverter) than it would have been had it bought only 19 computers at $795 each. The diverter could now profit by selling the computer to another retailer for something more than $600.

Today diverters are important members of the retailer's supply chain, especially in the grocery and computer fields. However, despite the problems discussed in Chapter 5 that some manufacturers have with diverters, not all manufacturers or retailers feel the same way about them. In fact, some manufacturers develop their pricing policies to enable diverters to function economically. By doing this they can increase sales by reaching markets they can't enter under normal operating conditions.

Retailers who understand how to negotiate the various discounts, especially quantity discounts, to their advantage will be more profitable.

Dollars & Sense

Promotional Discount

A third type of discount is a **promotional discount,** which is given when the retailer performs an advertising or promotional service for the manufacturer. For example, a vendor might offer a retailer 50 extra jeans if (1) the retailer purchases 1,250 jeans during the season and (2) runs two newspaper advertisements featuring the jeans during the season. One of the main reasons manufacturers offer such discounts is that the rates newspapers charge local retailers are often lower than the rates charged national manufacturers. These discounts are legal as long as they are available to all competing retailers on an equal basis.

promotional discount
Is a discount provided for the retailer performing an advertising or promotional service for the manufacturer.

Seasonal Discount

Retailers can earn a **seasonal discount** if they purchase and take delivery of the merchandise in the off-season (e.g., buying swimwear in October). However, this does not mean that all seasonal discounts result in the purchase of merchandise out of season. Retailers in resort areas often take advantage of these discounts since swimwear is never out of season for them. As long as the same terms are available to all competing retailers, seasonal discounts are legal.

seasonal discount
Is a discount provided to retailers if they purchase and take delivery of merchandise in the off season.

Cash Discount

The final discount available to the buyer is a **cash discount** for prompt payment of bills. Cash discounts are usually stated as 2/10, net 30, which means that a 2 percent discount is given if payment is received within 10 days of the invoice date and the net amount is due within 30 days.

Although the cash discount is a common method for encouraging early payment, it can also be used as a negotiating tool by delaying the payment due date. This future-dating negotiation may take many forms. Following are several of the most common:

1. **End-of-month (EOM) dating** allows for a cash discount and the full payment period to begin on the first day of the following month instead of on the invoice date. End-of-month invoices dated after the 25th of the month are considered dated on the first of the following month.
2. **Middle-of-month (MOM) dating** is similar to EOM except the middle of the month is used as the starting date.

cash discount
Is a discount offered to the retailer for the prompt payment of bills.

end-of-month (EOM) dating
Allows the retailer to take a cash discount and the full payment period to begin on the first day of the following month instead of on the invoice date.

middle-of-month (MOM) dating
Allows the retailer to take a cash discount and the full payment period to begin on the middle of the month.

receipt of goods (ROG) dating
Allows the retailer to take a cash discount and the full payment period to begin when the goods are received by the retailer.

extra dating (Ex)
Allows the retailer extra or interest-free days before the period of payment begins.

anticipation
Allows the retailer to pay the invoice in advance of the end of the cash discount period and earn an extra discount.

free on board (FOB) factory
Is a method of charging for transportation where the buyer assumes title to the goods at the factory and pays all transportation costs from the vendor's factory.

3. **Receipt of goods (ROG) dating** allows the starting date to be the date the retailer received the goods.
4. **Extra dating (Ex)** merely allows the retailer extra or free days before the period of payment begins.
5. A final discount form to be considered, but which is not widely used today, is anticipation. **Anticipation** allows a retailer to pay the invoice in advance of the expiration of the cash discount period and earn an extra discount. However, anticipation is usually figured at an annual rate of 7.0 percent, which is below the current cost of money.

Many vendors have eliminated the cash discount because retailers, especially department stores, have been taking 60 to 120 days to pay and still deduct the cash discount. In fact, many vendors are requiring new accounts to pay up front until credit is established.

Delivery Terms

Delivery terms are another factor to be considered in negotiations. They are important because they specify where title to the merchandise passes to the retailer, whether the vendor or buyer will pay the freight charges, and who is obligated to file damage claims. The three most common shipping terms are:

1. **Free on board (FOB) factory**. The buyer assumes title at the factory and pays all transportation costs from the vendor's factory.
2. **Free on board (FOB) shipping point**. The vendor pays the transportation to a local shipping point, but the buyer assumes title at this point and pays all further transportation costs.
3. **Free on board (FOB) destination.** The vendor pays all transportation costs and the buyer takes title upon delivery.

LO 6

In-store Merchandise Handling

What methods are available for handling the merchandise once it is received in the store, so as to control shrinkage, including vendor collusion and theft?

free on board (FOB) shipping point
Is a method of charging for transportation in which the vendor pays for transportation to a local shipping point where the buyer assumes title and then pays all further transportation costs.

The retailer must have some means of handling incoming merchandise. For some types of retailers (e.g., a grocery store), this need will be significant and frequent; for others (e.g., a jeweler), it will be relatively minor and infrequent. Frequent and large deliveries entail considerable planning of merchandise receiving and handling space. For instance, consider that a full-line grocery store must have receiving docks to which 40- to 60-foot semitrailers can be backed up. Similarly, space may be needed for a small forklift to drive between the truck and the merchandise receiving area to unload the merchandise. Subsequently, the merchandise will need to be moved from the receiving area, where it will be counted and marked, to a storage area, either on the selling floor or in a separate location.

The point at which incoming merchandise is received can be a high theft location. The retail manager needs to design the receiving and handling area to minimize this problem. Some thefts involve the retail employees themselves; others involve outsiders. The 2004 National Retail Security Survey found that the average shrinkage rate for the nation's largest retailers was 1.54 percent of their annual sales. This is the lowest number in the 14-year history of the survey. (**Shrinkage,** which is calculated "at retail," is the loss of merchandise due to theft, loss, damage, or bookkeeping errors.) This translates into an industry-wide net loss of $31 billion.[23] Therefore, several types of shrinkage caused by theft will be mentioned in the following discussion. While most discussions of shrinkage attribute theft to one

Retailing: The Inside Story

The Birds Did It

Alfred Hitchcock made a movie where the skies were full of birds wrecking havoc on the population. In the case of Bob Ridings of Spotsylvania, Virginia, just a few birds were causing his problems.

Bob, who with his wife, Kim, owned the Shop & Wash Carwash in nearby Fredericksburg, was taking his son to preschool one morning when he pulled into the carwash and noticed nearly a hundred quarters strewn all over his parking lot.

"I thought someone had hit my vending machines, so I checked the soft drink machine, but the locks were still on," he said. He was further confused the next day when he noticed a piece of straw sticking out of the change cup of the carwash's self-service coin-changing machine.

When he opened the front of the device and discovered some dandelions and the cellophane wrapper from a package of cigarettes stuffed in there, it occurred to him that his thief might be of the feathered variety. So he set up a surveillance camera. He trained his 35-mm Minolta on the coin machine and soon found his thief. The camera snapped 18 pictures of a small flock of starlings emptying coins out of the machine so they could build a nest in the change cup. They worked as a gang whereby one bird would go up inside the machine to jimmy coins loose and the other birds would grab them and fly off with them.

Attempting to put a stop to his shrinkage, Ridings plugged up the change chute with a paper towel to discourage the starlings. The birds simply pulled that out so he replaced the towel with black electrical tape. By the next morning the avian thieves had pecked through the tape. Ridings finally succeeded by stuffing a cloth into the coin chute. Unable to remove it, the birds eventually gave up and never returned.

Source: Based on conversations with Bob and Kim Ridings and used with their permission.

Courtesy of Robert Ridings

of three culprits—vendors, employees, and customers—the chapter's Retailing: The Inside Story box describes a rare case when it can come from a most unexpected source.

Vendor collusion includes the types of losses that occur when the merchandise is delivered. Typical losses involve the delivery of less merchandise than is charged for, removal of good merchandise disguised as old or stale merchandise, and the theft of other merchandise from the stockroom or off the selling floor while making delivery. This type of loss often involves both the delivery person and the retail employee who signs for the delivery with the two splitting the profit.

free on board (FOB) destination
Is a method of charging for transportation in which the vendor pays for all transportation costs and the buyer takes title on delivery.

shrinkage
Is the loss of merchandise due to theft, loss, damage, or bookkeeping errors.

vendor collusion
Occurs when an employee of one of the retailer's vendors steals merchandise as it is delivered to the retailer.

employee theft
Occurs when employees of the retailer steal merchandise where they work.

customer theft
Is also known as shoplifting and occurs when customers or individuals disguised as customers steal merchandise from the retailer's store.

Employee theft occurs when employees steal merchandise where they work. Although no one knows for sure how much is stolen annually from retailers (since all shrinkage statistics are based only on apprehensions), as many as 30 percent of American workers admit to stealing from their employers, even if they take only small items like a pen or pencil. Although some of the stolen goods come from the selling floor, a larger percentage is taken from the stockroom to the employee lounge and lockers, where it is kept until the employees leave with it at quitting time. Employee theft, which amounts to over $800 per apprehension, is most prevalent in food stores, department stores, and discount stores. Considering that these types of stores are usually larger in size, sales volume, and number of employees, the lack of close supervision probably contributes to this problem. Exhibit 9.6 shows 50 ways that an employee can steal from a bar.

Customer theft is also a problem. In fact, over a dozen shoppers are caught for every case of employee theft, although the average amount of merchandise recovered is less than $50. Stealing merchandise from the stockroom and receiving area may be easier than taking it from the selling floor for several reasons. First, much of the stockroom merchandise is not ticketed so it is easier to get it through electronic antishoplifting devices. Second, once the thief enters the stock area, there is very little antitheft security. Most security guards watch the exits and fitting rooms. Third, there is usually an exit in the immediate area of the stockroom through which the thief can carry out the stolen goods. Some retailers have wired these exits to set off an alarm when opened without a key, helping to reduce thefts somewhat. Another innovative retailer, after determining that employees were hiding merchandise in the compressed and discarded boxes that were left out as trash, started using a special spiked baler that punched holes in boxes to damage any stolen merchandise.

The retailer must be aware that the opportunities for receiving, handling, and storage thefts are numerous. Therefore, steps should be taken to reduce these crimes. The retailer cannot watch the employees every minute to see whether or not they are honest, but some surveillance is helpful. However, the retailer must consider the employees' and customers' rights to privacy versus the retailer's right to security. Legislation is currently being considered by several states that would, if approved, allow the use of electronic monitoring by video and audio systems only when advance notice is given. In effect, workers and shoppers must be informed when they are being monitored.

The amount of storage space the retailer needs is related to the physical dimensions of the merchandise and the safety stock level needed to maintain the desired rate of stock turnover. For example, furniture is bulky and requires considerable storage space; grocery items turn over frequently, so more merchandise is usually needed than can be displayed on the shelves. This excess inventory causes retailers to stack boxes and cartons on the floor of the stockroom. In most cases, however, this scenario is inefficient and costly given that the retailer is probably paying employees anywhere from $5 to $15 per hour to keep the storeroom in order. Thus, in most cases, some type of mechanized equipment will be used to increase productivity. For instance, rather than simply carry incoming merchandise, employees might use one of the numerous types of carts especially made for this purpose. Also, instead of stacking the cartons and boxes directly on the floor of the stockroom where they must remain packed and risk being damaged, the merchandise can be unpacked, checked, inventoried, and ticketed, then placed on shelves or in bins until needed. By doing this, one can increase the amount of merchandise stored per square foot by decreasing the amount of packing material. A tidy, well-ordered stock area is less tempting to dishonest employees. Trash compactors can be helpful to compress the packing clutter.

1. The "Phantom Register" trick: Set up an extra register in bar for use only during busy times. The income from this register is not totaled on master tape and funds are skimmed by the bartender.
2. Serve and collect while register is being read between shift changes.
3. Claim a phony walkout and keep money received from customer.
4. Pick up customer's cash when he or she isn't paying attention.
5. Fake a robbery of the night deposit on way to bank. It is difficult for owners to prove this fake occurred.
6. Add phantom drinks to a customer's "running tab."
7. The "Phantom Bottle" ploy: Bring your own bottle of liquor onto shift and pocket cash from its sale.
8. The "Short Pour" trick: Just pour less than shot to cover "giveaway" liquor costs.
9. Don't ring up any sale and keep the cash.
10. The "Short-ring" trick: Under-ring the correct price of item and pocket the difference.
11. The "Free-Giveaway" trick: Give drinks to friends in anticipation of larger tips.
12. Mislead the owner regarding the number of draft beers that can be poured from a keg.
13. Undercharge for drinks with the anticipation of a larger tip.
14. Reuse register drink receipts.
15. Trade drinks to the cook for meals.
16. Add water to liquor bottle to maintain inventory.
17. Substitute lower-priced liquor when asked for call brands.
18. Collude with the delivery person, sell "stolen" products that he or she provides, and split the profit.
19. Ask for kickbacks from liquor distributor.
20. Dispense and register one shot on computerized dispenser system, while short-shotting the liquor into two glasses.
21. Short-change a customer when he or she is a "little under the weather" and claim it was an "honest" mistake if caught.
22. Claim a returned drink: Extra drink produced and can be sold by bartender.
23. Count missing bottles as "to go sale" when bar is selling both liquor to go and by the drink.
24. The "Owner Is a Jerk" ploy: You, the bartender, are the only person in charge of liquor pickup, check-in, and stocking.
25. Maids sell complimentary cocktail or wine coupons from hotel room to bar personnel, which you can place in register for cash.
26. Add two different customer drinks together and charge both customers, claiming misunderstanding in who was purchasing the round.
27. Ring food items on liquor key to cover high liquor cost percent.
28. Sell "after-shift drinks" to customers, not having them consumed by other employees.
29. Pour not enough liquor into blended fruit drinks to cover other shortages.
30. Have customer sign credit card voucher in advance and then overcharge the ticket.
31. Claim opening bank was short.
32. Total out register in midshift. Start new tape. You keep both new tapes and cash.
33. Incorrect "overring" or "void" of register.
34. Make sales during tape changes.
35. Mistotal the amount on the credit card or change the amount after customer leaves.
36. Take money from the game machines or jukeboxes.
37. Accumulate the guest checks to ring up after customer leaves so as to change the amount or leave out items.
38. Run credit card through twice.
39. Sell empty kegs and returnable bottles to an off-premise retailer.
40. Place the tip jars next to cash register—easy to place cash in tip jar and ring "no sale" for register activity.
41. Falsify cumulative register readings and "losing" tape.
42. Add extra hours to your time card and split it with the shift manager.
43. Help the shift manager claim a fictitious employee on payroll.
44. Take home food or liquor or fake a burglary.
45. Take funds from vending machines.
46. Ring up sales at happy hour prices, but charge regular bar prices to the customer when he or she is keeping receipts.
47. Servers charge for happy hour hors d'oeuvres and bar snacks.
48. Hold back bank deposits for a couple days and invest or borrow money or just don't deposit money (or lesser amount) and keep difference.
49. Handwrite bar tabs and ring up lesser amounts on the register.
50. Wrap booze into garbage can for later retrieval.

Exhibit 9.6
50 Tricks for Bartenders

Although much theft results from in-store merchandise handling, retailers must also be aware of how theft in transit may influence their ability to have the appropriate amount of merchandise on hand. Therefore, retailers must not only plan to have the appropriate amount of merchandise on hand for customers, but also to ensure that the merchandise purchased for the store shelves actually arrives. Whether a retailer outsources its logistics or employs its own transportation force, ensuring that the merchandise makes it from the warehouse to the retail floor is critical for success.

So what can happen to merchandise in transit? Hijacking. A significant amount of shipment hijacking does occur in the United States, but the global playing field can be truly fraught with peril. Consider, for instance, the case of a truck carrying a load of consumer electronics bound for Paraguay. Deep in the heart of the Brazilian jungle the driver sees that the road ahead is blocked. As he comes to a stop, the driver realizes that his truck is about to be hijacked. Luckily, he has brought an off-duty Brazilian police officer with him to help protect the shipment. The police officer exits the cab of the truck and the driver immediately senses the feeling of familiarity between his security officer and one of the bandits. It seems that the bandit is also a police officer. After a brief discussion the truck is allowed to move on with its shipment. This may sound like fiction but it is a true story. And, although the shipment was consumer electronics, other high-value products, such as apparel, perfume, cigarettes, and alcohol, are also subject to hijacking. Whether on land, sea, or air, hijacking is a relatively common occurrence in the retail supply chain.

The probability of theft in transit varies considerably from region to region. Although relatively few shipments are hijacked in Canada, the United States, and Western Europe, regions such as Eastern Europe, Latin America, Russia, and Southeast Asia are the most dangerous. Deteriorating economic conditions in these regions has increased organized crime activity, resulting in increased theft of cargo. For many people in these regions, hijacking one shipment of consumer electronics can generate more cash than the average person in the area makes in a lifetime.

Although statistics related to the theft of cargo destined for retailers is difficult to obtain because few companies want to publicize their security problems, losses due to hijacking and the resulting disruption to retail operations are a major concern. However, losses due to hijacking are avoidable to a degree. Here are some tips that retailers and their supply chain partners can employ to minimize the threat of hijacking.

1. Eliminate the retailer's name from the side of containers carrying the cargo. For consumer electronics companies such as Best Buy, putting their name on the truck, signaling to all that a shipment of consumer electronics is inside, is tantamount to saying, "steal me."
2. Install electronic monitoring devices on all shipment vehicles. Whether shipping via land, sea, or air, being able to track the container in which the merchandise is shipped can help to determine its location when hijacked.
3. Carefully screen all internal transportation personnel as well as third-party logistics personnel in each global market. Given the nature of their jobs, these personnel are under loose supervision and higher security standards are therefore critical.
4. Hire security personnel for each shipment. It is much easier for a single person to collude with others than for multiple people to conspire.

As retailers continue to expand globally, the risks involved in international hijacking will continue to grow. However, by implementing a few security measures, retailers can minimize disruption to their supply of merchandise, thus increasing the level of satisfaction to customers by minimizing stockouts.

SUMMARY

Merchandise management is the analysis, planning, acquisition, and control of inventory investments and assortments in a retail enterprise. An understanding of the principles of merchandise management is essential to good retail management. A major part of merchandise management is planning. The retailer needs to plan, first, the dollars to invest in inventory and, second, when to purchase with these dollars.

What is the difference between the four methods of dollar merchandise planning used to determine the proper inventory stock levels needed to begin a merchandise selling period?

LO 1

In the section on dollar merchandise planning, we discussed how the basic stock (which is used when retailers believe that it is necessary to have a given level of inventory available at all times, plus a variable amount of inventory that is tied to forecasted sales for the period); percentage variation (which assumes that the percentage fluctuations in monthly stock from average stock should be half as great as the percentage fluctuations in monthly sales from average sales); weeks' supply (where the beginning inventory level should be set equal to a predetermined number of weeks' supply); and stock-to-sales (where the retailer wants to maintain a specified ratio of inventory to planned sales) inventory methods can be used in retailing today.

How does a retailer use dollar merchandise control and open-to-buy in the retail buying process?

LO 2

Once the buyer has planned the dollar merchandise to have on hand at the beginning of each month (or season), it is essential that the buyer does not make commitments for merchandise that would exceed the dollar plan. In short, the dollars planned for merchandise need to be controlled by a technique called open-to-buy. OTB represents the dollar amount that a buyer can currently spend on merchandise without exceeding the planned dollar stocks discussed previously.

The OTB figure should not be set in stone because it can be exceeded. Consumer needs are the dominant consideration. If sales exceed planned sales, additional quantities should be ordered above those scheduled for purchase according to the merchandise budget.

How does a retailer determine the makeup of its inventory?

LO 3

The dollar merchandise plan is only the starting point in determining a merchandise line, which consists of a group of products that are closely related because they are intended for the same end use, are sold to the same customer group, or fall within a similar price range. Once the retailer has decided how many dollars can be invested in inventory, the dollar plan needs to be converted into inventory. However, there seldom will be enough dollars to emphasize all three inventory dimensions: variety, breadth, and depth. Therefore, retailers must select a merchandise mix that appeals to the greatest number of profitable market segments.

How do retailers select proper merchandise sources?

LO 4

In addition to deciding what and how much to purchase, successful merchandise management must also consider vendor selection and negotiations. In this section, we reviewed the major factors (selling history, consumers' perception of the manufacturer's reputation, reliability of delivery, trade terms, projected markup, quality of merchandise, after-sale service, transportation time, distribution center processing time, inventory carrying cost, country of origin, fashionability, and net-landed

STUDENT STUDY GUIDE

cost) that are important in the selection of a vendor and how a buyer prepares for a buying trip.

LO 5

What is involved in the vendor-buyer negotiation process and what terms of the contract can be negotiated?

The climax of a successful buying plan is the active negotiation, which involves finding mutually satisfying solutions for parties with conflicting objectives, with those vendors that the retailer has identified as suitable supply sources. The effectiveness of this buyer-vendor relationship depends on the negotiation skills of both parties and the economic power of the firms involved. The retail buyer must negotiate price, delivery dates, discounts (trade, quantity, promotional, seasonal, and cash), delivery terms, and return privileges. All of these factors are significant because they affect both the firm's profitability and cash flow.

LO 6

What methods are available for handling the merchandise once it is received in the store, so as to control shrinkage, vendor collusion, and theft?

We concluded the chapter with a discussion on in-store merchandise handling as a means to control losses by theft.

TERMS TO REMEMBER

merchandise management
gross margin return on inventory
basic stock method (BSM)
percentage variation method (PVM)
weeks' supply method (WSM)
stock-to-sales method (SSM)
open-to-buy (OTB)
merchandise line
category management
variety
breadth (or assortment)
battle of the brands
depth
consignment
vendor profitability analysis statement
confidential vendor analysis
class A vendors
class B vendors
class C vendors
class D vendors
class E vendors
negotiation
trade discount
quantity discount
noncumulative quantity discount
cumulative quantity discount
free merchandise
promotional discount
seasonal discount
cash discount
end-of-month (EOM) dating
middle-of-month (MOM) dating
receipt of goods (ROG) dating
extra dating (Ex)
anticipation
free on board (FOB) factory
free on board (FOB) shipping point
free on board (FOB) destination
shrinkage
vendor collusion
employee theft
customer theft

REVIEW AND DISCUSSION QUESTIONS

LO 1

What are the differences between the four methods of dollar merchandise planning used to determine the proper inventory stock levels needed to begin a merchandise selling period?

1. If your annual turnover rate is 4 times, which inventory stock level method would you use and why?

2. The Corner Hardware Store is attempting to develop a merchandise budget for the next 12 months. To assist in this process, the following data have been developed. The target inventory turnover is 4.8 and forecast sales are as follows:

Month	Forecast Sales
1	$27,000
2	26,000
3	20,000
4	34,000
5	41,000
6	40,000
7	28,000
8	27,000
9	38,000
10	39,000
11	26,000
12	28,000

Develop a monthly merchandise budget using the basic stock method (BSM) and the percentage variation method (PVM).

How do retailer's use dollar merchandise control and describe how open-to-buy is used in the retail buying process? **LO 2**

3. What problems can occur to buyers open-to-buy if they misjudge planned sales?
4. What does the term "open-to-buy" mean? How can it be used to control merchandise investments?
5. A buyer is going to market and needs to compute the open-to-buy. The relevant data are as follows: planned stock at end of March, $319,999 (at retail prices); planned March sales, $149,999; current stock-on-hand (March 1), $274,000; merchandise on order for delivery, $17,000; planned reductions, $11,000. What is the buyer's open-to-buy?

How does a retailer use unit stock planning and model stock plans in determining the makeup of a merchandise mix? **LO 3**

6. What are the major constraints in designing the optimal merchandise mix?
7. How can merchandise lines have too much breadth, yet not enough depth?
8. Manufacturers of "third tier" brands argue that they are being squeezed out of many stores by the major brands. Do you agree with that statement? Why?

How does a retailer select proper merchandise sources? **LO 4**

9. What do you think is the most important criterion in selecting a vendor? Why?
10. Why should a new buyer look over the previous buyer's confidential vendor analysis before going to market?

What is involved in the vendor-buyer negotiation process and what terms of the contract can be negotiated? **LO 5**

11. If a vendor ships you $1,000 worth of merchandise on April 27 with terms of 3/20, net 30 EOM, how much should you pay the vendor on June 8?
12. A retailer purchases goods that have a list price of $7,500. The manufacturer allows a trade discount of 40-25-10 and a cash discount of 2/10, net 30. If the retailer takes both discounts, how much is paid to the vendor?

STUDENT STUDY GUIDE

13. How can cumulative quantity discounts be considered to be anticompetitive?
14. How can manufacturers stop retailers from diverting their brand name goods to discounters?

LO 6

What methods are available to the retailer for controlling loss through shrinkage, vendor collusion, and theft?

15. What is the worst type of shrinkage, employee theft, or customer theft? What is your reasoning?
16. Should retailers' right to security take precedence over the employee's and the customer's right to privacy when retailers set up an electronic monitoring system in their stores to curb losses from theft?

SAMPLE TEST QUESTIONS

LO 1

Determine the buyer's BOM for August, using the Percentage Variation Method, based on the following information: planned sales for August = $170,000; average monthly sales = $142,000; average stock for the season = $425,000.

a. $466,901
b. $390,000
c. $254,400
d. $425,000
e. $453,800

LO 2

The open-to-buy concept provides information about how much the buyer can order at:

a. the beginning of a merchandising period.
b. the middle of a merchandising period.
c. the end of a merchandising period.
d. anytime during the merchandising period.
e. anytime a vendor fails to ship merchandise on time.

LO 3

Which of the following factors is not a constraint on the retailer's optimal merchandise mix?

a. space
b. merchandise turnover
c. legal
d. dollar merchandise
e. market

LO 4

A vendor profitability analysis statement:

a. is a vendor's financial statement that is made available to all retailers.
b. is a retailer's analysis of the profitability of the different vendors and their lines from the prior year.
c. is a schedule maintained by the retailer which shows each vendor's initial data for new lines, shipment of orders, and gross margins.
d. is a retailer's financial statement used by the vendor for determining credit limits.
e. contains a list of who provided the retailer with discounts during the prior three years.

LO 5

A cumulative quantity discount is based on:

a. a single purchase.
b. the total amount of merchandise purchased over a period of time.
c. the total amount of merchandise purchased since you began dealing with a vendor.

d. the amount of free merchandise a vendor is offering.
e. cumulative discounts are only offered if a buyer is purchasing more than 50,000 units.

LO 6

Which two parties are usually involved in losses due to vendor collusion?
a. delivery people and customers
b. retail employee signing for the delivery and delivery person
c. vendor sales representative and retail employee signing for the delivery
d. customers and vendor sales representative
e. vendor sales representative and the retailer's accountant

WRITING AND SPEAKING EXERCISE

It is late August and the local economy is starting to slow, which is affecting sales in your department. In fact, your back-to-school sales were eight percent under plan. As the store's newest buyer, you just moved into your current position in early May, and you do not want to make any merchandising mistakes in your first Christmas season. Today, you receive a memo from the president stating, "I would rather lose sales, than get stuck with a tremendous overhang of merchandise and end up giving it away come December. So cut back your OTB by 25 percent." After reading this memo several times, you decide to respond to the president. What would your response say?

RETAIL PROJECT

Before leaving for the market, some buyers check Web sites, such as that run by Social Accountability International (http://www.cepaa.org), to check out products and manufacturers, as well as retailers, that are ranked high for having a responsible workplace environment.

Go to any Web site you choose, other than a manufacturer or retailer or other supplier-sponsored Web site, and examine for yourself how the Web site grades these issues. Do you agree or disagree with the statement that retail buyers should examine such Web sites before going to market and use this information to make their purchasing decision? Or should retailers merely check out this Web site to be prepared for any future problems involving manufacturers of products that they are selling? Finally, are some of these issues more important than others?

PLANNING YOUR OWN RETAIL BUSINESS

Alexia White is in the process of developing the merchandise budget for the gift shop she is opening next year. She has decided to use the basic stock method of merchandise budgeting. Planned sales for the first half of next year are $200,000, and this is divided as follows: February = 9 percent, March = 10 percent, April = 15 percent, May = 21 percent, June = 22 percent, and July = 23 percent. Planned total retail reductions are 9 percent for February and March, 4 percent for April and May, and 12 percent for June and July. The planned initial markup percentage is 48 percent. Alexia desires the rate of inventory turnover for the season to be two times. Also, she wants to begin the second half of the year with $90,000 in inventory at retail prices.

Develop a six-month merchandise budget for Alexia.

CASE

The Sizing Problem[24]

Pam Lewis, the owner of the up-scale Pam's Place in the Chicago suburb of Lincolnshire, had just entered what was to be the last vendor's showroom on her first day of this year's Dallas Apparel Market. She was excited about what she had seen that day and was already looking forward to a relaxing dinner with her former college roommate and the next two days of buying. This last vendor was new to Pam, but she had heard other buyers saying wonderful things about it at the food court earlier that afternoon. Since it was near one of her Class A vendors, she decided to stop by.

Upon entering the showroom, Pam uttered her usual "What's new?" to the manufacturer's sales rep.

"Depends on how important it is to you to make your customers very happy," was the quick reply. The salesperson then ushered Pam over to a display carrying slacks that featured a new fit technology. The key was the realization that a size 10 45- to 55-year-old women doesn't have the same shape as a size 10 25-year-old. Based on this fact, a new sizing system, called Fitlogic, is being used by the manufacturer. It is based on three body shapes that represent the most common female figures: straight silhouette, curvy, and pearlike. These shapes are labeled 1, 2, and 3. Thus the vendor showed Pam three different size 12 slacks, (12.1, 12.2, 12.3), one for each body shape.

The salesperson went on to explain that for women in the over-35 crowd, 40 percent are a 1 shape, 40 percent are a 3 shape, and only 20 percent are a 2 shape, the silhouette currently used as the standard for sizing.

Pam remembered recently seeing the developer of this system on television discussing why she thought it would revolutionize the way baby boomer women would purchase clothing. She even recalled an article in a trade journal about how a television shopping network, QVC, had great success with this concept. Still, she realized that the variety which would make the concept so appealing to her customers—multiple versions of the same size, each tailored to their body shape—would make it so unappealing to her as a buyer. After all, if she adopted the system for this line, she would have three times the number of items. They would require more display space and create a greater risk of future markdowns. It was a breadth versus depth issue to Pam because carrying the extra sizes would mean she would have to drop some other merchandise. Thus Pam, despite liking the fashions she saw in the showroom, was undecided as she left to meet her ex-roommate, Pat Marion, for dinner.

That night over dinner Pam described her day, especially this new fit technology. It hit her that there might be something to the system when Pat started telling her about Pat's troubles in taking back some clothes that didn't fit her correctly. They were either too tight or too loose. Pam remembered something said on that television show about how as women age, they not only change sizes but shapes. Twenty-five years ago, while in college, Pam and Pat were both a size 8 and often exchanged clothes. Now they were both size 12 but their shapes were entirely different. Maybe if she were able to offer a better fitting line of clothing, not only would sales increase but customer returns would decrease. Pam decided that she would revisit the showroom first thing the next morning and get more information about this sizing system.

Questions

1. What do you believe is most important to the average customer: fit, price, style, or quality of workmanship? Which one do you believe is the greatest cause of customer returns?
2. Is this really a breadth versus depth issue?
3. Should Pam adopt this new sizing system? Explain your reasoning.

chapter 10

Merchandise Pricing

Overview:

In this chapter, we examine the retailer's need to make pricing decisions. We begin with a discussion of the impact of a firm's objectives on its pricing policies and strategies. After reviewing several strategies, we look at why initial markups and maintained markups are seldom the same. We also discuss how a retailer establishes an initial markup. We conclude this chapter with a discussion of why and how a retailer takes markdowns during the normal course of business.

Learning Objectives:

After reading this chapter, you should be able to:

1. Discuss the factors a retailer should consider when establishing pricing objectives and policies.
2. Describe the differences between the various pricing strategies available to the retailer.
3. Describe how retailers calculate the various markups.
4. Discuss why markdown management is so important in retailing and describe some of the errors that cause markdowns.

Pricing Objectives & Policies

LO 1

What factors should a retailer consider when establishing pricing objectives and policies?

Although most retailers have gotten savvy about cutting costs, few have figured out how much money they have passed up by using outdated pricing strategies and tactics. After all, pricing is an important contributor to profitability. The price of an item multiplied by the quantity is the retailer's revenue and Chapter 8 illustrated the significance of revenue to profit. Nevertheless, retailers today tend to routinely overprice some products and underprice others. Pricing should not be a difficult decision if retailers have been performing their other activities correctly. Pricing, as we pointed out in our Retail Strategic Planning and Operations Management Model (Exhibit 2.5 on page 56), is an interactive decision made in conjunction with the firm's mission statement, its goals and objectives, its strategy, its operational management (i.e., merchandise planning, promotional mix, building and fixtures, and level of service), and its administrative management. However, as pointed out in this chapter's Retailing: The Inside Story box, too many retailers believe that the only way to attract consumers is by running a sale.

For retailers selling services, pricing is even more difficult. This higher degree of difficulty exists because services are intangible, not easily stored, and cannot be

Retailing: The Inside Story

Will Today's Sales Ultimately Hurt Tomorrow's Retailers?

According to a study by Opinion Research Corporation, the average American now considers 37 percent off the original price of an item to be a bargain. The study further found that 88 percent of Americans buy food items on sale versus 44 percent for toys; and that 44 percent of Americans comparison shop for brand-name products.

Based on this information, it can be concluded that the current level of price cutting is actually shortsighted because it has taught consumers to avoid anything that isn't on sale.

It seems that whenever a retailer experiences a slowdown in sales, that retailer often starts acting like a used-car salesman, offering shoppers two-for-one deals, "50 percent off" the entire stock, and direct-mail coupons. Ultimately, all the price cutting may give retailers what they want: revenues, but at what cost?

The long-term effects of too much discounting are expected to have a negative impact for future retailers. Deals and sales promotions may increase sales today, but for too many companies they've become a constant addiction. Too many retailers, especially grocery and department stores, are now relying on "promotional prices" to draw consumers into their stores without considering the impact on the income statement. Some experts blame Wal-Mart's **EDLP (everyday low prices)** strategy—whereby a retailer charges the same low price every day throughout the year and seldom runs out of the product—for this overemphasis on price. After all, the chain's sophisticated buying process and its Retail Link system, which was described in Chapter 5's What's New box, has allowed Wal-Mart to undercut competitors and still hold profit margins. Other retailers, such as Foot Locker, have controlled costs and lowered prices by selling just one category.

These low prices have forced competitors to use heavy promotions to keep up. It is little wonder that today's consumers expect a deal on almost everything they buy. Discounting strategies are used so regularly that consumers avoid any product that isn't marked down at least 25 percent.

Department stores, once considered single-destination meccas for clothing, appliances, and toys, have ceded precious market share to discounters and specialty shops. Big department store chains such as Federated, despite its recent merger with May Department Stores, account for just 16 percent of the nation's retail sales, down from nearly 20 percent a couple of decades ago.

Small grocery store operators are probably the worst offenders in this "markdown war" as they lower prices to either hold or win back market share when supercenters enter their trade area. But all these sales and special offers have confused customers and conditioned them to shop for deals. These retailers have forgotten one of the cardinal rules of retailing, which is to only compete on price on a short-term basis unless you are the low-cost operator. The small operators, such as Food4Less in Missouri, who have been successful in their battles with the supercenters have instituted the same buying processes as the big retail chains and have used their intimate size to more closely monitor their market. The losers have been those that lower prices to the point where they lose money on each sale. They have effectively taught their customers to value price as much as product selection and great service.

Retailers need only to look at the auto industry to see the repercussions of constant and deep discounting. Car buyers are now conditioned to expect $2,000 to $4,000 in factory rebates coupled with another 10–15 percent discount from the dealer. Whenever Ford or GM cuts off the rebates, consumers stay out of the showrooms even though the dealers continue to offer 10–15 percent discounts on most models. Over the short term, rebates allow carmakers to get their sales, but many industry analysts wonder what the real cost of those sales will be.

Retailers should know how to solve the problem. To sell more at full price, retailers must differentiate themselves from rivals and convince shoppers of the added value they can offer. One way to accomplish this is through brand building, a tactic many retailers have all but abandoned. The reason: A store can typically move two to three times the normal volume of a product during a week when it's on sale. Advertising and marketing are much slower to take effect and harder to measure—but they're critical to ensuring long-term survival. However, that is *NOT* easy to do when your competitors continue to cut prices.

Source: Based on information supplied by Dick Casey, President, Food4Less, Joplin, Missouri; "What's a Sale?" *Chain Store Age*, June 2003: 23; and conversations with many other retailers concerning this problem.

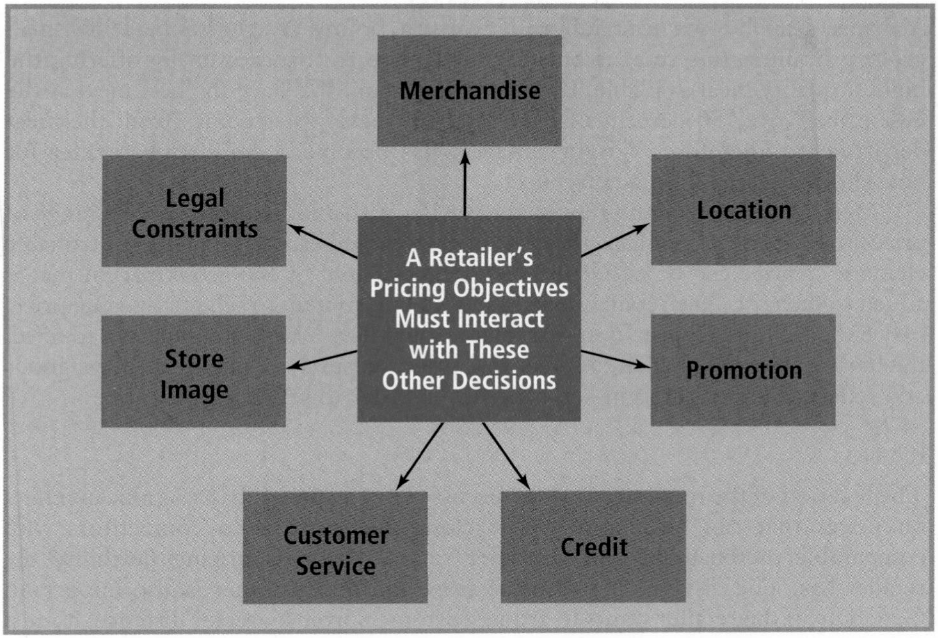

Exhibit 10.1
Interaction between a Retailer's Pricing Objectives and Other Decisions

returned to the vendor for credit. For example, a movie theater running a hit movie during a blizzard has the same fixed costs for being open as it would on any other night. The theater manager cannot resell the empty seats at a later date or increase attendance on the night of the blizzard by reducing ticket prices. It is no coincidence that, as discussed in Chapter 2's Service Retailing box on page 42, service retailers, airlines, hotels, golf courses, and now even universities are making smarter pricing decisions.

EDLP (everyday low prices)
Is when a retailer charges the same low price every day throughout the year and seldom runs the product on sale.

Interactive Pricing Decisions

As shown in Exhibit 10.1, decisions regarding pricing objectives should be interactive with other retail decisions. Specifically, the decision to price an item at a certain level should be related to the retailer's decisions on lines of merchandise carried, location, promotion, credit/check cashing, customer services, the store image the retailer wishes to convey, as well as the legal constraints discussed in Chapter 6.

Remember that just as each retailer is different, each retailer's pricing decision must be different.[1] After all, the pricing of an item is the easiest element of the retail mix for a competitor to copy. If, for example, one gas station lowers its price, that station should expect all the others stations in the immediate area to match or beat its price. This makes it very difficult, if not impossible, to use price to achieve a long-term differential advantage.[2] However, even with gasoline retailers, some creativity can help overcome this lack of differential advantage. For instance, some dealers will give a free car wash, candy bar, soda, or coffee refill with a 12 gallon fill-up.

Merchandise

Retailers should not set prices without carefully analyzing the attributes of the merchandise being priced. Does the merchandise have properties that differentiate it from comparable merchandise at competing retailers? What is the value of these attributes to the consumer? Consider, for example, Wright's Market in Opelika,

Alabama, a small town near Auburn University. Jimmy Wright has made his small grocery business (his store is only 22,000 square feet) successful by offering the highest quality meat available. By using the slogan "We have the best meat at the best price," over 50 percent of his $160,000 weekly sales comes from the meat department. Therefore, Wright's Market has become a destination retailer for households seeking high quality meat.

Merchandise selection presents the retailer with another decision: the range of prices to be made available to the consumer. Remember, the retailer's controllable element of price can be either the cost of goods sold or the gross margin that is added to the cost. The retailer, in deciding to buy an item to sell at a specific price, may either purchase lower-cost merchandise and have a high gross margin to offset the higher expenses needed to sell at that price, or purchase more expensive goods and reduce the gross margin and expenses in order to sell at a given price.

Location

The location of the retail store, as we discussed in Chapter 7, has a significant effect on prices that can be charged. The closer the store is to competitors with comparable merchandise and customer service, the less pricing flexibility the retailer has. The distance between the store and the customer is also important. Generally, if the retailer wants to attract customers from a greater distance, it must either increase its promotional efforts or lower prices on its merchandise. This is because of the increased travel costs (in both time and dollars) consumers incur when they are located farther from the store. Travel costs cut into the amount the customer is able or willing to pay for the merchandise, thus forcing the retailer to lower prices to attract those customers. For example, the lowest prices for many brand name products can usually be found at factory outlet malls, yet these locations usually have the highest travel costs. Thus, for many consumers it is cheaper to purchase the merchandise at a nearby retailer. The rising cost of

Old Navy has set its prices to be consistent with its store image and design and promotion, which all communicate good value for casual clothing.

© Robert Brenner/PhotoEdit

Factory outlet malls are known for their low prices. However, the typical consumer will incur high travel costs to reach these outlets.

gasoline over the past few years has had the net effect of encouraging customers to shop near where they live or work. This has benefited many small retailers and those located in neighborhood shopping centers. However, catalog and online retailers break down location barriers by providing a national and worldwide presence. Thus, pricing for these retailers is balanced between increases for providing greater customer convenience and decreases created through higher volume and lower overhead.

Promotion

The next chapter illustrates how promotion can increase demand for the retailer's merchandise. This chapter, however, will show how pricing can influence demand. This does not mean that pricing and promotion decisions are independent. If the retailer promotes heavily and is also very price competitive, the result may be an increase in demand greater than the high promotion and lower price strategies would produce independently. Imagine, for example, the retailer establishing low prices but not promoting them in the marketplace. How would consumers know of the price cuts? Or, imagine heavy promotion but no cut in prices. Obviously, each would generate demand, but the interactive and cumulative effect of both would be much greater.

Credit/Check Cashing

For a given merchandise price level, retailers selling on credit, even if they are only using bank cards, or offering a check cashing service will often be able to generate greater demand than retailers not offering credit or cashing payroll checks. Conversely, retailers providing these two financial services may be able to charge slightly higher prices than retailers not selling on credit and still generate the same demand as the noncredit retailers. Over the past decade, check cashing has become an extremely important decision for many retailers given that a large number of consumers don't have bank accounts. In particular, check cashing has been found to be an effective means to attract Hispanics. Though their cumulative wealth is soaring, nearly 60 percent of this market does not have a bank account.[3]

E-tailers targeting teens have a special problem regarding credit since teenagers under 18 are not legally liable for their credit card debts. But nothing prohibits an e-tailer from issuing a card to a minor. In fact, consumer advocates charge that banks and click-and-brick retailers are loosening the rules about who can obtain credit and are conveniently looking the other way when minors apply. This is because credit-granting retailers are able to develop a strong loyalty with those teenagers and they assume that the parents will bail out their child if he or she gets into credit trouble.

Customer Services

Retailers that offer many customer services (delivery, gift wrapping, alterations, more pleasant surroundings, sales assistance) tend to have higher prices. A decision to offer a multitude of customer services will automatically increase operating expenses and thus prompt management to increase retail prices to cover these additional expenses. Interestingly, such a policy may result in higher profits. Consider the case of women's dresses. Customer service used to be common in department stores that took 50 to 60 percent initial markups, but pricing pressure by discounters caused department stores to respond by cutting both markups and service. Women purchasing dresses began to feel neglected in department stores, especially when they had to pay for alterations. Specialty stores have picked up on this and, as a result, offer the consumer greater assistance in selecting and trying on dresses, something unheard of in the low-price stores. Another example of a retailer justifying a higher price by offering outstanding service is No Kidding. This small toy store is located in an affluent suburb just west of Boston and cannot compete with the retail megamarkets on either price or variety. Therefore, it does not carry the extremely popular items such as Xboxes, which everybody else discounts. However, it does stock items not available in the larger stores. What enables No Kidding to produce a profit at a time when most small toy shops fail are the composition and knowledge of its employees. This well-informed staff is primarily made up of moonlighting teachers who can discuss the finer points of play and inform the purchaser what is developmentally correct for a child of a certain age. In addition, the store wraps gifts at no charge, accepts returns without a receipt, and donates part of its profits to local schools and public television.[4] In fact, many consumers are willing to pay more for extra service. Obviously, it is important to remember that customer service decisions interact strongly with pricing decisions.

It is also important to note that service standards vary greatly by country. For example, Japan has extremely high service standards in their retail operations. In Japan, gift-wrapping is customary and retailers commonly accept merchandise for return even after the product has been well used. Alternatively, retailers in many countries throughout the world do not accept returns for any reason. In these retail operations once the product is sold, it is no longer the retailer's concern. This is truly a situation of *caveat emptor*—let the buyer beware. Given differences in expected service levels, retailers must adapt pricing levels accordingly.

Store Image

Prices aid the customer (either consciously or unconsciously) to develop an image of any given store. If an exclusive, high-fashion store such as Nordstrom began to discount its merchandise heavily, it simply would not be the same store in the eyes of the customers. The merchandise, store decor, and personnel might remain unchanged, but the change

© Dennis MacDonald/PhotoEdit

When floor-covering retailers offer free installation, the cost of providing this service must be factored into the prices the retailer charges.

in pricing strategy would significantly alter the overall store image. Thus, pricing policies and strategies interact with store image policies and strategies.

Legal Constraints

Pricing decisions must be made only after examining the legal environment. This is especially important if the retailer wants to operate in more than one state because state laws vary widely. In all cases, however, as discussed in Chapter 6, a retailer may not set a price in collusion with a competitor, may not offer different prices to different retail customers, may not sell below cost, and may not claim or imply that a price has been reduced unless it really has.

The other environmental factors we discussed in Part 2 of the text (consumer behavior, competitor behavior, channel relationships, the socioeconomic environment, and the technological environment) should also be considered when the retailer is developing its overall pricing and market strategy. Still, pricing decisions are fairly easy to make in the United States when compared to some other countries' retail environments. As pointed out in Chapter 6's Global Retailing box on page 101, laws in France require that products be sold to all retailers—big and small alike—for the same price, making it difficult for discounters to obtain any pricing advantage.

In the United States there are laws against monopolies and other restraints of trade in order to ensure fair competition. American consumers can buy from a full-price retailer or a discounter. American discounters depend on bulk-purchase discounts from manufacturers, rapid inventory turnover, private-label brands, relatively low-cost physical facilities and real estate, and price-conscious shoppers who are willing to perform some supply chain functions themselves.

Pricing Objectives

A retailer's pricing objectives should be in agreement with its mission statement and merchandising policies. Some objectives may be profit-oriented, some may be sales-oriented, and some may be to leave things just the way they are. However, by beginning with the proper pricing objectives, the retail manager can establish pricing policies that will complement the store's other decisions and help attract the desired target customers.

Profit-Oriented Objectives

Many retailers establish the objective of achieving either a certain rate of return or maximizing profits.

target return objective
Is a pricing objective that states a specific level of profit, such as percentage of sales or return on capital invested, as an objective.

profit maximization
Is a pricing objective that seeks to obtain as much profit as possible.

skimming
Is a pricing objective in which price is initially set high on merchandise to skim the cream of demand before selling at more competitive prices.

penetration
Is a pricing objective in which price is set at a low level in order to penetrate the market and establish a loyal customer base.

Target Return A **target return objective** sets a specific level of profit as an objective. This amount is often stated as a percentage of sales or of the retailer's capital investment. A target return for a supermarket might be 2 percent of sales (pre-tax).

Profit Maximization A **profit maximization** objective seeks to obtain as much dollar profit as possible. Some people claim that this pricing policy "charges all the traffic will bear." Retailers should know that if they follow such a policy, they are inviting competitors to enter the market. Thus, in general a retailer should seek to set prices at a level which builds customer loyalty, rather than getting as much as possible from each customer. However, in some cases, a retailer may have a temporary monopoly and decide to take advantage of it. The first video rental stores, knowing that others would follow shortly, often charged high rental fees, only to lower them when competition, such as Blockbuster, entered the market. This is known as **skimming,** or trying to sell at the highest price possible before settling at a more competitive level.[5] Other retailers may take the opposite approach and use **penetration,** which seeks to establish a loyal customer base by entering the market with a low price. For example, many locally owned coffee bars, knowing that Starbucks was coming, chose to charge low prices, hoping to make stopping at their shop a habit for their customers.

As the Global Retailing box illustrates, pricing aimed at achieving a certain profit objective is more difficult for retailers competing globally.

Sales-Oriented Objectives Sales-oriented objectives seek some level of unit sales, dollar sales, or market share, but do not mention profit. Two objectives most commonly used in retailing are growth in market share and growth in dollar sales. Although both of these objectives are used by many retailers, the achievement of either does not necessarily mean that profits will also increase. After all, if a retailer lowers prices, gross margin will go down. Sales may improve, but the retailer will not necessarily make more money.

Status Quo Objectives Retailers who are happy with their market share and level of profits sometimes adopt status quo objectives, or "don't rock the boat" pricing policies. Many supermarkets gave up on the extra profits and increases in market share that "double coupons" might have brought because they were afraid of what competitive actions might have resulted. It should be noted that pricing actions such as doubling coupons are not always effective and/or profitable. Many times, especially when other retailers match the promotion, only the retailer's regular customers take advantage of the special offer.

Some retailers prefer to compete on grounds other than price. Convenience stores, for example, seldom match the prices of nearby supermarkets. Still, retailers such as McDonald's and Burger King who want the consumer to focus on factors such as quality of food, service, and convenience of location rather than on price, are sometimes forced to drop prices in the face of mounting competition just to maintain status quo market share.

Global Retailing

While Markups Can Be Greater, Profits Can Be Lower

The largest 250 retailers in the world, combined, sell in 135 different countries. Selling in foreign markets is becoming an increasingly important part of retailers' growth strategies. For example, approximately 50 percent of U.K.-based retailer Tesco's square footage is now overseas. However, one of the most challenging issues for retailers as they expand globally is the widely divergent underlying factors influencing profits.

As one might imagine, one of the greatest factors affecting profits is a retailer's ability to achieve their desired markup (selling price–cost). Thus, setting an effective selling price is critical. This necessitates taking into account local competition, the retailer's global price positioning, exchange rates, inflation rates, additional supply chain costs, and differences in local taxes. However, even when retailers are able to obtain their desired selling price, underlying profits may diminish. One European retailer who was able to achieve its desired selling price with its European operations found compared to its worldwide operations, its European operations achieved significantly lower profits. Why? Labor and land costs are significantly higher in Europe.

Labor and land costs are extremely critical factors influencing a retailer's profits in their international operations. First, let's take a look at how labor costs will influence profits. Labor is typically the largest operating expense for retailers. In the United States many retailers employ a large number of either unskilled or semi-skilled laborers at low wages. In other countries, such as France, labor can be an even more significant cost for the retailer due to unionization and wages which are often two to three times those in the United States. The significant difference in underlying labor costs requires a retailer to adjust their overall retail mix. While simply raising prices would seem to be one way to offset these higher labor costs, increased local prices could change the retailer's positioning in the market. Toys "R" Us realized that in order to maintain its price positioning and achieve its desired level of profits in France it was necessary to reduce its labor force by one-third.

Second, the availability and resulting cost of real estate differs drastically from country to country. For years Tokyo has maintained the world's highest property values. Therefore, global retailers, such as the U.K.'s The Body Shop, need to make critical decisions regarding underlying cost adjustments to maintain pricing consistency. For example, how should The Body Shop adjust its overall retail mix when rents in Tokyo are ten times as high as in other markets? Some might argue that the retailer could just pass the higher costs on to its customers since all retailers in the local market have similar real estate costs. It would, therefore, maintain its price positioning relative to local competition. Ignoring the obvious global price positioning inconsistency this would create, there is another concern. While significant local price adjustments might have been effective 20 years ago, in today's age of print catalogs and e-tailing, a one-price pricing policy would surely cannibalize the local brick-and-mortar retailer. For instance, if The Body Shop were to increase their local prices in Tokyo significantly, many Japanese customers would simply purchase their product from The Body Shop's print catalog, thus further lowering the Tokyo store's profits.

While global retailers strive to maintain consistency, they must also be sensitive to local tastes, habits, customs, and demographic differences between markets. An error in any of these areas can damage a retailer's bottom line.

As you can imagine, pricing for a global retailer is fraught with challenges. To be successful on a global basis the retailer must balance global corporate profits while: (a) adjusting to local competitive pricing pressures, (b) maintaining a consistent global image and retail position in the face of widely diverse markets, and (c) managing underlying costs that can often be quite higher than normal.

Source: This box was prepared by Prof. Mark Fish, Marketing Department, Ohio University.

Pricing Policies

Pricing policies are rules of action, or guidelines, that ensure uniformity of pricing decisions within a retail operation. A large retailer has many buyers involved in pricing decisions. By establishing the store's overall pricing policies, the top merchandising executives provide these buyers with a framework for adopting specific pricing strategies for the entire organization.

A retail store's pricing policies should reflect the expectations of its target market. Very few retailers can appeal to all segments of the market. Low- and middle-income consumers are usually attracted to low-priced discount stores. The middle-class market often shops at moderately priced general merchandise chains. Affluent consumers are frequently drawn to high-priced specialty stores that provide extra services. Only supermarkets are able to cross the various income lines, and even then there is some basis for segmentation. Successful retailers carefully position themselves in a market and then direct their specific pricing strategies toward satisfying their target market. Many times the proper pricing policies influence consumers to patronize one store over another.

When establishing a pricing policy, retailers must decide whether they should price below market levels, at market levels, or above market levels.

Pricing Below the Market

below-market pricing policy
Is a policy that regularly discounts merchandise from the established market price in order to build store traffic and generate high sales and gross margin dollars per square foot of selling space.

Because a large segment of any trade area buys primarily on a price basis, a **below-market pricing policy** is attractive to many retailers, such as discounters and warehouse clubs. Such a policy doesn't mean that the retailer sells every item in its store at a price lower than can be found elsewhere in its trading area. Rather, the retailer is more intent on how its prices are perceived versus those of the competition. Remember that not even Wal-Mart will have the lowest price on every single item that a consumer will purchase during a week. However, the chain endeavors to have the lowest total cost for all the items purchased.

eBay's introduction of the cyber-auction and Priceline.com's "name-your-own-price" policy have led many to believe that all retailers will soon be forced to sell below market. (Never mind that it is impossible for all retailers to sell below the average selling price for all items.) However, for retailers to consistently price below the market and be profitable, they must concentrate on generating gross margin dollars per square foot of space, not the gross margin percentage. After all, profitability is not directly related to the gross margin percentage of the product sold but the amount of gross margin per unit sold times the number of units sold. Such retailers must always try to increase the sales per square foot because they have already reduced their markups.

A below-market retailer must buy wisely, which may include closeouts and seconds. Below-market stores stock fast-selling merchandise, curtail customer services, and operate from modest facilities. Also, some of them stock private label brands extensively and enhance their low-price image by promoting the price differences between their private brands and comparable national brands. That some retailers are successful with such a policy is evident by the fact that many local retailers, especially restaurants, now use below-market stores as their suppliers. Besides being known as a tough competitor, another benefit of using this policy is that some competitors may stay out of a given trading area so as to avoid head-to-head battles with a below-market operator.[6]

A growing number of retailers today are becoming increasingly concerned that the growth of the Internet will forever change the way retailers set prices. This is evidenced in the chapter's Retailing: What's New box, which illustrates that even the smallest of buyers and sellers can use cyberspace to learn what the market price is.

Pricing at Market Levels

Most merchants want to be competitive with one another. Retailers' use of comparison shoppers—that is, having employees visit competitive retail outlets in

What's New?

The Internet Has Come To Garage Sales

A decade ago when a relative of one of the authors passed away, the family had a garage sale to clear out some of the items that had accumulated after living in the same house for over 50 years. The author noticed that many of the early arrivals (some arrived before the sale opened) were professional antique dealers. One dealer purchased some very old Coca-Cola serving trays for 50 cents each. The family was happy to get $3 for the set of six trays until one day a family member walked by the dealer's storefront and saw four remaining trays selling for $45 each.

However, just recently, that same author was walking through his neighborhood and happened upon a garage sale. While looking over two full bookshelves, he noticed a set of books (in very good condition) that he enjoyed reading in the 1950s. These books were about a fictional hero named Baseball Joe who was loosely modeled after Babe Ruth. He read them while visiting his aunt and uncle's house during a summer vacation. His uncle had been given them as a boy 30 years earlier. While deciding if he wanted to pay $5 each for five books, a young man standing next to him who appeared to be a college student, put away his Blackberry and picked up the books. Later that night, the author went on Google and found that Baseball Joe books were selling for between $20 and $50 depending on their condition.

Next, just for the heck of it, the author searched Google for "buying at garage sales." In less than a second, over 19 million sites were listed, with the first one being *eBay Guide—Buying at a Garage Sale for eBay Resale*. Another title listed on that first page was *The Pocket Idiot's Guide to Garage and Yard Sales*.

Thus, what was once a casual family or neighborhood activity of cleaning out the closets and putting every unneeded item on the lawn, has been replaced by the frenzy of a free-market economy. Today everybody can be a professional. Small-scale e-tailers are now armed with global-positioning devices which allow them to quickly zoom from sale to sale. Special scanners and cell phones allow them do a quick price check on both new and vintage items.

The lesson to learn for garage-sale organizers is that they should start by using eBay as a guide for pricing their stuff so as to increase their revenue. A better question may be, "Has the Internet taken the fun out of the garage sale?"

---

order to compare prices—stems from this basic premise. Competitive pricing involves a **price zone,** a range of prices for a particular merchandise line that appeals to customers in a certain demographic group, such as Target selling women's tops for $14.99 to $29.99. Dillard's does not need to match the prices of Target. However, Dillard's should establish prices that are on a similar level with Macy's when they are competitors in the same mall. And Target should be competitively priced with Wal-Mart. Pricing at market levels is extremely important for e-tailers, given the ease of online price comparisons.

price zone
Is a range of prices for a particular merchandise line that appeals to customers in a certain market segment.

The size of a retail store affects its ability to compete on price. Small retailers usually pay more for their merchandise and have higher operating expenses (as a proportion of sales) than larger retailers. Although some small retailers have joined voluntary cooperative groups to reduce their expenses through quantity discounts, they continue to experience a cost disadvantage. For these reasons small retailers, such as mom-and-pop grocery stores and convenience stores, often stress convenience and service strategies rather than price in their retailing mix. Even in these cases, the price cannot be too far out of line.

Pricing above the Market

Some retailers, either by design or circumstance, follow an **above-market pricing policy.** Certain market sectors are receptive to high prices because nonprice factors are more important to some customers than price. Retailers such as Nordstrom,

above-market pricing policy
Is a policy where retailers establish high prices because nonprice factors are more important to their target market than price.

Bergdorf-Goodman, and Neiman Marcus offer such outstanding service that they have minimal price competition. Other retailers, such as small neighborhood drugstores and hardware stores, are forced to price above the market because of their high cost structure and low sales volume. Some other factors that permit retailers to price above market levels include:

- Merchandise Offerings. Some consumers will pay higher-than-average prices for specialty items, for an exclusive line, or for unusual merchandise. Prestige retailers such as Gucci or Neiman Marcus carry high-priced specialty items.
- Services Provided. In many communities there are service-oriented merchants with a loyal group of customers who are willing to pay higher prices to obtain an array of services ranging from wardrobe counseling to delivery. Nordstrom's clerks, for example, have a habit of doing special things such as dropping off purchases at a customer's home, sending thank-you notes to customers, or even ironing a newly purchased shirt so the customer can wear it that day.
- Convenient Locations. The convenient location of gift shops in hotels, airline terminals, and even downtown office buildings allows them to charge high prices. Knowing that consumers value time more than money, day spas and jewelry stores often select sites adjacent to residential areas.
- Extended Hours of Operation. By remaining open while other stores are closed, some merchants are able to charge higher-than-average prices. Service plazas on interstate highways justify their higher prices by never closing.

AP Photo/Beth A. Keiser

Retailers that use above-market pricing often offer exclusive merchandise lines coupled with high levels of customer service.

Specific Pricing Strategies

LO 2

What are the various pricing policies available to the retailer?

Various pricing strategies are adopted by traditional bricks-and-mortar retailers in their effort to achieve certain pricing objectives. The pricing strategies should be in accord with the other components of the store's retail mix: location, promotion, display, service level, and merchandise assortment.

Customary Pricing

Customary pricing occurs when a retailer sets prices for goods and services and seeks to maintain those prices over an extended period of time. Candy bars, newspapers, movies, and vending machine products are all items that use customary pricing. Retailers such as movie theaters with their $8 tickets, seek to establish prices for such products that customers can take for granted for long periods of time.

customary pricing
Is a policy in which the retailer sets prices for goods and services and seeks to maintain those prices over an extended period of time.

Variable Pricing

Variable pricing is used when differences in demand and cost force the retailer to change prices in a fairly predictable manner. Cut flowers tend to be higher priced when demand is greater around Mother's Day and Valentine's Day. It is a common practice for most resorts to increase their rates on premium rooms in June, a busy wedding season. Tuesday and Wednesday nights tend to have lower demand for movies and dining out, so many theaters and restaurants offer specials on those nights. Fresh produce tends to sell for less during its growing season when the retailer's costs are down. Many restaurants offer the same meal at lunch and at dinner but the lunch price is often discounted 10 to 20 percent to increase demand.

variable pricing
Is a policy that recognizes that differences in demand and cost necessitate that the retailer change prices in a fairly predictable manner.

Flexible Pricing

Flexible pricing means offering the same products and quantities to different customers at different prices. Retailers generally use flexible pricing in situations calling for personal selling. The advantage of using flexible pricing is that the salesperson can make price adjustments based on the customer's interest, a competitor's price, a past relationship with the customer, or the customer's bargaining ability. Most jewelry stores and automobile dealerships use this pricing policy, although not all customers like it.[7] Other retailers vary their prices by giving discounts to special consumer groups such as students, senior citizens, and the clergy. Interestingly enough, some analysts predict that because every eight seconds a person in America now turns 62, "senior citizen discounts" can be expected to disappear over the next decade. Today some employee groups, credit unions, and housing or neighborhood groups have negotiated price discounts with selected retailers. However, Americans are amateurs compared to how Chinese consumers negotiate lower flexible prices. To the dismay of many retailers, a portion of China's 1.3 billion consumers have started shopping in teams to haggle for bigger discounts. This team purchasing practice begins in Internet chat rooms, (such as 51tuangou.com—tuangou in Chinese means "I want to team buy") where people hatch plans to buy appliances, furnishings, food, and even cars in bulk. Next, they show up en masse at stores to demand discounts.[8]

flexible pricing
Is a policy that encourages offering the same products and quantities to different customers at different prices.

Flexible pricing can increase costs, as well as decrease revenues, as customers begin to bargain for everything, or find that they paid more than a friend did for the same product. As a result they may get mad at the retailer and take their business elsewhere. That is why the one-price policy is so popular in the United States.

One-Price Policy

one-price policy
Is a policy that establishes that the retailer will charge all customers the same price for an item.

Under the **one-price policy,** a retailer charges all customers the same price for an item. A one-price policy may be used in conjunction with customary or variable pricing. All people buying the same Quarter Pounder® at a McDonald's will pay the same price. Roland Hussey Macy, the founder of Macy's Department Store, is often credited with adopting the one-price policy, but recently the authors have found evidence that a Sacramento retailer, Weinstock & Lubin, was using this policy in 1875, nearly four decades earlier than Macy's.[9] This policy means efficiency and fairness in handling customer transactions in a large store where the selling activity is delegated to salespersons with varying degrees of loyalty to the retailer. If salespersons are permitted to bargain over price, customers who are shrewd and assertive could conceivably negotiate terms that are unprofitable to the retailer.

A one-price policy, therefore, speeds up transactions and reduces the need for highly skilled salespeople. Most catalog operators adopt a one-price policy since they are forced to retain their prices until the expiration date of the catalog, which can be six months from its issuance.

Today, after years of offering rebates to attract consumers, some automobile manufacturers such as GM (who already has had some success with this policy in its Saturn division), are encouraging their dealers to adopt the one-price policy as a means of regaining market share. However, such a pricing policy will work only if all the dealers voluntarily agree to stick to the plan. (Remember from Chapter 6's discussion, GM can't force dealers to adopt this policy.) Otherwise, the flexible price dealer will know the price it has to beat.

Price Lining

price lining
Is a pricing policy that is established to help customers make merchandise comparisons and involves establishing a specified number of price points for each merchandise classification.

trading up
Occurs when a retailer uses price lining and a salesperson moves a customer from a lower-priced line to a higher one.

trading down
Occurs when a retailer uses price lining, and a customer initially exposed to higher-priced lines expresses the desire to purchase a lower-priced line.

To simplify their pricing procedures and to help consumers make merchandise comparisons, some retailers establish a specified number of price lines or price points for each merchandise classification. Once the price lines are determined, these retailers purchase goods that fit into each line. This is called **price lining.** For example, in men's slacks the price lines could be limited to $29.95, $49.95, and $69.95. The monetary difference between the price lines should be large enough to reflect a value difference to consumers. This makes it easier for a salesperson to either trade up or trade down a customer. **Trading up** occurs when a salesperson moves a customer from a lower-priced line to a higher one. **Trading down** occurs when a customer is initially exposed to higher-priced lines but expresses the desire to purchase a lower-priced line.

Retailers select price lines that have the strongest consumer demand. By limiting the number of price lines, a retailer achieves broader assortments, which lead to increased sales and fewer markdowns. For example, a retailer who stocks 150 units of an item and has 6 price lines would have an assortment of only 25 units in each line. On the other hand, if the 150 units were divided among only 3 price lines, there would be 50 units in each line.

When retailers are limited to certain price lines, they become specialists in those lines. This permits them to concentrate all their merchandising and promotional efforts on those lines, thus defining their store image more clearly. In addition, they direct their purchases to vendors who handle those lines. The vendors, in turn, provide favored treatment to their large-volume retailing customers. Other advantages of price lining include buying more efficiently, simplifying inventory control, and accelerating inventory turnover. From the shopper's perspective, it is easier to shop when price lining is used because clear differences are perceived among the various price points.

An analysis of a store's best-selling price lines is essential prior to making any decision to alter them. Generally the middle-priced lines should account for the majority of sales. When the bulk of sales occurs at the extremes of the price lines, a retailer should take corrective actions. These include altering the assortments in the present price lines, changing the price lines, redirecting salespersons' efforts, developing more effective promotions, or adjusting the total marketing mix to a new target market.

Odd Pricing

The practice of setting retail prices that end in the digits 5, 8, or 9—such as $29.95, $49.98, or $9.99—is called **odd pricing**. A quick look at retail advertisements in newspapers will reveal that many retailers use an odd-pricing policy. Retailers feel that odd prices produce significantly higher sales. However, the effectiveness of using certain common odd-numbered prices based on the theory that $9.99 sounds lower to the customer than $10 and 49 cents sounds better than 52 cents has never been proven with any conclusive research.[10] Another theory suggests that the use of an odd price means the price is at the lowest level possible, thus encouraging the customer to purchase more units.

odd pricing
Is the practice of setting retail prices that end in the digits 5, 8, 9—such as $29.95, $49.98, or $9.99.

A more plausible explanation for the adoption of odd-numbered pricing is that in the early part of the 20th century, before there was a sales tax, merchandise was priced at even dollars. Because they did not have to make change for the customer, salesclerks could easily pocket an occasional one-, five-, or ten-dollar bill or gold piece. When Marshall Field caught on to this, he devised the first odd-numbered pricing system to stop the practice. Field ruled that, "We'll charge 99 cents instead of even dollars. This will force the clerks to ring up the sales, open the cash register, put the money in and give the customer a receipt and change." Maybe this explains why, despite the lack of supportive research, odd-numbered pricing is such a standard in retailing today.

Because odd prices are associated with low prices, they are typically used by retailers who sell either at prices below the market or at the market. Retailers selling above the market, such as Neiman Marcus and Nordstrom, usually end their prices with even numbers, which have come to denote quality. These retailers would likely sell an item for $90.00 rather than $89.99. Prestige-conscious retailers are not seeking bargain hunters as customers.

Multiple-Unit Pricing

With **multiple-unit pricing** the price of each unit in a multiple-unit package is less than the price of each unit if it were sold singly. Grocery retailers use multiple-unit pricing extensively in their sales of cigarettes, light bulbs, candy bars, and beverages. Apparel retailers often sell multiple units of underwear, hosiery, and shirts.

multiple-unit pricing
Occurs when the price of each unit in a multiple-unit package is less than the price of each unit if it were sold individually.

Retailers use multiple-unit pricing to encourage additional sales and to increase profits. The gross margin that is sacrificed in a multiple-unit sale is more than offset by the savings that occur from reduced selling and handling expenses. Generally multiple-unit pricing can be effectively employed for items that are either consumed rapidly or used together.

Bundle Pricing

bundling
Occurs when distinct multiple items, generally from different merchandise lines, are offered at a special price.

Bundling generally involves selling distinct multiple items offered together at a special price. Here the perceived savings in cost and/or time for the bundle justifies the purchase. At the same time, bundling can increase the retailer's revenue since the customer may actually purchase more items than originally planned. Many travel agencies use bundling for their vacation packages, by packaging airfare, hotel, transfers, and meals together. Before Congress recently deregulated the telecommunications industry, consumers had to shop separately for local, long distance, paging, cable television, Internet access, and cellular service. While the so-called major telecommunications companies were busy meeting various state and federal requirements to bundle these services, the previously unknown Frontier Corp. became an industry leader by making the bundle available a year before everybody else.

Today by providing baby-sitting services gratis or for a small fee, a small number of retailers are testing a form of bundling to encourage customers to patronize their establishments. Research by some movie theaters revealed that the main obstacle encountered by many parents in coming to the movies was finding child care. As a result, some theaters now offer either "Monday Night Is Baby's Night" for very young babies or child care for children aged 2 to 8. This latter bundling program seems to be going over well with parents who previously could only consider attending PG movies.

Grocery stores and physical fitness centers are also testing the addition of child care facilities. Such action shows that retailers are becoming more oriented toward their customers' needs, especially when child and adult activities significantly diverge (adult versus kiddie movies and working out). Some parents, especially single parents, believe that certain errands and tasks, such as trips to the grocery store, can be sharing activities. However, these parents are also aware that much of the time their youngsters get bored sitting in a shopping cart.

Conversely, as pointed out in the chapter's Service Retailing box, the economic conditions of recent years have caused some retailers, especially those selling services, to unbundle their services. These retailers hope that by unbundling their offerings they can increase revenues without offending their customers.

Leader Pricing

leader pricing
Is when a high-demand item is priced low and is heavily advertised in order to attract customers into the store.

In **leader pricing** a high-demand item is priced low and advertised heavily in an effort to attract consumers into a store. The items selected for leader pricing should be widely known and purchased frequently. In addition, information should be available that will permit consumers to make price comparisons. National brands of convenience goods, such as Crest® toothpaste, Mitchum® antiperspirant, Maxwell House® coffee, and Coca-Cola® are often designated as leader items.[11]

Leader pricing is usually part of a promotional program designed to increase store traffic. A successful program will produce additional sales for all areas of a store. In many instances the price of the leader item is reduced only for a specific promotion. However, some retailers such as supermarkets regularly feature leader items.[12] Today, many convenience stores use gasoline as a leader. These retailers reduce their gas price by a penny or two, just enough to get the customer into their store. Once in the store, they are exposed to fast-food sandwiches, groceries, fresh produce, beverages, and even fresh flowers. In such stores, the inside operations contribute over 70 percent of the store's gross margin dollars and subsidize the gasoline business. For customers who just want gas, these stores have pay-at-the-pump facilities.

A retailer using leader pricing should carefully evaluate its usefulness. If consumers are limiting their purchases to only the leader items, then the policy is ineffective. Because the leader items may be sold at or near a retailer's cost, higher-markup items

Service Retailing

The Latest Trend in Services: Unbundling

With dozens of search engines allowing price comparisons on products ranging from Nike athletic shoes to automobile tires, retailers have felt the need to keep their list prices low in order to survive. Today many retailers, especially those selling services, are achieving this goal by unbundling the products and services that were previously grouped together. Unbundling enables the retailer to keep the list price low while tacking on separate additional charges to the bottom of the bill. As a result, while the basic list price is unchanged, actual revenues are increasing.

Service retailers are more prone to use this approach, since direct comparisons between items such as hotel rooms are more difficult for consumers than comparisons of an established physical product such as Levi jeans.

This practice is especially evident near college campuses, where some landlords still charge the same apartment rent as last year, but may now add a fee for parking spaces. In the past, the cost of parking was "bundled" into a resident's rent. Thus, whether an apartment needed 0, 1, 2, 3, or more parking spaces, the amount for parking was included in the basic rent. Some may argue that separate prices for apartments and parking is fair for all residents and can result in lower prices for students without cars. Still, the fact remains that for most students, their expenses increased though the rent stayed the same. Universities are another example of this. They may leave the tuition rate fixed but will add a special fee per credit hour.

Motels are engaging in a similar practice. They once offered a free continental breakfast to their guests. Today they quote the same (or maybe even a slightly lower) room rate, but now charge for the breakfast. In addition, many hotels and motels now charge fees for using the exercise area and for having a coffee maker in the room. However, they will deduct 50 cents from a customer's bill if he or she declines the complimentary *USAToday*. Dry cleaners may still charge $1.69 for shirts, but will tack on a 15 cent environmental fee. Similar fees are also charged by dentists and auto repair shops. Airlines now add a fuel surcharge on their ticket prices. Phone companies have added various fees while maintaining their basic rate at the customary price.

Still, the wise shopper can sometimes take advantage of unbundling. After all, the basic price is set low and the surcharges may be negotiating points. Although unbundling is an attempt to increase revenues and profits, no retailer wants to lose business as result of it.

---

must also be sold to generate a profit for the retailer. An item that is sold below a retailer's cost is known as a **loss leader**. For example, every Thanksgiving many supermarkets sell turkeys at a loss in hopes of attracting consumers to their stores and making a profit on the rest of their purchases.

loss leader
Is an extreme form of leader pricing where an item is sold below a retailer's cost.

The pricing actions of discounters using below-market pricing have forced manufacturers into changing their pricing strategy, thus endangering another group of retailers' use of leader pricing. The use of everyday low prices (EDLP) has propelled Wal-Mart to the top spot in retail sales. Retailers using EDLP want vendors to offer them constant prices throughout the year by phasing out virtually all deep discounts and offering them the same low price every day. For example, instead of selling retailers a case of peanut butter for $20 one week and offering it on sale the next week for $15, they want it priced at $18 every week. Theoretically, this would limit the ability of leader pricers, such as supermarkets, to continue their use of high-low pricing. **High-low pricing** involves the use of high everyday prices and low leader specials on featured items for their weekly ads. However, Organizacion Soriana, a relatively little-known Mexican hypermarket, is becoming Wal-Mart's nemesis south of the border despite using high-low pricing. The retailer, which offers customers overhead covers to protect their cars from the blistering sun and in-store entertainment, also features low prices on a different category each day, such as Tuesday being fruit and vegetable day. The chain also guarantees that every day it will have the lowest price on at least 1,000 products.[13] Of course it didn't hurt Soriana that Wal-Mart so badly misunderstood the Mexican

high-low pricing
Involves the use of high everyday prices and low leader "specials" on items typically featured in weekly ads.

market, that it stocked ice skates.[14] JCPenney is a nonfood retailer who uses high-low pricing by having regularly scheduled sales every week.

Bait-and-Switch Pricing

The practice of advertising a low-priced model of a shopping good, such as a television or a computer, to merely lure shoppers into a store is called **bait-and-switch pricing**. Once the shoppers are in the store, a salesperson tries to persuade them to purchase a higher-priced model. Bait-and-switch pricing, which was discussed in detail in Chapter 6, is considered by the Federal Trade Commission to be an illegal practice when the low-priced model used as bait is unavailable to shoppers. Some in the industry describe the *bait* merchandise as being "nailed to the floor."

Private Label Brand Pricing

A private label item often can be purchased by a retailer at a cheaper price, have a higher markup percentage, and still be priced lower than a comparable national brand. Private brands also permit the retailer a large degree of pricing freedom because consumers find it difficult to make exact comparisons between private brands and national brands of similar goods. Marks & Spencer, Mervyn's, Sears, and others price their private brands below the market. Private labels can be used by a retailer to differentiate itself and its merchandise from competitors. At a time when everybody seems to be selling the same things, retailers are using their store's image to an advantage by developing their own exclusive private labels. Studio B, one of Bloomingdale's private labels, offers a women's trouser-and-vest outfit for $116. A look-alike designer-name outfit would cost over $300. Canada's Zellers, a division of the Hudson Bay Company, has relied on private labels to respond to Wal-Mart's invasion of its Canadian market. Backed by its motto, "The Lowest Price Is The Law," Zellers uses private labels to give it exclusivity and quality, especially in apparel, where 80 percent of its line is private.[15] Other retailers seeking to differentiate themselves from competitors are now using an above-market pricing approach for their private labels. Department stores that have been battered on price by discounters and specialty stores are now using private labels to improve their own image. Macy's, for example, uses its own "Hotel Collection by Charter Club" label to sell Italian-made $1,350 duvets and $275 pillowcases.[16] A variation of private labeling which is used by retailers selling products such as mattresses where customers have limited knowledge is not to use different brand names. These operators want the national brand's appeal, but instead, they use different coverings and model numbers. These differences or degrees of "blindness" prevent them from having to match a competitor's price.

Today some below-market retailers such as Wal-Mart are cutting back on their use of private labels. They prefer to use the national brands to convey the image of having lower prices.

LO 3

Using Markups

How does a retailer calculate the various markups?

A retail buyer should be able to calculate rapidly whether a proposed purchase will provide an adequate markup or gross margin. The markup can be expressed in dollars or as a percentage of either the selling price or the cost of the good. There are times, however, when a retail buyer needs to compute the markdown, which is a reduction in the selling price of the goods. Markdowns are made in order to move certain merchandise, especially when color or size assortments are no longer complete.

Calculating Markup

To calculate the selling price (or **retail price**), the retailer should begin with the following basic markup equation:

$$SP = C + M$$

where C is the dollar cost of merchandise per unit; M is the dollar markup per unit; and SP is the selling price per unit.

Thus, if the retailer has a cost per unit of $16 on a dress shirt and a dollar markup of $14, then the selling price per unit is $30. In other words, **markup** is simply the difference between the cost of the merchandise and the selling price, which is the same as gross margin.

markup
Is the selling price of the merchandise less its cost, which is equivalent to gross margin.

This markup is intended to cover all of the operating expenses (wages, rent, utilities, promotion, credit, and so on) incurred in the sale of the product and still provide the retailer with a profit. Occasionally, a retailer will sell a product without a markup high enough to cover these costs in order to generate traffic or build sales volume. For instance, many e-tailers originally expected high turnover to allow them to be profitable. However, low margins coupled with low traffic caused many to close before volume could make up for their low margins. This chapter, however, will only be concerned with using markup to produce a profit on the sale of each item.

Markup Methods

Markup may be expressed as either a dollar amount or as a percentage of the selling price or cost. It is most useful when expressed as a percentage of the selling price because it can then be used in comparison with other financial data such as last year's sales results, reductions in selling price, and even the firm's competition. The equation for expressing markup as percentage of selling price is

$$\text{Percentage of markup on selling price} = (SP - C)/SP = M/SP$$

Although some businesses, usually manufacturers or small retailers, express markup as a percentage of cost, this method is not widely used in retailing because most of the financial data the retailer uses are expressed as a percentage of selling price. Nevertheless, when expressing markup as a percentage of cost, the equation is

$$\text{Percentage of markup on cost} = (SP - C)/C = M/C$$

Several problems occur when we attempt to equate markup as a percentage of selling price with markup as a percentage of cost. Since the two methods use different bases, we really are not comparing similar data. However, there is an equation to find markup on selling when we know markup on cost:

$$\text{Percentage of markup on selling price} = \text{Percentage of markup on cost}/(100\% + \text{Percentage of markup on cost})$$

Likewise, when we know markup on selling price we can easily find markup on cost:

$$\text{Percentage of markup on cost} = \text{Percentage of markup on selling price}/(100\% - \text{Percentage of markup on selling price})$$

The preceding equations are conversions, converting percentage markup on cost to percentage markup on selling price, or vice versa. Exhibit 10.2 shows a conversion table for markup on cost and markup on selling price. Let's go back to our original example of the dress shirt and see how easy it is to determine markup on selling price when we know the markup on cost and vice versa.

The retailer purchased the dress shirt for $16 and later sold it for $30. The difference between the selling price and the cost is $14. This $14 as a percentage of selling price (markup on selling price) is 46.7 percent ($14/$30). This same $14, however, represents 87.5 percent ($14/$16) of the cost (markup). In this example, if all we knew was that the dress shirt had an 87.5 percent markup on cost, we could determine that this was the same as a 46.7 percent markup on selling price:

Percentage of markup on selling price = Percentage of markup on cost/(100% + Percentage of markup on cost) = 87.5%/(100% + 87.5%) = 46.7%

Likewise, if we knew we had a 46.7 percent markup on selling, we could easily determine markup on cost:

Percentage of markup on cost = Percentage of markup on selling price (100% – Percentage of markup on selling price) = 46.7%/(100% – 46.7%) = 87.5%

Exhibit 10.3 gives you the total picture of the relationships between markup on cost and markup on selling price. In Exhibit 10.3, you can see that dollar markup does not change as the percentage changes on cost or selling price. Dollar markup is presented as a percentage of a different base, cost, or selling price.

Exhibit 10.4 reviews the basic markup equations.

Exhibit 10.2
Markup Conversion Table

Markup Percentage on Selling Price	Markup Percentage on Cost	Markup Percentage on Selling Price	Markup Percentage on Cost
4.8	5.0	32.0	47.1
5.0	5.3	33.3	50.0
8.0	8.7	34.0	51.5
10.0	11.1	35.0	53.9
15.0	17.7	36.0	56.3
16.7	20.0	37.0	58.8
20.0	25.0	40.0	66.7
25.0	33.3	41.0	70.0
26.0	35.0	42.8	75.0
27.3	37.5	44.4	80.0
28.0	39.0	47.5	90.0
28.5	40.0	50.0	100.0
30.0	42.9	66.7	200.0

Exhibit 10.3
Relationship of Markups Expressed on Selling Price and Cost

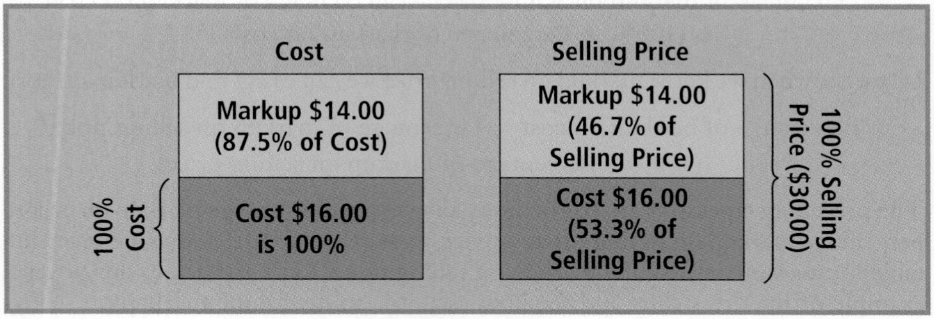

$$\text{\% Markup on Selling Price} = \frac{\text{Selling Price} - \text{Cost}}{\text{Selling Price}} = \frac{\text{Markup}}{\text{Selling Price}}$$

$$\text{\% Markup on Cost} = \frac{\text{Selling Price} - \text{Cost}}{\text{Cost}} = \frac{\text{Markup}}{\text{Cost}}$$

Finding % Markup on Cost when % Markup on Selling Price is Known:

$$\text{\% Markup on Cost} = \frac{\text{\% Markup on Selling Price}}{100\% - \text{\% Markup on Selling}}$$

Finding % Markup on Selling Price when % Markup on Cost is Known:

$$\text{\% Markup on Selling Price} = \frac{\text{\% Markup on Cost}}{100\% + \text{\% Markup on Cost}}$$

Finding Selling Price when Cost and % Markup on Cost Are Known:

$$\text{Selling Price} = \text{Cost} + \text{\% Markup on Cost(Cost)}$$

Finding Selling Price when Cost and % Markup on Selling Price Are Known:

$$\text{Selling Price} = \frac{\text{Cost}}{(1 - \text{\% Markup on Selling Price})}$$

Exhibit 10.4
Basic Markup Formulas

Using Markup Formulas When Purchasing Merchandise

Although quite simple in concept, the basic markup formulas will enable you to determine more than the percentage of markup on a particular item. Let's work with the markup on selling price formula to illustrate how an interesting and common question might be answered. If you know that a particular type of item could be sold for $8 per unit and you need a 40 percent markup on selling price to meet your profit objective, then how much would you be willing to pay for the item? Using our equation for markup on selling price, we have

$$\text{Percentage of markup on selling price} = (SP - C)/SP$$
$$40\% = (\$8 - C)/\$8$$
$$C = \$4.80$$

Therefore, you would be willing to pay $4.80 for the item. If the item cannot be found at $4.80 or less, it is probably not worth stocking.

Likewise, if a retailer purchases an item for $12 and wants a 40 percent markup on selling price, how would the retailer determine the selling price? Returning to our original equation ($SP = C + M$), we know that $SP = C + .40P$ since markup is 40 percent of selling price. If markup is 40 percent of selling price, cost must be 60 percent since cost and markup are the complements of each other and must total 100 percent. Thus, if

$$60\%\ SP = \$12$$

(divide both sides by 60 percent, then)

$$SP = \$20$$

Initial Versus Maintained Markup

Up to this point we have assumed that retailers have been able to sell the product at the price initially set when the product arrived at the store. We have assumed that the initial markup (the markup placed on the merchandise when the store receives it) is equal to the maintained markup or achieved markup (the actual selling price less the cost). Since in many cases the actual selling price for some of the firm's merchandise is lower than the original selling price, the firm's maintained markup is usually lower than the initial markup. Thus, maintained markup differs from initial markup by the amount of reductions:

Initial markup = (Original retail price – Cost)/Original retail price

Maintained markup = (Actual retail price – Cost)/Actual retail price

Thus, maintained markup (sometimes referred to as gross margin or just plain gross) is the key to profitability because it is the difference between the actual selling price and the cost of that merchandise.

Five reasons can account for the difference between initial and maintained markups. First is the need to balance demand with supply. Since most markup formulas are cost-oriented, rather than demand-oriented, adjustments in selling prices will occur. This is especially true when consumer demand changes and the only way for retailers to reduce their inventory and make their merchandise saleable is by taking a markdown or reduction in selling price. A second reason is stock shortages. Shortages can occur from theft by employees or customers, or by mismarking the price when merchandise is received or sold. In either case, the selling price received for the goods will be less than the price carried in the inventory records. In fact, clerical error probably accounts for more stock shortages than theft. Third, there are employee and customer discounts. Employees are usually given some discount privileges after they have worked for the firm for a specified period of time. Also, certain customer groups (e.g., religious and senior citizen groups) may be given special discount privileges.

The fourth reason is the cost of alterations. Some fashion apparel items require alterations before the product is acceptable to the customer. While men's clothing is often altered free of charge, there is usually a small charge for altering women's wear. Nevertheless, this charge usually does not cover all alteration costs and, therefore, alterations are actually a part of the cost of the merchandise.

A fifth and final reason that initial markup may be different from maintained markup is cash discounts. Cash discounts are offered to retailers by manufacturers or suppliers to encourage prompt payment of bills. Cash discounts taken reduce the cost of merchandise and therefore make the maintained markup higher than the initial markup. This is just the opposite of the first four factors.

Some large retailers ignore cash discounts in calculating initial markup because the buyer may have little control over whether or not the discount is taken. The reason for this is that achieving discounts through prompt payment is thought to be under the control of the financial operations group rather than merchandising personnel, and therefore the buyer should not be penalized if the discounts are not taken.

Planning Initial Markups

As the previous discussion illustrates, retailers do not casually arrive at an initial markup percentage. The initial markup percentage must be a carefully planned process. Markups must be large enough to cover all of the operating expenses and still provide a reasonable profit to the firm. In addition, markups must provide for markdowns, shortages, employee discounts, and alteration expenses (all of these together are referred to as total reductions), which reduce net revenue. Likewise, cash discounts taken, which increase net revenue, must be included.

Initial Markup Equation

To determine the initial markup, use the following formula:

Initial markup percentage = (Operating expenses + Net profit + Markdowns + Stock shortages + Employee and customer discounts + Alterations costs – Cash discounts)/(Net sales + Markdowns + Stock shortages + Employee and customer discounts)

We can simplify this equation if we remember that markdowns, stock shortages, and employee and customer discounts are all retail reductions from stock levels. Likewise, gross margin is the sum of operating expenses and net profit. This produces a simpler formula:

Initial markup percentage = (Gross margin + Alterations costs – Cash discounts + Reductions)/(Net sales + Reductions)

Because some retailers record cash discounts as other income and not as a cost reduction in determining initial markup, the formula can be simplified one more time:

Initial markup percentage = (Gross margin + Alterations costs + Reductions)/(Net sales + Reductions)

Regardless of which formula is used, the retailer must always remember the effect of each of the following items when planning initial markup: operating expenses, net profits, markdowns, stock shortages, employee and customer discounts, alterations costs, cash discounts taken, and net sales.

At this point, a numerical example might be helpful. Assume that a retailer plans to achieve net sales of $1 million and expects operating expenses to be $270,000. The net profit goal is $60,000. Planned reductions include $80,000 for markdowns, $20,000 for merchandise shortages, and $10,000 for employee and customer discounts. Alteration costs are expected to be $20,000, and cash discounts from suppliers are expected to be $10,000. What is the initial markup percentage that should be planned? What is the cost of merchandise to be sold?

The initial markup percentage can be obtained by using the original equation:

Initial markup percentage = ($270,000 + $60,000 + $80,000 + $20,000 + $10,000 + $20,000 – $10,000)/($1,000,000 + $80,000 + $20,000 + $10,000) = 40.54%

The cost of merchandise sold can also be found. We know that the gross margin is operating expenses plus net profit ($330,000). This gross profit is equivalent to net sales less cost of merchandise sold, where cost of merchandise sold includes alteration costs and where cash discounts are subtracted. Thus, in the problem at hand, we know that $1 million less cost of merchandise sold (including alterations costs and subtracting cash discounts) is equal to $670,000. Since the alterations costs are planned at $20,000 and cash discounts at $10,000, the cost of merchandise is equal to $660,000 ($670,000 – $20,000 + $10,000).

We can verify our result by returning to the basic initial markup formula: asking price minus cost divided by asking price. The asking price is the planned net sales of $1 million plus planned reductions of $110,000 ($80,000 for markdowns, $20,000 for shortages, and $10,000 for employee and customer discounts). The cost is the cost of merchandise before the alteration costs and prior to cash discounts, or $660,000. Using the basic initial markup formula, we obtain ($1,110,000 – $660,000)/$1,110,000, or 40.54 percent. This is the same result we achieved earlier.

The preceding computations resulted in a markup percentage on retail selling price for merchandise lines storewide. Obviously, not all lines or items within lines should be priced by mechanically applying this markup percentage, since the actions of competitors will affect the prices for each merchandise line. Thus, the retailer will want to price the mix of merchandise lines in such a fashion that a storewide markup percentage is obtained. To achieve this, some lines may be priced with considerably higher markups and others with substantially lower markups than the storewide average that was planned using the initial markup planning equation. It will be helpful to explore some of the common reasons for varying the markup percentage on different lines or items within lines.

Markup Determinants

In planning initial markups, it is useful to know some of the general rules of markup determination. These are summarized as follows:

1. As goods are sold through more retail outlets, the markup percentage decreases. On the other hand, selling through few retail outlets means a greater markup percentage.
2. The higher the handling and storage costs of the goods, the higher the markup should be.
3. The greater the risk of a price reduction due to the seasonality of the goods, the greater the magnitude of the markup percentage early in the season.
4. The higher the demand inelasticity of price for the goods, the greater the markup percentage.

Although these rules are common to all retail lines, other rules are unique to each line of trade and are learned only through experience in the respective lines, such as how much to mark up produce in a supermarket during different seasons.

LO 4

Markdown Management

Why is markdown management so important in retailing?

markdown
Is any reduction in the price of an item from its initially established price.

Although retailers would prefer to have their initial markup (the markup placed on the merchandise when the store receives it) equal to the maintained markup (the actual selling price less the cost), this seldom happens. **Markdowns**, which are reductions in the price of an item taken in order to stimulate sales, and other reductions result in a firm receiving a lower price for its merchandise than originally asked. The markdown percentage is the amount of the reduction divided by the original selling price:

$$\text{Markdown percentage} = \text{Amount of reduction/Original selling price}$$

For effective retail price management, markdowns should be planned. This is true in principle because pricing is not completely a science with a high degree of precision, but rather an art with room for error. If retailers could obtain complete information about demand and supply factors, they could use the science of economics to establish a price that would maximize profits and ensure the sale of all the merchandise. Unfortunately, retailers do not possess perfect information. As a result, the entire merchandising process is subject to error, which makes pricing a challenge. Four basic errors can occur: (1) buying errors, (2) pricing errors, (3) merchandising errors, and (4) promotion errors.

Buying Errors

Errors in buying occur on the supply side of the pricing question. They result when the retailer buys the wrong merchandise or buys the right merchandise in too large a quantity. The merchandise purchased could have been in the wrong styles, sizes, colors, patterns, or price range. Too large a quantity could have been purchased because demand was overestimated or a recession was not foreseen. Whatever the cause of the buying error, the net result is a need to cut the price to move the merchandise. Often the resulting prices are below the actual cost of the merchandise to the retailer. Thus, buying errors can be quite costly. Consequently, you might expect that the retail manager would wish to minimize buying errors. However, this is not the case. The retailer could minimize buying errors only by making extremely conservative purchasing decisions. Buyers would buy only what they knew the customer wanted and what they could be certain of selling. Buying errors would be minimized, but at the expense of lost profit opportunities on some riskier types of purchase decisions. Recall that when we reviewed the determinants of markups we mentioned that the greater the risk of potential price reductions, the higher the markup percentage. This is simply another way of recognizing that taking a gamble on some purchases can be profitable if initial markups are high. You may want to review the most common buying errors discussed in Chapter 9.

Chapter 3 explained that the demographics for baby boomers are different from those of Gen-X or Gen-Y consumers. These groups are not only different in age but also in their buying behavior. However, many retailers employ buyers who are members of the baby boomer generation. When boomers are buying for Gen-X and Gen-Y customers, it can be difficult for them to prevent buying errors unless they make an intentional effort to avoid such mistakes.

Pricing Errors

Errors in pricing merchandise can be another cause of markdowns. Errors occur when the price of the item is too high to move the product at the speed and in the quantity desired. The goods may have been bought in the right styles, at the right time, and in the right quantities, but the price on the item may simply be too high. This would create purchase resistance on the part of the typical customer.

An overly high price is often relative to the pricing behavior of competitors. Perhaps, in principle, the price would have been acceptable, but if competitors price the same item substantially lower, then the original retailer's price becomes too high.

Merchandising Errors

Although many new retailers believe that carrying over seasonal or fashion merchandise into the next merchandising season is the most common merchandise error, it really isn't. Failure by the buyer to inform the sales staff how the new merchandise relates to the current stock, ties in with the store's image, and satisfies the needs of the store's target market is the most common merchandising error. Another mistake is the failure to keep the department manager and sales force informed about the new merchandise lines, so that these goods will be available to the customer. Too many times, new merchandise is left in the storeroom or the salespeople are not informed of the key features of the new item, thus preventing the customer from becoming excited about the new merchandise. Another merchandising error is the improper handling of the merchandise by the sales staff or ineffective visual presentation of the merchandise. Mishandling errors include failure to stock the new merchandise behind old merchandise whenever possible or simply misplacing the merchandise. All too often a slow seller is a "lost" bundle of merchandise.

Promotion Errors

Finally, even when the right goods are purchased in the right quantities and are priced correctly, the merchandise often fails to move as planned. In this situation, the cause is most often a promotion error. The consumer has not been properly informed or prompted to purchase the merchandise. The advertising, personal selling, sales promotion activities, or in-store displays were too weak or sporadic to elicit a strong response from potential customers.

Markdown Policy

Retailers will find it advantageous to develop a markdown timing policy. In almost all situations, it will be necessary to take markdowns; the crucial decisions become when and how much of a markdown to take. In principle, there are two extremes to a markdown timing policy: early and late.

Early Markdown Policy

Most retailers who concentrate on high inventory turnover pursue an early markdown policy. Markdowns taken early speed the movement of merchandise and also generally enable the retailer to take less of a markdown per unit to dispose of the goods. One of the author's early bosses taught him early in his retailing career that "The first markdown is the cheapest to take. Therefore, once you take it, do not look back." In other words, when you as a buyer make a merchandising error, take your loss early and do not look back because taking that early markdown will allow the dollars obtained from selling the merchandise to be used to help finance more saleable goods. At the same time, the customer benefits, since markdowns are offered quickly on goods that some consumers find fashionable, and the store has the appearance of always stocking fresh merchandise. For example, the top 20 percent of women's apparel shoppers usually visit their favorite store three to four times a month. Thus, it is important for the retailer to always have the appearance of presenting new items. Many fashion retailers use the following set of rules when taking early markdowns.

- After the third week, mark it down 25 percent from the original price.
- After the seventh week, mark it down 50 percent from the original price.
- After the eleventh week, mark it down 75 percent from the original price.
- After the sixteenth week, sell it to an outlet store, give it to charity, or place it on an online auction.[17]

Another advantage of the early markdown policy is that it allows the retailer to replenish lower-priced lines with the higher-priced ones that have been marked down. For instance, many women's wear retailers will regularly take slow-moving dresses from higher-priced lines and move them down to the moderate- or lower-priced lines.

Late Markdown Policy

Allowing goods to have a long trial period before a markdown is taken is called a late markdown policy. This policy avoids disrupting the sale of regular merchandise by too frequently marking down goods. As a consequence, customers will learn to look forward to a semiannual or annual clearance, in which all or most merchandise is marked down. Thus, the bargain hunters or low-end customers will be attracted only at infrequent intervals.

Regardless of which timing policy a retailer follows, it must plan for these reductions. Remember, when preparing a merchandise budget, the retailer must estimate reductions for that time period.

Amount of Markdown

An issue related to the timing of markdowns is their magnitude. If the retailer waits until the last moment to use a markdown, then the markdown should probably be large enough to move the remaining merchandise. As was mentioned earlier in the chapter's Inside Story box, the average American now considers 37 percent off the original price of an item to be a bargain. Thus a late markdown should be at least this much. However, such a large amount is not necessary with an early markdown. An early markdown only needs to be large enough to provide a sales stimulant. Once sales are stimulated, the retailer can watch merchandise movement; when it slows, the retailer can provide another stimulant by again marking it down. Which strategy is more profitable depends on the situation. One rule of thumb for early markdowns is that prices should be marked down at least 20 percent in order for the consumer to notice. Recently, because consumers are no longer interested, large chains have begun to move away from chain-wide sales late in the selling season. They are now focusing on using early markdowns region by region based on supply and demand considerations.[18] Remember, however, that while some general rules regarding markdown percentage have been presented, the actual markdown percentage should vary with the type of merchandise, time of season, and competition.

Often retailers are able to have their suppliers supplement their markdown losses with "markdown money," or some other type of price allowances.[19] Here's how it works: Let's say Acme Clothing Company delivers 100 sweaters to Judy's Dress Shop at the wholesale price of $40 each. Judy in turn plans to take her customary markup of 50 percent on the selling price in order to sell each sweater for $80, thus producing a gross margin of $4,000.

However, after three months Judy still has 50 of the sweaters in stock, which she puts on sale for $50 each in order to move the merchandise. After selling the remaining sweaters, Judy's gross margin is only $2,500: [(50 × $80) + (50 × $50) − (100 × $40)].

The following month Judy goes to market and visits the Acme showroom. Judy wants Acme to pay her the $1,500 she lost in taking the markdowns on their sweaters. Judy threatens Acme with a loss of future orders if it does not cover her losses. Does this sound fair to you?

Actually, this type of scenario happens quite frequently when buyers go to market. Buyers maintain that manufacturers should share in the responsibility when the merchandise does not sell as promised. Buyers claim that if the supplier cannot deliver the gross margin desired, there is no reason to reorder from that supplier. From the retailers' standpoint, when the manufacturer contributes markdown money, the manufacturer is really asking for a second chance to prove the salability of their lines. This markdown money could be in the form of cash payment or of a discount on future purchases.

Now let's look at how the maintained markup percentage is determined. A retailer purchases a sweater for $16 with the intent of selling it for $25 (an initial markup of 36 percent). However, the sweater did not sell at that price and the retailer reduced it to $20 in order to sell it. This would result in a maintained markup of 20 percent:

$$\begin{aligned}\text{Maintained markup} &= (\text{Actual selling price} - \text{Cost})/\text{Actual selling price} \\ &= \$4/\$20 = 20\%\end{aligned}$$

The following formula can also be used to determine the maintained markup percentage:

$$\begin{aligned}\text{Maintained markup percentage} = {} & \text{Initial markup percentage} \\ & - [(\text{Reduction percentage})\ (100\% \\ & - \text{Initial markup percentage})]\end{aligned}$$

where

$$\text{Reduction percentage} = \text{Amount of reductions/Net sales}$$

In the preceding example,

$$\text{Maintained markup percentage} = 36\% - [(\$5/\$20) \times (100\% - 36\%)]$$
$$= 36\% - 16\% = 20\%$$

STUDENT STUDY GUIDE

SUMMARY

LO 1

What factors should a retailer consider when establishing pricing objectives and policies?

Pricing decisions are among the most frequent a retailer must make. They cannot be made independently, because they interact with the merchandise, location, promotion, credit/check cashing, customer service, and store image decisions the retailer has already made, as well as the federal and state legal constraints.

The pricing objectives the retailer ultimately sets must also agree with the retailer's mission statement and merchandise policies. These objectives can be profit oriented, sales oriented, or seek to maintain the status quo.

After establishing its pricing objectives, the retailer must next determine the pricing policies to achieve these goals. These policies must reflect the expectations of the target market.

LO 2

What are the various pricing strategies available to the retailer?

Among the strategies discussed were customary pricing, variable pricing, flexible pricing, one-price policies, price lining, odd pricing, multiple-unit pricing, bundle pricing, leader pricing, bait-and-switch pricing, and private label brand pricing.

LO 3

How does a retailer calculate the various markups?

The basic markup equation states that, per unit, the retail selling price is equal to the dollar cost plus the dollar markup. Markups can be expressed as either a percentage of selling price or a percentage of cost to the retailer. Since the initial selling price that the retailer puts on a newly purchased item may not be attractive enough to sell all the inventory of that item, the price may need to be reduced. When we talk of actual selling prices versus initial selling prices, we mean the difference between an initial and a maintained markup.

Initial markups should be planned. Next, the initial storewide markup percentage can be determined by using operating expenses, net profit, alterations costs, cash discounts, markdowns, stock shortages, employee and customer discounts, and sales. The retailer must recognize that not all items can be priced by mechanically applying this markup percentage. Some lines will need to be priced to yield a considerably higher markup and others, a substantially lower markup. The initial markup is seldom equal to the maintained markup because of three kinds of reductions: markdowns, shortages, and employee and customer discounts.

LO 4

Why is markdown management so important in retailing?

Because the retailer does not possess perfect information about supply and demand, markdowns are inevitable. Markdowns are usually due to errors in buying, pricing, merchandising, or promotion. Because markdowns are inevitable, the retailer needs to establish a markdown policy. Early markdowns speed the movement of merchandise and also allow the retailer to take less of a markdown per unit to dispose of the merchandise. Late markdowns avoid disrupting the sale of regular merchandise by too-frequent markdowns. The best policy from a profit perspective depends on the particular situation.

TERMS TO REMEMBER

EDLP (everyday low prices)
target return objective
profit maximization
skimming
penetration
below-market pricing policy
price zone
above-market pricing policy
customary pricing
variable pricing
flexible pricing
one-price policy
price lining
trading up
trading down
odd pricing
multiple-unit pricing
bundling
leader pricing
loss leader
high-low pricing
markup
markdown

REVIEW AND DISCUSSION QUESTIONS

What factors should a retailer consider when establishing pricing objectives and policies? LO 1

1. Some people think that retailers today are running too many sales. Do you agree with this statement? If you agree with the statement, how would you cut back on the sales without losing customers? If you disagree with the statement, explain why the same-store revenues for many retailers are growing at more than the current inflation rate.
2. Is pricing really an interactive decision? Provide an example of how pricing should interact with a retailer's location, merchandise selection, and services offered.
3. When should a retailer use the penetration pricing objective?
4. If a retailer wants to use an above-market pricing policy, how should that retailer's retailing mix be different from the competition?

What are the various pricing strategies available to the retailer? LO 2

5. Your mother's birthday is February 19. You notice that while a dozen roses cost almost $100 on Valentine's Day, they cost about half of that a week later. Is this fair? What would you do as a retail florist?
6. Despite the lack of supportive research, odd-numbered pricing is still used in retailing today. Shouldn't gas stations drop those .9 cents from their posted prices and round them to the nearest penny?
7. Would you prefer to buy a car from a dealer using a flexible or a one-price policy? Why?

How does a retailer calculate the various markups? LO 3

8. Compute the markup on selling price for an item that retails for $59.95 and costs $36.20.

9. Complete the following:

	Dress Shirt	Sport Shirt	Belt
Selling Price	$45.00	$49.99	$25.00
Cost	$24.00	$27.35	$13.50
Markup in Dollars			
Markup Percentage on Cost			
Markup Percentage on Selling Price			

10. A buyer tells you that he realizes a markup of $60 on a set of tires. You know that his markup is 25 percent based on the retail price. What did he pay for that set of tires?
11. If the markup on cost is 83 percent, what is the markup on selling price?
12. Which is more important to a retailer—initial or maintained markup?
13. Can an initial markup ever be equal to the maintained markup? Explain.
14. Intimate Apparel wants to produce a 9 percent operating profit this year on sales of $1,200,000. Based on past experiences, the owner made the following estimates:

Net Alteration Expenses	$ 8,100	Employee Discount	$15,400
Markdowns	141,000	Operating Expenses	375,000
Stock Shortages	43,200	Cash Discounts Earned	4,500

Given these estimates, what average initial markup should be asked for the upcoming year?

LO 4

Why is markdown management so important in retailing?

15. Why should a retailer plan on taking markdowns during a merchandising season?
16. Somebody once said, "Buyers only need to take a markdown when they make mistakes. Therefore, good buyers should never have to take markdowns." Do you agree with that statement? Explain your answer.
17. Using the following information, what is the maintained markup percentage? Planned sales = $214,000; planned initial markup = 40 percent; planned reductions = $16,000.
18. Which markdown policy would be best for sporting goods? Explain your reasoning. Would your answer be the same for a specialty apparel store?

SAMPLE TEST QUESTIONS

LO 1

What word best describes the relationship between a retailer's pricing decisions and the merchandise, location, promotion, credit/check cashing services, image, and legal decisions that retailers must make?

a. independent
b. separate
c. interactive
d. competitive
e. multifaced

LO 2

If a retailer is offering the same products and quantities to different customers at different prices, the retailer has what kind of pricing policy?

a. two-price
b. customary
c. flexible
d. leader
e. variable

LO 3

If a retailer buys a product for $25 and sells it for $45, what is the markup percentage if the markup is based on the selling price?

a. 44.4 percent
b. 80 percent
c. 75 percent
d. 100 percent
e. 55.5 percent

LO 4

An item was marked down to $19.99 from its original retail price of $29.99. What is the reduction percentage for this item?

a. 33.3 percent
b. 25 percent
c. 50 percent
d. 41.3 percent
e. 66.7 percent

WRITING AND SPEAKING EXERCISE

You have just been hired to be the merchandise manager of a small chain (three stores) of women's apparel stores. The chain caters to working women, and three of its four buyers have less than a year's experience. In looking over the records, you notice that these buyers seem to have been late in taking markdowns. As a result, the chain's profits have suffered. In talking with these young buyers, you detect a sense of fear in taking markdowns. They believe that a markdown is an admission of an error in their buying and that if they make too many errors, their jobs will be in jeopardy. You decide to write the buyers a memo regarding markdowns. What should you tell them?

RETAIL PROJECT

On your next trip to a mall, visit all the anchor stores and leading apparel stores. Look around at displays and notice if they are having sales. Now, based on the amount of merchandise on sale and the amount of reductions, determine if each store is using an early or late markdown policy. Explain your reasoning for each store and especially explain the reasoning for differences between the stores. (Note: You can also do this project for different Web sites.)

APPLICATIONS

PLANNING YOUR OWN RETAIL BUSINESS

The online retail operation you recently opened is doing well but you are uncertain of your pricing strategy. Currently the typical customer purchases four items at an average price of $11.71, for an average transaction size of $46.84. The cost of goods is 60 percent of sales, which yields a gross margin of 40 percent. You are considering lowering prices by 10 percent across the board so you can better compete with other music e-tailers. If you lower prices by 10 percent, you believe that the average number of items purchased per customer would rise by 25 percent. Assuming your assumptions are correct, should you lower prices by 10 percent across the board? If not, do you have an alternative pricing strategy to propose?

CASE

Some Buying Issues

PART A The buyer for the women's sweater department has purchased wool sweaters for $47.69. She uses an odd pricing policy and wants to sell them at a 47 percent markup on selling price. At what price should each sweater be sold?

PART B The buyer for men's shirts has a price point of $45 and requires a markup of 40 percent. What would be the highest price he should pay for a shirt to sell at this price point?

PART C The Men's Department buyer hopes to achieve net sales of $1,500,000 for the upcoming season. Operating expenses are expected to be $560,000 and retail reductions are $180,000. Management has set a profit goal of $110,000. What should the initial markup percentage be?

PART D A buyer submits the following plans to his general merchandise manager: Planned sales = $85,000; planned initial markup = 40%; planned reductions = $31,000. Based on these projections, what is the planned maintained markup percentage?

chapter 11

Advertising and Promotion

Overview:

Promotion is a major generator of demand in retailing. In this chapter, we will focus on the roles of advertising, sales promotion, and publicity in the operation of a retail business. Retail selling, another important element of promotion, will be discussed in Chapter 12. Our discussion here is directed at describing how retailers should manage their firm's promotional resources.

Learning Objectives:

After reading this chapter, you should be able to:

1. Name the four basic components of the retailer's promotion mix and discuss their relationship with other decisions.
2. Describe the differences between a retailer's long-term and short-term promotional objectives.
3. List the six steps involved in developing a retailer's advertising campaign.
4. Explain how retailers manage their sales promotion and publicity.

The Retail Promotion Mix

LO 1

What are the four basic components of the retailer's promotion mix and how are they related to other retailer decisions?

Retailers use **promotion** to generate sales by making their targeted customers aware, interested, and desiring of current offerings. This does not mean that sales cannot occur without using promotion. Some sales will always take place, even if the retailer spends no money on promotion. For example, households close to a retailer may shop there strictly for convenience, and a passerby might occasionally visit the store for an impulse purchase. Most retailers, however, use a combination of location, price levels, displays, merchandise assortments, customer service, and promotion as a means to generate store traffic and sales.

promotion
Is a means that retailers use to bring traffic into their stores, and it includes advertising, sales promotion, publicity, and personal selling.

Retailers make trade-offs between the elements of the retailing mix. Some retailers, such as Buckle, which operates in 320 mall locations in 38 states, prefer to use prime, high-traffic mall locations that participate in mall-sponsored promotions, rather than use their own promotions to generate customer interest. As a result, the Nebraska-based chain spends only one percent of its sales on promotions. Wal-Mart is another retailer that spends only a small percentage (0.3 percent) of its sales on promotion.[1] Wal-Mart believes that lower prices are more effective than location and heavy promotional expenditures in generating traffic levels. Thus, while direct promotional expenditures are not always a prerequisite to generating sales, they are a means of achieving sales above those that could be obtained merely from offering a lower price range, having a better location, or offering outstanding service. After all, without promotion how would consumers be aware of these retail offerings? Therefore, many of today's successful retailers use promotion to bring traffic into their stores, move the traffic to the various selling areas of the store, and entice the traffic into purchasing merchandise.

advertising
Is paid, nonpersonal communication through various media by business firms, nonprofit organizations, and individuals who are in some way identified in the advertising message and who hope to inform or persuade members of a particular audience; includes communication of products, services, institutions, and ideas.

sales promotion
Involves the use of media and nonmedia marketing pressure applied for a predetermined, limited period of time at the level of consumer, retailer, or wholesaler in order to stimulate trial, increase consumer demand, or improve product availability.

publicity
Is non-paid-for communications of information about the company or product, generally in some media form.

personal selling
Involves a face-to-face interaction with the consumer with the goal of selling the consumer merchandise or services.

Types of Promotion

Promotion has four basic components: advertising, sales promotion, publicity, and personal selling. Collectively, these components comprise the retailer's promotion mix. Each component is defined as follows and will be discussed from a managerial perspective.[2]

1. **Advertising** is "paid, nonpersonal communication through various media by business firms, nonprofit organizations, and individuals who are in some way identified in the advertising message and who hope to inform and/or persuade members of a particular audience; includes communication of products, services, institutions, and ideas." Retail advertising's function is primarily to inform potential buyers of the availability and price of a retailer's offering, with the objective of developing consumer preferences for a particular retailer. Retailers most commonly use the following advertising media: Internet, newspapers, radio, television, and printed circulars.
2. **Sales promotions** "involve the use of media and nonmedia marketing pressure applied for a predetermined, limited period of time at the level of consumer, retailer or wholesaler in order to stimulate trial, increase consumer demand, or improve product availability." The most popular sales promotion tools in retailing are premiums, frequent buyer programs, coupons, in-store displays, contests and sweepstakes, product demonstrations, and sampling.
3. **Publicity** is "non-paid-for communications of information about the company or product, generally in some media form." Popular examples are Macy's Thanksgiving Day Parade and local retail support of various civic and educational groups.
4. **Personal selling** is "selling that involves a face-to-face interaction with the consumer." Personal selling and other services provided by retailers, which will be discussed in detail in Chapter 12, occur when the retailer's promotional efforts cause a shopper to choose a specific selling area.

All four components of the retailer's promotion mix need to be managed from a total systems perspective. That is, they need to be effectively blended together to achieve the retailer's promotion objectives and reinforce each other. If the advertising conveys quality and status, so must the sales personnel, publicity, and sales promotion. Otherwise, the consumer will receive conflicting or inconsistent messages about the retailer, which will result in confusion and loss of patronage.

Dollars & Sense

Retailers who successfully integrate their promotional efforts with the other elements of the retailing mix will be higher profit performers.

The management of promotional efforts in retailing must also fit into the retailer's overall strategy. Promotion decisions relate to and must be integrated with other management decisions, such as location, merchandise, credit, cash flow, building and fixtures, price, and customer service. For example:

1. There is a maximum distance consumers will travel to visit a retail store. Thus a retailer's *location* will help determine the target for promotions. Retailers should direct their promotional dollars first toward households in their **primary trading area**, where the retailer can serve customers in terms of convenience and accessibility better than the competition, and then to **secondary trading areas**, where a retailer is still competitive even if some competitors have a locational advantage. However, e-tailers who are global in presence must determine specific areas, whether they be countries or communities, in which to focus their promotional efforts.
2. Retailers need high levels of store traffic to maintain rapid *merchandise* turnover. Promotion helps build traffic.
3. A retailer's *credit* customers are more store-loyal and purchase in larger quantities. Thus they are an excellent target for increased promotional efforts. Although the increased use of MasterCard, Visa, and Discover has impacted this retail advantage in recent years, many retailers have overcome this problem by developing their own co-branded cards.
4. A retailer confronted with a temporary *cash flow* problem can use promotion to increase short-run cash flow.
5. A retailer's promotional strategy must be reinforced by its *building and fixtures* decisions. Promotional creativity and style should coincide with building and fixture creativity and style. If the ads are exciting and appeal to a particular target market, so should the building and fixtures and store atmosphere.
6. Promotion provides customers with more information. That information will help them make better purchase decisions, because risk is reduced. Therefore, promotion can actually be viewed as a major component of *customer service*.

primary trading area
Is the geographic area where the retailer can serve customers, in terms of convenience and accessibility, better than the competition.

secondary trading area
Is the geographic area where the retailer can still be competitive despite a competitor having some locational advantage.

The retailer that systematically integrates its promotional programs with other retail decision areas will be better able to achieve high-performance results. One retailer developed a set of basic promotional guidelines that all retailers should follow:

- Try to utilize only promotions that are consistent with and will enhance your store image.
- Review the success or failure of each promotion to help develop better future promotions.
- Wherever possible, test new promotions before making a major investment by using them on a broader scale.
- Use appeals that are of interest to your target market and that are realistic to obtain. For example, doubling coupons offers everybody a reward; but a sweepstakes has only one winner.
- Make sure your objectives are measurable.
- Make sure your objectives are obtainable.
- Develop total promotional campaigns, not just ads.
- The lower the rent, the higher the promotional expenses generally needed.
- New stores need higher promotional budgets than established stores.
- Stores in out-of-the-way locations require higher promotional budgets than stores with heavy traffic.[3]

Promotion in the Supply Chain

The retailer is not the only member of the marketing supply chain who uses promotion. Manufacturers also invest in promotion for many of the same reasons retailers do; that is, to move merchandise more rapidly, to speed up cash flow, and to better retain customer loyalty. However, the promotional activities of the retailer's supply chain partners may sometimes conflict with the retailer's promotions. There are three major differences in the way retailers and manufacturers use promotion:

1. Product Image versus Availability: The manufacturer's primary goal is to create a positive image for the product itself and differentiate it from competing products. For example, when introducing a new product, a manufacturer will attempt to explain how the product works. Retailers, on the other hand, are primarily interested in announcing to their customers that they have the product available for purchase at a convenient location.
2. Specific Product Benefits versus Price: Manufacturers generally do not care where customers make their purchases as long as they buy their product. That is why they promote the benefits of their products. Retailers, on the other hand, do not care which brand the customer purchases. (Remember, retailers carry products from many different manufacturers.) Retailers just want the customer to make the purchase in their store. Thus, in addition to availability, retailers feature the product's price in their ads.
3. Focused Image versus Cluttered Ads: In comparison to manufacturers, most retailers carry a larger variety and breath of products, while manufacturers produce a greater depth than most retailers carry. Thus, retail ads, which are usually geared toward short-term results, tend to be cluttered with many different products as opposed to the manufacturer's ad, which focuses on a single product theme.

Dollars & Sense

Retailers who realize that there are major differences in the way retailers and manufacturers use promotion will be more profitable than those who do not understand these differences.

Sometimes a lack of promotional harmony by supply chain members results from other factors. Consider the case of the automobile channel. Assume that the country's rate of real economic growth has been flat for the past year and as a result the country's auto sales are 10 percent lower than last year. The manufacturer believes that this economic slowdown will be short-lived and therefore does not want to get into a price war by offering any price rebates or other special promotions from the factory. However, the automobile dealers believe that the country is in the beginning of a recession. They feel that the manufacturer's advertising should be increased and that special allowances should be given for increased local advertising. They would also like to see the manufacturer tie in this increased advertising program with cash rebates paid for by the factory. Because the manufacturer and dealer have different beliefs about the economy's future, serious disagreements could occur between them.

A second possible source of problems is when the supply chain members feel that the chain's promotional campaign is a mistake. Recently Wal-Mart introduced an in-store television network (WMTV), which allows its suppliers to advertise directly to the chain's customers. For a variety of reasons, ranging from the fact that

AP Photo/Damian Dovarganes

When fuel prices reached $3 per gallon during the summer of 2006, some auto dealers promoted their new cars by offering $1.99 a gallon fuel for one year after purchase.

many stores kept the volume down (or, in some cases, completely off) so as not to distract the customers to the perception that there wasn't enough testing of the system to prove it was a benefit, many suppliers didn't feel it was a good promotional investment. Nevertheless, most vendors signed up for the program to avoid angering the retail giant that controlled so much of their business.[4] Such different perceptions show why it is important for retailers to foster a cooperative relationship with their suppliers (discussed in Chapter 5) so that the conflict can be resolved.

Promotional Objectives

LO 2

What are the differences between a retailer's long-term and short-term promotional objectives?

To efficiently manage the promotion mix, retail managers must first establish their promotional objectives. These promotional objectives should flow from the retailer's overall objectives that were discussed in Chapter 2. They should be the natural outgrowth of the retailer's operations management plans. As such, all promotional objectives should ultimately seek to improve the retailer's financial performance, because this is what strategic and administrative plans are intended to accomplish.

Exhibit 11.1 shows how promotional objectives should relate to financial performance objectives. As this exhibit shows, promotional objectives can be established to help improve both long- and short-term financial performance.

institutional advertising
Is a type of advertising in which the retailer attempts to gain long-term benefits by promoting and selling the store itself rather than the merchandise in the store.

Long-Term Objectives

Institutional advertising is an attempt by the retailer to gain long-term benefits by selling the store itself rather than the merchandise in it. By doing this, the retailer is creating a positive image for itself in the consumer's mind. Retailers using institutional ads generally seek to establish two long-term promotion objectives: creating a positive store image and public service.

Exhibit 11.1
Possible Promotion Objectives in Retailing

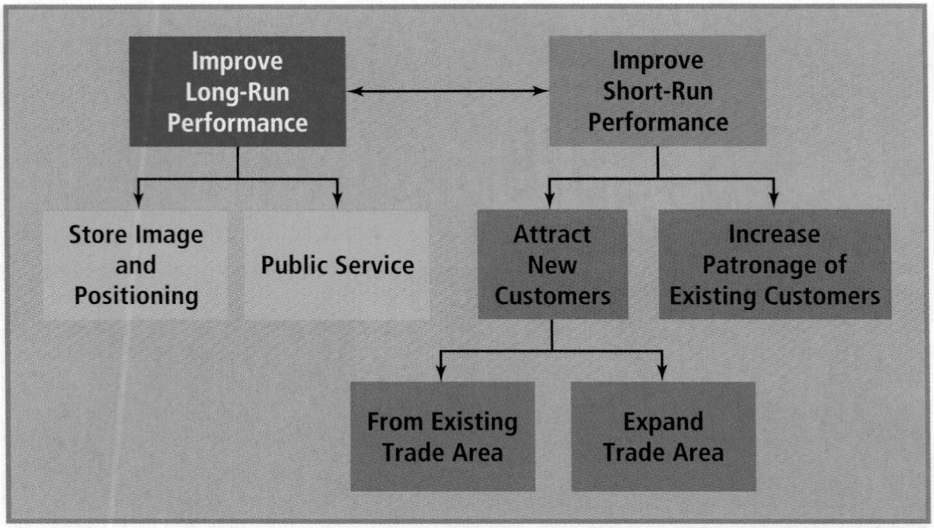

Creating a Positive Store Image

The first objective is intended to establish or reinforce in the consumer's mind the positive store image the retailer wants to convey relative to its competitors. Here the retailer seeks to gain a differential advantage by providing a clear favorable impression that is distinct from other retailers. By providing such an image, the retailer hopes to develop an on-going relationship with the customer. Promotion which fulfills this objective will improve the retailer's long-term financial performance. Two of the most successful retailers in this area have been Neiman Marcus and Nordstrom. Today, when consumers think of these retailers, they perceive elegantly designed store layouts featuring the top names in fashion backed by excellent service and a helpful, knowledgeable sales staff. However, as you might expect, this type of promotion will also assist the retailer in the short run, such as when a consumer is seeking to purchase a gift for a special friend and the retailer's ad suggests that "perfect" idea. A store's promotional efforts have been found to be a key predictor of store choice when gift shopping.

Public Service Promotion

The second long-term objective is directed at getting the consumer to perceive the retailer as a good citizen in the community. Retailers may sponsor public service advertisements to honor local athletes and scholars as well as provide cash and merchandise to local charities. For example, some retailers offer meeting rooms for use by local civic organizations; some supermarkets have begun publishing consumer newsletters with health, cooking, safety, and beauty tips; still others sponsor programs on public television stations.

promotional advertising
Is a type of advertising in which the retailer attempts to increase short-term performance by using product availability or price as a selling point.

Short-Term Objectives

Promotional advertising, on the other hand, attempts to bolster short-term performance by using product availability or price as a selling point. The two most common promotional objectives are increasing patronage of existing customers and attracting new customers.

Increased Patronage from Existing Customers

Increased patronage is probably one of the most common promotional objectives found in retailing. Simply stated, promotion expenditures are directed at current customers to encourage them to make more of their purchases at the retailer's store. In other words, promotion attempts to make present customers more store-loyal. Amazon.com, for example, in an effort to increase patronage from existing customers, offers a wide range of coupons. Within a few days of making a purchase one of the authors received a $50 coupon to purchase garden supplies from Amazon. Thus, Amazon.com's use of coupons to cross-sell is clearly an attempt to increase patronage from current customers.

Attraction of New Customers

A second major short-term promotional objective is to increase the number of customers that can be attracted to the store. One approach is to try to attract new customers from within the retailer's primary trading area. There are always some households included in this area that, for a variety of reasons, do not patronize the retailer. Perhaps they do their shopping at a retailer close to their place of employment or perhaps they simply do not think that the retailer's store is attractive to their tastes. Maybe they once had a bad experience while shopping there and vowed never to return. A second approach to gaining new customers is to attempt to expand the trading area by attracting customers from the secondary trading area. In this case the retailer might want to consider using different media so as to expand the geographic coverage of its promotional efforts. A third type of new customer is the customer just moving into the retailer's market area. Mobile consumers, for instance, are generally more prone to use national retailers because they are familiar with the stores, unless local retailers use promotions to inform them of their offerings.

Interdependence

The two-way arrow in Exhibit 11.1 suggests that although promotional objectives can be established to improve either long- or short-term financial performance, programs designed to achieve either objective will benefit the other as well. Promotional efforts to build long-term financial performance will begin to have an effect almost immediately, but will also have a cumulative effect over time. Similarly, efforts to promote short-term financial performance will carry over to affect the long-term future of the retailer.

Steps in Planning a Retail Advertising Campaign

LO 3

What six steps are involved in developing a retail advertising campaign?

What is involved in planning a retail advertising campaign? As we discussed in Chapter 2, the elements of the retailer's advertising campaign are just part of the total company's overall strategy. A retailer's advertising campaign is a six-step process:

1. Selecting advertising objectives
2. Budgeting for the campaign
3. Designing the message
4. Selecting the media to use
5. Scheduling of ads
6. Evaluating the results

Selecting Advertising Objectives

The advertising objectives should flow from the retailer's promotion objectives, but should be more specific because advertising itself is a specific element of the promotion mix. The objectives should be chosen only after the retailer considers several factors that are unique to retailing: Age of the store, its location, type of merchandise sold, the competition, the size of trading area, and what support is available from suppliers.

The specific objectives that advertising can accomplish are many and varied and the one(s) chosen depend on the target market the retailer is seeking to reach. Examples of common objectives include the following:

- Make consumers in your trading area aware that you offer the lowest prices (Wal-Mart's "Always Low Prices").

Brian Snyder/Reuters/Landov

The Neiman Marcus Christmas catalog features gifts for the super wealthy such as a personal Elton John concert.

- Make newcomers in your trading area aware of your existence (the "Welcome Wagon" coupons given to new residents of the area).
- Make customers aware of your large stock selection (Nordstrom's promise of a free shirt if it is out of stock on the basic sizes).
- Inform a specific target market of your product offering (Federated Department Stores' promotions as the exclusive retailer for Charter Club line of clothing).
- Increase traffic during slow sales periods (Subway sandwich shops' "Two for One Tuesdays").
- Move old merchandise at the end of a selling season (the after-Christmas clearance sales that all retailers use).
- Strengthen your store's image or reputation (Neiman Marcus's famous Christmas catalog which generates news stories around the world when it is mailed to customers).
- Make consumers think of you first when a need for your products occurs, especially if the product or service is not commonly purchased (this St. Louis service retailer's easy-to-remember jingle, "For a hole in your roof or a whole new roof—Frederick Roofing").
- Retain your present customers (supermarkets' use of a loyalty or frequent shopper card).

Although the ultimate goal of every advertising campaign is to generate additional sales, you will notice that increasing sales was not listed as an advertising objective. That is because other elements of the retail mix that are outside of advertising's control could negatively impact sales. The retailer could have, for example, selected the wrong merchandise for its target customers, charged too high a price for the merchandise in comparison to the competition, or improperly displayed the merchandise in the store. Therefore, since increasing sales is usually beyond the total control of just the advertising campaign, advertising should not be held solely accountable for increasing total sales.

Regardless of the objective chosen, it must be aimed at a specific market segment and be measurable over a given time period. For example, Wal-Mart recently sought to improve its image by first dropping the roll-back guy and then the smiley face. The chain's new "Look beyond the basics" campaign is directed at middle-class households and emphasizes that the retailer stocks fashionable clothing and home furnishings.[5] Thus, a good description of this campaign's objective may be "to increase the level of positive feelings among heads of middle-class households about Wal-Mart's improved fashion offerings by 30 percent over the next six months."

Budgeting for the Campaign

A well-designed retail advertising campaign requires money that could be spent on other areas (such as more merchandise or higher wages for employees). The retailer hopes that the dollars spent on advertising will generate sales that will in turn produce added profits, which can then be used to finance the other activities of the retailer.

When developing a budget, the retailer should first determine who is going to pay for the campaign; that is, will the retailer be the sole sponsor or will it get co-op support from other retailers and/or the manufacturer?

Retailer-Only Campaigns

If a retailer decides to do the campaign alone, it generally uses one of the following methods to determine the amount of money to be spent on the advertising campaign: the affordable method, the percentage-of-sales method, or the task and objective method.

1. *The affordable method.* Many small retailers use the **affordable method** by allocating all the money that they can afford for advertising in any given budget period. This method should be employed when the amount spent on advertising will add substantially more value to the retailer than an alternative use of the funds, such as increasing the sales force or adding more fixtures. Too much reliance on this method may lead to an inadequate advertising appropriation or to a budget that is not related to actual needs. A limitation of the affordable method is that the logic of this approach suggests that advertising does not stimulate sales or profits, but rather is supported by sales and profits. However, some retailers have little choice but to use this approach. A small retailer cannot go to the bank and borrow $100,000 to spend on advertising. This is unfortunate, because the small retailer might benefit more from advertising than from additional inventory or equipment. Thus, we can see that although the affordable method may not be ideal in terms of advertising theory, it is certainly defensible given the financial constraints that confront the small retailer.

affordable method
Is a technique for budgeting advertising in which all the money a retailer can afford to spend on advertising in a given time period becomes the advertising budget.

2. *Percentage-of-sales method.* The **percentage-of-sales method** of budgeting for advertising is a type of *benchmarking* whereby the retailer uses the industry's best practices as a standard. Here the retailer targets a specific percentage of forecasted sales to be used for advertising based on the assumption that successful, similar firms should be used as a guide.[6] Industry data, such as those shown in Exhibit 11.2, are often published by trade associations. These figures are averages, however, and do not reflect the unique circumstances and objectives of a particular retailer. A more suitable guide to the level of advertising expenditures is the retailer's past sales experience when the level of past expenditures has achieved management's objective. The average percentage of advertising expenditures to sales for the past several years can be applied to the current year.

percentage-of-sales method
Is a technique for budgeting in which the retailer targets a specific percentage of forecasted sales as the advertising budget.

One of the weaknesses of the percentage-of-sales method is that the amount of sales becomes the factor that influences the advertising outlay. In a correct cause-and-effect relationship, the level of advertising should influence the amount of sales. In addition, this technique does not reflect the retailer's advertising goals. One of the author's early retail mentors said that he "never saw business so bad that

Exhibit 11.2
Advertising as Percentage of Sales by Line of Trade

Line of Trade	NAICS	Ad Dollars as Percentage of Sales
Apparel and accessory stores	5600	6.6
Auto and home supply stores	5531	1
Bldg matl, hardwr, garden-retl	5200	4.2
Catalog, mail-order houses	5961	6.7
Cmp and cmp software stores	5734	0.1
Department stores	5311	3.6
Drug & proprietary stores	5912	0.8
Eating places	5812	3.6
Electronic parts,eq	5065	0.2
Family clothing stores	5651	2.5
Furniture stores	5712	4.6
Grocery stores	5411	1.2
Hardwr, plumb, heat eq	5070	1
Hobby, toy, and game shops	5945	1.2
Home furniture & equip store	5700	2.6
Lumber & oth bldg matl-retl	5211	0.5
Miscellaneous retail	5900	0.6
Misc Shopping goods stores	5940	3.5
Radio, tv, cons electr stores	5731	3.6
Record and tape stores	5735	1.9
Retail stores, nec	5990	5.6
Shoe stores	5661	2.6
Variety stores	5331	1
Women's clothing stores	5621	3.4

Source: From *Advertising Ratios & Budgets*, published by Schonfeld & Associates. Used with written permission, May 2006.

he couldn't buy all of it he wanted." By that he meant that when business slowed and all his competitors reduced their ad budgets, this retailer would then increase his ad expenditures. Without the clutter of competitor's ads, consumers became more aware of his ads and his sales increased, despite the general sales slowdown affecting the other local merchants.

Another weakness of this method is that it gives more money to departments that are already successful and fails to give money to departments that could be successful if given a little extra money. Percentage of sales does, however, provide a controlled, generally affordable amount to spend, and if spent wisely, it may work out well in practice. Most retailers, especially the smaller ones, do not use ad agencies and lack the sophistication required to adequately implement the task-and-objective approach. A percentage-of-sales guideline allows the retailer to follow objectives in an affordable, controlled manner. If the dollars are carefully applied in appropriate amounts over the year in such a way that they relate to expected sales percentages in each month, the percentage-of-sales method can work well.

task-and-objective method
Is a technique for budgeting in which the retailer establishes its advertising objectives and then determines the advertising tasks that need to be performed to achieve those objectives.

3. *Task-and-objective method.* With the preceding budgeting methods, advertising seems to follow sales results. With the **task-and-objective method**, the logic is properly reversed; here retailers can see the relationship between promotions that change attitudes and behavior. Thus, advertising leads to some other measure of financial performance, hopefully sales. Basically, the retailer prioritizes its advertising objectives and then determines the advertising tasks that need to be

performed to achieve those objectives.[7] Associated with each task is an estimate of the cost of performing the task. When all of these costs are totaled, the retailer has its advertising budget. In short, this method begins with the retailer's advertising objectives and then determines what it will cost to achieve them.

More and more retailers, as well as malls, are moving towards this method as they realize that their shrinking funds can no longer be wasted on promotions that don't pay off.[8] Exhibit 11.3 gives an example of the task-and-objective method. Notice that the retailer has five major advertising objectives and a total of 11 tasks to perform to accomplish these objectives. The total cost of performing these tasks is $99,020. While the task-and-objective method of developing the advertising budget is the best of the three methods from a theoretical and managerial control perspective, not all retailers have adopted it because it is difficult to implement.

Many of the major retailers use a combination of the percentage-of-sales method, which they use to keep pace with competitors, and the task-and-objective method, which reflects the different tasks they must accomplish to reach their objectives. Thus, as shown in Exhibit 11.4, while the percentages for close competitors are similar, they differ somewhat because of circumstances relating to the other elements of the retail mix. For example, Federated Department Stores recently spent 4.7 percent of its sales on advertising while rivals Saks Fifth Avenue, Dillards, and JCPenney's spent 3.3 percent, 2.9 percent, and 2.7 percent respectively; Target spent 2.2 percent while Wal-Mart spent only 0.3 percent; A&P spent 1.4 percent, while Safeway spent 1.2 percent and Publix only 0.7 percent.[9]

Exhibit 11.3
Task-and-Objective Method of Advertising Budget Development

	Objective and Task	Estimated Cost
Objective 1:	Increase traffic during dull periods.	
Task *A:*	15 full-page newspaper advertisements to be spread over these dates: February 2–16; June 8–23; October 4–18	$22,500
Task *B:*	Run 240 30-second radio spots split on two stations and spread over these dates: February 2–16; June 8–23; October 4–18	4,320
Objective 2:	Attract new customers from newcomers to the community.	
Task *A:*	2,000 direct-mail letters greeting new residents to the community	1,000
Task *B:*	2,000 direct-mail letters inviting new arrivals in the community to stop in to visit the store and fill out a credit application	1,000
Task *C:*	Yellow Pages advertising	1,900
Objective 3:	Build store's reputation.	
Task *A:*	Weekly 15-second institutional ads on the 10 P.M. television news every Saturday and Sunday	20,800
Task *B:*	One half-page newspaper ad per month in the home living section of the local newspaper	9,500
Objective 4:	Increase shopper traffic in shopping center.	
Task *A:*	Cooperate with other retailers in the shopping center in sponsoring transit advertising on buses and cabs	3,000
Task *B:*	Participate in "Midnight Madness Sale" with other retailers in the shopping center by taking out 2 full-page newspaper ads—one in mid-March and the other in mid-July	3,000
Objective 5:	Clear out end-of-month, slow-moving merchandise.	
Task *A:*	Run a full-page newspaper ad on the last Thursday of every month	18,000
Task *B:*	Run 3 30-second television spots on the last Thursday of every month	14,000
Total advertising budget		$99,020

Exhibit 11.4
Advertising Expenditures as Percentage of Sales for Some Leading Retailers

Line of Trade	Retailer	Ad Dollars as Percentage of Sales
Building materials & hardware		
	Tractor Supply	0.5
	Sherwin-Williams	4.6
	Fastenal	5.9
Department stores		
	Dillards	2.9
	Federated Department Stores	4.7
	JCPenney Co.	2.7
	Saks	3.2
Family clothing stores		
	Abercrombie & Fitch	2.1
	American Eagle Outfitters, Inc	3.4
	Gap Inc	3.1
	Pacific Sunwear Calf Inc	2.3
	Ross Stores	1.8
	TJX Companies	1.1
Grocery stores		
	Great Atlantic & Pacific Tea Co	1.4
	Kroger Co	1.1
	Pathmark Stores Inc	0.7
	Publix Super Markets Inc	0.7
	Safeway Inc	1.2
	Winn-Dixie Stores Inc	1.2
Variety stores		
	Dollar General	0.1
	Dollar Tree Stores Inc.	7.5
	Target Corp	2.2
	Tuesday Morning Corp	4
	Wal-Mart Stores	0.3
Women's clothing store		
	Charming Shoppes	2.2
	Dress Barn Inc	1.2
	Limited Brands	4.2
	Talbots Inc	4.3

Source: From *Advertising Ratios & Budgets*, published by Schonfeld & Associates. Used with written permission, May 2006.

This chapter's Service Retailing box discusses some of the creative methods used by new restaurants in the Dallas/Ft. Worth area to make consumers aware of them without spending a great deal of money.

Co-Op Campaigns

Although most retail advertising is paid for solely by the retailer, sometimes manufacturers and other retailers may pay part or all of the costs for the retailer's advertising campaign.

Service Retailing

Promoting a New Restaurant: Is There a Better, Less Costly Way?

For years, restaurant owners have tried to determine the cheapest way to promote a new restaurant effectively. Many restaurant managers have felt the same as John Wanamaker, the merchant prince of Philadelphia department store fame, when he was asked about his advertising budget. He answered that he knew that half of his money was wasted, but he just didn't know which half. Consider the changing trends that have occurred over the last two decades as restaurants have entered the Dallas, Texas market.

Twenty years ago, for example, when the Dallas-based sports bar/restaurant chain Dave & Busters first opened, most of its restaurants avoided advertising and relied on word of mouth. That strategy worked out just fine for Dave & Busters. Customers loved the games and good food and spread the word. This way, the restaurant used the money that might have been spent on advertising to ensure that every customer had a good experience. In fact, this strategy was so successful that it was widely copied and lost its effectiveness. As a result, Dave & Busters today advertises its new restaurants on local radio supported by direct mail and also conducts a nationwide campaign through radio and cable television outlets such as ESPN, TNT, TBS, the Comedy Channel, and Fox Sports.

A decade before Dave & Busters' arrival, another Dallas-based restaurant, Del Frisco's Double Eagle Steakhouse, also realized that word of mouth was no longer enough. Therefore, its co-founder, Dee Lincoln, used publicity as an alternative to advertising when she opened a new restaurant in the Denver market. Ms. Lincoln paid a record $80,000 for a 1,309-pound Maine-Anjou crossbreed at Denver's National Western Stock Show. When her winning bid was accepted an opposing bidder said, "Lady, you must either be really crazy or have too much money." Dee Lincoln got what she wanted—hundreds of thousands of dollars' worth of front-page newspaper coverage, not to mention radio and television publicity, for her high-quality steakhouses. It was no accident that all the media mentioned the newest restaurant in Denver. However, restaurant owners can't always be as lucky as Ms. Lincoln was to have a publicity-generating event available.

Recently, another five-star restaurant opened in Dallas and once again faced the dilemma of determining the best way to promote itself without wasting money. In spring 2003 New York-based Smith & Wollensky opened its tenth steakhouse in far north Dallas. S&W's original Manhattan location claims to be the highest grossing a la carte restaurant in the country, but it was not well known in Texas. What could S&W do to get its message out? This was especially important since it was located in an area of Dallas that is overrun with high-quality restaurants.

As luck would have it, the Dallas Mavericks were one of the hottest teams in the NBA that spring. However, advertising on their radio and television networks was very expensive. In addition, the expense of advertising on the rotating billboard beneath the scorer's table for Mavericks' home games was prohibitive. So S&W did what it had done in other NBA cities where it had restaurants. It purchased the space on the rotating board for Maverick road games in less-expensive cities at about a third of the cost, with the ads being visible for about six minutes a game on Maverick telecasts.

Thus, despite market changes over the last two decades, service retailers such as restaurants have come up with creative ideas for promoting their offerings. This is an especially difficult task for restaurants because a dining episode is essentially an experience, and the retailer's promotions must not promise an experience that cannot be delivered. Nevertheless, it must get the word out.

Source: Based on conversations with Dee Lincoln and 35 years of living in Texas.

Vertical cooperative advertising allows the retailer and other supply chain members to share the advertising burden. For example, the manufacturer may pay up to 40 percent of the cost of the retailer's advertising of the manufacturer's products, up to a ceiling of 4 percent of annual purchases by the retailer from the manufacturer. If the retailer spent $10,000 on advertising the manufacturer's products, then it could be reimbursed 40 percent of this amount, or $4,000, as long as the retailer purchased at least $100,000 during the last year from the manufacturer.

There is a strong temptation among retailers to view vertical co-op advertising money as free. Retailers forget, however, that good advertising, like a good investment, should increase revenues from customers, not just from vendors. That is, even if the

vertical cooperative advertising
Occurs when the retailer and other channel members (usually manufacturers) share the advertising budget. Usually the manufacturer subsidizes some of the retailer's advertising that features the manufacturer's brands.

supplier is putting up 50 percent of the expense, the retailer must still pay the other 50 percent. In addition, since the supplier often exercises considerable control over the content of the advertising and its objectives may be different from the retailer's, the retailer may actually be paying 50 percent of the supplier's cost of advertising rather than vice versa. Also, suppliers know that it is a common media practice to offer local retailers a discount on rates relative to national advertisers. Thus, suppliers often use local retailers to get this discount on their ads.

Retailers must prioritize their objectives to determine whether they can get a better return on their money by using vertical co-op dollars or by assuming total sponsorship of advertising a message with high priority. Remember, earlier in the chapter it was pointed out that retailers and their supply chain partners often have different objectives. As a result, sometimes it can be more profitable for the retailer to pass up the co-op deal on one product line and spend the money on another line, where the increased ad dollars will have a higher sales impact. Consider that for the past 50 years supermarket advertising has used vendor/supplier advertising funds that paid for retailers' advertising costs. However, due to the many recent mergers among manufacturers, there are fewer and fewer vendors using these "co-op" style funds to promote store brands. As a result, the more progressive retailers have figured out that their weekly ad should promote their brand—not vendors' offerings. The following example illustrates the logic behind such a strategy.

Assume that the retailer has $10,000 to spend on advertising and is considering the possibility of increasing advertising expenditures for either merchandise line A or line B. With line A, the vendor has offered a co-op deal, which roughly translates into the supplier's paying 50 percent of the cost of the advertising. This would allow the retailer to purchase $20,000 of advertising for a $10,000 investment. No co-op deal is being offered by the supplier of line B because it is the retailer's private label, but line B is just now becoming very popular with the retailer's customers, and the retailer believes it could benefit substantially from $10,000 in advertising. What should the retailer do?

The answer to the preceding question will depend on two major factors. First, how much will the sales of line A increase with $20,000 in advertising compared to the amount the sales of line B might increase with $10,000 in advertising? Second, what is the gross margin percentage for each line? Let's assume these are the facts; Line A has 50 percent gross margin and line B has 60 percent gross margin. Currently, line A has sales of $160,000, and it is expected that a $20,000 advertising program will push sales up to $220,000. At the present time, line B has sales of $36,000, but it is expected that a $10,000 advertising program will increase the sales volume to $120,000.

Notice that line B, although its current sales are relatively low, is very responsive to advertising expenditures as compared to the responsiveness of merchandise line A. Here is the numerical analysis:

	LINE A		LINE B	
	Before	After	Before	After
Sales	$160,000	$220,000	$36,000	$120,000
Cost of goods sold	80,000	110,000	14,400	48,000
Gross margin	80,000	110,000	21,600	72,000
Advertising	0	10,000[a]	0	10,000
Contribution to profit	$80,000	$100,000	$21,600	$62,000

[a]Actually, $20,000 was spent, but the net cost to retailer was $10,000 since the supplier paid the other $10,000.

As you can see, the numerical analysis suggests while the increase in line A's contribution to profit would be $20,000 ($100,000 versus $80,000), it would be $40,400 for line B ($62,000 versus $21,600). Therefore, it would be more profitable for the retailer to pass up the co-op deal on line A and spend the $10,000 on advertising line B, its private label brand.

Retailers can be more profitable if they pass up some co-op promotional deals.

Dollars & Sense

horizontal cooperative advertising
Occurs when two or more retailers band together to share the cost of advertising usually in the form of a joint promotion of an event or sale that would benefit both parties.

Horizontal cooperative advertising is when two or more retailers band together to share the cost of advertising. Significantly, this tends to give small retailers more bargaining power in purchasing advertising than they would otherwise have. Also, if properly conducted, it can create substantially more store traffic for all participants. For example, retailers in shopping malls will often jointly sponsor multi-page spreads in newspapers promoting special events such as "Santa Land" or "Moonlight Madness" sales, while downtown merchants usually jointly sponsor "Sidewalk Days" or "Downtown Days" sales. That these events are good traffic generators is evident by the many malls that have recently turned a very slow shopping night (Halloween) into a very successful "Dead Night." By having a store-to-store program that provides a safe place for trick-or-treating, a mall can pull significantly more people into each retailer's store than the retailers operating individually could expect to do for the same cost.

Designing the Message

The next step in developing an advertising campaign is to design a creative message and select the media that will enable the retailer to reach its objectives. In reality these decisions are made simultaneously. Creative messages cannot be developed without knowing which media will be used to carry the message to the target market. This text, however, will cover media selection after discussing how retailers design their message.

Creative decisions are especially important for retailers because their advertising messages generally seek an immediate reaction from the consumer while having a short life span. The development of such messages is one of retailing's major failings. If you have ever covered the retailer's name in a newspaper ad or tuned out the retailer's name in a broadcast ad, you know that all too often retailers lack originality in their ads. The chapter's Retailing: The Inside Story box provides a few examples of retailers who have demonstrated how using creativity in developing a promotional strategy can produce positive results.

Retail ads must accomplish three goals:

1. Attract attention and retain attention; that is, they must be able to break through the competitive clutter.
2. Achieve the objective of the advertising strategy.
3. Avoid errors, especially legal ones.

Accomplishing these goals is an extremely difficult task in today's marketplace given the limited attention span of the consumer. After all, newspaper and magazine readership is declining and more and more consumers use remote controls to block television commercials. Consumers now spend their time playing games on their Xboxes® and surfing the Internet instead of using mass media for entertainment.

Retailing: The Inside Story

Lack of Creativity In Retail Promotions

The late Stanley Marcus once lamented to a group of Retailing professors about the lack of creativity in retailing promotions. He said that if someone covered up the name of the retailer in most ads, consumers would have a difficult time identifying the sponsor. And that didn't even include those annoying locally produced automobile dealer promotions that dominate television.

However, some retailers, both large and small, have done an excellent job at developing promotions.

Consider how Papa John's used creativity to out-fox Domino's so that consumers would think of Papa John's first when they needed a particular type of pizza. Domino's once paid over $1 million to sponsor a task on "The Apprentice" where the teams competed to develop and sell a new type of pizza—meatball. In addition, Domino's wanted to use the episode as a vehicle to not only unveil its America Classic Cheeseburger pizza, but also introduce "The Donald" as the company's new pitchman. During one of the show's national commercial breaks, an ad ran with Mr. Trump saying, "It takes my two favorite foods—pizza and cheeseburgers—and blends them together. I've tried this product and it's fabulous."

However, remember, the show was about meatball pizzas and Papa John's took advantage of NBC's willingness to allow a rival to run a competing ad in 64 major markets. In that ad, Papa John's founder John Schnatter asked viewers, "Why eat a pizza made by apprentices when you can call the pros at Papa John's?"

Another great creative campaign aimed at getting consumers in the store, which in retailing means increased sales, was when IKEA first entered the U.S. market. Rather than engage in a price war, the foreign-based retailer started renting Christmas trees. IKEA ran newspaper advertisements stating, "The spirit of Christmas can't be bought, but for $10 you can rent it." The fine print explained that for $20 ($10 for the rental and a $10 deposit), IKEA would rent you a beautiful Douglas fir. (The going purchase price for similar trees in New York City was $50 and up.) "After the holidays, just return the tree, pick up your deposit and IKEA will mulch the tree for your garden or donate the mulch to the community. You will also receive a coupon for a free four-year-old Blue Spruce sapling to help save the environment. You can pick up your free tree the first week in April." In short, IKEA made it worthwhile to visit the store three separate times.

Even small, locally owned independent retailers can use creativity to break away from the crowd. T&M Appliance & TV of Clinton, MO, population 1,500, used a variation of the Christmas idea with decorating Halloween pumpkins. The four visits here involved picking up the free pumpkins with your parents, turning in the finished pumpkin, coming in to select the best pumpkin, and stopping by after the city-wide parade to see the store's decorations (including the pumpkins) and select the best costume.

Another creative idea was developed several years ago by Orville's Home Appliances in Lancaster, NY. Realizing that consumers always like a "deal," the store's owner ran an ad offering the first 2,500 customers to purchase an appliance a lifetime membership card in the store's "No Sales Tax for Life Club" which guaranteed that on all future purchases the member would not be charged sales tax. Sales more than doubled that first month of the promotion and even now about two or three sales per week involve the card. This promotion, which is really nothing more than a discount of less than 10 percent on merchandise with a large markup, has done what it was intended to do—draw customers into the store. (A follow up note about this promotion: The New York State Division of Taxation required Orville to put a disclaimer on its ads stating it was a discount equal to the amount of the tax and that current sales taxes had to be paid.)

Source: Stanley Marcus in a speech to the spring ACRA meeting, Dallas, TX, April 17, 1993; "The Worst," *Advertising Age*, October 3, 2005: 12; information supplied by Tom Drake of the North American Retail Dealers Association and Mickey Reali of Orville's.

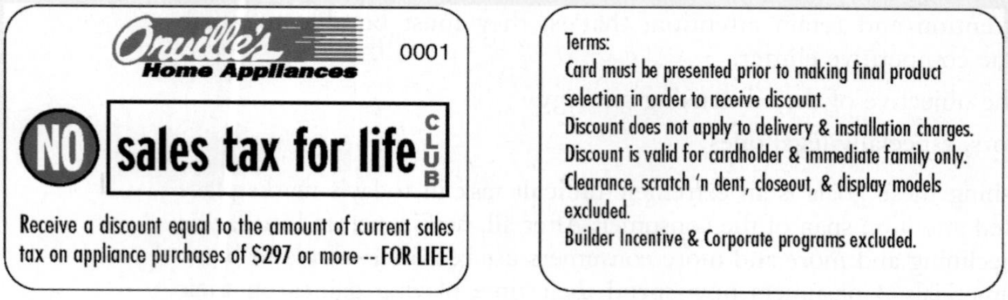
Orville's
Home Appliances
0001
NO sales tax for life
CLUB
Receive a discount equal to the amount of current sales tax on appliance purchases of $297 or more -- FOR LIFE!
Terms:
Card must be presented prior to making final product selection in order to receive discount.
Discount does not apply to delivery & installation charges.
Discount is valid for cardholder & immediate family only.
Clearance, scratch 'n dent, closeout, & display models excluded.
Builder Incentive & Corporate programs excluded.

Courtesy of Orville's Home Appliances

Therefore, as our Retailing: The Inside Story box pointed out, it is becoming imperative for retailers to find a unique way to break through the competitive clutter to get the consumer's attention and then to hold it. After all, if consumers have already seen or read the ad, why should they view it again? Following are some of the common approaches that retailers use to gain repeated viewing:

Lifestyle:	Shows how the retailer's products fit in with the consumer's lifestyle.
Fantasy:	Creates a fantasy for the consumer that is built around the retailer's products.
Humorous:	Builds a campaign around humor that relates to using the retailer's products.
Slice-of-life:	Depicts the consumer in everyday settings using the retailer's products.
Mood/Image:	Builds a mood around using the retailer's products.

Finally, before using the ad, the retailer should pretest it for mistakes. These mistakes could be either accidental or perhaps inserted by an unhappy employee. The authors have seen a promotion for an "early bird special" drawing where the customers could drop off their entries between 7 and 10 A.M. Unfortunately, the drawing was to be held at 9:30 A.M. In another case, a Sunday circular for a major retailer offered a special deal on Scrabble® games. However, the adjoining picture had two young boys playing the game and one had just spelled the word RAPE. A clothing store's ad had this heading; "SEMI-ANNUAL CLEARANCE SALE! SAVINGS LIKE THESE ONLY COME ONCE A YEAR," and a florist once advertised a "PRE-GRAND OPENING CLEARANCE."

Retailers who realize the importance of creative decisions in their advertising will have higher long-term profits.

Dollars & Sense

Although the above errors are serious, they should not present legal problems. Retailers can accidentally violate some advertising laws, even if they are not trying to deceive the consumer. Chapter 6 discussed some of the various federal laws governing retail advertising. All too often, however, the retailer runs into trouble with state or local laws. Some states limit promotions involving games of chance, others regulate the use of ads with price comparisons among retail stores, and others restrict the use of certain words in the description of merchandise. For example, the Pennsylvania Human Relations Commission has issued guidelines against the use of the following words in real estate ads because they tend to discriminate among consumer groups: *bachelor pad, couple, mature, older seniors, adults, traditional, newlyweds, exclusive, children, and established neighborhood.*

Internationally, individual countries, or in some cases groups of countries, such as the European Union, set specific guidelines for advertising content that must be adhered to. For instance, in the European Union, advertising that is directed at children or young people is generally allowed. However, the ad must not directly encourage children or young people to buy a product and must not exploit their inexperience and credulity. In addition, the ad must not cause them any physical or mental harm. Ads that could conceivably cause minors physical or mental harm must be broadcast between 11 P.M. and 6 A.M.

Media Alternatives

The retailer has many media alternatives from which to select. In the past, retailers generally categorized media as print, which included newspaper, magazines, direct mail, and broadcast, which lumped radio and television together. Now, however, retailers are beginning to classify media using a managerial perspective that recognizes that newspapers and television are mass media alternatives aimed at a total market, while radio, magazines, direct mail, and the Internet can be more easily targeted toward specific markets.

Newspaper Advertising

The most frequently used advertising medium in retailing is the newspaper. (Fashion magazines and newspapers are probably the only media that consumers will purchase specifically to see the advertising content.) Newspaper advertising is popular for the following reasons: (1) Most newspapers are local. This is advantageous since most retailers appeal to a local trading area. (2) A low technical skill level is required to create advertisements for newspapers. This is helpful for small retailers. (3) Newspaper ads require only a short interval between the time copy is written and when the ad appears. Because some retailers do a poor job of planning and tend to use advertising to respond to crises (poor cash flow, slackening of sales, need to move old merchandise), the short lead time for placing newspaper ads is a significant advantage.

Price-oriented retailers make heavy use of newspapers to promote sale events.

However, retail newspaper advertising also has its disadvantages: (1) The fact that a consumer was exposed to an issue of a newspaper does not mean the consumer read or even saw the retailer's ad. (2) The life of any single issue of a newspaper is short—it's read and subsequently discarded. (3) The typical person spends relatively little time with each issue, and the time spent is spread over many items in the newspaper. (4) Newspapers have poor reproduction quality, which leads to ads with little visual appeal. (5) If the retailer has a specific target market, much of its advertising money will be wasted since newspapers tend to have a broad appeal. In fact, seldom does the retailer's target market match the circulation of any newspaper. Still, despite these disadvantages, newspapers continue to be the number one form of advertising for retailers. Many of the large bricks-and-mortar retailers, such as Target and Mervyn's, use newspapers to deliver their own centrally produced inserts.

A new trend in newspaper advertising is "adazine" style format. In the past, many consumers simply ignored supermarket ads because they were simply lists of items on sale and many of the items don't pertain to their needs. However, since consumers enjoy reading magazines, grocers have evolved a new style of advertising. These lifestyle adazines, which are usually published quarterly, present meal ideas that incorporate items on sale with recipes, pictures and informational copy, such as holiday meal-planning ideas. Also, some retail observers believe that as a result of the recent crackdown on the use of Internet spam and consumers' dislike of pop-up ads on web pages, e-tailers will be forced to resort to using some newspaper advertising.

Television Advertising

Today many retailers are shifting out of newspapers and turning to television advertising as a means to reach the elusive full-price shopper. After all, for a brand to be viewed as credible and top-of-the-line, television is a more dynamic medium.[10] In addition, research suggests that, over time, the subtle and gradual effect from TV images on consumer memory is greater than the verbal messages received from media such as radio. However, even though television advertising is a great image-builder, it is expensive. A half-dozen well-designed television ads may use up the total ad budget. In addition, for the small or even intermediate-sized retailer, a television ad would reach well beyond its trading area. A final disadvantage of television advertising is that competition is high for the viewer's attention. During advertising periods, the viewer may take a break and leave the room, may be exposed to several ads, or may use the remote control to surf to other channels. In addition, overall time spent watching television has decreased in recent years as many younger consumers have switched over to the Internet.

In spite of the preceding drawbacks, television advertising can be a powerful tool for generating higher sales. The American public spends more time relaxing in front of the television than in any other recreational activity. Television has broad coverage; over 98 percent of homes in the United States have at least one television set. These sets offer the retailer a vehicle in which both sight and sound can be used to create a significant perceptual and cognitive effect on the consumer. It should be noted that television penetration rates differ across the world, and therefore its usefulness as a tool to reach consumers differs as well.

Further, the widespread development of cable television has made television attractive to small local retailers. Local cable operators have been selling advertising on cable channels which is quite competitive with newspaper advertising rates. However, retailers just beginning to use television advertising may be hard pressed to successfully locate a niche because so many others are also seeking to do so. The point to remember, as we mentioned earlier, is to sell both the products and store image at the same time. Television has also provided a new means of advertising—the 24-hour shopping channels.

Radio Advertising

Many retailers prefer to use radio because it can target messages to select groups. In most communities there are five or more radio stations, each of which tends to appeal to a different demographic group. Through the use of proper variations in volume and types of sounds, retailers can use radio to develop distinctive and appealing messages and to introduce a store and its image to current and potential customers. In short, there is a lot of flexibility. Also, many radio audiences develop strong affection and trust for their favorite radio announcers. When these announcers endorse the retailer, the audience is impressed.

Radio advertising also has its drawbacks. Radio commercials, especially the uncreative ones, are not saved or referred to again like print media ads. In fact, some media experts claim that radio's lack of innovation is a major shortcoming. All too often ad agencies and radio stations lack the creativity to help local retailers. The CBS radio network, claiming the last truly great radio campaign was Motel 6's "And we'll leave the light on for you," recently hired top creative people to stimulate better radio commercials, at both the national and local levels.[11] In addition, radio is frequently listened to during work hours and driving to and from work (drive time) and therefore tends, over time, to become part of the background environment. Since radio is nonvisual, it is impossible to effectively demonstrate or show the merchandise that is being advertised. Finally, satellite radio is pulling many consumers away from local radio offerings.

Magazine Advertising

Relatively few local retailers advertise in magazines, unless the magazine has only a local circulation. Nationally based retailers such as JCPenney will allocate some of their advertising budget to magazines. Usually, the retail ads that these retailers place in magazines are institutional.

Magazine advertising can be quite effective. In relation to newspapers, magazines perform well on several dimensions. They have a better reproduction quality; they have a longer life span per issue; and consumers spend more time with each issue of a magazine than the newspaper. For example, magazines have the unique quality of being shared among family and friends, thus extending the reach of the advertisement. An added benefit is that featured articles in a magazine can put people in the mood for a particular product class. For example, a feature article on home remodeling in *Better Homes and Gardens* can put people in a frame of mind to consider purchasing wallpaper, carpeting, tiling, draperies, paint, and other home improvement items. The major disadvantage of using magazines is that the long lead time required prevents advertising with price appeals or any urgency in its messages.

Direct Mail

Direct marketing can be a powerful addition to the retailer's promotional strategy. With direct mail, the retailer can precisely target its message to a particular group as long as a good mailing list of the target population is available. Macy's, for example, uses a customer database to select targeted recipients for each of its roughly 300 annual catalog and promotional mailings. In addition, direct mail provides retailers a personal contact with individual consumers who share certain valued characteristics. Thus, while all of Macy's customers receive the Christmas catalog, only those who recently purchased a men's suit will receive a postcard promoting a sale on shirts and ties. Such messages can reach the consumer without being noticed by the competition. Finally direct-mail results can generally be easily measured, thus providing the retailer with important feedback.

On the negative side, direct-mail advertising is relatively expensive per contact or message delivered. Also, the ability to reach the target market depends totally on the quality of the mailing list. If the list is not kept current, advertising dollars will be wasted. For example, the University of Phoenix regularly sends the authors a direct-mail advertisement suggesting that they could further their career prospects if they had a bachelor's degree in business. Given that the authors already have Ph.D.s, is this an instance of wasted ad dollars? A related problem is the incidence of unopened or unexamined mail, especially when it is addressed to "occupant" or is mailed using third-class postage.

Another negative is the increasing quantity of electronic direct mail, commonly known as "spam." Although most Americans tolerate direct-mail solicitations, the infestation of unsolicited e-mail irritates nearly everyone. At the present time, spammers and consumer groups are trying to settle this issue out of court without infringing on the spammers' right to free speech and their ability to conduct business. However, it appears only the legal system will be able to settle this issue.

Internet

As discussed in Chapter 4 in the discussion about myspace.com and facebook.com, clearly the Internet is playing an important role as a way for consumers to establish their identities. While TV ratings and newspaper circulation have declined at an accelerating rate in recent years, Internet traffic is growing nearly 25 percent per year. Therefore, the Internet should now be an important promotional tool for retailers. Projections indicate that the current 100 million unique American users will grow to over 200 million users in the next few years.

A key aspect of the Internet is in its ability to provide information-on-demand to customers. The communication elements of advertising, sales promotion, and public relations are all strategic options a firm can use when communicating with its various publics. For example, a firm may wish to provide online customers with samples of its advertising on its website, as Scottrade (http://www.scottrade.com) or The Gap (http://www.gap.com) have done. Or, a firm may wish to use sales promotions, such as online coupons, similar to those used by Harold's (http://www.harolds.com), a clothing retailer, and http://Amazon.com. A retailer can also use its website to share specific information on its good works through press releases or byline articles. Other uses include advising investors of financial policies and/or explaining the firm's position on a social issue. Excellent examples of websites used in this manner are Walt Disney Company (http://www.disney.com) and Target (http://www.target.com). In essence, the Internet provides a platform for a retailer to employ a relatively low cost integrated marketing communications mix, thus increasing shareholder value by enhancing the retailer's image by providing a variety of highly specialized information. Southwest Airlines' Web site (http://www.southwest.com) provides a good example of a fully integrated marketing communications mix. Southwest offers online ticketing, investor information, and advertising as well as sales promotions and public relations materials, thus effectively communicating with all of its relevant publics. Also, the Internet can pay off for smart shoppers. http://Ebates.com, http://yub.com, and http://fat-wallet.com, for example, offer visitors a cash-back refund when they register on the site and then make purchases at dozens of e-tailers.[12]

Equally important for the e-tailers is the fact that the various Internet providers offer so many tools to improve the effectiveness of their promotions. Not only can a search engine, such as Yahoo! provide the e-tailer with extremely detailed demographic information about the people who click on its ads, it can also predict the probable response rate to the ads. It knows what time of day the ads are likely to be most effective. And increasingly, by analyzing "click streams" on its network, a search engine can spot potential buyers at various stages of the consideration process. In other words, by looking at the billions of user clicks that flow through its servers every day, Yahoo! is getting better and better at figuring out that a given pattern—say, a user who's looked up scuba diving on Yahoo Sports, checked out romance movies on Yahoo Entertainment, and compared Key West hotel prices on Yahoo Travel—is interested in taking a trip and is just beginning to think about a purchase. Such information is invaluable to a retailer like Hyatt. Once Yahoo! knows when and where a potential customer is in the trip-buying process, it can serve up the appropriate hotel/resort ad.[13]

Internet pop-up banners are a completely different story. They provide one of the few sources of revenue for most websites, especially news and magazine sites. Most consumers do not view them in a positive light but at the same time they do not want to purchase subscriptions for every site they visit, or provide masses of personal information that can be sold to marketing companies to provide an income stream for the website. Until these problems are solved, it is doubtful that Internet advertising will play a major role in the retailer's promotional mix.

Miscellaneous Media

The retailer can advertise using media other than those previously identified: Yellow Pages, outdoor advertising, transit advertising (on buses, cabs, subways), electronic information terminals, specialty firms such as Welcome Wagon, and shopping guides (newspaper-like printed material, but containing no news). Each of these is usually best used to reinforce other media and should not be relied on exclusively unless the retailer's advertising budget is minimal. Most retailers look upon these media vehicles as geared mainly toward specific product advertising by manufacturers. However, that does not mean a retailer cannot make use of them because a new resident is still going to have to purchase food, clothing, and entertainment.

Dollars & Sense

Retailers who understand the advantages and disadvantages of the various media will be higher-profit performers.

Media Selection

To select the best media, the retailer needs to remember the strengths and weaknesses of each medium and determine the coverage, reach, and frequency of each medium being considered.

coverage
Is the theoretical maximum number of consumers in the retailer's target market that can be reached by a medium and not the number actually reached.

reach
Is the actual total number of target customers who come into contact with an advertising message.

cumulative reach
Is the reach that is achieved over a period of time.

frequency
Is the average number of times each person who is reached is exposed to an advertisement during a given time period.

cost per thousand method (CPM)
Is a technique used to evaluate advertisements in different media based on cost. The cost per thousand is the cost of the advertisement divided by the number of people viewing it, which is then multiplied by 1,000.

Coverage refers to the theoretical maximum number of consumers in the retailer's target market that can be reached by a medium—not the actual number reached. For example, if a newspaper is circulated to 35 percent of the 40,000 households in a retailer's trading area, then the theoretical coverage is 14,000 households.

Reach, on the other hand, refers to the actual total number of target customers who come into contact with the ad message. Another useful term is **cumulative reach**, which is the reach achieved over a period of time.

Frequency is the average number of times each person who is reached is exposed to an advertisement during a given time period.

Different media can be evaluated by combining knowledge of the ad cost for a medium and the medium's reach and cumulative reach. The most commonly used methods for doing this are the **cost per thousand method (CPM)** and **cost per thousand—target market (CPM-TM)**. The most appropriate way to compute the CPM is to divide the cost for an ad or series of ads in a medium by the total number of people viewing the ad, and then multiply by 1,000. For example, if a newspaper ad costs $500 and is distributed to 38,200 households, then the CPM is $13.09 [($500/38,200) × 1,000)]. However, the ad may reach only 13,860 customers in the retailer's target market; the cost per thousand for the target market is $36.08 [($500/13,860) × 1,000]. As you can see, CPM-TM only measures members of the retailer's target market who are reached by the ad.

Comparing CPM and CPM-TM for different media vehicles can also provide information on their effectiveness. For example, let's compare billboard to cable television advertising. Let's say that the billboard and cable both cost $1,000 a month and each reaches 1 million consumers. Here the CPM for both is $1.00. However, given the focused nature of cable, the retailer may hit 900,000 in its target market, thus having a $1.11 CPM-TM. The billboard, however, reaches only 500,000 of the retailer's targeted customers and as a result has a CPM-TM of $2.00. Comparing CPM-TMs, we can see that cable television (at $1.11), is more effective than the billboard (at $2.00) for the retail outlet. Thus, a medium such as television may cost more based on CPM, but if it has a significantly better CPM-TM, it may be the better buy.

Finally, **impact** refers to how strong an impression an advertisement makes and how well it ultimately leads to a purchase. As a result of the increase in media alternatives and the tendency of consumers to spend a stable amount of time on the various media, targeted ads have had a six-fold increase over the last decade.

Scheduling of Advertising

When should a retailer time its advertisements to be received by the consumer? What time of day, day of week, week of month, and month of year should the ads appear? No uniform answer to these questions is possible for all lines of retail trade. Rather, the following conventional wisdom should be considered.

cost per thousand—target market (CPM-TM)
Is a technique used to evaluate advertisements in different media based on cost. The cost per thousand—target market is the cost of the advertisement divided by the number of people in the target market viewing it, which is then multiplied by 1,000.

impact
Refers to how strong an impression an advertisement makes and how well it ultimately leads to a purchase.

1. Ads should appear on, or right before, the days when customers are most likely to purchase. If most people shop for groceries Thursday through Saturday, then grocery store ads might appear on Wednesday and Thursday.
2. Advertising should be concentrated around the times when people receive their payroll checks. If they get paid at the end of each month, then advertising should be concentrated at that point.
3. If the retailer has limited advertising funds, it should concentrate its advertising during periods of highest demand. For example, a muffler repair shop would be well advised to advertise during drive time on Thursday and Friday when the consumer is aware of his or her problem and has Saturday available for the repair work.
4. The retailer should time its ads to appear during the time of day or day of week when the best CPM-TM will be obtained. Many small retailers have discovered the advantages of late-night television.
5. The higher the degree of habitual purchasing of a product class, the more the advertising should precede the purchase time.

Many retailers use advertising to react to crises, such as an unexpected buildup of inventory due to slow sales. Of course, in these cases the timing of ads is not planned in advance and is an ineffective method of scheduling retail advertising. The preceeding rules are only suggestions based on conventional wisdom. Depending on the situation, a retailer may use a different scheduling plan to make the best use of its money. For example, earlier in the chapter it was mentioned that one of the author's retailing mentors suggested advertising when others were not and, to avoid getting lost in the crowd, cutting back on ads when competitors were advertising.

Evaluating the Results

Will the advertising produce results? It depends on how well the ads were designed and how well the advertising decisions were made. A consistent record of good retail advertising decision making can be made only if the retailer effectively plans its advertising program.

Some retailers try systematically to assess the effectiveness and efficiency of their advertising. **Advertising effectiveness** refers to the extent to which the advertising has produced the result desired (i.e., helped to achieve the advertising objective). **Advertising efficiency** is concerned with whether the advertising result was achieved with the minimum effort (e.g., dollars).

advertising effectiveness
Is the extent to which the advertising has produced the result desired.

advertising efficiency
Is concerned with whether the advertising result was achieved with the minimum financial expenditure.

The effectiveness or efficiency of advertising can be assessed on a subjective basis. Simply ask yourself: Are you satisfied with the results produced? Do you believe you achieved those results at the least cost? Most, but not all, ineffective advertising is due to one of 10 errors:

1. The retailer bombarded the consumer with so many messages and sales that any single message or sale tends to be discounted. A retailer that has a major sale every week will tend to wear out its appeal.

2. The advertising was not creative or appealing. It may be just more "me too" advertising in which the retailer does not effectively differentiate itself from the competition.
3. The advertisement didn't give customers all the information they need. The store hours or address may be absent because the retailer assumes that everyone already knows this information. Or, information may be lacking on sizes, styles, colors, and other product attributes.
4. Advertising dollars were spread too thinly over too many departments or merchandise lines.
5. There may have been poor internal communications among salesclerks, cashiers, stock clerks, and management. For example, customers may come to see the advertised item, but salesclerks may not know the item is on sale or where to find it, and cashiers may not know the sale price. Worst yet, for a variety of reasons, the advertised product may not be available when the consumer seeks to purchase it.
6. The advertisement was not directed at the proper target market.
7. The retailer did not consider all media options. A better buy was available, but the retailer did not take the time to find out about it.
8. The retailer made too many last-minute changes in the advertising copy, increasing both the cost of the ad and the chance for error.
9. The retailer took co-op dollars just because they were "free" and therefore presumably a good deal.
10. The retailer used a medium that reached too many people not in the target market. Thus, too much money was spent on advertising to people who were not potential customers.

LO 4

Management of Sales Promotions and Publicity

How do retailers manage their sales promotion and publicity?

Retailers also use sales promotions, which provide some type of short-term incentive, and publicity to increase the effectiveness of their promotional efforts. The role of sales promotions and publicity in the retail organization should be consistent with and reinforce the retailer's overall promotional objectives.

Role of Sales Promotion

Sales promotion tools are excellent demand generators. Many can be used on relatively short notice and can help the retailer achieve its overall promotion goals. Furthermore, sales promotions can be significant in helping the retailer differentiate itself from competitors. Retailers have long known that consumers will change their shopping habits and brand preferences to take advantage of sales promotions, especially those that offer something special, different, or exciting.

Retailers must remember that, since all stores are able to shop the same vendors, merchandise alone does not make a store exciting. In-store happenings of sales promotion can generate excitement. Because of their poor recordkeeping systems, many retailers fail to recognize that the role of sales promotion is quite large and may represent a larger expenditure than advertising. They know the cost of advertising because most of that is paid to parties outside the firm. However, the cost of sales promotions often includes many in-store expenses that the retailer does

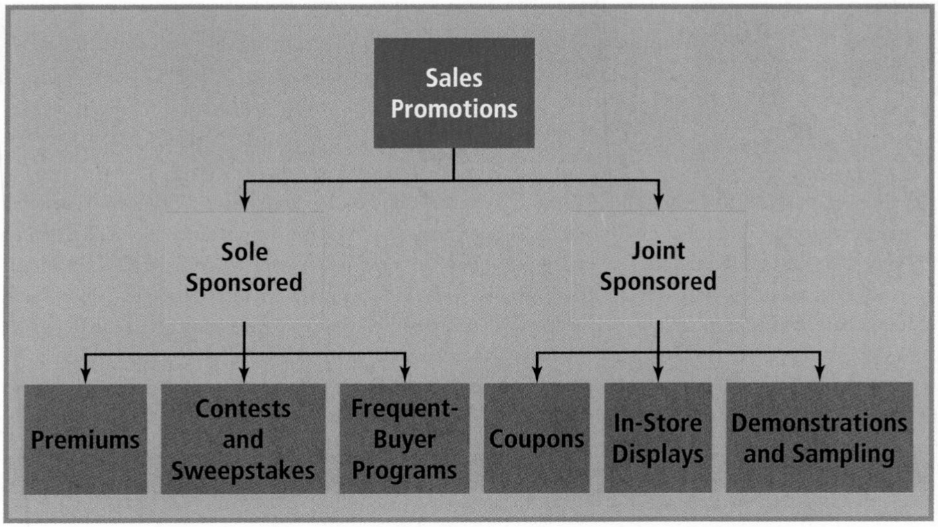

Exhibit 11.5
Types of Sales Promotion

not associate with promotion activities. If these costs were properly traced, many retailers would discover that sales promotions represent a sizable expenditure. Therefore, promotions warrant more attention by retail decision makers than is typically given.

Types of Sales Promotion

As a rule, successful retailers break sales promotions into two categories: those where they are the sole sponsors and those involving a joint effort with other parties. These are shown in Exhibit 11.5.

Sole-Sponsored Sales Promotions

Just like advertising, sales promotions are an expense to the retailer that may or may not be shared with others. With sole-sponsored sales promotions, the retailer has complete control over the promotion, but is also completely responsible for the costs. Although there may be some overlap in the sponsorship of these promotions, retailers generally consider the following sales promotions to be sole sponsored.

1. **Premiums** are extra items offered to the customer when purchasing a promoted product. Premiums are used to increase consumption among current consumers and persuade nonusers to try the promoted product. Generally the retailer is solely responsible for such programs, although some exceptions may occur. An example of a successful premium is the free toy McDonald's gives away with the purchase of a Happy Meal.
2. **Contests and sweepstakes**, which face legal restrictions in some states, are designed to create an interest in the retailer's product and encourage both repeat purchases and brand switching. Although such programs produce only one grand prize winner, the selection of a prize that will appeal to a large segment of the market and the addition of smaller prizes make such promotions very popular with consumers. Many local restaurants use weekly drawings not only to generate business, but also to track their customers.
3. **Loyalty programs**, or frequent shopper programs, are rapidly growing as retailers realize the importance of combining such promotions with their database system to

premiums
Are extra items offered to the customer when purchasing promoted products.

contests and sweepstakes
Are sales promotion techniques in which customers have a chance of winning a special prize based on entering a contest in which the entrant competes with others, or a sweepstakes in which all entrants have an equal chance of winning a prize.

loyalty programs
Are a form of sales promotion program in which buyers are rewarded with special rewards, which other shoppers are not offered for purchasing often from the retailer.

Global Retailing

Loyalty Cards in the U.K.

Back in 1995, despite press speculation that several competitors were about to launch their own customer relationship or loyalty cards, Tesco became the first United Kingdom supermarket chain to introduce a loyalty program with its Clubcard. The country's leading food chain, Sainsbury, called Tesco's introduction a gimmick, something akin to "electronic Green Shield stamps."

Using the Clubcard program Tesco has grown to become the U.K.'s market share leader despite Wal-Mart's arrival. In fact, the Clubcard has helped boost Tesco's market share in groceries to 31%, nearly double the 16% held by Wal-Mart's Asda chain. Many observers might conclude that it was the seemingly smooth and error-free development and implementation of Clubcard that was the major contributor to this success. However, while the loyalty program was strategically important to the retailer's growth, it wasn't a smooth ride. Early versions of the strategy used various forms of "reward currency or points" before settling on the simplest form (one point for one pound spent). Experiments with "loyalty levels" or thresholds of spending (similar to the gold or platinum cards offered by American hotels and airlines) were also abandoned early. In addition, a student version of the Clubcard was tried, but this proved to be too much effort for a valuable and dynamic, yet chaotically behaved, market segment. In 1999 a system of tiered additional rewards called "keys" was added to the Clubcard, allowing spending with selected outside business partners and focused on regular high-spending shoppers. This too quickly proved a failure and was withdrawn, mainly because its complexity turned consumers off. Like its American counterparts, Tesco also introduced the idea of business partners for its loyalty program. As a result, Clubcard members can not only achieve additional points when shopping with these partners, but their vouchers gain additional value when spent with these partners. However, the strategy for using and spending these tie-in points had to be simplified for ease of use.

Gimmick or not, Sainsbury and several other competitors soon introduced their own frequent shopper program. However, unlike Tesco's, many of these other loyalty cards have failed to achieve a following and other U.K. food retailers remain unconvinced about the importance of such loyalty strategies. Safeway (now taken over by Morrison's) withdrew their program in 2000, saying loyalty cards had lost their luster. Waitrose claimed that trying to analyze all the data was madness. Asda (which is now owned by Wal-Mart) argued that lower prices were the best driver of customer loyalty. Sainsbury gave up their stand-alone program and entered a co-branded multi-partner system called Nectar. Tesco's strategy, however, has prospered.

So why has Tesco's program been such a success?

From a customer perspective, Clubcard is easy to understand and to use. The expansion of the breadth of Tesco's products and services and thus the items on which customers can earn points has aided points collection. Every three months earned vouchers come in the mail with additional coupons to spend in store. As Tesco executives say, "Every little bit helps." Redemption choices are simple to make and the partner offers have proved valuable and achievable.

From the retailer's point of view, Tesco has furthered its advantage as it integrated its card with its strategic and tactical operations. The retailer's investment in analyzing and understanding the data and the improved understanding of the 12 million Britons who are members of the program have been significant. Their decision-making skills regarding both store development and general strategy have improved. At a tactical level, the data allow more accurate individual store-based marketing, as well as providing detailed understanding of local consumer behaviors and competitive effects. Without the knowledge mined from Clubcard, Tesco would have had more difficulty overtaking Sainsbury and successfully fighting off Asda/Wal-Mart. Today the retailer is not only the dominant food retailer in the U.K., but also one of the largest and fastest growing global food retailers.

In conclusion, it should be noted that Tesco has recently announced that they plan on entering the U.S. market by 2008. It should be interesting to see how they do.

Source: Leigh Sparks, Professor of Retail Studies at the Institute for Retail Studies, University of Stirling, Scotland, UK.

---

solidify their relationship with the customer. Some retailers, such as the Piggly Wiggly chain, credit loyalty programs for saving its customer base from attack by supercenters.[14] Other retailers think the benefits of using these two-tiered discount shopping cards are over-rated. The chapter's Global Retailing box looks at the development of loyalty cards in the United Kingdom.

Joint Sponsored Sales Promotions

Jointly sponsored sales promotions offer retailers the advantage of using "other people's money" (OPM). Although in some cases such promotions require the retailer to partially relinquish control, the co-sponsor's monetary offering to the retailer more than compensates. Retailers generally consider the following promotions to be jointly sponsored.

1. **Coupons** offer the retail customer a discount on the price of a specific item. Roughly 258 billion coupons are distributed annually in the U.S., and there are more of them every year, although less than 2 percent of coupons are redeemed. Coupons represent a windfall for retailers worth over $500 million since they receive, on average, a 10-cent coupon redemption fee from the manufacturers.

   For manufacturers, a coupon is a form of advertising to entice a consumer to try a product. People may forget their coupon, but buy the product anyway, because they remember seeing the coupon ad. Coupons are also used to maintain a loyal base of customers for older brands such as Kellogg's Raisin Bran and Wisk, as competitors attempt to get loyalists to switch brands by offering lower prices. Some manufacturers are testing the use of the Internet for coupon delivery. Currently, Internet sites such as http://www.valupage.com account for less than 1 percent of all redeemed coupons. Internet coupons do allow the manufacturer to benefit by obtaining vital demographic information on the consumer as well as the ability to track redemption rates.[15]

coupons
Are a sales promotion tool in which the shopper is offered a price discount on a specific item if the retailer is presented with the appropriate coupon at time of purchase.

2. **In-store displays** are promotional displays that seek to generate traffic, advertise, and encourage impulse buying. Displays such as **endcaps** (the shelving at the end of an aisle) and **register racks** at checkout offer manufacturers a captive audience for their products in the retailer's store. (Remember, the retailer does not care which brand the customer purchases, just as long as the purchase is made in its store.) As a result, the manufacturer is willing to pay for the right to "rent" the space necessary for this display from the retailer.

   The importance of these displays was illustrated by a recent study conducted by Mediaedge:cia that showed a strong correlation between shoppers noticing an in-store promotion and a resulting impulse purchase. However, not all forms of in-store media are equal, nor is the effectiveness the same with different shopper segments. For instance, endcaps and store flyers were the most noticed form of in-store advertising overall, while shopping cart ads and in-store TV ads were largely ignored by today's "on-the-go" shoppers.[16] Chapter 13 will provide a greater discussion on in-store displays.

in-store displays
Are promotional fixtures or displays that seek to generate traffic, highlight individual items, and encourage impulse buying.

3. **Demonstrations and sampling** are in-store presentations or showings whose intent is to reduce the consumer's perceived risk of purchasing a new product. These demonstrations, which accentuate ease, convenience, and/or product superiority, are paid for by the manufacturer at a price that is usually higher than the retailer's cost for providing that service.

   Joint demonstrations and sampling promotions can be undertaken with entities other than the retailer's suppliers or other retailers. Every spring, retailers, especially malls, invite landscapers and other lawn care experts onto their grounds to promote their own merchandise and services. Consumers are getting ready to prepare their lawns for the summer and appreciate the convenience of visiting with all the lawn experts at one location. In addition to bringing merchandise for sale, many lawn professionals also place samples of

demonstrations and sampling
Are in-store presentations with the intent of reducing the consumer's perceived risk of purchasing a product.

Exhibit 11.6
What Sales Promotion Can and Cannot Achieve

Tasks That Sales Promotions Can Accomplish
Get consumers to try a new product
Stimulate the sales of mature products
Neutralize competitive advertising and sales promotions
Encourage repeat usage by current users
Reinforce advertising
Tasks That Sales Promotions Cannot Achieve
Change the basic nonacceptance of an undesired product
Compensate for a poorly trained sales force
Give consumers a compelling reason to continue purchasing a product over the long run
Permanently stop an established product's declining sales trend

their work in mall hallways or parking lots. This is truly a case of using OPM (other people's money) since the retailer and malls bear no expense for this promotion; the lawn care folks are willing to do it as a form of self-promotion.

Evaluating Sales Promotions

As Exhibit 11.6 indicates, sales promotions are intended to help generate short-term increases in performance. Therefore, they should be evaluated in terms of their sales and profit-generating capability. As with advertising, sales promotions can also be evaluated with sophisticated mathematical models. However, the development and use of such models is usually not cost effective. A simpler approach is to monitor weekly unit volume before the sales promotion and compare it to weekly unit volume during and after the promotion.

Publicity Management

Publicity was defined at the outset of this chapter as non-paid-for communications of information about the company or products, generally in some media form. However, this definition is actually misleading because in many instances publicity is a contracted service. An example of this is the health reports on your local television news program. Sometimes these are in fact publicity, but at other times they may be part of the health provider's promotional contract with the station. Even when the retailer does not pay directly for publicity, it can be very expensive to have a good publicity department that plants commercially significant news in the appropriate places. It may be even more expensive to create news that is worth reporting. Consider Macy's Fourth of July fireworks display in New York, Lowe's and Home Depot's NASCAR sponsorship, McDonald's Ronald McDonald Houses, and Dee Lincoln's purchase of the crossbreed steer, described earlier in the chapter's Service Retailing box on page 365. All create favorable publicity; but all are expensive.

Recently some experts have suggested that publicity may be more important to a retailer than advertising. They claim that advertising can only maintain brands that have already been created by publicity. These experts cite examples of some successful modern retailers, including Starbucks and The Cheesecake Factory that have been built with virtually no advertising. Consider the case a few years back when Paris Hilton did an ad for Carl's Jr.'s Spicy BBQ Burger. The ad generated so much publicity across the country that many called the spicy ad nothing more than a naked publicity grab. Yet, the media coverage generated was what the restaurant chain wanted. While it is doubtful that publicity is more important than

What's New?

Internet Falsehoods

There isn't any doubt that the Internet is a great source of information for both the retailer and the consumer. However, what happens when that information is false?

Consider an e-mail that has been circulating around the country for the past couple of years about Starbucks Coffee. The e-mail accused "Starbucks of refusing to donate free coffee to U.S. Marines on the grounds that the company is against the Iraq war 'and anyone in it.'" There was just one problem—the e-mail wasn't true. It is unclear whether any Starbucks employee ever actually refused to donate coffee to Marines serving in Iraq. However, if they did, it wasn't because, as the above e-mail claims, "they don't support the war and anyone in it."

Starbucks PR people have explained that while the company has "the deepest respect and admiration for U.S. military personnel," corporate policy prohibits direct donations to U.S. troops because the military doesn't fall under the strict definition of a public charity. The PR spokesperson went on to explain that "individual employees are free to donate their weekly pounds of take-home coffee, however, and many have done so." Starbucks has put out its version of the story on its Web site and on its toll-free phone line.

Today, the Internet has made it possible for angry consumers to rapidly spread such false stories about any retailers. Unfortunately, only in rare circumstances do retailers ever find out who started the false rumors. There have been rumors about snakes found in overcoats, a fast-food chain using worms in its hamburgers, a global furniture retailer selling a cactus filled with a nest of deadly spiders, and another fast-food retailer slaughtering chickens inhumanely. You probably have heard some of these stories, as well as many others. Have you ever noticed that the events related in the stories never actually happened to the people sending you the e-mail, but rather to some "friend of a friend"?

For retailers to be able to handle these falsehoods, they must first be aware of them. Therefore, it is important for retailers to maintain a systematic program of monitoring the online rumor mill. This is what many fast-food chains were already doing in 2005 and 2006, in anticipation of the avian flu arriving in the United States.[17] For many retailers, simply checking general Web sites, such as urbanlegends.com or urbanlegands.about.com, may be effective. After all, once the rumor is known, appropriate remedies can be developed. However, some (ex)customers get so mad at retailers that they develop Web sites targeted directly at the retailer. These sites begin with the originator's complaints and soon generate both additional complaints and questionable events that, whether true or not, contribute to a negative public perception of the retailer. The most common names for these so-called complaint URLs are ihate(retailer's name).com or (retailer's name) sucks.com. There are currently 68 active Web sites with such names as ihatewalmart.com, bestbuysux.com, paypalsucks.com, radioshacksucks.com, and uhaul-sucks.com. There is even one for retail employees (retail-sucks.com) to share their frustrations and complaints with each other about their jobs. In other cases, individuals have created Web sites that work on misspellings of the retailer's name; examples include Untied Airlines: The Most Unfriendly Skies (untied. com) which is aimed at United Airlines and (unitedpackagesmashers.com) which targets United Parcel Services. Others use a play on the retailer's name, such as againstthewal.com, which focuses on Wal-Mart.

As a result, successful retailers who want to prevent such behavior have adopted a four-pronged plan:

1. Buy the URLs for their name followed by the word "sucks.com" or preceded by the word "ihate."
2. Locate the Web site's creator and determine why he or she is angry. If possible, apologize and then fix the problem before it irritates others.
3. Tell your side of the story on your Web site, as Starbucks has done.
4. When all else fails, take the hate site creators to court. Many will back away from a costly court battle. The courts will find in favor of the retailer if libel or slander can be proven. There are a couple of legal precedents to keep in mind. First, the 6th Circuit Court of Appeals has held that a domain name holder's use of another's trademark in a 'fan' site did not run afoul of Section 1114 of the Lanham Act because of the presence of both a prominent disclaimer on the site disavowing any affiliation with the mark owner, and a link to the plaintiff's official Web site. Second, the domain holder's use of the trademarks in conjunction with the word "sucks" in the domain names of non-commercial complaint sites did not violate Section 1114 of the Lanham Act because there was no likelihood of consumer confusion arising from that type of use, and because such speech is protected by the First Amendment of the U.S. Constitution.

Source: Taubman Company v. Webfeats, et al., Nos. 01-2648/2725 (6th Cir., February 7, 2003), Starbucks PR Department and all Web sites are current as of May 16, 2006.

advertising, as these experts claim, these examples do point out the importance of managing your firm's publicity.

Publicity (like other forms of promotion) has its strengths and weaknesses. When publicity is formally managed, it should be integrated with other elements of the promotion mix. In addition, all publicity should reinforce the store's image. Perhaps the major advantages of publicity are that it is objective and credible and appeals to a mass audience. Consider, for example the "Oprah Effect" that is generated when Oprah Winfrey mentions a book.[18] The Effect works for products as well. One of the author's favorite ice cream shops, Graeter's in Cincinnati, received nearly 500 orders via its toll-free phone number and Web site the day after Oprah called it the "best ice cream I've ever tasted" on her television show.[19] As the chapter's Retailing: What's New box points out in this age of the Internet, the major disadvantage of publicity is that it is difficult to control and schedule, especially when it involves falsehoods.

Dollars & Sense

Retailers who prepare for various types of negative publicity in advance will be more profitable.

STUDENT STUDY GUIDE

SUMMARY

LO 1

What are the four basic components of the retailer's promotion mix and how are they related to other retailer decisions?

A retailer's promotion mix comprises advertising, sales promotions, publicity, and personal selling. All four components need to be managed from a total systems perspective and must be integrated not only with each other but with the retailer's other managerial decision areas such as location, merchandise, credit, cash flow, building and fixtures, price, and customer service. In addition, the retailer must realize that its promotional activities may be in conflict with the way other supply chain members use promotion.

LO 2

What are the differences between a retailer's long-term and short-term promotional objectives?

A retailer's promotional objectives should be established to help improve both long- and short-term financial performance. Long-term, or institutional, advertising is an attempt by the retailer to gain long-term benefits by selling the store itself rather than the merchandise in it. Retailers seeking long-term benefits generally have two long-term promotion objectives: creating a positive store image and promoting public service.

Short-term, or promotional, advertising attempts to bolster short-term performance by using product availability or price as a selling point. The two most common promotional objectives are (1) increasing patronage of existing customers and (2) attracting new customers.

LO 3

What six steps are involved in developing a retail advertising campaign?

The six steps involved in developing a retail advertising campaign are: (1) selecting advertising objectives, (2) budgeting for the campaign, (3) designing the message, (4) selecting the media to use, (5) scheduling the ads, and (6) evaluating the results.

The advertising objectives should flow from the retailer's promotion objectives and should consider several factors that are unique to retailing such as the store's age and location, the merchandise sold, the competition, size of the market, and level of supplier support. The specific objectives that advertising can accomplish are many and varied and the ones chosen depend on these factors.

When developing a budget, retailers must decide whether they can get a better return on their money with co-op dollars or by total sponsorship of advertising. In budgeting advertising funds, retailers tend to use the affordable method, the percentage-of-sales method, or the task-and-objective method. While most retail advertising is paid for solely by the retailer, sometimes manufacturers and other retailers may pay part or all of the costs for the retailer's advertising campaign. For example, vertical cooperative advertising allows the retailer and other supply chain members to share the advertising burden while horizontal cooperative advertising enables two or more retailers to band together to share the cost of advertising.

Retailers must develop a creative retail ad that accomplishes three goals: attracts and retains attention, achieves its objective, and avoids errors. Some of the common approaches that retailers use to gain repeated viewing include showing how the retailer's products fit in with the consumer's lifestyle, creating a fantasy for the consumer that is built around the retailer's products, designing the campaign around humor that relates to the uses of the retailer's products, depicting the consumer in everyday settings using the retailer's products, and building a mood around using the retailer's products. Before publishing any ad, the retailer should pretest it with both consumer groups and legal experts for errors.

Once the budget is established, it should be allocated in such a way that it maximizes the retailer's overall profitability. In determining allocations, retailers can choose from a variety of media alternatives, primarily newspapers, television, radio, magazines, direct mail, and the Internet. Each medium has its own advantages and disadvantages. To choose among the media, the retailer should know their strengths and weaknesses, coverage and reach, and the cost of an ad.

After the retailer selects a medium, it must decide when the ad should appear. While there is no single "right" time to run an ad, conventional wisdom suggests that the ads should (1) appear on, or slightly precede, the days when customers are most likely to purchase, (2) be concentrated around the times when people receive their payroll checks, (3) be concentrated during periods of highest demand, (4) be timed to appear during the time of day or day of week when the best CPM (or CPM-TM) will be obtained, and (5) precede the purchase time, especially for habitually purchased products.

Advertising results can be assessed in terms of efficiency and effectiveness. Effectiveness is the extent to which advertising has produced the result desired. Efficiency is concerned with whether the result was achieved with minimum cost.

How do retailers manage their sales promotion and publicity? LO 4

Retailers use sales promotions, which provide some type of short-term incentive, and publicity to increase the effectiveness of their promotional efforts. The role of sales promotions and publicity in the retail organization should be consistent with and reinforce the retailer's overall promotional objectives.

Sales promotion tools are excellent demand generators. Many can be used on relatively short notice and can help the retailer achieve its overall promotion goals. Retailers usually break sales promotions into two categories: those where they are the sole sponsors (premiums, contests and sweepstakes, and loyalty programs) and those involving a joint effort with other parties (coupons, displays, and demonstrations and sampling).

Although retailers may not pay for publicity directly, the indirect cost can be quite significant. Most retailers do not have formal publicity departments or directors, but some of the larger, more progressive retailers do. The major advantages of publicity are that it is objective, credible, and appeals to a mass audience. The major disadvantage is that publicity is difficult to control and schedule.

TERMS TO REMEMBER

promotion
advertising
sales promotion
publicity
personal selling
primary trading area
secondary trading area
institutional advertising
promotional advertising
affordable method
percentage-of-sales method
task-and-objective method
vertical cooperative advertising
horizontal cooperative advertising
coverage
reach
cumulative reach
frequency
cost per thousand method (CPM)
cost per thousand—target market (CPM-TM)
impact
advertising effectiveness
advertising efficiency
premiums
contests and sweepstakes
loyalty programs
coupons
in-store displays
demonstrations and sampling

REVIEW AND DISCUSSION QUESTIONS

LO 1

What are the four basic components of the retailer's promotion mix and how are they related to other retailer decisions?

1. Why should a retailer feature price and not product features in its ads for national branded products?
2. How could the promotional efforts of other members of a retailer's channel affect the retailer's promotional decisions? Isn't the marketing supply chain supposed to be a partnership?

LO 2

What are the differences between a retailer's long-term and short-term promotional objectives?

3. Explain how a long-term promotional objective can affect the firm over the short run.
4. Should the promotional objectives for e-tailers be the same as those for bricks-and-mortar retailers, such as a department store? Explain your answer.

LO 3

What six steps are involved in developing a retail advertising campaign?

5. What factors that are unique to retailing should be considered before selecting an advertising objective? Which one of these factors is most important?
6. Describe the three methods available to the retailer for determining the amount to spend on advertising. Which one is the best one to use? Which one is most commonly used by small retailers?

7. Some retailers decline a vendor's offer of cooperative advertising; is this smart? After all, aren't they passing up "free" money?
8. An old proverb claims that "Doing advertising without planning is like running a giant manure spreader; your advertising department throws words out the back faster than you can shovel money in the front." Do you agree or disagree with this statement? Explain your reasoning.
9. What methods should a retailer use in selecting ad media?
10. How should a small town retailer use the Internet?

How do retailers manage their sales promotion and publicity? LO 4

11. What is sales promotion? How is it different from advertising?
12. What is publicity? Isn't this always free to the retailer? How does publicity fit into a retailer's promotional efforts?
13. You own a small chain of music stores, Ben's House of Music, serving three nearby towns. Earlier this morning an employee came into your office and said that while surfing the Web last night he came across a Web site called Ihatebenshouseofmusic.com. What should you do?

SAMPLE TEST QUESTIONS

Which of the following areas should not be taken into consideration by a retailer when formulating a promotional strategy? LO 1

a. the retailer's credit customers
b. the price level of the merchandise
c. merchandise/inventory levels
d. the retailer's building and fixtures
e. the retailer's net worth

The two objectives of institutional advertising include: LO 2

a. Creating a positive store image and public service promotion
b. Increasing patronage from existing customers and attracting new customers
c. Publicity and sales promotion
d. Advertising a sale and generating store traffic
e. Using "other people's money" and using "co-op" money

Which of the following should not be part of The Campus Shoppe's advertising campaign's objectives. The Campus Shoppe desires to increase LO 3

a. awareness of its two locations
b. sales among incoming freshmen
c. sales to 40 percent
d. sales over the next three months.
e. All of the above belong in the retailer's advertising objectives.

Consumer premiums are considered to be a form of: LO 4

a. joint-sponsored sales promotion
b. publicity that utilizes OPM
c. advertising
d. personal selling
e. sole-sponsored sales promotion

WRITING AND SPEAKING EXERCISE

As the summer intern for your uncle's 30,000 square foot grocery store in a town of 5,000, you have been approached by your uncle to discuss some nagging retailing issues. The town has three convenience stores, but no other grocery store. There is a supercenter in the county-seat 19 miles away.

As a member of a wholesale-sponsored voluntary group, your uncle's store participates in the group's loyalty club card program. Overall, he seems happy with the program but recently two events have caused him to ask you for advice.

The first occurred about two months ago, when one of his regular customers mentioned as she presented her loyalty card to him at the cash register that it was her birthday; then she asked if she got a gift or discount. Your uncle seemed surprised at the remark and asked, "What gives you that idea?" She explained that since the loyalty card application asked for her birthday, she just assumed that she would get something. Actually, the out-of-town company running the program never shared that information with your uncle.

The second issue was whether he should continue running coupons in the weekly newspaper. The frequent shopper/loyalty program is focused on offering low prices to regular customers. Hasn't its growth eliminated the need for coupons? Isn't a frequent shopper program designed as an alternative to coupons? By using both, isn't the store double rewarding the same customers? Since the loyalty card strategy enables him to target precisely the customers he wants to reach with a special offer, is it still cost effective to offer newspaper coupons?

Given this information, prepare a memo for your uncle with your recommendation.

RETAIL PROJECT

Find two current advertisements using the same medium (newspaper, television, radio, Internet, etc.) that you feel are effective in achieving their objectives and two that you do not feel are effective.

Explain what you understand each ad's objectives to be and why you categorized them as you did.

In reviewing the ineffective ads, was something wrong with the creative design? Did they fail to hold the consumer's attention, or did they use the wrong medium to reach their intended market? How would you improve these ads?

PLANNING YOUR OWN RETAIL BUSINESS

Your Uncle Nick has agreed to sell you his supermarket where you have worked for seven years, since graduating from college. Uncle Nick is 72 years old and is ready to step down from day-to-day management.

After operating the Crest Supermarket on your own for six months, you begin to analyze how you can increase store traffic and, consequently, annual sales and profitability. During a recent trip to the Food Marketing Institute convention you ran across several successful grocers. Some of them competed largely on price, while others competed more on promotion and advertising.

You decide to pursue a heavy promotion-oriented strategy. Consequently, you budget to increase advertising by $20,000 monthly or $240,000 annually and to also have a weekly contest where you give away $100 in groceries to 25 families. This will cost you $130,000 (52 × $100 × 25) annually.

Currently Crest Supermarket serves a trade area with a 2-mile radius and a household density of 171 per square mile. Seventy percent of these households shop at Crest an average of 45 times per year. Of those that visit Crest, 98 percent make a purchase that averages $24.45. Crest operates on a 25 percent gross margin.

You estimate that with your new promotion program, the radius of Crest's trade area will increase to 2.5 miles. Assuming that all other relevant factors remain constant (171 households per square mile, 70 percent of households shop Crest, 98 percent closure rate, $24.45 average transaction size, 25 percent gross margin percent), is the planned promotion program and investment of an additional $370,000 annually a profitable strategy?

Hint: Assume the trade area is circular and thus its size in square miles can be computed as pi (22/7) times the radius of the circle squared. The total square miles of the trade area can be multiplied by the number of households per square mile to obtain total households in the trade area. This in turn can be multiplied by the percentage that shop at Crest, which in turn can be multiplied by the average number of trips annually to Crest, which will yield total traffic. This traffic statistic can be multiplied by the percent of visitors that make a purchase, which will yield total transactions. You should be able to figure out on your own the rest of the computations that are needed to determine if the promotional strategy is profitable.

CASE

The Bandanna*

The following letter was sent to a mall recently.

Alison Stiles
5319 Walnut Hill Drive
Indianapolis, Indiana 46202
aestiles@hotmail.com
October 4, 2006

To Whom It May Concern:

Last weekend, I drove four hours from my home in Indianapolis, Indiana to visit my boyfriend, a grad student at Washington University, St. Louis. It wouldn't have been a noteworthy trip, except that the last time I came to St. Louis I ended up at Barnes-Jewish Hospital for a week with a dangerous infection. I have breast cancer and am undergoing chemotherapy, so my immune system is not what it once was. After that scare I decided to wait until my immune system was up before making the trip again. I had my final infusion last month, the drugs ran their course, and so at long last I packed my weekend bag. My bag probably has a somewhat different style than most women with breast cancer—mine is usually filled with low-rise jeans and baby-tees. Did I mention that I'm 29? I'm 29.

Like most other women with breast cancer, my hair called it quits when the chemotherapy started. So, I'm a hip bald chick. I'll admit that around friends and family I'm pretty comfortable showing scalp, but in public I try to cover up—fewer stares that way. But, I've found that most traditional headscarves and hats cramp my style. I prefer a simple bandanna. Classic.

On the Saturday of my grand return to St. Louis, my boyfriend and I hit the town. We did some shopping, visited the Landing, saw the Arch, and then were going to cap off a great day with a trip to Riverside. I was having a perfect day—the kind of day when I can forget, for a few hours or so, that I am 29 and have cancer. That day, I was just a normal, healthy 29-year-old visiting her boyfriend.

We had been wandering around Riverside Mall for about a half an hour or so when I was approached by a security guard. At first I didn't realize he was speaking to me—my boyfriend and I had been waiting for the show at the Fudgery to begin, not bothering anyone, not creating anything resembling a disturbance. Why would he be speaking to me? Once he got my attention, he told me that I would have to take off my bandanna.

And then—whomp!—I remembered. I have cancer. Reality. I took a step towards him and, trying not to draw attention, lifted the bandanna just enough that he could see the few wisps of hair left on my scalp. I then had to say the words I have come to hate: "I have cancer."

I thought that would be enough; that he might apologize and leave me be. But he didn't. He told me that my condition didn't matter—there were no bandannas allowed. Never mind that I have never been asked to remove my chosen headwear before; not anywhere in Indianapolis, not anywhere in Chicago; not anywhere in Louisville. If I wanted to continue wearing it I would have to put on a medical bracelet. He very kindly offered to have a bracelet provided to me for my bandanna-wearing purposes.

So, now I was 29, had cancer, and was being tagged. Don't get me wrong; I can guess why bandannas are prohibited mall attire. I imagine it would have something to do with gangs and gang violence. Now, St. Louis may have a problem with gang violence of which I am unaware. But I am aware that those of us in the "Breast Cancer Gang" are less inclined to violence than your average gang member. We're a rather peaceful bunch, really. Something about the unending fatigue, the humiliation of losing much of your dignity (not to mention your hair), and the regular vomiting just drives the urge to hurt others right out of you.

Which is why, when I felt the tears in my eyes at the thought of having to put on a stupid medical bracelet to walk through a stupid mall instead of taking out the months of humiliation, loss of dignity, frustration, fear, and plain old anger out on the guard who was just trying to enforce a policy that he didn't institute but was paid to enforce, I left your mall. But I also promised myself that I would never, ever return—and that I would send out this letter voicing how the experience made me feel. An overreaction? Maybe. But, the way I see it, I've already had to put up with quite a lot. Arbitrary and ineffective mall rules cross the line. And, I hate to say it, but in my mind St. Louis is no longer the city I thought I knew. I grew up in St. Louis, but now instead of thinking of the old neighborhood and the Arch and the Botanical Gardens and the Cardinals, I'll think of cancer and gangs and insensitivity, all thanks to the policies of a place which calls itself "the number one attraction in St. Louis."

Ironically, October is "Breast Cancer Awareness Month." And believe me, I am aware. I hope that others become aware, too, and that the proud women who follow me in treatment and survival wear whatever they damn well please on their bald heads and go wherever they damn like. I hope Riverside and any other public place which has any policy against any type of headwear rethinks that policy, or at least makes an exception for women who are engaged full-time with a battle for their lives and have other things to worry about. And, I hope that someday, no woman will have to say at any age, to a mall security guard or anyone else, "I have cancer."

Sincerely,
Alison Stiles

cc: Riverside Mall
Mayor Francis G. Slay
KSDK-TV, St. Louis
Fox 2, St. Louis
St. Louis Post Dispatch
Susan G. Komen Foundation
Young Survival Coalition
American Cancer Society

The mall responded with the following e-mail letter.
From: "Stacy Barnes" <stacybarnes@stlus.com>
To: <aestiles@hotmail.com>
Subject: response letter
Date: Fri, 14 Oct 2006 16:37:42 -0500

Dear Ms. Stiles,
Thank you for expressing your thoughts and concerns regarding our code of conduct. We appreciate your comments and regret any hard feelings.

It is important that you know that our primary goal at Riverside Mall is to offer a safe and comfortable shopping environment for all of our visitors. We are committed to treating our shoppers in a fair, consistent and sensitive manner and are upset that you felt that you were treated unfairly.

Our policy was put in place five years ago to ensure the safety of our more than 6 million shoppers annually and this is the first time that a reaction of this type has occurred. The policy is quite specific in its language so that it addresses only those types of apparel that are worn to support gang activity. Unfortunately, your head covering fell into that category. The dress code does have an exception for those with medical conditions, such as yourself.

In an effort to accommodate every person and every kind of situation with sensitivity, when those with medical conditions such as cancer are stopped for non-compliance with the dress code, they are asked to wear a small wristband to enable them to continue to shop without being stopped again by the public safety officers. The intention is not to single out any individual, but to avoid any further interruption to your visit.

We regularly review the policies and the code to make sure they are up to date and are appropriate for the current environment.

We thank you again for your comments and we assure you that we will review our policies in the near future with your situation in mind.

Sincerely,

Stacy L. Barnes
Marketing Director
Riverside Mall
314-555-5555 ext. 7032
314-555-5556 fax

Questions

1. If you were the marketing director for a retailer and received such a letter, would you have replied the same way that Ms. Barnes did?
2. Does a retailer's imposition of hard-and-fast rules cause bad PR? (After all, a breast cancer victim wearing a bandanna could hardly be mistaken for a gang member. The lack of hair, missing eyelashes, and a pale complexion should have been a clue.)
3. Since the press was copied on Ms. Stiles' letter, should the mall copy them on its reply?

* While the names of the individuals and the mall have been changed, everything else is as it occurred.

chapter 12

Customer Services and Retail Selling

OVERVIEW:

In this chapter, we demonstrate how customer services, including retail selling, generate additional demand for the retailer's merchandise. We also examine the determination of an optimal customer service level. We conclude the chapter by looking at the unique managerial problems that retailers must address.

LEARNING OBJECTIVES:

After reading this chapter, you should be able to:

1. Explain why customer service is so important in retailing.
2. Describe the various customer services that a retailer can offer.
3. Explain how a retailer should determine which services to offer.
4. Describe the various management problems involved in retail selling, salesperson selection, and training and evaluation.
5. Describe the retail selling process.
6. Understand the importance of a customer service audit.

LO 1

Customer Service

Why is customer service so important in retailing?

The old rules about customer loyalty are obsolete. Today's customers are tired of making a series of wishes (see the shopper's wish list in Exhibit 12.1) before embarking on their planned purchases. Now customers define loyalty on their terms, not the retailer's. Little wonder then, the average firm loses half of its customers every five years.[1] And as Exhibit 12.2 illustrates, even those customers who continue to shop with a particular retailer—in this case Wal-Mart—are not always loyal. Without exception, it is a fact of life that all retailers must give consideration to the service level and services they offer their customers.

high-quality service
Is the type of service that meets or exceeds customers' expectations.

High-quality service is defined as delivering service that meets or exceeds customers' expectations. In this definition there is no absolute level of quality service, but only service that is perceived as high quality because it meets and exceeds the expectations of customers. For example, suppose a consumer has lunch at a restaurant at which he or she expects to have slow service and is served in 10 minutes. The next day at lunch, the same consumer eats at another restaurant where he or she expects to have fast service and again is served in 10 minutes. Even assuming that other factors such as cleanliness, friendliness, and food quality are equal, this consumer might report the service quality to be better in the first

Exhibit 12.1
A Shopper's Wish

Please . . .

- Let me find a parking place near the store.
- Do not let me pay too much.
- Have the sales staff pretend that they care.
- Do not make me have to return anything.
- Get me in and out as fast as possible.
- Do not make me wait in line to make my purchase.
- Let this experience be somewhat enjoyable.
- Do not make me have to deal with other obnoxious shoppers.

Exhibit 12.2
The Cross Shopping Trend, 2006

	Monthly Shoppers at Retailer		
Monthly Shoppers at Retailer	**Kmart/Big Kmart**	**Target**	**Wal-Mart**
Kmart/Big Kmart	100.00%	17.04%	15.03%
Target	39.20%	100.00%	30.52%
Wal-Mart	56.41%	49.80%	100.00%
Small-Format Value Retailers	55.92%	36.21%	44.47%
Drug Store/Pharmacies	56.18%	54.94%	52.05%
JCPenney	21.27%	16.67%	13.37%
Kohl's	16.43%	20.29%	12.45%
Sears	18.51%	11.28%	9.29%
Apparel Specialty Stores	44.14%	48.52%	33.67%

Source: Retail Forward ShopperScape™, January 2006–September 2006

restaurant, because the 10-minute service was faster than expected, and report lower service quality in the second restaurant, because the 10-minute service was slower than expected. On an absolute basis, the service was the same in each case—good food in 10 minutes—but the customer's evaluation was different due to different expectations. Just the opposite may be expected at dinner. Here you will want to enjoy the time you are having with friends and family, and 10-minute service may be perceived as an unsatisfactory rush job because it prevents you from visiting with your friends. Another illustration of this concept is regarding customers who have a problem with a purchase. If these problems are handled swiftly and politely (above their expectations), these customers will end up being more loyal to the retailer than customers who never encountered a problem.

In an attempt to offer the high-quality service expected and to reduce these defections, retailers are now engaging in relationship retailing programs.[2] **Relationship retailing** includes all the activities designed to attract, retain, and enhance customer relationships. Retailing will no longer be driven by the expansion of large, homogeneous, big-box chains offering only low prices. Profitable retailers of the future will be those who concentrate on building long-term relations with loyal customers by promising and consistently delivering high-quality products, enhanced by high-quality

relationship retailing Comprises all the activities designed to attract, retain, and enhance long-term relationships with customers.

service, shopping aids to ease the purchase process, and honest pricing to build and maintain a reputation for absolute trustworthiness. Loyal customers are less prone to shop other retailers selling the same merchandise mix and are less price conscious.[3] In addition, an Office of Consumer Affairs study found that it costs a retailer five times as much money to attract a new customer as it does to convince a former customer to return.[4] As a result, today's retailers are not trying to maximize the profit on each transaction, but are instead seeking to build a mutually beneficial relationship with their customers. The new operating maxim for retailers is: Proper management of relationships will produce a satisfied customer who will become a repeat customer. And repeat customers produce long-term profits. Leo Shapiro, a well-known retail consultant, claimed that the "dollars that walk out of a store every day to be spent at a competitor's store represent the most immediate, major source of potential sales and profit growth."[5] Robert Kahn, another retail consultant discussed earlier in the text, often argued that just reducing the amount of customer defections by as little as 10 percent could often double a retailer's profits.

Dollars & Sense

Successful retailers are those who realize that the longer a customer stays with a retailer, the more profitable that customer is to their operations.

Profitable retailers can develop these relationships with their customers by offering two benefits:

1. *Financial benefits* that increase the customer's satisfaction, such as the frequent purchaser discounts or product upgrades already offered by some supermarkets, airlines, and hotels.
2. *Social benefits* that increase the retailer's interaction with the customer. Chapter 13 will discuss how shopping can be a pleasant experience for the customer. Retailers must not forget that their stores must offer customers a combination of excitement and entertainment.

Exhibit 12.3 highlights retailing's three most basic tasks: getting consumers from your trading area into your store, converting these consumers into loyal customers, and doing so in the most efficient manner possible. Chapter 7 described how retailers determine their trading area. The earlier chapters of Part 4, Chapters 8 through 11, discussed the first task: how retailers budget for and select their merchandise, and then price and promote this merchandise. In addition, Chapter 8

Exhibit 12.3
Three Basic Tasks of Retailing

covered the third task by describing the basic method for controlling inventory cost. The next two chapters will discuss the second and most important task—converting the consumer from your trading area who has decided to try your store into a loyal (and thus profitable) customer.

Due to significant cost cutting following the recent period of retailer consolidation and retrenchment, this second task is even more difficult. Retailers today are so standardized in either their physical layout or Web site design, with each one carrying the same merchandise styles and colors, that customers cannot tell them apart. More importantly, many current retailers have an indifferent and poorly or inadequately trained sales force. As a result, there is a complete breakdown of what is essential for a successful retailer: exciting merchandise backed up by outstanding service, and personal selling that generates loyal customers. In recent years, intense competition from discounters caused many retailers to lower customer service levels as a means of staying price competitive. These retailers felt that reduced service levels would lower their operating costs, thus allowing increased price competitiveness. No wonder that for most customers, shopping trips do not always meet their expectations and result in an unsatisfying experience.[6]

Retailers must differentiate themselves by meeting the needs of their customers better than the competition. Thus, successful retailers have again come to realize that customer service is a strength. Instead of frustrating the customer by not having the necessary stock on hand or the proper selling support on the sales floor, today's profitable retailers realize that customer service is a major demand generator. However, it is important that retailers also remember that when they encourage high customer expectations, the slightest disappointment in service can be a catastrophe. Even Nordstrom, the retailer most famous for its outstanding service, cannot please all its customers all the time. One study quoted an unhappy customer as saying: "Never during our visit did she ask me how much money I wanted to spend, who my favorite designers were . . . or what fashion pet peeves I had."[7] Although the Nordstrom salesperson really did not make any mistake, the retailer nonetheless failed to live up to the very high expectations that it had trained its customers to expect.

Customer service consists of all those activities performed by the retailer that influence (1) the ease with which a potential customer can shop or learn about the retailer's offering, (2) the ease with which a transaction can be completed once the customer attempts to make a purchase, and (3) the customer's satisfaction with the transaction. These three elements are the pretransaction, transaction, and posttransaction components of customer service. Some common services provided by retailers include alterations, fitting rooms, delivery, gift registries, check cashing, in-home shopping, extended shopping hours, gift wrapping, charge accounts, parking, layaway, and merchandise return privileges. One must remember that none of these services are altruistic offerings; they are all designed to entice the customers with whom the retailer is seeking to develop a relationship. After all, successful retailers don't try to satisfy customers just because the customers deserve it. Rather, they do it because "firms that actually achieve high customer satisfaction also enjoy superior economic returns."[8]

customer service
Consists of all those activities performed by the retailer that influence (1) the ease with which a potential customer can shop or learn about the store's offering, (2) the ease with which a transaction can be completed once the customer attempts to make a purchase, and (3) the customer's satisfaction with the transaction.

Retailers should design their customer service program around pretransaction, transaction, and posttransaction elements of the sale in order to obtain a differential competitive advantage. After all, in today's world of mass distribution, most retailers have access to the same merchandise and, therefore, retailers can seldom differentiate themselves from others solely on the basis of merchandise stocked. The same can be said regarding location and store design advantages. Retailers can, however, obtain a high degree of differentiation through their customer service programs.

A retail shopping experience is more than negotiating your way through the retailer's store, Web site or catalog, finding the merchandise you want, interacting (or not interacting) with the staff, and paying for the merchandise. It also involves your actions before and after the transaction. Therefore, serving the customer before, during, and after the transaction can help to create new customers and strengthen the loyalty of present customers. If customer service before the transaction is poor, the probability of a transaction occurring will decline. If customer service is poor at the transaction stage, the customer may back out of the transaction. And if customer service is poor after the transaction, the probability of a repeat purchase at the same store will decline. The customer who visits a retailer and finds the service level below expectations or the product "out of stock" will become a **transient customer**. This transient, or temporary, customer will seek to find a retailer with the level of customer service he or she feels is appropriate. At any given moment, for all lines of retail trade, there are a significant number of transient customers. The retailer with a superior customer service program will have a significant advantage in turning these transients into loyal customers. Thus, customer service can play a significant role in building a retailer's sales volume.

transient customer
Is an individual who is dissatisfied with the level of customer service offered at a store or stores and is seeking an alternative store with the level of customer service that he or she thinks is appropriate.

Customer service cannot happen all by itself, but must be integrated into all aspects of retailing. That is why the profitable retailers of the future will know that the demand for their merchandise is not simply price elastic, as economists would have us believe. It is also *service elastic*, which means that an increase in service levels of 1 percent will result in more than a 1 percent increase in sales.

Merchandise Management

Chapter 9 discussed the importance of merchandise management since one of the best ways a retailer can serve a customer is by having what the customer wants in inventory. There are few things more disturbing to a customer than making a trip to a store for a specific item only to discover that the item is out of stock. This is why Nordstrom offers its customers a free dress shirt if it is ever out of stock on any of the basic sizes. This retailer wants the customers to be confident of locating any style, color, or size. Basically, the better the store is at allocating inventory in proportion to customer demand patterns, the better the customer will be served.

Building and Fixture Management

Retailers' decisions regarding building and fixtures can also have a significant effect on how well the customer is served. For example, consider how the following noncomprehensive list of building and fixture dimensions might influence customer service: heating and cooling levels; availability of parking space; ease of finding merchandise; layout and arrangement of fixtures; placement of restrooms and lounge areas; location of check-cashing, complaint, and returns desks; level of lighting; and width and length of aisles.

Promotion Management

Promotion provides customers with information that can help them make purchase decisions. Therefore, retailers should be concerned with whether the promotion programs they develop assist the consumer. The following questions can help the retailer assess whether its promotion is serving the customer:

1. Is the advertising informative and helpful?
2. Does the advertising provide all the information the customer needs?
3. Are the salespeople helpful and informative?

4. Are the salespeople friendly and courteous?
5. Are the salespeople easy to find when needed?
6. Are sufficient quantities available on sales promotion items?
7. Do salespeople know about the ad and what's being promoted and why?

This list is not comprehensive, but rather is intended only to show that customer service issues need to be considered in designing promotional programs.

Price Management

Price management will also influence how well the customer is served. Are prices clearly marked and visible? Is pricing fair, honest, and straightforward? Are customers told the true price of credit? These questions suggest that the pricing decision should not be isolated from the retailer's customer service program.

Credit Management

The management of credit, both in-house and bank card, should also be integrated into the customer service program. Credit, along with the retailer's layaway plans, is a significant aid in both encouraging loyalty and helping consumers purchase merchandise. Retailers' credit policies influence the customers' perception of how well they are being serviced. Some retailers have recently begun issuing their own co-branded credit cards. Today, Target is one of the top 10 credit card issuers in the United States. The retailer hopes that these cards, in addition to increasing exposure, awareness, and store loyalty to Target, will aid the retailer in tracking customer purchases and obtain data, as well as make a healthy profit on the credit transactions.[9]

Michael Nagle/Bloomberg News/Landov

Starbucks has a co-branded credit card with Visa that provides an additional revenue stream as well as valuable information on its customers.

A Recap

Integration between the elements of the retail mix is important when retailers develop their customer service programs. Much of what has already been discussed in this book relates, either directly or indirectly, to one of the three broad categories of customer service: pretransaction, transaction, and posttransaction. Successful retailers view customer service as a way to gain an advantage over the competition. As a result, even discounters are beginning to empower all their employees, not just management, to do whatever is reasonable to take care of the customer.

Dollars & Sense

The more profitable retailers will integrate customer service decisions with their merchandise, promotion, building and fixtures, price, and credit management decisions.

LO 2

Common Customer Services

What are the various customer services that a retailer can offer?

Much of the discussion in previous chapters on location, merchandise, pricing, and promotion had implications for serving the customer. However, many of the more popular types of customer service have not been mentioned or have received sparse coverage. Let us review some of them.

Pretransaction Services

pretransaction services
Are services provided to the customer prior to entering the store.

The most common **pretransaction services**, which are provided to the customer prior to entering the store, are convenient hours and information aids. Each of these makes it easier for the potential customer to shop or to learn of the retailer's offering.

Convenient Hours

The more convenient the retailer's operating hours are to the customer, the easier it is for the customer to visit the retailer. Convenient operating hours are the most basic service that a retailer should provide to its customers. Retailers must ascertain what their customers want and weigh the cost of providing those wants against the additional revenues that would be generated. If a retailer's target customers, because of their work schedules want longer hours, the retailer should do so provided it is profitable. Some retail entrepreneurs are now serving their time-deprived customers with round-the-clock food service, auto-repair, and medical services. Some merchant groups have started banding together to start a concierge service at the local commuter train station which, for a fee paid by the merchants, will return video rentals, handle dry cleaning, pick up prescriptions, and do other shopping chores for the commuter.

A retailer's operating hours also depend on the competition. If a competitor is willing to stay open until 9 P.M. six nights per week to serve customers, it would probably not be wise to close every night at 6 P.M. unless a lease provision requires it. Many bricks-and-mortar retailers are transforming themselves into bricks-and-click retailers to compete with retailers who offer the most convenient hours—24/7.

The retailer must also remember that local and national laws, which were described in Chapter 6, may restrict the retailer's ability to set their hours of operation. For example, some states employ blue laws to restrict certain types of retailers from operating on Sundays. In Oklahoma and Texas, for example, new car dealers must be closed one day each weekend.

Information Aids

As already mentioned, the retailer's promotional efforts help to inform the customer. Many retailers offer customers other information aids that help them enter into intelligent transactions. Today, for example, with the click of a mouse, consumers can not only search for products or services, but more importantly can determine what choices are available in local stores, the location of specific stores, and directions on how to get there. Consumers can also get information about return policies, credit policies, merchandise availability, and even merchandise prices on the Web sites of most major retailers. There are even Web sites where consumers experience firsthand a virtual walk through the store. Other Web retailers, such as the Gap, (www.gap.com) and Lands' End (www.landsend.com), let consumers move images of the latest fashions around on the screen to get a feel for how the different outfits will mix and match.

AP Photo/Ted S. Warren

Web sites have become popular information aids for consumers.

In addition, retailers regularly offer demonstrations that instruct the customer on how to use, operate, or care for a product. For example, as a means of by-passing price competition, the Dorothy Lane Market in Dayton, Ohio developed a reputation for pampering its upscale customer base. One of its stores offers weekly cooking classes. Customers can also choose recipes from recipe cards and find placards in the wine section that describe the various wines and the food dishes they complement. Not surprisingly, retailers that offer these demonstrations can increase their market share because many customers are afraid to buy a new item without first knowing how to use it. If the store offers classes or specific instruction on the use of a product, the customer will be less resistant to trying and ultimately purchasing the product. For many items that are technologically sophisticated or represent significant departures from traditional ways of doing something, the customer will tend to buy from the retailer that offers instruction.

The chapter's Global Retailing box shows examples of information aids that were *not* too beneficial to the customer because something was lost in translating from a retailer's native language into English.

Transaction Services

In the past, retailers believed that transaction services meant employing salespeople who would personally take care of an individual customer. But for the profitable retailers of the future, the term **transaction services** will mean offering the conveniences customers need and then helping them get out of the store as fast as possible with their purchases. The most important *transaction services* are credit, layaway, gift wrapping and packaging, check cashing, gift cards, personal shopping, merchandise availability, personal selling, and the sales transaction itself. These services help to facilitate transactions once customers have made a purchase decision.

transaction services
Are services provided to customers when they are in the store shopping and transacting business.

Credit

One of the most popular transaction-related services offered by retailers is consumer credit. Offering credit can be of great service to the customer because it enables shopping without the need to carry large sums of money. In addition, it allows the

Global Retailing

International Information Aids Mistakes

There are usually significant differences between domestic and foreign retail markets. However, nowhere have international retailers had more problems than when their employees try to write signs and instructions in a foreign language, such as English, and don't check these signs for errors. Frequently, poor knowledge of the customer's language results in unintentional but highly "interesting" signage. Consider the following errors by foreign retailers trying to translate into English:

Cocktail lounge in Norway:	LADIES ARE REQUESTED NOT TO HAVE CHILDREN IN THE BAR.
In a Nairobi restaurant:	CUSTOMERS WHO FIND OUR WAITRESSES RUDE OUGHT TO SEE THE MANAGER.
Hotel in Vienna:	IN CASE OF FIRE, DO YOUR UTMOST TO ALARM THE HOTEL PORTER.
Mexico City discount store:	AMERICAN WELL SPEAKING HERE.
Paris dress shop:	DRESSES FOR STREET WALKING.
Tokyo hotel's rules and regulations:	GUESTS ARE REQUESTED NOT TO SMOKE OR DO OTHER DISGUSTING BEHAVIORS IN BED.
Hong Kong dentist:	TEETH EXTRACTED BY LATEST METHODISTS.
Rome laundry:	LADIES, PLEASE LEAVE YOUR CLOTHES HERE AND SPEND THE AFTERNOON HAVING A GOOD TIME.
French hotel:	PLEASE LEAVE YOUR VALUES AT THE FRONT DESK.
Athens hotel:	WE EXPECT OUR VISITORS TO COMPLAIN DAILY AT THE OFFICE BETWEEN THE HOURS OF 9 AND 11 A.M.
Tokyo hotel:	THE FLATTENING OF UNDERWEAR IS THE JOB OF THE CHAMBERMAID—TO GET IT DONE, TURN HER ON.
Paris hotel:	SLENDID VIEWS AND A FRENCH WIDOW IN EVERY ROOM.
Bangkok dry cleaner:	DROP YOUR TROUSERS HERE FOR BEST RESULTS.
Amsterdam hotel:	YOU ARE ENCOURAGED TO TAKE ADVANTAGE OF OUR CHAMBERMAIDS.
Hotel in Acapulco:	THE MANAGER HAS PERSONALLY PASSED ALL THE WATER SERVED HERE.
Swiss restaurant:	SPECIAL TODAY . . . NO ICE CREAM.
Hong Kong tailor shop:	ORDER YOUR SUMMER SUIT NOW. BECAUSE OF BIG RUSH WE EXECUTE CUSTOMERS IN STRICT ROTATION.
Hotel room notice in Thailand:	PLEASE DO NOT BRING SOLICITORS INTO YOUR ROOM.
Hotel brochure in Italy:	THIS HOTEL IS RENOWNED FOR ITS PEACE AND SOLITUDE. IN FACT, CROWDS FROM ALL OVER THE WORLD FLOCK HERE TO ENJOY ITS SOLITUDE.
Hotel lobby in Bucharest:	THE LIFT IS BEING FIXED FOR THE NEXT DAY. DURING THAT TIME WE REGRET THAT YOU WILL BE UNBEARABLE.
Supermarket in Hong Kong:	FOR YOUR CONVENIENCE, WE RECOMMEND COURTEOUS, EFFICIENT SELF-SERVICE.
Hotel in Zurich:	BECAUSE OF THE IMPROPRIETY OF ENTERTAINING GUESTS OF THE OPPOSITE SEX IN THE BEDROOM, IT IS SUGGESTED THAT THE LOBBY BE USED FOR THIS PURPOSE.
Laundromat in Italy:	AUTOMATIC WASHERS: PLEASE REMOVE ALL YOUR CLOTHES WHEN RED LIGHT GOES ON.
Department store in London:	BARGAIN BASEMENT UPSTAIRS

customer to buy now and pay later. Credit can be a benefit to the retailer also: It increases sales by increasing both impulse buying and purchases of expensive items. Of course, in-house credit can decrease profits if the credit policy is too lenient.

Layaway

When a layaway service is offered, the customer can place a deposit (usually 20 percent) on an item, and in return the retailer will hold the item for the customer. The customer will make periodic payments on the item and, when it is paid for in full, can take it home. In a sense, a layaway sale is similar to an installment credit sale; however, the retailer retains physical possession of the item until the bill is completely paid.

A negative aspect of using layaways is that many times customers never pick up the items they have in layaway. The retailer then has to return a "dated" item to regular inventory, where a markdown, which is usually larger than the first customer's initial payment, is required.

Gift Wrapping and Packaging

Customers are typically better served if their purchase is properly wrapped or packaged. The service may be as simple as putting the purchase into a paper bag or as complex as packaging crystal glassware in a special shatterproof box to prevent breakage.

The retailer must match its wrapping service to the type of merchandise it carries and its image. A discount grocer or hardware store does quite well by simply putting the merchandise into a paper sack. Specialty clothing stores often have dress and suit boxes that are easy to carry home. Some upscale retailers even put the purchased merchandise in decorated shopping bags or prewrapped gift boxes. This considerably reduces the number of packages that must be gift wrapped.

Many larger department stores and most gift shops offer a gift-wrapping service. Often there is a fee for gift wrapping unless the purchase price exceeds some limit, usually \$10 or \$25. Many other retailers also offer a courtesy wrap, which consists of a gift box and ribbon, or a store wrap that identifies the place of purchase. This type of wrap is not only a goodwill gesture, but also a form of advertising.

Check Cashing

Most retailers offer some form of check-cashing service. The most basic type consists of allowing customers to cash a check for the amount of purchase. Most retailers now have online acceptance systems on their registers, which make check cashing as easy as using a credit card. Other retailers provide their customers with an identification card that entitles them to pay for merchandise with a personal check. More generous check-cashing retailers allow qualified customers to cash checks for amounts above the purchase price, usually not for more than \$20.

Another form of check cashing is accepting third-party checks from either the customers' employers or from the government. As pointed out in Chapter 10, check cashing has been found to be an effective means of attracting certain market segments and is based on the premise that consumers will spend more if they have cash in their pockets. This trend has resulted in some supermarket chains becoming the biggest check-cashing operators in some cities, oftentimes bigger than the banks.[10]

Gift Cards

For most Americans, the popularity of gift cards, especially during the holiday season, is at an all-time high. Many view gift cards as the perfect present because they are fun to receive and they make shopping for that perfect gift easier. According to the National Retail Federation, these cards rank third on consumers' Christmas wish lists and there is no sign that the craze is slowing down. In fact, one in every six dollars of Christmas sales is for a gift card.

Still, gift cards are a year-round service being sold by retailers ranging from Macy to Starbucks and from Amazon.com to The Home Depot. One of the key reasons for the popularity of today's plastic gift card is that it is a "stored value" card as opposed to an old fashioned gift certificate. Thus, when a consumer spends \$33 from a \$100 plastic card, the card automatically updates the balance. This is more efficient, and much less time consuming than making the retailer reissue a new gift certificate for the \$67 balance.

The major impact of gift cards on retailers is the postponement of sales since retailers can't count a gift card as a sale at the time of purchase. Instead, they must wait until the gift card is redeemed for merchandise. As a result, most of the \$20 + billion spent on gift cards in November and December will not show up in holiday sales, but instead as sales in January or February, when the gift card is redeemed.

Personal Shopping

As discussed in Chapter 3, recent changes in family lifestyles have left many Americans without enough time to accomplish all they need and want to do. Other shoppers hate browsing in stores more than they hate doing household chores. Successful retailers have sought to aid these consumers by offering personal shopping services. **Personal shopping** is the activity of assembling an assortment of goods for a customer. This can be as varied a service as picking out clothing, filling a nonstore order (many retailers now offer key customers an 800 number or a Web site address), assembling a supply of groceries and sending them to the customer's home, or selecting a wedding gift. Personal shopping services are one of the best ways to build a relationship with the customer.

personal shopping
Occurs when an individual who is a professional shopper performs the shopping role for another; very upscale department and specialty stores offer personal shoppers to their clients.

Today, the newest type of personal shopper is the health advocate. Working most often for busy affluent consumers who are suffering from illnesses, these advocates research new treatments, cut through medical bureaucracy, and frame medical decisions more objectively than stressed-out patients and their family members.[11]

Merchandise Availability

Merchandise availability as a service simply relates to whether the customers can easily find the items they are looking for. A customer might be unable to find an item for one of three reasons: (1) The item is out of stock, (2) it is not located where the customer looks for it, or (3) the customer does not know what is really needed. The retailer can minimize out-of-stock conditions by good merchandise management although some out-of-stock situations are inevitable. The customer's ability to locate a needed item in the store can be increased by having proper in-store signage, displays, helpful and informative employees, and a well-designed layout. The problem of not knowing "what is really needed" is more difficult to overcome. Most major retailers have a bridal registry, both in-store and online, with easy-to-remember phone numbers to help solve one such problem. For example, at Chicago's old Marshall Field's (which has been renamed Macy's, after the merger between Federated and May), the number is 1-800-2-I DO I DO; at JCPenney it is 1-800-JCP-GIFT; and at Target it is 1-800-888-WEDD.

Merchandise availability is an element of customer service that many retailers take for granted, but they should not. When customers do not find items they are looking for in a store—regardless of the cause—they will remember their bad experiences and will probably tell their friends.

Personal Selling

Another important transactional service that retailers can offer is a strong, customer-oriented retail sales staff. A good job of personal selling or even skilled suggestive selling, resulting in a need-satisfying experience, will greatly enhance customer satisfaction. One study found that in 73 percent of the cases where the customer had the "best ever shopping experience," there was sales force involvement. The same study also pointed out the dangers of ineffective sales personnel—81 percent of the time when a customer had the "worst ever shopping experience," there was direct employee involvement.[12] Personal selling will be discussed in detail later in this chapter.

Sales Transaction

The final service to be discussed is the sales transaction itself or the interaction between the retailer, its employee, and the customer. Some discounters, seeking to invoke a positive, personal touch made headway with a greeter, who acknowledges customers when they enter the store. Probably the two most overlooked problems involving transaction services are having clean restrooms and minimizing dwell time, which is the amount of time a consumer must spend waiting to complete a purchase. The majority of all shopping experiences should be recreational and entertaining. This is especially true for retailers selling nonessential products such as books. Therefore, the retailer should never do anything that might drive the consumer away. Leonard Riggio, the feisty CEO of Barnes & Noble, recognized this truth in offering customers Starbucks coffee, comfy chairs, a clubby atmosphere, and yes, public restrooms.[13] Sam Walton believed that his restrooms should be the best in town so that a woman would never want to leave his stores to rush home for a bathroom visit. In fact, whenever Sam visited a store, he and his wife, Helen, always checked the restrooms.[14]

As noted above, all retailers face unique challenges in determining how to deal with customers in their stores. However, as the chapter's Service Retailing box illustrates, these decisions are far more complex for those retailers whose interaction with the customer is conducted in the customer's home.

Another issue facing the retailer is how to handle dwell time. **Dwell time** refers to the amount of time a consumer must spend waiting to complete a purchase. This time greatly influences the customer's expectations and evaluations of the retailer. Customers understand that certain waiting periods are required, especially for services, which cannot be produced ahead of demand. However, they must perceive that the line or waiting time is shortening.

dwell time
Refers to the amount of time a consumer must spend waiting to complete a purchase.

It may seem like a simple thing, but for any retailer serving hundreds of customers daily, the decision on how to line them up can have a major impact on customer satisfaction. This decision affects all retailers, from the U.S. Post Office to fast-food operations to hotels to banks. Currently, most retailers are moving away from multiple lines and opting for the single, serpentine line. This type of line, which was first made popular at amusement parks, got its name because of its long, snake-like shape. Multiple lines cause customer frustration because other lines inevitably move faster. In recent years, the frustration of waiting to complete the transaction—the dwell time—has become a threat to retailers, according to a study by America's Research Group. Eighty-three percent of women and 91 percent of men say that long waits, what they call "register rage," has caused them to stop patronizing a particular store.[15]

Service Retailing

Etiquette Guidelines for Service Retailers

Many service retailers don't work from their own location, but must go to the customer. Some, such as lawn care specialists, work outside the customer's home but others, such as home improvement/repair contractors, must enter the customer's home to complete the assigned job. Anytime a service provider enters a private home, there is the possibility of being put in an awkward situation.

Most of the major service franchisors try to avoid these situations by having all franchisees follow a detailed operating policy manual. This manual covers hiring and training procedures as well as providing operational and financial guidance. One common guideline is to require the franchisee to obtain a police background check on applicants before making the hiring decision. Many service franchisors now insist that all "service techs" be bonded, that they wear uniforms with collared shirts and slacks, and that they wear plastic protective shoe coverings when entering a home. Despite these and other similar upgrades in professionalism, not every unfortunate contingency can be anticipated. How does a service retailer prepare its employees for that "once-in-a-million" situation?

One service provider who provides outstanding training in this sensitive area is Ted Tenenbaum, the owner of the Mr. Handyman franchise in Los Angeles. Mr. Tenenbaum's employees provide all types of home maintenance including electrical, plumbing, drywall repair, painting, tilling, and so on. Like all Mr. Handyman franchisees across America, Tenenbaum's workers specialize in jobs that are too small for most general contractors. Because his employees spend the bulk of their time inside customers' homes, Tenenbaum's training sessions focus on teaching a "common sense" level of business etiquette which is specific to the nature of the work. Because every situation is different, these guidelines are neither written in stone nor posted for employees to memorize. Instead, Tenenbaum attempts to instill the idea that a combination of common sense and basic etiquette will forestall many of the problems that service retailers might encounter. Here is an overview of Ted Tenenbaum's unwritten rules:

WHATEVER YOU SEE, PRETEND YOU DON'T SEE IT. Whether it is a pair of racy underwear in the middle of the floor or the homeowner walking around in flimsy clothing, the worker didn't see it.

DON'T STARE TOO LONG AT ANYTHING. After all, if you followed the first guideline, you didn't see anything.

NEVER GET IN THE MIDDLE OF ANY DOMESTIC ARGUMENT and *AGREE WITH EVERYONE AND THEN SWITCH THE CONVERSATION TO SOMETHING ELSE.* Feuding parties often like to involve a neutral third party. The third party can never win—so always try to avoid such situations.

NEVER BE ALONE IN A ROOM WITH A CHILD. What would happen if a child were to stumble and fall, start crying, and a parent walks in the room to see a "service tech" with an arm around the child trying to provide comfort? Or what if the child cuts himself on a tool or replacement part?

BE SURE TO COMPLIMENT AT LEAST ONE ITEM OR FEATURE IN THE CUSTOMER'S HOME. You always want to get on the customer's good side.

Mr. Tenenbaum's final guideline and probably most important is

CALL ME IF YOU ARE EVER FRIGHTENED.

With etiquette guidelines such as these, it is little wonder that the Academy Awards has chosen the Mr. Handyman system, with Mr. Tenenbaum's franchise representing the L.A. area, to be a part of their official gift basket given to all Oscar presenters. But don't ask Ted or his "techs" about these celebrities. All they will say is that among their celebrities/customers this past year were 16 Oscar nominees and four statuettes. And a lot of newly repaired walls, doors, and faucets.

Based on "Handyman Etiquette: Stay Calm, Avert Eyes," *The Wall Street Journal*, May 10, 2005: B1 and information provided by Ted Tenenbaum.

This is such an important issue that before introducing sandwiches to its menu, Starbucks had to first determine, "How long is too long to wait for a vanilla latte or a Venti Double Chocolate Chip Frappuccino Blended Crème?" After all, the Seattle-based coffee retailer didn't want to see any of its 33 million worldwide weekly customers switch to Dunkin' Donuts or some other rival who could beat them on the clock. As a result, the chain stopped requiring signatures with credit card purchases under $25 because this had become the longest part of the transaction at the cash register, taking an average 30 seconds.[16]

What's New?

E-Tailers' Two Major Posttransaction Problems

Two of the three major consumer concerns regarding online purchasing are posttransaction services: slow delivery and handling returns. (The other concern is the inability to see and touch items before purchase.) These concerns are particularly important if e-tailers want to attract repeat business. It seems that e-tailers with the biggest problems are those with little experience in catalog retailing and those who hand off the function to outside companies that are not closely supervised for quality control.

Two of the major benefits offered by online retailers are lower prices and convenience. Convenience means that consumers can shop from their home or office 24 hours a day, 7 days a week. However, the ease and speed of ordering products online has raised expectations for an equally speedy delivery and return.

For example, the same customer who would wait ten days for a catalog order will begin to complain only three days after placing an online order. Actually, 70 to 80 percent of all online customers will make more than one where-is-my-order (WISMO) call to an 800 number, at a cost to the e-tailer of $2.80 to $7. Little wonder that Lands' End finds the extra cost for UPS's second-day delivery worth it. (By the way, the Federal Trade Commission's mail and telephone-order rule mandates that when a date is not promised, shipment must occur within 30 days. If the merchant cannot ship as promised, shoppers must be informed and a new shipping date set so a customer can accept the delay or cancel the order.) However, most experts believe that this is one of the simplest problems for retailers to overcome.

Returns may be the biggest headache for online merchants. The problem is not the number of returns, but rather how they are handled. Delayed exchanges or mishandled returns are the most common complaints. Consumers especially dislike having to pay high return postage because of their inability to return the item to a nearby store.

Most retail consultants have always believed Internet shoppers would buy more online if they could return items more easily. As a result, many online retailers are copying catalog retailers in offering free shipping on returns. However, many bricks-and-clicks do not allow items ordered online to be returned to their bricks-and-mortar locations. In contrast, The Gap and Macy's do accept store returns of merchandise purchased online. Estee Lauder allows the return of Clinique merchandise to stores that carry its products if the store allows this policy.

To reduce returns, retailers are trying to better educate customers by providing more information about the item and responding to other possible questions or problems. Companies such as Lands' End allow the customer to view the items from all sides and include a request for customer measurements in order to determine the best fit. Realizing that every computer monitor displays colors slightly differently, Furniture.com uses the M&Ms test. If the colors of the M&M candies you see on the computer screen don't look the same as they do in real life, the e-tailer has the customers adjust their monitors' brightness and contrast. Alternatively, because Furniture.com has a tie-in with local furniture dealers, the customer can visit these dealers to see the items. These same dealers will then deliver the merchandise directly. In addition, all merchandise returns are handled by the retailer who delivered the item. Since each local retailer has their own policies, the customer is advised of the policies for a particular order under the "Policies" section on each page of the checkout process.

Posttransaction Services

The relationship between the retailer and the consumer has become more complex in today's service-oriented economy. Many products, such as computers, automobiles, and travel and financial services, require an extended relationship between the retailer and consumer. The longer this period of time can be extended by ensuring the customer's satisfaction with the product, the greater the chances that future sales will result. The most common **posttransaction services**, which are provided after the sale has been made, are complaint handling, merchandise returns, merchandise repair, servicing, delivery, and post-sale follow-ups. Posttransaction services are especially important for online retailers, as pointed out in the chapter's What's New box.

posttransaction services
Are services provided to customers after they have purchased merchandise or services.

Complaint Handling

Customer dissatisfaction occurs when the customer's experience with a retailer or a product fails to live up to expectations. The proper handling of customer complaints can mean a big difference in retail performance. Dealing with customers is a sensitive issue because it involves employees who make human errors dealing with customers who make human errors. In essence, this doubles the chance of misunderstanding and mistakes between the two parties. Unfortunately, these mistakes and misunderstandings often lead to a poor image of the retailer, no matter whose fault they might be. Therefore, it is essential that retailers try to solve customer complaints effectively. If retailers solve the customer's problem the right way, then the customer will not only continue to shop with the retailer, but by word of mouth may influence others to shop there also.[17]

Dollars & Sense

Highly profitable retailers place a very high emphasis on responsive complaint-handling systems. They recognize that the cost of fixing mistakes is less than the cost of an unhappy customer.

There are several ways of handling and solving customer complaints. Regardless of the method used, retailers should follow the six rules shown in Exhibit 12.4. For a large retailer, the central complaint department is most efficient. Here, a staff that is specifically trained for this task handles all customer complaints. This method leaves the sales force free to do its job and allows the customer to deal with someone who has the authority to act on most complaints. Many large retailers have even established an 800 number so that they may properly handle complaints with minimal effort on the part of the customer.

Some retailers have the individual salesperson handle complaints. They believe that a friendly, sympathetic attitude exhibited by the salesperson will have a positive effect on future sales, especially if the complaint is about a product, rather than the retailer or sales force. This method does, however, have several disadvantages. First, the individual salesperson often does not have the authority to settle problems and must call in someone else to handle the situation, forcing the customer to restate the problem. A second drawback of this system is the fact that a salesperson who is listening to a past customer complain cannot serve present customers who, incidentally, are overhearing the complaints.

Some retailers are making an all-out effort to stop complaints before they occur. Ohio's Sun Television & Appliances has hired an outside marketing firm to do daily computerized price checks on all comparable merchandise. If somebody beats Sun's price within 30 days of any customer's purchase, the customer automatically gets a check in the mail for the difference.[18] Other retailers seek to stop complaints before they happen by using guarantees. Costco, for example, has what many consider the greatest guarantee in retailing. Its "diamond guarantee" promises to pay a member $100 if a gem it sells is appraised for less than double the Costco price.[19]

Regardless of the complaint-handling system, the retailer needs to remember three things when handling complaints: The customer deserves courteous treatment, a fair settlement, and prompt action. Remember, even if the sale is lost, the customer need not be. The proper handling of complaints has a substantial payback for the smart retailer. Sometimes, however, the customer makes it difficult for even the best retailer to handle a complaint and make the customer happy. Luckily for frontline employees,

Exhibit 12.4
Six Rules to Follow When Handling a Customer's Complaint

1. Acknowledge the importance of the customer. Before the customer even begins to explain his or her problem, acknowledge that the customer is important by telling him or her that you are there to help. Try to ease the customer's frustration.
2. Understand the customer's problem. Ask all the questions needed to completely understand the situation. Determine the responsibilities of each party and what went wrong. Do not assign any fault at this stage.
3. Repeat the problem (as you understand it) to the customer. Without interrupting the customer, paraphrase the problem as you understand it.
4. Think of all possible solutions. Using your creative powers, think of all possible, even wild, solutions that could remedy the problem.
5. Agree on the solution. Determine the solution that is fair to both parties and then have both parties agree to it.
6. Above all, make sure the customer leaves feeling as you would want to feel if you were the customer. If you would not be satisfied with the solution if you were the customer, start over. Remember, it is better to lose a little now than to take a chance on losing a customer for life.

there are online support groups: http://www.customerssuck.com and http://www.retail-sucks.com. Through these Web sites employees can share and vent their frustrations regarding unruly and sometimes just plain stupid customers.

Merchandise Returns

A return policy can range from "no returns, no exchanges" to "the customer is always right." The handling of merchandise returns is an important customer service, sometimes making the difference between turning a profit and losing money. As was pointed out earlier, successful retailers are well aware that it costs five times as much money to get a customer into your store as it does to make a sale to someone already there. Therefore, since "customer retention" is so important, why would a retailer ever seek to lose one due to the mishandling of a return. Retailers, therefore, need to decide if they want to use either of the extreme policies mentioned above or a more moderate one. Few services build customer goodwill as quickly as a fair return policy. It is important that the retailer's return policy be consistent with its image. A mistake that some retailers make is to follow the policies, such as "No receipt, no return" or 30-day limits on returns, established by the competition. Because a retailer is trying to differentiate itself from the competition, adopting a return policy similar to their competitor's isn't the best strategy.

Fraudulent returns and abuses are currently estimated to be a $16 billion per year problem for American retailers.[20] Some common examples of this fraud/abuse are:[21]

Renting, Not Buying: Buying merchandise, such as a laptop computer to use for a semester with intent of returning it. A customer service representative of a hardware store told the authors that one of the most commonly returned items is a plunger: "It wouldn't be so bad, but usually they come back in a plastic bag just after they have been used." However, what is probably the most abused return policy is that of an electronic retailer getting back a large screen television set the Monday after the Super Bowl.

Fraudulent Employee Actions: Returning merchandise stolen by employees for cash. This may also involve using falsified, stolen, or reused receipts to return the merchandise.

Shoplift Returns: Shoplifting with intent to return for cash.
Price switching: Putting lower priced tags on merchandise with intent to return for full retail price with the original price tag back on the item.

Research has also shown that approximately 75 percent of all shoppers never return purchases and that only one percent of consumers are responsible for fraudulent or abusive returns.[22] Even so, it is important that a retailer set a return policy that considers the effect on both sales and expenses. Thus, retailers must estimate the salvage value of returned merchandise that is probably out of its peak selling season, the probability of losing a customer, and the transaction costs of returning merchandise. There is also an opportunity cost—the foregone interest or return on investment dollars. This money is tied up in merchandise that is in the possession of the customer but will be returned.

One innovative approach to dealing with the one percent of abusers is a new technology used by retailers such as Target and Wal-Mart that tracks the buying and return activity of shoppers, especially those returns without a receipt. After a shopper reaches the retailer's return limit within a given time period,[23] they are informed that they cannot make another exchange at any of the retailer's stores for up to year. Such actions allow retailers to offer the other 99 percent of consumers a more lenient/flexible return policy.

Servicing, Repair, and Warranties

Any new product with more than one moving mechanical part is a candidate for future servicing or repair. In fact, even items without moving parts such as clothing, coffee tables, and paintings are candidates for repair. Retailers who offer merchandise servicing and repair to their customers tend to generate a higher sales volume. And if the work

AP Photo/Tyler Morning Telegraph, Brad Smith

Merchandise returns are a major cost to retailers but also an important form of customer service.

they perform is good, they can also generate repeat business. For example, if the service department of a TV and appliance store has a reputation for doing good work at fair prices, customers will not only purchase TVs at the store but will also tend to purchase radios, stereos, and washers.

Repair servicing, especially repairs involving warranties, is perhaps one of the most difficult customer services to manage. While good repair service can stimulate additional sales, many customers will never be satisfied because it is difficult to schedule appointments. In today's urban environment, it is virtually impossible for retailers to schedule a repair call or delivery within even a three-hour time frame. Traffic, parking, and the inability to predict exactly how long each call will take make scheduling uncertain. These factors often make it difficult for today's dual-income families to be home when the retailer's personnel arrive. In addition, in many cases, buyers are confused by warranties, especially since some involve free replacement parts, but not labor. (The legal issues pertaining to warranties were discussed in Chapter 6.) These disgruntled customers will tell their friends, relatives, and acquaintances of their experiences.

Delivery

Delivery of merchandise to the customer's home can be a very expensive service, especially because of the high cost of fuel. Retailers such as florists can offer free delivery (which is actually absorbed in slightly higher prices) or they can charge the customer a small fee to help offset the cost. Nonetheless, the extra business derived from providing delivery may be worth the expense if the merchandise and customer characteristics warrant it. For example, when consumers think of delivery, they usually think of Domino's Pizza. When Thomas Monaghan started the company, pizza already enjoyed widespread popularity. He soon realized that success could come by focusing on fast, free delivery, something no one else did.[24] However, with higher gasoline prices, the days of free pizza delivery for Americans may soon end. Despite the risk that extra charges will alienate customers, Pizza Hut, Domino's, and Papa John's have been testing the addition of a delivery fee in an attempt to bolster their bottom line.

The final step of the delivery process is installation. As products become more technically advanced, more people are looking for someone who can actually install it for them. This was described in Chapter 3 as the "do-it-for-me" (DIFM) age. The chapter's Retailing: The Inside Story box discusses how one retailer, Best Buy, has taken this delivery and installation process to the next level with its Geek Squad.

Post-Sale Follow-Up

Retailing's job is not over when the cash register rings. It is only starting. Many retail salespeople spend a great deal of time and energy to get a customer to say yes, but most don't spend enough time trying to keep that purchaser as a loyal customer. Earlier in the chapter it was pointed out that it costs a retailer five times as much to attract a first-time customer as it does to persuade a former customer to return. Therefore, it is important that the retailer care for its current customers. This may involve just a follow-up phone call to see how the product is working, or remind a customer about an upcoming sale, or that it might be time to reorder. Southwest Airlines, for example, sends out special deals to its Rapid Rewards (loyalty club) members who haven't flown with them over the past few months.

Retailing: The Inside Story

Geek Squad to the Rescue

Got problems installing your new computer or just adding software? Call the Geek Squad. They will immediately send a "geek" who will arrive in a "Geekmobile" (a black-and-white Volkswagen Beetle) wearing a white shirt, white socks, black tie and black pants. Don't let the looks fool you—these geeks are the experts that Best Buy customers can call any time of the day or night. An agent will be at their home, in many cases, within the day. The geeks can repair, set up, and train consumers to run Microsoft Windows, Macintosh, and in some areas, Linux operating systems. They even will set up and service computers purchased at other retailers.

The Geek Squad was founded by Robert Stephens in 1994 in Minneapolis, Minnesota. Eight years later it was acquired by Best Buy. Today, the Geek Squad can be found in every Best Buy store (in Geek language they are called precincts) plus a selected number of Office Depot locations in North America. The squad's basic proposition is: "Wherever you need service and support for computing, we're there for you." Despite the fact that the majority of homes now have computers, the Geek Squad has relatively little competition. While there are firms that specialize in aiding large corporations, Geek Squad is the only nationally available 24-hour in-home customer support retailer. Basic PC setup service costs start at $129. In addition to normal services, squad members are often able to suggest other ideas and components for getting the most out of the customer's home computer.

The name itself, Geek Squad, is an attempt to inject a little humor. Call its toll-free number—(800) Geek-Squad—and you will hear the "Mission Impossible" theme song. Its agents have titles like CIA agents:

"Counter Operations Agents" (COAs) perform many administrative tasks for the precincts, but do not primarily work on computers.

"Counter Intelligence Agents" (CIAs) offer customer assistance at the counter and perform repairs inside their local stores or "precincts."

"Cadets" perform a dual role: when not on a service call, they can be found at the precinct assisting in repairs. In addition, Cadets are authorized to provide follow-home service for customers with newly purchased PCs and can also handle special customer situations, on a case-by-case basis, that arise at the store.

"CIA Seniors" are responsible for the supervision and training of CIAs, COAs, and Cadets in addition to managing the normal operations of a precinct.

"Deputy of Counter Intelligence" is the title given to the supervising Agent within a precinct.

"Double Agents," as the name would imply, have two roles. They are based out of a Geek Squad Precinct and work primarily at the client's site, but also come to the precinct to provide training, additional field-tested knowledge, and to coordinate strategies with the Deputy of Counter Intelligence.

"Special Agents" provide corporate support to business customers, large and small, with Microsoft Windows server-based networks.

"Precinct Chief" is the title earned when an Agent is promoted to manage a free standing Geek Squad Store not inside a Best Buy location.

"Covert Operations Agents" provide telephone support for technology problems.

"Mission Controllers" assist clients in scheduling appointments.

"Guidance Engineers" schedule Agents in the field and provide them with support and backup, if needed.

There are also "Secret Agents" who embark on extended/long-term covert missions for special "classified" clients. Some of the Geek Squad's recently declassified clients include celebrities such as Larry King, The Rolling Stones, Ice Cube, U2, and Vanilla Ice.

Based on information supplied by Best Buy.

LO 3 Determining Customer Service Levels

How should a retailer determine which services to offer?

It is not easy to determine the optimal number and level of customer services to offer. Theoretically, however, one could argue that a retailer should add customer services until the additional revenue that is generated by higher service levels is equal to the additional cost of providing those services. In the short run, cutting back on costly customer services can usually increase profits. However, such action may present serious long-run problems as customers may shop elsewhere seeking better services.

Deciding what specific customer services to offer in order to increase sales volume is a difficult question for any retailer. Exhibit 12.5 lists six factors to be considered when determining the customer services to offer: the retailer's characteristics, the services offered by the competition, the type of merchandise handled, the price image of the retailer, the income of the target market, and the cost of providing the service. It is the retailer's job to study these six areas to arrive at the service mix that will increase long-run profits by retaining present customers, enticing new customers, and projecting the right image. Above all else, retailers must remember to be realistic and not expect to satisfy the wants and needs of all customers. No strategy could be less profitable than trying to satisfy everybody. What the retailer is really trying to do is to use its sales staff as the conduit between the vendor's expectations and the customer's expectations, as shown in Exhibit 12.6.

Retailer's Characteristics

Retailer's characteristics include store location, store size, and store type. It is especially important to look at these three characteristics when considering adding a service.

Services offered in the downtown area of a large city would probably be different from those offered by a similar store in a suburban shopping center. For example, a drugstore in the downtown area might offer free delivery of prescriptions as a service

Exhibit 12.5
Factors to Consider When Determining Customer Services to Offer

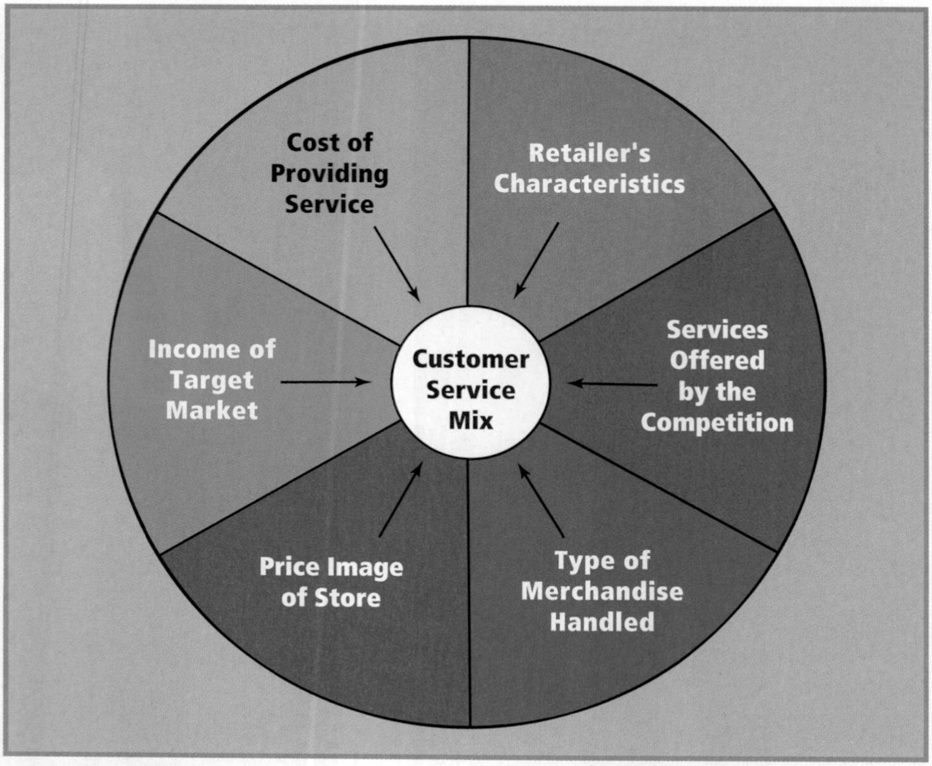

Exhibit 12.6
How the Retailer's Sales Force Meets the Expectations of Both Vendors and Customers

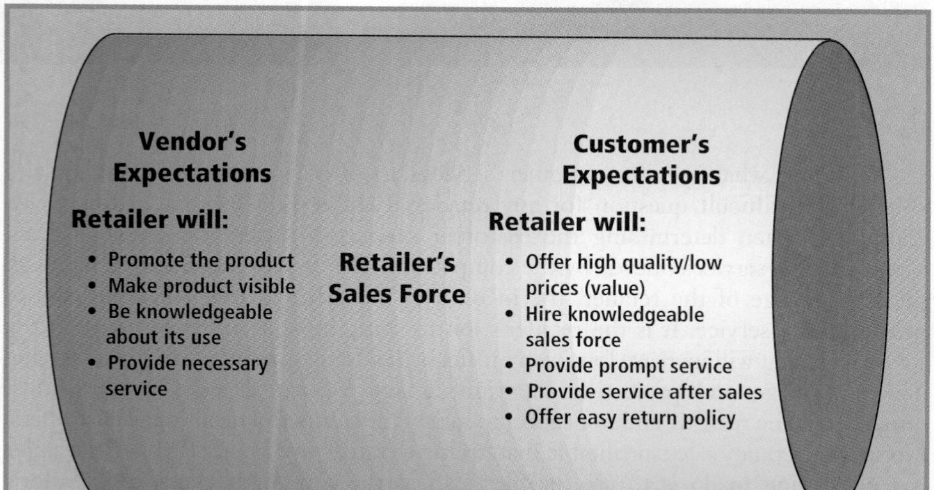

to its clientele. This service would be of great benefit to city dwellers without cars and businesspeople who do not want to wait at the drugstore for a prescription. This same service in a suburban shopping center would not be as important. This druggist might get a better return on investment by offering such services as check cashing, credit, and a drive-through window rather than free delivery of prescriptions.

The size and type of store also determine which services to offer. A major department store would offer a different assortment of services than a supermarket. There would also be a difference between large and small stores of the same type, or among bricks-and-mortar, clicks-and-mortar, and e-tail stores as well.

Competition

The services offered by competitors will have a significant effect on the level and variety of customer services offered. A retailer must also provide these services or suitable substitutes, or offer lower prices.

Suppose there are three clothing stores of the same general type, price range, and quality within a given area. Store A and Store B offer free gift wrapping, standard alterations, bank-card credit, and a liberal return policy. Store C, on the other hand, offers only standard alterations and has an exchange-only return policy. Customers who are shopping for gifts will generally prefer Stores A and B to Store C because they feel confident that whatever they purchase will ultimately be just right. It can even be gift wrapped at the store. If the gift is not suitable, the receiver can exchange it or get a cash refund. In this situation, Store C can do two things to compete: add different services or decrease prices.

Type of Merchandise

The merchandise lines carried can be an indication of the types of services, especially personal selling, to offer. The principle reason is that certain merchandise lines benefit from knowledgeable sales personnel; for example, would you want a less-than-knowledgeable salesperson to assist you in purchasing an engagement ring for the woman of your dreams? Or worse, would you want your boyfriend buying your engagement ring at a self-service discounter, even if it offers a "diamond guarantee" that it will appraise for double the selling price. In addition, other products benefit from coupling them with complementary services: bicycles and free assembly, major appliances and delivery, and sewing machines and free sewing lessons.

Price Image

Customers usually expect more services from a retailer with a high-price image than from a discounter. When a customer perceives a retailer as having high prices, it also sees the retailer as possessing an air of luxury. Therefore, the services rendered by this retailer should reinforce the image of luxury or status. Some of the typical luxury services include personal shopping, a home design studio, free gift wrapping, free delivery, free alterations, and sales personnel who are more professional in both appearance and manner.

On the other end of the scale, discounters need not offer luxury services because customers who shop there are seeking low prices, not pampering. A discounter or store with a low-price image might offer such basic services as free parking, layaway, bank-card credit, and convenient store hours.

Target Market Income

The higher the income of the target market, the higher the price that consumers will pay. The higher the prices consumers will pay, the more services the retailer can profitably provide. Some customers may expect more services than retailers can afford, and retailers must avoid the strong temptation of providing costly services to such consumers. In the long run, the retailer will have to raise prices to pay for the services and then it will most likely lose customers at the lower income boundary of its target market.

Cost of Services

It is important that retailers know the cost of providing a service so that they can estimate the additional sales needed to pay for the service. For example, a customer service expected to increase costs by $20,000 per year for a store operating on a gross margin of 25 percent would have to stimulate sales by at least $20,000/0.25, or $80,000. In this sense, customer services are evaluated in a manner similar to promotional expenditures. The key criterion becomes the financial effect of adding or deleting a customer service. As a result, some national retailers have started charging for their catalogs after decades of providing them free. Research determined that although nearly 20 percent fewer customers received the catalog, those who did felt that they had made an investment ($5). As a result, these customers increased their purchases by 25 percent.

Another way of expressing the cost of having poor service is to examine what the costs would be if a store did not offer good service. If a 100-store supermarket chain alienated only one customer per day per store, the chain would lose $100 million in annual revenue. This is based on the assumption that grocery business is repeat business, and that the real revenue loss is the $60-$75 that customers spend weekly at that chain.

LO 4

Retail Sales Management

What are the various management problems involved in retail selling, salesperson selection, and training and evaluation?

Retail salespeople and the service they provide are a major factor in consumer purchase decisions. For example, if the retail salesperson is rude or unhelpful, customers often walk out of the store empty-handed. The salesperson is a major determinant of a retailer's image. When the salesperson is available, friendly, appropriately dressed and helpful, customers are often influenced to enter into a transaction with the retailer. The management of the retail sales force plays a crucial role in the success or failure of retail operations.

Types of Retail Selling

In many retail settings, the employees are called salespersons or order takers. For example, consider the role of salespeople in a typical fast-food restaurant such as McDonald's, Burger King, or Wendy's. Most order takers simply ask the customers, "Can I take your order?" Little if anything related to the actual sale occurs. Similarly, in a discount department store, such as Target, Kohl's, or Wal-Mart, salespeople may show a customer where a specific product is or, if the product is not on the shelf, may go to the storeroom to attempt to locate the item. However, seldom do they attempt to sell merchandise or demonstrate its use. In fact, one discounter's policy is to provide "next-to-no-sales-help." Some discounters do not want to get into the business of person-to-person selling. Retailers that employ order takers are appealing to those customers who want value instead of service. Nonetheless, one must recognize that these order takers can influence demand, especially in a negative manner. If you stand at the counter of a McDonald's and no one asks you for your order, you may get frustrated and leave the store without making a purchase.

Retail employees who are most appropriately labeled salespersons should be order getters, rather than order takers. Order getters are involved in conversations with prospective purchasers for the purpose of making a sale. They will inform, guide, and persuade the customer to culminate a transaction either immediately or in the future. For example, in many restaurants whether or not the customer chooses to order a dessert is related to the relationship they have established with their host/hostess.

The degree of emphasis the retailer places on its employees' being order getters depends on the line of retail trade and the retailer's strategy. Retailers that concentrate on the sale of shopping goods (e.g., automobile dealers, furniture retailers, computer retailers, and appliance retailers) want their salespeople to both get and take orders. In lines of retail trade where predominantly convenience goods are sold (gasoline service stations and grocery retailers), the role of the salesperson (or what many call the retail clerk) is that of an order taker. In terms of strategic orientation, it is generally true that retailers with high margins and high levels of customer service place more emphasis on order getting. Those with low margins and a low customer service policy tend to emphasize order taking. Clearly, however, regardless of the line of retail trade and the retailer's strategic thrust, all retail enterprises must carefully evaluate the role of the salesperson in helping to generate demand.

Salesperson Selection

Selecting retail salespeople should involve more than casually accepting anyone who answers an ad or walks into the retailer seeking a job. In fact, the casualness with which many retailers have selected people to fill sales positions is one cause of poor productivity.

Criteria

To select salespeople properly, retailers must decide on their hiring criteria. What is expected from retail salespeople? Are retailers looking for a sales force that has low absenteeism and a willingness to work nights and weekends or the ability to generate a high volume of sales? Are they seeking other qualities or a combination of factors? Unless retailers know what they are looking for in salespeople, they will not acquire a sales force that possesses the proper qualities.

However, good results are dependent not only on the salesperson's characteristics but also on how satisfied the salesperson is with the job and how the sales job was designed. Retail selling jobs should be designed to have high levels of variety (the opportunity to perform a wide range of activities), autonomy (the degree to which an employee determines the work procedures), task identity (the degree to which an employee is involved in the total sales process), and feedback from supervisors and customers.

Predictors

Once retailers determine the hiring criteria, they must then identify the potential predictors to meet the chosen criteria. The most commonly used predictors in selecting retail salespeople are demographics, personality, knowledge and intelligence, and prior work experience. We will discuss criteria for selecting managerial trainees later in the chapter.

Demographics. Depending on the specific line of retail trade, demographic variables can be important in identifying good retail salespeople. For example, a music store appealing to teens will probably benefit from having retail salespeople less than 30 years of age. A high-fashion women's apparel store appealing to 30- to 50-year-old, career-oriented, and upwardly mobile females would probably not desire inexperienced salespeople just out of high school. Interestingly enough, a famous study by J.D. Power & Associates of over 33,000 new car buyers has shown that female salespersons scored higher or at least equal to men in 13 of the 15 categories evaluated. The two items where men scored best were knowledge of "models and features" and "competitive vehicles." Women, however, scored substantially higher in "sincerity," "honesty," and "concern for the buyer's needs."[25] Obviously, there are exceptions to the preceding cases, but the essential point is that demographics play an important role in the retail sales process.

Personality. An applicant's personality can reflect on his or her potential as a retail salesperson. Most retailers prefer salespeople who are friendly, confident, consistent, and understanding of others. These personality traits can be identified either through a personal interview with the applicant or by personality inventory tests. In most lines of retail trade the personal interview is sufficient.

Knowledge and Intelligence. Many products that retailers sell are technically complex. Consider, for example, camcorders, plasma screens, TiVos, DVDs, and Xboxes. Salespeople with knowledge of these products will be better able to sell them. Similarly, to be able to respond competently to customer inquiries, retail employees need to possess a level of education and intelligence compatible with the job description.

Experience. One of the most reliable predictors of success as a salesperson is prior work experience, especially selling experience. If applicants have performed well in prior jobs, there is a good chance that they will perform well in the future. However, many applicants for retail selling jobs are young and have no prior work experience of any magnitude. These applicants are better assessed on their personal character and apparent ambition, drive, and work ethic. This could be indicated by leadership positions in clubs or student organizations, timely graduation, and the display of ambition during the interview process.

Salesperson Training

After salespeople are selected, they will need some form of training. This is true even if they have selling experience. In training programs retailers can explain their own policies. Furthermore, retailers usually want inexperienced salespeople to become familiar with and knowledgeable about their merchandise, warranties and return policies, the different customer types they may have to deal with, and the selling strategies appropriate for these different customers. Even order takers need training in greeting a customer, thanking customers, and using a point-of-sale terminal. Best Buy does an extremely good job of training new sales employees. Relative to sales, Best Buy now spends more on employee training than any other retailer. In 2005 Best Buy increased spending on employee training to 5% of its payroll, from 4.1% the previous year.[26]

As illustrated earlier in the chapter's Service Retailing box on page 402, probably the most important skill the retailer can teach the new sales staff is common customer etiquette and courtesy. Office Depot's employee training manual, for example, says that employees are to offer fanatical customer service by "doing, with truth and compassion, whatever it takes and then some, to win the customer's heart forever." A discount chain insists that its sales staff carry with them at all times when they are on the sales floor the following "crib sheet" about being customer friendly.

Customer Friendly Means
Smiling
Greeting the customer
Being as helpful as you would want somebody to be to you
Using the customer's name (if possible)
Saying "Thank You"

The importance of being customer friendly can be shown in studies from the medical field. These studies found that the doctor's competence and prescribed method of treatment played a very small role in determining if a malpractice suit would be filed. Rather, it was the interpersonal skills that the doctor used with the patient that was the determining factor.[27]

Retailer's Policies

In most situations, the salesperson provides the interface between the customer and retailer. It is thus important for the salesperson to become familiar with the retailer's policies, especially those that may involve the customer directly. Some of these policies relate to merchandise returns and adjustments, shoplifting, credit terms, layaway, delivery, and price negotiation. In addition, the retail salesperson should be knowledgeable about work hours, rest periods, lunch and dinner breaks, commission and quota plans, nonselling duties, and standards of periodic job evaluation. Sales employees should also be informed about criteria used for promotion and advancement, as well as dismissal and termination, within the retail enterprise.

Merchandise

If the merchandise includes shopping goods, the retailer will want to familiarize its salespeople with the strengths and weaknesses of the merchandise so they can advise customers on the best items to meet their needs. The retailer may also suggest that the salesperson become knowledgeable of the competitor's merchandise offerings and their strengths and weaknesses.

Successful retailers make sure all their salespeople know the strengths and weaknesses of the competition's offerings.

Dollars & Sense

Increasingly, retail salespeople need to be familiar with the warranty terms and serviceability of merchandise the retailer handles. This implies that the salesperson know something about the reputation of each manufacturer the retailer represents.

Customer Types

Many retailers have recognized that an important way to increase customer satisfaction is by having their salespeople identify and respond to certain customer types.[28] Various customer types are described in Exhibit 12.7. By knowing how to handle each of these customers, the salesperson can generate additional sales. Too many times retailers dwell on handling the technical details of the job rather than the feelings of a customer. One retail salesperson (who should go online at the customerssuck.com Web site mentioned earlier in the chapter) said this about her training program: "The computer training was real good. I know how to do all this technical stuff, but nobody prepared me for dealing with all these different types of people."

Customer Choice Criteria

The retail salesperson should also learn how to identify the customer's choice criteria and how to respond to them.[29] There are four choice criteria situations: (1)

Characteristics	Basic Types	Recommendations
Don't trust any salesperson. Resist communication as they have a dislike of others. Generally uncooperative and will explode at slightest provocation.	**Defensive** 	Avoid mistaking their silence for openness to your ideas. Stick to basic facts. Tactfully inject product's advantages and disadvantages.
Intense, impatient personality. Often interrupt salespersons and have a perpetually "strained" expression. Often driven and successful people who want results fast.	**Interrupter** 	Don't waste time; move quickly and firmly from one sales point to another. Avoid overkill since they know what they want.
Confident in their ability to make decisions and stay with them. Open to new ideas but want brevity. Highly motivated by self-pride.	**Decisive** 	No canned presentations. The key is to assist. Don't argue or point out errors in their judgment.
They worry about making the wrong decision and therefore tend to postpone all decisions. Want salesperson to make decision for them.	**Indecisive** 	Avoid becoming frustrated yourself. Determine as early as possible the need and concentrate on that. Avoid presenting customer with too many alternatives. Start with making decisions on minor points.
Friendly, talkative types who are enjoyable to visit with. Many have excess time on their hands (e.g., retirees). They usually resist the close.	**Sociable** 	You may have to wait out these customers. Listen for points in conversation where you can interject product's merits. Pressure close is out. Subtle friendly close needed.
Quick to make decision. Impatient, just as likely to walk out as they were to walk in.	**Impulsive** 	Close as rapidly as possible. Avoid any useless interaction. Avoid any oversell. Highlight product's merits.

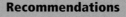

Exhibit 12.7
Customer Types

the customer has no active product choice criteria; (2) the customer has product choice criteria but they are inadequate or vague; (3) the customer has product choice criteria but they are in conflict; and (4) the customer has product choice criteria that are explicit and well defined. For each situation there is an appropriate selling strategy that the salesperson should learn.

No Active Product Choice Criteria. The best sales strategy when the customer does not have a prior criteria set is to educate the customer on the best choice criteria and how to weigh them. For example, a prospective customer enters an automobile dealership to purchase a used automobile but does not know what criteria to use in selecting the best car. The salesperson may present convincing arguments for considering four criteria in the following order of importance: warranty, fuel economy, price, and comfort. Once the salesperson and customer agree on this list, they can work together at finding the used car that best fits the criteria.

Inadequate or Vague Choice Criteria. When the criteria are inadequate or vague, the range of products that will satisfy them is often wide. Perhaps the easiest thing for the salesperson to do is to show that a particular product fits a customer's choice criteria. Because the choice criteria are vague, this would not be difficult and little actual selling may be involved. However, the customer may have trouble believing that the product the salesperson selected is the best one to meet his or her needs. The customer may therefore choose to shop around at other locations.

If the salesclerk is interested in building repeat business and customer goodwill and has a wide range of products to sell, a preferable strategy would be to help the customer define his or her problem in order to refine the choice criteria. The customer and salesclerk can work together in defining the criteria of a good product and then select the product that best fits the criteria.

Choice Criteria in Conflict. Prospective customers with choice criteria that are in conflict frequently have trouble making purchase decisions. There are two basic ways in which choice criteria can be in conflict. First, the customer may want a product to possess two or more attributes that are mutually exclusive. For example, a person purchasing a mountain bike may wish it to be of high quality and low price. This person will quickly find that these two attributes do not co-exist. The best strategy in this situation is for the salesperson to downplay one of the attributes and play up the other. A second way the choice criteria can be in conflict is when a single attribute possesses both positive and negative aspects. Consider a person thinking of purchasing a high-performance automobile. High-performance automobiles have both positive aspects (status, speed, and pleasure fulfillment) and negative aspects (high insurance rates and low mileage per gallon). For this type of conflict, the best selling strategy is to enhance the positive aspects and downplay the negative aspects.

Explicit Choice Criteria. When the customer has a well-defined, explicit choice criteria, the best selling strategy is for the salesperson to illustrate how a specific product fits these criteria. "The salesclerk guides the customer into agreeing that each attribute of his product matches the attributes on the customer's specification. If, at the end of the sales talk, the customer does not agree to the salesclerk's proposition, he appears to be denying what he has previously admitted."[30]

Evaluation of Salespeople

Evaluation of salespeople seeks to determine each salesperson's value to the firm. That determination is important as a basis for salary adjustments, promotions, transfers, terminations, and sales reinforcement. The retailer should develop a systematic method for evaluating both individual salespeople and the total sales staff. Rather than subjectively evaluating performance, the manager should develop explicit performance standards.

Performance Standards

Several standards can be developed to measure a salesperson's performance. Some standards apply only to individual efforts, whereas others assess both individual and total sales force effort.

conversion rate
Is the percentage of shoppers that enter the store that are converted into purchasers.

Conversion Rate. The **conversion rate** is the percentage of all shoppers who make a purchase—that is, who are converted into customers. This is a measure of the sales force's performance; not the individual salesperson's.

A poor conversion rate can be caused by a variety of factors. Perhaps there were not enough clerks on hand when customers needed them. This could have resulted in numerous unassisted searches and long customer waits, causing many customers to exit the store without making a purchase. Or the number of salesclerks could have been adequate to handle the flow of customers, but the salespeople may not have done a good selling job. A poor selling job could have several causes, such as giving inadequate product information, disagreeing or arguing too strongly with the customer, demonstrating the product poorly, having an unfriendly attitude, or giving up on the sale too early. However, all of these factors are really related to poor training, which is the underlying reason for poor sales. A low conversion rate might also have been due to factors beyond the salesperson's control, such as inadequate merchandise levels. The important point is that when a substandard conversion rate exists, the retailer should identify the causes and remedy the situation, because even a small increase in the conversion rate can have a major impact on retail sales.

Marvin Rothenberg, a retired retail consultant, studied what happened in four chains operating a total of 68 department stores.[31] He found that 131,328,000 sales opportunities a year (that is, 2.4 million shoppers who averaged 1.9 shopping visits per month and 2.4 departments per trip) produced only 38 million sales transactions. Thus, 93 million departmental shopping visits resulted in "no sale."

In fact, 49 million of the departmental shoppers who made no purchase did not even have contact with a salesperson or a cashier. Another 44 million had contact with a salesperson but did not buy anything. And among these two segments of 93 million shoppers already in the departments, 28 million came into the department with the intent to make a specific purchase! In total, 71 percent of all the departmental shopping visits resulted in shoppers either having no contact with sales personnel or having the wrong kind of contact, and as a result they made no purchase. No wonder Rothenberg, in another study, found that one-third of customers who entered a store with the expressed intent of making a specific purchase walked out without making any purchase. It is obvious that a small increase in converting these nonpurchasing consumers into customers could increase sales dramatically, even if the shopper is only in the store as a means to combat loneliness.

For example, if these retailers did nothing more than just contact half the 49 million customers who had no sales contact, and if the conversion rate among this group was only half of what it was among those who had sales contact, the number of sales transactions, currently 38 million, would increase by 15 percent (half of 49 million who had no contact multiplied by half of the conversion rate for those who had contact equals 5.6 million more sales transactions). That's an opportunity to add 15 percent to sales by doing nothing more than what is already being achieved when customers contact a salesperson. Yet for many retailers this is a lost opportunity as they either do not want to (or do not know how to) train their sales staff in the proper methods of approaching and assisting customers and more generally providing customer service. Worse yet are those retailers who view their sales force as an operating expense and not as an investment. As such they want to cut back on expenses and end up with too few salespeople on duty. Either way, the retailer is missing out on a great opportunity to increase sales.

High salesperson productivity is one of the hallmarks of high-profit retailers. These retailers do a better job selecting, training, and evaluating their salespeople.

Dollars & Sense

Sales Per Hour. Perhaps the most common measure of sales force performance is sales per hour. Sales per hour is computed by dividing total dollar sales over a particular time frame by total salesperson or sales force hours. A retailer can compute this simple measure for each salesperson, any group of salespeople, or the entire sales force. It can also be computed for various days, weeks, or months.

When employing this measure, remember that standards should be specific to the group or person being evaluated for a particular time period. For example, in a department store the sales per hour of selling effort cannot be expected to be the same for the toy department as for the jewelry department. Nor could one expect the same sales per hour during July and December, because of the heavy Christmas demand for toys and jewelry. In some lines of retail trade, particularly those selling high-ticket items such as automobiles, the key performance measure is gross profit generated per salesperson.

Use of Time. Standards can be developed for how salespeople should spend their time. A salesperson's time can be spent in four ways:

1. Selling time is any time spent assisting customers with their needs. This could be time spent talking, demonstrating a product, writing sales receipts, or assisting the customer in other potentially revenue-generating ways.
2. Nonselling time is any time spent on nonselling tasks such as marking or straightening up the merchandise.
3. Idle time is time the salesperson is on the sales floor but is not involved in any productive work.
4. Absent time occurs when the salespeople are not on the sales floor. They may be at lunch, in the employee lounge, in another part of the store, or in some inappropriate place.

The retailer may develop standards for each of these ways to spend time. For example, the standard time allocation may suggest that salespeople spend 60 percent of their time selling, 28 percent of their time on nonselling activities, 5 percent idle, and 7 percent absent. Any deviation from these standards should be investigated and corrective measures should be taken if necessary.

Data Requirements

To establish proper standards of performance, the retailer needs data. What are good standards for the conversion rate? Sales per hour? Time allocation? Only data will help answer these questions. For bricks-and-mortar retailers, data can come from retail trade associations, consulting firms, or the retailer's own experience.

Once the retailer obtains the data on which to base standards, it must collect additional data continually or at least periodically on actual performance. For example, an increasing number of retailers today survey their customers and use other programs, such as mystery shoppers, to evaluate their salespeople. In fact, a whole service industry specializing in mystery shopping has developed. The results of mystery shopper surveys, along with the employee's actual conversion rate, sales per hour, and time allocation must be compared to their respective standards. If the actual data differ significantly from the standard, an investigation of the cause is warranted. Both favorable and unfavorable variances should be investigated, because a retailer may learn just as much from unusually good performance as from unusually poor performance.

LO 5

The Retail Sales Process

What steps are involved in the retail selling process?

Several basic steps occur during the retail selling process. The length of time that a salesperson spends in each one of these steps depends on the product type, the customer, and the selling situation. Exhibit 12.8 details the sales process model.

Dollars & Sense

Successful retail salespeople do a better job at prospecting, approaching, sales presentation, and closing the sale.

Prospecting

prospecting
Is the process of locating or identifying potential customers who have the ability and willingness to purchase your product.

Prospecting is the search process of finding those who have the ability and willingness to purchase your product. Prospecting is particularly important when the store is full of customers. A salesperson should be aware that good prospects generally display more interest in the product than poor prospects that are "just looking." Salespeople should take advantage of the behavioral cues shown earlier in Exhibit 12.7 on page 416.

Approach

The salesperson may meet hundreds of customers a day, but the customer is only going to meet the salesperson once that day. Therefore, it is extremely important that the first 15 seconds set the mood for the sale. Never begin the sales presentation with "May I help you?" or any other question to which the customer may respond negatively. A simple good morning (afternoon, evening) or any other greeting acknowledging the customer's presence should do. Nordstrom's trains its sales force to mention an item the customer is wearing as an approach, if something better is not evident.

The key to a successful approach is discerning the customer's needs as soon as possible by asking the right questions and listening. What the salesperson hears about the customer's problem or need is more important than anything the salesperson can possibly contribute at this point. The salesperson should ask only a few well-chosen questions to find out more about the need or problem to be solved. The salesperson should also find out if the user of the product is someone different from the customer. Remember the salesperson should ask only as many questions as needed, and let the customer do the talking. One well-known retail sales trainer

Exhibit 12.8
Selling Process in the Retail Environment

Step 1—Prospecting

Decide who can benefit from your product.

a. Find prospects.
b. Qualify prospects (determine whether a prospect has the ability, buying power, and willingness to make a purchase).

Step 2—Approach

The first 15 seconds are the key as they set the mood for the sale.

a. Never say, "May I help you?"
   A single "Hello," "Good morning," or "What may I show you?" makes the customer realize that you are glad they are in your store.
b. Determine the customer's needs as early as possible.
   Listen—*What you hear* is more important than anything you could possibly tell your customer. Ask a few well-chosen questions—What do I need to know?
   1. Product needed or problem to be solved.
   2. User of the product (tell me about so-and-so).

Step 3—The Sales Presentation

Get the customer to want to buy your product/service.

a. Pick the right price level.
   If uncertain, ask, "Is there a price range you have in mind?" Remember, you can't pick out the *right product* for the uncertain customer if the price is wrong.
b. Pick the right product.
   Match user and need with product. Show the customer at least two items.
c. Show the merchandise in an appealing manner.
   1. Make the merchandise stand out.
   2. Show the item so that its good points will be seen.
   3. Let the customer handle the merchandise.
   4. Stress the features of the product.
   5. Explain the benefits of these features.
   6. Appeal to the customer's emotions.
d. Help the customer decide.
   1. Handle objections.
   2. Replace unneeded items.
   3. Watch for unconscious clues.
   4. Stress features and benefits of "key" product.

Step 4—Closing the Sale

Reach an agreement.

a. What is going on in the customer's mind?
b. Four effective ways to close.
   1. Make the decision for the customer.
   2. Assume the decision has already been made.
   3. Ask the customer to choose.
   4. Turn an objection around.

Step 5—Suggestion Selling

Follow up leads to other sales.

was famous for telling her trainees that you can close more sales with your ears than with your mouth. Listening to the voice of the customer is KEY.

Sales Presentation

Once the initial contact has been established and the salesperson has listened to the customer's problems and needs, the salesperson is in a position to present the merchandise and sales message correctly. How the salesperson presents the product or service depends on the customer and the situation. The key, however, is to get the customer to want to buy your product or service. The salesperson might begin by determining the right price range of products to show the customer. A price too high or too low will generally result in a lost sale. If uncertain, the salesperson should ask the customer about the price range desired.

Next, the salesperson should pick out what he or she believes will be the right product or service to satisfy the customer's needs. The salesperson should be careful not to show the customer too many products so as to avoid confusing the customer.

The salesperson should tell the customer about the merchandise in an appealing way, stressing the features that are the outstanding qualities or characteristics of the product, and have the customer handle the merchandise. The salesperson can then help the customer decide on the product or service that best fulfills the customer's needs. The salesperson should handle any objection that the customer might have, replace the unneeded items, and continue to stress the features and benefits of the product the customer seems most interested in.

Closing the Sale

closing the sale
Is the action the salesperson takes to bring a potential sale to its natural conclusion.

Closing the sale is a natural conclusion to the selling process. However, for most salespeople closing the sale is the most difficult part of the job. In fact, by some estimates almost three-quarters of all lost sales occur during this stage of the selling process because the salesperson didn't ask for the sale. The salesperson was either afraid of rejection or, worse, was unaware that the customer was ready to make the purchase. Remember, the salesperson is there to help the customer solve a problem, and so should not be afraid to ask for the sale. The key to closing the sale is to determine what is going on in the customer's mind. Exhibit 12.9 lists some of the things a salesperson should watch for at this stage of the selling process. If the salesperson waits too long or is too impatient in completing this step, the customer will be gone before the salesperson realizes it. There are four effective ways to close a sale: (1) make the decision for the customer, (2) assume that the decision has been made and ask if the sale will be cash or charge, (3) ask the customer to select the product or service, and (4) turn an objection around by stressing a positive aspect of the product. For example, a salesperson might suggest that although the initial cost of a product might be high, its longer life span will reduce total cost.

In Chapter 3's discussion of the Consumer Behavior Model post-purchase resentment was described. This can occur whether the consumer is buying a car, a sport coat, or spring break get-a-way. Usually, the more expensive the purchase, the greater the doubt and the higher the risk of dissatisfaction. Over the years, good salespeople selling expensive products have found the following three steps to be effective when dealing with this problem:

1. Always congratulate the customer for making a wise decision. As soon as customers agree to a purchase, assure them that others have been happy with their decision to purchase the same item, and you know they will be equally satisfied.

Exhibit 12.9
Closing Signals the Salespeople Should Watch For

The customer reexamines the product carefully.
The customer tries on the product (i.e., trying on a sport coat or strapping on a wristwatch).
The customer begins to read the warranty or brochure.
The customer makes the following statements:
- I always wanted a compact disc player.
- I never realized that these were so inexpensive.
- I bet my wife would love this.

The customer asks the following questions:
- Does this come in any other colors?
- Do you accept Discover cards?
- Can you deliver this tomorrow?
- Do you have a size 7 in this style?
- Do you accept trade-ins?
- Do you have any training sessions available?
- Do you have it in stock?
- What accessories are available?
- Where would I take it to get it serviced?
- Is it really that easy to operate?

2. Always send a thank-you note. Nordstrom's system has shown everyone the value of these notes by the positive customer responses and referrals.
3. Get the customer in possession of the product as quickly as possible. If the products can't be delivered immediately, send updates on the progress of those orders, even if it is only a phone call or e-mail.

Suggestion Selling

An effective salesperson continues to sell even after the sale has been completed. An additional sale is always the possibility. The salesperson should find out if the customer has any other needs or if the customer knows of anybody else with needs that can be solved with the salesperson's product line. Many retailers refer to suggestion selling as filling the basket. A couple of examples would be selling a Valentine's gift to a college student for his girlfriend and then asking if he needs help with a gift for his mother or suggesting an extra ink cartridge to a customer that just purchased a printer (because most cartridges in printers are only half-full).

Many customers appreciate suggestion selling because it often eliminates a second shopping trip. However, it may also decrease a consumer's satisfaction with the retailer as some customers view suggestion selling as an annoyance.

The Customer Service and Sales Enhancement Audit

LO 6

What is involved in a customer service audit?

Up to this point, we have discussed the level and type of sales personnel needed in a retail operation; the types of retail selling; the selection, training, and management of the sales force; the factors to consider when evaluating individual salespeople, and how to sell in a retail store. These are microapproaches to improving the productivity of an individual. How do we get macro answers for the performance of a whole department or a whole store? Remember the example earlier in this chapter of those retailers who had 49 million possible buyers walk out of their stores without any salesperson contact. One solution is an audit of the retailer's customer services and sales enhancement programs.[32]

Such an audit, which can easily be performed by the retailer's own staff or by a consultant, provides the direction that enables retailers to capture the unrealized potential of customers who walk out with no salesperson contact. It analyzes current levels of performance by selling area within each store, revealing how customers shop the store and the extent of the service they receive. It is *not* an attempt to learn what the customers want (e.g., "friendly and competent salespeople," "low prices," "free assembly"); instead, it concentrates on the facts of their shopping experience.

The audit is usually performed by having the retailer's staff, or hired researchers, intercept customers as they leave the store and ask about their experience in the store. The number of customers interviewed should reflect the size and shopping patterns of each store. The objectives of the audit are to:

- Identify the service, salesmanship, and sales enhancement methods that will produce more sales from the existing shopping traffic.
- Target the methods by store and selling area that will produce the most significant improvements.
- Determine the added sales that can be generated by improving the accepted service level, salesmanship, and sales enhancement programs.

Upon completion, the audit provides management with a detailed analysis of current sales activity by location and by selling area. It identifies how and where additional sales volume is available. It measures, analyzes, and reports on the specific factors.

BASIC SERVICE

1. *Customer contact.* In stores that purport to offer service, there can be no sale if the shopper has no contact with a salesperson or a cashier. Increasing the number of shoppers who are approached increases the number of shoppers who are likely to buy.
2. *Salesperson-initiated contact.* Motivated salespeople—those who do not wait for customers to approach them—can prevent walk-outs and generate more sales from shoppers who otherwise might have to spend shopping time looking for a salesperson.
3. *Customer acknowledgment.* Greeting customers within a short time frame also prevents walk-outs and provides more shopping time. It keeps the shopper in a favorable buying mood.

SALESMANSHIP

4. *Merchandise knowledge.* A salesperson with product knowledge can answer a shopper's questions, enhance the transaction, help to consummate the sales, prevent lost sales, and even add to the purchase.
5. *Needs clarification.* Asking the proper questions enables the salesperson to present and show the proper merchandise.
6. *Active selling.* Actively selling the merchandise and volunteering advice about the use and care of the goods, as well as stating the advantages of ownership, helps to consummate the sale.

7. *Suggestion selling.* Suggesting additional and/or complementary merchandise may increase the value of the sale. (The audit should also measure the number of times that suggestion selling resulted in an additional purchase.)

SALES ENHANCEMENT

8. *Impulse purchasing.* Proper selection of merchandise, packaging, location within a department, presentation, and then servicing the transaction will increase the productivity of shopping traffic.
9. *Walkouts.* Retaining sales that would otherwise be lost is one of the most direct and immediate routes to sales improvement. Offering the desired goods in easy-to-find locations is the most obvious method for reducing walkouts. However, customer contact and salesmanship can be a major deterrent of walkouts among those who come to buy.

These elements of service, salesmanship, and sales enhancement are measured and reported by selling area within each store, enabling management to apply targeted training programs. It is usually not necessary to spend the money to train or retrain all personnel in each store for each of the techniques. However, when applied, the method can add significantly to the value of each transaction. For example, for the four chains cited in our earlier example, the incremental sales transactions for the average salesperson after the audit were:

10%	when the salesperson initiated the contact with the shopper.
3%	when the salesperson acknowledged the customer's presence in a timely manner.
12%	when the salesperson was able to answer the customer's questions.
14%	when the salesperson asked questions to clarify the shopper's needs.
18%	when the salesperson actively "sold" the merchandise.
48%	when the salesperson suggested additional or complementary merchandise and the suggestion was taken.

No incremental addition to the average salesperson can be calculated for increasing contacts with shoppers, for improving the rate of impulse buying, or for reducing walkouts. The reason is obvious: when these techniques are applied and are successful, an entirely new transaction is created!

To provide management with an action program, the **customer service and sales enhancement audit** includes a series of exception reports showing specifically what improvement is necessary within each selling area at each company store. The dollar value also is listed, so that management can know the added volume that is available by applying targeted retraining programs. The report should list the causes of walk-outs for each selling area at each location. Management therefore receives an analysis of current performance by selling area at each company location and the specific action necessary to capture unrealized potential. The dollar opportunity is also calculated to highlight the value of each improvement. Exception reports make it easy to implement the program.

customer service and sales enhancement audit
provides management with a detailed analysis of current sales activity by location and by selling area.

Every day, within all types of stores, there are "acres of diamonds in their own backyards." Shoppers are continuing to visit stores in large numbers, many of them willing, able, and anxious to be converted into buyers. Management's task is to identify where and how that can be accomplished. That is the function of the audit.

STUDENT STUDY GUIDE

SUMMARY

LO 1

Why is customer service so important in retailing?

This chapter emphasizes that customer service is a key revenue-generating variable for the retailer. To properly manage the customer service decision area, the retailer needs to build a customer relationship by integrating customer service with merchandise, promotion, building and fixtures, price, and credit management. Only an integrated customer service program will allow the retailer to achieve maximum profits.

LO 2

What are the various customer services that a retailer can offer?

Customer services are classified into pretransaction, transaction, and posttransaction services. Pretransaction services make it easier for a potential customer to shop at a retailer's location or learn about the retailer's offering. Common examples are convenient hours and informational aids. Transaction-related services make it easier for the customer to complete a transaction. Popular transaction-related services are consumer credit, gift wrapping and packaging, check cashing, gift cards, personal shopping, merchandise availability, personal selling, and the transaction itself. Posttransaction services influence the customer's satisfaction with the merchandise after the transaction. The most frequently encountered are handling of complaints, merchandise returns, servicing, repairing and warranting, delivery, and post-sale follow-up.

LO 3

How should a retailer determine which services to offer?

Conventional wisdom suggests that in establishing the mix of customer services the retailer should consider six factors: retailer's characteristics, competition, type of merchandise, price image, target market income, and cost of the service.

LO 4

What are the various management problems involved in retail selling, salesperson selection, and training and evaluation?

This chapter also illustrates the role of managing the retail salesperson. Regardless of whether salesclerks are primarily order getters or order takers, they play an important role in the demand for a retailer's products. However, the role played by the order getter is obviously more important in this regard.

Various criteria to be used in the selection of a selling staff and its training program were discussed. The section ended by reviewing performance evaluation of retail salespeople.

LO 5

What steps are involved in the retail selling process?

The retail selling process consists of five steps—prospecting, approach, presentation, close, and suggestion selling. The length of time a salesperson spends on each step depends on the product type, customer, and selling situation.

LO 6

What is involved in a customer service audit?

An audit of the retailer's customer services and sales enhancement programs enables retailers to capture the unrealized potential of customers who walk out without salesperson contact. It analyzes current levels of performance by selling area within each company store, revealing how customers shop the store and the extent of the service they receive. It is *not* an attempt to learn what the customers want, but concentrates on the facts of their shopping experience.

TERMS TO REMEMBER

high-quality service
relationship retailing
customer service
transient customer
pretransaction services
transaction services
personal shopping
dwell time
posttransaction services
conversion rate
prospecting
closing the sale
customer service and sales enhancement audit

REVIEW AND DISCUSSION QUESTIONS

Why is customer service so important in retailing?

LO 1

1. Your store manager just told you that since profits have been falling over the past year, he has recommended to the owners that they could increase profits by cutting back further on customer services. After all, customers don't really expect service anymore. Agree or disagree with this statement and explain your reasoning.
2. It is said that the first two tasks in retailing are getting consumers from your trading area into your store and then converting these consumers into loyal customers. Which is the easiest and most cost-effective task?
3. Should online customers expect the same type of service that bricks-and-mortar customers get from retailers selling similar merchandise? Explain the reasoning behind your answer.

What are the various customer services that a retailer can offer?

LO 2

4. A major discounter was recently quoted as saying that he "no longer worries about dwell time. After all, low price is the only factor that drives sales." Do you agree or disagree with this statement? What is your reasoning?
5. Are posttransaction services more important for bricks-and-mortar retailers or online retailers? What do you feel accounts for the differences between these two types of retailers?

How should a retailer determine which services to offer?

LO 3

6. How does the type of customer affect the level of customer service a retailer should offer?
7. Shouldn't all retailers seek to exceed their competition's level of customer service? Explain the reasoning behind your answer.

What are the various management problems involved in retail selling, salesperson selection, and training and evaluation?

LO 4

8. Develop a list of predictor variables you would use to screen applicants for a sales position in (a) a jewelry department in a high-prestige department store, (b) a used-car dealership, (c) a health club, and (d) an antique shop.
9. A men's clothing store chain has analyzed the annual sales per salesperson in ten of its stores nationwide. The sales per salesperson range from a low of $91,000 to a high of $178,000. Develop the list of factors that might help to explain this wide variation.

LO 5

What is involved in the retail selling process?

10. When you are shopping for yourself, do you appreciate it when the salesperson uses suggestion selling techniques? Does the type of merchandise make a difference in your answer?
11. Provide examples of suggestion selling in a home improvement store.
12. Why is selling so much more important for retailers of services than it is for retailers selling physical products?

LO 6

What is involved in a customer service audit?

13. Why is it so important that a retailer's sales personnel be taught that each customer must be contacted by a sales associate each time the customer enters the store? Don't some customers just want to be left alone to look around?

SAMPLE TEST QUESTIONS

LO 1

A transient customer is a consumer who visits a retailer:

a. and finds the item desired in a matter of minutes
b. only when his/her regular retailer is closed
c. that does not meet his/her customer service expectations
d. while on vacation
e. and then visits all the other retailers in the neighborhood

LO 2

Merchandise availability is an example of a(n):

a. cost of sales
b. pretransaction service
c. operating cost
d. posttransaction service
e. transaction service

LO 3

Which of the following is not a factor in determining the service level to offer?

a. income of target market
b. price image of the retailer
c. services offered by the competition
d. firm's management structure
e. retailer's characteristics

LO 4

Which one of the following factors is not one of the elements that need to be considered when designing a sales job?

a. feedback from supervisors
b. the number of complaints a salesperson should have to handle
c. the amount of variety involved
d. the appropriate degree of autonomy
e. the level of task identity present

LO 5

What is the first step that a salesperson should take during the sales presentation?

a. Inform the customer about the merchandise in an appealing manner.
b. Select the right product or service that he/she believes will satisfy the customer's needs.
c. Greet the customer.
d. Help the customer to decide on the product that best fulfills the customer's needs.
e. Determine the right price range of products.

Which of the following is not an objective of a customer service audit?

LO 6

APPLICATIONS

a. It is an attempt to learn what are the most important considerations for customers when choosing a store, i.e., low prices or ease of the transaction.
b. It identifies the service, salesmanship, and sales enhancement methods that the retailer can use to produce more sales from the existing shopping traffic.
c. It targets which methods can be used to produce significant customer service improvement.
d. It helps determine the added sales that can be generated by improving the current level of customer service.
e. All of the above are customer service audit objectives.

WRITING AND SPEAKING EXERCISE

As manager for a fast-food hamburger chain, you have been approached by your counterpart at a rival Mexican food chain two blocks away. He wants to know if you would be willing to extend your chain's employee discount to his employees. In return, he would do the same for your employees.

Currently, both chains offer their employees a 50 percent discount on all purchases. However, the employees tire of eating from the same menu all the time and as a result they usually go to other nearby restaurants when working long (six or eight hours) shifts.

At first the idea appeals to you since it is a means of aiding your employees to stretch their limited earnings and provide them with some variety in food selection. It may even benefit you, as your employees will witness how a competitor operates. Thus, they can see how they compare in terms of their strengths and weaknesses versus the competition. However, the thought of them being seen by customers in the Mexican restaurant while wearing your chain's uniform does worry you.

Prepare a response to the other manager outlining your position on this subject.

RETAIL PROJECT

As you are approaching graduation you decide that you need a new suit for interviewing. In considering your shopping alternatives, you decide to compare online clothing stores versus bricks-and-mortar stores.

Determine the difference in the amount of time involved in shopping between the two types of retailers, the time it would take for you to obtain the clothing from each, and price. Which would you choose to use?

PLANNING YOUR OWN RETAIL BUSINESS

Donnelly's Jewelers, a family business your grandfather started in 1952, had annual sales last year of $900,560. Your parents, who purchased this business from your grandfather in 1981, have asked you to help them develop a strategy to improve sales. Since you plan to open a second Donnelly's Jewelers store upon graduation, with your family's support, you want to use this opportunity to impress your parents with your business and retail marketing skills.

In reviewing the records of the store you were surprised to find that a record had been kept of how many shoppers visited the store on a daily basis. For the most recent year you computed that there were 15,000 visitors and that 2,803 of these made a purchase. You also have spent the last few weeks observing the salespeople (including your parents) make sales presentations. Your observation is that they do a good job of approaching shoppers and making a sales presentation, but, they are quite weak and passive on closing a sale. You also have observed little effort is made to cross-sell merchandise.

Your recommendation is to have a local professor who teaches a course in personal selling conduct a sales training workshop. This two-day workshop would cost $5,000. After consulting with the professor, you both believe the training should produce an increase in average transaction size of $30 and an increase in the conversion rate of 5 percent.

Based on the preceding information, show the impact on annual sales of the proposed training program.

CASE

The Internship

Back in February Kim Wake interviewed with JoBeth Brenholtz for a Summer Internship with Reed's. Ms Brenholtz's family has owned Reed's, a locally owned women's apparel store located in a neighborhood center near the campus, for over a half-century. Kim explained to Ms. Brenholtz that she really wasn't sure if a career in retailing was what she wanted to do with her college education. JoBeth told her not to worry, that this was what the internship was for—to learn about and experience what was actually involved in a retailing career.

The Reed's internship would last twelve weeks and during that time she would spend five weeks working on the sales floor, two weeks in the buying office, and one week each in display, receiving, and advertising promotion. The final two weeks would entail a special project.

In late July, Ms. Brenholtz's secretary called Kim while she was on the sales floor and asked if she could stop by JoBeth's office before the store opened the next morning. Kim guessed it would be about the special project.

Just before the store's 10 A.M. opening, Kim was ushered into the executive office suite. Kim was here once before, on her first day on the job. In fact, while she had seen Ms. Brenholtz occasionally walking the store over the past eight weeks, she really hadn't talked to her since that earlier visit. Kim had noticed that Ms. Brenholtz seldom did anything more than exchange pleasantries with the store's lower-level employees as she walked through the store.

After visiting with Kim about her internship experiences thus far, Ms. Brenholtz explained that Kim's project would be to review the store's operation. She realized that Kim was only going to be a college senior and had rather limited retailing experience. However, Kim's lack of long-held beliefs was appealing. The store needed a fresh analysis because after years of steady growth, sales had declined slightly the past three years. The meeting ended with Kim asking if she could wait until the end of August to complete the report.

That night Kim started thinking about what she should say in her report. She remembered from her retailing class that the first two tasks of any retailer were to get consumers into the store and then convert them into customers. Despite her rather abbreviated retailing career, Kim was already aware that the common retail excuse for poor sales was lack of traffic. Still Kim wasn't sure that this was the real problem. So she started a list based on her observations over the past two months at Reed's:

- In conversations with employees, no one had mentioned that store traffic had been declining over the past few years.
- She estimated that the store's conversion rate was around 20 percent.
- In reviewing her own training, she really didn't think that Reed's spent more than an hour covering store policies and procedures. When she went on the sales floor, the area manager spent time explaining the scanner and cash register, but nobody taught her about selling. She assumed that his was the way it was with all new salespeople.
- Kim heard that over the past few years, the store had experienced a high amount of employee turnover. While she wasn't sure of the actual number, she had observed that a significant number of sales positions were filled by part-timers.
- Over the past two months, she felt that the employees were doing a good job on what they were told to do. In fact, after her third week on the floor, the assistant store manager congratulated her for not having any errors cashing out of the register at the end of her shifts.

Questions

1. Should JoBeth Brenholtz spend more time on the sales floor? Why?
2. If Reed's was willing to spend more money to increase sales, should the retailer spend it on promotions to increase traffic or on training to increase the conversion rate?
3. Is it a mistake to have too many part-time employees? Does this situation impact customer service? How?
4. Do you agree or disagree with the statement that "Reed's seems to be a typical example of a retailer that doesn't evaluate employees on their ability to serve the customer, but on their ability to cash out correctly." What should be done about this?
5. What should be the key point for Kim to address in this memo?

chapter 13

Store Layout and Design

Overview:

In this chapter we discuss the place where all retailing activities come together—the retail store. The store can be the most meaningful form of communication between the retailer and its customers. Most important, the store is where sales happen—or fail to happen. We will see that despite its hundreds of elements, the store has two primary roles: creating the proper store image and increasing the productivity of the sales space. We identify the most critical elements in creating a successful retail store and describe the art and science of store planning, merchandise presentation, and design.

Learning Objectives:

After reading this chapter, you should be able to:

1. List the elements of a store's environment and define its two primary objectives.
2. Discuss the steps involved in planning the store.
3. Describe how various types of fixtures, merchandise presentation methods and techniques, and the psychology of merchandise presentation are used to increase the productivity of the sales floor.
4. Describe why store design is so important to a store's success.
5. Explain the role of visual communications in a retail store.

LO 1

Introduction to Store Layout Management

What are the elements of a store's environment?

The previous chapter discussed how customer service and personal selling can be used to develop a relationship with the customer. This chapter examines another method retailers can use to initiate and continue this relationship—the retail store itself. Retailers must never forget the old axiom that "we all sell discretionary merchandise; therefore, we must package it with theater and excitement." Today's finicky customers demand sizzle with their steak. *Setting* and *presentation* are now critical factors in serving the customer. All too often the retailer, realizing the importance of getting customers into a store, develops an excellent promotional campaign only to have the customer become turned-off upon entering the store. Successful retailers today use their stores as a means to excite their customers so they will spend more time looking and thus view more merchandise. A positive first impression is particularly important when customers enter the store with a negative attitude or emotion because, in the current economy of time poverty, they have other things they would rather be doing.[1] In fact, no other variable in the retailing mix influences the consumer's initial perception of a bricks-and-mortar retailer as much as the store itself. Profitable retailers today are spending a great deal of time and effort making sure the right things happen in their store and that the right customers enter the store, shop, and spend money. Simply put, for retailers the store is "where the action is," and this includes such seemingly minor details as the placement of merchandise.

Although this chapter is concerned with the physical store, the same factors may be used to develop an e-tailer's "virtual store." Just as with a bricks-and-mortar location, the first impression is most important. After all, most consumers spend less than five seconds at a Web site the first time they visit. Therefore, there is a limited window of opportunity to capture the attention of an online user. Although there is no strict list of do's and don'ts, given that the online "rules" are constantly changing, a few underlying fundamentals have been identified that can drive repeat visits and encourage purchasing:

- *Keep content current.* Online consumers browse frequently and therefore it is very important to continually update information on the site. Two aspects should be considered.
    1. Merchandise presentation: The web offers e-tailers a plethora of merchandise presentation options. Not limited by physical restraints, e-tailers can provide consumers with 3D presentations that allow a 360-degree view of merchandise.
    2. Merchandise description: Write in Web-ese. Online consumers scan information as opposed to reading it.
- *Make the site easy and enjoyable to use.* Ease of use is a primary concern for online consumers. Ease of use means that users with little or no experience either online or with your product category should easily be able to move about the site and find the information they desire. Much like signage in a bricks-and-mortar world, e-tailers must clearly show the way for online consumers.
- *Structure an online community where consumers can interact with one another or contribute to the site's content.* The virtual world allows for new methods of integrating customers into a retailer's business. Offering potential consumers an opportunity to become involved in the site can build a loyal clientele.

store image
Is the overall perception the consumer has of the store's environment.

space productivity
Represents how effectively the retailer utilizes its space and is usually measured by sales per square foot of selling space or gross margin dollars per square foot of selling space.

Although a store is composed of literally thousands of details, the two primary objectives around which all activities, functions, and goals revolve are **store image** and **space productivity**. However, before discussing these two objectives, it is important to identify the elements that compose the store environment (shown in Exhibit 13.1), each of which will be discussed in detail in this chapter.

Elements of the Store Environment

Successful retailers, whether operating traditional or virtual stores, place a heavy emphasis on designing their physical facilities or Web sites so as to enhance image and increase productivity. — Dollars & Sense

The first decision the retailer must make in planning a store is how to allocate the scarce resource, space. The retailer creates a store layout that shows the location of all merchandise departments and the placement of circulation aisles to allow

Exhibit 13.1
Elements That Compose the Store Environment

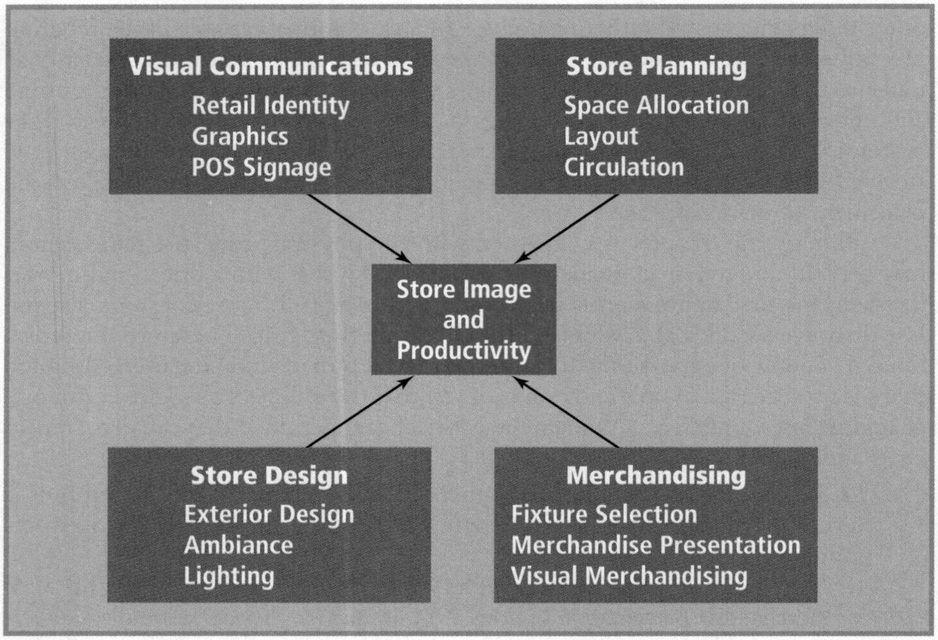

customers to move through the store. As discussed above, the merchandise presentation must be exciting so as to catch and hold customers' attention, be easy to understand, and encourage shoppers to browse, evaluate, and buy. Therefore, the presentation of the merchandise is a critical factor in the selling power of a store and has a significant effect on the store image. A bookstore with a high percentage of face-outs, for example, can create the image of being a specialty book boutique that carries a limited selection of exclusive titles and is, therefore, a rather pricey place to shop. A bookstore with virtually all spine-outs is often perceived as cramming in a huge selection of titles sold at low prices. Thus, merchandise presentation is a critical factor in determining both store image and productivity.

© Michelle D. Bridewell/PhotoEdit

Bookstores that display books using face-outs create a specialty and higher price store image.

Most shoppers are accustomed to noticing the layout and design of a store, which is composed of all the elements affecting the human senses of sight, hearing, smell, and touch. An effective store layout and design, including the storefront, creates a comfortable environment that enhances the merchandise and entices shoppers to browse and buy. Lighting is an important element that should not be overlooked. Both display and in-store lighting help create the proper image and also draw customers' eyes around the store, onto merchandise, and ultimately encourage them to purchase the product.[2] Likewise, in-store graphics such as art, photography, and signs form an important visual communication link between the store and its customers by providing much-needed information on how to shop in the store. The chapter's Retailing: The Inside Story box gives a description of how supermarket managers have perfected the art of store design and layout.

Sometimes retailers tend to forget the lessons in the Retailing: The Inside Story box. For example, many managers ignore their own 25-25-50 rule on endcaps. This rule states that 25 percent of all endcaps should be advertised "sale" merchandise that the customer will seek out and another 25 percent should be unadvertised "sale" items that will cause the customer to be alert when looking at an endcap. The remaining 50 percent should be regular priced seasonal or impulse merchandise. Retailers tend to violate this rule when manufacturers offer money for the right to set up their own displays. While the managers will gain a short-term profit by renting out most of their endcap space, they often destroy the long-term profits that a well-defined endcap policy generates.

Bookstores that display books using spine-outs create a high-volume, low-price store image.

Objectives of the Store Environment

The two primary objectives of creating the desired store image and increasing space productivity amount to a simple description of the three basic tasks of retailing described in Exhibit 12.3 on page 392:

- Get customers into the store (*market image*)
- Once inside the store, convert them into customers buying merchandise (*space productivity*)
- Do this in the most efficient manner possible

The retailer must constantly balance the first two elements of the model, as they are sometimes at odds. After all, some customers may be attracted because they expect a nice clean uncluttered shop with low prices. However, store management realizes that low prices are the result of high turnover and high turnover often means a congested shopping environment.

Developing a Store Image

The starting point in creating this image is, of course, the merchandise carried in the store, along with the retailer's promotional activities, customer service, cleanliness, and sales force. That the store image serves a critical role in the store selection process is best illustrated by research in the supermarket industry showing that overall cleanliness is the most important criterion in deciding where to shop.[3] Other important criteria were low prices, accurate price scanning, pleasant and accurate checkout clerks, clearly labeled prices, and well-stocked shelves.[4]

To further illustrate the importance of store image, consider for a moment the words *7-Eleven*. For most people, these words represent more than just two numbers. Together, they form the name of one of the most familiar retailers, the worldwide chain with more than 27,000 convenience stores.

Retailing: The Inside Story

Consumer Behavior: Supermarket Style

While it is unknown how many supermarket managers took a consumer behavior class in college, they sure know how to practice the art.

OBSERVE:

Most consumers not only are right-handed, they think right-headed.

- Since supermarkets make more money on their store's private label brands, they stock the store brands to the right of the name brands so that the consumer has to reach across the store brand to grab the name brand.
- Since shoppers are more prone to look right, supermarkets display the higher gross margin merchandise on the right side of an aisle, as gauged from the predominant direction of cart traffic. Also, displays should be set so that they are visible on the right side as shoppers travel the predominant path.
- Since 90 percent of all customers entering a store turn right, that area is the most valuable for the store. Thus it is no accident that produce, a deli, or a bakery is the first section that a customer will reach. That is because they can see, feel, and smell the merchandise. This in turn will get their mouths watering and make them hungry. Any supermarket manager will tell you that their best customer is a hungry customer.
- When customers enter a store and begin to turn right, they tend to scan the entire store from left to right and then fix their eyes on an object (sign or merchandise) at a 45 degree angle from the point of entry.
- Grocers also use the most recognizable brand to lead off the product category as the consumer is walking towards it. That is, they use Coca-Cola to lead off soft drinks, Fusion to lead off razors, and Secret to lead off deodorants.

Most consumers think "neatness" counts.

- Merchants sometimes try to make their point-of-purchase displays look like a mess. These so-called "dump displays" which are affectionately known by some grocers as "organized chaos" are deliberately arranged in a haphazard fashion so the items inside look cheap and are, therefore, perceived as a great bargain. The same thought process works for merchants leaving out open cartons piled on top of another. Usually the items are not on sale, they merely look "hot" or such a "great deal" that the retailer can not keep the merchandise in stock.
- For the same reason, handwritten (as long as they are legible) signs create the impression of recently lowered prices (i.e., there has not been time to get the printed signs). Thus, even though they do not always look great, handwritten signs move the merchandise faster than standard printed signs.

Most consumers are likely to focus on a large central display.

- The point-of-purchase displays at the end of each supermarket aisle that are known in the trade as endcaps are usually the focus of customers' attention as they wheel their carts through the store. Thus, a smart retailer knows to follow the 25-25-50 rule.

Consumers are creatures of habit and when something is out of place they become more sensitive to their environment.

- Every supermarket will make regularly scheduled display changes for staple items, such as cake mixes, salad dressings, and cereals. They do not want to move the items to new locations because that may upset time-pressed customers. However, by changing shelf displays of these staples, the grocer draws the attention of the customer, thereby increasing the chances of an impulse sale.

There is a little bit of greed in every one of us.

- Supermarket managers may put a limit on the purchase of a sale item, by advertising "Limit 4 to a Customer." Not only will consumers think that the limit restrictions mean it's a great deal, but they will often buy the limit, even if they don't need that many.
- Another version of the above is the special "10 for $x" where x is an even dollar amount, such as 10 for $9, or 10 for $6. Many of these promotions are "mix and match" deals where the customer can choose among several different items. In many cases, the new "sale" price is slightly higher than the typical sale price. Retailers have found that selling an item on sale at $0.79 each usually results in one sale. However, at 10 for $8, or even $9, many consumers will stock up and buy more than one unit.
- Similarly, many customers will get so excited by finding a great price on a staple like peanut butter, they will fail to notice that the item's complimentary products—in this case, jelly and bread—may have had their prices increased.

Source: Based on insights provided Jim Lukens, Paul Adams, Zack Adcock, and Paul Easter.

The thoughts and emotions this logo evokes in customers constitute 7-Eleven's store image. Regardless of what its managers would like its market image to be, regardless of what image they have tried to create, the store's actual image exists only in the heads and hearts of consumers. Many factors influence that image.

First, the name itself has a great influence. If the stores were called "8-Twelve," we all might have a different image in our heads. The name was created in 1946 to stress the stores' operating hours, 7 A. M. to 11 P. M. every day, then unheard-of in retailing.[5] The rhythm and rhyme of *seven* and *eleven* allow the name to roll easily off the tongue and be memorable, even if the customer does not shoot craps. (In craps a 7 or 11 on the shooter's first roll is a winner.) The orange and green colors of the logo suggest quality. The storefront, historically a large black mansard roof, conveys a heavy, masculine appearance, and the windows plastered with price savings signs suggest a promotional environment. When you walk in the store, a buzzer warns clerks of entering shoppers, suggesting a concern about safety and theft. The smell of cheese nachos and the sight of sausages and hot dogs rolling around on the hot dogger create a certain atmosphere. Even the uniforms worn by the store clerks leave an impression, which joins all other impressions to create 7-Eleven's store image in our minds. The consumer's image of a store is, therefore, a combination of out-of-store factors—location (Chapter 7), advertising and publicity (Chapter 11), and the various services offered (Chapter 12)—plus the dozens of in-store variables perceived by the consumer.

In fact, 7-Eleven has conducted experiments to change its store image to that of a high-quality food service provider. Managers have altered not only the merchandise mix but also such store variables as colors, layout, light levels, and aisle widths to affect the consumer's perception of a 7-Eleven store.

This is why planning the store environment is so important to a retailer. Although advertising and other promotional activities are important in establishing a desired store image, the store itself makes the most significant and lasting impression on our collective consciousness and it is here that the retailer must focus great energy. Today, McDonalds, after 30 years without a major design overhaul, is tempting fate by testing a change in its appearance. The redesign (comfortable armchairs, cool hanging lights, funky graphics, photos on the walls, and Wi-Fi access) is risky and has many franchisees up in arms over the high costs of a makeover. But company officials believe the overhaul is needed to conform to its revamped menu of healthier items aimed at attracting a new breed of customer. After all, McDonalds seeks to be a "forever young" brand and the new layout is another way of delivering on that promise.[6] Layout makeovers are complicated by the knowledge that consumers are extremely fickle, able to change their feelings about retailers at any time for little substantive reason, and the fact that today there are more stores than ever vying for limited consumer dollars. It is not surprising that image engineering—the ability to create and change a store's image—becomes more important every day for a retailer's survival.

Increasing Space Productivity

The store's image attracts customers. However, when customers are visiting the store or its Web site, the retailer must also convince them to make a purchase. Therefore, a store must increase its space productivity, a goal that is summarized in a simple but powerful truism in retailing: *The more merchandise customers are exposed to that is presented in an orderly manner, the more they tend to buy*. The typical shopper in a department store goes into only two or three shopping areas per trip. By carefully planning the store environment, the retailer can encourage customers to flow through the entire store, or at least through more shopping areas, and see a wider variety of merchandise. The proper use of in-store advertising and displays will let the customer know what's happening in other departments and encourage a visit to those areas. Conversely, however, the retailer does not want to have merchandise pushed into every conceivable nook and cranny of the store so that customers cannot get to it.

Dollars & Sense

Successful retailers design their stores to expose shoppers to as much merchandise as possible, displayed in a safe and orderly manner, while creating an uncongested shopping environment.

As will be discussed later in the chapter's What's New box, many retailers are focusing more attention on in-store marketing, based on the theory that marketing dollars spent inside the store, in the form of store design, merchandise presentation, visual displays, or in-store promotions, should lead to significantly greater sales and profit increases than marketing dollars spent on advertising and other out-of-store vehicles such as public relations and promotions. After all, it is easier and more cost effective to get a consumer who is already in your store to buy more merchandise than planned than to persuade a new consumer to come into your store.

shrinkage
Represents merchandise that cannot be accounted for due to theft, loss, or damage.

One factor that detracts from space productivity is shrinkage, or the loss of merchandise through theft, loss, and damage, which was discussed back in Chapter 9. It is called **shrinkage** because retailers usually do not know what happened to the missing items, only that the inventory level in the store has somehow shrunk. Even stores that move customers through the entire space and effectively use in-store marketing techniques to maximize sales can fall victim to high shrinkage. Remember, when a store sells an item for $1.29, it earns only a small percentage of that sale, perhaps ranging from 15 to 60 cents. When that item is stolen, lost, or damaged, however, the store loses the cost of that $1.29 item—for example 69 cents, in the case of a $1.29 item—and this loss is deducted from the store's overall sales. Shrinkage ranges from 1 to 4 percent of retail sales. Although this may seem like a small number, consider that after-tax profit for many retailers is little more than 4 percent, so high shrinkage alone can make the difference between a profit and a loss.

Therefore, to enhance space productivity, retailers must incorporate planning, merchandise presentation, and design strategies that minimize shrinkage by avoiding hidden areas of the store. They should also seek to reduce the number of times merchandise must be moved, during which damage and loss can occur.

LO 2 Store Planning

What is involved in store planning?

Planning an effective retail store resembles planning an effective piece of writing, and moving through a store as a customer is similar to reading an article or a chapter in a book. The merchandise, like text, is there for you to review, understand, and consume. But just as a book needs more than words to make sense, a store needs more than merchandise to be shopable.

The store's layout and design can be compared to the organization of chapters, sections, and subsections in this book. Grouping the words and thoughts into mental "chunks" makes the book easier to digest and understand. Unless a store specializes in only one product type, for example, candles, it would be impossible to shop if that store were not broken into departments and categories. The books would be mixed in with the shovels, the DVDs would be found among the garden plants, and you wouldn't know where to begin.

Signs and graphics are similar to the headings and punctuation, which give you cues to understanding the organization of both a book and the merchandise in a store. Without headings and subheadings, this chapter would be a stream of words, very difficult and, worse, boring, to read and understand. Similarly, without signs, a store would seem like an endless sea of racks and merchandise, annoying to understand and shop.

Finally, the photos, exhibits, charts, and boxes in this book are the retail equivalent of the visual displays and focal points, where merchandise is pulled off the shelf or racks and displayed in theatrical vignettes. Successful retailers use these settings to break up the store space, illustrate merchandise opportunities in the store, and visually demonstrate how certain merchandise goes together or can work in the consumer's life. Like photos and exhibits in a book, these visual displays elaborate on the text, or the bulk of merchandise on the racks, to make statements.

Most important, a retail store and a piece of writing are very similar in the way they affect the consumer. Many writing coaches teach aspiring writers that each time an uncommon word is used or a punctuation mark is missing, the reader hits a "speed bump" in the writing and must mentally pause to consider what is meant. After hitting three speed bumps, the reader may conclude that the writing is too difficult to understand and quit reading.

The same is true in a retail store. All cues must work subliminally to organize the merchandise and guide shoppers effortlessly through the store. Each time shoppers become a bit confused as to where they are, where they need to go, how much an item costs, or where certain merchandise is, they become frustrated. The first or second instance may not even be consciously noticed, but shoppers may quickly become frustrated and walk out, concluding that the store is too hard to shop. Exhibit 13.2 is a list of warning signs that managers should look for, because each warning sign indicates a speed bump waiting to drive customers away from a store.

Most shoppers cannot consciously identify the elements of a good store, but they certainly know when these elements are missing. We have all experienced the feeling that a store seems to "really have it together." It's easy to shop, fun, and exciting; the merchandise is easy to understand; the associates seem friendly. You conclude that this store is a "good shop" and, with any luck, are completely oblivious to the thousands of little details that have guided you through the shopping experience.

floor plan
Is a schematic that shows where merchandise and customer service departments are located, how customers circulate through the store, and how much space is dedicated to each department.

In retailing, the term **floor plan** indicates where merchandise and customer service departments are located, how customers circulate through the store, and how much space is dedicated to each department. The floor plan, which is based around the predicted demands of the store's targeted customer, serves as the backbone of the store and is the fundamental structure around which every other

Exhibit 13.2
These Warning Signs May Indicate a Space Problem

Open spaces on the selling floor, even if the product is on hand
Cluttered and disorganized aisles, hallways, and stockrooms
Excessive time required to put away new receipts
Insufficient staging space for large shipments of advertised products
Sales associates continually required to leave the sales floor to locate additional merchandise
Poor utilization of vertical space and excessive time required to retrieve products stored on high shelves
Sales lag expectations for specific locations where space or fixtures are a known issue
Off-site storage or multiple stockrooms required for a single commodity

element of the store environment takes shape. Successful retailers, such as Wal-Mart with its Retail Link, analyze their sales along with the demographics of the store's trading area when developing a floor plan. These retailers then structure the merchandise to the needs of each store. Thus it is not uncommon for two Targets or Best Buys in the same city to be different in both merchandise carried and in its presentation. This is called **microretailing**, and it means that each store's offerings are tailored to the trading area being served.

microretailing
Occurs when a chain store retailer operating over a wide geographic area, usually nationally, tailors its merchandise and services in each store to the needs of the immediate trading area.

In addition, successful retailers place merchandise in key strategic locations. For example, H.E.B. Grocery Company places the jelly next to the peanut butter, facial tissues next to the cold medicines, and chocolate syrup next to the ice cream. (Next time you are in a supermarket, see if it locates such items together.) Other profitable retailers know that toys and movies are kid magnets and thus display snacks right next to them. Another simple rule to follow is to think of the age of the consumer. For example, a retailer should never put a child's toy on the top shelf where kids can't reach it or denture cream on the bottom shelf where seniors can't easily bend down and get it. Therefore, the store's layout and design, including merchandise location, must be carefully planned to meet the retailer's merchandising goals, make the store easy to understand and shop, and allow merchandise to be effectively presented. The importance of merchandise location can be observed the next time you visit a supermarket. Notice, for instance, that some products are displayed by keeping all the brands from one manufacturer together (cereals, frozen pizzas, and salad dressings) while other products are grouped by category (canned vegetables and fruit, bars of soap, and baking aids, such as flour and sugar).[7] One retailing format that is an exception to such rules is the warehouse club. Costco, for example, uses crazy product positioning as part of its selling formula. The retailer has found that putting toothpaste next to golf clubs and cereals next to computer tables not only increases impulse purchasing but provides customers with a "thrill-of-the-hunt" psychological lift when they find something.[8] Such positioning tends to make customers more alert as to what is available, and retailers know that 30-50 percent of all brick-and-mortar purchases are impulse buys.[9]

stack-outs
Are pallets of merchandise set out on the floor in front of the main shelves.

Almost as important as the placement of merchandise is the reduction of **stack-outs**, those pallets of merchandise set on the floor in front of the main shelves. Although stack-outs may improve the short-run sales of the featured product, their negative impact may offset these marginal sales. As Robert Kahn, the late editor of *Retailing Today* and highly regarded retail consultant, pointed out many times in his newsletter, when there is a stack-out and the customer does not have a specific need on that aisle, then the customer will skip that aisle. This phenomenon is known in retailing as the dreaded "butt-brush," which holds that the likelihood of a woman being converted from a browser to a buyer is inversely proportional to the likelihood of her being brushed on her backside while she is examining merchandise.[10] Thus, any item that requires extensive examination by a woman should never be placed in a narrow aisle. Also, since 30 to 50 percent of all purchases are impulse, the retailer may actually lose sales when shoppers ignore certain aisles, especially when the product being considered requires some type of examination or inspection.

Allocating Space

The starting point for developing a floor plan is analyzing how the available store space, usually measured in square footage, should be allocated to various departments. This allocation can be based on mathematical calculation of the returns generated by different types of merchandise. However, before describing this process, we must understand the various types of space in the store.

Types of Space Needed

Shoppers are most familiar with the sales floor, but this is not the only element in a retail store with which the planner must contend. There are five basic types of space needs in a store: (1) back room; (2) office and other functional spaces; (3) aisles, service areas, and other nonselling areas of the main sales floor; (4) wall merchandise space; and (5) floor merchandise space. The retailer must balance the quest for greater density of merchandise presentation with the shopability and functionality of the store. Since space is the retailer's ultimate scarce resource, rarely can the retailer fully achieve all of its desired goals. Rather, most retailers find themselves compromising on one or more dimensions, carefully weighing priorities, strategies, and special constraints. In reviewing each of these space categories, keep in mind that the overall goal is to make the largest possible portion of the space available to hold merchandise and be shopable.

Back Room. To operate virtually any type of retail store, some space is required as back room, which includes the receiving area to process arriving merchandise and the stockroom to store surplus merchandise. The percentage of space dedicated to the back room varies greatly depending on the type of retailer, but the amount of space is shrinking for all types. Historical back room percentages have ranged from nearly 50 percent in some department stores to as little as 10 percent in some small specialty and convenience stores. General-merchandise stores have historically dedicated about 15 to 20 percent of their store space to the back room. The need to squeeze more sales out of expensive retail space, coupled with new distribution methods allowing smaller, more frequent merchandise deliveries from suppliers (called *quick response inventory* or *efficient consumer response*, depending on the industry involved), have allowed retailers to shrink their back rooms, with department stores cutting back to about 20 percent, and others reducing theirs to 5 percent or even less.

Some recent retail formats, such as warehouse clubs, have receiving areas but virtually no back room stock capacity. In these stores, the store fixtures are usually large "warehouse racks" that carry shopable inventory at reachable heights (up to 84 inches) and large pallets or cartons of excess inventory at higher levels. These racks can be as tall as 15 feet.

By using this strategy, warehouse clubs are taking advantage not only of the width and depth of the store, but also the height. In other words, while retailers pay expensive rents for their store space, as measured in *square* footage, the store and the merchandise can be stacked as high as possible at little additional cost, using the *cubic* footage of the store. The ability of shoppers to reach does limit the height at which *shopable* merchandise can be stacked, but it does not limit the use of this high space to carry excess inventory. The same inventory carried in the back room would require additional square footage, causing either higher rent or reducing the amount of shopable space. Essentially, the sales floor doubles as the back room. This stocking method visually creates a dramatic low-cost image in the store, which can be advantageous to value-oriented retailers, but detrimental to fashion or high-end retailers.

Offices and Other Functional Spaces. Every store must contain a certain amount of office and other functional space. This often includes a break room for associates, a training room, offices for the store manager and assistant managers, a cash office, bathroom facilities for both customers and employees, and perhaps other areas. Though necessary, the location of such functional spaces receives a lower priority than the location of the sales floor and stockroom. Often they are located on mezzanines over the front of the store or over the back stockroom, or in side spaces too small to be stockrooms.

Aisles, Service Areas, and Other Nonselling Areas. Even on the main sales floor, some space must be given up to nonselling functions, the most obvious of which is moving shoppers through the store. The retailer's first step, particularly in larger stores, is to create main aisles through which shoppers will flow on their way through the store, and secondary aisles that draw customers back into the merchandise. These aisles must be large enough to accommodate peak crowds, and in bigger stores may be as wide as 15 feet. The amount of space dedicated to aisles can be significant. For instance, a 15-foot aisle running around the perimeter of an 80,000 square-foot store (the size of a typical discount store) may consume 12,000 square feet, or 15 percent of the entire space!

In addition to aisles, space must be given to dressing rooms, layaway areas, service desks, and other customer service facilities that cannot be merchandised. While the retailer always attempts to minimize the amount of nonmerchandisable space, customer service is an equally important part of a store and should not be shortchanged.

Wall Merchandise Space. The walls are one of the most important elements of a retail store. They serve as fixtures holding tremendous amounts of merchandise as well as providing a visual backdrop for the merchandise on the floor.

Floor Merchandise Space. Finally, we come to the store space with which we as shoppers are most familiar, the floor merchandise space. Here, many different types of fixtures are used to display a wide variety of merchandise. Generally speaking, retailers use bulk fixtures on the floor to carry large quantities of merchandise. But increasingly, retailers are realizing that the best goal is not to just cram the largest possible amount of merchandise on the floor, but to attractively and effectively display the largest amount customers can understand and shop.

Space Allocation Planning

To determine the most productive allocation of space, the retailer must first analyze the profitability and productivity of various categories of merchandise. According to one study, around 20 percent of the average retailer's inventory is either obsolete or not wanted by the retailer's target market.[11] Such a number indicates the importance to retailers of analyzing the profitability and productivity of all merchandise.

There are several methods for measuring these variables. Regardless of the method used, the results must relate some type of output performance measure (e.g., net sales, net profit, or gross margin) to the amount of space used in the store in order to get a productivity figure to help determine the best allocation of the square footage. Two situations may cause a retailer to perform these tasks: revising the space allocation of an existing store and planning a new store.

space productivity index
Is a ratio that compares the percentage of the store's total gross margin that a particular merchandise category generates to its percentage of total store selling space used.

Improving Space Productivity in Existing Stores. A retailer that has been in business for some time can develop a sales history on which to evaluate merchandise performance, refine space allocations, and enhance space productivity. One easy measure to use is the **space productivity index**, which compares the percentage of the store's total gross margin dollars for a particular merchandise category to its percentage of space utilized. An index rating of 1.0 would be an ideal department size. If the index is greater than 1.0, the product category is generating a larger

Category	Total Sales	Sales as % of Total	Total Sq. Ft.	Sq. Ft. as % of Total	Sales per Sq. Ft.	Total G.M. $	G.M. $ as % of Total	Space Productivity Index
Softlines								
Juniors	259,645	3.9	1,602	2.9	162.08	211,497	4.57	1.58
Dresses	47,829	0.7	608	1.1	78.67	33,426	0.72	0.66
Misses	512,458	7.7	3,702	6.7	138.43	429,403	9.29	1.39
Womens	170,819	2.6	1,934	3.5	88.33	148,899	3.22	0.92
Boys	184,485	2.8	2,542	4.6	72.58	144,866	3.13	0.68
Mens	751,604	11.3	3,591	6.5	209.30	603,330	13.05	2.01
Infants	204,983	3.1	1,658	3.0	123.63	142,545	3.08	1.03
Toddlers	47,829	0.7	497	0.9	96.24	43,261	0.94	1.04
Girls	191,318	2.9	2,542	4.6	75.27	157,573	3.41	0.74
Lingerie	273,311	4.1	2,431	4.4	112.43	262,548	5.68	1.29
Accessories	245,980	3.7	1,602	2.9	153.55	238,735	5.16	1.78
Jewelry	129,823	1.9	829	1.5	156.60	123,484	2.67	1.78
Total Softlines	3,020,084	45.2	23,537	42.6	128.31	2,539,566	54.92	1.29
Hardlines								
Domestics	498,792	7.5	4,531	8.2	110.08	407,745	8.82	1.08
HBA	464,628	7.0	1,989	3.6	233.60	153,153	3.31	0.92
Housewares	457,795	6.8	3,591	6.5	127.48	254,979	5.51	0.85
Cosmetics	75,160	1.1	608	1.1	123.62	55,913	1.21	1.00
Tobacco	140,187	2.1	221	0.4	634.33	37,349	0.81	2.02
Candy	144,944	2.2	387	0.7	374.53	88,179	1.91	2.72
Sporting Goods	184,485	2.8	2,652	4.8	69.56	129,948	2.81	0.59
Stationery	307,475	4.6	2,763	5.0	111.28	254,150	5.50	1.10
Furniture	75,160	1.1	1,547	2.8	48.58	60,333	1.30	0.47
Home Entertainment	601,284	9.0	2,265	4.1	265.47	255,973	5.54	1.35
Toys	300,642	4.5	2,431	4.4	123.67	143,429	3.10	0.70
Seasonal	145,333	2.2	2,652	4.8	54.80	90,168	1.95	0.41
Hardware/Paint	163,986	2.5	2,100	3.8	78.09	111,274	2.41	0.63
Pet Supplies	13,666	0.2	55	0.1	248.47	13,094	0.28	2.83
Auto Accessories	81,993	1.2	1,271	2.3	64.51	29,227	0.63	0.27
Total Hardlines	3,655,480	54.8	29,061	52.6	125.79	2,084,914	45.08	0.86
Nonselling	—	—	2,652	4.8	—	—	—	—
Total Scores	6,675,564	100.0	55,250	100.0		4,624,480	100.00	1.00

Exhibit 13.3
Merchandise Productivity Analysis

percentage of the store's gross margin than the percentage of store space it is using, and the retailer should consider allocating additional space to this category. If the index falls below 1.0, the product category is underperforming relative to other merchandise, and the retailer might consider reducing its space allocation. The merchandise productivity analysis shown in Exhibit 13.3 indicates that in this store, softlines (apparel and apparel accessories) categories, with an index of 1.29, are performing very well and perhaps should be given more space, and hardlines (nonapparel products), with an index of 0.86, are underperforming and should be considered for downsizing.

Of course, as with all financial analysis, the space productivity index is simply a tool to help management make decisions, not a decision-making formula. Even though a certain category may have a low index, senior management may retain its full space because a new buyer has just been hired, or because the category is an important image builder. A high-index category might not be given more space if management expects a hot fashion trend to cool off soon and believes the space productivity index for that category will drop accordingly.

Space Allocations for a New Store. When a retailer is creating a new store format, no productivity and profitability data are available on which to base the allocation of space. In these situations, the retailer bases space allocation on industry standards, previous experience with similar formats, or more frequently, the space required to carry the number of items specified by the buyers. Kroger, for example, used information obtained from existing stores to revamp its beverage section at new locations. In its newer stores, one side of a 48-foot-long aisle was committed to bottled waters and new energy drinks—some 150 different types. At the same time, Kroger reduced the space normally allocated for traditional colas.

Once a detailed assortment plan has been created, typical stock levels are estimated based on minimum and maximum quantities. The retailer can then determine the amount of shelf space required to carry this merchandise. By determining the space for each item, then for each category, then for each department, the retailer can develop the floor plan for the store. As you can imagine, optimizing a store's space is a grueling process.

Robert Kahn, who was also a member of Wal-Mart's board of directors, once explained to Sam Walton that one of the problems with retailers was that they thought the best way to get higher sales per square foot (which they recognized was an important factor in store profitability, since higher sales would reduce operating expenses as a percentage of sales) was to run more ads and add more merchandise displays. Thus, retailers at the time reduced their aisle space and stacked the merchandise so high that many customers either could not reach the top or were afraid to touch the display.[12]

Kahn, however, had his own ideas about customer behavior in the store and explained that there was a better formula for higher sales per square foot:

$$\text{Sales per square foot} = f(\text{Number of customers}) \times (\text{Length of time they spend in the store})$$

Therefore, according to Kahn's theory, retailers should concentrate on the time customers spend browsing and experiencing the store (this doesn't include the dwell time of waiting in line to checkout), not how much merchandise they are exposed to. Based on this concept, Kahn outlined four things that Wal-Mart should do:

1. Ensure that in every aisle, a customer with a cart can comfortably pass another customer with a cart without having to ask that customer to move.
2. Make the restrooms the best in town so that a customer will never leave the store and rush home to use the bathroom.
3. Put at least one bench in each store, in the alcove at the front door. When Wal-Mart opened the first American hypermarket, discussed in the chapter's Global Retailing box, Kahn went to the Grand Opening. Afterward, he kiddingly told Sam to put ten to twelve benches inside each hypermarket and have a vendor

Global Retailing

Hypermarkets: A Retailing Lesson

The hypermarket is a retailing format which first integrated a supermarket with a department store. At 250,000 square feet, it is one and a half times larger than the traditional 140,000 to 160,000 square foot supercenter. These enormous retail outlets, which often carry over 200,000 SKUs, are able to provide a seemingly endless array of products from apparel to electronics to fresh groceries in one stop. The first hypermarket, located near Paris, France, was opened in 1962 by Carrefour.

The original idea behind this format was to offer a wide variety of products in one location, thereby lowering operating costs and passing the savings along to the consumers. Consumers would be offered the convenience of a one-stop, self-service shopping area with weather protection and adequate parking. In the beginning, European hypermarkets were typically located on the edge of town, near major access roads and residential areas so that customers could reach the facility without spending time commuting. Prior to hypermarkets, European consumers had to travel to larger metropolitan areas to have convenient, one-stop access to all their shopping needs.

Soon after their introduction, European lawmakers became skeptical of hypermarkets, especially their effect on small retail businesses. Therefore, in parts of Europe, legal statutes limiting their development were passed. Still, despite these regulations, today the number of hypermarkets continues to increase slightly (0.6% per year). Also impacting their growth in Western Europe is the demographic change towards smaller households. Thus, while hypermarkets continue to appeal to multi-person households, they don't offer the same attraction for single-person households, the most rapidly growing market segment.

Given the restrictive regulatory climate and the demographic changes in Western Europe, the hypermarket format sought new locales. Central and Southern European consumer markets provided great opportunities since these nations were relatively new to "free" market economies and had little experience with modern retail formats. Former Communist bloc countries such as the Czech Republic, Hungary, Poland, and Slovakia were particularly attractive to the hypermarket chains. The dynamically growing countries in Central and South America were also receptive to the hypermarket.

However, despite the success of the hypermarket in Europe and Central and South America, it didn't meet the same level of success in U.S. markets. In 1987, Wal-Mart introduced its first Hypermart USA, with 220,000 square feet, in Garland, Texas, and soon expanded to six other locations. While the U.S. hypermarkets were similar to the European model, with restaurants, full-scale grocery sections, and general merchandise, they never achieved consumer acceptance. Whether the downfall of hypermarkets was caused by their sheer size (stockers wore roller skates to move around the store quickly) or the lack of excitement these warehouse-type stores provided is still open to debate. However, Wal-Mart immediately recognized its mistake and scaled down the format into our present-day supercenters.

Hypermarkets illustrate the important lesson that not every form of retail presentation can be easily transferred from country to country. Rather, in order to be successful, retailers must adapt their marketing strategies to fit the specific consumer markets they enter. Despite the current endless discussion of "global villages," it is evident that a single, uniform marketing strategy cannot be successfully exported from one country to another.

Source: Prepared by Professor Deborah Whitten, University of Houston-Downtown.

---

sponsor (pay for) each bench. Sam Walton thought this was a dumb idea because as he told Kahn "if they (the customers) are sitting, they ain't buying."

4. In all large stores, install a coffee stand catty-corner from the snack bar so that customers can recharge themselves in order to spend more time and money shopping.

All these ideas seemed to agree with Sam Walton's concept that a retailer was a failure if, after getting customers to come into the store, the retailer did not do everything possible to satisfy all their needs and not force them to go elsewhere for merchandise.

As an experiment, Wal-Mart built ten new 85,000-square-foot stores and ten new 115,000-square-foot versions. The stores had identical amounts of fixtures and merchandise. The larger stores used the extra 30,000-square-feet for wider aisles and extra space at the increased number of checkouts (obviously the time spent in the store was to reflect shopping or browsing time and NOT the dwell time spent waiting to checkout), and to project an open, friendlier image. Also, the new restrooms, which were checked every two hours for cleanliness, had tile, not cement, floors; diaper-changing shelves in both the men's and women's restrooms; and easy-to-clean vinyl-covered walls. Eight to ten benches were placed in the main aisles. However, Wal-Mart dropped Kahn's coffee bar idea.

The first indication of the success of the larger store was that their parking lots were always full because shoppers were spending so much more time in the store. Sales figures showed that the larger stores not only had higher sales but were also producing higher sales per square foot of store space than the smaller stores despite all that "wasted" aisle space. Wal-Mart did not know exactly what the customers were doing in these larger stores, just that they were spending more time and money. As a result, Wal-Mart went with the larger store model and increased the parking spaces from five to six per 1,000 square feet of store space. However, the benches were dropped because as mentioned earlier Sam felt if the customers were sitting, they weren't buying.

Kahn used the experience as the basis in 1998 for his work as an expert witness supporting a suit by two disabled individuals under the Americans with Disabilities Act (ADA). The case involved R. H. Macy Company, which purchased an O'Connor, Moffat & Co. store in San Francisco during the 1940s. Despite three expansions, the store still had inadequate-sized aisles. Macy's, along with the California Retailers Association, and its own expert witnesses, claimed, "It's pretty basic in retail. Inventory per square foot drives sales per square foot, which drives profit." Kahn used the Wal-Mart experience to show that a "reduction in nonaisle space permitted greater access to merchandise, which in turn leads to an increase in sales. If Macy's was correct, why didn't all retailers eliminate all aisles and stack merchandise to the ceiling to maximize profit? "[13] While this case was settled out of court, five years later a California court ruled that the Mervyn's department store chain didn't have to expand its aisles to ease shopping for disabled customers because Mervyn's would lose $30 million a year in profits due to remodeling expenses, causing them to shut down some of their 126 California operations.[14] Despite the rather general guidelines of the ADA, it is important that retailers not lose sight of the fact that 21 percent of the U.S. population has some type of disability. Today, profitable retailers need to understand the relationship between "the store needs and objectives and those of disabled customers."[15]

Circulation

The circulation pattern not only ensures efficient movement of large numbers of shoppers through the store, exposing them to more merchandise, but also determines the character of the store. Disney Stores, for example, are designed to communicate the fun and excitement of the theme parks and famous characters and to entice customers to walk to the back wall. After all, chances are good that when customers get to the back, they will return using a different route. This will expose them to more merchandise and increase the chance of a sale. Four basic types of layout are used today (free flow, grid, loop, and spine), each of which is described in the following discussion. Shoppers have been trained to associate certain circulation patterns with different types of stores, so in reading these descriptions, try to

Zigy Kaluzny/Stone

The ability of disabled shoppers to navigate aisles and shop a store should be considered in all aspects of store design.

think of how they are used in the various stores you shop and the store image they evoke in your mind.

Free Flow

The simplest type of store layout is a **free-flow layout** (Exhibit 13.4), in which fixtures and merchandise are grouped into free-flowing patterns on the sales floor. Customers are encouraged to flow freely through all the fixtures, since there are usually no defined traffic patterns in the store. This type of layout works well in small stores, usually less than 5,000 square feet, in which customers wish to browse through all of the merchandise. Generally, the merchandise is of the same type, such as fashion apparel, perhaps categorized only into tops and bottoms. If there is a greater variety of merchandise (for instance, men's and women's apparel, bedding, and health and beauty aids), a free-flow layout fails to provide cues as to where one department stops and another starts, confusing the shopper.

free-flow layout
Is a type of store layout in which fixtures and merchandise are grouped into free-flowing patterns on the sales floor.

Grid

Another traditional form of store layout is the **grid layout**, in which the counters and fixtures are placed in long rows or "runs," usually at right angles, throughout the store. In a grid layout (Exhibit 13.5), customers circulate up and down through the fixtures, and, in fact, the grid layout is often referred to as a maze. The most familiar examples of the grid layout are supermarkets and drugstores.

grid layout
Is a type of store layout in which counters and fixtures are placed in long rows or "runs," usually at right angles, throughout the store.

The grid is a true shopping layout, best used in retail environments in which the majority of customers wish to shop the entire store. In supermarkets, for instance, many shoppers flow methodically up and down all the fixture runs, looking for everything they might need along the way. However, if the shopper wishes to find only several specific categories, the grid can be confusing and frustrating, because it is difficult to see over the fixtures to other merchandise (especially today, as fixtures have become higher). For example, Service Merchandise placed discounted Black & Decker power tools at the rear of the store to lure customers into purchases of high-margin jewelry, which was

Exhibit 13.4
Free-Flow Layout

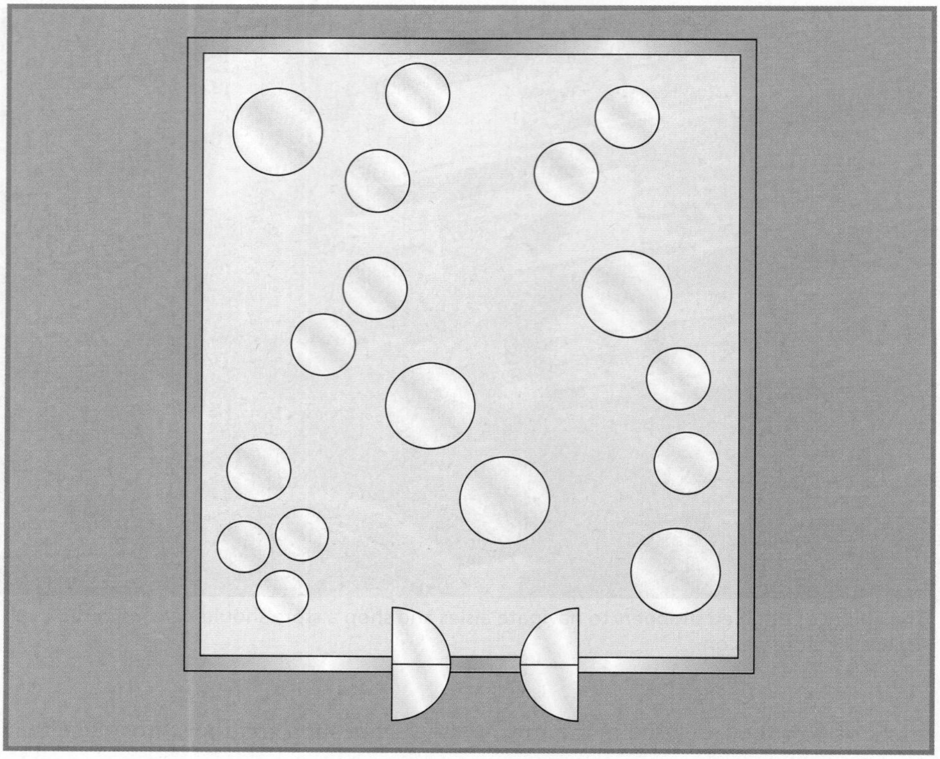

Exhibit 13.5
Grid Layout

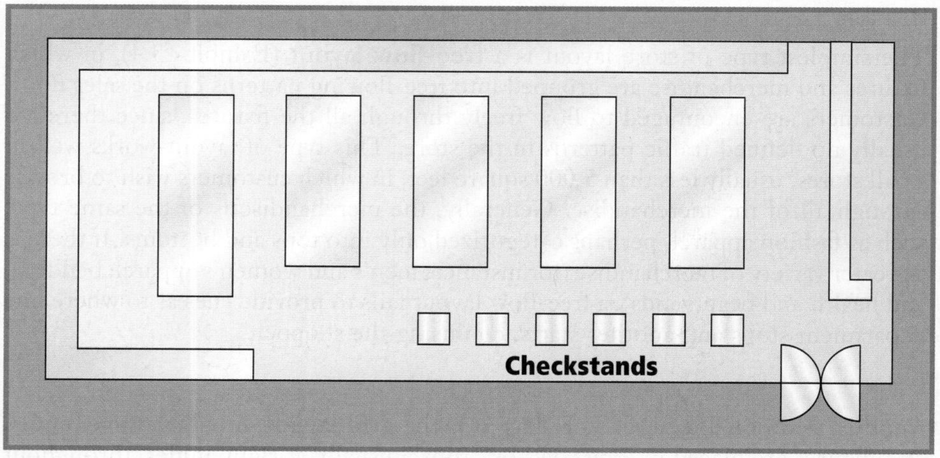

located near the entrance.[16] Supermarkets move customers through the entire store by placing the meats, dairy goods, and other frequently purchased items at the rear of the store. However, retailers should employ this strategy carefully. Forcing customers in a hurry all the way to the back of a large store will frustrate many customers and lead some to go elsewhere for merchandise.

loop layout
Is a type of store layout in which a major customer aisle begins at the entrance, loops through the store—usually in the shape of a circle, square, or rectangle—and then returns the customer to the front of the store.

Loop

Over the past two decades, the **loop layout** (sometimes called a racetrack layout) has become a popular tool for enhancing the productivity of retail stores. A "loop," as shown in Exhibit 13.6, provides a major customer aisle that begins at the entrance, loops through the store—usually in the shape of a circle, square, or

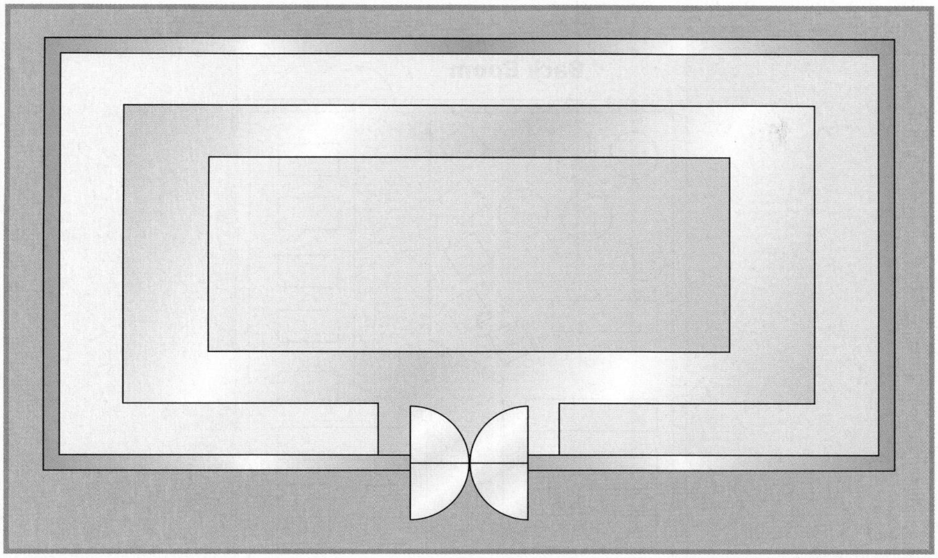

Exhibit 13.6
Loop Layout

rectangle—and then returns the customer to the front of the store. While this seems like a simple concept, the loop can be a powerful space productivity tool.

The major benefit of the loop layout is that it exposes shoppers to the greatest possible amount of merchandise. An effective circulation pattern must first guide customers throughout the store to encourage browsing and cross-shopping. Along the way, shoppers must be able to easily see and understand merchandise to the left and right, so ideally the main aisle should never stray more than 60 feet from any merchandise. The way to simultaneously accomplish these two goals is to create a main circulation loop that mirrors the configuration of the outside walls of the store and is never more than 60 feet from the outside wall. In larger stores, the interior island of the loop can itself be too large to easily see across, and internal walls may be created to shorten sightlines to merchandise.

Spine

The **spine layout**, which is shown in Exhibit 13.7, is essentially a variation of the free-flow, grid, and loop layouts and combines the advantages of all three in certain circumstances. A spine layout is based on a single main aisle running from the front to the back of the store, transporting customers in both directions. On either side of this spine, merchandise departments branch off toward the back or side walls. Within these departments, either a free-flow or grid layout can be used, depending on the type of merchandise and fixtures in use. The spine is heavily used by medium-sized specialty stores, either hardlines or softlines, ranging in size from 2,000 to 10,000 square feet. Often, especially in fashion stores, the spine is subtly set off by a change in floor coloring or surface and is not perceived as an aisle, even though it functions as such.

spine layout
Is a type of store layout in which a single main aisle runs from the front to the back of the store, transporting customers in both directions, and where on either side of this spine, merchandise departments using either a free-flow or grid pattern branch off toward the back or side walls.

Shrinkage Prevention

When planning a store's layout and design, the prevention of shrinkage due to theft, damage, and loss must be considered. Some layouts will minimize vulnerability to shoplifters. One of the most important considerations when planning the layout is visibility of the merchandise. Most shoplifting takes place in fitting rooms, blind spots, aisles crowded with extra merchandise, or behind high displays. Fitting rooms, one of the most common scenes of the shoplifting crime, should be placed in visible areas that can be monitored by associates. Historically, display fixtures have been kept no higher

Exhibit 13.7
Spine Layout

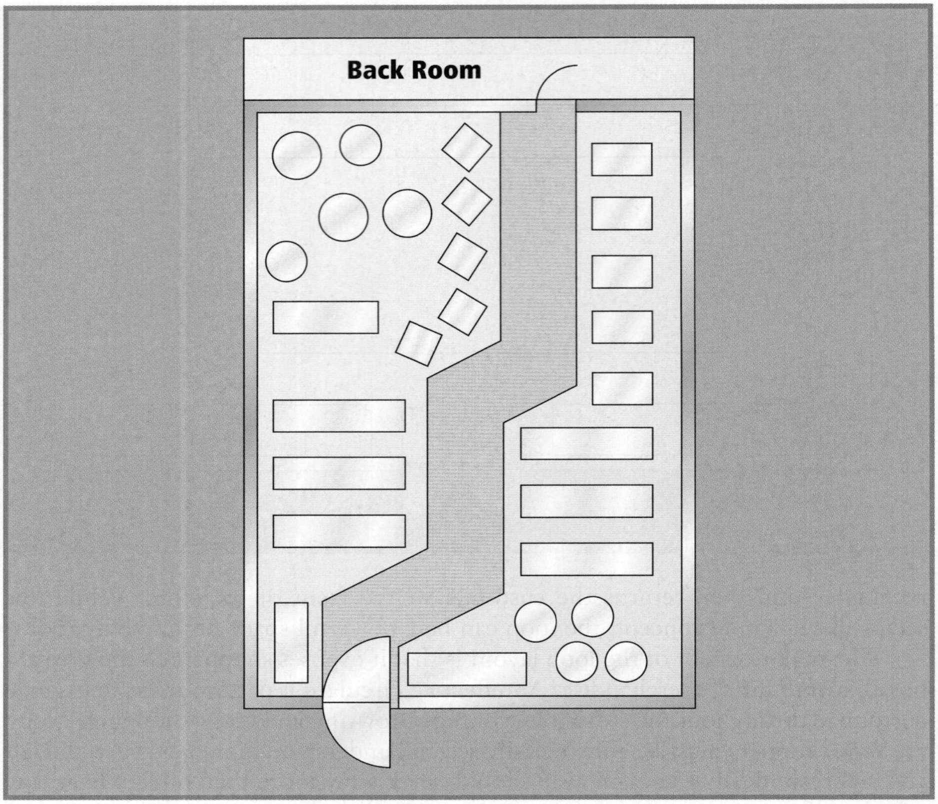

than eye level to allow store associates to monitor customers in other aisles. Recently, mass merchandisers have found that increased sales from the greater merchandise intensity of higher fixtures outweighs the increase in shoplifting due to reduced visibility. This depends greatly on merchandise type, however. Expensive items that are easily placed into pockets and handbags, such as compact discs, are high-theft items, and are usually kept on low fixtures to discourage shoplifting. The manager's office and other security windows can be an excellent deterrent to shoplifting if they are placed in an obvious area above the sales floor level, where managers can easily see the entire store. Electronic security systems, including sensor tags and video cameras, have become very popular, and are usually in a highly visible location to serve as a deterrent.

LO 3

Planning Fixtures and Merchandise Presentation

How are the various types of fixtures, merchandise presentation methods and techniques, and the psychology of merchandise presentation used to increase the productivity of the sales floor?

Retailing is theater, and in no area is that more true than in merchandise presentation. Recently retailers have been increasing their emphasis on presentation, as competition has grown and stores try to squeeze more sales out of existing square footage. There are two basic types of merchandise presentation, visual merchandising and on-shelf merchandising. In thinking of retailing as theater, visual merchandising is analogous to the stage props that set scenes and serve as backdrops.

In Chapter 3 the text discussed the behavioral differences between Gen Xers and baby boomers. Many retailers have begun to redesign their store layouts to reflect these differences. Probably nowhere is this more evident than, as this chapter's Service Retailing box illustrates, in the way hotels have begun to repackage themselves to attract Gen-X travelers.

Service Retailing

Hotel Fixtures Are About to Change

For the last two decades, hotels have catered to the wishes of the traveling baby boomer. After all, boomers—those 78 million Americans born in the years from 1946 to 1964—accounted for the majority of their business. However, today another demographic group has begun to impact the industry. Though boomers, because of their sheer size, will still continue to fill more rooms than Gen Xers, hotel and motel operators have become aware of the importance of the Gen Xers. In fact, Gen Xers already spend more on rooms annually per capita than boomers. Thus as boomers age and reduce their travel, hotels are offering new brands with a new concept in fixtures as a means to bridge the generational divide.

Boomers, who grew up with the likes of Holiday Inn, desire a room that offers utility. They basically want a clean room where they can sit, have a clean bed and access to room service, and watch TV. Plus, they are more likely to be loyal, lifelong customers. Gen Xers, on the other hand, are more at home in boutique hotels where, instead of relaxing in their room, they can meet others in an energetic bar. For them the sameness of a Holiday Inn, with its traditional floral bedspread, is a turn-off. They demand not only a clean room, but it must be modern-looking, sleek, high-tech with extras like a CD with relaxation music or XM or Sirius satellite radio. Comforters or duvets must accompany pillow top mattresses, and Starbucks coffee, rather than generic coffee, must be available.

Seeking to attract this new generation of customers, the hotel chains have introduced new brands of hotels in the higher half of the price scale. For example, Starwood, the parent company of Westin, Sheraton, and Four Points, has developed the high-end W hotel. Modern in decor and style, the W features the latest in wireless technology, 24-hour massage, pillow-top beds, and "spa bath products." Special events, called W Happenings, which offer guests film screenings, wine tastings, and celebrity book signings, are also common occurrences at W hotels. Asian-influenced furniture and candles are common in its lobbies. However, in addition to design and layout changes, what really sets the W apart from the competition are the services. Consider the one the chain calls "Whatever/Whenever" service. If it's legal, the folks at W will get it done for you. As the chain's Web site states, "From wish to whim, from work quandary to wedding emergency, where there's a W, there's a way. There are no orders too tall, no deadlines too short, nothing too absurd—who knew that a phone call transforms your dreams into reality?" Another service has the hotel packing your bags and shipping them to you, so you don't have any hassles traveling with luggage.

Starwood is currently testing a lower-priced version of W that is more limited in service. This new brand, which like W will target Gen Xers, will offer loft-like rooms with high ceilings and lobbies where guests can expect frequent lounge parties.

Competitors such as Marriott, Hilton, and InterContinental are not ignoring Starwood's strategy. Marriott is revamping lobbies of Courtyard hotels, turning them into flexible open spaces with wireless Internet access and "grab and go" food pantries where food is available 24 hours a day. InterContinental has introduced rooms with hardwood floors, "spa-style" showers, a wide-open foyer and "pub-style social areas."

Source: "Hotels Spend Big to Lure Guests," *USAToday*, September 27, 2005: 1D–2D; "To Bed or to Bar," *New York Times*, September 20. 2005: C1; http://www.welcometowhotels.com; and based on the author's experience staying at a W on a business trip.

Merchandise presentation is a complex activity best learned on the retail floor. While this text will not attempt to teach the art and science of merchandise presentation, you should be familiar with a number of basic components of merchandise presentation and their potential impact on store image and sales, including fixture type and selection and certain techniques and methods of on-shelf merchandising.

on-shelf merchandising
Is the display of merchandise on counters, racks, shelves, and fixtures throughout the store.

On-shelf merchandising, which describes the merchandise that is displayed on and in counters, racks, shelves, and fixtures throughout the store, represents the stars on our theater stage. This is the merchandise that the shopper actually touches, tries on, examines, reads, understands, and hopefully buys. Therefore, on-shelf merchandising must not only present the merchandise attractively; it must also display the merchandise so it is easy to understand and accessible. Further, it must be reasonably easy to maintain, with customers themselves able to replace merchandise so it is equally appealing to the next shopper. It must not be so overwhelming that the customer is afraid to touch the merchandise. After receiving more than 25,000 complaints a year regarding injuries from falling merchandise, Wal-Mart has sought to reduce the height level of merchandise displays in every store. Despite the efforts of top management, many managers still falsely believe the best way to improve sales (and their year-end bonus) is to cram as much merchandise as possible into the store.

Fixture Types

Store fixtures fall into three basic categories: hardlines, softlines, and wall fixtures.

Hardlines Fixtures

The workhorse fixture in most hardlines departments is known as the gondola, so named because it is a long structure consisting of a large base and a vertical spine or wall sticking up as high as eight feet, fitted with sockets or notches into which a variety of shelves, peghooks, bins, baskets, and other hardware can be inserted. The basic gondola can hold a wide variety of merchandise by means of hardware hung from the vertical spine. Think of your last trip to a discount store or supermarket. The long, heavy-duty fixtures fitted predominantly with shelves are gondolas. In addition to the gondola, a few other types of fixtures are in common use today: tables, large bins, and simple flat-base decks. These fixtures are commonly used in promotional aisles to display advertised or other special-value merchandise.

Softlines Fixtures

The bulky gondola is inappropriate for fashion-oriented softlines merchandise. A large array of fixtures has been developed to accommodate the special needs of softlines, which are often hung on hangers. As shown in Exhibit 13.8, the four-way feature rack and the round rack are the two fixtures most heavily used today. These smaller, specialized fixtures have replaced the straight rack, a long pipe with legs on each end from which rows of apparel were hung, and which for generations was the most prevalent softlines fixture. Although it held a great quantity and was easy to maintain, the straight rack provided few opportunities to differentiate one style or color of garment from another, which merchants have found is the key to selling more. A straight rack is like the hanger rod in your closet, and what you see when you open your closet is nothing more than sleeves. You know your own clothes, so sleeves are enough to tip you off to what the rest of the garment looks like. When you are shopping, however, the more of the garment you are exposed to and the more varieties of size, silhouette (shape), and color, the more you are apt to buy. So merchants prefer "face-out" presentations over "sleeve-out" presentations. Of course, face-outs take up more space than sleeve-outs, so it is impractical to face out all or even a high percentage of the total merchandise on the floor.

bulk or capacity fixture
Is a display fixture that is intended to hold the bulk of merchandise without looking as heavy as a long, straight rack of merchandise.

feature fixture
Is a display that draws special attention to selected features (e.g., color, shape, or style) of merchandise.

The round rack is known as a **bulk or capacity fixture** and is intended to hold the bulk of merchandise without looking as heavy as a long straight rack of merchandise. Although it is smaller than the straight rack, it too allows only sleeve-outs unless fitted with special hardware. The four-way rack, on the other hand, is considered a **feature fixture**, because while it holds fewer items it presents merchandise in a manner that permits the shopper to glimpse a garment's style and key characteristics (such as color or shape). The ingenious design also allows it to hold a large quantity of merchandise on the hanger arms behind the four face-outs.

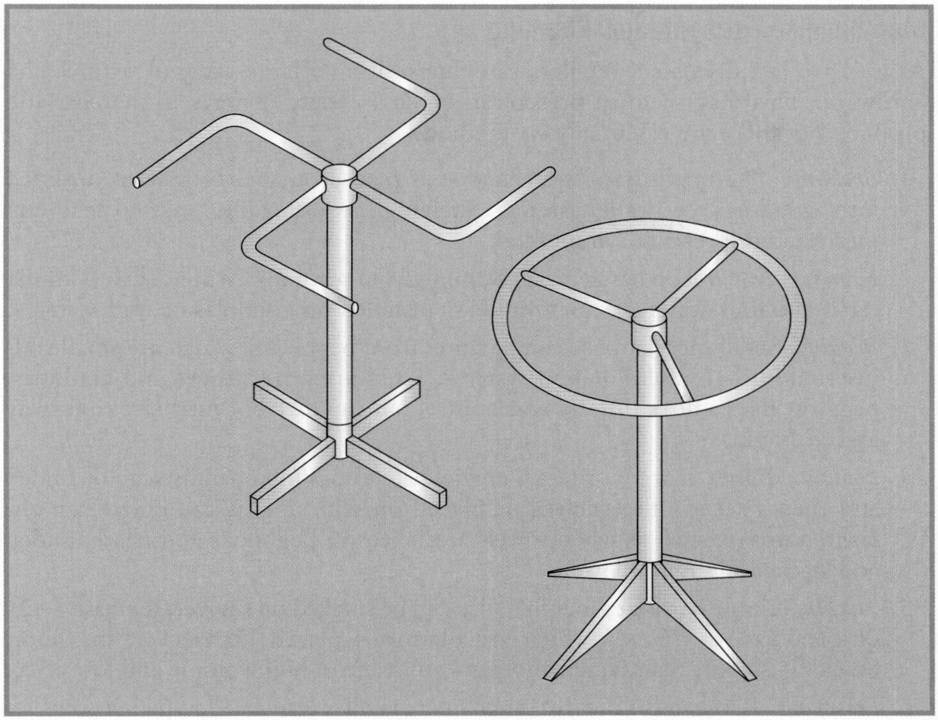

Exhibit 13.8
Four-Way Feature Rack and Round Rack

However, to be easily shopped, all the merchandise on one arm must be the same type of garment with variations only in color and size. In its recent effort to attract a more upscale consumer, Wal-Mart is moving away from its old mantra of "stack it high, watch it fly" towards a greater use of these fixtures.[17] However, the retailer should be warned that when poorly merchandised so that the front garment does not match those behind it, the four-way leaves the customer in the same quandary as the straight rack.

Wall Fixtures

The last type of fixture is designed to be hung on the wall. To make a store's plain wall merchandisable, it is usually covered with a skin that is fitted with vertical columns of notches similar to those on the gondola, into which a variety of hardware can be inserted. Shelves, peghooks, bins, baskets, and even hanger bars can be fitted into wall systems. Hanger bars can be hung parallel to the wall, much like a closet bar, so that large quantities of garments can be "sleeved out," or they can protrude perpendicularly from the wall, either straight out (straight-outs) or angled down (waterfalls), to allow merchandise to be faced out. The primary quality to remember about wall systems is that walls can generally be merchandised much higher than floor fixtures. On the floor, round racks are kept to a maximum of 42 inches so that customers can easily see over them to other merchandise, but on the wall garments can be hung as high as customers can reach, which is generally about 72 inches. This allows walls to be "double hung" with two rows of garments, or even "triple hung" with smaller children's apparel. Therefore, walls not only hold large amounts of merchandise, but also serve as a visual backdrop for the department.

Merchandise Presentation Planning

As we have just discussed, retailers can choose from a large array of fixtures and hardware. This may seem to present an endless variety of ways to merchandise product, but there are essentially six methods:

1. *Shelving*. The majority of merchandise is placed on shelves that are inserted into gondolas or wall systems. Shelving is a flexible, easy-to-maintain merchandise presentation method.
2. *Hanging*. Apparel on hangers can be hung from softlines fixtures, such as round racks and four-way racks, or from bars installed on gondolas or wall systems.
3. *Pegging*. Small merchandise can be hung from peghooks, which are small rods inserted into gondolas or wall systems. Used in both softlines and hardlines, pegging gives a neat, orderly appearance, but can be labor intensive to display and maintain.
4. *Folding*. Higher-margin or large, unwieldy softlines merchandise can be folded and then stacked onto shelves or placed on tables. This can create a high-fashion image, such as when towels are taken off peghooks and neatly folded and stacked high up the wall.
5. *Stacking*. Large hardlines merchandise can be stacked on shelves, the base decks of gondolas, or "flats," which are platforms placed directly on the floor. Stacking is easily maintained and gives an image of high volume and low price.
6. *Dumping*. Large quantities of small merchandise can be dumped in bins or baskets inserted into gondolas or wall systems. This highly effective promotional method can be used in softlines (socks, wash cloths) or hardlines (batteries, grocery products, candy), and creates a high-volume, low-cost image.

The method of merchandise presentation can have a dramatic impact on image and space productivity. Different merchandise presentation methods have been shown to strongly influence buying habits and stimulate consumers to purchase more. There is a certain "psychology of merchandise presentation," which must be carefully considered in developing merchandise presentation schemes. Only between a third and half of store shoppers make an impulse (unplanned) purchase, and these purchases are made by only 60 percent of the shoppers who actually enter the store with an intent to make a specific purchase. Thus, 40 percent of the shoppers who enter a store to make a purchase are "wasted" because the store failed to use merchandise presentation to generate additional purchases.[18] This is why department store design incorporates a gauntlet of goodies to stimulate impulse buys. For example, cosmetics, usually the store's most profitable department, is always near the main entrance. Typically, the department is leased to cosmetic companies who use their own salespeople to sell the perfume, lipstick, and eye shadow. Other high-impulse items (e.g., jewelry, handbags, and shoes) are usually nearby, while the "demand" products (e.g., furniture) are on upper floors. These stores would be unprofitable if they failed to induce a significant amount of impulse buying.

The following are three key psychological factors to consider when merchandising stores:

1. *Value/fashion image*. One of merchandise presentation's most important psychological effects is to foster an image in the customer's mind of how trendy, exclusive, pricey, or value-oriented the merchandise is. For each of the merchandise presentation methods mentioned previously, we discussed its effect on price image. By changing the merchandise presentation method, we can change the perception of our towel display from common, high-volume,

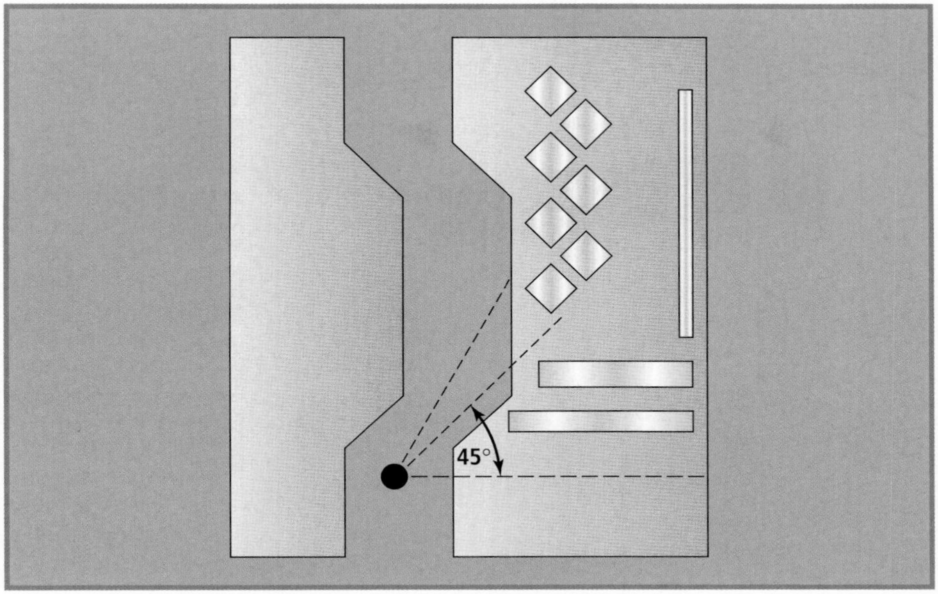

Exhibit 13.9
45-Degree Customer Sightline

and high-value to an exclusive selection of high-fashion merchandise, which presumably will be at higher prices.

2. *Angles and sightlines*. Research has shown that as customers move through a retail store, they view the store at approximately 45-degree angles from the path of travel, as shown in Exhibit 13.9, rather than perpendicular to their path. Although this seems logical, most stores are set up at right angles because it is easier and consumes less space. Therefore, merchandise and signage often wind up being at a 90-degree angle to the main aisle. Exhibit 13.9 also shows how four-way feature racks can be more effectively merchandised by being turned to meet the shoppers' sightlines head-on.
3. *Vertical color blocking*. To be most effective, merchandise should be displayed in vertical bands of color wherever possible. As customers move through the store, their eyes naturally view a "swath" approximately two feet high, parallel to the floor, at about eye level. This is shown in Exhibit 13.10. This visual swath of merchandise will be viewed as a rainbow of colors if each merchandise item is displayed vertically by color (e.g., the vertical columns represent different colors and within these colors could be different sizes). This method of merchandise presentation creates such a strong visual effect that shoppers are exposed to more merchandise, which in turn increases sales. In addition, when shopping for clothing, customers most often think first of color. Thus, they can easily find the column of color on display and locate their size.

Selecting Fixtures and Merchandise Presentation Methods

Proper fixtures emphasize the key selling attributes of merchandise while not being overpowering. A good guideline for selecting fixtures—although it is not always possible to follow—is to *match the fixture to the merchandise, not the merchandise to the fixture*. This means you should only use fixtures that are sensitive to the nature of the merchandise, but all too often, retailers are forced to put merchandise on the wrong fixture.[19]

Exhibit 13.10
Vertical Color Blocking

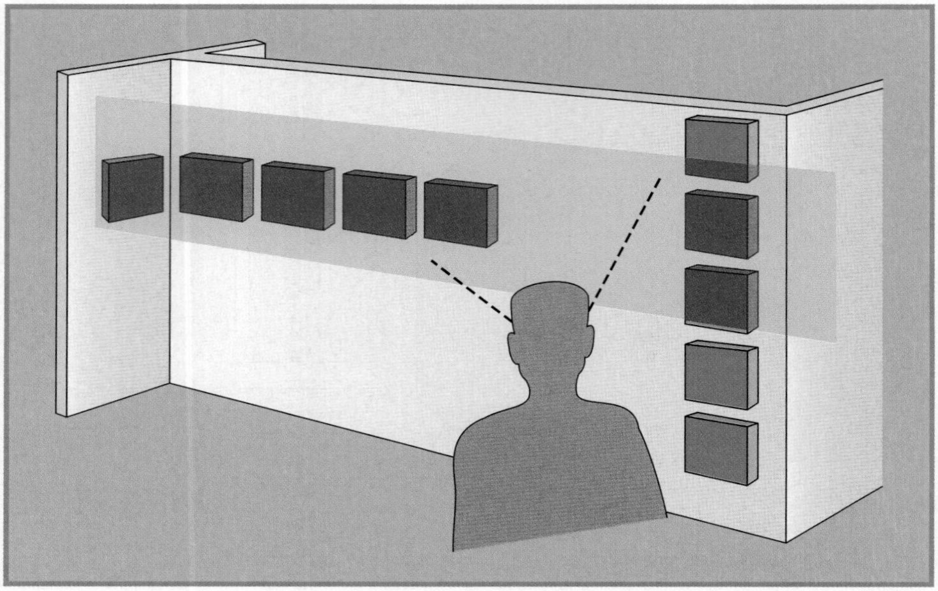

Consider intimate apparel, for instance. This is a fast-selling, high-margin merchandise category that can enhance a retailer's image in fashion merchandising. Though retailers entering this business might be tempted to place intimate apparel on existing shelves of a gondola, they would be well served to consider special fixtures to enhance the delicate qualities of intimate apparel. A large, metal, bulky gondola will overpower a small, delicate intimate apparel item, and therefore reduce sales potential. More delicate fixtures made of softer materials will enhance sales. Likewise, it would not be effective to bulk-stack fragile merchandise, because the weight of items might damage those lower in the stack. It would not make sense to peghook large, bulky items, because they take up too much room and might be too heavy for the peghook.

Visual Merchandising

visual merchandising
Is the artistic display of merchandise and theatrical props used as scene-setting decoration in the store.

The second type of merchandise presentation, **visual merchandising**, is the artistic display of merchandise and theatrical props used as scene-setting decoration in the store. While on-shelf merchandising must be tastefully displayed to encourage shopping, a store with just on-shelf merchandising would be dreary. Many low-price stores contain little visual merchandising and they do appear more boring than their upscale cousins in fashion retailing, who concentrate heavily on visual merchandising displays, or "visuals," as they are often called.

An effective visual merchandising display has several key characteristics. Visual displays are not typically associated with a shopable fixture, but are located in a focal point, feature area, or other area remote from the on-shelf merchandising and perhaps even out of reach of the customer. Their goal is to create a feeling in the store conducive to buying merchandise.

Another characteristic of visual merchandising is its use of props and elements in addition to merchandise. In fact, visuals do not always include merchandise—they may just be interesting displays of items somehow related to the merchandise or to a mood the retailer wishes to create. A prop might be a wooden barrel, a miniature airplane, or a mock tree with autumn leaves. Visuals are like the illustrations and design elements in a book that make it interesting; they tell the customer whether this is an upscale, serious shopping experience; a frivolous, fun shopping experience; or a down and dirty, low-price shopping experience. Claire's stores, for example, make shopping fun for tweens, teens, and young adults. The stores are clean, bright, and easy to shop with an inviting image set off by purple-and-pink carpeting, white ceiling tiles and accent lighting that attracts attention even across a crowded mall corridor. The merchandise is easily accessible so even the youngest girls can hold up an item to see how it looks.[20]

To be most effective, however, visuals should incorporate relevant merchandise. In apparel retailing, mannequins or figure forms are used to display merchandise as it might appear on a person, rather than hanging limply on a hanger. This helps the shopper visualize how these garments will enhance her or his appearance. Good fashion visuals include more than just one garment, to show how tops and bottoms go together and how belts, scarves, and other accessories can be combined to create an overall fashion look. This is called accessorization. When successful, visuals help the shopper translate the merchandise presentation from "garments on a rack" to "fashionable clothes that will look good on me."

The retailer should be careful in setting visuals to make sure that the displays do not create walls that make it difficult for shoppers to reach other areas of the store. In addition, the retailer should carefully consider the placement of signs. A popular fast-food restaurant increased sales when it changed the sign placement featuring its specials from being visible to patrons on their way to the restrooms. Now the signs are visible as the customers exit the restrooms and are more relaxed.[21]

Store Design

LO 4

Why is store design so important to a store's success?

Store design is the element most responsible for the first of our two goals in planning the store environment: creating a distinctive and memorable store image. Store design encompasses both the exterior and the interior of the store. On the exterior, we have the storefront, signage, and entrance, all of which are critical to attracting passing shoppers and enticing them to enter. On the inside, store design includes the architectural elements and finishes on all surfaces, such as wall coverings, floor coverings, and ceilings. There are literally hundreds of details in a store's design, and all must work together to create the desired store **ambiance**, which is the overall feeling or mood projected by a store through its aesthetic appeal to the human senses. For instance, Warren Buffett's Nebraska Furniture Mart uses noncomposite panels, which not only lower heating and cooling costs, but also create an upscale look.[22]

ambiance
Is the overall feeling or mood projected by a store through its aesthetic appeal to human senses.

Highly profitable retailers employ exterior designs that pull shoppers into the store and interior designs that stimulate sales.

Dollars & Sense

Storefront Design

If the retail store can be compared to a book, then the storefront, or store exterior, is like the book cover. It must be noticeable, easily identified by passing motorists or mall shoppers, and memorable. The storefront must clearly identify the name and general nature of the store and give some hint as to the merchandise inside. Generally, the storefront design includes all exterior signage and the architecture of the storefront itself.

In many cases, the storefront includes display windows, which serve as an advertising medium for the store. Store windows must arrest the attention of passing shoppers, enticing them inside the store. Therefore, windows should be maintained with exciting visual displays that are changed frequently, are fun and exciting, and reflect the merchandise offering inside. Always remember that in those few seconds that the customer is approaching the store, he or she is already forming an opinion about the store and the merchandise in it.

Interior Design

Unless you have ever been responsible for redecorating a house or room, you may be unaware of the dozens of design elements that go into a physical space. We can break interior design into two types of elements: the finishes applied to surfaces and the architectural shapes. Think of all the elements from the floor to the ceiling. First, we have some type of floor covering placed over a concrete or wood floor. At the least this finish is stain or paint, but vinyl, carpet, ceramic tile, or marble are more frequently used. Each of these different surfaces creates a different impression on the shopper. An unpainted concrete floor conveys a low-cost, no-frills environment. A color-stained floor can convey a rustic yet sophisticated look and feel. Vinyl floor covering makes another statement, which, depending on its quality, sheen, color, and design pattern, can vary from very downscale to very upscale. Carpet suggests a homelike atmosphere conducive to selling apparel. Ceramic tile, travertine, and especially porcelain or marble suggest an upscale, exclusive, and probably expensive shopping experience.

Retailers have even more options for covering the walls, from paint and wallpaper to hundreds of types of paneling. The ceiling must also receive a design treatment, whether it is finished drywall (a very upscale image because it is an expensive process), a suspended ceiling (very common and economical, though not distinctive), or perhaps even an open ceiling with all the pipes and wires above painted black (which suggests a low-price warehouse approach). Then, there are thousands of types of moldings that can be applied to the transitions from floor to wall to ceiling, and hundreds of architectural design elements that can be incorporated.

Lighting Design

Another important, though often overlooked, element in a successful store design is lighting. Retailers have come to understand how lighting can greatly enhance store sales. One of the early keys to success for Blockbuster Video was its move away from the 100-watt bulbs used by its competitors to brighter lights. Brighter lighting in a wine store also influences shoppers to examine and handle more merchandise. Department stores, on the other hand, have found that raising lighting levels in fashion departments can actually discourage sales, because bright lighting suggests a discount store image.

Lighting design, however, is not limited to simple light levels. Contemporary lighting design requires an in-depth knowledge of electrical engineering and the effect of light on color and texture. Retailers have learned that different types and levels of lighting can have a significant impact on sales.[23] In addition, the types of light sources available have multiplied quickly. Today, there are literally hundreds of light fixtures and lamps (bulbs) from which to choose.

Many retailers are actually using too much outdoor lighting today, probably because of the increasing risk of accidents and/or lawsuits. Lighting is measured in foot-candles. One foot-candle is a unit of illuminant equal to one lumen per square foot. Research findings suggest that customers in urban areas feel safest in parking lots lighted to the level of five foot-candles, while those in suburban parking lots prefer three foot-candles. (By comparison, one foot-candle lights most roadways, and full moonlight is 1/100th of one foot-candle.) However, most businesses, especially gas stations, restaurants, and convenience stores, are now lighting at 100 to 150 foot-candle levels. This not only substantially increases costs but causes "light pollution" for the neighborhood.[24]

Sounds and Smells: Total Sensory Marketing

Effective store design appeals to the human senses of sight, hearing, smell, and touch. Obviously, the majority of design activity in a retail store is focused on affecting sight. For example, have you ever gone into a Wal-Mart store and had the greeter say "Hello" to you? Sam Walton's wife, Helen, suggested the idea of the greeter as a way to put customers in a better mood and to convey a feeling of warmth toward the retailer. However, Sam Walton soon came to realize another benefit of greeters—they slowed customers down as they entered the store. The first 20 feet inside a store is a decompression chamber for customers as they adjust to the different lighting and climate of the store. Customers are often unable to pick up visual cues until they adjust to their new environment. Thus greeters allowed Wal-Mart to not only convey a positive message but also forced customers to slow down to return the greeting, and then become aware of the merchandise at the front of the store. Sam Walton actually added 30 feet to this effective selling area. Today, supermarkets and other retailers are using a similar tactic with the area between the parking lot and the front door to the store. For this critically important area they are incorporating "plazas," thus allowing their customers to enter the store through an attractively designed area, as opposed to older stores which typically have shopping carts and soda machines at their front doors. Some of the more progressive retailers now have water fountains, plants, and seating areas directly in front of their stores. Others slow down the consumer with a community area near the front of the store even incorporating small stage areas for local bands to play on the weekends. Thus, rather than a Coke or Pepsi machine parked in the front of the store, they have a BBQ grill with burgers and hotdogs, music, and happy and entertained customers entering the store.

Research has shown that senses other than sight can also be very important, and as a result many retailers are beginning to engineer the smells and sounds in their stores. Despite some recent academic research to the contrary,[25] smell is believed to be the most closely linked of all the senses to memory and emotions. Bakeries, coffee shops, popcorn vendors in movie theaters, and specialty shops that sell coffee or tobacco often attract customers through the smells that emanate from the products. Retailers hope that using smells as an in-store marketing tool will put consumers "in the mood." Victoria's Secret has deployed potpourri caches throughout its stores, and in fact now sells them, to create the ambiance of a lingerie closet. The Walt Disney Company uses the smell of fresh-baked cookies on Main Street in

Courtesy of Zimmerman Architecture

Shopping at the Ballard Market is a total sensory experience.

Courtesy of Zimmerman Architecture

Everything about Central Market from its lighting, exterior and interior design, and merchandise displays both, inside and outside, create a coherent and memorable store atmosphere.

the Magic Kingdom to relax customers and provide a feeling of warmth. Regardless of the smell used, it must be consistent with the store's image. For example, a natural foods store should employ natural scents such as potpourri or sandalwood rather than artificial scents that are typical of modern floor cleansers. A large department or grocery store should also create islands within the store with distinct smells. For example, shoppers may find it natural to move from fresh produce, to bakery, to coffee, and then to meats and to seafood. A store should also have neutral zones where shoppers can recover their olfactory senses. Some believe that a strong coffee scent actually serves as a powerful neutralizer. However, the type of aroma to use depends on the merchandise being sold and the target customer. You may want to use a floral aroma for men because it will remind them of their mothers and trigger a happy memory or feeling of security. For teenagers, some retailers have used smells that resemble airplane or automobile exhaust. Nike has discovered that putting customers in a room with the odor of old sneakers had a positive effect on their desire to buy new ones.[26]

Retailers have piped music, such as Muzak, into their stores for generations, believing that a musical backdrop will create a more relaxing environment and encourage customers to stay longer.[27] Increasingly, music is being seen as a valuable marketing tool, because the right music can create an environment that is both soothing and reflective of the merchandise being offered. For example, a jeans retailer might play hip-hop near baggies and classic rock over by the Dockers. Researchers believe that while the tempo of music affects how long shoppers stay in a store, the type of music may be just as influential on how much they purchase.[28] For instance, although classical music is soothing and has been shown to encourage customers to shop longer[29] and select more expensive merchandise,[30] it may be inconsistent with the desired ambiance of a trendy fashion store catering to college-age women. Today, some retailers are experimenting with placing advertisements into the background music. Other retailers have found a different use for this canned music. A shopping mall in Australia plays Bing Crosby music to drive out the kids who want to hang out after school. In addition, the mall uses pink fluorescent lights, which supposedly highlight pimples. The New South Wales train service in Australia uses canned music at stops in high crime areas to keep the undesirable element away.[31]

LO 5 Visual Communications

What is the role of visual communications in a retail store?

The last chapter was devoted to the retail selling process. However, sales associates cannot always be available to assist customers, particularly in this era of increased competitive pressure and reduced gross margins, which have caused many retailers to cut costs by reducing their sales staffs. Even department stores, which staked their reputations on high levels of personal customer service, have had to reduce their service levels and learn to rely on alternative service strategies. How, then, can retailers provide good selling communications and high customer service while controlling labor costs?

The answer is visual communications, in the form of in-store signage and graphics. The chapter's What's New box describes how retailers can plan the store environment to incorporate signs, large photopanels, and other visual devices that serve as silent salespersons, providing shoppers with much-needed information and directions on how to shop the store, evaluate merchandise, and make purchases. Because these visual communications are inanimate objects that stay permanently in place, they require only a one-time installation cost and low maintenance, and can be relied on to perform their function, the same way, for every shopper. Unlike sales associates, visual communications are never late for work, are never in a bad mood, and never mistreat customers. Of course, neither are they as effective as a good sales associate who provides the personal touch that makes customers feel welcome and comfortable. But when carefully balanced with personal service, visual communications, with their reliability and low cost, can create an effective selling environment and are therefore becoming an important tool in the store designer's toolbox.

Earlier we likened a retail store to a well-written book. Visual communications are akin to the headlines, subheads, illustrations, and captions that give the reader direction and illustrate the written descriptions. These visual communications must address the questions of the shopper: What is it? Where is it? Why should I buy it? How much does it cost?[32] Without visual communications, a store would resemble a newspaper full of words but no headlines, a jumbled, incomprehensible mess of merchandise. An effective visual communications program includes a range of messages, from large and bold directives, used sparingly to provide cues to the gross organization of the space, to the smaller, more specific, and plentiful messages that describe actual merchandise. A visual communications program includes the following important elements.

Name, Logo, and Retail Identity

The first and most visible element in a comprehensive visual communications program is the retailer's identity, composed of the store name, logo, and supporting visual elements. The name and logo are seen not only on the storefront and throughout the interior, but also in advertising and all communications with consumers, and therefore they must be catchy, memorable, and most of all, reflective of the retailer's merchandising mission. Historically, many retail companies have taken the names of their founders, as is the case with most department stores. That practice has fallen out of vogue, however, as retailing has become a game of crafty store images and catchy retail identities. A founder's name rarely captures the merchandising spirit of a company as well as names such as Bath & Body Works, The Home Depot, and Toys "R" Us. Given the ever-increasing barrage of advertising messages and the waning effectiveness of each message, retailers have found it necessary to choose names that are highly distinctive as well as descriptive of their unique offerings. Today's hottest logos, reflecting "American values," include Starbucks, L. L. Bean, Cheesecake Factory, and Old Navy.

Once a name has been chosen, a logo is developed to visually portray the name in a creative and memorable manner. Again, the key is to keep the logo simple and easy to understand, while making it exciting enough to leave a lasting image in the customers' minds. The logo is often accompanied by taglines that provide more description of the store concept, such as Wal-Mart's "Always Low Prices—Always."

What's New?

Retailing and the First Moment of Truth

In the discussion on in-store promotions in Chapter 11, it was pointed out that there is a strong correlation between shoppers noticing an in-store display or signage and impulse purchases. However, the study cited noted that in-store TV ads were largely ignored by today's "on-the-go" shoppers.

This lack of interest is about to change as leading manufacturers, such as Procter & Gamble, and innovative retailers, such as Pierce's Northside Market in Madison, Wisconsin, are increasingly using sophisticated in-store marketing to power sales. Gone is the traditional in-store marketing, typically signs posted at the end of supermarket aisles and TV sets hanging from the ceilings near the checkstands with Pepsi ads. In are large flat-panel plasma televisions placed strategically throughout the store and special electronic shelf displays. This ensures that each time a shopper visits a particular department, they will see new, fresh content versus outdated print signage. All this is aimed at creating positive impressions that will attract and inform customers.

This first impression is what P&G refers to as the "first moment of truth" or the three to seven seconds that someone first notices an item on a store shelf. This is the time that P&G believes shoppers make up their mind about a product. Given today's fragmentation of television among hundreds of broadcast and cable networks and the multitude of print ad opportunities, the giant manufacturer now touts its brands directly to consumers where they're most likely to be influenced: the store. Supporting this strategy is evidence that shoppers are more likely to recall an ad seen in a retail location than one seen at home. As a result, when P&G's Gillette division introduced Venus Vibrance, a women's razor, in 2005, its first TV ad ran on just one network—Wal-Mart's in-store satellite network.

Retailers are now incorporating these same ideas, not only to enhance the customer's shopping experience but also to increase store sales. Pierce's Northside Market recently placed three large-screen plasma TVs in its 25,000 square foot store. One was placed in the back of the store near the frozen foods so that shoppers who are buying frozen foods could see, for example, shish kabobs on the grill. Hopefully, this screen image will lead customers to the meat department and produce department to buy ingredients for their own shish kabobs. The plasma near the produce department features the orchards and farms that produced the grocer's fruits and vegetables. The sitting area adjacent to the deli has a fireplace, comfortable seats, and even some wireless PC desks. Over the fireplace is the third 60″ plasma TV—with photos of farms surrounding Madison, local landmarks, and of course, more "beauty" shots of items available in the store.

The premise behind three televisions in a small grocery store is that people "eat with their eyes." How many times have you heard someone say that you shouldn't shop when

Pierce's Northside Market-Madison, WI

Plentiful use of fresh flowers and plants at Pierce's Northside Market reinforce a fresh food image.

What's New? *(continued)*

Pierce's Northside Market Madison, WI

Highly focused soft lighting gives Pierce's Northside Market the ambiance of a high-end specialty store.

you're hungry? With time-starved shoppers pushing shopping carts, why not show them some great prepared meal ideas and get them to visit the meat department to buy some T-bones? Other grocers are using large format (10 feet high by 40 feet wide) cinema sized projections of the same content. In place of the typical styrene letters "Farm Fresh Produce" that customers never look at, is a large screen showing still photos and short movies with fresh produce ideas. After all, this is the MTV video generation.

Source: Phil Lempert, *Facts, Figures, & The Future*, August 2005; "In a Shift, Marketers Beef up Ad Spending Inside Stores," *The Wall Street Journal*, September 21, 2005: A1 & A8; and based on information supplied by Jim Lukens, DW Green Company, and Jim Maurer, Pierce's Northside Market.

The logo's most prominent placement is on the outside of the store. This is critical to attracting customers and creating high store traffic. Another reason the store name and logo should be succinct and descriptive is that they often play to motorists passing by at 45 miles per hour.

Institutional Signage

Inside the store, the first level of visual communications is known as institutional signage, or signage that describes the merchandising mission, customer service policies, and other messages on behalf of the retail institution. This signage is usually located at the store entrance, to properly greet entering customers, and at service points such as the service desk, layaway window, and cash registers. In addition, some retailers place customer service signage throughout the store, to reinforce special policies several times during the shopping trip. This signage might include messages such as "Lowest Price Guaranteed" or "All Major Credit Cards Accepted."

Directional, Departmental, and Category Signage

Directional and departmental signage serve as the highest level of organization in an overall signage program. These signs are usually large and placed fairly high, so they can be seen throughout the store. They help guide the shopper through the

directional and departmental signage
Are large signs that are usually placed fairly high, so it is be seen throughout the store.

store and locate specific departments of interest. Not all stores use directional signage. It is not necessary in smaller stores, but in virtually all stores larger than 10,000 square feet, some type of departmental signage is used. Once a shopper locates and moves close to a particular department, category signage is used to call out and locate specific merchandise categories. **Category signage** is usually smaller, since it is intended to be seen from a shorter distance and is located on or close to the fixture itself. For instance, the departmental sign might say "Sporting Goods," be two feet high and six feet wide, and hang from the ceiling. On the other hand, the category signage might be only six inches high and two feet wide, affixed to the top of the gondola, and read "Hunting," "Tennis," or "Fitness."

category signage
Is smaller than directional and departmental signage and is intended to be seen from a shorter distance; it is located on or close to the fixture itself where the merchandise is displayed.

Point-of-Sale (POS) Signage

The next level of signage—even smaller, and placed closer to the merchandise—is known as **point-of-sale**, or **POS** signage. Because POS signage is intended to give details about specific merchandise items, it usually contains more words and is affixed directly to fixtures. POS signage may range in size from 11 by 17 inches to a 3-by-5-inch card with very small type describing an item. Always, however, the most important function of POS signage is to clearly state the price of the merchandise being signed.

point-of-sale signage (POS)
Is relatively small signage that is placed very close to the merchandise and is intended to give details about specific items.

POS signage includes a set of sign holders used throughout the store, along with a variety of printed signs that can be inserted into the hardware. Store associates mix and match the signage and hardware as directed by management, so that POS signage changes frequently. Special POS signs for sales, clearance, and "as advertised" are often different colors than the normal price signage to highlight these special values.

Lifestyle Graphics

Visual communications encompass more than just words. Many stores incorporate large graphics panels showing so-called lifestyle images in important departments. These photo images portray either the merchandise, often as it is being used, or simply images of related items or models that convey an image conducive to buying the product. In a high-fashion department, lifestyle photography might show a scene of movie stars arriving at a nightclub in very trendy fashions, suggesting that similar fashions are available in that department. In sporting goods, a lifestyle image might show an isolated lake surrounded by autumn-colored trees, with mist rising off the water and the sun rising in the background.

Retailers must be careful when choosing lifestyle photography, for as the saying goes, "beauty is in the eye of the beholder." One person's lifestyle is not necessarily another's, so lifestyle photography must be kept very general so as to be attractive to the majority and offensive to none. Increasingly, photopanels and lifestyle imagery, which can be expensive to create, are being provided free of charge to retailers by merchandise vendors, who are looking to gain an advantage for their products on the retail floor.

Dollars & Sense

Retailers can use visual communications, such as institutional signage, directional and departmental signage, category and POS signage, and lifestyle graphics to communicate more effectively with shoppers and increase space productivity.

SUMMARY

LO 1

What are the elements of a store's environment?

In this chapter, we focused on the retail store; a key factor influencing the consumer's initial perception of the retailer. It must effectively convey the store image desired by the retailer and provide a shopping environment that is conducive to high sales. The guiding principle in effective store planning, merchandise presentation, and design is that the more merchandise customers are exposed to, the more they tend to buy. This depends largely on planning the name, logo, and visual appearance of the store to convey a desired market positioning image. Although retailers work diligently to influence their images, true store image is an amalgam of all messages consumers receive, from advertising, to stories they hear from friends, to the store itself.

LO 2

What is involved in store planning?

Store planning refers to developing a plan for the organization of the retail store. First, the retailer must decide how to allocate the available square footage among the various types of selling and non-selling space needed. This is usually accomplished by conducting a mathematical analysis of the productivity of various merchandise categories. By comparing the sales and/or gross margin produced by various categories with the space they use, the retailer can develop a plan for the optimal allocation of available space. Next the floor plan is created, showing the placement and circulation patterns of all merchandise departments. Finally, thought must be given as to how the floor plan can help reduce shrinkage.

LO 3

How are the various types of fixtures, merchandise presentation methods and techniques, and the psychology of merchandise presentation used to increase the productivity of the sales floor?

Fixture selection and merchandise presentation are critical to exposing customers to the maximum amount of merchandise. There are many types of store fixtures, as well as specific methods of merchandise presentation, that have been shown to maximize merchandise exposure and lead to increased sales. Particularly, there is a psychology of merchandise presentation that utilizes customers' natural shopping behaviors and adopts merchandise presentation to match them. In addition to maximizing sales, fixture selection and merchandise presentation must conform to operational constraints and be easy to maintain.

LO 4

Why is store design so important to a store's success?

The most visible elements of the store are the design of its storefront and the interior decor. The storefront or exterior must be eye-catching, inviting, and reflective of the merchandise inside. The interior design must be comfortable, put the shopper in the proper buying mood, and provide a backdrop that enhances but does not overpower the merchandise. The store designer must always remember that shoppers are there to look at the merchandise, not the store design.

LO 5

What is the role of visual communications in a retail store?

A successful selling environment is based on effective visual communications with the customers. Since shoppers require information even when sales associates are not available, visual communications must be used throughout the store to provide direction, specific information, and prices. A visual communications program begins with the store name and logo and includes a range of interior signage that walks the customer through the buying experience.

Finally, there are literally hundreds of details in a successful retail store, and all must be carefully coordinated to create a cohesive, targeted store image that reflects the retailer's mission.

TERMS TO REMEMBER

store image
space productivity
shrinkage
floor plan
microretailing
stack-outs
space productivity index
free-flow layout
grid layout
loop layout
spine layout
on-shelf merchandising
bulk or capacity fixture
feature fixture
visual merchandising
ambiance
directional and departmental signage
category signage
point-of-sale signage (POS)

REVIEW AND DISCUSSION QUESTIONS

LO 1

What are the elements of a store's environment?

1. Discuss the two primary objectives of the store environment and how these are achieved.
2. What is merchandise presentation and how does it impact sales?
3. Why are store layout and design makeovers, such as the one McDonalds is attempting, so dangerous for a retailer? Do you think McDonalds will be successful? Why?
4. If shrinkage detracts from space productivity, why don't retailers keep all merchandise under lock and key and eliminate their emphasis on display?

LO 2

What is involved in store planning?

5. What lessons can store planners draw from an effectively written book?
6. Discuss the various types of space in a retail store, describing the role of each.
7. Identify the four main types of store layouts, discussing their differences and impact on customers.

LO 3

How are the various types of fixtures, merchandise presentation methods and techniques, and the psychology of merchandise presentation used to increase the productivity of the sales floor?

8. In the theater of retailing, discuss the differences between the "props and visual backdrops" and the "stars."
9. If retail space is such a scarce resource, what is wrong with the mantra of "stack it high, watch it fly" so as to stock more merchandise in the limited available space?
10. What is the psychology of merchandise presentation and how is it used? Can it be used by e-tailers?

LO 4

Why is store design so important to a store's success?

11. What are the goals of interior and exterior design?

12. Why is lighting design important to store planners?
13. Can sounds and smell influence store performance?

What is the role of visual communications in a retail store? LO 5

14. What is the first moment of truth and how does it impact a retailer's visual communications strategy?
15. Why is the retailer's logo so important? Why isn't the founder's name a good choice for the name of a retail store?

SAMPLE TEST QUESTIONS

The two primary objectives of the store environment are LO 1

a. effective sales management and creating a distinctive ambiance.
b. creating the store image and increasing space productivity.
c. creative merchandise presentation and effective store traffic control.
d. maximizing impulse purchase opportunity and effective shelf space allocation.
e. maintaining market share and effective merchandise control.

The goal of store layout and design in store planning should be to LO 2

a. maximize customer access to high-profit items.
b. evenly divide floor space between the five functional areas of a retail store.
c. make the store easy to understand and shop and allow the merchandise to be effectively presented.
d. allow for the rapid restocking of valuable shelf space in low-turnover merchandise categories.
e. design a store which maximizes back room stock capacity.

The psychology of merchandise presentation refers to the fact that LO 3

a. different merchandising methods can strongly influence the store's image and its sales.
b. psychologists should always be hired as merchandisers.
c. merchandise presentation teaches consumers how to shop effectively.
d. social factors strongly influence shopping behavior.
e. shoppers can be classified according to psychological tests.

Store design does all but which of the following: LO 4

a. creates a distinctive and memorable store image
b. maximizes sales transactions per customer visit
c. includes the architectural elements and finishes on all surfaces
d. seeks to attract passing shoppers and entice them to enter the store
e. encompasses the store's exterior and interior

Which of the following is not part of a visual communications program? LO 5

a. store name and logo
b. institutional signage
c. directional and category signage
d. lifestyle graphics
e. television advertising

WRITING AND SPEAKING EXERCISE

While in school you work part-time for a clothing store. The suburban store, which is located in a neighborhood shopping center near a high school, has been experiencing a high rate of shoplifting. Shrinkage is running over 5 percent of sales, or two and a half times the national average. Part of the problem is the students feel it is a lark to get "something for nothing." In fact, several shoplifters who were recently caught had more than enough money on them to pay for the merchandise. They explained that they got "points" toward membership in a social club for every dollar's worth of merchandise they could steal.

No matter how the store layout has been redesigned, the theft rate has remained constant. Now the owner wants to use those "high-tech" tags that set off an alarm at the door if not deactivated at the checkout counter. You worry about what might happen if you, or some other associate, forgot to deactivate a tag from a paying customer. After all, this would be an embarrassing situation.

After suggesting this to your department manager, the two of you feel that moving the checkout counter to block the exit would be a better solution. However, that would mean that even customers who don't purchase anything would have to go through the line. This may upset some customers.

Your manager suggests that you think out all the possible consequences of these alternatives and write a memo with your solution. He promises to copy the memo to the boss.

RETAIL PROJECT

Let's look more closely at some of the attributes that often influence supermarket choice decisions. Nine frequently cited attributes are:

1. Low prices
2. Choice of national versus private labels
3. Physical characteristics (including decor, layout, and floor space)
4. Fast checkouts
5. Produce quality
6. Convenience (including hours, location, ease of entrance and parking, ease of finding items)
7. Services (including credit, delivery, return policy, and guarantees)
8. Store personnel (including helpfulness, friendliness, and courtesy)
9. Advertised "specials" in stock

For your assignment, you are to rank these attributes in order of importance to you. After ranking them, take the most important attribute and assign it the value of 10, take the second most important attribute and assign it the value of 9. Continue to do this for your top five attributes, with your fifth attribute getting a value of 6.

Now visit two supermarkets or supercenters and assign a value (1 being very poor, 10 being very good) to the stores' performance on your five attributes. Next multiply your rank value by their performance value for each attribute and sum the total. Is the store with the highest total points your favorite? If not, why is there a difference?

If you were planning to shop on the Internet for clothing, what "store" attributes would be the most important?

PLANNING YOUR OWN RETAIL BUSINESS

After graduation from college, you opened a swimwear store, called the ZigZag, on South Padre Island. The building you located is 400 square feet and had been vacant for 18 months. Because of the limited amount of startup capital you had to invest in the business, you moved into the building without remodeling either its exterior or its interior.

During the first year the ZigZag had 13,400 visitors, of whom 3,350 made a purchase. The average transaction size was $38. The ZigZag operates on a gross margin of 55 percent and has annual fixed operating expenses of $30,000. Variable costs were 15 percent of sales. The two primary fixed expenses are rent of $1,100 a month and salaries of $1,200 a month. You keep all profits in the business to reinvest in inventory and other immediate business needs.

Because your first year was profitable, you are now considering remodeling the store. Your landlord will not help with these expenses. To paint the exterior would cost $1,400. For the interior, you are thinking of tiling the floor in a zigzag pattern, which will cost $1,600. In addition, new lighting and some new fixtures would cost $4,000.

You believe these changes will increase traffic by 10 percent and that your closure or conversion rate will increase to 30 percent. Will your proposed changes pay for themselves the first year?

CASE

The Unique Shop

You are the facilities manager for a chain of six women's apparel stores called the Unique Shop. The chain, which targets younger women, has its flagship store in the strip center near a college campus in a city of 120,000. The 15,000-square-foot store, which was last remodeled twelve years ago, has experienced consistent sales increases in recent years. However, the company president believes the store is missing even more sales since many competitors have left the campus area for one of two malls on the outskirts of the city.

Hoping to take advantage of this lack of competition, the president has budgeted about $400,000 for expansion next year. She plans on leasing the 5,000-square-foot empty storefront next door and increasing the aisle widths and number of dressing rooms while maintaining the same level of inventory. The merchandise manager, however, recommends that the $400,000 be used to buy new fixtures to increase the merchandise capacity of the existing store. His idea is to shrink the width of all aisles, fit more bulk fixtures on the floor, and double-stack all merchandise. After all, without these new racks and shelves, customers won't be able to see the merchandise. And if customers can't see the merchandise, they can't buy it.

When walking the store last week, you noticed that the merchandise is already crammed in too tightly and that customers were having trouble putting unwanted merchandise back on the racks and shelves. You also felt that there were too few feature presentations to support your fashion apparel. Finally, it bothered you that there was not a clear distinction between the various departments within the store.

The president and the marketing and merchandising personnel must understand their target customer groups to make the expansion plans most effective. If the store adds more merchandise, what type of merchandise should be added, targeting which types of customers? Even if little new inventory is added, what types of departments should be made distinctive?

Questions

1. What do you feel is more important for customers: increasing store space, which will take longer, and be more difficult, or adding more racks to the present store? Why?
2. If increasing total sales is the goal, which plan would you recommend? Explain your reasoning.
3. Describe some of the market segments that can be found in the customer category ''young women.'' How do their lifestyles influence different clothing needs? How could you use your customer base to help you decide which new merchandise categories to carry?
4. Could the president consider subleasing parts of a larger store to a compatible merchant? For example, should the store consider a coffee bar or a vintage clothing shop? What are some of the considerations in this decision?

Source: This case was prepared by Jan Owens, Carthage College, Kenosha, WI, and used with her written permission.

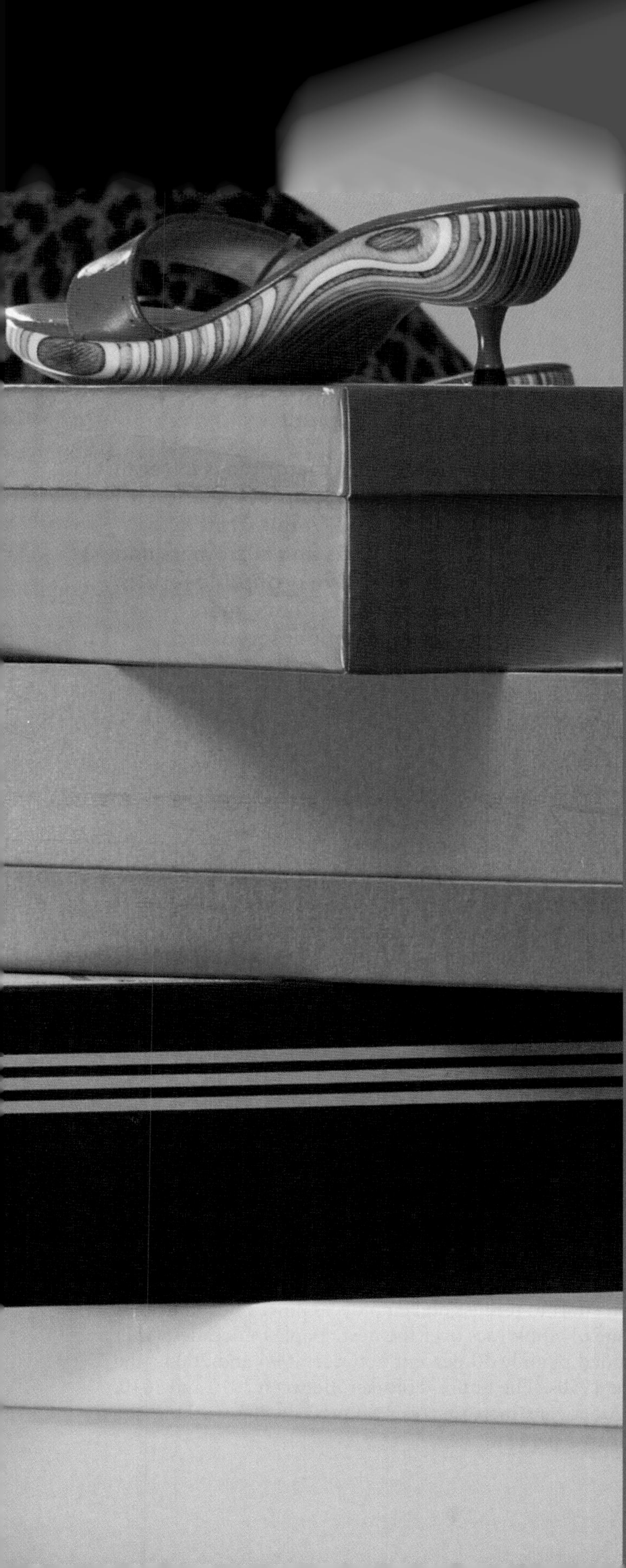

5

Retail Administration

Chapter 14
Managing People

chapter 14

Managing People

Overview:

In this chapter we examine the role that the human factor plays in retail firms. In retailing the human factor is composed of employees and customers. Both are critical to carry out a successful retail strategy. Retailers therefore must recruit the right employees and customers and then manage these relationships if they are to achieve profitable results. Both outstanding employees and desirable customers have many options; thus, employees must be competitively compensated and customers must be offered more compelling value than they can achieve from competing retailers.

Learning Objectives:

After reading this chapter, you should be able to:

1. Explain why intangible people resources can provide a more competitive advantage than tangible resources.
2. Describe how to recruit both the right employees and the right customers to be the store's partners.
3. Explain how to manage employees and customers to develop long-term profitable relationships.
4. Discuss how to compensate employees and offer customers a compelling value proposition.

LO 1

Intangible People Resources Make the Difference

Why are intangible people resources more important than tangible resources to a retailer's competitive advantage?

A dominant theme in this chapter is that a retailer's *people* resources are more important than its *tangible* (bricks-and-mortar) resources. "People," as used in this text, refers to both customers and employees. The earlier chapters have already discussed the importance of customers. However, many retailers fail to give equal significance to employees.

The demographic data suggest that the successful retailers of the future will be those that devote the maximum effort to hiring good employees now. The sad truth is that retailers will face a shortage of employees over the next couple of decades. After all, the total labor force expanded by only 10 percent between 1996 and 2006—the slowest rate of growth since the 1950s. The future is bleaker. Between 2010 and 2030, while the number of elderly Americans increases over 80 percent, the working-age population will grow by less than 2 percent.[1]

The preceding information has caused some retailers to start using tangible resources to either substitute for people resources or to improve the productivity of people with additional tangible resources. Retailers have already begun to use technologies as replacements for some employees. Hilton Hotels is using guest self-service kiosks at some of its wholly owned properties. Hilton believes that the kiosks will improve guest service by reducing time spent in lines, thereby increasing customer convenience, and reducing transaction costs (labor costs). Although the kiosks are built to be user-friendly, hotel staff will be available to answer questions and assist guests. Your neighborhood supermarkets and discount stores may already be offering a similar concept with self-checkouts. Other examples of retailers using technology to replace people include the increased usage of RFID (radio frequency identification) and the placement of in-store kiosks to allow customers to look up information themselves.

AP Photo/John Amis

Successful retailers realize that both employees and customers need to be recruited, motivated, and compensated for their efforts.

It is important, however, that retailers realize that all these investments in tangible assets (land, building, technology, equipment and fixtures, and merchandise) will not produce a profitable return unless the retailer is willing to invest in recruiting, motivating, and retaining the right people. These people are the retailer's employees and customers because a store without employees and customers cannot generate sales.[2]

Too many retailers are shortsighted. As a result, they often fail to give the same care to their investments in intangible assets, such as employees and customers that they do to their tangible investments. This is myopic because it is easy for a competitor to copy or replicate the tangible. Land, buildings, technology, equipment and fixtures, and merchandise are all easy to buy and sell in the marketplace, so in the end, retailers gain little relative advantage by their tangible presence. An Office Depot and Staples look very similar, as do competing Lowe's and The Home Depot stores. However, a retailer with superior employee and customer resources will enjoy a differential advantage over the competition. To be successful, retailers must view labor costs, as well as the expenses of attracting and retaining customers, not as *costs* but as *investments* in obtaining a sustainable competitive advantage. The fact that interacting with an unhappy and disgruntled employee often makes co-workers and customers unhappy should not be overlooked. Some estimate that disengaged workers, "those that have quit, but forgot to tell you," cost American firms in excess of $250 billion annually.[3]

Similarities Between Employees and Customers

While everyone can make the distinction between a retail employee and a retail customer, few choose to focus on their similarities. These similarities far outweigh the differences, and the inability to realize this can limit retail success. After all, whether an individual is an employee or a customer, that individual must perform some task in the economic exchange process so as to create value. Lacking a complete knowledge of the retail process, many consumers fail to see themselves as performing a retailing task. Yet, as the demand for labor outstrips supply, many retailers are being forced to follow the example of Hilton Hotels. Another service retailer group, the airlines, has also shifted some retailing tasks, i.e., ticketing and issuing boarding passes, to the customer. This is the result of staff cutbacks caused by the industry's multiple bankruptcies. Airlines are now at the point where they have more tasks to perform than employees to perform them, thus they must pass them off to the customer.

Just like employees, *customers need to be recruited, motivated, and compensated for their efforts*. In this sense, clearly the customer is similar to an employee, but what about the employee as a customer? Some forward-thinking retailers have begun to refer to employees as "internal customers." Retailers must remember that all employees are part of the service delivery chain where each, in turn, performs some task in the economic exchange process. With a division of labor, each employee performs microspecializations that are combined with the work of other microspecialists to create value along a service chain. Consider, for example, a JCPenney store. Before a customer purchases a pair of Arizona jeans, a number of microtransactions between the firm's associates have already occurred. As described in Chapter 5, a buyer has contracted with an apparel manufacturer in Asia to produce the jeans, which are then shipped to a distribution center. At the distribution center there are receivers, stockers, and retrievers. Each of these individuals is a customer of another employee. For example, the retriever of merchandise is a customer of the stocker. If the stocker places the jeans in the wrong bin location, then the retriever may pick the wrong jeans. If the wrong jeans are picked, they are likely to be sent to a store that does not need them, and thus the store manager or active wear merchandise manager is not served well. This service chain continues until the customer purchases an item from the store.

Actually, the division of labor and development of microspecialists within retailing is the cause of many customer service problems. Have you ever experienced a problem with a salesclerk? The clerk may proclaim, "Well, I need to check with my boss." This person is another microspecialist who may then need to check with his or her boss (also a microspecialist), and the buck keeps being passed. For this reason, many retailers are trying to *empower* employees to better serve not only external customers but also internal customers, or other employees.

One successful retailer whose excellent service has already been discussed several times in this text is Nordstrom's. Nordstrom's employees, as well as the employees of other great retailers, are able to provide great service because they have been empowered by their employers to take care of the customer. **Empowerment** simply means giving the employee the "power to make things right for the customer." An empowered retail employee

empowerment
Occurs when employees are given the power in their jobs to do the things necessary to satisfy and make things right for customers.

1. Seeks to understand the customer's problem.
2. Desires to develop a relationship with the customer.
3. Understands the value of customer loyalty.
4. Is allowed or encouraged by management to solve the customer's problem.

Dollars & Sense

The more profitable retailers empower their employees to solve internal and external customer problems.

The profit impact of empowering employees is dramatic. For many retailers providing good customer service can make the difference between success and failure. Because retailers operate on a low net profit margin, even a small increase in sales force productivity—whether measured in sales per employee hour or gross margin per employee hour—often translates directly into an improvement in profits. Consequently, retailers are now expanding their efforts to improve labor's productivity, especially that of the sales force, by training and empowering employees. Consider the following situation: A customer comes in to an appliance dealership to purchase a specific clothes dryer and the only unit left is the display model on the sales floor. Unfortunately, this model has a scratch on the left side panel that will probably not be seen when placed in the customer's home. The dryer is priced at $600, so in order to not lose the sale, the salesperson offers a $50 reduction in price. The end result is higher self-esteem among employees because they have been trained and are permitted to "make things right" without having to seek the permission of a higher authority. In addition, the lower price has also increased the customer's satisfaction. Combined, these two factors will reduce employee turnover because happy situations don't cause conflicts.

Another retailer who has done an excellent job of keeping customers and employees happy is privately-held Wegmans Supermarkets which was #1 on *Fortune's* "The 100 Best Companies to Work for." This Rochester, New York, based chain has an employee turnover rate less than one-third the industry average and a customer base that has bonded with the store and its employees. Little wonder then that the chain has determined that shoppers who are emotionally attached to a supermarket spend 46 percent more than shoppers who were satisfied but lacked that bond with the store and its employees.[4]

In summary, what customers and employees have in common is that they both perform retail tasks and they both serve the other. It is important to remember that employees must not only serve customers, but also other employees (internal customers). Recognizing that employees and customers must always serve each other is the beginning point of servant leadership. With **servant leadership**, employees recognize that their primary responsibility is to be of service to others. Many of the great retail leaders of the past century epitomized this attitude of servant leadership. These included James Cash Penney (founder of the JCPenney Company), Stanley Marcus (former chairman of Neiman Marcus), Sam Walton (founder of Wal-Mart), Leslie Wexner (founder of The Limited), Merv Morris (founder of Mervyns'), and Bernie Marcus and Arthur Blank (co-founders of The Home Depot).

servant leadership
An employee's recognition that their primary responsibility is to be of service to others.

Employees and Customers are Profit Drivers

This chapter began by emphasizing that retailers must view their employees and customers as investments. Therefore, an important question becomes how much a retailer should be willing to invest in recruiting an employee and/or a customer. Unfortunately, there is no single correct answer for this question. The answer depends on how much value the retailer thinks an employee or customer can contribute to the firm's bottom line by directly or indirectly causing revenue to increase more than their cost. If a retailer takes an investment versus an expense, or cost perspective, then that retailer is addressing this issue from a long-term perspective.

Consider these two examples. New-car salespersons should generate sufficient profit on their sales that they more than pay for their salary. Similarly, the amount Amazon spends on direct marketing efforts to a household should result in profit on sales that exceeds the cost of the marketing efforts. Of course, these are simple examples, but the basic point is clear: The gross profit generated by an employee or customer must exceed the cost of servicing these employees and customers. Employees and customers whose gross profit generated greatly exceeds their cost to the retailer will be the people who are most important to the retailer's success. In the case of customers, as a rule, retailers have found that 20 percent of the customers generate 80 percent of the sales. These are the frequent and heavy shoppers who comprise the most loyal core of customers. The same 80/20 rule holds for retail salespeople. Furniture, jewelry, auto, and insurance salespeople all generally follow the 80/20 rule: Eighty percent of retail sales come from 20 percent of the salespeople.

As previously mentioned, when some retailers think of people, they usually think of employees. However, this chapter also considers how customers can be managed with some of the same processes used in managing employees. The authors feel that retail managers must be encouraged to think of their customers as employees and to treat their employees like customers. Retailing is an exchange relationship, and in exchange relationships people want to be "treated right." This means being treated honestly, fairly, and with respect. Only by treating people right will retailers be able to have enduring and profitable relationships with their employees and customers.

Good customer and employee relationships are more than additive in their effect on a retailer's performance; the effect is synergistic. Think about it. Recall a time when you were treated rudely by a retail employee. Most likely this person did not have a good relationship with his or her employer; perhaps the employee was upset about working conditions or treatment by a supervisor. Or maybe it was that disengaged worker discussed earlier who "quit, but forgot to tell the boss." In return, because employees are only human, this person took out these bad feelings on other employees (internal customers) and on customers—like you. This unfair treatment made you mad, and you in turn got mad at the employee and the store, which only increased the employee's unhappiness. Such behavior can be said to have a multiplying effect as the unhappy employee takes out his or her frustrations on the next customer.

Dollars & Sense

Retailers that foster good employee and customer relationships will achieve dramatically improved performance.

LO 2 Obtaining the Right People

What is the process for recruiting the right employees and customers?

Retailers must remember that human resources are acquired in a competitive marketplace. Good employees are not waiting around to be hired, and seldom will they come knocking at the door. In fact, when talented workers or managers are looking for employment, they seldom think of contacting retail firms because of the reputation, sometimes unwarranted, many retailers have for low starting wages. Therefore, retailers must aggressively seek out and recruit good employees; in so doing, they must compete with other industries for labor resources.

Perhaps even more competitive is the marketplace for customers. In any community in the United States with a population over 50,000, an individual consumer has many choices. And if the choices in the immediate community are limited, the consumer can shop on the Internet, through the mail, or perhaps traveling 20 to 40 miles to a larger city. These alternatives allow individuals to expand their shopping options immensely. To recruit the most profitable customers, a retailer must offer a compelling **value proposition** and build long-term relationships with these customers.

value proposition
The promised benefits a retailer offers in relation to the cost the consumer incurs.

Customer Relationship Management

An increasingly popular technology for cultivating and maintaining the right customers is **customer relationship management (CRM)**. CRM is composed of an integrated information system where the fundamental unit of data collection is the customer, supplemented by other relevant information about the customer including purchasing behavior. Customer data at the most micro level is captured, including merchandise and services purchased, store location, time of purchase, demographic information, and satisfaction data such as customer complaints.

customer relationship management (CRM)
Is comprised of an integrated information system where the fundamental unit of data collection is the customer, supplemented by relevant information about the customer.

Historically, retailers have thought of their business in terms of merchandise. As a result, merchandise management became so fundamental that every unique item of merchandise had its own identifier, or stock-keeping unit (SKU). However, retailers do not develop relationships with SKUs but with customers. Customers—not merchandise—are the ultimate source of profitability. Despite knowing this, almost all retailers can tell you how many SKUs they have in their store, as well as the dollar value of their inventory, but few retailers know how many unique customers they have that patronize their store. Following are some fundamental questions that a CRM system can answer.

1. How many unique customers patronize the store over a given time frame (week, month, year)?
2. What is the average transaction size in terms of dollars and units purchased by type of customer? For instance, do customers between the ages of 21 and 33 have a different transaction profile than those aged 34 to 54?
3. What is the profitability of groups of customers or the profitability of a particular customer?
4. Is the customer profile at a retailer's stores in one region or part of a city different from the profile in another area?
5. Was the recent direct mail promotion cost effective? This analysis can be broken down to the level of the specific customer.
6. Which customers purchase the same items repeatedly versus trying new items? For predictable purchase items, the retailer can notify the customer when they may need to restock. The retailer can also notify a more opportunistic customer of new merchandise items.

Of course, CRM can help the retailer answer literally hundreds of other questions. After all, with each customer I.D., the retailer has data on the time of day, location, price paid, and any other important information about every purchase. Those retailers who are on the leading edge of CRM are the ones that have integrated their CRM system with their suppliers, advertising agencies, and other members of the supply chain. This collaborative effort can enable the entire supply chain to be more customer-focused. For example, Tesco's integration of a CRM program to its "Clubcard" has been cited as the main reason that it has been able to withstand Wal-Mart's U.K. invasion.[5] However, this Tesco example (Chapter 11's Global Retailing box) also illustrates that the overall goal of CRM is not just to generate reports or data. Rather, its goal is to provide the retailer with a tool to develop a long-term profitable relationship—target marketing—with a customer that is mutually beneficial. How can this be done? Here are a few examples.

1. A retailer could analyze transactional data by time of day and day of week, find the times of day when its most profitable customers shop, and schedule key associates to better serve these customers at these hours.

2. A retailer might find that sales or visits from a customer have been declining. In such cases, the retailer could target specific marketing programs toward that customer. These special programs could be direct mail, coupons, or a special call from the customer's most frequently used sales associate.
3. CRM can help the retailer identify the type of merchandise to stock during certain seasons, based on customer preferences. If a customer has been purchasing toddler's clothing for a year or so, the retailer may want to alert the customer about its children's clothing department. Based on past purchases and the family demographic information in the CRM system, the retailer can predict future purchases, and the next size up from toddlers' is children's.
4. A retailer's customer service personnel can see a complete record of the customer's purchase history and prioritize the special treatment the customer may deserve based on their profitability to the retailer. In short, knowing the cost of losing a customer can be a strong motivator for doing everything in terms of customer service to retain that customer.

Employee Sources

Where does a retailer obtain employees? The eight employee sources shown on the left side of Exhibit 14.1 are the most common: competitors, walk-ins (both in person at the store and online at the retailer's Web site), employment agencies (including online at Web sites such as monster.com), schools and colleges, former employees, advertisements, recommendations, and customer referrals. Perhaps the most innovative source is customer referral. In such a case, the retailer would use its CRM system to contact its frequent customers (after all, they know the store best) and ask them to refer potential employees to the store. Who knows, perhaps some frequent shoppers themselves may want to be employed by the retailer.

Customer Sources

The second column of Exhibit 14.1 lists sources of customers. These include competitors, walk-ins (again in the store or on the Web site) advertisements, employees, and referrals from other customers. Essentially these sources are not that different from the sources used for gathering employees. Many customers can be obtained from competitors that have stockout problems or other failures in customer service. In fact, retail patronage research has demonstrated that many customers do not go about selecting which stores to patronize, but which stores to avoid. After a customer has decided where *not* to shop, the remaining options become the ones that win the customer's patronage. As discussed in Chapter 7,

Exhibit 14.1
Employee and Customer Sources

Employees	Customers
Competitors	Competitors
Walk-ins	Walk-ins
Employment agencies	Advertisements
Schools and colleges	Employees
Former employees	Customer referrals
Advertisements	Affinity programs
Recommendations	Customer agency
Customer referrals	

traffic is also a major source of customers. High levels of consumer traffic passing by a store will result in more walk-ins. Finally, satisfied employees will promote the store to their family and friends. Employees who praise the store where they work are especially credible because they should know the store best. This is particularly true for service retailers. Many hospital workers tell negative stories about their environment and the level of patient care and service, and this can have a very negative effect on the health provider's ability to attract patients (if the patients have a choice). Conversely, of course, satisfied customers can become enthusiastic about the retailer resulting in referrals to friends and acquaintances. But even though an enthusiastic customer may demonstrate a strong commitment to the retailer, an unhappy customer is likely to tell more friends and potential customers than a satisfied customer will.[6]

In addition to the preceding traditional sources of customers, retailers are recognizing the potential value of two other sources. Affinity programs are membership programs that offer participants special discounts, such as the lifetime membership card in a retailer's "No Sales Tax for Life Club" that was discussed in Chapter 11's Inside Story box. Similarly, the American Automobile Association (AAA) provides members with discounts at many motels, hotels, restaurants, and other retailers that cater to the automobile traveler. And the American Association of Retired Persons (AARP) offers member discounts on travel, financial services, lodging, prescription drugs, and many other products and services (see http://www.aarp.org/aarp_benefits). AARP currently offers discounts on rental cars (Avis, Hertz, and National Car Rental, among others), hotels (AmeriSuites, Best Western, Days Inn, Holiday Inn, and Sheraton), and many other products.[7] It is interesting to note that this program doesn't just attract older consumers. Anyone, even students, as long as they list their correct date of birth on their AARP application, can obtain an associate AARP membership card and the good deals on travel.[8]

Another unusual source for capturing customers is the equivalent of an employment agency but is more akin to a customer agency, which is used for some products and services where the typical customer may not have the knowledge and information to make an informed decision. One such example is the selection of a college, especially for a first-generation student. There are more than a thousand choices in the United States for a four-year undergraduate education. Prices range from less than $7,000 per year to more than $45,000 per year. Consequently, many parents are retaining college consultants who provide a good match between the demands of colleges for students and the desires and needs of various students. (Perhaps some of you used such a service when you were selecting your college.) Another example relates to major household redecorating and/or renovation. It is not unusual for a couple who purchased a 2,500-square-foot house in 1979 for $65,000 to decide after the last child has gone off to college to redecorate and renovate the house. Many people prefer to renovate in order to stay in a well-liked neighborhood. However, a major redecorating and renovation of a house that cost $65,000 in 1979 may cost $100,000 or more. For most such major projects, the house owner would retain an interior designer and a general contractor who would guide the couple in what to purchase and where. Consequently, the interior design consultant is a major gatekeeper and source of customers for many home improvement retailers.

Screening and Selection of Employees

Hiring the wrong person is costly in terms of both time and money. Making a hiring mistake can lead to turnover of both employees (the mis-hired individual and maybe other good employees) and customers. Therefore, before beginning the discussion of human resource issues, it is important to point out that these issues are extremely complex—too much so for retailers without special training in that area. The authors strongly recommend working with HR professionals. However, retailers must still understand and implement basic procedures for selecting employees.[9] Regardless of the specific source, in today's environment all job applicants should be subject to a formal screening process to sort the potentially good from the potentially bad employees. As with any judgment process, some mistakes will happen. But fewer errors occur when *potential* employees are screened.

Retailers tend to vary in the amount of screening they use. In addition, to the outside verification just discussed, there are four other types of screens: application forms, personal interview, testing, and references. The total applicant pool for a particular job is progressively reduced as the applicants are subjected to each screen.

Application Form

As a matter of procedure, all applicants should be asked to fill out an application form. The application form should conveniently and compactly capture the individual's identity, training, and work history that relates to his or her performance of the job tasks. Title VII of the Civil Rights Act of 1964 prohibits employers from discrimination in employment on the basis of race, color, religion, sex, or national origin; the Age Discrimination in Employment Act of 1967 (ADEA) prohibits employers from discrimination in employment on the basis of age; and the Americans with Disabilities Act of 1990 (ADA) prohibits employers from discrimination in employment on the basis of handicap/disability. Thus, the employer is effectively prohibited from asking any questions whose answer could be used to discriminate between two different groups of applicants.[10] Many times a resume is substituted for an application form. The chapter's What's New box provides some ideas on using a resume to differentiate yourself from other applicants.

From the list of qualified applicants who filled out an application or submitted a resume, the retailer must select the best possible subset of candidates for each job.

Adrian Brown/Bloomberg News/Landov

An increasing number of job seekers use monster.com to search for and apply for jobs.

What's New?

Does Your Resume Have a Differential Advantage?

Today many college students post their resumes with their school's Career Center or on the Internet in hopes of finding that "special" job or internship. Yet, just as retailers must have a differential advantage over their competition, students must create an advantage with their resumes. How can your resume persuade a recruiter, who has spent hours looking over a hundred other resumes, call *you* for an interview?

Most employers are looking for new team members who will "fit" with the culture of their organization. They have spent a great deal of time and resources identifying the attributes that they need. So before you write or revise your resume, you also need to know what attributes they are seeking and integrate them into your resume. In many cases this information can be found on the company Web site, usually under the employment section. Some companies even have a space dedicated to college recruiting on their Web site! Your objective is to "match" your resume to the attributes that the organization is looking for in order to create your differential advantage. The key is to do this in an honest and ethical manner.

For most students, one typed page is enough. A resume should not detail your whole life history. Rather, it should outline your education and other pertinent experience. It should be positive and should accentuate the positive traits that you possess as a young professional making the transition to the world of work. For example, if your grades are good, mention that. If not, refer to other achievements, such as being elected fraternity president or having had an interesting internship.

A good predictor of future success is often the past success that an individual has achieved. As a potential candidate for a job, you need to highlight your accomplishments and emphasize that what you have done during your years in college. Many employers look for a balance between academics, leadership and work experience when making hiring decisions.

To achieve this, start your resume with a statement that summarizes what you are seeking. This summary should state why you are the perfect candidate. Don't use vague, fluffy objectives like "To work in the field in which I am striving to earn a degree, retailing." Companies want to read resumes that say: "I want to work at Nordstrom." Just make sure that you do not send this same version of the resume to Macy's or Neiman Marcus!

In addition to mentioning your work experience during college, include any volunteer work. Don't sell yourself short here. Recruiters want to know what *you* made happen, rather than see a list of the usual duties of, say, a waiter. So, a student with waitressing experience should highlight things that would not be obvious from the job title, such as "the city's most exclusive restaurant with demanding clientele."

Don't fill your resume with extraneous information, such as "references available upon request," your height and weight, and commonly used computer skills. Remember, you only want to use one page.

When your resume is complete, reread it and ask yourself these questions:

- Is it promotionally oriented? (Remember that your resume is a tool in your personal sales campaign.)
- Does it accurately reflect my background? (Remember, ethics count!)
- Does it emphasize my accomplishments?
- Can the reader easily find the information that she or he will be looking for? (Remember the balance of academics, leadership, and work experience.)
- Is it complete? Concise? Neat?
- Are all words spelled correctly and are the statements grammatically correct?

Finally, be creative, but don't go overboard. There are as many different types and styles of resumes as there are people. Choose the approach that will represent you most effectively for the job you are pursuing.

Source: Prepared by Dr. Robert Shindell, Director of the Rawls Career Management Center, Texas Tech University.

Personal Interview

Those applicants who possess the basic characteristics needed to perform the job should be personally interviewed. This important step allows the retailer to assess how well qualified the applicants are for the job. By its very nature an interview is subjective, but in a well-structured interview a retailer can obtain information or at least gain insight into the attitudes, personality, motives, and job aspirations of the interviewee.

Many interviewers overlook the fact that the interview should be a two-way communication process. Not only does the retailer want to gather information about the applicant, but also the applicant may desire information about the retailer. Allowing time for the interviewee to ask questions is essential if the retailer is competing for the talents of highly desired applicants. In fact, the interviewer may actually use part of the interview time to try to sell the applicant on working for the retailer as well as honestly explain what the job entails and thus avoid job dissatisfaction or possible legal complications based upon misunderstandings.

As pointed out in the chapter's Service Retailing box, many retailers are now using online placement companies to aid them in locating applicants. However, the Internet may also be used to gather information about the applicant either before or after the interview phase.

A final note about the interview is that while it may be explicitly discriminatory to eliminate appearance-challenged candidates during the interview stage, many employers may be implicitly doing it.[11] Research has found men ranked high in appearance earn 5 percent more than average looking males and that those in the lowest category were paid 9 percent below the average.[12] However, other factors may explain this wage difference. Today, many employers may subconsciously discriminate against overweight applicants for fear that they are more prone to health problems and will raise the company's insurance premiums. After all, the United States has the highest percentage of those over age 15 that are overweight or obese.[13] The same may probably be said about smokers.

Testing

Sometimes formal tests are administered to applicants who received favorable ratings in their personal interviews. These tests may look for certain characteristics, such as intelligence, leadership potential, particular interests or personality traits, or honesty. The Home Depot, for example, uses kiosks to test the applicant. This way The Home Depot can obtain more information more cheaply. Also, because the responses are made to the computer directly rather than on paper or to an interviewer, respondents feel that the information is more readily subject to instant checking and verification with other databases. Thus, to avoid potential embarrassment, applicants are assumed to be more truthful. As a result, these tests have an excellent record at screening out the low-integrity applicants, thereby avoiding the type of irresponsible and counterproductive behavior that drives managers crazy: disciplinary problems, disruptiveness on the job, chronic tardiness, and excessive absenteeism. A big advantage of this system for The Home Depot is that prior to its use, the retailer hired only one or two of 30 or more applicants who completed the application/interview process. Now the figure may be as high as 20 out of 30.[14]

Other assessments used by retailers include credit checks with local credit bureaus. Most applicants are unaware that their chances of getting that job can be destroyed by a bad credit score. These credit checks not only include your payment history, but also include unpaid parking fines, library fines, unpaid speeding tickets, and any other bill more than 30 days old.[15] Currently over 42 percent of all employers check out an applicant's credit history.[16] (By the way, over 50 percent of the retailers check out the applicant's driving history.)[17]

References

As a general rule, retailers should not ask for or check the references the applicant has provided until the applicant has been screened or filtered through the preceding

Service Retailing

The Internet: Friend or Foe to the Retail Job Seeker?

The Internet has created an amazing opportunity for job seekers and employers alike. As job seekers, college students now have the resources to visit and learn about any company on the planet from the comfort of their own home. Employers are also now using the Internet as a resource to find out more about those that are seeking jobs with their companies.

As a job seeker, research is an important part of the job search process. When looking for a job or internship, students should do research into the industry they are interested in, the specific company they are applying with, and the job position they are seeking. In-depth research into these three areas will show the company that the applicant has taken that extra step and has gone above and beyond in preparing for the interview. There are several helpful Web sites that can help in the research process, including: www.hoovers.com, www.vault.com, and www.careeronestop.com.

In addition to the availability of research about companies, the Internet also provides resources to help students connect with employers looking for great employees. The most popular of these is monster.com (www.monster.com). This international site has listings from thousands of companies for internships and full-time positions. Students have found it a good idea to use sites like these to assist them in making the connection to an employer. Other sites like this include www.hotjobs.com, www.careers.msn.com, and www.careerbuilder.com.

It is important for students to remember that they can never create too many avenues to help them land that "perfect job." The Internet sites are certainly one avenue, but students should not put all of their eggs in one basket! Personal networking and college career centers are also great ways to land that dream job or internship.

Unfortunately, the Internet can also be a very dangerous place, especially for the job seeker. The popularity of online profile and networking sites has increased over the past couple of years, especially with college students. MySpace.com, Facebook.com, and Yahoo.profiles.com have created a virtual world in which people can communicate information about themselves for a variety of reasons. These sites can be an amazing way to keep in touch with your friends, especially ones at a distance. They can also be extremely detrimental to a student's employment future if they aren't careful about what information they post on their site.

One thing that students sometimes do not think about is who else, other than their friends, is viewing the information that has been posted online. Many times employers will use these sites for background checking of potential employees. This is becoming common practice in the area of internship recruiting. Some students make the mistake of posting information about excessive drinking, gambling, sexual conquests, etc. and mistakenly feel that no harm can come from their posting of what used to be regarded as private behavior. Remember, anything that is posted online, even to a site that offers limited password protection such as Facebook and Myspace, is information that can potentially be accessed by anyone at anytime and forever!

A good piece of advice in regards to using these types of sites is that the student should only post information that they would feel comfortable sharing with their grandmother. If a student's grandmother would not want to hear about or see, through posted digital pictures, what the student did last Thursday night, then it shouldn't be posted anywhere online. Posting information online is like getting a tattoo. There's nothing inherently wrong with posting information online or getting a tattoo, but in both cases you need to be prepared for the fact that it will be out there forever. And some people that you didn't want to see it will see it. If the student isn't prepared to live with that, they shouldn't do it.

Source: Prepared by Dr. Robert Shindell, Director of the Rawls Career Management Center, Texas Tech University.

---

stages. If references were obtained and verified on all initial applicants, the cost would be excessive.

Negligent hiring is a major issue in current employment law. The premise is that an employer can be held responsible for an employee's unlawful actions if it did not reasonably investigate an employee's background and then placed the employee in a position where he or she caused harm to a customer. After all, with the average verdict in a negligent hiring case reaching $2 million, the time and money spent here is a good investment. Whether it is sales, service, delivery, or administration, the failure to investigate a new hire's background is a major mistake.[18] Some retailers even use a screening service that provides bi-weekly updates on current employees to protect themselves from future legal problems.[19] When references are obtained and checked, the retailer should try to assess the honesty and reliability of the applicant. The reason for leaving the prior place or places of employment should also be investigated. The retailer should be interested in finding out what type of person will vouch for the prospective employee. Although most references provided by the applicant can be expected to give a neutral or favorable recommendation (if they give one at all), the reference check does give the retailer a means to verify the accuracy and completeness of the application. Also, many retailers have found greater success using telephone interviews instead of asking for written recommendations. This method enables retailers to gather more complete and honest evaluations than do letters, even if it is only in what the reference does *not* say about the applicant. The chapter's Inside Story box points out one of the major problems faced by writers of such letters of recommendation.

One final comment on checking references: The retailer must tread carefully here to avoid breaking federal and state laws. The personnel manager is well advised to visit the firm's legal staff yearly to determine the firm's and the applicant's legal rights. New laws are regularly being enacted in Congress and state legislatures and interpreted daily in court cases throughout the country.

Screening and Selecting Customers

Retailers compete aggressively for customers, and you might believe it is unusual for a retailer to not want to do business with a customer. In a general sense, this is true. Retailers that are successful are both market- and customer-oriented and are always recruiting and welcoming new customers. However, the screening and selection of customers is more common than you might think. Bars and gambling establishments must screen for underage customers. A Porsche mechanic may not take customers with non-Porsche autos. Perhaps most predominant are universities, who screen out and select the most desirable students.

A personal interview is an important part of screening and selecting applicants for retail positions.

When retailers screen or select customers they must be sure not to violate any equal opportunity or discrimination laws. However, there are very legitimate reasons for screening and selecting customers. The most common include

1. The inability to adequately service certain customers; for example, not accepting older children for a preschool.
2. The deterioration of a retailer's atmosphere if customers of a certain type are admitted, such as allowing individuals in bathing suits or T-shirts to enter a fine dining establishment.

Retailing: The Inside Story

An Ambiguous Lexicon for Job Recommendations

Every once in a while a person requests a letter of recommendation from a previous employer, professor, or family friend about whom the letter writer has serious reservations. Does the writer send a moderately favorable letter and live with his or her conscience or write a frank, unfavorable letter and risk a lawsuit when the person finds out about it? (Remember, under certain circumstances, such letters are no longer confidential.)

Professor Robert J. Thornton at Lehigh University has developed the following guidelines for handling such a dilemma.

To describe a candidate who is not particularly industrious, here is what the writer can say (and what the writer really meant):

- "You will be very fortunate to get this person to work for you." (She's not very industrious.)
- "He could not have done a better job for us if he had tried." (He's not only incompetent, but he's lazy as well.)
- "I think it's safe to say that his true interests were lying in the stockroom." (He used to sneak naps there.)
- "No job is too much for this man to handle." (He just can't seem to deal with any kind of responsibility.)
- "She works effortlessly." (She doesn't expend much energy.)
- "You will never catch him asleep on the job." (He's too crafty to get caught.)
- "He always found his work challenging." (It was hard for him to get going.)
- "She doesn't think twice about attacking a difficult problem." (In fact, she doesn't think about it at all.)
- "He spared no effort in his work." (He did as little as possible.)

To describe a candidate who is incompetent:

- "I recommend this man with no qualifications whatsoever." (He's woefully inept.)
- "I understand that she would very much like to work with you if possible." (She just can't seem to get herself moving, though.)
- "No amount of praise would suffice for the job that he's done for us." (He's bungled everything he ever tried to do.)
- "Her former buyer was always raving about her work." (Her mistakes nearly drove him insane.)
- "He would always ask if there was anything he could do." (And we would always ask ourselves the same question.)
- "He has completed his schooling, and is now ready to strike out in a career." (I expect his batting average to be .000.)
- "I wouldn't hesitate to give her an unqualified recommendation." (She just doesn't have the skills for the job.)

To describe a person who has no ambition:

- "Once she got started on a project she wouldn't stop until it was finished." (It's the only thing she actually did in all the years she was with us.)
- "He couldn't care less about the number of hours he had to put in." (We just wish he could have cared more about them.)
- "He is not the type to run away from responsibility." (He'll walk very quickly, though.)
- "From the moment he arrives at work, he is ready to go." (. . . home.)
- "She didn't think much of the extra time she had to work." (In fact, she didn't do much thinking during her regular work hours.)

For the person who has mediocre work habits or credentials and should never be hired:

- "Waste no time in making this candidate an offer of employment." (She's not worth further consideration.)
- "All in all, I cannot recommend this person too highly." (He has lackluster credentials.)
- "You can't offer this man too high a salary." (You're better off saving your money.)
- "We were forever asking him for new ideas." (We were sick and tired of the old ones.)
- "She has made immeasurable contributions to our firm." (Far too minor to be measured.)

In addition, Thornton also demonstrates the use of the "questionable" or "missing" comma. Which applicant would you hire?

- "He won't do anything, which will lower your high regard for him" or "He won't do anything which will lower your high regard for him."
- "The job required very few skills, which he lacked" or "The job required very few skills which he lacked."

Source: Based on material in Robert Thornton's *Lexicon of Intentionally Ambiguous Recommendations,* revised 2nd ed. (Sourcebooks Chicago:, 2004). Used with the written permission of Professor Robert Thornton, Lehigh University.

3. The inability to profitably service customers. For example, Sam's Club and Costco charge a minimum annual fee to discourage customers who purchase only small quantities.

However, one must never use these screening criteria to illegally discriminate against certain groups. For instance, the Americans Disabilities Act (ADA) requires that all businesses have access for handicapped individuals. A retailer cannot simply conclude that it is unprofitable to admit customers who are in a wheelchair or are blind and therefore choose not to serve them. However, it is perfectly legitimate for a retailer to decide with the aid of its CRM system that certain customers do not meet their purchase transaction standards. For instance, some restaurants set a minimum order. Each table is a valuable revenue-generating tool; if two people sit and converse for two hours and spend only $12, then considerable revenue may be foregone.

LO 3

Managing People

How do retailers manage employees and customers?

Employees and customers need to be managed. Many retailers have policies for managing their employees, but seldom think of managing their customers. While customer management is not something to be ignored, this section begins with a discussion of managing employees.

The retailer must prepare programs for training employees to meet current or future job requirements, evaluating employees, and motivating them. After all, in an economy with a low unemployment rate, if an employee does not like something about the job, its training, or even his or her coworkers, that employee can easily go elsewhere. Therefore, the most critical job for retailers today is retaining current employees. A study of the supermarket industry by The Coca-Cola Retailing Research Council, for example, found that the median retention rate of hourly supermarket employees was 97 days. That is, one-half of all new supermarket hires terminate their employment within 97 days of starting work.[20] The study further found that the cost (including both direct and opportunity cost, which are described in Exhibit 14.2) of replacing this hourly employee was $4,291 for a union

Exhibit 14.2
Types of Employee Turnover Costs

Direct: These costs are reflected on the retailer's financial statements.

- Cost of recruiting applicants
- Cost of evaluating applicants (including interviews, reference checks, and any testing)
- Cost of training classes (including management's time)
- Pay (including benefits) during period when new employee is taking training course
- Part of supervisor's pay (including benefits) to cover time spent helping new employee during first few weeks of job

Indirect: These activities cause a reduction in the firm's revenue. Thus, while they are not shown on the retailer's financial statements, they are still a cost.

- Loss of customers who were "loyal" to former employee
- Lost sales resulting from the employee's initial lack of product knowledge
- Lost sales and potential profits missed from alienated customers resulting from inexperience in retail selling
- Decrease in employee morale caused by the departure of an employee
- Effect of the employees' lower morale on customers

store and $3,372 for a nonunion store.[21] In all, employee turnover costs the average supermarket almost $190,000 annually in direct and opportunity costs.[22] Turnover is thought to be an even more serious problem in specialty stores since they typically hire part-timers at entry-level positions.

Turnover is a problem and a major cost not only in the realm of retail employees; a similar problem exists regarding customers. In Chapter 3, it was noted that on average it costs a retailer five times as much to recruit a new customer as it does to retain an existing customer. However, most retailers fail to recognize this obvious fact. One of the authors was consulting with an auto dealer on retail advertising and promotion. The dealership was selling over 1,200 new cars and more than 300 used cars a year, and had a very successful service and body shop. The dealership spent over $1 million annually on advertising. Research revealed that the dealership received approximately one complaint letter a week about warranty claims and/or the service and body shop. The typical complaint protested a charge that ranged from less than $200 to $1,500, with the average being $425. In short, the total complaints for a year were around $22,000. One of the recommendations was to allow the service manager to waive charges at his discretion and charge these to the general marketing expense of the dealership (up to $30,000 per year). This meant that the waiver of the fees would not influence the profitability of the service and body shop. The following year the dealership won a regional award from Ford Motor Company for outstanding customer service in the auto service and body shop area of the business. However, the more interesting thing was that the general manager was now receiving about one letter a month from customers praising the service area. And you can bet these customers told their friends. If the dealership had taken the equivalent amount of money and spent it on advertising to attract new customers, it would not have yielded these results.

Training and Developing Employees

Retailers wanting the best return on their human resource investment should provide training and development for both new and existing employees. Training and development are consistent with the concept of human resource planning. After all, there is no such thing as a "natural" salesperson or manager. Like any other talent, this ability must be carefully taught and monitored with a training program.

Training is not a one-time event. It must be ongoing because without the necessary knowledge to perform their assigned tasks, employees will not enjoy their jobs. When employees aren't happy at work, they switch jobs. Therefore, retailers today must view training as a process of continuing education. For example, many of the country's most successful retailers, such as Target and McDonalds, invest a great deal of money in order to maintain their competitive position. Thus, as an individual's responsibilities increase, so does the training and development. Employees are taught not just technical skills but administrative and people skills, such as functioning as a team, as well. Each phase of development is built on the training that preceded it and includes training in merchandising, operations management, motivation, decision making, problem analysis, and time management.

In addition to developing a pool of future managers and assisting employees with present duties, training and development programs enable the employees to know their status within the firm; that is, where they stand and how they are doing. Generation Yers, in particular, provide a wealth of potential to employers because of their vigor, enthusiasm, talent, early experience, and high expectations.[23] Retail managers must remember that a career in their field is different from careers in other business fields. In the beginning retailing is like a pyramid, as the employee

Retailers that invest in training and developing both new and existing employees will achieve higher profit levels.

becomes increasingly specialized in working toward the goal of being a buyer—the ultimate specialist. Afterward, the objective is to increase breadth, not specialty, with the goal of becoming a store or division manager. The chapter's Global Retailing box describes one of the best methods for employees to increase their long-term worth to their employer—taking an assignment in a foreign country.

Today there is a new type of training tool available to retailers. Online training is one of the fastest-growing ways of training employees at small retailers who cannot afford to have a complete training staff. For example, many of these smaller retailers use services such as http://www.videomedia.net to train their employees in sexual harassment and thus minimize their liability. In the event of any future claims, these retailers can prove that their employees were required to participate in this training and the retailers made an effort to eliminate such harassment from the workplace. Unless other circumstances prevail, the retailer would probably not be liable.

The best training and development program devised is useless unless management adopts a philosophy of complete support. In the past, many retail executives got so tied up in merchandising concerns, they forgot about human resources—a big mistake.

Training and Developing Customers

Once again, the typical mindset of the retailer or general businessperson is that they train employees but not customers. Such thinking is myopic. Two retailers that have made training and educating of customers a core part of their value proposition are The Home Depot and PetSmart. Both retailers provide short courses that instruct customers how to use their products and/or engage in do-it-yourself projects. Other examples involve new vehicle dealers (especially Porsche and Harley-Davidson) that provide vehicle care clinics and driving schools, and local supermarkets that offer cooking classes.

Global Retailing

Taking a Global Assignment to Build Your Long-Term Performance

Too many employees in retailing and other businesses tend to focus on their short-term careers and performance. In a sense they are similar to organizations that obsess on short-term financial gains. However, if you want to truly distinguish yourself shortly after you graduate and if you happen to work for a retailer with operations in multiple countries (such as Aldi, Benneton, Papa John, Carrefour, The Home Depot, McDonald's, 7-Eleven, Starbucks, Tesco, Wal-Mart, and Yum! Brands), then consider positioning yourself for an international retailing assignment.

Two broad options can present themselves and provide you an invaluable experience and enhance your promotion possibilities with your employer but also make you more valuable to other employers. One option is to be an *expatriate*. You become an expatriate if you work for a retailer in their home country, such as working for Carrefour in your native France, and take an assignment in a foreign country, such as Korea. A second option is to be an *inpatriate*. This occurs when you work in a foreign subsidiary of the retailer and take an assignment in the home country of the retailer. An example of this would be if you are a U.S. citizen working for Aldi in the United States and they transferred you to the home office in Germany. With the rapid growth of multinational retailers, both of these options are readily available. However, because they can be great platforms for future advancement, there is stiff competition from young aspiring retailing professionals.

How do you set yourself up for one of these assignments? First, you need to understand the key factors that may prevent you from gaining such an opportunity or put you in an unfavorable light. These include

1. *Family Issues.* Is your spouse willing to relocate with you? What about your school age children? Are they up to this challenge of relocating into a different culture?
2. *Dual Career Issues.* This is related to the preceding, however, it warrants separate mention. If both you and your spouse work for the same retailer this problem may actually end up being an advantage. However, if you both have separate employers can you arrange for an opportunity that advances both careers? If so, what about when it is time to return home? Will both firms be ready to transfer you and your spouse back at the same time?
3. *Willingness to Take on Relocation.* If you have turned down domestic transfers, then you may not be immediately considered for an international transfer. Most firms find that younger employees are more willing to relocate because as they get older the two prior issues become major obstacles.
4. *Lack of Language Skills.* To be productive on your foreign assignment you need to be conversant in the native language of the host country. Even if English is increasingly the business language spoken worldwide, knowledge and fluency in the requisite foreign language can make your assignment more productive for both you and your employer.

On the positive side, what are some of the factors that can favorably influence your ability to get the foreign assignment you desire?

1. Perhaps the biggest factor is your personality. Do you have empathy and respect for others? Are you tolerant and flexible in new situations and willing to learn? Are you sociable and possessing a positive self-image? All of these personality or soft skills make you much more of the type of person that senior management will want to have represent them on a foreign assignment.
2. Do you have an interest in the local culture? Perhaps because of your ethnic background or family heritage you have a particular interest in the foreign assignment. Or perhaps you studied abroad in the country and developed friendships and an interest in the culture. You should make that known to your superiors so they can factor that into consideration.
3. Do you have extensive foreign travel experience? This is a good indicator to management that you enjoy visiting foreign countries.
4. Do you have an excitement and commitment to spending several years in a foreign country? Even if you lack knowledge of the language and extensive foreign travel experience, you can be a top candidate if you have an excitement and willingness to experience and adapt to a new culture.

Why is taking a foreign assignment so valuable to your career progression? The answer can be summed up as social capital. Social capital is the relationships one develops with others. Think of it as your network of relations; friends, business associates, and other contacts. As you take on a foreign assignment you increase

(continued)

Global Retailing *(continued)*

this network. Of particular value are the contacts you make with employees of the company you work for but in a new country that you have not experienced. Imagine working for Benneton in the United States, then going to their headquarters in Italy, and then back to the United States a few years later. The contacts you develop will be invaluable and thus over the long-term will enhance your career progress and economic compensation.

Source: M. G. Harvey, N. M. Novicevic, and C. Speier, "Inpatriate Managers: How to Increase the Probability of Success" *Human Resource Management Review,* (1999) vol. 9 no. 1: 51–81; M. G. Harvey, C. Speier, and M.M. Novicevic, "A Theory-Based Framework for Strategic Global Human Resource Staffing Policies and Practices," *International Journal of Human Resource Management,* (2001) vol. 12 no. 6: 898–915; and author's familiarity with past students that have taken foreign retail assignments.

Evaluating Employees

performance appraisal and review
Is the formal, systematic assessment of how well employees are performing their jobs in relation to established standards and the communication of that assessment to employees.

Performance appraisal and review is the formal, systematic assessment of how well employees are performing their jobs in relation to established standards, and the communication of that assessment to employees. Employees place a great deal of importance on appraisals, and the way the appraisal system operates affects morale and organizational climate in significant ways. Moreover, the appraisal system also has an impact on other human resource processes, such as training and development, compensation, and promotion.

Informal appraisals tend to take place on an ongoing basis within the retail firm as supervisors evaluate their subordinates' work on a daily basis and as subordinates appraise each other as well as their supervisors. However, the formal, systematic appraisal of an individual is likely to occur at certain intervals throughout the year or when the employee is being considered for a wage increase, a promotion, a transfer, or an opportunity to improve job skills.

Retailers of all sizes should try to use objective criteria for the appraisal and review process whenever possible. Criteria for the objective review and appraisal of salespeople are shown in Exhibit 14.3. However, not every item that the retailer might want to evaluate can be quantified. Larger retail operations use a committee, frequently consisting of the vice president of human resources/personnel and one or two other executives, to evaluate each employee. Some retailers, especially smaller ones, sometimes forego the formal evaluation process and judge a salesperson on the basis of dollar sales, number of transactions, errors, on-time performance, ratio of returned merchandise, and customer complaints.

It is important to recognize several key factors in conducting performance appraisals. First, evaluation should be an ongoing process, not just a periodic review. Regularly scheduled review times should not keep supervisors from appraising or coaching their subordinates whenever necessary. Second, employees seek feedback, or information about how well they are doing their jobs, and this feedback should be provided on a timely and relevant basis. Third, the person doing the review should know what the job being reviewed entails and what the performance standards are. Employees can justifiably become upset with the review process when the reviewer is not aware of the problems and limitations of the job under review. Fourth, different supervisors are likely to rate personnel with different degrees of leniency or severity. Therefore, not only should the person conducting the review understand the performance standards, but at least two people should contribute to the evaluation. Finally, research has shown that the particular method of reviewing the employee does not matter. Retailers have found success with various types of measures, including the rating scale, checklist, free-form essay, and rankings.

Merchandise Procedures:	Is accurate in counting and inventorying merchandise.
	Prevents merchandise shrinkage due to mishandling of merchandise.
	Keeps merchandise in a neat and orderly manner on sales floor.
	Knows the design and specification of warranties and guarantees of the merchandise groups.
	Gets merchandise on sales floor quickly after merchandise arrival.
Customer Service Ability:	Provides courteous service to customers.
	Handles customer complaints and/or service problems as indicated by store procedure.
	Follows proper procedure concerning merchandise returns and layaways when conducted through credit transactions.
	Suggests add-on or complementary merchandise to customers.
Sales Ability:	Has strong ability to close the sale.
	Promotes sale of merchandise items having profit margins.
	Acts as a resource to other departments or other salespeople needing assistance.
	Works well with fellow workers in primary merchandise department.
Product/ Merchandise Knowledge:	Knowledgeable of design, style, and construction of merchandise group.
	Knowledgeable of special promotions and/or advertised sale items.
	Knowledgeable of material (fabrics), color coordination, and complementary accessories.
Store Policy:	Provides accurate and complete paperwork related to returned merchandise.
	Provides accurate and complete paperwork related to work schedules.
	Provides accurate and complete paperwork for cash and credit transactions.
	Shows up on time for work, sales meetings, and training sessions.
	Accurately follows day-to-day instructions of immediate supervisor.
	Employee's overall job-related attitude.

Source: Robert P. Bush, Alan J. Bush, David J. Ortinau, and Joseph F. Hair, Jr., "Developing a Behavior-Based Scale to Assess Retail Salesperson Performance," *Journal of Retailing,* Spring 1990: 119–136.

Exhibit 14.3
Criteria Used in the Appraisal and Review Process

Evaluating Customers

It is important for employers not only to evaluate employees on their performance, but also to evaluate customers for their contributions to the retailer's financial objectives. A variety of retailers, including Neiman Marcus, Safeway, American Airlines, and Fidelity Investments, have detailed profiles on their most profitable customers. However, increasingly CRM is allowing the retailer to evaluate the profitability of each of its customers.

Retailers doing this have discovered some interesting information about their "Top-Shoppers" (that 10 to 20 percent of customers who account for nearly 80 percent of their sales). For example, these shoppers are very loyal; many have been your customers for over two decades. They tend not to read your competitors' ads, but instead look for good deals among the various products in your store. For them price shopping is a decision made in the store about what brand to buy and not a decision about where to shop. They really wish you would use your CRM-developed loyalty program to make them feel special. And they focus on people, relating to store employees far more than other shoppers do.[24] Therefore, the critical building blocks for CRM include some type of customer identification process coupled to product or service identification codes. Consider how grocery stores can do it. Here virtually 100 percent of the merchandise has a uniform product code (bar code) that is scanned at the time of checkout. If this data can be coupled with customer data when the customers use their loyalty cards, the grocer can compute sales and profit for each customer and do this by any time period (weekly, monthly, annually) desired. (Remember that point above about making loyal customers feel special?) *Thus retailers should use this data to decide which customers should be offered special services or special prices.* Delta Airlines, for example, offers its frequent fliers who travel more than 25,000 miles annually preferred boarding, free upgrades to better seating, and a special phone line for customer service. Recently a sister of one of the authors was trying get back home after a busy trip. Her flight was canceled and she was told that she would have to take a connecting flight home. Worse yet, she was also informed that she would have to settle for a center seat in coach. Because she travels two to three round trips a week, she had averaged over 100 round trips a year on that airline over the past couple of years. The author's sister asked the gate agent to check her CRM file. After looking at it, the agent asked, "Would you like a window or aisle in first class?" The agent realized that this customer had her choice of airlines, and the agent wasn't going to be responsible for her switching carriers.

Motivating Employees

motivation
Is the drive that a person has to excel at activities, such as a job, that he or she undertakes.

content theories
Refer to theories on motivation that ask, "What motivates an individual to behave?"

process theories
Refer to theories on motivation that ask, "How can I motivate an individual?"

hierarchy of needs model
Theorizes that individuals have lower-level physiological and safety and security needs, which are first satisfied before higher-level needs of belongingness or social esteem and selfactualization are pursued.

Human resource management goes beyond selecting, training, and compensating employees. It also involves motivating them to improve current performance. A successful retailer today must constantly motivate all employees to strive for higher sales figures, decrease expenses, communicate company policies to the public, and solve problems as they arise.

Motivation is what drives a person to excel at the activities he or she undertakes, such as a job. Several theories on motivation have been developed. These can be divided into **content theories**, which ask, "What motivates an individual to behave?" and **process theories**, which ask, "How can I motivate an individual?" Among the content theories to be discussed are Maslow's hierarchy of needs and McGregor's Theory X and Theory Y. This discussion of the process theories will look at two of the most widely used: expectancy theory and goal setting.

Content Theories

Abraham Maslow, a noted psychologist, developed a **hierarchy of needs model**, shown in Exhibit 14.4, which suggests people have different types of needs and that they satisfy lower-level needs before moving to higher levels. The first level is the basic physiological need, which can be satisfied by the employee's cash wages. In some cases money alone can't guarantee happy employees. One incentive offered all JetBlue reservation phone agents is to work at home in their everyday clothes and maybe even fluffy slippers.[25] Once employees become content at this level, they become concerned with safety and security needs. Retailers have satisfied these needs with such benefits as security-patrolled parking and health insurance benefits. The third level, the need to belong and other social needs, can be satisfied with "employee or salesperson of the month" awards. However, perhaps the best indication of fulfilling this need is when customers return to the store and ask for an employee by name. A similar approach can be used at the fourth level of needs, esteem, whereby the employee gains confidence by achieving a level of competency or mastery of a task. A classic example is offering fancier offices and job titles. The highest need level is self-actualization or "becoming all you can be." Here retailers can provide seminars to help broaden the horizons of their employees. Maslow's hierarchy thus provides retailers with ideas that can address the basic needs of their employees.

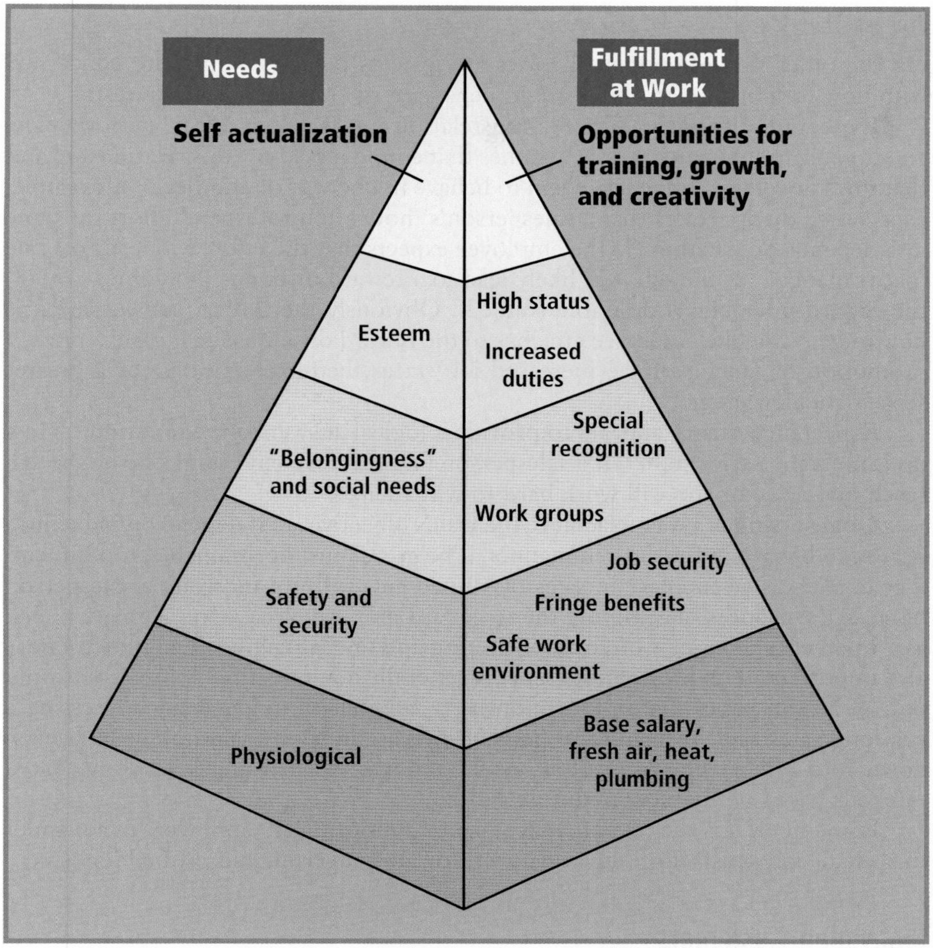

Exhibit 14.4
How Retailers Can Use Maslow's Hierarchy of Needs

Sometimes retailers make coming to work entertaining for everyone by using fun titles for their job descriptions. Chipotle Mexican Grill, for example, calls its marketing director the "Director of Hoopla, Hype, and Ballyhoo" and its restaurants "burrito joints." Its Web site has over two dozen photos of employee dogs. All this is an attempt to promote a laid-back culture where everyone fits in and has fun with each other.[26]

Another content theory is McGregor's Theory X and Theory Y. **Theory X** assumes that employees must be closely supervised and controlled and that economic inducements (salaries and commissions) motivate employees to perform. This theory assumes that employees need to be induced or coerced to work since they are inherently lazy. **Theory Y**, on the other hand, assumes that employees are self-reliant, enjoy work, and can be delegated authority and responsibility. Over the past decade, some small independent retailers have been forced by economic conditions to substitute a share of management for traditional wage increases. These "employee-managed" retail stores have generally experienced an increased organizational effectiveness, thus supporting Maslow's and the Theory Y contention that money alone is not a primary motivator.

theory X
Is a theory of management that views employees as unreliable and thus must be closely supervised and controlled and given economic inducements to perform properly.

theory Y
Is a theory of management that views employees as self-reliant and enjoying work and thus can be empowered and delegated authority and responsibility.

Process Theories

On the other side of content theories are process theories, which are concerned with how to motivate an employee to behave in the retailer's best interest.

expectancy theory
Suggests that an employee will expend effort on some task because the employee expects that the effort will lead to a performance outcome that will lead in turn to a reward or bonus that the employee finds desirable or valued.

Expectancy theory addresses the relationship between effort, performance, and organizational outcomes. It assumes that employees know this relationship and that this knowledge influences them to behave in one way or another. For example, expectancy theory states that a salesperson's motivation to expend effort on some task depends on whether (1) the employee expects that the effort will lead to a sale (performance), (2) the sale will likely lead to a reward or bonus (outcome), and (3) the reward or bonus is desirable (valued). Obviously the critical consideration is how much value the employee attaches to the reward or bonus, be it cash, a prize, a promotion or fancier office, increased job status, better conditions, or a greater sense of achievement.

Expectancy theory appears to provide a logical answer to the question, "How do I motivate a sales staff?" If a salesperson likes to travel and thinks he or she can reach quota, he or she will work hard to win a trip.

goal setting
Is the process in which management and employees establish goals that become the basis for performance appraisal and review.

Goal setting is a way to achieve the firm's objectives that depend on inducing a person to behave in the desired manner. The goals must be attainable; too difficult a goal, such as an increase in sales of 50 percent, will not motivate a salesperson because the chances of achieving the target are slim. Likewise, too easy a goal, such as a 1 percent increase, is often demotivating and unchallenging. The time frame is also important. Too long a time frame is generally demotivating. Just as you would put off a term paper due in four months, a salesperson might delay addressing a yearlong sales goal. Instead, a 10 percent increase in yearly sales might be broken down into either the two seasons or 12 months, with changes made at stated intervals based on market conditions.

Remember, it is the retail manager's job to motivate all employees in a manner that yields job satisfaction, low turnover, low absenteeism, and profitable results.

Motivating Customers

Retailers use a variety of demand stimulation tools to motivate customers to purchase or purchase greater quantities. Most of these programs are based on the assumption that customers are motivated primarily by economic incentives, such as price, free merchandise, and so on. However, innovative retailers are recognizing that other factors can motivate customers. For instance, Sewell Auto in Texas and Click Automotive in Arizona and California, with their state-of-the-art CRMs, are able to stay in contact with their customers and send them birthday cards, special notes, coupons, and other marketing materials to motivate continued patronage.

Customers cite many of the things that a retailer controls as the motivator for their purchases. However, major life changes, such as a new baby, new job, and/or a new home, would also be examples of factors (outside of the retailer's influence) that would motivate a purchase. Nevertheless, it is surprising how much motivation can be stimulated or triggered by the retailer. Here is a list of the key nonprice elements that can either motivate customers to make a purchase or deter them from using a retailer.

1. *Merchandise* (including quality, style and fashion, assortment, national versus private labels). Motivating example: A Safeway customer is positively motivated by the high quality assortment of fresh vegetables and fruit. Demotivating example: A customer shopping at a local women's apparel store is demotivated by the large number of out-of-season dresses and outdated (last year's) color selection.

2. *Physical characteristics* (including decor, layout, and floor space). Motivating example: A family on its first trip to Disney World is highly motivated to purchase gift items due to the high-impact decor and layout of the on-site gift shops. Demotivating example: A shopper visits a newly opened hardware store and is turned off by the very narrow and poorly lit aisles. The shopper is actually driven to get out of the store as quickly as possible rather than linger, explore, and potentially purchase more products. Compare this store's image to one of an open and well-lit Lowe's home improvement store.
3. *Sales promotions*. Motivating example: A customer is relaxing on a Friday afternoon and notices a special sales promotion at the local mall that starts at 8 A.M. on Saturday morning. The first 100 shoppers will receive a free $25 gift certificate. The customer awakens early and is in line by 7:15 A.M. and is happily one of the first 100; by 7:45 A.M. there are 300 people lined up to shop at the mall. Demotivating example: A department store customer who lives 50 miles from the store is attracted to visit because of a special sales promotion. The customer arrives the first day of the "sale" only to find that the sale merchandise has already been sold. This is a disincentive to travel for future purchases at this store.
4. *Advertising*. Motivating example: A customer shopping for an auto develops a positive image of the dealership and is motivated to patronize the dealership due to the professional way it advertises autos and showcases compelling features of the autos as well as its high level of customer service. Demotivating example: A customer shopping for a new car is afraid to enter a new dealership whose slick, fast-talking TV salesperson promises the best deal in town if you will only visit their dealership.
5. *Convenience* (including hours, location, ease of entrance and parking, ease of finding items). Motivating example: A family stops along the interstate to refuel and finds that the service station has a new food court with a McDonald's and a Dunkin' Donuts shop. In a 15-minute stop, four stomachs are refueled as well. Demotivating example: A once-popular family-style restaurant no longer seems safe to clientele because the neighborhood around the restaurant has deteriorated into a high crime area. Many of the restaurant's old customers are now forced to drive several miles out of the neighborhood to other restaurants.
6. *Services* (including credit, delivery, return policy, and guarantees). Motivating example: Knowing that most people have trouble envisioning how new furniture will look in their home, a furniture store has a liberal return policy. Customers can return furniture within 72 hours if they don't like the way it fits their decor. Even if a small return fee is charged, most customers find it very reasonable. Demotivating example: A retailer's signage throughout the store repels customers because it boldly proclaims that all sales are final and there are no returns.
7. *Store personnel* (including helpfulness, friendliness, and courtesy). Motivating example: Nordstrom sales associates go out of their way to help a visiting customer from out of town. The customer is very uncertain about how to dress for a special event and the salesperson coaches the young man through the entire purchasing process. The customer ends up with a new business suit, shoes, furnishings, and a level of satisfaction seldom achieved in retailing today. Demotivating example: An elderly lady new to the community walks into what appears to be a very upscale women's apparel store but is ignored by the store personnel, who are busy helping younger, more fashionably dressed customers.

The sales associates do not even acknowledge the elderly lady's presence. The lady walks out determined to never return.

LO 4 Compensation

What methods can retailers use in compensating their employees and customers?

As all business people know, human resources are not free goods. They are expensive, and in retailing, employee costs (including benefits) typically represent 50 percent of operating expenses. However, as we illustrated at the beginning of this chapter, customers can also perform work activities. The key point to keep in mind is that the more work you ask the customer to perform, the lower the price they will be willing to pay. In short, their price savings become a way of compensating them for their work. Very simply that is why self-service retailers can sell at lower prices.

Employee Compensation

Compensation is one of the major variables in attracting, retaining, and motivating human resources. The quality of employees that can be attracted, whether as salesclerks or executives, is directly proportional to the compensation package offered. Naturally, other things besides compensation are important to employees. According to a report by Deloitte & Touche's Human Resource Strategies Group, "more flexible, portable benefits systems with fewer links to age and service" are desired by today's retail associates. In addition, these benefits should be compatible with the employee's lifestyle choices.[27]

compensation
Includes direct dollar payments (wages, commission, bonuses) and indirect payments (insurance, vacation time, retirement plans).

fixed component
Typically is composed of some base wage per hour, week, month, or year.

Here the term **compensation** includes direct dollar payments (wages, commissions, and bonuses) and indirect payments (insurance, vacation time, retirement plans). Compensation plans in retailing can have up to three basic components: a fixed component, a variable component, and a fringe benefit component. The **fixed component** typically is composed of some base wage per hour, week, month, or

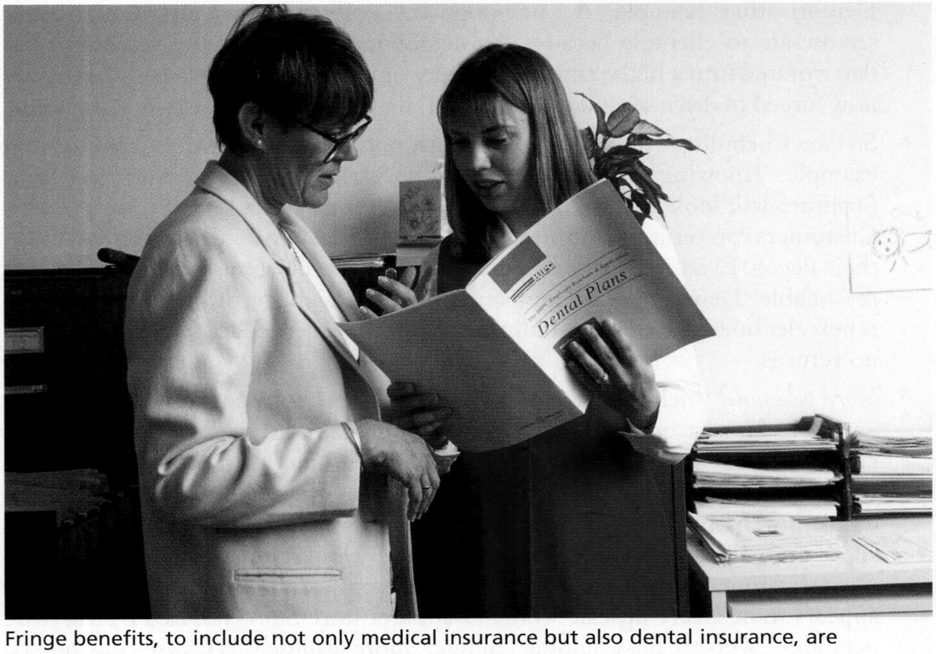

© Michael Newman / PhotoEdit

Fringe benefits, to include not only medical insurance but also dental insurance, are increasingly needed to recruit high-performance employees.

year. The **variable component** is often composed of some bonus that is received if performance warrants. Salesclerks may be paid a bonus of 10 percent of sales above some established minimum; department managers may receive a bonus based on the profit performance of their department. Workers in restaurants often receive tips, a variable component that the retailer does not control. Finally, a **fringe benefit package** may include such things as health insurance, disability benefits, life insurance, retirement plans, the use of automobiles, and financial counseling.

variable component
Is often composed of some bonus that is received if performance warrants.

fringe benefit package
Is a part of the total compensation package offered to many retail employees and may include health insurance, disability benefits, life insurance, retirement plans, child care, use of an auto, and financial counseling.

Each of the three components helps the retailer to achieve a different human resource goal. The fixed component helps to ensure that employees have a source of income to meet their most basic financial obligations. This helps to fulfill the employees' physiological needs. The variable component allows the retailer to offer employees an incentive for higher levels of effort and commitment, which helps to fulfill a "belongingness" and social need among employees for special recognition in return for high performance. The fringe benefit component allows the retailer to offer employees safety and security. Retail employees have a need to be protected and cared for when they are faced with difficult times or when they become too old to provide for themselves. Also, certain employees (especially executives) have a need for prestige and status.

The best combination of fixed, variable, and fringe benefit compensation components depends on the person, the job, and the retail organization. There is no set formula. Some top retail executives prefer mostly salary, others thrive on bonuses, and still others would rather have more pension benefits. The same holds for salesclerks. Therefore, the compensation package needs to be tailored to the individual. We now focus our attention on compensation of the sales force, but the same principles will apply to managers.

Common Types of Compensation Programs for a Sales Force

Retail sales force compensation programs can be conveniently broken into three major types: (1) straight salary, (2) salary plus commission, and (3) straight commission. Each of these methods has its advantages and disadvantages.

Straight Salary

In the straight salary program, the salesperson receives a fixed salary per time period (usually per week) regardless of the level of sales generated or orders taken. However, over time, if the salesperson does not help generate sales or take enough orders, he or she will likely be fired for not performing adequately. Similarly, over time, if the salesperson helps to generate more than a proportionate share of sales or fills more than a proportionate number of orders, the retailer will be unable to retain the employee without a raise.

Many small retailers use this compensation method, because they typically assign tasks such as stock rearranging, merchandise display, and other nonselling duties to their salespeople. Therefore, if the employees were paid on a commission basis they would spend little if any time on their nonselling duties, and the retail organization would suffer. Many promotional and price-oriented chain stores whose salespeople are merely order takers will use the straight salary method because the salesperson is not much of a factor in generating sales. Also, most clerks and cashiers, as well as other lower level retail personnel, are almost always paid straight salaries.

The salesperson may view this plan as attractive because it offers income security or as unappealing because it gives little incentive for extraordinary effort and performance. Thus, for this method, which is also the easiest plan for the employee to understand, to be effective it must be combined with a periodic evaluation so that superior salespeople can be identified and singled out for higher salaries.

Salary Plus Commission

Sometimes the salesperson is paid a fixed salary per time period plus a percentage commission on all sales or on all sales over an established quota. Because merchandise lines and items can vary in terms of gross margins, some retailers pay commissions on gross margin dollars generated. The fixed salary is lower than that of the salesperson working on a straight salary plan, but the commission structure gives one the potential to earn more than the person on the straight salary plan. In fact, most salespeople on the salary plus commission program earn more than their counterparts on a straight salary program.

This plan gives the employees a stable base income—and thus incentive to perform nonselling tasks—but it also encourages and rewards superior effort. Therefore, it represents a good compromise between the straight salary and the straight commission programs. In many cases, top management generally receives a salary and a bonus based on overall store or department performance.

Straight Commission

Income of some salespeople is limited to a percentage commission on each sale they generate. The commission could be the same percentage on all merchandise or it could vary depending on the profitability of the item.

The straight commission plan provides substantial incentive for retail salespeople to generate sales. However, when the general business climate is poor, retail salespeople may not be able to generate enough volume to meet their fixed payment obligations (mortgage payment, auto payment, food expenses). Because of that problem, most retailers slightly modify the straight commission plan to allow the salesperson to draw wages against future commissions up to some specified amount per week.

A major problem with the straight commission plan is that it may provide the retail salesperson with too much incentive to sell. The employee as a result of the income insecurity features of this plan may begin to use pressure tactics to close sales, hurting the retailer's image and long-run sales performance. Similarly, the employee may not be willing to perform other duties such as helping customers with returned merchandise or helping to set up displays. After all, compensation is paid to sell and not to handle customer complaints or displays. Generally, sales personnel for high-priced merchandise, or high ticket items, such as automobiles, real estate, jewelry, and furniture, as well as those items requiring the sales personnel to prospect or seek out potential customers, i.e., insurance and door-to-door selling, are paid this way.

An Ernst & Young survey reported that 51 percent of the retailers polled used a salary plus commission plan and 38 percent used straight commission.[28] Exhibit 14.5 summarizes the attributes of each of these plans. During the late 1990s, some retailers began to reduce the commission portion of employee compensation plans and increase the salary portion. This was an attempt to reduce consumer distaste for what was perceived to be "high pressure selling." However, as retailers have faced a tight labor market and the need to increase productivity in recent years, the trend has begun to reverse.

Supplemental Benefits

In addition to regular wages (salary, commission, or both), retail salespeople also can receive four types of supplementary benefits: employee discounts, insurance and retirement benefits, child care, and push money (or spiffs).

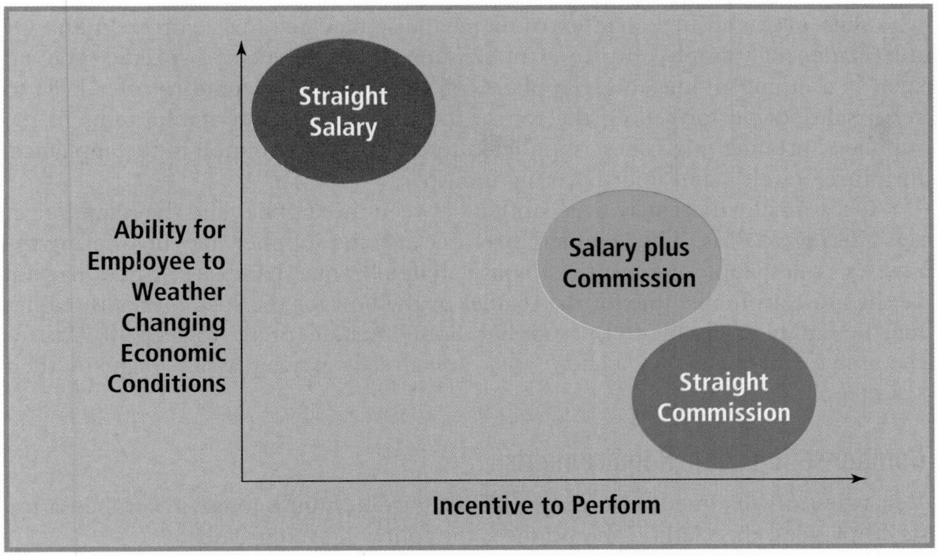

Exhibit 14.5
Attributes of Compensation Plans

Employee Discounts

Almost all retailers offer their employees discounts on merchandise or services they purchase for themselves or their immediate family. About the only line of trade where these discounts are not offered is grocery retailing, because grocery retailers operate on relatively thin gross margins.

Insurance and Retirement Benefits

Historically, retail personnel were not provided any insurance or retirement benefits. However, with recent changes in the federal employment laws this is no longer the case. In addition, many retailers are providing their part-time employees with either free or low-cost group health and life insurance. Still others are making profit sharing, stock ownership, and retirement programs available to salespeople and all other employees.

Child Care

In an effort to attract employees from two-wage-earner families, some U.S. businesses have begun to provide child care for employees' children during working hours. Retailers have just started providing child care, a program that experts agree will be a necessity in upcoming years. However, with health-care costs rapidly increasing, some retailers have delayed plans to add child care due to the added expenses.

Push Money

A final type of supplementary benefit is "push money," which some may call "prize money," "premium merchandise," or just plain "PM." Retailers commonly called it by another name, "spiffs." The PM, paid to the salesperson in addition to base salary and regular commissions, is said to encourage additional selling effort on particular items or merchandise lines.

PMs can be offered by either retailer or supplier. A retailer may give a PM in order to get salespeople to sell old or slow-moving merchandise. The salesperson who sells the most may win a free trip to Hawaii or some other prize, or everyone who sells an established quantity of merchandise may get a prize or premium. Or the retailer may simply offer an extra $25 bonus for the sale of a specific product, such as a dining room table. Suppliers, on the other hand, tend to offer PMs to retail salespeople for selling the top-of-the line or most profitable items in the suppliers' product mix. These supplier-offered PMs are common in the appliance, furniture, jewelry, and floor covering industries.

Occasionally there may be a conflict between the supplier and the retailer over the offering of PMs. This conflict arises because the supplier may be offering the retailer's salespeople an incentive to push an item or merchandise line that may not be the most profitable line for the retailer or the best for the customer, although it may be highly profitable to the supplier. Some retailers prefer to keep all PMs for themselves, because they believe they are already paying a fair wage to their salespeople.

Compensation Plan Requirements

Regardless of what method a retailer ultimately determines to use in compensating its employees, the method should meet the following requirements:

1. *Fairness*: The plan does not favor one group or division over any other group or division or enable such a group to gather disproportionate reward in relation to contribution. It must also keep compensation costs under control so that they do not put the store at a competitive disadvantage.
2. *Adequacy*: The level of compensation should enable the employee to maintain a standard of living commensurate with job position and to maintain job satisfaction.
3. *Prompt and regular payments*: Payments should be made on time and in accordance with the agreement between employer and employee. In incentive plans, greater stimulation is provided when reward closely follows the accomplishment.
4. *Customer interest*: The plan should not reward any actions by an employee that could result in customer ill will.
5. *Simplicity*: The plan must be easy to understand so as to prevent any misunderstandings with the resultant ill will. This should also enable management to minimize the man-hours needed to determine compensation levels.
6. *Balance*: Pay, supplemental benefits, and other rewards must provide a reasonable total reward package.
7. *Security*: The plan must fulfill the employee's security needs.
8. *Cost effective*: The plan must not result in excessive payments, given the retailer's financial condition.

While none of the three plans we discussed above satisfies all of these requirements to the maximum level, awareness of these requirements will aid in the selection of the best plan given the individual circumstances. In fact, it is not uncommon for the same retailer to use more than one plan in the same store as different divisions or departments have different needs.

job enrichment
Is the process of enhancing the core job characteristics of employees to improve their motivation, productivity, and job satisfaction.

Job Enrichment

A planned program for enhancing job characteristics is typically called job enrichment. **Job enrichment** is the process of enhancing the core job characteristics for the purpose of increasing worker motivation, productivity, and satisfaction. There are five core job characteristics that should be increased:

1. *Skill variety*: The degree to which an employee can use different skills and talents.
2. *Task identity*: The degree to which a job requires the completion of a whole assignment that has a visible outcome.
3. *Task significance*: The degree to which the job affects other employees.
4. *Autonomy*: The degree to which the employee has freedom, independence, and discretion in achieving the outcome.
5. *Job feedback*: The degree to which the employee receives information about the effectiveness of his or her performance.[29]

Job enrichment programs have their base in motivation theory, which suggest that job factors themselves, such as job challenge, independence, and responsibility, are powerful motivators.

Retail management has long recognized that paying attention to job characteristics and descriptions, work scheduling, job sharing, and employee input programs will have a positive effect on employee productivity and satisfaction. Retailers using the job enrichment program must be careful in presenting it to the employees; otherwise, the employees may feel that they are being asked to do too many tasks without being compensated for the extra workload.

Customer Compensation

The best way to think of customer compensation is in terms of the concept of value proposition. (Remember that earlier in the chapter a value proposition was defined as the promised benefits a retailer offers in relation to the cost the consumer incurs.) Each of the eight attributes mentioned above for motivating customers (price, merchandise, physical characteristics, sales promotions, advertising, convenience, services, and store personnel) is part of the value proposition. These attributes represent benefits and costs and the better the value equation (benefits versus costs), the more compelling the retailer's value proposition. Stated alternatively, if the consumer is expected to do more work—for example, search for merchandise in the store, travel a large distance to an inconvenient store, and assume the risk of a no-return policy—then that customer will want to be compensated with a lower price. When retailers ask customers to perform more work they must adjust their value proposition by lowering prices.

If retailers ask customers to perform more work and do not offer a corresponding drop in price, then the retailer's value proposition will suffer and profitability will decline.

Dollars & Sense

The value proposition notion, however, also illustrates that a firm does not have to use low prices to compensate customers. Alternatively, it can offer more benefits. In fact, if the retailer wants more pricing power (the ability to maintain or raise prices), it can only do this by offering the customer more benefits, such as Starbucks does when it offers its customers a relaxing store atmosphere, convenient locations, reading material, and a wide variety of coffee drinks.

SUMMARY

LO 1 **Why are intangible people resources more important than tangible resources to a retailer's competitive advantage?**

It is relatively easy for competing retailers to duplicate the tangible resources of each other. They can all purchase the same merchandise, equipment, and fixtures. People, however, are more difficult to replicate and thus become a source of differential competitive advantage. Employees can be even more valuable if they are empowered to make things right for the customer. Because intangible people resources are central to competitive advantage, the retailer should view employee costs and the cost of attracting and retaining customers as an investment. This investment can pay high dividends because the best employees and customers are profit drivers; often 20 percent of the customers or employees generate 80 percent of the retailer's profit.

LO 2 **What is the process for recruiting the right employees and customers?**

To recruit the best employees and customers requires considerable effort; however, the payoff can be enormous. Consequently, retailers are more systematically recruiting employees and customers. A popular technology to cultivate and maintain the right customers is customer relationship management. A retailer must screen and select employees as well as customers. Just as some potential employees should be avoided, it is also true that some customers are not appropriate for the retailer.

LO 3 **How do retailers manage employees and customers?**

Once an employee is hired or a customer obtained, the retailer must still continue to train, develop, evaluate, and motivate the employee.

Expenditures on training and development are an attempt by the retailer to increase the productivity of human resources. Employees can be trained to increase their productivity and customers can be trained and developed to help establish long-term relationships.

The employee's performance should be subjected to an ongoing, formal, systematic review process. This process will enable the employer to make better decisions concerning wage increases, promotions, transfers, or improvement in job skills. At the same time, the customer should be evaluated. CRM helps the retailer evaluate the profitability of single customers and groups of customers. This evaluation is critical to determining where to allocate future resources.

Employee motivation is also a topic of great importance. In our discussion, we looked at two schools of thought: content theories and process theories. Although both theories are extremely important to retailers, more retailers actively use the process models to link together the task, the outcome, and the reward. We also showed how seven key offerings of the retailer (merchandise, physical characteristics of the store, sales promotions, advertising, convenience, services, and store personnel) can serve as motivators of positive patronage behavior but also can demotivate the customer if not appropriately managed.

LO 4 **What methods can retailers use in compensating their employees and customers?**

Compensation is crucial to attracting, retaining, and motivating retail employees. A good compensation program includes a fixed component to provide income, a variable component to motivate employees, and a fringe benefit component to provide security and prestige. Special attention was paid to the advantages and disadvantages of the three types of compensation plans: straight salary, straight commission, and a combination of both.

Job enrichment is the process of increasing the skill variety, task identity, task significance, autonomy, and feedback from the job in an effort to improve worker motivation, productivity, and satisfaction and thereby reduce turnover.

A retailer's value proposition is the most important way to compensate customers. The retailer must offer benefits that exceed the costs (price and nonprice) that the customer incurs. If the value proposition is not sufficiently high, then customers will patronize other retailers where they can get a better overall deal (value).

TERMS TO REMEMBER

empowerment
servant leadership
value proposition
customer relationship management (CRM)
performance appraisal and review
motivation
content theories
process theories
hierarchy of needs model
theory X
theory Y
expectancy theory
goal setting
compensation
fixed component
variable component
fringe benefit package
job enrichment

REVIEW AND DISCUSSION QUESTIONS

Why do intangible people resources provide more competitive advantage than tangible resources? LO 1

1. Should a retailer view its employees as a "cost" or as an "investment?" Support your reasoning.
2. What is meant by the concept of "internal customers?" Give several examples of internal customers in a retail store you are familiar with.
3. In retailing, customers and employees are distinct groups and have little in common. Agree or disagree and explain your answer.
4. What does it mean to "empower" a retail employee? Give examples from your personal experience of situations where you felt a retail employee was not properly empowered.

What is the process involved in hiring the right employees and recruiting the right customers? LO 2

5. What are the sources that a department store could use to recruit customers? Do you see any potential for the use of "affinity" programs by department stores? Explain or suggest examples.
6. What would be some embarrassing things that employers doing a computer search might find out about a job applicant? Do you feel employers have the right to conduct such a search? Should job applicants ask employers during the interview if they conduct such searches?
7. Do a search on Google using your name and school (or hometown). Did you find anything that might embarrass you? What can you do about it? Now do the same on Myspace.com.

STUDENT STUDY GUIDE

LO 3 **How do retailers manage employees and customers for long term profitability?**

8. Explain why turnover is costly in retailing regardless if it is employee turnover or customer turnover.
9. How can a retailer expect consumers to buy its products when its own employees shop elsewhere? As a result of this question, some clothing retailers have considered requiring that their employees only wear store brands when working. Disregarding any possible legal issues, what would this do to employee motivation? How would you handle this problem?
10. What is customer relationship management (CRM) and how can it be used to develop more profitable customer relationships?

LO 4 **What are the methods retailers can use in compensating their employees and offering customers a compelling value proposition?**

11. If you were to go to work for a retailer today, what would be the most important supplemental benefit the retailer could offer you? Would this benefit change as your lifestyle changed?
12. What factors under the retailer's control have a positive effect on employee productivity?
13. What is a "value proposition"?
14. How does a retailer's value proposition relate to creating long term profitable customer relationships? Give an example.

SAMPLE TEST QUESTIONS

LO 1 **When retailers grant their employees "empowerment," they are giving them**

a. the power to set their own hours.
b. the power to kick improperly dressed customers out of the store.
c. the power to determine what products should be featured in the retailer's weekly ad.
d. the power to make things right with the customer.
e. all of the above powers.

LO 2 **Which of the following questions may a women's apparel store ask on an employment application?**

a. What is your marital status?
b. What is your age?
c. Have you ever been arrested?
d. Are you handicapped?
e. The retailer is not allowed to ask any of the above questions since each of them can be used to discriminate against a minority or group of minorities.

LO 3 **Training and development programs should**

a. be concerned with new employees only.
b. get rid of the least productive employees within the first two years.
c. be an ongoing process.
d. rely heavily on senior management's teaching skills.
e. focus on operational skills only.

For an individual who does not care about security, but only wants to maximize his/her current earnings, the _______ compensation plan would be best.

a. straight commission
b. straight salary
c. salary plus commission
d. fringe plus salary
e. teamwork salary

WRITING AND SPEAKING EXERCISE

While working at your parents' appliance dealership over the past summer, your father approached you with a problem. It seems a sales rep had approached him to ask if she could offer to pay push money to the store's four salespeople. At the time, the store had no set policy on the subject. According to your father, the only reason there wasn't a policy was because no one had ever offered to pay push money before. Your father thought it might be a good idea because it would be an extra incentive for the sales force to close the sale. Your mother wasn't in favor. She felt that since The Home Depot, the leading appliance retailer in the town, didn't permit its sales force to accept spiffs, your parents' store should not do it either. Neither of your parents knew for sure what the two other locally owned stores would do about the offer, though they knew that the other stores would be made the same offer.

Since you were the only member of the family to have formal training in retailing (this class), your parents asked you to describe the pros and cons of spiffing and prepare a response for the sales rep. Explain the reasoning behind your policy recommendation.

RETAIL PROJECT

Since retailers often lack legal expertise when making human resource decisions, it is a good idea to review the current laws before doing anything in this area. For your assignment, go to the Equal Employment Opportunity Commission (EEOC) Web site (http://www.eeoc.gov). List five circumstances where sexual harassment may occur. Also, explain how an individual may waive his/her rights under the Age Discrimination in Employment Act.

PLANNING YOUR OWN RETAIL BUSINESS

During the planning process for starting a gift shop in a local resort town you began to question and consider different compensation plans for the retail clerks. It was fairly standard in the area to pay retail clerks $6.25 an hour. However, as you visited gift shops that were paying these rather low wages you noticed that the clerks simply took orders and did not sell or try to answer any questions for customers. In a visit to a gift shop in Ft. Lauderdale last spring you struck up a conversation with the owner. She was more than willing to share her experiences about retail clerks. After a lot of trial and error she decided to pay wages in the top 25% of those paid to retail clerks in the area. This consisted of a base wage of $9.50 an hour and a 3 percent commission on all sales. She mentioned that when she went to this type of system her average transaction size increased by 20 percent and that closure went from 28 percent to 40 percent. More importantly, she found that her bottom line profit rose by 32 percent. In short, by paying more for retail clerks she increased employee productivity and the profits of her store.

For the gift shop you are planning you initially estimated that traffic would be 30,000 visitors annually and that closure would be 24 percent. You estimated your average transaction size at $32. Your gross margin percent would be 60 percent and fixed operating expenses would be $60,000 annually. Variable operating expenses would be 20 percent of sales. Under this plan you would pay two full-time clerks $6.25 an hour and you would fill in when things got busy.

Your new plan, which you want to evaluate, calls for paying the clerks $9.00 per hour plus 4 percent commission on all sales. Thus, your fixed operating expenses would go up by $3,000 and variable operating expenses would rise to 24 percent of sales. You believe that closure would rise to 32 percent and average transaction size would rise to $36. Which compensation strategy should you pursue? Provide reasons for your decision.

CASE

The Cliff Problem

Over the past twenty years, Carrie Taylor had taken a passing interest in her parents' furniture and appliance store. She had worked there part time as an interior designer. However, she had no interest in the day-to-day operations of the store. After all, her college major was design and not business.

All that suddenly changed nine months ago when a drunk driver killed her father and seriously injured her mother. She was now in charge of the family business. She soon became somewhat comfortable handling the daily management tasks, but was unsure of what to do about one of her employees. Thus, as she prepared to leave for the High Point Furniture Market, a merchandise market where independent retailers meet with furniture manufacturers and wholesalers, she was determined to seek the advice of other independent retailers about how to handle the situation.

One of the first things that Carrie had done upon taking over the business was to establish a Saturday morning meeting during which she could discuss the store's operations with all the employees. At her first meeting, she explained to everyone that they were a team and that she needed their help and support to carry out her parents' legacy. She asked what she could do to improve things. After listening to everyone and trying to solve all the issues, Carrie decided to bring in an outside speaker once a month to motivate the staff. One of the first speakers was a sales consultant who offered selling tips. Another early session involved a local high school instructor who was seeking to place an intern with the store. This morning the speaker was from the local Chamber of Commerce. He spoke on the Chamber's plans and promotions to draw customers to the downtown business district over the next year.

Ever since the first meeting, however, Carrie's superstar salesperson, Cliff Cochran, had not come to a meeting. Cliff, besides being a long-time employee of the store, had also been a close friend of her father. In addition to missing the meeting, Cliff was often late coming to work.

Carrie began to worry that Cliff's behavior was going to affect the morale of the other five members of the sales team. However, he was the store's top seller, accounting for over a third of the store's sales.

On her first night at the High Point Market, Carrie attended a reception and was seated at a table with three other independent owners and a sales rep for a major furniture line. She asked them for advice on her "Cliff problem."

One of the owners asked Carrie about feedback from others about the Saturday meetings. Were these meetings beneficial enough to justify coming to work a half-hour early on Saturday? The owner asked if many of the housekeeping announcements at the meeting could have been replaced with e-mails or postings on the employee bulletin board.

The sales rep suggested that maybe the situation was a good thing, rather than a problem. Perhaps the other sales people would realize that if they increased production, they could miss the meetings also. Besides, what was Cliff like once he got to work? Was he a leader by example? Did he take care to neatly arrange the merchandise displays and follow up on sales leads with phone calls or e-mail?

Another owner asked if Carrie tried to involve Cliff in the Saturday meetings. She felt that Cliff needed special "atta-boy" treatment. She suggested that Carrie feed his ego by asking him to develop a training session on closing the sale or some other topic. Everyone knows he is at the top of the sales ladder, so use his skills.

The third owner wondered if maybe Cliff was merely rebelling against the person who replaced his long-time friend. Maybe Carrie should go out of her way to help Cliff through this difficult period.

Questions

1. What criteria should be used to judge the importance and necessity of having a weekly Saturday morning training meeting? Do these meetings really motivate a sales force?
2. If Cliff's problem were really one of motivation, what would you recommend that Carrie should do? Why?
3. Should Carrie ever think about firing Cliff? After all, his behavior in recent months had become intolerable. Support your reasoning.

Source: This case is based on an idea from the "Strategy Zone," *NARDA Independent Retailer,* December 2005: 14 & 26.

ANSWERS TO SAMPLE TEST QUESTIONS

Chapter 1

1. D is the correct answer since these nations really didn't have a great selection and the stores were the size of a large room. All the other answers were true.
2. A is the true statement, and all the other possible answers were false statements.
3. E is the correct answer. It was stated on page 11 that all the ways of categorizing retailers are useful, depending on the situation.
4. B is the correct answer. However, we would hope that a retailer possesses the other four possible characteristics as well as being a leader.
5. C is the correct answer, as the manager investigated both sources of supply and competition before making her decision.

Chapter 2

1. B is the correct answer because market performance objectives seek to establish the retailer's dominance against the competition. A and C are wrong because they are made-up terms. D is wrong because societal performance is concerned with the broader issues of the world, and E is wrong because financial objectives are internally number-oriented and deal with profit or productivity.
2. C is the correct answer. A and B are wrong because price is the poorest way to differentiate yourself. D is wrong because this action would restrict you from selling many of the top brands. E is wrong because the customers really don't see planning, only the results of planning.

Chapter 3

1. B is the correct answer. Americans do move about a dozen times in their lifetime. A is wrong because some baby boomers are already in their 50s. C is wrong because small markets still represent great opportunities for retailers if they satisfy the consumers' wants and needs. D is wrong because the U.S. growth rate is expected to be about 1 percent. E is wrong because the growth rate has been declining in recent years.
2. C is the correct answer: the "boomerang effect" is a relatively new phenomenon that describes something many of today's students will face that previous generations did not have to face—returning home to live with their parents. A, B, and D are at least true statements, but they have nothing to do with the "boomerang effect." E may or may not be true at the time you are reading this, but it also has nothing to do with the question asked.
3. D is correct since discretionary income is disposable income (which is all personal income minus personal taxes) minus the money needed for necessities. E is wrong because as we just noted, it is the definition of disposable income. The other three possible choices are just made-up definitions.
4. D is the correct answer. A is an incorrect answer because such resentment may have a long-term negative impact on the retailer's ability to regain that consumer as a customer. B is wrong because if the retailer is proactive with its customer satisfaction program and responds quickly to the problem, the resentment can be overcome. C is incorrect because most unhappy consumers don't make the retailer aware of their dissatisfaction. Therefore, it is up to the retailer to be vigilant and monitor customer satisfaction. E is not correct either. Retailers must measure customer satisfaction on an ongoing basis and compare customer service ratings against preestablished benchmarks.

Chapter 4

1. B is the correct answer. E is true in rare cases, but the question asked for what structure MOST retailers are involved in. D, while it is a type of market structure, is wrong because retailers don't operate in environments with

horizontal demand curves. A and C, while sounding good, are made-up terms.

2. D is the correct answer because this involves different types of retailers competing with each other with similar products. B is wrong because intratype refers to cases where the same types of retailers compete with each other and Wal-Mart is a general merchandise store and not a grocer. C (scrambled merchandising) can be used to describe what Wal-Mart is doing but this term does not refer to a type of competition. E refers to a situation where a retailer dominates a single line of merchandise, not many lines as Wal-Mart is doing with its supercenters. A is wrong because it is a made-up nonsense term.
3. D is the correct answer. Some might say that the retail accordion theory describes this pattern—that the small original hamburger stand expanded to the large McDonald's and Burger Kings of today and will get smaller as customers rebel. However, this isn't entirely accurate. Nevertheless, we didn't include the accordion theory as a possible answer. B is wrong because it describes a stage of growth that institutions pass through and not why they change formats. The other three possible answers used made-up terms.
4. D is the correct answer. A is wrong because retailing is more diverse around the world. B is wrong because success in one country doesn't guarantee success in other countries; witness the hypermarkets in the United States or the fact that Kmart, Sears, and JCPenney have abandoned their foreign expansion plans. C is wrong because the size of the average retailer is diverse. E is wrong because other countries have also developed successful new retailing formats—witness IKEA.

Chapter 5

1. E is the correct answer since facilitating institutions aid the supply chain by performing tasks at which they are more capable of doing than the current supply chain members. A is wrong since, though some facilitating institutions may take possession of the merchandise, none of them take title. B is wrong since facilitating institutions do not take title to the goods. C is wrong since they do not manage the supply chain; besides, the goal of a supply chain is to minimize "sub-optimization" since they cannot operate at 100 percent efficiency. D is wrong since they cannot do all eight functions without taking title; besides, the text mentions that no one firm would want, or be able, to perform all eight functions.
2. E is the correct answer. A and C are wrong since conventional channels, due to their loose alignment, are by their very nature not efficient. B is wrong because contractual channels are not loosely aligned since the contract directs each member's duties and responsibilities. D is wrong since there is not any feeling of partnership and cooperation in a conventional channel.
3. B is the correct answer. A is wrong even though it may be true that each member wants all the power; a supply chain member is still dependent on the other members. C is wrong because no member can perform all eight functions. D is wrong because a partnership should be committed to the life of the supply chain. E is wrong since if everybody wanted to work independently of each other, there would not be a supply chain in the first place.
4. A is the correct answer since to be successful, all channel members must work as a team. B is wrong because in some cases, especially those involving a small retailer and a larger manufacturer, it doesn't make sense to have a retailer direct the channel. E is wrong for the same basic reason; a small manufacturer would never tell Wal-Mart how to act. C is incorrect because at times coercive power is necessary to make some members realize that their actions hurt other members. D is not the correct answer because it doesn't work to set an arbitrary profit level. Profit should be based on the tasks performed.

Chapter 6

1. E is the correct answer since the major price discrimination law, the Robinson-Patman Act, is meant to protect competition by making sure that retailers are treated fairly by suppliers. The other possible answers pertain to laws covering other situations.
2. E is the correct answer since it involved a deceitful action (using another firm's trademark) that caused damage to the other firm. A is wrong because it did not cause damage to the competitor. B is wrong because it was not

deceitful; the retailer told the truth. C is wrong because it involves deceptive pricing. D is perfectly legal since you did not do anything wrong.

3. A is the correct answer since an implied warranty of fitness for a particular purpose arises when the customer relies on the retailer to assist or make the selection of goods to serve a particular purpose. B is wrong because an implied warranty of merchantability means that the retailer implies that the merchandise is fit for the ordinary purpose for which the product is usually purchased. C is wrong because it is a made-up answer. D and E are wrong because no verbal or written guarantee was mentioned in the question.
4. B is the correct answer since the purchase of the cat food was tied to the purchase of the unpopular product—litter. The other answers have nothing to do with the question.
5. B is the correct answer. While there are federal laws governing franchise operations, the most stringent laws are usually state laws since the state government wants to protect its citizens and locally owned franchise businesses, as well as voters, from unfair practices of out-of-state franchisors.
6. A is the correct answer since it is a merchandising decision regarding the success or failure of merchandise. The other four answers pertain to the ethical decisions discussed in the chapter.

Chapter 7

1. C is the correct answer. It is not essential that a market segment create high sales, however, it should be profitable. A, B, C, and E are all criteria used to successfully reach a target market and thus are incorrect answers.
2. A is the correct answer. Since freestanding retailers are not part of a shopping center or CBD they do not have direct competition. B is not correct since it is an advantage of retailers in shopping centers. C is incorrect since freestanding retailers have more difficulty in attracting customers for the initial visit. D is incorrect because freestanding retailers are not able to share advertising costs with other retailers as in a shopping center. E is incorrect because freestanding stores can be either leased or purchased.
3. E is the correct answer. A, B, C, and D are all purposes of geographical information systems and thus any one of these answers is not the single best choice.
4. B is the correct answer. The three steps presented are exactly as discussed in the textbook. A is wrong because the first step is incorrect. C is wrong because the second step is incorrect. D is wrong because all three steps are incorrect. E is wrong because the third step is incorrect.
5. E is the correct answer. A and B by themselves are not the best answer because both are needed to do a site analysis. C and D are incorrect because they are irrelevant to site analysis.
6. C is correct because alternative investments available to the retailer should not be a consideration in the selection of a site. A, B, D, and E are incorrect because they are all important considerations in selecting the best site.

Chapter 8

1. B is the correct answer since current liabilities are listed on the balance sheet, but are not included in the merchandise budget. The other answers are all included in the merchandise budget.
2. D is the correct answer since the income statement is a summary of the sales and expenses for a given time period. A is wrong because an expense report, while not mentioned in the chapter, would cover only expenses. B is wrong because although the inventory valuation will affect the retailer's expenses, it also does not include sales. C is wrong because the cash flow statement only deals with the inflow and outflow of cash. E is wrong because gross margin only considers sales and cost of goods sold and does not include operating expenses.
3. C is the correct answer since the cost ($120,000) divided by sales ($200,000) is 0.6.

Chapter 9

1. A is the correct answer since $\$425{,}000 \times 1/2[1+(\$170{,}000/\$142{,}000)] = \$466{,}901$. E would be the correct answer if the question asked for the basic stock method, not the PVM. D is the average stock for the season, but not the correct answer. The other two answers are made-up numbers.
2. Since the key feature of OTB is that it can be determined at anytime during the merchandise

period, D is the correct answer. The other answers are wrong because they are time-specific.

3. C is the correct answer as the other four are the constraints listed in the text.
4. B is the correct answer since it best describes what is involved in a vendor profitability analysis statement, which was defined in the text as "the record of all purchases you made last year, the discounts granted you by the vendor, transportation charges paid, the original markup, markdowns, and finally, the season-ending gross margin on that vendor's merchandise." A is wrong because it is about the vendor's financial statements, which are seldom provided to retailers. C is wrong because it deals with new lines of merchandise. D is wrong because it deals with the retailer's line of credit granted by the vendor. E is wrong because it covers only one factor (discounts) covered by the vendor profitability analysis statement.
5. B is the correct answer. A is wrong because it describes a noncumulative quantity discount. C is wrong because it assumes the discount period starts with the beginning of the year, something that is not always true. D is wrong because it describes a different type of discount. E is wrong because it is based on a specific quantity that may be too high or too low given the circumstances of the sale.
6. B is the correct answer since it is the combination of vendor and retail employees that are most often involved in collusion. A and D are wrong because customers are not involved in vendor collusion. C and E are wrong because while the sales representative or accountant may be involved, the people involved with delivery must also be included.

Chapter 10

1. C is the correct answer since the retailer's pricing objectives must be interactive with all the other decision areas of the firm. A is incorrect since pricing cannot be independent of these other decision areas. B is incorrect since pricing cannot be separate from these other areas. D is wrong because the retailer's pricing objectives should not be in competition with these other areas. E is incorrect since multifaced has nothing to do with the question.
2. C is the correct answer because in this case the retailer offered the same merchandise to different customers at different prices. E is incorrect because variable pricing means that the prices for all customers may change as differences in either demand or costs occur. Nevertheless, all customers will pay the same price unless the retailer also uses a flexible policy. A is wrong because there is no such policy as "two-price." B is incorrect because with customary pricing, the retailer seeks to maintain the same price for an item over an extended period of time. D is incorrect because leader pricing involves taking a popular item and offering it for sale to everybody as a means of drawing these consumers into a store.
3. A is the correct answer since markup on selling price is SP – C/SP [($45 – 25)/$45 = 44.4%]. B is incorrect because the question asked for markup on selling price and 80% is the markup on cost. The other answers are merely made-up numbers.
4. This question was chosen because many students get confused about reduction percentage. C is the correct answer because reduction percentage is the amount of the reduction ($29.99 –$19.99 = $10) divided by net sales ($19.99). A is the markdown percentage, which is the amount of the reduction divided by the original selling price ($10/$29.99). The other answers are made-up numbers, although E is the result of dividing the new selling price by the original selling price.

Chapter 11

1. E is the correct answer. Even though the retailer may have a low net worth, this should not be taken into consideration when developing a promotional strategy. After all, the objectives will still be the same. The other four alternatives (credit customers, price level, merchandise, and building and fixtures) are managerial decisions that must be integrated into the retailer's overall plan.
2. A is the correct answer. Institutional, or long-term, advertising tries to create a positive store image and provide public service. B lists the objectives for short-term, or promotional, advertising. C lists the two other types of promotion. D lists how a retailer might seek to obtain short-term results. E lists two other

topics covered in this chapter that have nothing to do with the question.

3. E is the correct answer as all four of the alternatives belong as part of an ad's objectives.
4. E is the correct answer. Premiums are the extra items offered to customers when they purchased the promoted item. When in a limited number of cases premiums could be joint-sponsored sales promotions (Alternative A), such promotions would not be beneficial to the retailer since the consumer could purchase the product from another retailer. The other three alternatives (B, C, and D) are other forms of promotion.

Chapter 12

1. C is the correct answer since the text explained that a transient customer is an individual who visits a retailer and finds the service level below expectations or the product "out of stock. This transient, or temporary, customer will seek to find a retailer with the level of customer service he or she feels is appropriate. A is wrong because, even though the dictionary defines "transient" as short-lived or not long-lasting, the term does not refer to length of time spent shopping. The other choices are wrong because they have nothing to do with a transient customer.
2. E is the correct answer since merchandise availability is a transaction service that helps build the relationship with the customer thus making B and D wrong. A and C are wrong because personal shopping is a service not a cost, despite the fact that there might be some additional cost involved.
3. D is wrong because as shown in Exhibit 12.5 the other alternatives are factors that must be considered when determining the service levels to offer.
4. B is the correct answer since complaint handling is most often a centralized customer service function. Retail selling jobs should be designed to have high levels of variety (C), autonomy (D), task identity (E), and feedback from supervisors and customers (A).
5. E is the correct answer since once the approach has been completed, the salesperson is in a position to present the merchandise and sales message correctly. The key to the presentation, however, is to get the customer to want to buy your product or service. Therefore, you must have the right price range of products to show the customer. A is wrong because if the price is too high or too low, the sale will already be lost. B is wrong because you cannot select the right product unless you know the right price. C is wrong because the greeting occurs in the approach stage. D is wrong because helping the customer to decide is the last step of the presentation.
6. A is the correct answer. The audit isn't an attempt to learn what the customers want; rather it concentrates on the facts of their shopping experience and Answers B, C and D all concern that shopping experience.

Chapter 13

1. B is the correct answer since the two primary objectives around which all activities, functions, and goals in the store revolve are store image and space productivity. Alternatives C & D have two worthwhile activities (merchandise presentation and traffic control; opportunities for impulse buying and shelf management) but by themselves they will not produce high performance results. A and E are wrong because while its activities are also good traits, sales management (A) and maintaining market share (E) are not objectives of the store environment.
2. C is the correct answer since the store's layout and design must allow the store to be shopable and the merchandise to be effectively presented. A is wrong because even though the retailer would like all the customers to see every high-profit item, this is not always possible and nothing was said about presentation of the merchandise. B is obviously wrong since it would be foolish to give offices, the back room, wall, and aisles as much space as the selling floor since these areas are not where sales are generated. D is wrong because a retailer would not care to have rapid replacement in a low-turnover area. E is wrong because retailers today want to minimize the space given to back rooms.
3. A is the correct answer since the method of merchandise presentation has an impact on the store's image and space productivity. B is obviously wrong since it would be foolish to hire a psychologist to do the store's displays.

C is wrong because by shopping effectively, the customer might not make any impulse purchases. D is wrong because while social factors may influence our behavior, this alternative has nothing to do with the question. E is another obviously wrong choice because it would be foolish for this to be done.

4. B is the correct answer since store design is most responsible for developing a store image, which the other four alternatives are concerned with doing. B, however, would not increase the productivity of the store.
5. E is the correct answer since visual communications is concerned with messages within the store, which are covered by the other four possible answers, and not those external to the store.

Chapter 14

1. D is the correct answer as empowerment gives the employee the power to make decisions in order to take care of the customer. A is wrong because it is the concept of teamwork, not empowerment, that lets the employees adjust their hours. B is wrong because empowerment is concerned with satisfying customers' problems, not enforcing dress codes. C is wrong because while the employees may make suggestions for featuring products in the weekly ads, this decision is made by the buyer and department manager.
2. E is the correct answer. As noted in the text, none of these would be a valid reason for not hiring an applicant.
3. C is the correct answer since training and development must be viewed as a process of continuing education. A is wrong because existing employees must also undergo training to remind them of how things are done and to teach and inform them of new items. B is wrong because even though employee turnover is expensive, it is better to get rid of unproductive employees as soon as possible. D is wrong because senior management should be involved in the training process; their time will be more efficiently spent in their areas of expertise, such as store management, buying, and finance. E is wrong because training should cover all retail activities.
4. A is the correct answer because straight commission offers the greatest potential for instant income. B is wrong because straight salary cannot be influenced in the short run by an individual's performance. C is wrong because the commission in a salary plus commission plan will be lower than the straight commission to compensate for the employer taking some of the risk. D is wrong because it is not a compensation plan. E is wrong because a teamwork salary is based on the entire team's performance, not just an individual.

Glossary

A

above-market pricing policy Is a policy where retailers establish high prices because nonprice factors are more important to their target market than price.

accounts and/or notes receivable Are amounts that customers owe the retailer for goods and services.

accounts payable Are amounts owed vendors for goods and services.

active information gathering Occurs when consumers proactively gather information.

administered vertical marketing channels Exist when one of the channel members takes the initiative to lead the channel by applying the principles of effective interorganizational management.

advertising Is paid, nonpersonal communication through various media by business firms, nonprofit organizations, and individuals who are in some way identified in the advertising message and who hope to inform or persuade members of a particular audience; includes communication of products, services, institutions, and ideas.

advertising effectiveness Is the extent to which the advertising has produced the result desired.

advertising efficiency Is concerned with whether the advertising result was achieved with the minimum financial expenditure.

affordable method Is a technique for budgeting advertising in which all the money a retailer can afford to spend on advertising in a given time period becomes the advertising budget.

ambiance Is the overall feeling or mood projected by a store through its aesthetic appeal to human senses.

anchor stores Are the stores in a shopping center that are the most dominant and are expected to draw customers to the shopping center.

anticipation Allows the retailer to pay the invoice in advance of the end of the cash discount period and earn an extra discount.

asset Is anything of value that is owned by the retail firm.

asset turnover Is total sales divided by total assets and shows how many dollars of sales a retailer can generate on an annual basis with each dollar invested in assets.

B

bait-and-switch Advertising or promoting a product at an unrealistically low price to serve as "bait" and then trying to "switch" the customer to a higher-priced product.

basic stock method (BSM) Is a technique for planning dollar inventory investments and allows for a base stock level plus a variable amount of inventory that will increase or decrease at the beginning of each sales period in the same dollar amount as the period's expected sales.

battle of the brands Occurs when retailers have their own products competing with the manufacturer's products for shelf space and control over display location.

below-market pricing policy Is a policy that regularly discounts merchandise from the established market price in order to build store traffic and generate high sales and gross margin dollars per square foot of selling space.

breadth (or assortment) The number of merchandise brands that are found in a merchandise line.

break-even point Is where total revenues equal total expenses and the retailer is making neither a profit nor a loss.

bricks-and-click approach An approach that involves a tangible retail store that also offers its merchandise on the Internet.

bricks-and-mortar retailers Retailers that operate out of a physical building.

bulk or capacity fixture Is a display fixture that is intended to hold the bulk of merchandise without looking as heavy as a long, straight rack of merchandise.

bundling Occurs when distinct multiple items, generally from different merchandise lines, are offered at a special price.

buying The retailing career path whereby one uses quantitative tools to develop appropriate buying plans for the store's merchandise lines.

buying power index (BPI) Is an indicator of a market's overall retail potential and is composed of weighted measures of effective buying income (personal income, including all nontax payments such as social security, minus all taxes), retail sales, and population size.

C

cash discount Is a discount offered to the retailer for the prompt payment of bills.

catalog sales Retail sales that occur through catalogs mailed to households.

category killer Is a retailer that carries such a large amount of merchandise in a single category at such good prices that it makes it impossible for the customers to walk out without purchasing what they need, thus killing the competition.

category management (CM) Is a process of managing all SKUs within a product category and involves the simultaneous management of price, shelf space, merchandising strategy, promotional efforts, and other elements of the retail mix within the category based on the firm's goals, the changing environment, and consumer behavior.

category manager Is an employee designated by a retailer for each category sold in their store. The category manager leverages detailed knowledge of the consumer and consumer trends, detailed point-of-sales information, and specific analysis provided by each supplier to tailor a store's offerings to the specific needs of each market. The category manager works with the suppliers to plan promotions throughout the year.

category signage Are smaller than directional and departmental signage and are intended to be seen from a shorter distance; they are located on or close to the fixture itself where the merchandise is displayed.

central business district (CBD) Usually consists of an unplanned shopping area around the geographic point at which all public transportation systems converge; it is usually in the center of the city and often where the city originated historically.

channel Used interchangeably with supply chain.

channel advisor or **channel captain** Is the institution (manufacturer, wholesaler, broker, or retailer) in the marketing channel that is able to plan for and get other channel institutions to engage in activities they might not otherwise engage in. Large store retailers are often able to perform the role of channel captain.

class A vendors Are those from whom the retailer purchases large and profitable amounts of merchandise.

class B vendors Are those that generate satisfactory sales and profits for the retailer.

class C vendors Are those that carry outstanding merchandise lines but do not currently sell to the retailer.

class D vendors Are those from whom the retailer purchases small quantities of goods on an irregular basis.

class E vendors Are those with whom the retailer has had an unfavorable experience.

clicks-and-mortar retailers Retailers that sell both online and via physical stores.

closing the sale Is the action the salesperson takes to bring a potential sale to its natural conclusion.

coercive power Is based on B's belief that A has the capability to punish or harm B if B doesn't do what A wants.

compensation Includes direct dollar payments (wages, commission, bonuses) and indirect payments (insurance, vacation time, retirement plans).

confidential vendor analysis Is identical to the vendor profitability analysis but also provides a three-year financial summary as well as the names, titles, and negotiating points of all the vendor's sales staff.

consignment Is when the vendor retains the ownership of the goods and usually establishes the selling price; it is paid only when the goods are sold by the retailer.

content theories Refer to theories on motivation that ask, "What motivates an individual to behave?"

contests and sweepstakes Are sales promotion techniques in which customers have a chance of winning a special prize based on entering a contest in which the entrant competes with others, or a sweepstakes in which all entrants have an equal chance of winning a prize.

contractual vertical marketing channels Use a contract to govern the working relationship between channel members and include wholesaler-sponsored voluntary groups, retailer-owned cooperatives, and franchised retail programs.

conventional marketing channel Is one in which each channel member is loosely aligned with the others and takes a short-term orientation.

conversion rate Is the percentage of shoppers that enter the store that are converted into purchasers.

corporate vertical marketing channels Exist where one channel institution owns multiple levels of distribution and typically consists of either a manufacturer that has integrated vertically forward to reach the consumer or a retailer that has integrated vertically backward to create a self-supply network.

cost method Is an inventory valuation technique that provides a book valuation of inventory based solely on the retailer's cost of merchandise including freight.

cost of goods sold Is the cost of merchandise that has been sold during the period.
cost per thousand method (CPM) Is a technique used to evaluate advertisements in different media based on cost. The cost per thousand is the cost of the advertisement divided by the number of people viewing it, which is then multiplied by 1,000.
cost per thousand—target market (CPM-TM) Is a technique used to evaluate advertisements in different media based on cost. The cost per thousand per target market is the cost of the advertisement divided by the number of people in the target market viewing it, which is then multiplied by 1,000.
coupons Are a sales promotion tool in which the shopper is offered a price discount on a specific item if the retailer is presented with the appropriate coupon at time of purchase.
coverage Is the theoretical maximum number of consumers in the retailer's target market that can be reached by a medium and not the number actually reached.
cue Refers to any object or phenomenon in the environment that is capable of eliciting a response.
culture Is the buffer that people have created between themselves and the raw physical environment and includes the characteristics of the population, humanly created objects, and mobile physical structures.
cumulative quantity discount Is a discount based on the total amount purchased over a period of time.
cumulative reach Is the reach that is achieved over a period of time.
current assets Are assets that can be easily converted into cash within a relatively short period of time (usually a year or less).
current liabilities Are short-term debts that are payable within a year.
current ratio Current assets divided by current liabilities.
customary pricing Is a policy in which the retailer sets prices for goods and services and seeks to maintain those prices over an extended period of time.
customer relationship management (CRM) Is comprised of an integrated information system where the fundamental unit of data collection is the customer, supplemented by relevant information about the customer.
customer satisfaction Occurs when the total shopping experience of the customer has been met or exceeded.
customer service Consists of all those activities performed by the retailer that influence (1) the ease with which a potential customer can shop or learn about the store's offering, (2) the ease with which a transaction can be completed once the customer attempts to make a purchase, and (3) the customer's satisfaction with the transaction.
customer service and sales enhancement audit provides management with a detailed analysis of current sales activity by location and by selling area.
customer theft Is also known as shoplifting and occurs when customers or individuals disguised as customers steal merchandise from the retailer's store.

D

deceptive advertising Occurs when a retailer makes false or misleading advertising claims about the physical makeup of a product, the benefits to be gained by its use, or the appropriate uses for the product.
deceptive pricing Occurs when a misleading price is used to lure customers into the store; usually there are hidden charges or the item advertised may be unavailable.
demand density Is the extent to which the potential demand for the retailer's goods and services is concentrated in certain census tracts, ZIP code areas, or parts of the community.
demonstrations and sampling Are in-store presentations with the intent of reducing the consumer's perceived risk of purchasing a product.
depth Is the average number of stock-keeping units within each brand of the merchandise line.
direct selling Engaging in the sale of a consumer product or service on a person-to-person basis away from a fixed retail location.
direct supply chain Is the channel that results when a manufacturer sells its goods directly to the final consumer or end user.
directional and departmental signage Are large signs that are usually placed fairly high, so they can be seen throughout the store.
discretionary income Is disposable income minus the money needed for necessities to sustain life.
disposable income Is personal income less personal taxes.
diverter Is an unauthorized member of a channel who buys and sells excess merchandise to and from authorized channel members.
divertive competition Occurs when retailers intercept or divert customers from competing retailers.
domain disagreements Occur when there is disagreement about which member of the marketing channel should make decisions.

drive Refers to a motivating force that directs behavior.

dual distribution Occurs when a manufacturer sells to independent retailers and also through its own retail outlets.

dwell time Refers to the amount of time a consumer must spend waiting to complete a purchase.

E

ease of access Refers to the consumer's ability to easily and quickly find a retailer's Web site in cyberspace.

EDLP (everyday low prices) Is when a retailer charges the same low price every day throughout the year and seldom runs the product on sale.

employee theft Occurs when employees of the retailer steal merchandise where they work.

empowerment Occurs when employees are given the power in their jobs to do the things necessary to satisfy and make things right for customers.

end-of-month (EOM) dating Allows the retailer to take a cash discount and the full payment period to begin on the first day of the following month instead of on the invoice date.

ethics Is a set of rules for human moral behavior.

exclusive distribution Means only one retailer is used to cover a trading area.

expectancy theory Suggests that an employee will expend effort on some task because the employee expects that the effort will lead to a performance outcome that will lead in turn to a reward or bonus that the employee finds desirable or valued.

expertise power Is based on B's perception that A has some special knowledge.

explicit code of ethics Consists of a written policy that states what is ethical and unethical behavior.

expressed warranties Are either written or verbalized agreements about the performance of a product and can cover all attributes of the merchandise or only one attribute.

extended problem solving Occurs when the consumer recognizes a problem but has decided on neither the brand nor the store.

extra dating (Ex) Allows the retailer extra or interest-free days before the period of payment begins.

F

facilitating marketing institutions Are those that do not actually take title but assist in the marketing process by specializing in the performance of certain marketing functions.

feature fixture Is a display that draws special attention to selected features (e.g., color, shape, or style) of merchandise.

FIFO Stands for first in, first out and values inventory based on the assumption that the oldest merchandise is sold before the more recently purchased merchandise.

financial leverage Is total assets divided by net worth or owners' equity and shows how aggressive the retailer is in its use of debt.

financial performance Represents the profit and economic performance a retailer desires.

fixed component Typically is composed of some base wage per hour, week, month, or year.

flexible pricing Is a policy that encourages offering the same products and quantities to different customers at different prices.

floor plan Is a schematic that shows where merchandise and customer service departments are located, how customers circulate through the store, and how much space is dedicated to each department.

franchise Is a form of licensing by which the owner of a product, service, or business method (the franchisor) obtains distribution through affiliated dealers (franchisees).

free merchandise Is a discount whereby merchandise is offered in lieu of price concessions.

free on board (FOB) destination Is a method of charging for transportation in which the vendor pays for all transportation costs and the buyer takes title on delivery.

free on board (FOB) factory Is a method of charging for transportation where the buyer assumes title to the goods at the factory and pays all transportation costs from the vendor's factory.

free on board (FOB) shipping point Is a method of charging for transportation in which the vendor pays for transportation to a local shipping point where the buyer assumes title and then pays all further transportation costs.

free-flow layout Is a type of store layout in which fixtures and merchandise are grouped into free-flowing patterns on the sales floor.

free-riding Is when a consumer seeks product information, usage instructions, and sometimes even warranty work from a full-service store but then, armed with the brand's model number, purchases the product from a limited-service discounter or over the Internet.

freestanding retailer Generally locates along major traffic arteries and does not have any adjacent retailers to share traffic.

frequency Is the average number of times each person who is reached is exposed to an advertisement during a given time period.

fringe benefit package Is a part of the total compensation package offered to many retail employees and may include health insurance, disability benefits, life insurance, retirement plans, child care, use of an auto, and financial counseling.

G

geographic information system (GIS) Is a computerized system that combines physical geography with cultural geography.

goal incompatibility Occurs when achieving the goals of either the supplier or the retailer would hamper the performance of the other.

goal setting Is the process in which management and employees establish goals that become the basis for performance appraisal and review.

goals and objectives Are the performance results intended to be brought about through the execution of a strategy.

goodwill Is an intangible asset, usually based on customer loyalty, that a retailer pays for when buying an existing business.

gray marketing Is when branded merchandise flows through unauthorized channels.

grid layout Is a type of store layout in which counters and fixtures are placed in long rows or "runs," usually at right angles, throughout the store.

gross margin Is the difference between net sales and cost of goods sold.

gross margin percentage A measure of profitability derived by dividing gross margin by net sales.

gross margin return on inventory Is gross margin divided by average inventory at cost; alternatively, it is the gross margin percent multiplied by net sales divided by average inventory investment.

gross sales Are the retailer's total sales including sales for cash or for credit.

H

habitual problem solving Occurs when the consumer relies on past experiences and learns to convert the problem into a situation requiring less thought. The consumer has a strong preference for the brand to buy and the retailer from which to purchase it.

hierarchy of needs model Theorizes that individuals have lower-level physiological and safety and security needs, which are first satisfied before higher-level needs of belongingness or social esteem and self-actualization are pursued.

high-low pricing Involves the use of high every day prices and low leader "specials" on items typically featured in weekly ads.

high-margin/high-turnover retailer Is one that operates on a high gross margin percentage and a high rate of inventory turnover.

high-margin/low-turnover retailer Is one that operates on a high gross margin percentage and a low rate of inventory turnover.

high-performance retailers Are those retailers that produce financial results substantially superior to the industry average.

high-quality service Is the type of service that meets or exceeds customers' expectations.

home page Is the introductory or first material viewers see when they access a retailer's Internet site. It is the equivalent of a retailer's storefront in the physical world.

horizontal cooperative advertising Occurs when two or more retailers band together to share the cost of advertising usually in the form of a joint promotion of an event or sale that would benefit both parties.

horizontal price fixing Occurs when a group of competing retailers (or other channel members operating at a given level of distribution) establishes a fixed price at which to sell certain brands of products.

I

impact Refers to how strong an impression an advertisement makes and how well it ultimately leads to a purchase.

implicit code of ethics Is an unwritten but well understood set of rules or standards of moral responsibility.

implied warranty of fitness Is a warranty that implies that the merchandise is fit for a particular purpose and arises when the customer relies on the retailer to assist or make the selection of goods to serve a particular purpose.

implied warranty of merchantability Is made by every retailer when the retailer sells goods and implies that the merchandise sold is fit for the ordinary purpose for which such goods are typically used.

income statement Is a financial statement that provides a summary of the sales and expenses for a given time period, usually a month, quarter, season, or year.

index of retail saturation (IRS) Is the ratio of demand for a product (households in the geographic area multiplied by annual retail expenditures for a particular line of trade per household) divided by available supply (the square footage of retail facilities of a particular line of trade in the geographic area).

indirect supply chain Is the channel that results once independent channel members are added between the manufacturer and the consumer.

informational power Is based on A's ability to provide B with factual data.

institutional advertising Is a type of advertising in which the retailer attempts to gain long-term benefits by promoting and selling the store itself rather than the merchandise in the store.

in-store displays Are promotional fixtures of displays that seek to generate traffic, highlight individual items, and encourage impulse buying.

intensive distribution Means that all possible retailers are used in a trade area.

intertype competition Occurs when two or more retailers of a different type, as defined by NAICS codes in the Census of Retail Trade, compete directly by attempting to sell the same merchandise lines to the same households.

intratype competition Occurs when two or more retailers of the same type, as defined by NAICS codes in the Census of Retail Trade, compete directly with each other for the same households.

inventory turnover Refers to the number of times per year, on average, that a retailer sells its inventory.

J

job enrichment Is the process of enhancing the core job characteristics of employees to improve their motivation, productivity, and job satisfaction.

L

leader pricing Is when a high-demand item is priced low and is heavily advertised in order to attract customers into the store.

legitimate power Is based on A's right to influence B, or B's belief that B should accept A's influence.

liability Is any legitimate financial claim against the retailer's assets.

LIFO Stands for last in, first out and values inventory based on the assumption that the most recently purchased merchandise is sold first and the oldest merchandise is sold last.

limited problem solving Occurs when the consumer has a strong preference for either the brand or the store, but not both.

location Is the geographic space or cyberspace where the retailer conducts business.

long-term liabilities Are debts that are due in a year or longer.

loop layout Is a type of store layout in which a major customer aisle begins at the entrance, loops through the store—usually in the shape of a circle, square, or rectangle—and then returns the customer to the front of the store.

loss leader Is an extreme form of leader pricing where an item is sold below a retailer's cost.

low-margin/high-turnover retailer Is one that operates on a low gross margin percentage and a high rate of inventory turnover.

low-margin/low-turnover retailer Is one that operates on a low gross margin percentage and a low rate of inventory turnover.

loyalty programs Are a form of sales promotion program in which buyers are rewarded with special rewards, which other shoppers are not offered, for purchasing often from the retailer.

M

markdown Is any reduction in the price of an item from its initially established price.

markdown money Markdown money is what retailers charge to suppliers when merchandise does not sell at what the vendor intended.

market performance Represents how a retailer desires to be compared to its competitors.

market segmentation Is the dividing of a heterogeneous consumer population into smaller, more homogeneous groups based on their characteristics.

market share Is the retailer's total sales divided by total market sales.

markup Is the selling price of the merchandise less its cost, which is equivalent to gross margin.

merchandise budget Is a plan of projected sales for an upcoming season, when and how much merchandise is to be purchased, and what markups and reductions will likely occur.

merchandise line Is a group of products that are closely related because they are intended for the same end use (all televisions); are sold to the same customer group (junior miss clothing); or fall within a given price range (budget women's wear).

merchandise management Is the analysis, planning, acquisition, handling, and control of the merchandise investments of a retail operation.

merchandising Is the planning and control of the buying and selling of goods and services to help the retailer realize its objectives.

metropolitan statistical areas Are freestanding urban areas with populations in excess of 50,000.

micromarketing Is the tailoring of merchandise in each store to the preferences of its neighborhood.

microretailing Occurs when a chain store retailer operating over a wide geographic area, usually nationally, tailors its merchandise and services in each store to the needs of the immediate trading area.

middle-of-month (MOM) dating Allows the retailer to take a cash discount and the full payment period to begin on the middle of the month.

mission statement Is a basic description of the fundamental nature, rationale, and direction of the firm.

monopolistic competition Occurs when the products offered are different, yet viewed as substitutable for each other and the sellers recognize that they compete with sellers of these different products.

motivation Is the drive that a person has to excel at activities, such as a job, that he or she undertakes.

multiple-unit pricing Occurs when the price of each unit in a multiple-unit package is less than the price of each unit if it were sold individually.

mutual trust Occurs when both the retailer and its supplier have faith that each will be truthful and fair in their dealings with the other.

N

negotiation Is the process of finding mutually satisfying solutions when the retail buyer and vendor have conflicting objectives.

neighborhood business district (NBD) Is a shopping area that evolves to satisfy the convenience-oriented shopping needs of a neighborhood, generally contains several small stores (with the major retailer being a supermarket or a variety store), and is located on a major artery of a residential area.

net profit Is operating profit plus or minus other income or expenses.

net profit margin Is the ratio of net profit (after taxes) to total sales and shows how much profit a retailer makes on each dollar of sales after all expenses and taxes have been met.

net sales Are gross sales less returns and allowances.

net worth (owner's equity) Is total assets less total liabilities.

noncumulative quantity discount Is a discount based on a single purchase.

noncurrent assets Are those assets that cannot be converted to cash in a short period of time (usually 12 months) in the normal course of business.

nonstore-based retailers Intercept customers at home, at work, or at a place other than a store where they might be susceptible to purchasing.

O

odd pricing Is the practice of setting retail prices that end in the digits 5, 8, 9—such as $29.95, $49.98, or $9.99.

off-price retailers Sell products at a discount but do not carry certain brands on a continuous basis. They carry those brands they can buy from manufacturers at closeout or deep one-time discount prices.

oligopolistic competition Occurs when relatively few sellers, or many small firms who follow the lead of a few larger firms, offer essentially homogeneous products and any action by one seller is expected to be noticed and reacted to by the other sellers.

100 percent location Is when there is no better use for a site than the retail store that is being planned for that site.

one-price policy Is a policy that establishes that the retailer will charge all customers the same price for an item.

one-way exclusive dealing Occurs when the supplier agrees to give the retailer the exclusive right to merchandise the supplier's product in a particular trade area.

online only approach An online only approach is when the retailer only offers merchandise or services via the Internet and not through a tangible retail store.

on-shelf merchandising Is the display of merchandise on counters, racks, shelves, and fixtures throughout the store.

open-to-buy (OTB) Refers to the dollar amount that a buyer can currently spend on merchandise without exceeding the planned dollar stocks.

operating expenses Are those expenses that a retailer incurs in running the business other than the cost of the merchandise.

operating profit Is gross margin less operating expenses.

operations management Deals with activities directed at maximizing the efficiency of the retailer's use of resources. It is frequently referred to as day-to-day management.

optional stock list Is a merchandising method in which each store in a retail chain is given the flexibility to adjust its merchandise mix to local tastes and demands.

other income or expenses Includes income or expense items that the firm incurs which are not in the course of its normal retail operations.

outshopping Outshopping occurs when a household leaves their community of residence to shop in another community; it usually occurs when people leave a smaller community to shop in a larger community.

overstored Is a condition in a community where the number of stores in relation to households is so large that to engage in retailing is usually unprofitable or marginally profitable.

P

palming off Occurs when a retailer represents that merchandise is made by a firm other than the true manufacturer.

passive information gathering Is the receiving and processing of information regarding the existence and quality of merchandise, services, stores, shopping, convenience, pricing, advertising, and any other factors that a consumer might consider in making a purchase.

penetration Is a pricing objective in which price is set at a low level in order to penetrate the market and establish a loyal customer base.

percentage variation method (PVM) Is a technique for planning dollar inventory investments that assumes that the percentage fluctuations in monthly stock from average stock should be half as great as the percentage fluctuations in monthly sales from average sales.

percentage-of-sales method Is a technique for budgeting in which the retailer targets a specific percentage of forecasted sales as the advertising budget.

perceptual incongruity Occurs when the retailer and supplier have different perceptions of reality.

performance appraisal and review Is the formal, systematic assessment of how well employees are performing their jobs in relation to established standards and the communication of that assessment to employees.

personal objectives Are those that reflect the retailers' desire to help individuals employed in retailing fulfill some of their needs.

personal selling Involves a face-to-face interaction with the consumer with the goal of selling the consumer merchandise or services.

personal shopping Occurs when an individual who is a professional shopper performs the shopping role for another; very upscale department and specialty stores offer personal shoppers to their clients.

planning Is the anticipation and organization of what needs to be done to reach an objective.

point of indifference Is the extremity of a city's trading area where households would be indifferent between shopping in that city or in an alternative city in a different geographical direction.

point-of-sale signage (POS) Is relatively small signage that is placed very close to the merchandise and is intended to give details about specific items.

population variables Include population growth trends, age distributions, and geographic trends.

post-purchase resentment Arises after the purchase when the consumer becomes dissatisfied with the product, service, or retailer and thus begins to regret that the purchase was made.

posttransaction services Are services provided to customers after they have purchased merchandise or services.

power Is the ability of one channel member to influence the decisions of the other channel members.

predatory pricing Exists when a retail chain charges different prices in different geographic areas to eliminate competition in selected geographic areas.

premiums Are extra items offered to the customer when purchasing promoted products.

prepaid expenses Are those items for which the retailer has already paid, but the service has not been completed.

pretransaction services Are services provided to the customer prior to entering the store.

price discrimination Occurs when two retailers buy an identical amount of "like grade and quality" merchandise from the same supplier but pay different prices.

price lining Is a pricing policy that is established to help customers make merchandise comparisons and involves establishing a specified number of price points for each merchandise classification.

price zone Is a range of prices for a particular merchandise line that appeals to customers in a certain market segment.

primary marketing institutions Are those channel members that take title to the goods as they move through the marketing channel. They include manufacturers, wholesalers, and retailers.

primary trading area Is the geographic area where the retailer can serve customers, in terms of convenience and accessibility, better than the competition.

private label branding Also often called store branding, occurs when a retailer develops its own brand name and contracts with a manufacturer to produce the merchandise with the retailer's brand on it instead of the manufacturer's name.

problem recognition Occurs when the consumer's desired state of affairs departs sufficiently from the actual state of affairs, placing the consumer in a state of unrest.

process theories Refer to theories on motivation that ask, "How can I motivate an individual?"

product liability laws Deal with the seller's responsibility to market safe products. These laws invoke the foreseeability doctrine, which states that a seller of a product must attempt to foresee how a product may be misused and warn the consumer against the hazards of misuse.

productivity objectives State the sales objectives that the retailer desires for each unit of resource input: floor space, labor, and inventory investment.

profit maximization Is a pricing objective that seeks to obtain as much profit as possible.

promotion Is a means that retailers use to bring traffic into their stores, and it includes advertising, sales promotion, publicity, and personal selling.

promotional advertising Is a type of advertising in which the retailer attempts to increase short-term performance by using product availability or price as a selling point.

promotional discount Is a discount provided for the retailer performing an advertising or promotional service for the manufacturer.

prospecting Is the process of locating or identifying potential customers who have the ability and willingness to purchase your product.

public warehouse Is a facility that stores goods for safekeeping for any owner in return for a fee, usually based on space occupied.

publicity Is non-paid-for communications of information about the company or product, generally in some media form.

pure competition Occurs when a market has homogeneous products and many buyers and sellers, all having perfect knowledge of the market, and ease of entry for both buyers and sellers.

pure monopoly Occurs when there is only one seller for a product or service.

Q

quantity discount Is a price reduction offered as an inducement to purchase large quantities of merchandise.

quick response (QR) systems Also known as **efficient consumer response (ECR) systems,** are integrated information, production, and logistical systems that obtain real-time information on consumer actions by capturing sales data at point-of-purchase terminals and then transmitting this information back through the entire channel to enable efficient production and distribution scheduling.

R

rasm The revenue per available seat mile calculation used by airlines.

reach Is the actual total number of target customers who come into contact with an advertising message.

receipt of goods (ROG) dating Allows the retailer to take a cash discount and the full payment period to begin when the goods are received by the retailer.

recycled merchandise retailers Are establishments that sell used and reconditioned products.

referent power Is based on the identification of B with A.

Reilly's law of retail gravitation Based on Newtonian gravitational principles, explains how large urbanized areas attract customers from smaller rural communities.

relationship retailing Comprises all the activities designed to attract, retain, and enhance long-term relationships with customers.

retail accordion Describes how retail institutions evolve from outlets that offer wide assortments to specialized stores and continue repeatedly through the pattern.

retail gravity theory Suggests that there are underlying consistencies in shopping behavior that yield to mathematical analysis and prediction based on the notion or concept of gravity.

retail inventories Comprise merchandise that the retailer has in the store or in storage and is available for sale.

retail life cycle Describes four distinct stages that a retail institution progresses through: introduction, growth, maturity, and decline.

retail method Is an inventory valuation technique that values merchandise at current retail prices, which is then converted to cost based on a formula.

retail mix Is the combination of merchandise, price, advertising and promotion, location, customer service and selling, and store layout and design.

retail store saturation Is a condition where there are just enough store facilities for a given type of store to efficiently and satisfactorily serve the population and yield a fair profit to the owners.

retailer-owned cooperatives Are wholesale institutions, organized and owned by member retailers, that offer scale economies and services to member retailers, which allows them to compete with larger chain buying organizations.

retailing Consists of the final activities and steps needed to place merchandise made elsewhere into the hands of the consumer or to provide services to the consumer.

return on assets (ROA) Is net profit (after taxes) divided by total assets.

return on net worth (RONW) Is net profit (after taxes) divided by owners' equity.

returns and allowances Are refunds of the purchase price or downward adjustments in selling prices due to customers returning purchases, or adjustments made in the selling price due to customer dissatisfaction with product or service performance.

reward power Is based on B's perception that A has the ability to provide rewards for B.

S

sales promotion Involves the use of media and nonmedia marketing pressure applied for a predetermined, limited period of time at the level of consumer, retailer, or wholesaler in order to stimulate trial, increase consumer demand, or improve product availability.

same-store sales Compares an individual store's sales to its sales for the same month in the previous year.

scrambled merchandising Exists when a retailer handles many different and unrelated items.

seasonal discount Is a discount provided to retailers if they purchase and take delivery of merchandise in the off season.

secondary business district (SBD) Is a shopping area that is smaller than the CBD and that revolves around at least one department or variety store at a major street intersection.

secondary trading area Is the geographic area where the retailer can still be competitive despite a competitor having some locational advantage.

selective distribution Means that a moderate number of retailers are used in a trade area.

servant leadership An employee's recognition that their primary responsibility is to be of service to others.

set of attributes Refers to the characteristics of the store and its products and services.

shopping center (or mall) Is a centrally owned or managed shopping district that is planned, has balanced tenancy (the stores complement each other in merchandise offerings), and is surrounded by parking facilities.

shrinkage Represents merchandise that cannot be accounted for due to theft, loss, or damage.

site analysis Is an evaluation of the density of demand and supply within each market with the goal of identifying the best retail site(s).

skimming Is a pricing objective in which price is initially set high on merchandise to skim the cream of demand before selling at more competitive prices.

slotting fees (slotting allowances) Are fees paid by a vendor for space or a slot on a retailer's shelves, as well as having its UPC number given a slot in the retailer's computer system.

societal objectives Are those that reflect the retailer's desire to help society fulfill some of its needs.

solidarity Exists when a high value is placed on the relationship between a supplier and retailer.

space productivity Represents how effectively the retailer utilizes its space and is usually measured by sales per square foot of selling space or gross margin dollars per square foot of selling space.

space productivity index Is a ratio that compares the percentage of the store's total gross margin that a particular merchandise category generates to its percentage of total store selling space used.

spine layout Is a type of store layout in which a single main aisle runs from the front to the back of the store, transporting customers in both directions, and where on either side of this spine, merchandise departments using either a free-flow or grid pattern branch off toward the back side walls.

stack-outs Are pallets of merchandise set out on the floor in front of the main shelves.

standard stock list Is a merchandising method in which all stores in a retail chain stock the same merchandise.

stimulus Refers to a cue that is external to the individual or a drive that is internal to the individual.

stock-keeping units Are the lowest level of identification of merchandise.

stock-to-sales method (SSM) Is a technique for planning dollar inventory investments where the amount of inventory planned for the beginning of the month is a ratio (obtained from trade associations or the retailer's historical records) of stock-to-sales.

stock-to-sales ratio Depicts the amount of stock to have at the beginning of each month to support the forecasted sales for that month.

store compatibility Exists when two similar retail businesses locate next to or nearby each other and they realize a sales volume greater than what they would have achieved if they were located apart from each other.

store image Is the overall perception the consumer has of the store's environment.

store management The retailing career path that involves responsibility for selecting, training, and evaluating personnel, as well as in-store promotions, displays, customer service, building maintenance, and security.

store positioning Is when a retailer identifies a well-defined market segment using demographic or lifestyle variables and appeals to this segment with a clearly differentiated approach.

store-based retailers Operate from a fixed store location that requires customers to travel to the store to view and select merchandise or services.

strategic planning Involves adapting the resources of the firm to the opportunities and threats of an ever-changing retail environment.

strategy Is a carefully designed plan for achieving the retailer's goals and objectives.

supercenter Combine a discount store and grocery store and carry 80,000 to 100,000 products in order to offer one-stop shopping.

supply chains Is a set of institutions that moves goods from the point of production to the point of consumption.

T

target market Is the group of customers that the retailer is seeking to serve.

target return objective Is a pricing objective that states a specific level of profit, such as percentage of sales or return on capital invested, as an objective.

task-and-objective method Is a technique for budgeting in which the retailer establishes its advertising objectives and then determines the advertising tasks that need to be performed to achieve those objectives.

territorial restrictions Are attempts by the supplier, usually a manufacturer, to limit the geographic area in which a retailer may resell its merchandise.

thematic maps Use visual techniques such as colors, shading, and lines to display cultural characteristics of the physical space.

theory X Is a theory of management that views employees as unreliable and thus must be closely supervised and controlled and given economic inducements to perform properly.

theory Y Is a theory of management that views employees as self-reliant and enjoying work and thus can be empowered and delegated authority and responsibility.

total assets Equal current assets plus noncurrent assets plus goodwill.

total liabilities Equal current liabilities plus long-term liabilities.

trade discount Is also referred to as a **functional discount** and is a form of compensation that the buyer may receive for performing certain wholesaling or retailing services for the manufacturer.

trading area Is the geographic area from which a retailer, or group of retailers, or community draws its customers.

trading down Occurs when a retailer uses price lining, and a customer initially exposed to higher-priced lines expresses the desire to purchase a lower-priced line.

trading up Occurs when a retailer uses price lining and a salesperson moves a customer from a lower-priced line to a higher one.

transaction services Are services provided to customers when they are in the store shopping and transacting business.

transient customer Is an individual who is dissatisfied with the level of customer service offered at a store or stores and is seeking an alternative store with the level of customer service that he or she thinks is appropriate.

two-way communication Occurs when both retailer and supplier communicate openly their ideas, concerns, and plans.

two-way exclusive dealing Occurs when the supplier offers the retailer the exclusive distribution of a merchandise line or product in a particular trade area if in return the retailer will agree to do something for the manufacturer, such as heavily promote the supplier's products or not handle competing brands.

tying agreement Exists when a seller with a strong product or service requires a buyer (the retailer) to purchase a weak product or service as a condition for buying the strong product or service.

U

understored Is a condition in a community where the number of stores in relation to households is relatively low so that engaging in retailing is an attractive economic endeavor.

V

value proposition A clear statement of the tangible and/or intangible results a customer receives from shopping at and using the retailer's products or services.

variable component Is often composed of some bonus that is received if performance warrants.

variable pricing Is a policy that recognizes that differences in demand and cost necessitate that the retailer change prices in a fairly predictable manner.

variety Refers to the number of different merchandise lines that the retailer stocks in the store.

vendor collusion Occurs when an employee of one of the retailer's vendors steals merchandise as it is delivered to the retailer.

vendor profitability analysis statement Is a tool used to evaluate vendors and shows all purchases made the prior year, the discount granted, the transportation charges paid, the original markup, markdowns, and finally the season-ending gross margin on that vendor's merchandise.

vertical cooperative advertising Occurs when the retailer and other channel members (usually manufacturers) share the advertising budget. Usually the manufacturer subsidizes some of the retailer's advertising that features the manufacturer's brands.

vertical marketing channels Are capital-intensive networks of several levels that are professionally managed and centrally programmed to realize the technological, managerial, and promotional economies of a long-term relationship orientation.

vertical price fixing Occurs when a retailer collaborates with the manufacturer or wholesaler to resell an item at an agreed-on price.

virtual store Is the total collection of all the pages of information on the retailer's Internet site.

visual merchandising Is the artistic display of merchandise and theatrical props used as scene-setting decoration in the store.

W

weeks' supply method (WSM) Is a technique for planning dollar inventory investments that states that the inventory level should be set equal to a predetermined number of weeks' supply, which is directly related to the desired rate of stock turnover.

wheel of retailing theory Describes how new types of retailers enter the market as low-status, low-margin, low-price operators; however, as they meet with success, these new retailers gradually acquire more sophisticated and elaborate facilities, and thus become vulnerable to new types of low-margin retail competitors who progress through the same pattern.

wholesaler-sponsored voluntary groups Involve a wholesaler that brings together a group of independently owned retailers and offers them a coordinated merchandising and buying program that will provide them with economies like those their chain store rivals are able to obtain.

Y

yield management The understanding, anticipating, and reacting to changing customer needs in order to maximize the revenue from a fixed capacity of available services.

Endnotes

Chapter 1

1. "Wal-Mart Sets Seminar to Assess Economic Impact," *The Wall Street Journal*, November 4, 2005: B2.
2. "America's Most Admired Companies," *Fortune*, March 7, 2005: 67–70.
3. "One Nation Under Wal-Mart," *Fortune*, March 3, 2003: 64–76.
4. *Ibid.*
5. "Wal-Mart Is the Best! No, Wait, It's the Worst!" *Advertising Age*, June 13, 2005: 14.
6. "Bloc buster," *Shopping Centers Today*, October 2005: 66–68.
7. *Ibid.*
8. "LeadershipIQ Study: Mismanagement, Inaction Among the Real Reason Why CEOs Get Fired," a study by LeadershipIQ.com released June 21, 2005.
9. A shortcoming of using Census Bureau data is that it fails to reflect all retail activity. The Census Bureau definition equates retailing only with the sale of "tangible" goods and does not include the selling of services to the final consumer. This excludes businesses such as barber/beauty shops, health clubs, dry cleaners, banks, insurance agencies, funeral homes, movie theaters, amusement parks, maid services, medical and dental clinics, and one-hour photo labs. Counting service retailers, there are over 3 million retail establishments in the United States.
10. U.S. Bureau of Census, *Statistical Abstract of the United States: 2004–2005*, Tables # 11, 56, 728, 1019, 1020, 1026, and author calculations.
11. "Google This: Amazon Plans to Sell Portions of Books Online," *The Wall Street Journal*, November 4, 2005: B1, B5.
12. "In the Driver's Seat," *The Wall Street Journal*, May 12, 2003: R12.
13. From a list compiled by Robert Kahn.
14. "One Nation Under Wal-Mart": 72.
15. "Why Costco Is All Pumped Up," *Business Week*, September 12, 2005: 13.
16. "Restoring Sparkle to the Golden Arches," *Stores*, March 2003: 28–32, and "McDonald's Announces Plans to Revitalize Its Worldwide Business and Sets New Financial Targets," a McDonalds' press release on April 7, 2003.
17. "Bigger and Bigger," *Fortune*, September 5, 2005: 104–107.
18. "Supermarkets Slimming Down," *Shopping Centers Today*, December 2004: 38.
19. "Toy Story III: The Toys 'R' Us Story," a presentation by Rebecca Caruso at the *Establishing a Distinctive Identity in a Changing Global Marketplace Conference* at Notre Dame University, September 7, 2001.
20. "Toys 'Were' Us," *The Wall Street Journal*, August 12, 2004: B1, B2.
21. "Forbes 400—The Top Ten," *Forbes*, October 10, 2005: 100.
22. U.S. Bureau of Census, *Statistical Abstract of the United States: 2004–2005*, Tables # 1017, 1019, and author calculations.
23. The Census Bureau no longer compiles data on chain store sales as a percentage of total retail sales. This information is based on estimates from various industry experts and older government data.
24. "Taxing Times at H&R Block," *Fortune*, March 21, 2005: 181–184.
25. "U.S. Airport Shops Go High-End," *The Wall Street Journal*, December 20, 2005: D1, D3, and "High-Flying Retail: JFK's The Shops Raises Bar for Airport Retail with Posh Purveyors," *Shopping Centers Today*, May 2005: 213–214.
26. "Retailers Try to Fill Urban Gap," *Houston Chronicle*, January 26, 2003: 1D.
27. "Albertsons Leads the Way For Women," *The Idaho Statesman*, January 16, 2005: 1–2 of the Business section.
28. *Ibid.*
29. "Running the Show," *The Wall Street Journal*, November 8, 2004: R3, and "50 Most Powerful Women," *Fortune*, November 14, 2005: 125–136.
30. "At Sears, a Great Communicator," *Business Week*, October 31, 2005: 50–52.
31. "Americans Can't Get No Satisfaction," *Fortune*, December 11, 1995: 194.
32. "Can the Body Shop Shape Up?" *Fortune*, April 15, 1996: 118–120.
33. Roger Dickinson, "Creativity in Retailing," *Journal of Retailing* (Winter 1969–1970): 4.
34. *Ibid.*

Chapter 2

1. "Bigger and Bigger," *Fortune* September 5, 2005: 104–107.

2. "Its Sales in a Funk, Gap Makes a Big Bet on Store Makeover," *The Wall Street Journal*, January 6, 2006: A1, A6; "Bridging the Gap," *Shopping Centers Today*, December 2005: 45–48; and "Yes, We Have a New Banana," *Business Week*, May 31, 2004: 70–72.
3. "Internet Grocery Quietly Grows to $2.4 Billion Industry," *USA Today*, May 17, 2004: 1B.
4. "Supermarkets Flex In-Line Muscle," *Stores*, February 2003: 28–32.
5. This information was provided to the authors by Robert Kahn.
6. Reprinted with permission of Record World.
7. Taken from Borders's Web site, November 13, 2005.
8. "What New Economy?" *Forbes*, April 17, 2000: 478.
9. Sidney Schoeffler, "Nine Basic Findings on Business Strategy," *PIMS Letter, No. 1, The Strategic Planning Institute, 1977.*
10. For a detailed discussion of this material with examples, see "The Profit Wedge: How Five Measure Up," *Chain Store Age*, May 1998: 60–68.
11. "Fair trade: A Major Trade Expands," *Facts, Figures & the Future*, a newsletter by Phil Lempert, June 13, 2005: 4–5.
12. "Ksears Hedging on Longtime Charitable Giving," *MorningNewsBeat*, November 22, 2005.
13. "Cautiously, Starbucks Puts Lobbying on Corporate Menu," *The Wall Street Journal*, April 12, 2005: A1, A10.
14. *Dollar General, Annual Report to Shareholders, 1996.*
15. "Attention, Shoppers: Bored College Kids Competing in Aisle 6," *The Wall Street Journal*, February 23, 2005: A1, A14.
16. "Winning Back Lost Customers," *Retail Issues Letter*, March 2001.
17. Jay Fitzsimmons, senior vice president and treasurer of Wal-Mart, quoted in MorningNewsBeat.com, March 24, 2003.

Chapter 3

1. "Commentary by Professor Claes Fornell," *ACSI February 21, 2006 Report*. Used with the author's permission.
2. If you want to see the most recent ACSI data for the nation's leading retailers, go to the University of Michigan's American Customer Satisfaction Index at http://www.bus.umich.edu/research/nqrc. The index for retailers is updated every February.
3. U.S. Bureau of Census, *Statistical Abstract of the United States: 2004–2005*, Table 3.
4. U.S. Bureau of Census, *Statistical Abstract of the United States: 2004–2005*, Tables 1318, 1319, 1320; and author calculations.
5. U.S. Bureau of Census, *Statistical Abstract of the United States: 2004–2005*, Tables 16 and 46.
6. "Love Those Boomers," *Business Week*, October 24, 2005: 94–102.
7. "I Inherited My Money the Hard Way: I Earned It," *AARP Bulletin*, December 2005: 6.
8. U.S. Bureau of Census, *Statistical Abstract of the United States: 2004–2005*, Table 16.
9. "Generation Y," *USA Today*, November 7, 2005: 1B, 2B; and "Hey Dude, This Sure Isn't the GAP," *The Wall Street Journal*, February 12, 2002: B1, B4.
10. HaeJung Kim, Dee K. Knight, and Christy Crutsinger, "Generation Y Employees' Work Experience in the Retail Industry: The Impact on Job Performance, Job Satisfaction and Career Intention," a paper presented at the ACRA 2006 Spring Conference, Springdale, Arkansas, April 7, 2006.
11. "Half of Boomers Hit the 50 Mark, but Spending Not Likely to Slow Down," *Advertising Age*, July 4, 2005: 18.
12. "Malls Woo Back Older Shoppers," *Advertising Age*, July 2004: 1, 56–57.
13. "Helping Boomers Chart Their Course," *The Wall Street Journal*, June 6, 2005: R1, R3.
14. "Older Consumers Don't Believe You," *Advertising Age*, August 14, 1995: 14.
15. "Bob's 'Get Real' with Carhart," *DSN Retailing Today*, April 7, 2003: 5, 53.
16. "Marriott Hip? Well, It's Trying," *Business Week*, September 26, 2005: 70–72.
17. "Bling Is the Thing," *Advertising Age*, January 2, 2006: 16–17; and "Putting Generation Y in Focus," *Facts, Figures, & the Future*, May 16, 2005: 1–2.
18. "A Walk on the Mild Side," *Advertising Age*, January 2, 2006: 12–13.
19. "Just How Deep Are Those Teen Pockets?" *Business Week*, July 30, 2001: 39; and "'Tweeners' Latest Must Market," *Lubbock Avalanche-Journal*, April 8, 2003: 9D.
20. "To Lure Teenage Mall Rats, You Need the Right Cheese," *Business Week*, June 7, 2004: 96–97.
21. "Turn Signals," *Advertising Age*, May 9, 2005: 8.
22. U.S. Bureau of Census, *Statistical Abstract of the United States: 2004–2005*, Table 25.
23. U.S. Bureau of Census, *Statistical Abstract of the United States: 2004–2005*, Tables 28, 29 and author calculations.
24. "A Bigger Family Stays Closer to the Nest," *The Wall Street Journal*, April 1, 1994: B1.
25. U.S. Bureau of Census, *Statistical Abstract of the United States: 2004–2005*, Tables 212 and 213.
26. U.S. Bureau of Census, *Statistical Abstract of the United States: 2004–2005*, Tables 213.
27. "U.S. Consumer—Like No Other on the Planet," *Advertising Age*, January 2, 2006: 3–5.
28. "My Daughter, the PhD," *Business Week*, March 27, 2000: 30.

29. U.S. Bureau of Census, *Statistical Abstract of the United States: 2004–2005*, Table 214; and author calculations.
30. U.S. Bureau of Census, *Statistical Abstract of the United States: 2004–2005*, Table 53.
31. "Data on Marriage and Births Reflect the Political Divide," *New York Times*, October 13, 2005: A14.
32. U.S. Bureau of Census, *Statistical Abstract of the United States: 2004–2005*, Table 53.
33. For a complete discussion of the consumer's behavior, especially differences between male and female shoppers, see Paco Underhill, *Why We Buy* (New York: Simon Schuster, 1999).
34. U.S. Bureau of Census, *Statistical Abstract of the United States: 2004–2005*, Table 61.
35. U.S. Bureau of Census, *Statistical Abstract of the United States: 2004–2005*, Table 57.
36. U.S. Bureau of Census, *Statistical Abstract of the United States: 2004–2005*, Table 57.
37. "Mom? Dad? I'm Home," *Business Week*, June 5, 2006: 126.
38. U.S. Bureau of Census, *Statistical Abstract of the United States: 2004–2005*, Tables 586, 587; and author calculations.
39. U.S. Bureau of Census, *Statistical Abstract of the United States: 2004–2005*, Table 590.
40. U.S. Bureau of Census, *Statistical Abstract of the United States: 2004–2005*, Table 592.
41. "Turnover Costs Sack Retailers," *Chain Store Age*, March 2000: 100–102.
42. U.S. Bureau of Census, *Statistical Abstract of the United States: 2004–2005*, Table 671; and author calculations.
43. U.S. Bureau of Census, *Statistical Abstract of the United States: 2004–2005*, Table 650.
44. "U.S. Households Wealthier, Thanks to Property Values," *Shopping Centers Today*, August 2005: 5.
45. "Our Hidden Savings," *Business Week*, January 17, 2005: 34–36.
46. "Age Before Beauty. No, Really," *Business Week*, April 26, 2004: 14.
47. U.S. Bureau of Census, *Statistical Abstract of the United States: 2004–2005*, Table 571.
48. U.S. Bureau of Census, *Statistical Abstract of the United States: 2004–2005*, Table 579.
49. U.S. Bureau of Census, *Statistical Abstract of the United States: 2004–2005*, Table 588.
50. U.S. Bureau of Census, *Statistical Abstract of the United States: 2004–2005*, Table 674; and author calculations.
51. "Not Tonight, Honey: The Plight of the Dual-Income, No-Sex Couple," *The Wall Street Journal*, April 3, 2003: D1.
52. "Crushed by . . . Savings," *Fortune*, March 6, 2006: 60.
53. U.S. Bureau of Census, *Statistical Abstract of the United States: 2004–2005*, Table 1186.
54. U.S. Bureau of Census, *Statistical Abstract of the United States: 2004–2005*, Table 1166 and 1186.
55. "No Kidding," *Forbes*, July 21, 2003: 20.
56. "Hamburger Joints Call Them 'Heavy Users'—But Not to Their Face," *The Wall Street Journal*, January 12, 2000: A1, A10.

Chapter 4

1. "Family Dollar Takes a Second Look at Urban Store Strategy," *Shopping Centers Today*, December 2005: 68–72.
2. Based on information provided in a speech by Brad Anderson, Best Buy's CEO, at Texas Tech University, November 8, 2005.
3. "Supermarkets," *Shopping Centers Today*, May 2005: 16–35.
4. Fred Crawford and Ryan Mathews, *The Myth of Excellence: Why Great Companies Never Try to Be the Best at Everything* (Crown Business: New York, 2001): 21–39.
5. However, in real life retailers are not confronted by such a curve because they face a three-dimensional demand function. The three dimensions are (1) quantity demanded per household, (2) price at the retail store, and (3) distance from the individual's residence or place of work to the store. The quantity demanded by a household is inversely related to the price charged and distance to the store. This discussion is, however, beyond the scope of this text.
6. Anthony J. Capraro, Susan Broniarczyk, and Rajendra K. Srivastava, "Factors Influencing the Likelihood of Customer Defection: The Role of Consumer Knowledge," *Journal of the Academy of Marketing Science*, Spring 2003: 164–175.
7. "Retailers Demanding New Products Carry Category," *KPMG Consumer Markets Insiders Focus*, (http://www.kpmginsiders.com), May 28, 2003.
8. "45 Reasons to Choose a Supermarket," *Progressive Grocer*, April 2005: 58.
9. "Drugstores Wage a Pricey Online Battle," *Advertising Age*, August 30, 1999: 26.
10. "Supermarkets, Warehouse Clubs Gas Up," *Shopping Center Today*, November 2005: 9.
11. "Eddie's Master Stroke," *Business Week*, November 29, 2005: 34–36.
12. "A Million Marketers," *Advertising Age*, June 26, 2006: 1, 71.
13. Malcolm P. McNair, "Significant Trends and Developments in the Postwar Period," in A.B. Smith (ed.), *Competitive Distribution in a Free High-Level Economy and Its Implications for the University* (University of Pittsburgh Press: Pittsburgh, PA, 1958).
14. Michael Levy, Dhruv Grewal, Robert Peterson, and Bob Connolly, "The Concept of the 'The Big Middle,'" *Journal of Retailing*, 81 (2, 2005): 83–88.

15. "Conquer And Divide," *Fortune*, October 17, 2005: 175–186.
16. Stanley C. Hollander, "Notes on the Retail Accordion," *Journal of Retailing*, Summer 1966: 29–40, 54.
17. For a complete discussion of this theory see Shelby D. Hunt, *A General Theory of Competition* (Thousand Oaks, CA: Sage Publications 2000).
18. Shelby D. Hunt and Robert M. Morgan, "The Resource-Advantage Theory of Competition: Dynamics, Path Dependencies, and Evolutionary Dimensions," *Journal of Marketing*, October 1996: 107–114.
19. *Vision for the New Millennium* (Atlanta: Kurt Salmon Associates, 1997).
20. The information in this section was provided by Karen Garrett of the Direct Selling Association, Washington D.C. and "China's New Rules Open Door to Amway, Avon, Others," *USA Today*, December 1, 2005: 9B.
21. "News Corp. Goal: Make MySpace Safer for Teens," *The Wall Street Journal*, February 17, 2006: B1, B2; "AOL: MySpace Invader," *Business Week*, January 30, 2006: 24; and "The MySpace Generation," *Business Week*, December 12, 2005: 86–96.
22. "IKEA Prefers Stores," *Shopping Centers Today*, February 2004: 9.
23. "Going Offline," *Shopping Centers Today*, December 2005: 9.
24. "Dress For Less," *Shopping Centers Today*, June 2004: 29–30.
25. "Used Products Are Hot as Japanese Discover the Joy of Buying Second-Hand," *The Wall Street Journal*, June 22, 2000: A1.
26. "Repo Men of Retailing," *The Wall Street Journal*, November 28, 2001: B1, B10.
27. *Wal-Mart's 2006 Annual Report:* 51
28. "With Profits Elusive, Wal-Mart to Exit Germany," *The Wall Street Journal*, July 29, 2006: A1, A6.
29. Michael J. O'Connor, "Global Marketing: A Retail Perspective," *International Trends in Retailing*, December 1998: 19–35.
30. "Name Brands Are OK, But We Want Style," *Shopping Centers Today*, May 2005: 13.
31. The above information was supplied in an information kit supplied by Target.

Chapter 5

1. For a more complete discussion of this subject, see the special report, "Managing the Trading-Partner Link Is the Key to Success," *Chain Store Age*, June 2003: 1A–12A.
2. For a more complete discussion on this subject, the reader should consult Robert Buzzell and Gwen Ortmeyer, "Channel Partnerships Streamline Distribution," *Sloan Management Review*, Spring 1995: 85–96.
3. F. Robert Dwyer and Sejo Oh, "A Transaction Cost Perspective on Vertical Contractual Structure and Interchannel Competitive Strategies," *Journal of Marketing*, April 1988: 21–34.
4. "Your Ticket to a New Career?" *Business Week*, May 12, 2003: 100–101.
5. Bert C. McCammon, Jr., "Perspectives for Distribution Programming," in Louis P. Bucklin, ed., *Vertical Marketing Systems* (Glenview, IL: Scott, Foresman, 1970): 45. Reprinted with permission of the author.
6. "U.S Consumer Companies Brace for Wal-Mart's Pinch," *Lubbock Avalanche Journal*, March 22, 2006: B9.
7. "Franchisees Turn On Crispin's King," *Advertising Age*, October 24, 2005: 1, 42.
8. "Quizno's Axes Spongmonkey Spokesthing," *Advertising Age*, August 2, 2004: 6.
9. "In a Clash of the Sneaker Titans, Nike Gets Leg up on Foot Locker," *The Wall Street Journal*, May 13, 2003: A1, A10.
10. "A Deal with Target Put Lid on Revival at Tupperware," *The Wall Street Journal*, February 18, 2004: A1, A9.
11. "Behind GM's Slide: Bosses Misjudge New Urban Tastes," *The Wall Street Journal*, March 8, 2006: A1, A10.
12. "Lawsuits Filed Over Auto Prices," *USAToday*, February 20, 2003: 1B; and "Same Cars Can Cost Oodles Less in Canada," *USAToday*, May 6, 2003: 1B.
13. "The Reimportation Blues," *The Wall Street Journal*, October 11, 2004: 18.
14. Robert Morgan and Shelby Hunt, "The Commitment-Trust Theory of Relationship Marketing," *Journal of Marketing*, July 1994: 20–38.
15. Jan B. Heide and George John, "Do Norms Matter in Marketing Relationships?" *Journal of Marketing*, April 1992: 32–44; and James C. Anderson and James A. Narus, "A Model of Distributor Firm and Manufacturer Firm Working Partnerships," *Journal of Marketing*, January 1990: 42–58.
16. "P&G's Gillette Edge: The Playbook It Honed at Wal-Mart," *The Wall Street Journal*, January 31, 2005: A1, A12.
17. "Toys 'R' Us Suppliers Pitch in Retailer, on Auction Block, Approaches Holiday Season with an Arsenal of Exclusives," *The Wall Street Journal*, November 10, 2004: B1, B3.
18. The authors want to acknowledge the contributions of many of their ex-students in this sections. These students are now buyers, suppliers/vendors, and category managers. In addition, we want to give special credit to Wally Switzer, President of the 4 R's of Retailing, Inc., and Kevin Blackwell, General Manager of Sales & Marketing–Analytic Solutions, Bristol Technology Inc., for their suggestions in this section.

Chapter 6

1. Sherman Act, 26 Stat, 209 (1890) as amended, 15 U.S.C. articles 1–7.
2. "Free Becomes Fighting Word," *Advertising Age*, January 24, 2005: 14.
3. "Fakes," *Business Week*, February 7, 2005: 54–64.
4. "Black Market," *Fortune*, April 3, 2006: 21.
5. "Media Counter Piracy in China in New Ways," *The Wall Street Journal*, September 26, 2005: B1, B3.
6. "Piracy Fight Strains U.S.-China Ties," *The Wall Street Journal*, January 27, 2005: A2.
7. "Fake-Jewelry Lawsuit Shakes Big Discounters, Customers," *The Wall Street Journal*, May 11, 2004: B1, B4.
8. *Ibid.*
9. "Shop Wins Round in Victoria's Secret Case," *USAToday*, April 5, 2003: 5B.
10. Fred W. Morgan and Allen B. Saviers, "Retailer Responsibility for Deceptive Advertising and Promotional Methods," paper presented at the Retail Patronage Conference, Lake Placid, NY, May 1993.
11. 227 F.3d 489, 497 (5th Cir). Section 43(a) of the Lanham Act states in part: "Any person who . . . in commercial advertising or promotion, misrepresents the nature, characteristics, quality, or geographic origin of his or another person's goods, services, or commercial activities, shall be liable in a civil action by any person who believes that he or she is likely to be damaged by such act."
12. Morgan and Saviers, *Ibid.*
13. Based on information supplied by Susan Busch, director, public relations-corporate for Best Buy, January 23, 2006.
14. *N. C. Freed Co., Inc. v. Board of Governors of Federal Reserve System* (CA2 NY) 473 F. 2d 1210.
15. Consumer Product Safety Act, U.S. Public Law 92-573 (1972).
16. "Wal-Mart Settlement," *MorningNewsBeat.com*, April 28, 2003.
17. "How To Right Retailing Wrongs," *Consumer Reports*, May 2006: 5.
18. Magnuson-Moss Warranty Federal Trade Commission Act, Public Law 93-637, 93rd. Congress (1975).
19. *Burger King v. Weaver*; United States Court of Appeals, Eleventh Circuit, 96-5438, 1999.
20. *Eastman Kodak Company v. Image Technical Services (1992)*, 112 S. Ct. 2072.
21. For a detailed analysis of the changes taking place in this area of government regulation, consult, "Antitrust Enforcers Drop the Ideology, Focus on Economics," *The Wall Street Journal*, February 27, 1997: A1, A8.
22. *Kelo v. City of New London*, 125 S. Ct. 2005.
23. "Don't *Kelo* My House," *The Wall Street Journal*, February 25, 1006: A16.
24. "Oklahoma Death Grip," *The Wall Street Journal*, March 18, 2005: W15.
25. "Supermarkets, Warehouse Clubs Gas Up," *Shopping Centers Today*, November 25, 2005: 9.
26. "For States, the Sales-Tax-Hemorrhage Continues," *The Wall Street Journal*, August 12, 2004: D2.
27. "Best Buy Increases Third-Quarter Net Earnings to $138 Million," press release issued by Best Buy, December 13, 2005; and "Form 10-Q," quarterly report issued by The Home Depot on June 2, 2005.
28. "Gap Offers Unusual Look at Factory Conditions," *The Wall Street Journal*, May 12, 2004: A1, A12.
29. K. Sudhir and Vithala Roa, "Do Slotting Allowances Enhance Efficiency or Hinder Competition?" *MSI Reports*, 2005 working paper series, issue four.
30. "Uninhibited, Uncut, Unrated DVDs Fly Off Shelves," *Advertising Age*, October 31, 2005: 9.
31. Information supplied by Bob Kahn to the authors.
32. "Companies That Serve You Best, *Fortune*, May 31, 1993: 74–88.
33. "Best Buy's Giant Gamble," *Fortune*, April 3, 2006: 68–75.
34. Richard Hollinger and Lynn Langton, *2004 National Retail Security Survey*, 2005, p. 6; used with permission.
35. This case is based on information supplied by William Davidson and the late Robert Kahn, the two individuals to whom the 3rd edition of this textbook was dedicated.
36. Letter from Sam Walton to Robert Kahn dated July 6, 1990.

Chapter 7

1. Albertson's 1998 Annual Report: 5.
2. "Growing Opposition Frowns On Wal-Mart," *USAToday*, December 5, 2005: 1B–2B.
3. Information taken from http://www.sprawl-busters.com on February 19, 2006.
4. The Opinion Page from *The Otago Daily Times*, November 26–27, 2005.
5. "Gotham Power Center," *Shopping Centers Today*, December 2004: 42–44; and "Big-box Stores Squeeze into Big Apple," *USAToday*, October 19, 2004: 3B.
6. "In The New Economy," *Inc.*, May 1999: 50; and "Striking Gold in the Nation's Urban Core," *Fortune*, May 10, 1999: 152.
7. "Lease Land Mines," *Shopping Centers Today*, September 2005: 1, 11.
8. "Airports Try Harder to Please Travelers' Palates," *USAToday*, Tuesday, March 22, 2005: 8B; and "Happier Landings," *Shopping Centers Today*, January 2004: 13–15.
9. "Check-in Time," *Shopping Centers Today*, November 2003: 17–20.
10. "Hot Kiosks and Carts," *Shopping Centers Today*, February 2003: 14–16.

11. "Shoppers Prefer Internet Retailers Made of Bricks," *Shopping Center Today*, December 2002: 13.
12. "Big Boxes Dig for Their Own Data," *Shopping Centers Today*, December 2005: 9.
13. Based on information from McDonald's Web site (http://www.mcdonald. com), February 19, 2006.
14. Based on information from Retail Forward's *Retailing in China* industry report dated January 2006.
15. William J. Reilly, *Methods for the Study of Retail Relationships*, (Austin, Texas: Bureau of Business Research, The University of Texas 1929), Research Monograph, No. 4.
16. P.D. Converse, "New Laws of Retail Gravitation," *Journal of Marketing*, January 1949: 379–384.
17. "For States, the Sales-Tax-Hemorrhage Continues," *The Wall Street Journal*, August 12, 2004: D2.
18. Bernard LaLonde, "The Logistics of Retail Location," *American Marketing Proceedings*, William D. Stevens (ed.), (Chicago: American Marketing Association, 1961): 572.
19. "Home Depot," *Business Week*, February 13, 1995: 65.
20. Mobility can be viewed as both a household characteristic and a community characteristic. We chose to treat it as a community characteristic because the design of the community, the availability of public transportation, and the cost of operating an auto in any given area are determinants of mobility and are themselves characteristic of the community.
21. The essence of Applebaum's work, plus contributions from several of his students, can be found in "William Applebaum and Others," in *Guide to Store Location Research with Emphasis on Supermarkets*, Curt Korhblau (ed.), sponsored by the Supermarket Institute, (Reading, MA: Addison-Wesley, 1968).
22. *MapInfo's PSYTE USA Handbook*, a CD-rom (Troy, N.Y., MapInfo, 2001): 360.
23. *Ibid:* 343-347.
24. Richard L. Nelson, *The Selection of Retail Locations*, (New York: F.W. Dodge, 1958): 66.
25. "Big-box Bedfellows," *Shopping Centers Today*, December 2005: 9.
26. *Ibid.*

Chapter 8

1. "Getting Ahead of the Weather," *Fortune*, February 7, 2005: 87–94.
2. Based on information contained in a letter from Sam Walton to Robert Kahn, November 30, 1989.
3. "The Only Lifeline Was the Wal-Mart," *Fortune*, October 3, 2005: 74–80.
4. "What's Really Inside Krispy Kreme?" *Business Week*, August 16, 2004: 72; and "Ovens Are Cooling at Krispy Kreme As Woes Multiply," *The Wall Street Journal*, September 3, 2004: A1, A5.
5. IRS Revenue Procedure 97–37.
6. Based on information supplied by the late Robert Kahn, a retail consultant and editor of *Retailing Today*.

Chapter 9

1. "Gap Net Falls 17% As Sales Slump Poses Challenges," *The Wall Street Journal*, May 19, 2006: B3.
2. For a more detailed discussion of the effect of any retail holiday on retail sales, visit the National Retailing Federation Web site at http://www.nrf. com and click on "Pressroom" on the left side of the home page. Then look under "Holiday/Special Occasion Retail Information."
3. "The Best Investor of His Generation. So What Is He Doing with Sears?" *Fortune*, February 20, 2006: 90–104.
4. Itamar Simonson, "The Effect of Product Assortment on Buyer Preferences," *Journal of Retailing*, Fall 1999: 347–370.
5. "A Blueprint for Local Assortment Management," *Chain Store Age*, February 1997: 27–34.
6. "P&G Slams Inefficient Marketing," *Marketing Week*, November 8, 1996: 26–27.
7. Susan Broniarczyk, Wayne Hoyer, and Linda McAlister, "Consumers' Perceptions of Assortment Offered in a Grocery Category: The Impact of Item Reduction," *Journal of Marketing Research*, May 1998: 166–176; and S. Iyengar, M. Lepper, "When Choice Is Demotivating: Can One Desire Too Much of a Good Thing?" *Journal of Personality and Social Psychology*, 6, 2000: 995–1006.
8. "For Plus-Size Women, Clothes Turn Chicer," *The Wall Street Journal*, September 13, 2005: B1, B4.
9. "Most Clothing," *Business Week*, February 20, 2006: 14.
10. Information supplied by Retail Forward, Inc. and used with their permission.
11. "Strong Suits," *Shopping Centers Today*, May 2004: 65–70.
12. *Ibid.*
13. "The Times They Are a-Changing," *The Wall Street Journal*, January 18, 2006: D1, D4.
14. "Weak Barbie Sales Hurt Mattel Net," *The Wall Street Journal*, October 18, 2005: B2; "Barbie Hits the Skids," *Advertising Age*, October 31, 2005: 1, 33; and "The Barbie Bust," *Forbes*, March 28, 2005: 64–66.
15. "How Dream Works Misjudged DVD Sales of Its Monster Hit," *The Wall Street Journal*, May 31, 2005: A1, A9.
16. "Managing for Results," *Wal-Mart's 1998 Annual Report*: 14.
17. "P&G's Soap Opera," *The Wall Street Journal*, May 3, 2006: C1; and "Wal–Mart Aims to Sharply Cut

Its Inventory Costs," *The Wall Street Journal*, April 20, 2006: B2.
18. Rockney G. Walters, "An Empirical Investigation into Retailer Response to Manufacturer Trade Promotion," *Journal of Retailing*, Summer 1989: 253–272.
19. Rajeev Batra and Indrajit Sinha, "Consumer-Level Factors Moderating the Success of Private Label Brands," *Journal of Retailing*, Summer 2000: 175–191.
20. Company annual reports for 2005 and conversations with vendors.
21. This example is based on "Unauthorized Channels of Distribution: Gray Markets," by Roy Howell, Robert Britney, Paul Kuzdrall, and James Wilcox, *Industrial Marketing Management*, 15 (November 1986): 257–263. Used with the permission of the authors.
22. "The Only Company Wal-Mart Fears," *Fortune*, November 24, 2003: 158–166; and "Inside the Cult of Costco," *Fortune*, September 6, 1999: 185–190.
23. Richard C. Hollinger and Lynn Langton, *2004 National Retail Security Survey*, Department of Criminology, Law and Society, University of Florida, 2005: 4–5.
24. This case is based on information supplied by Cricket Lee, CEO of Fit Technologies, Inc. (http://www.fitlogic.net) and used with her permission. Some readers may want to visit this Web site to determine what size would work best for them.

Chapter 10

1. For more details on how consumers process price information, see Sangkil Moon, Gary J. Russell, and Sri Devi Duvvuri, "Profiling The Reference Price Consumer," *Journal of Retailing*, (2006) Vol. 82; issue 1: 1–11.
2. Roger Dickinson, "Pricing At Retail," *Pricing Strategy & Practice*, Vol. 1, No. 1, 1993: 24–25.
3. "Tapping a Market That Is Hot, Hot, Hot," *Business Week*, January 17, 2005: 36.
4. "A Small Toy Store Manages to Level the Playing Field," *The Wall Street Journal*, December 20, 1996: A1, A8.
5. It should be noted that some academics consider skimming and even the use of couponing to be a form of price discrimination because it causes different groups of customers to pay different prices depending upon what they are willing to pay. Remember, as was pointed out in Chapter 6, price discrimination is not always illegal.
6. Dickinson, *ibid.*
7. "No-Haggle Pricing Climbs Higher, Finds Fans Among Affluent, Educated," *Advertising Age*, August 1, 2005: 23.
8. "Chinese Consumers Overwhelm Retailers with Team Tactics," *The Wall Street Journal*, February 28, 2006: A1, A14.
9. Based on material found in the Robert Kahn Collection, University of Oklahoma.
10. Zarrel V. Lambert, "Perceived Prices as Related to Odd and Even Price Endings," *Journal of Retailing* Fall 1975: 13–21, 78; and "Strategic Mix of Odd, Even Prices Can Lead to Increased Retail Profits," *Marketing News*, March 7, 1980: 24.
11. For a more complete discussion of a store manager's ability to use this strategy, see Joel E. Urbany, Peter R. Dickson, and Alan Sawyer, "Insights Into Cross- and Within-Store Price Search: Retailer Estimates vs. Consumer Self-Reports," *Journal of Retailing*, (2000) vol 76, issue 2: 243–258.
12. For a more complete discussion of grocery pricing, see James Binkley and John Connor, "Grocery Market Pricing and the New Competitive Environment," *Journal of Retailing*, Summer 1998: 273–294.
13. "One Hot Tamale," *Forbes*, December 27, 2004: 137–147.
14. "Innocents Abroad?" *The Wall Street Journal*, May 16, 2006: B1, B4.
15. "Zellers Fights Back," *Discount Merchandiser*, January 1996: 24–30.
16. "Going Private (Label)," *The Wall Street Journal*, June 12, 2003: B1, B3.
17. Charles M. Wood, Bruce L. Alford, Ralph W. Jackson, and Otis W. Gilley, "Can Retailers Get Higher Prices For 'End-of-Life' Inventory Through Online Auctions?" *Journal of Retailing*, (2005) Vol. 81; issue 3: 181–190.
18. "Sales May Go Out Like Last Year's Winter Coat," *Advertising Age*, April 25, 2005: 16.
19. "Marked Down," *Fortune*, August 22, 2005: 103–108.

Chapter 11

1. *Advertising Ratios & Budgets*, published by Schonfeld & Associates, 2006.
2. The definitions of the four types of promotion are from *Dictionary of Marketing Terms* (Chicago: American Marketing Association, 1988) and reprinted with permission of the American Marketing Association.
3. This list was developed by the late Louis Bing, Bing Furniture Company, Cleveland, Ohio.
4. "Is Wal-Mart TV a Smart Buy or Defensive One?" *Advertising Age*, September 19, 2005: 3, 49; and "Wal-Mart TV's Bad Reception," *Advertising Age*, September 19, 2005: 24.
5. "Wal-Mart Shows a Similar Side to Sears," The *New York Times*, March 31, 2006: C1, C3.

6. Myron Gable, Ann Fairhurst, Roger Dickinson, and Lynn Harris, "Improving Students' Understanding of the Retail Advertising Budgeting Process," *Journal of Marketing Education*, 2000 Vol. 22 No. 2: 120–128.
7. *Ibid.*
8. "Winds Of Change," *Shopping Centers Today*, October 2005: 43–48.
9. This information was provided by Schonfeld & Associates, Inc. in May 2006 and is used with the firm's written permission.
10. "Stores Shift Out of Newspapers to TV," *Advertising Age*, June 28, 2004: S–16.
11. "King of All Radio," *Fortune*, April 14, 1997: 110–114.
12. "Finding Extra Discounts Online," The *Wall Street Journal*, November 26, 2005: B1.
13. Based on an illustration in "Yahoo's Brilliant Solution," *Fortune*, August 8, 2005: 42–52.
14. "Piggly Wiggly," *Progressive Grocer*, January 1, 2002: 55–58; and "Pigging Out," *Chain Store Age*, July 1999: 77–82.
15. The information used in this section was accessed from Phil Lempert's Web site (http://www.supermarketguru.com) and used with his permission.
16. Based on information from the August 2005 *Facts, Figures, & The Future* newsletter, Phil Lempert, editor. Used with the permission of Phil Lempert.
17. "KFC Preps Bird-flu Plan,"*Advertising Age*, November 7, 2005: 1, 58; "McD's, Subway Attack Avian-flu Panic Head-on," *Advertising Age*, May 8, 2006: 1, 87; and "McDonald's Prepares Bird-Flu Ad Effort," *The Wall Street Journal*, May 26, 2006: B3.
18. "Why Oprah Opens Readers' Wallets," *Business Week*, October 10, 2005: 46.
19. "Oprah's Fans Scoop Up Graeter's," *Cincinnati Enquirer*, June 4, 2002: C1.

Chapter 12

1. "Learning From Customer Defections," *Harvard Business Review*, March-April 1996: 56–69.
2. For a detailed discussion of this topic, see Pratibha Dabholkar, David Shepherd, and Dayle Thorpe, "A Comprehensive Framework for Service Quality: An Investigation of Critical Conceptual and Measurement Issues Through a Longitudinal Study," *Journal of Retailing*, Summer 2000: 139–173.
3. Christian Homburg, Nicole Koschate, & Wayne D. Hoyer. "Do Satisfied Customers Really Pay More? A Study of the Relationship Between Customer Satisfaction and Willingness to Pay," *Journal of Marketing*, Vol. 69, No. 2 (April 2005): 84–96.
4. "After All You've Done For Your Customers, Why Are They Still *Not Happy?*" *Fortune*, December 11, 1995: 178–182.
5. Leo J. Shapiro, "How to Increase Sales by 20 Percent Without Attracting Any New Customers," *International Trends in Retailing*, December 1998: 37–49.
6. University of Michigan's American Customer Satisfaction Index at http://www.bus.umich.edu/research/nqrc. This survey, which is updated quarterly, was discussed in Chapter 3.
7. "Americans Can't Get No Satisfaction," *Fortune*, December 11, 1996: 186–194.
8. Eugene W. Anderson, Claes Fornell, and Donald R. Lehmann, "Customer Satisfaction, Market Share, and Profitability: Findings from Sweden," *Journal of Marketing*, Vol. 58, No. 3 (Jul., 1994): 53–66.
9. "Guess Who Made Top 10 Credit-Card List? Target," *Advertising Age*, June 5, 2006: 3, 50.
10. "Tapping A Market That Is Hot, Hot, Hot," *Business Week*, January 17, 2005: 36.
11. "Your Guide To The Medical Maze," *Business Week*, October 24, 2005: 120–122 and "New Services Cater to Affluent Patients," *The Wall Street Journal*, February 9, 2005: D1, D3.
12. SIRS presentation at National Retail Federation (NRF) Annual Convention 2000, January 18, 2000.
13. "Speaking Volumes," *Dallas Morning News*, April 16, 2000: 1H, 5H.
14. Based on a letter from Sam Walton to Robert Kahn, June 5, 1991.
15. "Big Retailers Try to Speed Up Checkout Lines," *The Wall Street Journal*, March 13, 2000: B1.
16. "Coffee on the Double," *The Wall Street Journal*, April 12, 2005: B1, B7.
17. James G. Maxham III and Richard G. Netemeyer, "Modeling Customer Perceptions of Complaint Handling Over Time: The Effects of Perceived Justice on Satisfaction and Intent," *Journal of Retailing*, Fall 2002: 239–252.
18. "The Latest Weapon in the Price Wars," *Fortune*, July 7, 1997: 200.
19. "Inside the Cult of Costco," *Fortune*, September 6, 1999: 185–190.
20. *Second Annual Customer Returns in the Retail Industry*, a study conducted by King Rogers International, September 2004.
21. The following is based on information published in the King Rogers International study cited in the previous endnote.
22. "Return Fraud and Abuse: How to Protect Profits," *Texas A&M Retailing Issues Letter*, Vol. 17, No. 1 (2005).
23. The actual number of returns and the time period involved is confidential and varies by retailer.
24. Domino's press release, dated September 25, 1998.
25. "Customers Like Buying Cars from Women, Survey Finds," *USA Today*, November 8, 1994: B1.
26. "Teaching the Teachers," *Forbes*, December 12, 2005: 115–118.

27. W. Levinson, et al., "Physician-Patient Communication. The Relationship With Malpractice Claims Among Primary Care Physicians and Surgeons," *JAMA*, February 19, 1997: 553–559; Gerald B. Hickson, et al, "Obstetricians' Prior Malpractice Experience and Patients' Satisfaction with Care," *JAMA*, November 23/30, 1994: 1583–1587; Stephen S. Entman et al., "The Relationship Between Malpractice Claims History and Subsequent Obstetric Care," *JAMA*, November 23/30, 1994: 1588–1591.
28. For a more complete discussion of this subject, see Anne W. Magi, "Share of Wallet in Retailing: The Effects of Customer Satisfaction, Loyalty Cards, and Shopper Characteristics," *Journal of Retailing*, Spring 2003: 97–106; and Arun Sharma and Michael Levy, "Categorization of Customers by Retail Salespeople," *Journal of Retailing*, Spring 1995: 71–82.
29. Much of the following is based on John O'Shaughnessy, "Selling as an Interpersonal Influence Process," *Journal of Retailing*, Winter 1971–72: 32–46.
30. *Ibid*: 41.
31. The following information was provided the authors by Marvin J. Rothenberg and is used with his written permission.
32. *Ibid.*

Chapter 13

1. Haim Mano, "The Influence of Pre-Existing Negative Affect on Store Purchase Intentions," *Journal of Retailing*, Summer 1999: 149–172.
2. "Lights On: Study Shows Display Lighting Boosts Sales at GNC," *Chain Store Age*, June 2003: 78.
3. "45 Reasons To Choose a Supermarket," *Progressive Grocer Annual Report*, April 2004: 38.
4. *Ibid.*
5. Alan Liles, *Oh Thank Heaven! The Story of the Southland Corporation* (Dallas: The Southland Corporation, 1977).
6. "Mickey D's McMakeover," *Business Week*, May 15, 2006: 42–43.
7. This information was provided to the authors by Paul Adams, a supermarket consultant, June 3, 2006.
8. "Out of the Box Thinking," *Newsweek*, May 12, 2003: 40–41.
9. Angela Hausman, "A Multi-method Investigation of Consumer Motivations in Impulse Buying Behavior," *Journal of Consumer Behavior*, (2000) Vol. 17, No. 5: 403–419.
10. "The Science of Shopping," *The New Yorker*, November 4, 1996: 66–75.
11. John Rutherford, director of Kmart's vendor relations, in a speech titled "The Evolution of Profitability" given at the University of Arizona Southwest Retail Center's 4th Annual Global Retail Symposium, March 5, 1999.
12. Based on a November 30, 1989, letter from Sam Walton to Robert Kahn and numerous conversations on the subject with Robert Kahn.
13. Based on conversations with Robert Kahn.
14. "Mervyn's Doesn't Have to Widen Aisles," *Lubbock Avalanche-Journal*, November 6, 2003: D12.
15. Carol Kaufman-Scarborough, "Reasonable Access for Mobility-Disabled Persons Is More Than Widening the Door," *Journal of Retailing*, Winter 1999: 479–508.
16. "I Screwed It Up," *Forbes*, December 6, 1993: 144.
17. "Looking Upscale, Wal-Mart Begins a Big Makeover," *The Wall Street Journal*, September 17, 2005: A1, A10.
18. The preceding material was provided for the authors' use by Marvin J. Rothenberg.
19. For a more detailed discussion of this topic, the reader should consult the latest edition of Martin M. Pegler's *Stores of the Year* published by Retail Reporting Corporation, New York.
20. "Girls Just Wanna Have Fun," *Shopping Centers Today*, September 2004: 21–22.
21. Based on an example in Paco Underhill, *Why We Buy: The Science of Shopping*, (Simon & Schuster: New York: 2000).
22. "Form and Function," *Chain Store Age*, June 2003: 76.
23. "Blinded by the Light," *Progressive Grocer*, August 2000: 57–58.
24. *Ibid.*
25. Paula Fitzgerald Bone and Pam Scholder Ellen, "Scents in The Marketplace: Explaining a Fraction of Olfaction," *Journal of Retailing*, Summer 1999: 243–262.
26. D. Douglas Graham, "Sell More with Store Design," *NARDA Independent Retailer*, February 2004: 6–10.
27. Charles Areni and David Kim, "The Influence of Background Music on Shopping Behavior: Classical Versus Top-Forty Music in a Wine Store," *Advances in Consumer Research*, 1993: 336–340.
28. Gordon C. Bruner II, "Music, Mood, and Marketing," *Journal of Marketing*, October 1990: 94–104.
29. Ronald E. Milliman, "Using Background Music to Affect Behavior of Supermarket Shoppers," *Journal of Marketing*, Summer 1982: 86–91.
30. Charles Areni and David Kim, "The Influence of Background Music on Shopping Behavior: Classical Versus Top-Forty Music in a Wine Store," *Advances in Consumer Research*, 1993: 336–340.
31. Based on information supplied by Charles Areni, University of Sydney.
32. Randahl Ramos, "Enhancing Your Customer's Shopping and Learning Experience," *NARDA Independent Retailer*, February 2005: 24.

Chapter 14

1. "Monthly Labor Review," *Bureau of Labor*, November 2005.
2. "Satisfaction Not Guaranteed," *Business Week*, June 19, 2006: 32–36.
3. Terri Kabachnick, "I Quit But I Forgot to Tell You," *Retailing Issues Letter*, (2004) Vol. 16, No. 1.
4. "The 100 Best Companies To Work For," *Fortune*, January 25, 2005: 62–68.
5. "No. 1 Retailer in Britain Uses 'Clubcard' to Thwart Wal-Mart," *The Wall Street Journal*, June 6, 2006: A1, A12.
6. David M. Szymanski, "Forget about Satisfied Customers, You Need Enthusiastic Customers," *Retailing Issues Letter*, Summer 2003.
7. Based on information found on AARP's Web site, June 11, 2006.
8. "AARP Skews Younger," *Fortune*, May 15, 2006: 36–40.
9. For a more complete discussion of this topic, the reader may want to consult a textbook on the subject. The authors recommend William Anthony, Pamela Perrewe, and Michele Kacmar, *Human Resource Management*, (Cincinnati: South-Western Publishing Co., 2006).
10. Section 703(e) of Title VII.
11. "The Ugliness Problem," *Forbes*, August 15, 2005: 96.
12. Daniel S. Hamermesh and Jeff E. Biddle, "Beauty and the Labor Market," *American Economic Review*, (December 1994) Vol. 84(5): 1174–94.
13. "World Heavyweights," *Advertising Age*, May 15, 2006: 43.
14. "Retailers Using Computers to Screen Applications," *Shopping Centers Today*, October 1999: 50.
15. "A New Threat to Your Credit Rating," *The Wall Street Journal*, January 3, 2006: D1, D2.
16. Richard C. Hollinger and Lynn Langton, *2004 National Retail Security Survey*, Department of Criminology, Law and Society, University of Florida, 2005: 15.
17. *Ibid.*
18. Robert Goldberg, "Pre-Employment Background Screening," *NARDA Independent Retailer*, December 2005: 12, 30.
19. "Background Checks That Never End," *Business Week*, March 20, 2006: 40.
20. *New Ideas for Retaining Store-Level Employees*, a study for The Coca-Cola Retailing Research Council by Blake Frank, PhD, University of Dallas, 2000: 10.
21. *Ibid:* 6.
22. *Ibid:* 5.
23. HaeJung Kim, Dee K. Knight, and Christy Crutsinger, "Generation Y Employees' Work Experience in the Retail Industry: The Impact on Job Performance, Job Satisfaction and Career Intention," a paper presented at the ACRA 2006 Spring Conference, Springdale, Arkansas, April 7, 2006.
24. "Understanding Your Top Shoppers: The Fuel That Drives Your Business!" a presentation by Glenn Hausfater at the 2006 FMI Show, Chicago, May 9, 2006.
25. "The Slipper Solution," *Forbes*, May 24, 2004: 64.
26. "Hot Tamale," *The Wall Street Journal*, January 28, 2006: B2.
27. *Ibid.*
28. *An Ernst & Young Survey: People in Retail*, September 1990: 11.
29. J. Richard Hackman and Greg R. Oldham, *Work Redesign*, (Reading, MA: Addision-Wesley, 1980): 77–80.

Subject Index

URL INDEX

Company Name	Ticker Symbol	Website	Parent Co.
7-Eleven	Tokyo(3382)	http://www.7-eleven.com	Seven and Eleven holdings Co., Ltd.
A&P	NYSE: GAP	http://www.aptea.com	The Great Atlantic & Pacific Tea Co., Inc.
AAMCO Transmission	NASDAQ(GS): ACAS	http://www.aamco.com	American Capital Strategies
Abercrombie & Fitch	NYSE: ANF	http://www.abercrombie.com	
Ace Hardware	Private-Cooperative	http://www.acehardware.com	Ace Hardware Coproration
Addidas	OTD:ADDDY[ADR], Ger.: ADS	http://www.adidas-group.com	Adidas AG
Aeropostale, Inc.	NYSE: ARO	http://www.aeropostale.com	
Albertson's	Private	http://www.albertsons.com	Supervalu, CVS, Cerberus Capital Management, Kimco Realty
Aldi	Private	http://www.aldi.com	ALDI Group
Amadeus	Private	http://www.amadeus.com	Amadeus IT Group SA
Amazon.com	NASDAQ(GS): AMZN	http://www.amazon.com	Amazon.zom, Inc.
Ameri Suites	Private	http://www.amerisuites.com	Global Hyatt Corporation
American Airlines	NYSE: AMR	http://www.aa.com	AMR Corporation
American Association of Retired Persons	Private-Association	http://www.aarp.org	
American Automobile Association	Private-Not-for-Profit	http://www.aaa.com	
American Eagle Outfitters	NASDAQ(GS): AEOS	http://www.ae.com	Americal Eagle Outfitters, Inc.
Amway	Subsidiary-Private	http://www.amway.com	Alticor, Inc.
Ann Taylor	NYSE: ANN	http://www.anntaylor.com	Ann Taylor Stores Corporation
Ann Taylor Loft	NYSE: ANN	http://www.anntaylor.com	Ann Taylor Stores Corporation
ASDA	Subsidiary (NYSE:WMT)	http://www.asda.co.uk	Wal-Mart Stores, Inc.
Auchan	Private	http://www.auchan.com	Auchan, S.A.
Auto Nation	NYSE: AN	http://www.autonation.com	Auto Nation, Inc.
Autobytel.com	NASDAQ(GM): ABTL	http://www.autobytel.com	Autobytel Inc.
Avis (Avis Group Holdings, Inc.)	Subsidiary (NYSE: CD)	http://www.avis.com	Cendant Corporation
Avon	NYSE: AVP	http://www.avoncompany.com	Avon Products, Inc.
Banana Republic	Subsidiary (NYSE: GPS)	http://www.bananarepublic.com or gap.com	Gap Inc.
Barnes & Noble	NYSE: BKS	http://www.barnesandnobleinc.com	Barnes & Noble, Inc.
Baskin-Robbins	Private	http://www.dunkinbrands.com	Dunkin' Brands, Inc.
Bass Pro Shops	Private	http://www.basspro.com	Bass Pro Shops, Inc.
Bath and Body Works	Subsidiary (NYSE: LTD)	http://www.bathandbodyworks.com	Limited Brands, Inc.
Bed Bath & Beyond	NASDAQ(GS): BBBY	http://www.bedbathandbeyond.com	Bed Bath & Beyond, Inc.
Benetton	NYSE: BNG[ADR]; Italian: BEN	http://www.benetton.com	Benetton Group, S.p. A.
Bergdorf-Goodman	Subsidiary	http://www.bergdorfgoodman.com	The Neiman Marcus Group, Inc.
Best Buy	NYSE: BBY	http://www.bestbuy.com	Best Buy Co., Inc.
Best Western	Private-Association	http://www.bestwestern.com	Best Western International, Inc.
Big Lots	NYSE: BLI	http://www.biglots.com	Big Lots, Inc.
BJ's	NYSE: BJ	http://www.bjs.com	BJ'S Wholesale Club
Blockbuster Video	NYSE: BBI	http://www.blockbuster.com	Blockbuster, Inc.
Bloomingdale's	Subsidiary (NYSE: FD)	http://www.bloomingdales.com	Federated Department Stores, Inc.
Borders	NYSE: BGP	http://www.bordersgroupinc.com	Borders Group, Inc.
Brooks Brothers	Business Segment	http://www.brooksbrothers.com	Retail Brand alliance, Inc (Private)
Buckle	NYSE: BKE	http://www.buckle.com	The Buckle, Inc.
Burger King	NYSE: BKC	http://www.burgerking.com	Burger King Holdings, Inc.
Burlington Coat Factory Warehouse Corp.	Private	http://www.coat.com	Acquired by Bain Capital in 2006
Canyon Ranch	Private	http://www.canyonranch.com	Canyon Ranch Enterprises, Inc.
Car Max	NYSE: KMX	http://www.carmax.com	Car Max, Inc.
Careerbuilder.com	Joint Venture	http://www.careerbuilder.com	Tribune, Gannett, & McClatchy Company

Company Name	Ticker Symbol	Website	Parent Co.
Carl's Jr.	NYSE: CKR	http://www.ckr.com	CKE Restaurants, Inc.
Carrefour	Euronext Paris: CA	http://www.carrefour.com	Carrefour
Carson Pirie Scott	NASDAQ(GS): BONT	http://www.carsons.com	The Bon Ton Stores, Inc.
Century 21	NYSE: H	http://www.century21.com	Realogy Corporation
Charming Shoppe	NASDAQ(GS): CHRS	http://www.charmingshoppes.com	Charming Shoppes, Inc.
Cheesecake Factory	NASDAQ(GS): CAKE	http://www.thecheesecakefactory.com	The Cheesecake Factory, Inc.
Chevrolet	NYSE: GM	http://www.gm.com	General Motors Corporation
Chico's	NYSE: CHS	http://www.chicos.com	Chico's FAS, Inc.
Chipotle Mexican Grill	NYSE: CMG	http://www.chipotle.com	Chipotle Mexican Grill, Inc.
Circle K	Private	http://www.circlek.com	Circle K, Stores
Circuit City	NYSE: CC	http://www.circuitcity.com	Circuit City Stores, Inc.
Claire's Stores	NYSE: CLE	http://www.clairestores.com	Claire's Stores, Inc.
Coach	NYSE: COH	http://www.coach.com	Coach, Inc.
Coca-Cola	NYSE: KO	http://www.cocacola.com	The Coca-cola Company
Coldwater Creek	NASDAQ(GM): CWTR	http://www.coldwater-creek.com	Coldwater Creek, Inc.
Community Health Systems	NYSE: CYH	http://www.chs.net	Community Health Systems, Inc.
Comp USA	Private	http://www.compusa.com	Mexican holding company, U.S. Comercial
Continental	OTC: CTTAY[ADR]	http://www.conti-online.com	Continental AG
Continental Airlines, Inc.	NYSE: CAL	http://www.continental.com	Continental Airlines, Inc.
Costco	NASDAQ(GS): COST	http://www.costco.com	Costco Wholesale Corporation
Crate & Barrel	Private	http://www.crateandbarrel.com	Euromarket Designs, Inc.
CUTCO Corp	Private	http://www.alcas.com	Alcas Corporation
CVS Drugstores	NYSE: CVS	http://www.cvs.com	CVS Corporation
Dave & Busters	Private	http://www.daveandbusters.com	Dave & Buster's, Inc.
Days Inns Worldwide, Inc.	Subsidiary, NYSE: WYN	http://www.daysinn.com	Wyndaham Worldwide Corporation
Del Frisco's	NASDAQ(GS): STAR	http://www.lonestarsteakhouse.com	Lone Star Steakhouse & Saloon, Inc.
Dell	NASDAQ(GS): DELL	http://www.dell.com	Dell Inc.
Delta Airlines	Pink Sheets: DALRQ	http://www.delta.com	Delta Air Lines, Inc.
Dick's Sporting Goods	NYSE: DKS	http://www.dickssportinggoods.com	Dick's Sporting Goods, Inc.
Dillard's	NYSE: DDS	http://www.dillards.com	Dillard's, Inc.
Disney	NYSE: DIS	http://www.disney.go.com	The Walt Disney Company
DKNY	Subsidiary, Euronext Paris: MC	http://www.dannakaran.com	Donna Karan International Inc. Subisdiary of LVMH Moet Hennesy Louis Vuitton SA
Dollar General	NYSE: DG	http://www.dollargeneral.com	Dollar General Corporation
Dollar Tree	NASDAQ(GS): DLTR	http://www.dollartree.com	Dollar Tree Stores, Inc.
Domino's Pizza	NYSE: DPZ	http://www.dominos.com	Domino's Pizza, Inc.
Driver's Mart	Private-Partnership	http://www.ffpmarketing.com	FFP Operating Partners L. P.
DSW Shoes	NYSE: RVI	http://www.retailventuresinc.com	Retail Ventures, Inc.
Dunkin' Donuts	Private	http://www.dunkinbrands.com	Dunkin' Brands, Inc.
eBay	NASDAQ(GS): EBAY	http://www.ebay.com	eBay Inc.
Embassy Suites	NYSE: HLT	http://www.hiltonworldwide.com	Hilton Hotels Corporation
Enron	Private	http://www.enron.com	Enron Corporation
Escape	Private	http://www.steakescape.com	Escape Enterprises, Ltd.
Esprit	Hong Kong: Full Quote	http://www.esprit.com	Esprit Holdings Limited
Estee Lauder	NYSE: EL	http://www.elcompanies.com	The Estee Lauder Companies Inc.
E*TRADE	NYSE: ET	http://www.etrade.com	E*TRADE Financial Corporation
Expedia	NASDAQ(GS): EXPE	http://www.expediainc.com	Expedia, Inc.
Family Dollar	NYSE: FDO	http://www.familydollar.com	Family Dollar Stores, Inc.
Federated Department Stores	NYSE: FD	http://www.federated-fds.com	Federated Department Stores, Inc.
Fidelity Investments	Private	http://www.fidelityacquisitions.com	Fidelity Capital Investors
Firestone	Bus.Seg. OTC: BRDCY[ADR]	http://www.firestonecompleteautocare.com/	Bridgestone/Firestone Retail & Commercial Operations LLC. Segment of Bridgestone Corporation
Food 4 Less of Southern Califonia, Inc.	Subsidiary, NYSE: KR	http://www.food4less1.com	The Kroger Company
Foot Locker	NYSE: FL	http://www.footlocker-inc.com	Foot Locker, Inc.
Ford	NYSE: F	http://www.ford.com	Ford Motor Company
Forth & Towne	NYSE: GPS	http://www.gap.com	Gap Inc.
Fresh Direct	Private	http://www.freshdirect.com	Fresh Direct, LLC.
Furniture.com	Private	http://www.furniture.com	Furniture.com, Inc.

Company Name	Ticker Symbol	Website	Parent Co.
Galileo	Subsidiary, NYSE:CD	http://www.galileo.com	Cendant Corporation
Geek Squad, Inc.	Bus.Seg., NYSE: BBY	http://www.geeksquad.com	Best Buy Co., Inc.
General Electric	NYSE: GE	http://www.ge.com	General Electric Company
Giant	NYSE: GI	http://www.giant.com	Giant Industries, Inc.
Giant Food	NYSE: AHO[ADR]	http://www.giantfood.com	Royal Ahold N.V.
Godiva	Subsidiary, NYSE: CPB	http://www.godiva.com	Godiva Chocolatier, Inc, Subdidiary of Campbell Soup Company
Google	NASDAQ(GS): GOOG	http://www.google.com	Google Inc.
Graeter's	private	http://www.graeters.com	Graeter's
Great Indoors	Subsidiary, NASDAQ(GS): SHLD	http://www.sears.com	Sears Holdings Corporation
Gristede's	Private	http://www.gristedes.com	Gristede's Foods, Inc.
Gucci	Subsid., EuronextParis: PP	http://www.guccigroup.com	PPR SA
Guess	NYSE: GES	http://www.guess.com	Guess?, Inc.
Gymboree	NASDAQ(GS): GYMB	http://www.gymboree.com	The Gymboree Corporation
H & R Block	NYSE: HRB	http://www.hrblock.com	H & R Block, Inc.
H.E.B. Grocery	Private	http://www.heb.com	H. E. Butt Grocery Company
Haagen Dazs	Subsid. OTC: NSRGY[ADR]	http://www.haagen-dazs.com	Nestle SA
Hallmark	Private	http://www.hallmark.com	Hallmark Cards, Inc.
Handy Hardware	Private-Cooperative	http://www.handyhardware.com	Handy Hardware Wholesale, Inc.
Hannaford's	Subsid., NYSE: DEG[ADR]	http://www.hannaford.com	Delaize Group
Harley-Davidson	NYSE: HOG	http://www.harley-davidson.com	Harley-Davidson, Inc.
Harrod's	Private	http://www.harrods.com	Harrods Holdings
Harry & David	Private (NYSE: HND Proposed)	http://www.bco.com	Harry & David Holdings, Inc.
Herbalife Int'l	Private	http://www.herbalife.com	Herbalife International, Inc.
Hertz	Private (NYSE: HTZ Propsed)	http://www.hertz.com	Hertz Global Holdings, Inc.
Hilton Hotels	NYSE: HLT	http://www.hiltonworldwide.com	Hilton Hotels Corporation
Holiday Inn	Subsid., AMEX: LGN	http://www.lodgian.com	Lodgian, Inc.
Home Depot	NYSE: HD	http://www.homedepot.com	The Home Depot, Inc.
Home Interiors & Gifts Inc.	Private	http://www.homeinteriors.com	Home Interiors & Gifts Inc.
Hoovers.com	Subsid., NYSE: DNB	http://www.hoovers.com	Dun & Bradstreet
Hotjobs.com	Subsid., NASDAQ(GS): YHOO	http://www.hotjobs.com	Yahoo!
Hudson Bay Co.	Private	http://www.hbc.com	Hudson's Bay Company
Hyatt	Private	http://www.hyatt.com	Global Hyatt Corporation
IKEA	Private	http://www.ikea.com	IKEA International A/S
IMAX	NASDAQ(GM): IMAX	http://www.imax.com	IMAX Corporation
Intercontinental	NYSE: IHG	http://www.ihgplc.com	Intercontinental Hotels Group PLC
J. Alexander's	NYSE: JAX	http://www.jalexanders.com	J. Alexander's Corporation
J.C. Penney	NYSE: JCP	http://www.jcpenney.com	J. C. Penney Company, Inc.
Jet Blue	NASDAQ(GS): JBLU	http://www.jetblue.com	Jet Blue Airways Corporation
Jewel/Osco	Bus. Seg., NYSE: SVU	http://www.jewelosco.com	Supervalu, Inc.
Jiffy Lube	Subsid., NYSE: RDS'A[ADR]	http://www.jiffylube.com	Royal Dutch Shell Plc.
Jos. A Bank	NASDAQ(GS): JOSB	http://www.josbank.com	Jos A. Bank Clothiers, Inc.
Kayak.com	Private	http://www.kayak.com	Kayak.com
KFC	Subsid., NYSE: YUM	http://www.kfc.com	Yum! Brands, Inc.
Kmart	Subsid., NASDAQ(GS): SHLD	http://www.kmartcorp.com	Sears Holdings Corporation
Kohl's	NYSE: KSS	http://www.kohls.com	Kohl's Corporation
Krispy Kreme	NYSE: KKD	http://www.krispykreme.com	Krispy Kreme Doughnuts, Inc.
Kroger	NYSE: KR	http://www.kroger.com	The Kroger Company
L.L. Bean	Private	http://www.llbean.com	L.L. Bean, Inc.
Land's End	Bus. Seg., NYSE: SHLD	http://www.landsend.com	Sears Holdings Corporation
Lane Bryant	Subsid., NASDAQ(GS): CHRS	http://lanebryant.charmingshoppes.com	Charming Shoppes, Inc.
Levi Strauss	Private	http://www.levistrauss.com	Levi Strauss & Company
Linens 'n Things	Private	http://www.lnt.com	Linens 'n Things, Inc.
Liz Claiborne	NYSE: LIZ	http://www.lizclaiborne.com	Liz Claiborne, Inc.
Loblaw	Toronto: L	http://www.loblaw.com	Loblaw Companies Limited
London Fog	Subsid., NASDAQ:ICON	http://www.iconixbrand.com	Iconix Brand Group

Company Name	Ticker Symbol	Website	Parent Co.
Lowe's	NYSE: LOW	http://www.lowes.com	Lowe's Companies, Inc.
Laura Ashley	London: ALY	http://www.lauraashley.com	Laura Ashley Holdings, plc.
Macy's	NYSE: FD	http://www.macys.com	Federated Department Stores, Inc.
Marks & Spencer	PinkSheets: MAKSY.PK[ADR]	http://www.marksandspencer.com	Marks & Spencer Group, p.l.c.
Marriott	NYSE: MAR	http://www.marriott.com	Marriott International, Inc.
Mary Kay	Private	http://www.marykay.com	Mary Kay, Inc.
McDonald's	MYSE: MCD	http://www.mcdonalds.com	McDonald's Corporation
McLane's (Berkshire Hathaway)	NYSE: BRK	http://www.berkshirehathaway.com	Berkshire Hathaway, Inc.
Meijer's	Private	http://www.meijer.com	Meijer Inc.
Merry Maids	Subsid., NYSE: SVM	http://www.servicemaster.com	The Service Master Company
Mervyn's	Private	http://www.mervyns.com	Mervyn's, LLC
Metro AG	German: MEO	http://www.metro.com	Metro AG
Midas Mufflers	NYSE: MDS	http://www.midasinc.com	Midas, Inc.
Monster.com	NASDAQ(GS): MNST	http://www.monsterworldwide.com	Monster Worldwide, Inc.
Motel 6	Bus.Seg., EuronextParis: AC	http://www.motel6.com	Accor
Mothercare	London: MTC	http://www.mothercare.com	Mothercare, plc.
MP3.com	NASDAQ(GS): CNET	http://www.cnetnetworks.com	CNET Networks, Inc.
Mr. Handyman	Private	http://www.mrhandyman.com	Mr. Handyman, LLC
Music Go Round	NASDAQ(GM): WINA	http://www.winmarkcorporation.com	Winmark Corporation
National Car Rental	Subsid., NYSE: VCG Proposed	http://www.nationalcar.com	Vanguard Car Rental Group, Inc.
Nebraska Furniture Mart	Subsid., NYSE: BRK	http://www.nfm.com	Berkshire Hathaway, Inc.
Neiman Marcus	Private	http://www.neimanmarcus.com	The Neiman Marcus Group, Inc.
Nike	NYSE: NKE	http://www.nikebiz.com	Nike, Inc.
Nordstrom's	NYSE: JWN	http://www.nordstrom.com	Nordstrom, Inc.
Northwest Airlines	Pink Sheets: NWACQ	http://www.nwa.com	Northwest Airlines Corporation
Nuskin Enterprises	NYSE: NUS	http://www.nuskinenterprises.com	Nuskin Enterprises, Inc.
Office Depot	NYSE: ODP	http://www.officedepot.com	Office Depot, Inc.
Office Max	NYSE: OMX	http://www.officemax.com	OfficeMax Incorporated
Old Navy	Bus.Seg., NYSE: GPS	http://www.gap.com	Gap, Inc.
Olive Garden	NYSE: DRI	http://www.dardenrestaurants.com	Darden Restaurants, Inc.
Once Upon A Child	NASDAQ(GM): WINA	http://www.winmarkcorporation.com	Winmark Corporation
Orbitz	Subsid., Private	http://www.orbitz.com	Travelport
Organizacion Soriana	Mexican: SORIANA	http://www.soriana.com.mx	Organizacion Soriana, S.A. de C.V.
Orville's Home Appliances	Private	http://www.orvilles.com	Orville's Home Appliances
Outback	NYSE: OSI	http://www.osirestaurantpartners.com	OSI Restaurant Partners, Inc.
Papa John's	NASDAQ(GS): PZZA	http://www.papajohns.com	Papa John's Inaternational, Inc.
Parisian	Bus.Seg., NYSE: SKS/Private	http://www.parisian.com/	Saks Incorporated has agreed to sell Parisian to Belk, Inc.
Pathmark	NASDAQ(GM): PTMK	http://www.pathmark.com	Pathmark Stores, Inc.
Peapod	Subsid., NYSE: AHO[ADR]	http://www.peapod.com	Royal Ahold N.V.
Pepsi-Cola	NYSE: PEP	http://www.pepsico.com	Pepsi Co., Inc.
Petco	NASDAQ(GS): PETC	http://www.petco.com	PETCO Animal Suppliers. Inc.
Pets Mart	NASDAQ(GS): PETM	http://www.petsmart.com	PetsMart, Inc.
PF Chang's	NASDAQ(GS): PFCB	http://www.pfcb.com	P F Chang's China Bistro, Inc.
Pier 1	NYSE: PIR	http://www.pier1.com	Pier 1 Imports, Inc.
Piggly Wiggly	Private	http://www.thepig.net	Piggly Wiggly Carolina Company, Inc.
Pizza Hut	Subsid., NYSE: YUM	http://www.pizzahut.com	Yum! Brands, Inc.
Plato's Closet	NASDAQ(GM): WINA	http://www.winmarkcorporation.com	Winmark Corporation
Play It Again Sports	NASDAQ(GM): WINA	http://www.winmarkcorporation.com	Winmark Corporation
Polo Ralph Lauren	NYSE: RL	http://www.polo.com	Polo Ralph Lauren Corporation
Pottery Barn	NYSE: WSM	http://www.williams-sonomainc.com	Williams-Sonoma, Inc.
Priceline.com	NASDAQ(GS): PCLN	http://www.priceline.com	priceline.com, Incorporated
Princess House Inc.	Private	http://www.princesshouse.com	Princess House Inc.
Promodes	Euronext Paris: CA	http://www.carrefour.com	Carrefour SA, Promodes merged with Carrefour in 2000
Publix	Private	http://www.publix.com	Publix Supermarkets, Inc.
Quizno's	Private	http://www.quiznos.com	The Quiznos Master, LLC
Reebok	Subsid., OTC: ADDDY [ADR]	http://www.reebok.com	Adidas AG, Reebok International Ltd. was bought by adidas AG in 2006

Company Name	Ticker Symbol	Website	Parent Co.
Ross Dress For Less	NASDAQ(GS): ROST	http://www.rossstores.com	Ross Stores, Inc.
Ross-Simon	Private	http://www.ross-simons.com	Ross-Simons
Sabre	NYSE: TSG	http://www.sabre.com	Sabre Holdings Corporation
Safeway	NYSE: SWY	http://www.safeway.com	Safeway, Inc.
Sainsbury	OTC: JSNSY[ADR]	http://www.j-sainsbury.co.uk	J. Sainsbury plc.
Saks Inc.	NYSE: SKS	http://www.saks.com	Saks Inc.
Salvation Army	Private-Not-for-Profit	http://www.salvationarmyusa.org	The Salvation Army National Corporation
Sam's Club	Bus.Seg., NYSE: WMT	http://www.samsclub.com	Wal-Mart Stores, Inc.
Scottrade	Private	http://www.scottrade.com	Scottrade, Inc.
Sears	NASDAQ(GS): SHLD	http://www.sears.com	Sears Holdings Corporation
See's Candy	Subsid., NYSE: BRK	http://www.sees.com	Berkshire Hathaway, Inc.
Sewell Auto	Private	http://www.sewell.com	Sewell Automotive Companies
Shaklee Corp	Private	http://www.shaklee.com	Shaklee Corporation (80% is owned by Ripplewood Holdinga and Activated Holdings)
Sharper Image	NASDAQ(GM): SHRP	http://www.sharperimage.com	Sharper Image Corporation
Sheraton	Bus.Seg., NYSE: HOT	http://www.sheraton.com	Starwood Hotels & Resorts Worldwide, Inc.
Sherwin Williams	NYSE: SHW	http://www.sherwin-williams.com	The Sherwin Williams Company
Sirius	NASDAQ(GS): SIRI	http://www.sirius.com	Sirius Satellite Radio, Inc.
Smith & Wollensky	NASDAQ(GM): SWRG	http://www.smithandwollensky.com	The Smith & Wollensky Restaurant Group, Inc.
Southern States Cooperative	Private-Cooperative	http://www.southernstates.com	Southern States Cooperative Incorporated
Southwest Airlines Company	NYSE: LUV	http://www.southwest.com	Southwest Airlines Company
Spiegel	Pink Sheets: EBHC	http://www.eddiebauer.com	Eddie Bauer Holdings, Inc.
Sports Authority	Private	http://www.sportsauthority.com	The Sports Authority, Inc.
Staples	NASDAQ(GS): SPLS	http://www.staples.com	Staples, Inc.
Starbucks	NASDAQ(GS): SBUX	http://www.starbucks.com	Starbucks Corporation
Starwood	NYSE: HOT	http://www.starwoodhotels.com	Starwood Hotels & Resorts Worldwide, Inc.
Stein Mart	NASDAQ(GS): SMRT	http://www.steinmart.com	Stein Mart, Inc.
Sterling Optical	OTC: ISEE	http://www.emergingvision.com	Emerging Vision, Inc.
Stop & Shop	Subsid., NYSE: AHO[ADR]	http://www.stopandshop.com	Royal Ahold N.V.
Subway	Private	http://www.subway.com	Doctor's Associates Inc.
Super Valu	NYSE: SVU	http://www.supervalu.com	Super Valu
Supercuts	Bus.Seg., NYSE: RGS	http://www.supercuts.com	Regis Corporation
Sutherlands	Private	http://www.sutherlands.com	Sutherlands
Swatch	Pink Sheets: SWGAF	http://www.swatchgroup.com	The Swatch Group Ltd.
Sylvan Learning	NASDAQ(GS): EEEE	http://www.educate-inc.com	Educate, Inc.
Sysco	NYSE: SYY	http://www.sysco.com	SYSCO Corporation
T.J. Maxx	Subsid., NYSE: TJX	http://www.tjx.com	The TJX Companies, Inc.
Taco Bell	Bus.Seg., NYSE: YUM	http://www.tacobell.com	Yum! Brands, Inc.
Talbot's	NYSE: TLP	http://www.talbots.com	The Talbot's, Inc.
Target	NYSE: TGT	http://www.target.com	Target Corporation
Tesco	OTC: TSCDY.PK[ADR]	http://www.tesco.com	Tesco Plc.
The Body Shop	OTC: LORLY[ADR]	http://www.the-body-shop.com	L'Oreal S.A. (Body Shop sold to L'Oreal mid-2006)
The Container Store	Private	http://www.containerstore.com	The Container Store
The Gap	NYSE : GPS	http://www.gap.com	Gap, Inc.
The Limited	NYSE: LTD	http://www.limitedbrands.com	Limited Brands, Inc.
The Pamper Chef Ltd.	Subsid., NYSE: BRK	http://www.pamperedchef.com	Berkshire Hathaway, Inc.
The UPS Store	NYSE: UPS	http://www.ups.com	United Parcel Service, Inc.
Tiffany & Company	NYSE: TIF	http://www.tiffany.com	Tiffany & Company
Tommy Hilfiger	Private	http://www.tommy.com	Tommy Hilfiger Corporation
Toys 'R' Us	Private	http://www.toysrus.com	Toys "R" Us, Inc.
Tractor Supply	NASDAQ(GS): TSCO	http://www.tractorsupplyco.com	Tractor Supply Company
Trader Joe's	Private	http://www.traderjoes.com	Trader Joe's Company, Inc.
Travelocity	Subsid., NYSE: TSG	http://www.travelocity.com	Sabre Holdings Corporation
Tru Serv	Private-Cooperative	http://www.truevaluecompany.com	True Value Company
Tupperware	NYSE: TUP	http://www.tupperware.com	Tupperware Brands Corporation
United Airlines	NASDAQ(GS): UAUA	http://www.united.com	UAL Corporation
University of Phoenix	NASDAQ(GS): APOL	http://www.apollogroup.com	Apollo Group, Inc.

Company Name	Ticker Symbol	Website	Parent Co.
UPS	NYSE: UPS	http://www.ups.com	United Parcel Service, Inc.
US Airways	NYSE: LCC	http://www.usairways.com	US Airways Group, Inc.
Vault.com	Private	http://www.vault.com	Vault, Inc.
Victoria's Secret	Subsid., NYSE: LTD	http://www.limitedbreands.com	Limited Brands, Inc.
Vons	Bus.Seg., NYSE: SWY	http://www.vons.com	Safeway, Inc.
Waitrose	Subsid., Private	http://www.waitrose.com	John Lewis Partnership plc.
Walgreens	NYSE: WAG	http://www.walgreens.com	Walgreen Company
Wal-Mart	NYSE: WMT	http://www.walmartstores.com	Wal-Mart Stores, Inc.
Wegmans Supermarkets	Private	http://www.wegmans.com/	Wegmans Supermarkets
Wells Fargo	NYSE: WFC	http://www.wellsfargo.com	Wells Fargo & Company
Wendy's	NYSE: WEN	http://www.wendys.com	Wendy's International, Inc.
Wet Seal	NASDAQ(GM): WTSLA	http://www.wetsealinc.com	The Wet Seal, Inc.
Whole Foods	NASDAQ(GS): WFMI	http://www.wholefoodsmarket.com	Whole Foods Market, Inc.
Wild Oats	NASDAQ(GM): OATS	http://www.wildoats.com	Wild Oats Markets, Inc.
Williams-Sonoma	NYSE: WSM	http://www.williams-sonomainc.com	Williams-Sonoma, Inc.
Worldspan	Subsid.,(NYSE: WS Proposed)	http://www.worldspan.com	Travel Transaction Processing Corporation
XM Radio	NASDAQ(GS): XMSR	http://www.xmradio.com	XM Satellite Radio Holdings, Inc.
Yahoo	NASDAQ(GS): YHOO	http://www.yahoo.com	Yahoo!
Yum Brands	NYSE: YUM	http://www.yum.com	Yum! Brands, Inc.
Zara	Subsid., Spanish ITX	http://www.inditex.com	Industria de Diseno Textil, S.A (Inditex)
Zellers	Subsid., Private	http://www.hbc.com/zellers	Hudson's Bay Company